Introduction to
Investment Management

Introduction to Investment Management

C. Ronald Sprecher

Southern Illinois University, Carbondale

Houghton Mifflin Company   Boston

Atlanta   Dallas   Geneva, Illinois
Hopewell, New Jersey   Palo Alto   London

Printed in the U.S.A.

Library of Congress Catalog Card Number: 74–12896

ISBN: 0–395–18706–0

To Carol and Steven

Contents

Preface

This text is designed to give the student an overview of the field of investment management. To achieve this goal, it has three distinct areas of concern. First, it views the investment decision in terms of its setting, in particular the inter-relationships among the financial markets, investor needs and preferences, and the economic environment. In this connection, it also describes the evolution of the financial world and the practices of security analysts and portfolio managers. Second, investment management is a classic example of decision-making under conditions of uncertainty. Hence, the focus is on the analytical techniques necessary for dealing with this risk and uncertainty. Finally, the text interweaves some basic theory with actual practice to provide a foundation for the procedures used in investment management. In an introductory course the theoretical developments cannot be too rigorous, but the theory underlying the actual practice can be shown at an intuitive level.

Investment management has undergone a marked change in recent years with the emergence of a vast amount of research on the securities markets and portfolio management. This research has opened new avenues for analyzing the processes of security analysis and portfolio management and has led to a re-evaluation of many of the existing practices. Probably the major benefit of this research has been to focus on portfolio composition as the essential question of investment management. Historically the focus has been on security analysis, but recent developments in the fields of business and finance have illustrated the central importance of portfolio management in reconciling the needs of the investor with existing conditions in the money and capital markets.

In organizing the text, I have divided the investment process into security analysis and portfolio management. Various aspects of security analysis are covered in Parts II and III, although some topics covered in Part I, on the investment setting, will have important implications for security analysis as will other aspects for portfolio composition. Portfolio management is covered in Parts IV and V. Part IV deals with methods of constructing portfolios of securities. Within this area the traditional approaches to portfolio composition are discussed as well as some of the more recent developments. Although some of these recent developments are fairly complex, I felt that much of the theory surrounding them should be presented to give a fairly complete treatment of the subject. The instructor may very well choose to omit some of this material from class discussion. For example, it may not be feasible to introduce capital market theory and the wealth-maximization model into class discussions. Omission of such material should not affect the overall course development since subsequent chapters do not rely heavily on these topics.

This text requires a minimum of preparatory courses. It assumes that the student has had college algebra, introductory statistics, accounting, and economics. Many colleges and universities now require one or two semesters of calculus of their undergraduates. This prerequisite is not essential for this text, but for those who do have the training or interest, some of the more advanced topics are treated in appendices at the ends of some chapters.

A number of people have been influential in making this text a reality, and it is a pleasure to acknowledge their contributions. First, I would like to express my appreciation to my colleague D. E. Vaughn for his advice and counsel in developing this text. In addition, I would like to thank my colleagues John Booker and Adam Gehr for their helpful comments on various chapters of this text. I would also like to express my appreciation to James Hugon, Charles Kroncke, and Richard McEnally for their helpful advice on various chapters of an earlier draft of this text. In compiling the final draft Phillip Cooley, John Walter McKibben, and Charles Rini provided much valuable assistance for which I am greatly indebted.

In addition, let me express my appreciation to Barbara Hodge and her staff, which included Susan Hudock and Michelle Landes, for their untiring efforts of typing and editing. Finally, I must express my appreciation to my wife, Carol, and son, Steven, for their understanding and patience while I was working on this text.

C. Ronald Sprecher

Introduction to
Investment Management

I

The Investment Setting

Chapter 1

An Introduction

Securities investment has a long and somewhat glamorous history. Many fortunes have been made and lost by investing in securities, and the events surrounding these activities represent some of our best nonfiction literature. For most of us, however, securities investment is the mundane undertaking of investing our savings. The purpose for saving varies from individual to individual; whatever the purpose, securities offer an investment outlet that can meet a wide range of needs and preferences. For the investor who wants to invest in high-quality, short-term instruments, there are Treasury bills, bankers' acceptances, certificates of deposit, and commercial paper. For the investor who wants to invest in long-term instruments, there are bonds and debentures, common stock, preferred stock, and warrants. In addition, there are other kinds of investments, such as real estate and commodity futures.

Having all these alternatives raises the inevitable question about the appropriate course of action. With every investment decision there is not only an anticipated return, but also a certain amount of risk associated with that return. The investment decision, therefore, may be characterized as a tradeoff between risk and return; it is generally assumed that the larger the amount of risk the larger the anticipated return must be to compensate for this risk. For securities this means that the risk and return associated with various securities must be estimated. At the same time, the appropriate level of risk for the individual investor must also be determined. Just as the risk associated with various securities varies widely, the ability and willingness to accept risk also varies substantially from investor to investor. Consequently, the portfolio of securities that is finally constructed represents the optimal tradeoff between the perceived risk and expected return.

Role of Financial Assets

Once an economy passes beyond the subsistence level, the majority of transactions are facilitated by the use of financial assets. The most notable example is the exchange of commodities for money. Following closely behind the development of money as a medium of exchange are the use of credit and the formation of a banking system. These developments mark the beginning of a financial system; as the economy grows and develops, the financial system becomes more complex. The major function of the financial system, however, is to facilitate economic growth. This function is accomplished by gathering small pools of savings and channeling them into investment in tangible assets, such as commercial plant and equipment. Because of the increased complexity of modern economics, the financial systems of the developed countries of the world have become quite complex, with a wide range of institutions, markets, and instruments.

Individual wealth can be held in the form of either tangible assets or financial assets, or in some combination of the two. Tangible assets normally take the form of such producers' goods as land, plant, and equipment, or such commodities as inventories. Financial assets, on the other hand, represent claims against tangible assets, such as bankers' acceptances, bonds, preferred stock, and common stock. Tangible assets are fundamental to economic well-being; but economic growth depends to a large extent on the efficiency of the financial system in gathering and channeling savings into new tangible investment. Financial theory may, therefore, be defined as the analysis of the interrelationship between tangible assets and financial assets.

Both firms and households have real and financial assets in their asset portfolios, but the mix may vary considerably. Table 1-1 indicates the types of tangible and financial assets a typical firm may have on its balance sheet. Liabilities and net worth are also shown, since these represent financial claims against the firm. Whenever a firm creates a liability, someone has a financial asset. Consequently, financial assets and liabilities cancel one another out

TABLE 1-1 *Assets and Liabilities of a Typical Firm*

Tangible assets	Liabilities
Land	Accounts payable
Building	Notes payable
Inventories	Bonds and debentures
Durables	Mortgages
Financial assets	Net worth
Currency	
Demand deposits	
Receivables	
Bonds and debentures	

when viewed in the aggregate. The type of business conducted normally plays a major role in determining the asset mix of a firm. For example, finance companies have a significantly different asset mix than public utilities. Many other factors, such as liquidity, profitability, firm size, and anticipated growth prospects also play an important role. Reconciling the many factors that affect the asset mix and the asset size of the firm is the problem that corporate financial managers must wrestle with.

The firm's problem of determining the asset mix is well recognized—it is the material of courses in managerial finance. What is not so well recognized is that households face the same decisions; this is illustrated in Table 1-2. A household, like a firm, must determine its investment in tangible assets, such as a house, furniture, and automobile, as well as its investment in financial assets, such as cash, stocks, bonds, and time deposits. A household, too, creates liabilities such as home mortgages and consumer loans that become financial assets of others within the economic system.

Both households and firms can invest in many different combinations of tangible and financial assets. This explains why the term *investment* can refer to the acquisition of either tangible or financial assets, depending upon the context in which it is being used. In economics, for example, investment commonly refers to the acquisition of tangible assets. In finance, on the other hand, investment, or the term *investment management,* can refer solely to the acquisition and administration of securities. These securities generally include stocks, bonds and debentures, and warrants, because these securities are usually traded in organized markets. Investment management does not include all financial assets. Mortgages are not considered part of investment management because they are not traded actively in organized markets. Time and savings deposits also are not given explicit consideration, although they may be used as short-term liquidity instruments. The main thrust of investment management is directed toward stocks and bonds and, to some extent, warrants, since these securities represent the more common investment media.

TABLE 1-2   *Assets and Liabilities of a Typical Household*

Tangible assets	Liabilities
Land	Consumer debt
Building	Mortgages
Durables	
	Net worth
Financial assets	
Currency	
Demand deposits	
Time deposits	
Bonds, debentures, and notes	
Stocks and equity	

A Brief History of Investment Management

The history of securities investment dates back to 1725, when securities were believed to be traded in an auction market in lower New York at the foot of Wall Street.[1] The market, however, was actually for agricultural commodities such as wheat and tobacco. The first definite mention of a market for securities appears in the *Diary* or *London's Register,* which was published in 1792.[2] For our purposes, the historical events of interest occurred in the twentieth century. World War II provides a convenient point of departure, since the pre–World War II period was markedly different from the post–World War II period.

Pre–World War II Period In the period from the turn of the century up to World War I, the prevailing investment attitude was fairly conservative. Bonds were considered the primary investment media. Some common stocks were considered to be of investment quality, but most common stocks were considered much too speculative for the average investor. The attitude prevailing during this period can be illustrated by reference to the generally accepted requirements for investment-grade common stocks.[3] First, they had to have stable if not increasing dividends that would be maintained throughout depression periods. In addition, the firm had to have a sound capital structure and an adequate amount of working capital. Second, the market price had to be near the book value per share. This gave evidence that the shares were backed by tangible assets. Investment-grade common stocks, therefore, were treated much like bonds.

For many reasons, the 1920s marked a dramatic change in the attitude of investors toward common stocks. The use of liberty bonds in the financing of World War I introduced many to the process of investment. This form of war financing brought millions of people into contact with the process of investing in securities. Another reason was the increased confidence in the stability of the economy. Prior to the formation of the Federal Reserve System in 1913, there were numerous liquidity crises which resulted in financial panics. Formation of the Federal Reserve System led many to believe that the financial sector could now be controlled, and that these financial panics were a thing of the past. Finally, the publication of a study by Edgar Lawrence Smith in 1924 gave impetus to common stock investment.[4] Smith's study demonstrated that a representative list of common stocks had consistently outperformed bond investments in the period since the Civil War. As a result, investment interest began shifting toward common stocks. This shift culminated in the stock market "crash" of 1929.

[1] George L. Leffler and Loring C. Farwell, *The Stock Market,* 3d ed. (New York: The Ronald Press, 1963), p. 81.
[2] Ibid.
[3] Benjamin Graham, David L. Dodd, and Sidney Cottle, *Security Analysis and Techniques,* 4th ed. (New York: McGraw-Hill, 1962), pp. 405–7.
[4] Edgar Lawrence Smith, *Common Stocks As Long-Term Investments* (New York: MacMillan, 1924).

The second half of the 1920s marked a speculative binge that was practically unrivaled in history. With the growing interest in common stocks, it was not surprising that the market would experience a speculative period. The financial machinery of the period, however, was not able to cope with the widespread abuses that occurred. Margin trading was widely used and was a major reason for the debacle of 1929. Investors could borrow up to 90 percent of the market value of stocks. In rising markets, such low margin requirements would lead to substantial profits. In declining markets these low margin requirements brought margin calls and many times necessitated the subsequent selling of securities to pay off the borrower's indebtedness. When a market falls somewhat, the widespread use of low margins leads to the snowballing effect that occurred in 1929.

Manipulation was widespread, and the use of corners and pools was commonplace. Graham, Dodd, and Cottle report that manipulation was so flagrant that brokers would gather in a leading manipulator's office to learn which stocks were to be run up on the following day.[5] A corner was a situation in which the shares were concentrated in the hands of a few people. It was a device to trap the unsuspecting speculator, who would sell the stock short as the stock rose in price on the assumption that it was too high and would fall. Those who had "cornered" the market would readily lend to the speculator and then immediately buy the stock the speculator sold short. At some point the speculator would have to cover his position, and the only stock available would be that held by the controlling group. At that point, the only alternative open to the speculator was to reach an accommodation with the controlling group, which normally meant a substantial profit for the members. Corners were not an important form of manipulation in the market of the 1920s. Probably the last important corner was the Piggly Wiggly Corner in 1923; breaking this corner probably marked the end of corners as a major form of market manipulation.

Pools, on the other hand, were widely used up to the time of the "crash" in 1929 and beyond. Pools were usually cooperative ventures, sometimes with as many as seventy members, but such individual operators as Drew, Gould, and Vanderbilt also successfully carried on this type of manipulation. The first step in the pool operation required that stock be accumulated for subsequent operations. In some cases this stock would be acquired in the open market. More often it was acquired directly from the firm through the use of options, since normally some of the directors and executive officers were members if not initiators of the pool. Once the pool had an adequate supply of stock, the next step was to "unload" the stock on the unsuspecting public by generating interest. This was done through publicity such as "inside tips" and a rising price and volume as members of the pool sold to one another. This activity would draw attention to the stock, and soon the public would begin buying it. At this point, the manager of the pool would attempt to unload the pool's holdings quietly and at a substantial profit. These pools were very successful, the profits

[5] Graham, Dodd, and Cottle, op. cit., p. 408.

of publicized pools ranging from about $200,000 to almost $13 million. They continued to flourish until the Securities Exchange Act of 1934 was put into effect.

Another form of abuse involved the excessive use of leverage by firms. Leverage was the watchword of the era. Two new types of firms, investment companies and public utility holding companies, utilized large amounts of leverage to obtain above-average returns for their stockholders. For example, some of the public utility holding companies were pyramided to the extent that equity made up only 11 percent of the capital structure.[6] Consequently, as long as the return on the total assets did not decline, these firms earned a substantial return on equity. Once the return on total assets did decline, however, reverse leverage magnified the effect. Investment companies faced a similar situation. As long as the prices on common stocks were increasing, the return on equity was substantial, and stocks of these investment companies sold at substantial premiums above book value. Once stock prices began to fall, the leverage in their capital structures worked to their disadvantage.

In the 1930s, it became evident that major steps were needed to restore confidence in the financial sector of the economy before progress could be made in the production of goods and services. To accomplish this, it was decided that the excesses of the 1920s could not be allowed to occur again. In 1933 and 1934, the Senate's Committee on Banking and Currency made an exhaustive study of the nation's financial institutions. This study led to the major legislation that provides the basis for the current regulation: the Banking Act of 1933, the Securities Act of 1933, the Securities and Exchange Act of 1934, and the Public Utility Holding Company Act of 1935.

Another important development of this period was the publication in 1934 of Benjamin Graham and David L. Dodd's classic text entitled *Security Analysis*.[7] This text was the first major work in the field of security analysis and laid the groundwork for the profession that developed. Graham and Dodd's approach emphasized evaluating the fundamentals of the firm to determine the value of its securities. For common stock this meant determining its intrinsic value; for bonds this meant estimating the assurance that one could place on receiving principal and interest. Since the publication of Graham and Dodd's work, the techniques for evaluating securities have been refined, but their basic tenets are still widely followed by security analysts.

Post–World War II Period   Much of the machinery of the current financial environment was developed prior to World War II, but its efficacy was not really tested until after World War II. The regulations and agencies formed during the depression were not really tested under "normal" conditions until the 1950s, and it was not until 1959 that it became evident that the tools existed

[6] Arthur Stone Dewing, *Financial Policy of Corporations*, 5th ed. (New York: The Ronald Press, 1953), Vol. 2, p. 992 footnote.
[7] Benjamin Graham and David L. Dodd, *Security Analysis* (New York: McGraw-Hill, 1934).

to control the financial and economic environment. After 1959, most skeptics were reasonably convinced that the tools were available to stabilize the business cycle.

The reason for this delay can be traced to several factors. First, during the entire decade of the 1930s, the economy was operating substantially below its potential. Consequently, this period provided no concrete evidence that fiscal and money policy could effectively combat economic slowdowns, or slow rapid expansion and the resultant inflation that would follow. Second, the decade of the 1940s provided little additional evidence, since the first part of the decade was influenced essentially by World War II. After the war, the economy experienced a slowdown as the economy was converted from wartime to peacetime. However, the Korean conflict brought this recession to an end, and again there was little evidence of the effect fiscal and monetary policy could exert. It was only after the Korean conflict that the operation of fiscal and monetary tools could be evaluated, and it was the period 1956–60 that constituted the first real test of these tools.

Figure 1-1 shows the Gross National Product for the period 1929–73 and allows the comparison of economic activity after World War II with that prior to World War II. The magnitude of the Great Depression is apparent from the decline in the GNP from approximately $100 billion in 1929 to less than $60 billion in the period 1932–33. Moreover, it did not reach its 1929 level until 1940. In contrast, the post–World War II period has had few declines in the GNP, and those that have occurred have been short-lived. The experience of the post–World War II period has led many to question whether a business cycle in the usual sense tends to exist now, but the experience of the 1970s may shed more light on this question.

In investment management, many important developments have occurred during this period. The fundamental approach to security analysis developed by Graham and Dodd still provides the basis for security analysis, but a clearly recognized division has developed between security analysis and portfolio management. For a number of reasons, much more emphasis is being placed on portfolio management than was the case previously. One important reason is that there was an increased interest in common stock investment and, consequently, the benefits that could be derived from diversification. Common stock investment represents a classic example of decision-making under conditions of uncertainty. The classic study completed by Harry M. Markowitz in 1959 provided a framework for the evaluation of portfolio decisions under conditions of uncertainty.[8] Much of the current theory on portfolio composition is an outgrowth of this study.

Note that the use of fundamentals is not the only approach to determining the value of common stocks. Technical analysis emerged as an alternative approach and has been a source of considerable controversy. An important reason for the prominence of technical analysis is the classic study published by Robert D.

---

[8] Harry M. Markowitz, *Portfolio Selection: Efficient Diversification of Investments* (New York: John Wiley & Sons, 1959).

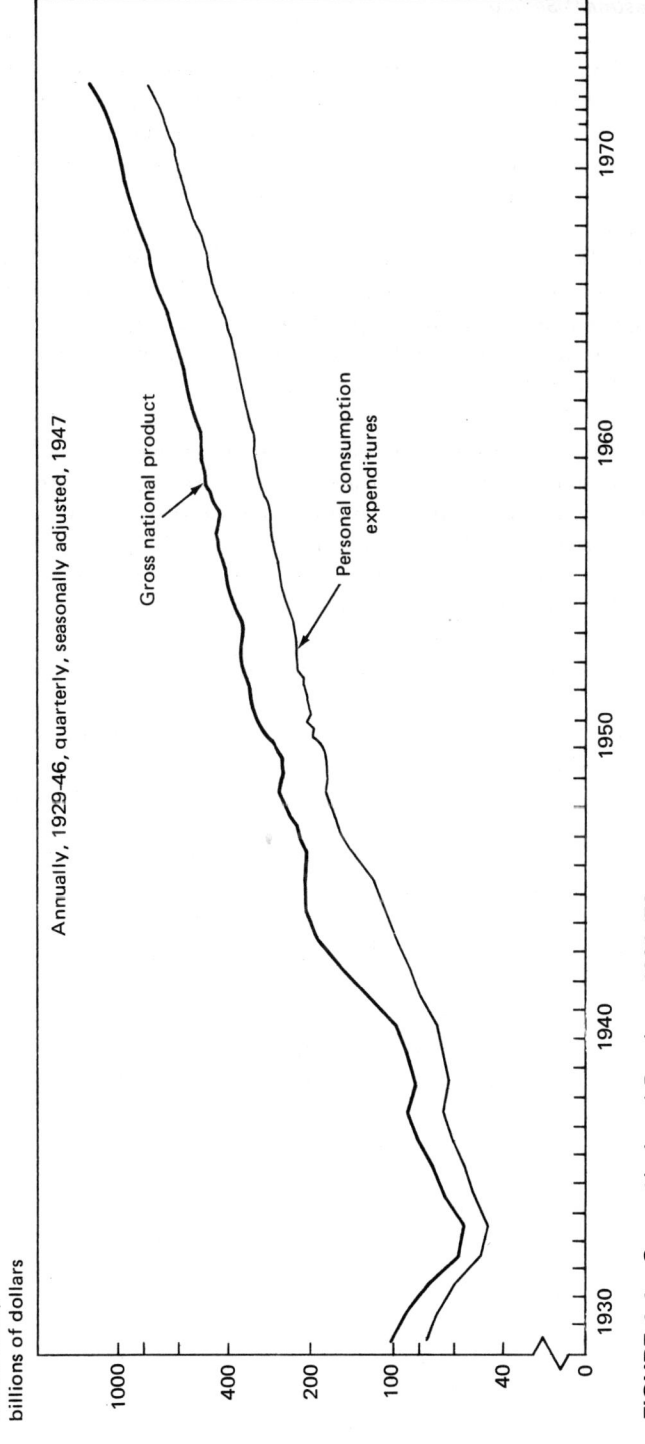

FIGURE 1-1 *Gross National Product, 1929–73*

Source: Board of Governors of the Federal Reserve System *Historical Chart Book,* 1973.

Edwards and John McGee in 1948.[9] Technical analysis holds that the value for a particular stock or stocks in general can be determined by the use of market statistics. For example, trends in prices and share volume are believed to have predictive value. The technician is basically a trader who is attempting to profit on short-term swings in the market. Fundamentalists, on the other hand, generally do not recommend trading on the short-term swings of the market, but attempt to evaluate the longer-term developments. As a result, technical analysis and security analysis represent diametrically opposed viewpoints.

An important development of the post–World War II period is the return to favor of common stocks. After 1929, common stocks fell into disfavor, and it was not until 1954 that the Dow-Jones Industrial Average reached its 1929 level. There are a number of reasons for the increased interest in common stocks; a general explanation is found in people's desire to participate in the economic growth of the nation. Common stocks are a means of doing this, especially if the business cycle can be controlled within reasonable limits. As a result, the number of shareowners has increased significantly. In 1951 the number was estimated to be 6.5 million. In 1962 the number had increased to 17 million, and by 1972 the number had increased to over 30 million.[10] Such estimates are subject to substantial error because of the difficulty of obtaining reliable information, but they nonetheless illustrate the resurgence of common stock investment.

Another aspect of the increasing interest in common stock investment is the activity of large financial institutions in the stock market. It is generally recognized that financial institutions dominate the bond market, but the influence of these institutions is steadily being felt in the stock market as well. Table 1-3 shows that financial institutions' holdings of stocks listed on the New York Stock Exchange grew from approximately 13 percent in 1949 to over 29 percent in 1972. These institutions account for approximately 70 to 80 percent of the trading on the major exchanges. Much of this growth can be attributed to the tremendous growth of open-end investment companies (mutual funds) and noninsured pension funds. Mutual funds have grown largely because of a concerted sales effort sustained by the rising level of the stock market. However, 1972 may mark a reversal of this trend, since it appears as if the industry is not receiving the market acceptance it once did. Private pension fund growth has resulted from the widespread introduction of employee pension plans by firms. Common stocks became an important vehicle because of the higher return that could be earned on diversified portfolios of common stock.

During this period, Harry M. Markowitz developed a quadratic programming model to deal with the question of portfolio composition that had nearly as much impact on investment management as the earlier work of Graham and Dodd.[11] This work had a much wider impact on finance than just portfolio

[9] Robert D. Edwards and John McGee, *Technical Analysis of Stock Trends* (Springfield, Mass.: John McGee, 1948).
[10] "Shareowners in Public Corporations," *New York Stock Exchange 1973 Fact Book* (New York: New York Stock Exchange), p. 49.
[11] Markowitz, op. cit.

TABLE 1-3 *Estimated Holdings of Stocks Listed on the New York Stock Exchange by Financial Institutions*

Type of institutions	Selected years (in $ billions)			
	1949	*1958*	*1967*	*1972*
Insurance companies				
Life	1.1	2.7	7.7	20.3
Nonlife	1.7	5.4	11.0	19.7
Investment companies				
Open-end	1.4	10.2	33.2	51.3
Closed-end	1.6	4.4	4.9	6.3
Noninsured Pension Funds				
Corporate	0.5	9.4	40.6	90.4
Other private	*	0.6	2.5	5.4
State & Local Govt.	*	0.3	3.6	17.4
Nonprofit institutions				
College & university endowments	1.1	2.8	6.0	8.7
Foundations	1.1	5.0	11.3	18.7
Other	1.0	4.0	8.6	11.8
Common trust funds	*	1.3	3.5	6.4
Mutual savings banks	0.2	0.3	0.6	1.8
Total	9.7	46.4	133.3	258.3
Market value of all NYSE stocks	76.3	276.7	605.8	871.5
Percent held by financial institutions	12.7%	16.8%	22.0%	29.6%

* Less than $50 million
Source: *New York Stock Exchange Fact Books.*

composition because it was one of the first attempts to quantify the measurement of risk. As a first step, the Markowitz approach hypothesized that the investor wanted to maximize his expected return but was constrained from doing so by his preferences for risk. Therefore, a tradeoff between risk and expected return was explicitly recognized. For a given level of risk, the investor would prefer that portfolio which provided the largest return. The Markowitz approach uses quadratic programming to determine the locus of all portfolios that will give a maximum return for a given level of risk. Once these are selected, the investor selects the portfolio that meets his risk preferences.

Probably the most important contribution of the Markowitz approach was the interest generated in portfolio theory. This applies to portfolios not only of securities but also of tangible assets and other financial assets. As indicated earlier, household and firms hold a wide range of tangible and financial assets. The question then is, what should be the mix of assets between real and financial assets? Further, what will be the divisions within these categories? The Markowitz approach provided a framework in which the process of diversification and portfolio composition could be conceptualized and studied.

Objectives of the Investor

The ultimate objective of the investor is to derive a portfolio of securities that meets his preferences for risk and expected return. Consequently, the utility of various payoffs becomes the central focus. The investor is believed to select the portfolio that maximizes his expected utility. Securities represent a spectrum of risk ranging from virtually risk-free debt instruments to highly speculative bonds, common stocks, and warrants. From this spectrum, the investor will select those securities that maximize his utility. Consequently, the objective of the investor can be stated as an optimization problem—that is, the investor attempts to maximize his expected return subject to certain constraints.

To illustrate the nature of this decision consider the situation given in Figure 1-2. Suppose the curve ABCDE represents the expected risk-return tradeoff for a number of portfolios. These portfolios may be selected from a universe of securities ranging from relatively risk-free to highly risky securities. Further, suppose each of these portfolios represents a mix of securities that will give the

FIGURE 1-2   *Hypothetical Expected Risk-Return Tradeoff*

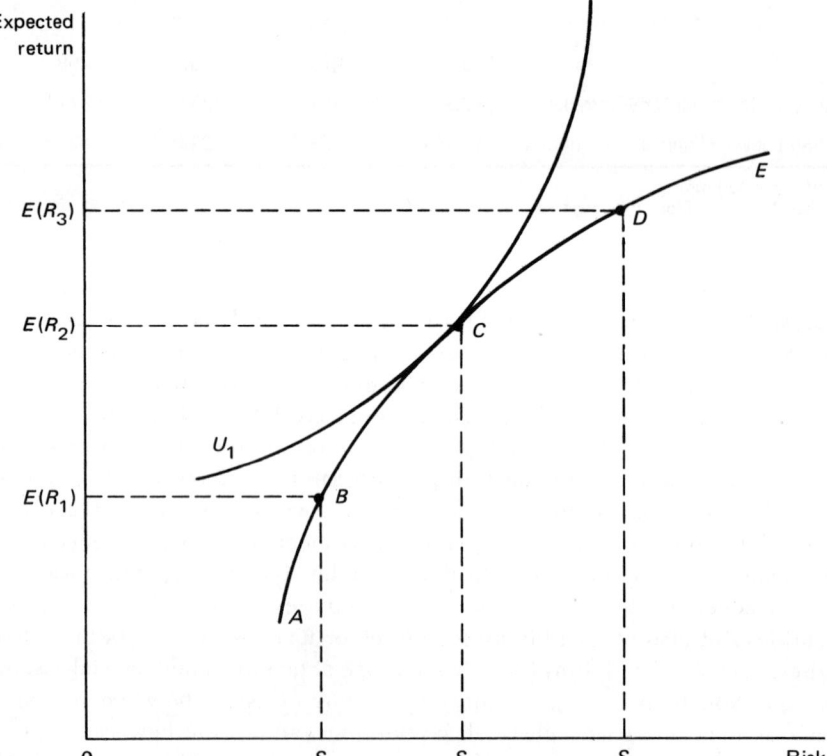

maximum expected return for a given level of risk. If an investor has the indifference curve represented by the curve U_1, he will prefer portfolio C to all other portfolios represented by the curve ABCDE. For example, portfolio B has a lower risk, but it also has a lower expected return, $E(R_1)$. This investor is evidently willing to accept more risk to obtain a higher return. On the other hand, portfolio D offers a higher expected return, $E(R_3)$, but its risk, S_3, is also higher. Evidently, our investor is unwilling to accept the risk associated with portfolio D.

Figure 1-2 illustrates that there is a wide range of investor objectives. These result from the various constraints that the investor faces. To illustrate, consider two extreme situations. First, an investor may face an extreme liquidity constraint. An example of this situation is the secondary reserves that many firms hold to meet unexpected exigencies. Whenever an investor faces a severe liquidity constraint, the securities portfolio may have to be liquidated on short notice. As a result, such portfolios are made up of high-quality, short-term instruments, usually Treasury bills. These securities minimize the loss of principal in the event of forced sale. At the same time, however, the investor must also sacrifice a higher expected return to obtain this greater safety. For example, in Figure 1-2 the investor's utility function may touch the curve ABCDE at point B instead of point C. At point B, the risk is lower than for points to the right on the curve ABCDE, but the expected return is considerably lower as well.

An example of the opposite extreme is the situation in which there are few constraints. In such circumstances, an investor is able to undertake fairly aggressive investment policies. To illustrate, consider an investor who is 28 years old, independently wealthy, and a highly successful lawyer. His net worth is placed at about $4 million, and his annual income is about $200,000. Such an individual still faces investment constraints, but they are not particularly severe. For example, this young lawyer may face a management constraint. The demands on his time may be such that he cannot manage a risky portfolio, such as a portfolio of growth stocks. This constraint can easily be overcome by the use of an investment counselor. A more important constraint may be psychological. This investor must have a temperament that will permit investing in fairly risky securities. Not everyone is willing to accept fairly high levels of risk, even though there is the possibility of a high return. Once these constraints are evaluated, the appropriate amount of risk may be determined. For example, it may be determined that this investor can invest in growth stocks. As a result, he is able to accept the higher risk that is coincident with attempting to attain a higher expected return.

It is not possible, therefore, to set forth one specific objective in investment management as is commonly done in managerial finance. The investment decision is an optimizing problem, but the objective function varies from investor to investor. The portfolio manager faces a very complex problem. It is not simply a matter of constructing a portfolio that will promise the highest expected return.

It becomes a matter of constructing a portfolio that will satisfy the needs and preferences of the investor. This may mean that a bond portfolio will be required for one investor, whereas a portfolio of blue chip common stocks is appropriate for another.

Organization of the Text

This text views the focal point of investment management as the construction and management of securities portfolios. The emphasis throughout the text will be on common stock, since investors have tended to favor it. This approach is feasible from a technical point of view because evaluating bonds is somewhat easier than common stock. Therefore, bonds and debentures will not receive as much attention as common stock.

Managing securities portfolios may be viewed as comprising two functional areas. First, the risk and return coincident with individual securities must be determined. This is the familiar area of security analysis. Second, after the security analysts have made their estimates, these estimates must be used to form portfolios that best meet the needs of the investor. This decision involves the tradeoff between risk and expected return. To arrive at this tradeoff, certain questions must be answered. Will the portfolio contain only bonds or only common stock? If a combination, what mix of the two types of securities? What stocks or what bonds? Additionally, this decision area concerns attempting to predict market behavior in order to improve the return of the investor. The investor, therefore, must decide whether to attempt to time his investments or to ignore this aspect of investment management completely. If investment timing is pursued, several different policies may be followed, ranging from trading to buying and selling at major turning points in the market. Consequently, investment timing offers several different courses of action.

Portfolio management is subject to the dynamics of constantly changing conditions. The portfolio manager's job is not finished after the portfolio is constructed. Some securities that have been included in the portfolio will not do as well as anticipated. A decision must be made as to what to do about such securities. Should they be held or sold? This decision will be based on new information provided by security analysts. In addition, if the portfolio manager attempts to improve the return on the portfolio by attempting to predict market swings, securities will be bought and sold on the basis of this policy.

This text is divided into five basic parts. Parts I, II, and III are concerned with various aspects of security analysis. Parts IV and V are concerned with portfolio management. Part I deals with the investment setting. Investment in securities takes place within the larger context of the financial and real sectors of the economy. This requires an understanding of certain institutional aspects of the financial environment, such as the operations of the securities markets, the economic environment, and current accounting conventions. In addition, security analysis commonly focuses on four different elements: economic analysis, industry anlysis, firm analysis, and market analysis. Part I, therefore, fulfills two purposes. First, it provides a necessary backdrop for investment management. Second, it provides the rudiments of economic and industry analysis.

Part II focuses on the evaluation of common stock, and Part III focuses on the evaluation of bonds and debentures. Common shares, bonds, and debentures have quite different features; therefore, the analysis of these securities will stress different aspects. The risk connected with bonds and common stocks may be divided into firm-related and market-related risks. In common stock analysis, uncertainty exists as to the level of return that may be expected. With bonds and debentures, there is little doubt about the level of the return; the uncertainty surrounds the assurance of obtaining *any* return. Firm-related and market-related risks aid in making these estimates for both bonds and common shares.

Part IV deals with the subject of constructing portfolios. There are several different approaches to this problem. The so-called traditional approach has been the mainstay of portfolio managers and is currently in widespread use. However, Markowitz's study has led to considerable research into the question of portfolio composition. Out of this research has emerged the wealth-maximization model. Chapter 13 will discuss the traditional approach and its application. Chapters 14, 15, and 16 will outline the development of more contemporary portfolio models, and Chapter 17 will complete Part IV by indicating the problems connected with measuring actual portfolio performance.

The final decision area of investment management involves the policy decision on investment timing, which is the topic of Part V. At the most basic level, this involves developing a policy of whether to attempt to predict market swings. If the portfolio manager does attempt to take advantage of market swings, he must then decide whether to deal with major market swings or shorter-term market swings. Chapter 18 contrasts the approaches that attempt to ignore investment timing. Chapter 18 also discusses techniques involving purchases and sales not related to investment timing. Chapter 19 sets forth methods which can be used to predict major swings in the securities markets. Chapters 20 and 21 deal with the important considerations involved in trading to take advantage of short-term or intermediate swings in the securities markets.

Summary

The investment environment and investment practices have changed considerably in the last 60 years. Regulation of the investment environment has increased significantly as a result of the experience of the 1920s. It has attempted to obtain full disclosure to enable the investor to make better decisions. The experience of the post–World War II period provides evidence that the economic managers are able to control the swings in the business cycle. For various reasons, common stock investment has gone through two phases. In the late 1920s there was a great surge of popularity with the subsequent catastrophic result. The post–World War II period has seen a great resurgence in the popularity of common stock investment.

Against this backdrop, the individual investor must decide what investments he wishes to undertake. Investment management is divided into two different functions: securities analysis and portfolio management. Security analysis is by far the better known of the two functions, dating back to Graham and Dodd's classic text, *Security Analysis,* published in 1934. Portfolio management is a more recent development. Security analysis deals with the function of estimating the expected return from securities over some time horizon and the risk associated with that return. Portfolio management is more general in nature. It attempts to determine the needs and preferences of the investor and then select the securities that satisfy these needs and preferences in light of current conditions. Even after the portfolio of securities is selected, the portfolio manager is required to continually re-evaluate the portfolio.

Questions

1. An individual can hold his wealth in many different forms.
   a. Contrast tangible assets with financial assets. Give several examples of each.
   b. Define economic behavior.
   c. Define financial theory.
2. How would you characterize the prevailing attitude to securities investment in the early part of the twentieth century, up to 1920?
3. How do you explain the sudden popularity of common stocks during the late 1920s? The resurgence in the 1950s?
4. What were some of the factors that led to the stock market "crash" of 1929?
5. What would you consider the major developments in investment management during the 1950s?
6. Suppose that you are considering investing $10,000 and you have the following alternatives:
   a. Treasury bills that will yield only 4 percent on the average, with an assured principal value.
   b. AA bonds to yield 7.5 percent to maturity.
   c. Common stock that currently does not pay a dividend and is selling for $25 per share. The firm's prospects hinge on a new copier. If sales materialize as expected, the price of the stock is expected to reach $75 in five years. If the copier is not successful, the price of the stock is expected to fluctuate within a range of $15–$25.
   d. Warrants to buy stock at $40 per share for the next five years. Currently these are selling at $8.

Which alternative would you select? Why? What type of investor characteristics are necessary to invest in each one of these alternatives?

7. Contrast security analysis with portfolio management.

Selected References

Eiteman, Wilford J., Charles A. Dice, and David K. Eiteman. *The Stock Market*, 4th ed. New York: McGraw-Hill, 1964. Chapters 1, 2, and 29.

Graham, Benjamin, and David L. Dodd. *Security Analysis*. New York: McGraw-Hill, 1934.

Graham, Benjamin, David L. Dodd, and Sidney Cottle. *Security Analysis: Principles and Technique*, 4th ed. New York: McGraw-Hill, 1961. Chapters 1, 4, and 30.

Jones, Lawrence D. "Some Contributions of the Institution Investor Study." *Journal of Finance*, vol. 27, no. 2 (May, 1972), pp. 305–19.

Krooss, Herman E., and Martin R. Blyn. *A History of Financial Intermediaries*. New York: Random House, 1971. Chapter 8.

Leffler, George L., and Loring C. Farwell. *The Stock Market*, 3rd ed. New York: The Ronald Press, 1963. Chapters 5, 27, and 28.

Markowitz, Harry M. *Portfolio Selection: Efficient Diversification of Investments*. New York: John Wiley and Sons, 1962.

Moore, Basil J. *An Introduction to the Theory of Finance*. New York: The Free Press, 1968. Chapter 1.

Smith, Keith V., and Maurice B. Goudzwaard. "Survey of Investment Management: Teaching Versus Practice." *Journal of Finance*, vol. 25, no. 2 (May, 1970), pp. 329–49.

Smith, Edgar Lawrence. *Common Stocks as Long-Term Investments*. New York: MacMillan, 1924.

Chapter 2

The Securities Markets

The term *securities markets* refers to the markets for the purchase and sale of securities; but this term has four different dimensions that must be distinguished. These are the capital market, the money market, the primary market, and the secondary market. Since these markets are not mutually exclusive, it may be useful to view them as cells of a matrix.

Market	Primary	Secondary
Capital	A	B
Money	C	D

The distinction between the capital market and the money market is that the capital market is the market in which long-term financial assets are traded, whereas the money market is the market for short-term instruments. Examples of capital market instruments are preferred and common stock, bonds, and debentures. Money market instruments include Treasury bills, bankers' acceptances, and commercial paper. These two markets have developed to permit the trading of long-term and short-term instruments of both firms and government bodies.

In addition to the distinction between the capital and money markets, there is also the distinction between the primary and secondary markets. These two markets are closely related, but their operation is quite different. The primary market refers to the new issues market, whereas the secondary market refers to the trading of securities after their initial sale. When a firm issues securities, either bonds or common stock, the securities are sold in the primary market, since they are new issues. Once the security issue has been sold, any future sales occur in the secondary market. In terms of the above matrix, the initial sale is represented by cell A; subsequent trading of the issue is represented by cell B. A primary and secondary market also exists for the money market, as illustrated by cells C and D. In a primary issuance, security issues may be marketed in a number of ways. These include negotiated underwriting, competitive bidding, best-efforts basis, and a rights offering. In the secondary market, securities may be listed, and traded on the stock exchanges; or they may not be listed, and traded in the over-the-counter market.

There is a substantial interrelationship between the capital market and the money market and also between the primary market and the secondary market. The interrelationship between the money market and the capital market results because users and suppliers of funds have access to both markets. Suppliers of funds have the option of either lending in the short-term market or in the long-term market. The actual decision will depend to some extent on the perceived risk and return, as well as other institutional factors. Users also have access to both markets. The reason for acquiring the funds is an important factor in determining which market is used. Generally, long-term funds are used to finance fixed assets, permanent inventories, and permanent accounts receivables, while short-term funds are used to finance seasonal needs. But firms do have the option of financing in either market depending upon their expectations. Consequently, these markets are not mutually exclusive from either the user or the supplier side.

The primary markets develop to facilitate capital formation. Secondary markets for financial assets develop only for securities with specific characteristics. The reasons for wanting to sell security holdings vary from investor to investor. For example, the investor's expectations may change. He may want to hold cash or switch to other securities. Or, he may need the funds for other purposes. He may need to liquidate some of his security holdings to make other expenditures. However, not all securities have a viable secondary market in which they can be easily sold. Mortgages are the most notable example of a financial instrument that does not have a flourishing secondary market.

In general, three characteristics must be present before a viable secondary market will develop. First, the securities must have the features that are generally desired by a fairly large portion of the investing public. These features include maturity, liquidity, marketability, and quality. There is a wide range of needs and preferences within the marketplace, and securities need to develop to satisfy all of these needs. An examination of the instruments available to the investor illustrates the complexity of this feature of the security markets.

Second, to evaluate the desirability of purchasing a particular security requires that information about the firm be readily available at low cost. A viable market for securities will not exist if costly credit investigations and negotiations are necessary. The mortgage market provides a good example. A potential out-of-state purchaser of a conventional mortgage will not initiate any action until the credit standing of the borrower is established. Such a credit check, however, may be expensive and time consuming, making the sale of the mortgage highly unlikely.

Finally, a regular secondary market depends upon a large supply of securities, so that enough securities are bought and sold to provide some continuity in the marketplace. This means that the secondary market is sufficiently viable so that one can buy and sell securities as needs dictate. It also implies that the market for a particular security is sufficiently broad to permit the development of expectations. This factor is an important reason for the extensive development of the markets for bonds and stocks.

As with the capital market and the money market, there is an interrelationship between the primary and secondary markets. The secondary market provides liquidity for the primary market by providing a readily available marketplace for securities. A secondary market facilitates the primary market in other ways as well. A viable secondary market greatly facilitates the issuance of new securities. If a secondary market did not exist, the issuer of the securities would have to seek out the potential buyers and negotiate the terms of the security issue. Obviously, this would be a time-consuming and costly process. Secondary markets, therefore, provide a valuable sounding board which can be used in the primary issuance of securities. For example, the secondary market indicates whether bonds or common stock will receive a better reception in the market, and what the terms should be. Consequently, there is a substantial amount of interrelationship between the primary and secondary markets, with the secondary markets acting as a form of barometer for the primary markets.

In investment management, the major concern is the secondary markets for long-term securities. It is well recognized that there is an interrelationship between the capital market and the money market, and the movement of funds from one market to the other is viewed as a rational part of managing securities portfolios. However, the purchase of short-term securities is normally a temporary measure. In some cases the funds are designated for a particular expenditure, or these investments may be the result of switching out of long-term securities because of a change in expectations. The interrelationship between the secondary and primary markets is also recognized, but as previously indicated, the secondary market acts as an indicator for the primary market. As a result, these two markets are closely related. It follows, therefore, that by focusing on the secondary markets for long-term instruments, we are focusing on the predominant market for securities.

Role of the Capital Markets

The capital markets play a vital role in the process of financial intermediation and capital formation. The wealth of a nation includes structures, equipment, inventories, land, monetary metals, and net foreign assets. Structures, equipment, inventories, and land are generally referred to as capital goods; they represent the allocation of income to investment for future production rather than current consumption. These capital goods combined with labor become the means for generating future income. Financial assets, however, are necessary to facilitate the process of wealth and capital accumulation. The most fundamental financial asset is money, which is necessary for the development of any form of advanced economic system because it is necessary to facilitate the exchange of economic goods. Other forms of financial assets, such as stocks and bonds, are necessary to aggregate the small pools of savings and channel these into real investment. This channeling is accomplished by financial intermediation.

Financial intermediaries, therefore, are firms whose assets consist almost exclusively of financial claims against others. Typical financial intermediaries include the following types of firms.

Deposit Institutions
Commercial banks
Mutual savings banks
Savings and loan associations
Investment Institutions
Life insurance companies
Property and casualty companies
Investment companies
Noninsured pension funds
Government pension funds
Merchandisers
Investment bankers

The assets of commercial banks, for example, consist almost entirely of financial claims against others. The only real assets a commercial bank has are its bank premises and office equipment. Much the same is true of the other financial institutions, with the possible exception of those life insurance companies that make some investments directly in real estate development.

Figure 2-1 shows the process of financial intermediation as funds flow from savers into capital formation undertaken by firms and government agencies. The financial intermediaries gather the savings of households and invest these funds in such financial assets as stocks, bonds, short-term debt instruments, and mortgages. Many financial institutions are highly specialized. For example, savings and loan associations and mutual savings banks invest heavily in mortgages, while life insurance companies invest heavily in high-quality debt instruments. In addition, as noted by the arrow at the top of Figure 2-1, some

FIGURE 2-1 *Process of Financial Intermediation*

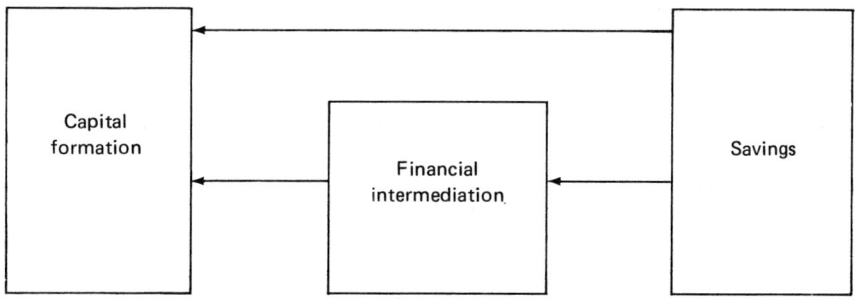

funds are converted into capital formation without the aid of the financial intermediaries. These funds come from internal sources for the firm, such as retained earnings, depreciation allowances, and contributions by owner-operators of the firm.

In the process of capital formation depicted in Figure 2-1, the secondary markets do not appear. And indeed the secondary markets do not play a direct role in the formation of capital and wealth. In the process of capital and wealth formation, it is the process of investing in real assets, such as plant and equipment, that leads to an increase in the nation's income and wealth. However, most of the transfers that take place in the capital markets actually represent the transfer of existing claims, not the creation of new capital. Table 2-1 gives an approximation of the amounts of various types of capital market instruments outstanding at selected dates since 1950. The magnitude of these outstanding claims explains why the secondary markets have taken on such importance.[1] For example, in 1972 the combined value of bonds and stocks outstanding was $1,480 billion. Not all of these securities are traded in a given year, but even a small proportion is substantial.

The Secondary Markets

The trading of securities may be accomplished in the over-the-counter market, through an organized exchange, or directly without the aid of a broker. The over-the-counter (OTC) market refers to the sale of securities off the floor of an exchange. This market generally may be viewed as a process for selling unlisted securities. However, listed securities may be sold over the counter; indeed, this was the way in which the so-called third market developed. It developed as a result of the over-the-counter trading of listed securities by large financial institutions.

TABLE 2-1 *Amount of Selected Capital Market Instruments Outstanding During 1965–73* (Market Values in $ Billions)

	1965	*1970*	*1972*
United States Government debt			
Total	$321	$389	$449
Marketable	215	248	270
State and local government debt	100	145	173
Corporate long-term debt	126	206.3	252.1
Listed corporate stock	749	902	1,228
Mortgage debt	326	452	569

Source: *Federal Reserve Bulletin,* September, 1973.

[1] Of the instruments cited in Table 2-1, the bonds and common stocks constitute the major portion of the transactions in the secondary markets. A secondary mortgage market has not developed substantially for two reasons. First, prior to the establishment of the Federal Housing Authority to insure mortgages, the costs of the credit investigation precluded the extensive trading of mortgages. Second, those who purchase mortgages tend to hold them until maturity.

The organized exchanges are institutions whose function is to facilitate buying and selling in securities listed on the exchanges. These exchanges follow an auctioning procedure in the purchase and sale of securities; in essence, they represent a large number of auction blocks. In the United States there are 13 registered exchanges and 4 unregistered exchanges. These are shown in Table 2–2. Of these 17 exchanges, the New York Stock Exchange (NYSE) is by far the largest, with the American Stock Exchange (AMEX) ranking second. In 1972, for example, the NYSE handled approximately 72 percent of the shares traded and 80 percent of the market value. The AMEX handled approximately 18 percent of the number of shares traded and approximately 10 percent of the market value of the shares traded, leaving a relatively small amount for the other exchanges. Since the NYSE is the predominant exchange in the nation, it is useful to consider it as a model of the typical operation of a stock exchange.

New York Stock Exchange

The NYSE has a history dating back to 1792, when the Buttonwood Tree Agreement was drawn up. Although there was trading in securities prior to 1792, much of this activity is unrecorded. The first dealers in securities were initially merchants and auctioneers. However, speculation in government securities led to a separation of the securities dealers from the commodity dealers, the former taking up trading at 68 Wall Street. The securities brokers were still unhappy with this arrangement because they were subject to a monopoly created by the auctioneers who sold the securities. In March of 1792, the brokers drew up the famed Buttonwood Tree Agreement. In essence, this agreement provided (1) that the brokers to the agreement would only deal with each other, and (2) that a commission of ¼ of 1 percent would be charged. This agreement broke the monopoly of the auctioneers and was the basis for the NYSE as it later developed.

TABLE 2-2 *Registered and Unregistered Stock Exchanges*

Registered exchanges	
New York Stock Exchange	Cincinnati Stock Exchange
American Stock Exchange	National Stock Exchange
Midwest Stock Exchange	Spokane Stock Exchange
Pacific Coast Stock Exchange	Chicago Board of Trade
Boston Stock Exchange	Philadelphia—Baltimore—Washington Stock
Pittsburgh Stock Exchange	Exchange
Detroit Stock Exchange	

Unregistered (exempt) exchanges	
Colorado Springs Stock Exchange	Richmond Stock Exchange
Honolulu Stock Exchange	Wheeling Stock Exchange

In subsequent years, the NYSE had many locations and went through many phases before it finally settled in its current location on Wall Street. The NYSE is neither a corporation nor a partnership. It is an association and may best be described as a voluntary association. It is similar to a corporation in that the existence of the association is not affected by the death of one of its members. On the other hand, it has many features of a partnership. First, the members are subject to unlimited liability. In other words, the liability of the members of the NYSE is not limited to the cost of a seat on the exchange; it may be substantially more. This fact explains why the difficulties of the brokerage houses during the early 1970s were so serious. Second, right of ownership of a seat is not freely transferable. Prospective members must be acceptable to the existing membership. Consequently, becoming a member of the NYSE requires more than just the sufficient funds to buy a seat.

Organization   To become a member of the NYSE requires the purchase of a seat on the exchange and acceptance by the membership. When the original signers of the Buttonwood Tree Agreement agreed to deal with those who were party to the agreement, they were supplanting one monopoly with another. At one time the NYSE was run exclusively by its members. However, after the debacle of 1929 and the new regulatory machinery of the 1930s, the NYSE dropped some of the trappings that had made it seem like a private club. In 1938 the NYSE reorganized, adopting an organizational structure that resembles a modern corporation. There is a Board of Governors whose function is similar to that of the board of directors of a corporation. The Board of Governors formulates policies subject to the provisions of the Exchange's constitution and bylaws. The actual operation of the Exchange is carried out by a staff of executive officers. During the period from 1938 until early 1972, there were 33 members of the Board of Governors. Of this group 30 members were connected with the securities industry and only three were public members. In early 1972 the composition of the Board was changed to include 10 public members and 11 Exchange members. The management of the Exchange is carried on by a President and six executive officers, all of whom are full-time salaried employees of the Exchange. This organization is shown in Figure 2–2. There are three line officers and three staff officers. The three staff officers, who report directly to the President, are the Economist, the Special Assistant to the President, and the Assistant to the President who is responsible for civic and government controls. The line departments include the Executive Vice President, Operations, the Vice President, Administration and Finance, and the Vice President, Public Relations and Market Development. Under each of these officers there are a number of functions, as shown in Figure 2-2. Operations is by far the largest department, having control of the operation of the trading floor.

Membership   The membership of the Exchange is restricted to 1,366. The members may perform different functions, which basically fall into two categories. One group of members act on behalf of their customers. A second group of members deal with other brokers or act on their own behalf.

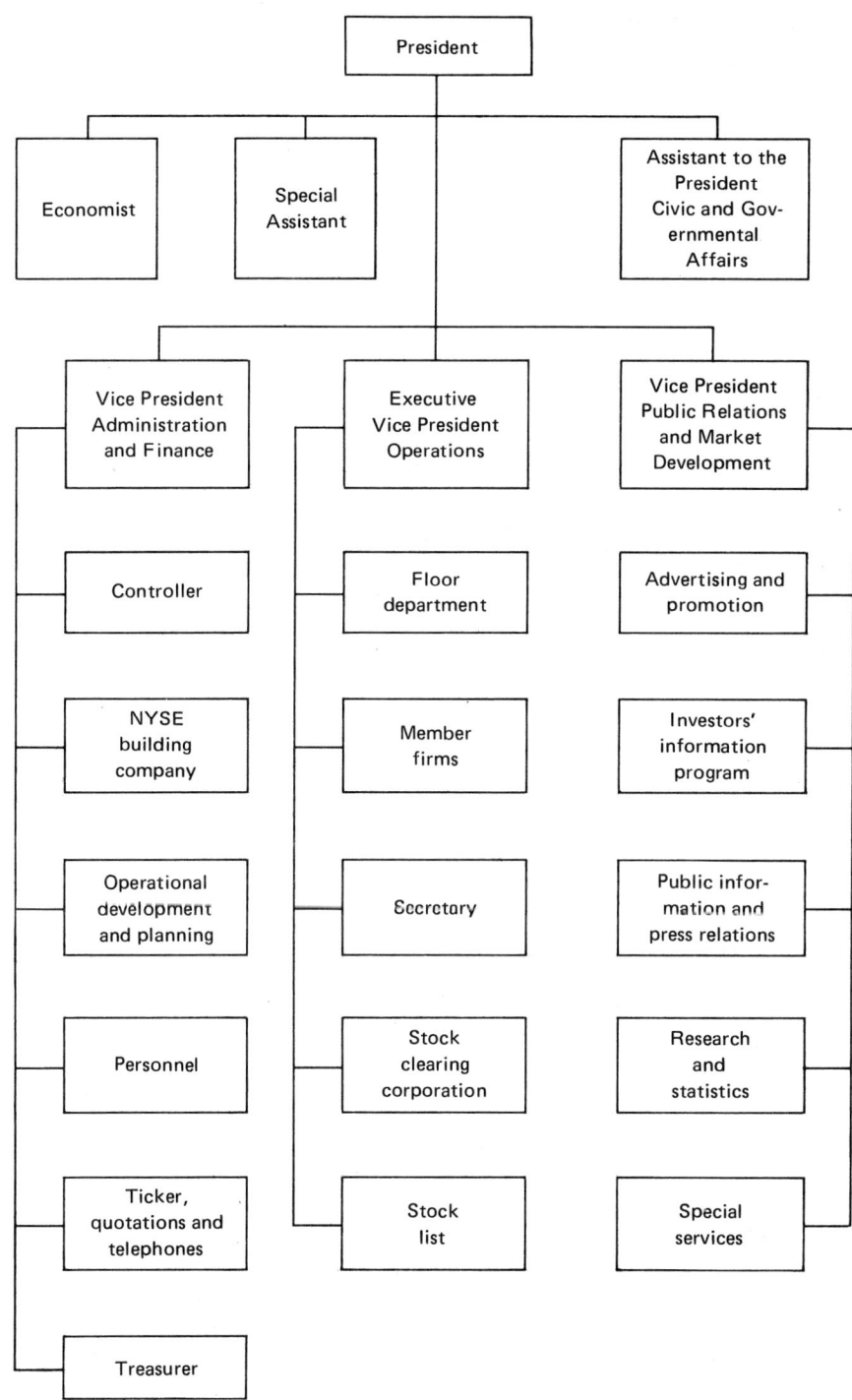

FIGURE 2-2 *Executive Organization of the New York Stock Exchange*

There are six types of membership on the NYSE. These are:

1. Commission broker
2. Bond broker
3. Floor broker
4. Odd-lot dealer
5. Specialist
6. Floor trader

The commission brokers constitute the majority of the members of the NYSE. Their function is to buy and sell on behalf of their clients. Brokerage firms like Merrill Lynch, Pierce, Fenner and Smith, Inc., and Bache and Company are examples of commission brokers. This type of membership constitutes over 40 percent of the total membership of the NYSE.

The bond broker buys and sells bonds for his customers in the same fashion that the commission broker buys and sells securities for his clients. Perhaps it is surprising that bonds are bought and sold on the NYSE, but bonds have been an integral part of the NYSE since its beginning. Bond listings appeared to reach a peak in 1930 with 1,543 issues being listed. This number declined substantially in the subsequent 20-year period, but after 1951 the number of issues listed began to increase until by the early 1970s approximately 2,000 issues were listed.

The floor broker and the odd-lot dealer represent highly specialized functions performed by the members. The floor broker normally does not belong to a member firm but owns his seat and acts on his own behalf. The floor broker's function is to execute orders on behalf of the commission brokers. In this sense, the floor broker acts on behalf of other brokers who may be too busy to execute orders. In return the floor broker receives a portion of the commission firm's brokerage fee. At times when orders are extremely heavy, the floor broker acts to reduce the work load of the commission brokers and speed up transactions. Moreover, the floor broker enables the smaller commission firms to operate with fewer memberships, since these firms can rely on his services.

The odd-lot dealer specializes in buying and selling odd-lots of securities. An order can be for either a round lot or an odd-lot. What constitutes a round lot is a matter of definition. Generally, an order in multiples of 100 is a purchase of round lots. Odd-lots are orders of less than 100. For example, a purchase of 140 shares of Du Pont stock would constitute a round-lot order and an odd-lot order for 40 shares. Round lots are not always multiples of 100. For some inactive stocks and some high-priced stocks, a round lot is 10 shares.

Most of the odd-lot business on the NYSE is done by the two firms of De Coppet and Doremus, and Carlisle and Jacqueline. Both of these firms are old and established members of the Exchange. The odd-lot dealers operate solely as dealers and never as brokers. When an odd-lot is purchased or sold, the odd-lot dealer charges an odd-lot differential. This differential varies with the price of the stock. For stocks selling at less than $55 per share, the odd-lot differential is $\frac{1}{8}$ of a point. For stocks selling at more than $55 per share, the differential is $\frac{1}{4}$ of a point. Consequently, if someone purchased 40 shares of a stock selling at 56, the odd-lot differential would be $\frac{1}{4}$ of a point, and the price of the stock before transactions costs would be $56\frac{1}{4}$. If it were a sale rather than a purchase, then the individual would receive $55\frac{3}{4}$ less transactions costs. The appropriate price to charge is determined by the most recent trade on the floor of the exchange.

Probably the most controversial type of membership is the specialist. About 90 members are specialists. These members specialize in a small number of stocks, perhaps three to five, but some deal in more. The specialist's function is twofold. First, he maintains an orderly market in those stocks in which he deals. This normally means that he should buy if the price of one of his stocks is falling rapidly, and sell if the price is rising rapidly. If one of the specialist's stocks were rising very rapidly, the specialist would meet part of the demand from his own inventory. On the downside, of course, he would buy. This action by the specialist tends to blunt sharp breaks in the market and in individual stocks, although it does not prevent them. The specialist's second function is that of a broker. He executes orders for other brokers, particularly limit orders.

To conduct his functions, the specialist must have sufficient capital. Generally, he must be able to assume a position of 1,200 shares in each 100-share unit stock that he deals. For 10 unit stocks, he must be able to take a position of 120 shares. Furthermore, he must have $50,000 in liquid assets available. One factor that tends to aid the specialist is that he is subject to special margin requirements of only 25 percent.

The specialists are obviously in a very unique position, and they have been subjected to much criticism. They have a unique opportunity to engage in manipulative practices; however, there has been little evidence of specialists actually engaging in these practices. Another criticism is that the specialists have access to inside information because of the information carried in their books. Specialists record all of the stop and limit orders placed with them, and this gives them information on the expectations of investors that is not readily available to the investing public. Whether or not the specialists use this information profitably is impossible to determine.

The floor trader is a member who acts solely for his own account. He buys and sells securities for the trading profit he can earn. He has the particular advantage of not being required to pay brokerage fees, but he still must pay transfer fees, clearing fees, and Securities and Exchange Commission fees. Consequently, the trading activity of the floor trader is not without certain costs. Trading profits of the floor traders must be sufficient to cover these and to justify the expense of a seat. The number of floor traders has declined in recent years, mainly because of higher costs and stricter regulations on floor traders.

Listing   To be listed on the NYSE is very prestigious, because the NYSE only accepts established firms. Therefore, the listing requirements for the NYSE are the most demanding of all the exchanges. The actual process of listing is conducted by the President of the Exchange and a full-time staff in the Department of Stock List. Negotiating for listing on the Exchange involves two phases. The first phase involves preliminary discussions between the firm and the staff of the Department of Stock List. The staff members of the Exchange attempt to determine whether any weaknesses exist in the firm's proposed application. If any are found, then the firm will be so advised, and the proposed application will be dropped. During this stage the firm's interest in being listed on the NYSE is not made public. Consequently, if obstacles to the firm's listing are apparent, the firm will be notified without harmful effects. On the other hand, if no obstacles are apparent, a formal application for listing may be made.

Once the listing representative is satisfied that the firm meets the listing requirements of the Exchange, the application is brought before the Board of Governors of the Exchange. The Board votes to accept or reject the application, but generally it will accept the recommendation of the Department of Stock List. A standard format for the application does not exist, but it normally includes information about the firm's business operations, financial condition, management, organization, accounting practices, and principal stockholders. In addition, supplemental information is required, including such items as the firm's charter and bylaws, prospectus under the Securities Act of 1933, and certified financial statements.

It is difficult to outline adequately the requirements for listing on the NYSE. The NYSE lists only well-established, well-known firms, and therefore it is not interested in listing speculative ventures or new firms. The NYSE prefers that such firms list their securities on other exchanges or trade over-the-counter until they have established themselves. There are five requirements that must be met before listing can take place. Two of these requirements are fairly general tests of the firm's position:

1. National interest in the company
2. Prospects of the company

The first requirement means that only firms that have generated a national following will be listed. A firm must be well-known throughout the nation, not just within a region. The second requirement is that a firm must be able to maintain its position within the industry. Just as important is the industry's position within the economy.

In addition to these two general tests, three specific tests are applied. These are:

1. Demonstrated earning power
2. Substantial assets
3. Broad distribution of stock

The demonstrated earning power is defined as income of not less than $2.5 million in the most recent year and $2 million in the previous two years. This minimum represents profits before federal income taxes. Moreover, the earning power must be demonstrated over a number of years, and it cannot include nonrecurrent sources.

The substantial assets requirement means that the firm must have at least $16 million in net tangible assets; in other words, the market value of the common stock must be $16 million. Net tangible assets are the total tangible assets of the firm minus the liabilities of the firm as shown on the firm's balance sheet. The substantial assets requirement is emphasized more than the demonstrated earning power requirement.

Finally, the broad distribution of stock normally means that 1,000,000 shares should be outstanding among the general public, and there should be at least 2,000 stockholders, each with holdings of 100 shares or more. This requirement is consistent with the requirement that the firm have a national following and should lead to a good market for the firm's stock.

Beyond these rather general provisions little can be said about the listing requirements. Much of the process involves qualitative considerations; therefore, the actual process cannot be spelled out too clearly. The preliminary negotiations between the Exchange and the firm are invaluable to the firm. The firm can raise the question of listing without any concern about the detrimental effects of refusal by the Exchange. Once the proposed application has been reviewed, the firm can confidently make a formal application with the assurance that it will be accepted.

Security Transactions

In undertaking an investment program, the initial step, of course, is to open an account, and the brokerage houses are required to take certain precautions in setting up new accounts. The brokerage houses collect certain information, particularly credit references, so that accounts of irresponsible parties are not accepted. The actual buying and selling requires a basic knowledge of the orders that may be placed as well as the use of borrowing.

Orders   There are three basic types of orders. These are as follows:

1. Market orders
2. Limit orders
3. Special orders

The simplest type of order is the market order, which simply instructs the broker to buy or sell at market. This means that the order is executed on the floor of the exchange at the best possible price at the time the order is placed. The major advantage of this type of order is the speed by which the transaction may be executed.

Limit orders generally have two dimensions. First, the investor has decided on a price at which he is willing to undertake a transaction before he contacts his broker. For example, a corporation's common stock may be selling for $35 a share. If the investor believes that it may fall to $30 per share, and if he believes that it is a good buy at that price, he may place a limit order to buy at $30 per share. The broker then must attempt to buy at $30 per share or less. The investor expects not to pay over $30 per share for the stock. Conversely, if the broker were given a limit order to sell at $38 per share for the stock, he would not execute the order for less than $38 per share.

The second dimension of a limit order is time. There are four time limits on limit orders:

1. Day orders
2. Week orders
3. Month orders
4. Open orders

Day orders expire automatically at 3:30 P.M. on the day entered. This type of order is used when conditions are expected to change from day to day. Any order for which a time period is not specified is considered to be a day order. Week orders expire at 3:30 P.M. on Friday of the week in which the order was placed. Similarly, month orders expire at 3:30 P.M. on the last trading day of the month in which the order was placed. There appears to be little advantage in placing either week orders or month orders over an open order, and specialists are not permitted to accept these orders on the floor. Brokers may accept these orders. In practice, however, week and month orders are not widely used.

Open orders have no time limit, but the investor must specify that it is an open order. The order then remains in effect until it is canceled or until the broker fails to confirm the order to the specialist. At one time open orders were carried indefinitely, but this practice led to a number of difficulties. As a result, confirmation is now required every six months and has been routinized to the point that confirmation is required on specific trading days in April and October. An open limit order is normally used whenever an investor is fairly confident about his predictions and is willing to wait until his judgment is confirmed.

Special orders take a number of forms, but the following are some of the more common forms:

1. Stop orders
2. Stop-limit orders
3. Discretionary orders

Stop orders are similar to limit orders. With a stop order, a price at which the transaction is to take place is determined by the investor. The difference arises in two ways. First, a stop order becomes a market order as soon as the market price reaches the stop price. This means that if the market price briefly reaches the stop price then the stop order becomes a market order, and the broker obtains the best price at the point in time. Second, the motives for using a stop order are somewhat different, since stop orders are normally used to protect a gain or minimize a loss.

To illustrate, consider the ways a stop order may be used to protect a gain. A gain on a long position occurs when one buys a security and its price rises. It is also possible to sell short, which means selling a security that one does not own. A gain on a short sale occurs when the security is sold and its price falls. A stop order can be used in both situations. Suppose the investor has purchased 100 shares of a certain corporation at $40 per share, and suppose these shares have appreciated to $125 per share. In addition, suppose that market conditions are uncertain. The investor would place a stop order at, say, $115 per share. If the market price begins to fall, once it reaches $115 per share, the stop order becomes a market order and the investor has preserved most of his appreciation. A difficulty always arises in selecting the right stop price. The price could drop temporarily and then bounce back up.

A short sale involves borrowing stock and selling it in anticipation of a decline in the stock's selling price. If the stock's price does decline, the person who originally sold short will enter the market and buy the same number of shares that he sold short originally. These shares are then returned to the lender and the difference between the selling price and the buying price less transactions costs is profit. A stop order may be used to portect a gain in a short sale. Suppose the particular stock is selling for $125 per share and for various reasons it is expected to decline. This stock can be sold short. Now, if it does decline in price to, say, $95 per share, a profit of $30 per share will be involved. One way to protect this gain is to place a stop order slightly above its current price, perhaps at $100 per share. If the market price of the stock begins to rise, once it gets up to $100 per share the broker will purchase the stock to fill the original short sale. The person selling short has preserved $25 of his profit, less transactions costs.

Stop orders may also be used to limit the size of the loss in both a long position and a short position. In a long position, the concern may be the price falling instead of rising as originally believed. To minimize a loss caused by error, a stop order may be placed somewhat below the current market price. If the price does fall, the broker will sell, and the amount of the loss is minimized. Conversely, in a short sale, the concern is that the stock price will rise instead of fall. Consequently, a stop order may be placed somewhat above the price at which the short sale was consummated. If the price of the stock does go up instead of down, the broker will buy at the stop price, minimizing the investor's loss.

A special type of stop order is the stop-limit order. These orders are unusual in that they combine the advantages of a stop order with the advanatges of a limit order. Normally, anyone using a stop-limit order wants to know exactly what price is involved in the transaction. He will not be satisfied with the uncertainty of a stop order. A stop-limit order may be illustrated by considering the following situation. Suppose an investor holds 100 shares of stock selling at $60 per share. There are some indications that the market may break. He could, therefore, place an order to sell at 56, stop and limit. This would mean that the broker would have to execute the order as soon as the stock reaches 56, but a price of 56 or better must be obtained. A variation of this approach is to use two prices, for example, a stop of 56 and a limit of 55. As soon as the price fell to 56, the stop order would become a market order, but in no case could the broker sell for less than $55 per share.

A stop-limit order may appear to be advantageous. However, there is one major weakness, especially in falling markets. That is, by imposing a limit order, the broker may be unable to execute the order. In falling markets the most important consideration may be to sell out and not to haggle over a half or a quarter of a point. Consequently, the stop-limit order is not widely used because it does not permit the flexibility of an ordinary stop order.

Discretionary orders give the broker discretionary power, the degree of which may vary from complete discretion to limited discretionary powers. Complete discretionary power usually means that the broker has the right to make all of the decisions connected with the buying and selling of securities. For example, the broker would have the right to select the securities to be bought and sold, the number of shares, and the time of execution. Limited discretion normally means the right to make decisions with respect to the price and the time of execution. Discretionary power is normally given to a broker on the assumption that the broker has more knowledge and experience and therefore can obtain a higher return for the investor.

Much controversy surrounds the use of discretionary orders, since there is substantial potential for abuse. The most common abuse is "churning," which means the broker is undertaking sales and purchases to generate commissions. In addition, from the investor's point of view, it is questionable whether discretionary orders are really desirable. There is some question whether the broker can devote the time necessary to actually obtain a better-than-average return. Moreover, it is debatable whether the broker really wants discretionary accounts. If he does obtain a better-than-average return for his client, his payoff is still his commissions. He receives nothing in payment for the additional work of managing the portfolio.

Short Selling   The term *short selling* was used in the previous discussion, but without a precise explanation. By definition, a short position, or short sale, means that the investor is selling a borrowed security. In contrast, a long position means that one is buying with cash. The basic assumption behind a short sale is that the market price of the particular stock is going to fall. Hence, the investors borrows the security and sells it, hoping that the future price will fall and he will be able to buy the security at a lower price and return it to the lender. The difference between the selling price and the purchase price less transactions costs represents the profit from the transaction.

There are several important considerations in any short sale. The first concern is where the borrowed stock comes from. Although this may appear to be a problem, in actual practice the broker can readily obtain the stock because he can borrow stock left with him in the "street name," from his customers, or from other brokers. Once the stock is sold, the proceeds do not go to the short seller, the borrower; they go to the lender as his collateral. This explains why individuals and firms are willing to lend their stock. They usually do not charge an interest for lending their stock, but by lending their stock they have in effect made an interest-free loan with their stock as collateral. Within certain restrictions placed by the Federal Reserve Board and the NYSE, they are able to do whatever they wish with these funds.

There are two restrictions on the use of the funds from lending securities. The Federal Reserve Board, which sets the margin requirements, has certain requirements for lenders who plan to use these funds for further investment in securities. If the lender intends to use the funds for investment in securities, Regulation T restricts the amount that can be invested in securities to the current margin requirements. Regulation T does not apply to other uses of the funds. The NYSE, however, restricts the amounts that may be turned over to the lender to 75 percent of the market value of the stock.

In addition, three other situations may emerge. First, what happens if the borrowed stock pays a dividend? If an individual borrows stock, and while it is borrowed it pays a dividend, the individual who sold short returns not only the stock when he covers his position but he also returns any dividends that have been paid. Second, what happens if the lender wants his stock back? This does not actually pose much of a problem, since the broker will simply borrow from someone else on his list and return the stock to the original lender. Finally, do margin requirements apply to short sales as they do to a long position? In the following section, margin requirements will be discussed. However, since short selling involves borrowing, the margin requirements also apply to short sales. The mechanics of applying margin requirements to short sales will be discussed below.

Margin Requirements   Margin requirements refer to the amount of cash the investor must put up when he purchases securities. For example, if the margin required is 25 percent, the investor must put up 25 percent of the purchase price of the securities in cash and he can borrow the remaining 75 percent. Borrowing funds to buy securities has a long history. The impact of margin purchases was probably the greatest in 1929. Until 1933, there were no specific rules on the amount of borrowing that may be used in connection with the purchase of securities. Before 1914 margins were probably about 10 percent, and by 1929 they had increased from 20 to 25 percent. It was not until 1933 that the NYSE introduced a margin requirement; in 1934 the Securities Exchange Act finally gave the Federal Reserve Board the power to control the amount of borrowing that may be undertaken.

Currently there are two margin requirements that affect the investor. The margin requirements set by the Federal Reserve Board are commonly referred to as the initial margin, and the NYSE's margin requirements are referred to as the maintenance margin. These two margin requirements complement each other. The initial margin only applies at the time of purchase. It is computed simply by multiplying the market value of the securities being purchased by the margin requirement. The difference between the margin requirement and the market value of the securities is the amount that may be borrowed. For example, suppose that an individual buys $3,000 worth of stock, and the margin requirement is 70 percent. If transaction costs are $45, then the individual must put up 0.7 × $3,045 = $2,131.50, and he may borrow the remaining $913.50.

The NYSE maintenance margin applies to the difference between the market value of the securities and the amount borrowed, and continues to apply as long as an account is margined. On long positions, the minimum margin is 25 percent of the market value of the securities. On short positions, the maintenance margin is 30 percent. Determining the maintenance margin is rather straightforward, and may be represented notationally as follows:

$$M = 100 \left(\frac{V - B}{V} \right) \tag{2-1}$$

where V is the market value of the securities which are collateral for the loan, and B is the debit balance. This formula may also be used to determine the initial margin.

To illustrate, suppose that an individual purchased $10,000 worth of stock subject to a 70 percent margin requirement.[2] As we would expect, the margin, determined by Equation 2-1, would be 70 percent. That is

$$M = 100 \left(\frac{10,000 - 3,000}{10,000} \right)$$

$$= 70 \text{ percent}$$

Now suppose that the stock fell substantially to $50 per share. The question is, does this mean that account is undermargined, which is the term used to denote an account which does not meet the maintenance margin requirements? Simply substituting into Equation 2-1 indicates that it is not. That is

$$M = 100 \left(\frac{5,000 - 3,000}{5,000} \right)$$

$$= 40 \text{ percent}$$

Even after this substantial decline, this stock still meets the maintenance margin requirement. In fact, as long as the stock did not fall below $40 per share, it would not be undermargined. If the stock price did fall below $40 per share, this would necessitate a margin call, meaning that the investor would need to put up additional cash or be sold out.

Short sales also are subject to the margin requirements of the Federal Reserve Board and the NYSE. The initial margin is not difficult to calculate, but the maintenance margin is not so straightforward. With the margin on long positions, the concern is falling stock prices and the resulting margin calls. With short sales, it is just the opposite. The concern is the price going up instead of down. Therefore, the following formula may be used:

$$M = 100 \left(\frac{N + X}{V} - 1 \right) \tag{2-2}$$

[2] We will deliberately ignore transactions costs, but they are added in before determining the margin.

where N is the net proceeds of the sale, X is the initial margin, and V is the market value of the securities.

To illustrate, suppose the initial margin is still 70 percent and the individual sells short 100 shares of a stock selling for \$100. The margin initially will be, as expected, 70 percent. That is

$$M = 100 \left(\frac{10{,}000 + 7{,}000}{10{,}000} - 1 \right)$$

$$= 70 \text{ percent}$$

Suppose the price of the stock increases to \$135 per share. The margin would be

$$M = 100 \left(\frac{10{,}000 + 7{,}000}{13{,}500} - 1 \right)$$

$$= 25.93$$

The margin now is 25.93 percent, which is less than the required 30 percent. As a result, this account would be undermargined and would necessitate a margin call.

On the other hand, if the price of the stock fell as anticipated, the maintenance margin would increase as expected. Suppose the price of the stock in the above example fell to \$80 per share. The margin would be

$$M = 100 \left(\frac{10{,}000 + 7{,}000}{8{,}000} - 1 \right)$$

$$= 112.5 \text{ percent}$$

There would be no difficulty with the maintenance margin in this case.

Over-the-Counter Market

The over-the-counter market is a rather misleading term, since it implies a place rather than a mechanism for buying and selling securities. It is not an organized market like the exchanges; it is a nebulous market made up of brokers and dealers. In this market the brokerage houses may be acting as either brokers or dealers. On the one hand, a brokerage house may act as an agent (broker) in filling an order for a client. The third party in this transaction would normally be another brokerage house acting as a dealer. On the other hand, the brokerage house may act strictly as a dealer selling directly from its inventory. As a result, the brokerage houses are said to make the market, since certain houses generally deal in specific securities. The OTC market performs three closely related functions:

1. It provides a market for outstanding securities.
2. It provides a market for new issues.
3. It provides a market for secondary distributions.

The focus in this chapter is on the secondary markets, but the process involved is not markedly different for primary issues.

The OTC market is a loosely knit organization of dealers and brokers who communicate by means of telecommunications networks. The National Association of Securities Dealers is the common association for these brokers and dealers. Although it lacks formal organization, the OTC market is quite pervasive. It constitutes the major market for government securities and corporate bonds. All government securities—federal, state, and local—are sold in the OTC market. In addition, a majority of the corporate bonds are also sold in this market. As a result, the OTC market is the largest market of all, undoubtedly much larger than generally realized. Most common stocks, however, are sold on the organized exchanges. The substantial interest in common stocks explains in part the widespread attention given to the exchanges.

There are usually two reasons for a firm's stock trading in the OTC market. First, the firm may not be well-known and may only have a small number of shares that are traded from time to time. Such issues may have difficulty getting listed on an exchange. Second, well-known firms may choose to have their stocks traded in the OTC market because of some of its inherent advantages. Two of these advantages are:

1. Less restrictive reporting standards are required for OTC trading
2. The firm only has a regional interest

Obtaining data on the OTC market may be difficult. Since the market is loosely knit, market quotations must be gathered from many different sources. Most large daily newspapers carry OTC market quotations, at least on a weekly basis, and the *Wall Street Journal* carries similar data on a daily basis. The chief source of information for the wholesale market is the National Quotation Bureau, Inc. This organization collects quotes on thousands of bonds and stocks. Each day these price sheets are made up and sent to thousands of subscribers. Of course, these publications only give the bid and asked price for round lots; consequently, the quote sheets on the OTC market only give an indication of the market range. An actual transaction may vary somewhat from the quoted price.

Regulation of the Capital Markets

Currently the capital markets are subject to substantial regulation. Before 1934 the exchanges were self-regulated, and firms were not subject to uniform reporting requirements. The "crash" of 1929 and its aftermath led to a complete review of the nation's financial system. The ultimate objective was to restore confidence in the nation's economy, and this required restoring confidence in the nation's financial system. An important step in this direction was the Securities Act of 1933. This act only applies to new issues, but it does set forth the reporting requirements for new issues of securities. The act with the greatest impact on the securities exchanges was the Securities Exchange Act of 1934. One other act which should be mentioned is the Maloney Act of 1938, which permits the organization of OTC market associations.

Securities Act of 1933

The Securities Act of 1933 was the first important act to regulate the securities industry, and it set the tone for subsequent regulation. Its principal purpose was to obtain fair and full disclosure of the nature of securities sold in interstate commerce. The fair and full disclosure provision has become the touchstone of securities regulation. The implication of this provision was that investors should and could make reliable decisions about securities given full and accurate disclosure of relevant information.

The registration statement filed by the firm is the first step in issuing new securities. This statement is a substantial document, sometimes over 100 pages, which provides detailed information so that the investing public may determine the investment worth of the security being issued. Much information is included in this document, but the following are some of the items contained in it.

First, it states the type of business the firm is engaged in and presents a brief historical survey of the firm's circumstances. This historical survey normally stresses the events that led to the need to issue new securities. Second, detailed information is presented about the terms of the securities to be issued. This information is particularly important in the issuance of fixed-income securities. Third, a vast amount of financial data is presented. This data focuses on various accounting statements, such as intercompany accounts, and specialized accounting schedules. Fourth, all contracts are presented in detail. This applies particularly to those between the firm and its personnel. Finally, a summary of the relationship between the firm, its directors and executives, and the underwriters is required.

Generally, a 20-day waiting period is required between filing the registration statement and actually putting the issue on the market. Obviously, the registration statement is too voluminous and technical for the average investor to use. Therefore, a summary of the information available in the registration statement is made available in the form of the prospectus. The purpose of this document is to provide information about the issue during the waiting period, and is available to all potential investors during this waiting period. Security salesmen may not contract or accept definite orders during this period. Sales can only occur after the waiting period when the security is registered for sale.

When the Securities Act of 1933 was passed, the Federal Trade Commission administered the act. However, with the formation of the Securities and Exchange Commission in 1934, the administration of the act was transferred to the SEC.

Securities Exchange Act of 1934

The Securities Exchange Act of 1934 was passed to regulate the security exchanges and the over-the-counter market. Previously, the securities markets were self-regulated, but the experience of the 1920s and early 1930s indicated that self-regulation was not sufficient. This act had four objectives.

1. To regulate the securities markets
2. To limit the amount of speculative credit
3. To control unfair practices in the organized and unorganized markets
4. To insure that sufficient information on the market is available

Administration of the Act was provided for by the formation of the Securities and Exchange Commission. This commission was made up of five men, and it was given the authority to administer the provisions of the Act, with the exception of controlling speculative credit. This power was given to the Federal Reserve Board.

The regulation of the exchanges takes two forms. First, securities must be registered with the SEC unless specifically exempted. Exempt securities basically include two types. All government securities are exempt from registration. This exemption includes securities of the federal government, state and local governments, and securities of government agencies or firms in which the government has an interest. The other type comprises securities of small intrastate firms, or firms that the SEC may deem necessary to exempt. The second form of regulation is the requirement that all exchanges involved in interstate or foreign commerce must register with the SEC. The procedure involves submitting data on the organization, constitution, bylaws, rules of procedure, and membership. Further, registration is not granted unless the exchange indicates a willingness to discipline its members. If there is some doubt, the SEC will not permit registration, or if it appears that the exchange is unwilling to control its membership, it may revoke its registration.

The importance of the firm registering its securities with the SEC is seen by the fact that members of registered exchanges cannot undertake transactions in unregistered securities on these exchanges. Consequently, if a firm wants its securities traded on an exchange, it must register with the SEC. Registering involves submitting substantial data to the SEC each year. This process has become so formalized that the same information is required for listing on the NYSE.

The other aspect of the SEC's regulation of the exchanges is its attempt to eliminate manipulation. Some manipulative practices were discussed briefly in Chapter 1. What is not always realized is that such practices as pools continued up until the introduction of the Securities Act of 1934 and the formation of the SEC. To prevent this type of manipulation, the following activities were completely barred:

1. Wash sales
2. Matched orders

3. Artificial market activity
4. Circulating false and misleading information
5. Circulating manipulative information for remuneration

In addition, certain other types of activities were brought under stricter controls, but these were not barred completely. These are

1. Pegging and price stabilization
2. Stop orders
3. Short sales
4. Puts, calls, and straddles

In attempting to control manipulation, the SEC was given the power to formulate any rules or guidelines necessary to achieve this objective.

Maloney Act of 1938

This act was an outgrowth of an early association of securities dealers, which attempted to formulate a code of fair practices for the industry. This first association was declared unconstitutional in 1935. The Maloney Act permitted the formation of OTC associations to organize for the purposes of self-regulation. As such, these associations become registered members with the SEC. Only one OTC association, the National Association of Securities Dealers, has registered. The Association is permitted to formulate rules to protect the public interest, to prevent unreasonable profits and commissions, and to prevent manipulation and fraud. As with the registered exchanges, the Association must be willing to discipline its members with fines, censure, or expulsion.

The National Association of Securities Dealers has a membership numbering in the thousands, and it has become highly organized. It has a Board of Governors and committee organizations in at least 13 districts. It has drawn up an extensive code of conduct. The securities brokers-dealers in the OTC market appear to have banded together successfully in the formation of the NASD. However, critics of the Maloney Act and the NASD question the concept of self-regulation. Undoubtedly there are strong arguments on both sides, but at this time there appears to be little impetus to change the fundamental approach.

Efficiency of the Capital Markets

Efficiency in the process of financial intermediation refers to the allocational and operational efficiency of the nation's financial institutions. If the nation's financial markets allocate funds in an efficient fashion, the participants will not reap abnormal profits. Operational efficiency refers to the costs of channeling funds from savers to the users of funds. The greater the allocational efficiency of the financial markets, the smaller the chance of earning an above-average return from the investment in securities.

Recent studies of the efficiency of the capital markets have focused on whether the market is efficient to the point where the investor cannot earn an above-average return on the basis of currently available information. This hypothesis is commonly referred to as the "fair game model," and it holds that the current price of a security reflects all of the available information about the security and the investment outlook. Empirical studies seem to indicate that the markets are quite efficient. The first tests were conducted to test the usefulness of the technical analysis as a method of obtaining an above-average return in the stock market. Technical analysis uses market statistics, such as stock prices and volume, to forecast trends in stock prices. For technical analysis to be valid, predictable imperfections have to exist in the stock markets. For example, an important part of Wall Street lore is that seasonality exists in stock prices. If this is true, the shrewd investor can obtain an above-average return by trading on the basis of this seasonal pattern. Another example is that short-term trends are believed to persist in stock prices. If the stock market is efficient, these imperfections could not exist.

The first tests of the efficiency of the stock markets led to what is popularly known as the random walk hypothesis (RWH). More will be said about this hypothesis and subsequent developments in Chapter 21; briefly, the hypothesis holds that changes in stock prices are random and therefore cannot be predicted with any certainty. Notationally, the RWH may be represented as follows:

$$P_{it} = P_{it-1} + \epsilon_{it} \tag{2-3}$$

where P_{it} is the price of stock i at time t, P_{it-1} is the price of stock i at time $t-1$, and ϵ_{it} is a normally distributed error term. In other words, Equation 2-3 indicates that the price of a stock today is equal to the price yesterday plus a change in price that is purely random. When empirical studies found this model approximated reality closely, it meant that the market was quite efficient, and that any attempts to obtain an above-average return on the assumption that certain imperfections existed would fail.

Subsequent empirical studies, however, led to a slight modification of the RWH. Empirical studies of stock price changes found that the changes did not quite meet the requirements of a normal distribution. Therefore, the RWH has been modified to the efficient markets hypothesis, which simply states that the current price of a share of stock reflects all currently available information. The only way for an investor to earn an above-average return, therefore, is to have inside information.

The bond market, on the other hand, is not believed to be as efficient as the stock market. The major reason is that the markets are dominated by large financial institutions. These institutions have certain characteristics that affect the nature of the bond market. For example, some of these institutions are tax-exempt, or at least subject to special tax laws. Most of these institutions pay cash for their purchases and thus do not buy on margin. These characteristics permit unusually profitable opportunities to emerge in the bond market.[3]

---

[3] "Stealing in the Bond Market," *Fortune's Guide to Personal Investing* (New York: Time Inc., 1968–69), p. 133.

Summary

When the term *securities markets* is used, it can refer to any one of four securities markets; that is, the capital market, the money market, the primary market, or the secondary market. It is common to associate the securities markets with the stock exchanges, particularly the New York Stock Exchange; actually, from an economic point of view, the stock exchanges and the secondary markets in general are kind of a side show. The primary markets channel funds into new real investment, whereas the secondary markets involve trading in already outstanding securities. Since most of the activity of security analysts involves evaluating securities already outstanding, the focus in this chapter was on the secondary markets. This does not mean that the markets are mutually exclusive. On the contrary, funds flow back and forth among the various markets. However, focusing on the secondary markets—in particular, on the capital markets—provides the broadest insight into the nation's securities markets.

The NYSE can be used as a model of the major exchanges in the nation, since the regional exchanges and the American Stock Exchange are all patterned after it. It has a long history, and it ascended to pre-eminence along with the emergence of New York as the leading trading center in the nation. In contrast, the over-the-counter market is an ill-defined process made up of broker-dealers. Just as the stock exchanges dominate in the handling of common stock transactions, the OTC market dominates in the handling of bond transactions. The major reason for this is that all government securities are traded in the OTC market, as are the majority of corporate bonds and debentures. As a result, it is not surprising that the OTC market is the larger of the two markets.

Appendix A: The Popular Stock Market Indexes

There are a number of stock market indexes in current use. The purpose of these is to provide a means for comparing levels of the market over time. Indexes are a well-known and reliable way of comparing time series data. The index permits a comparison of the current index level with a base period. In the construction of stock market indexes, two considerations emerge:

1. The sample used
2. The relative proportion or weight given to each stock in the index

Sampling is a problem in constructing stock market indexes, because the stocks in the index should be representative of the market as a whole or of the segment being measured. The weighting scheme becomes important because the relative importance given to particular stocks in the index will affect the values of the index.

In the subsequent discussion, the only two general types of indexes considered are the arithmetic mean indexes and the aggregate indexes, which include the four most popular indexes. The arithmetic mean types of indexes include the Dow-Jones indexes, while aggregate indexes include the Standard and Poor's indexes, the New York Stock Exchange indexes, and the American Stock Exchange Market Value Index.

Dow-Jones Indexes

The Dow-Jones indexes are probably the best known of all the stock indexes. This group of indexes includes the Dow-Jones Industrial Average, the Dow-Jones Transportation Average, the Dow-Jones Utility Average, and the Dow-Jones Composite Average. The Industrial Average is made up of 30 "blue chip" firms and is sometimes referred to as the blue chip average. There are 20 firms in the Transportation Average, and 15 firms in the Utility Average. These 65 firms then make up the Composite Average.

The Dow-Jones indexes date back to 1884, when Charles Dow began compiling these indexes. The first index was composed almost entirely of railroad issues and constituted 11 stocks. The Industrial Average which is so widely followed was developed in 1897 and consisted of 12 stocks. Initially the Dow-Jones indexes were arithmetic averages of the sum of the prices of the stocks included in the index. Notationally, this may be represented as:

$$I_{Dt} = 1/n \sum_{i=1}^{n} P_{it} \tag{2-4A}$$

where I_{Dt} is the Dow-Jones index value at time t, and P_{it} is the price of stock i at time t.

In this scheme, every stock is weighted according to its market value. In other words, high-priced stocks will have a greater effect on the index than low-priced stocks. Empirical studies seem to indicate that such a weighting scheme does not introduce any inherent bias into the index. However, bias does enter in the method of adjusting for stock splits and dividends. The basic formulation of the Dow-Jones indexes would be satisfactory if stock splits and stock dividends did not occur. However, whenever a firm whose stock is in the index splits or issues a stock dividend, an adjustment must be made. Two methods available for making such adjustment are multiplying the price of the stock by a factor or reducing the divisor.

To illustrate, consider a three-stock arithmetic mean index in which the stocks A, B, and C have respective values of $50, $60, and $70 at a point in time. The index value is given by Equation 2-4A, where n equals 3:

$$I = \tfrac{1}{3} [50 + 60 + 70]$$

$$= 60$$

At this point in time, the value of the index is 60. Now suppose that stock B is split 2 for 1. The value of the index now is *not* $\tfrac{1}{3}$ the sum of the three stock prices, or

$$I = \tfrac{1}{3} [50 + 30 + 70]$$

$$= 50$$

The correct value, 60, can be given by multiplying the price of stock B by 2, or by reducing the divisor from 3 to 2.5. In other words, if we choose to multiply by 2, the index becomes

$$I = \tfrac{1}{3} [50 + (2)30 + 70]$$

$$= 60$$

On the other hand, if the divisor is reduced, the new divisor becomes 2.5.

$$I = \frac{[50 + 30 + 70]}{2.5}$$

$$= 60$$

Either of these methods will give the same answer, but the implications are very much different.

Reducing the divisor was the method used by the Dow-Jones Averages. Bias is consequently introduced, because by reducing the divisor the relative contribution of each stock in the index is in effect being redistributed. In the above example, the contribution of stocks A, B, and C to the index before the split was

$$I = 16.67 + 20.00 + 23.33$$

$$= 60$$

After reducing the divisor to reflect the split, the contribution is

$$I = 20.00 + 12.00 + 28.00$$

$$= 60$$

Now it is clear that stock B's contribution has been reduced as a result of reducing the divisor relative to stocks A and C. This is sometimes referred to as the growth stock bias. This bias is introduced because it follows that stock B was appreciating rapidly, leading to the split. Yet by reducing the divisor, the Dow-Jones index has in effect dampened the effect of this appreciation on the index.

It is clear that the Dow-Jones Averages have a major weakness in their composition, and this explains why these indexes are criticized and why they are not widely used in research work. The divisor has now been reduced over the years, so that at mid-year in 1973 it was 1.661.

A second criticism is that the Dow-Jones Averages ignore small stock dividends. These effects are not reflected in the indexes at all. Finally, the Dow-Jones Industrial Average is criticized because it is only made up of 30 blue chip stocks and therefore is not representative of the total market. Although this observation is true, a comparison of the Dow-Jones Industrial Average with other market indexes indicate that it is a fairly good indicator of market conditions.

Aggregate Indexes

Aggregate indexes include not only the price of the stock but also the number of shares outstanding. The term *aggregate* is applied because the indexes are based on the aggregate market values of the issues included in the index. There are two well-known aggregate indexes. These are the Standard and Poor's indexes and the New York Stock Exchange indexes.

Standard and Poor's Indexes   There are four Standard and Poor's index series. These are the industrial, the utility, the transportation, and the composite. The industrial index is made up of 425 industrial stocks, the utility index is made up of 50 utilities stocks, and the transportation index is made up of 25 transportation stocks. These 500 stocks then compose the Standard and Poor's Composite Index. The construction of the S & P's indexes is accomplished by comparing the aggregate value of the stocks in the index series with the base period aggregate value, which is the average aggregate value for the period 1941–43. Notationally this can be represented as follows:

$$I_{st} = \left(\frac{\sum_{i=1}^{n} N_{it}P_{it}}{\sum_{i=1}^{n} N_{io}P_{io}} \right) \times 10 \qquad (2\text{-}5A)$$

where N_{it} is the number of shares of stock i outstanding at time t, P_{it} is the price of stock i at time t, N_{io} is the number of shares of stock i outstanding in the base period, and P_{io} is the price of stock i during the base period. The base period aggregate value, for the period 1941–43, was set equal to 10.

To illustrate the mechanics of the S & P's indexes, suppose that the aggregate value for a particular day is 10,000. That is, the number of shares outstanding for the stocks in the index times the prices of the stocks on that day equals 10,000. Further, suppose that the base period aggregate value is 1,000. The index value is

$$I_s = \left(\frac{10,000}{1,000} \right) \times 10$$

$$= 100$$

Thus, the S & P's index value is 100

It is clear that a major advantage of this type of index is that it automatically adjusts for stock splits and stock dividends. This factor was a major problem in the Dow-Jones indexes. However, the S & P's indexes do require an adjustment whenever a firm issues additional stock or when a firm is replaced in an index for one reason or another. Notationally, this adjustment process may be represented as follows:

$$BP_N = BP_o \left(\frac{M_A}{M_B} \right) \qquad (2\text{-}6A)$$

where BP_N is the new base period aggregate market value, BP_o is the old base aggregate market value, M_A is the current aggregate market value after the change in the firm's capitalization, and M_o is the aggregate market value before the change in capitalization.

To illustrate, suppose a firm in one of the S & P's indexes issued new stock in a negotiated underwriting worth \$50 million. Suppose the old base period aggregate value was \$100 million, and the current aggregate market value before the issuance of the new common stock was \$1 billion. Substituting into Equation 2-6A gives

$$B_N = 100 \left(\frac{1,050}{1,000}\right)$$

$$= 105$$

Thus, the new base period aggregate value becomes \$105 million.

The advantages of the S & P's indexes are that they are broad, covering a large number of prominent stocks, and they are not subject to the splitting bias of the Dow-Jones indexes. However, these indexes are subject to a weighting bias. That is, these indexes are weighted by the relative capitalization of each firm in the index. Hence, not only do price changes affect the index values, but this impact is weighted by the size of the firm. Large firms can be expected to have a larger impact on the index than small firms, simply because of their size.

New York Stock Exchange Index The NYSE developed its indexes in 1965. There is a composite index, and industrial index, a transportation index, a utility index, and a financial index. The method of calculating these indexes parallels that of the S & P's indexes. The only difference is the number of securities in the indexes. The NYSE Composite Index is made up of all stocks listed on the Exchange. In this manner the sampling problem is avoided. A similar approach is taken for the other indexes; they are fairly inclusive. The NYSE Composite Index is constructed by using all of the common stocks listed on the NYSE. Notationally this may be represented as follows:

$$I_{Nt} = \left(\frac{\sum_{i=1}^{n} N_{it}P_{it}}{\sum_{i=1}^{n} N_{io}P_{io}}\right) \times 50 \qquad (2\text{-}8A)$$

where the terms are as previously defined. Unlike the S & P's indexes, the base period value of the index was set equal to \$50. This was the approximate average value of shares listed on the NYSE on December 31, 1965.

In late 1973, the American Stock Exchange developed a new index to be used in place of its existing index. The index being replaced was an arithmetic index that added and subtracted the average change in price of all stocks listed on the AMEX. The new index appears to be an aggregate index including all of the stocks listed on the AMEX. In this sense it is very similar to the NYSE Composite Index. The only apparent difference is that its base period is referenced in terms of 100, instead of 50 as in the NYSE Composite Index.

These indexes have the same advantages and weaknesses as the S & P's indexes. They automatically account for stock splits and stock dividends, and they both include the weighting bias. The NYSE and AMEX indexes must adjust the base period aggregate value for changes in capitalization, new listings, and delistings in the same fashion as the S & P's are adjusted. However, there are many more changes for the AMEX and NYSE indexes than for the S & P's.

Which Index to Use

The question of which index series gives the best indication of the stock market level has caused a great deal of interest. At one point or another there have been advocates of all of the major indexes. The general consensus is that the indexes tend to move together. This is not surprising when it is recalled that the market value of the securities included in S & P's Composite Index comprise better than 90 percent of the value of the NYSE common stock issues. Even the stocks included in the DJIA constitute over 30 percent of the market value of the NYSE common stock issues. Since stocks in general tend to be positively correlated, it is logical that the indexes tend to move together. Generally, long-term trend of all the indexes is fairly consistent. It is in the short-run that the indexes may diverge. Turning points may be different, and some indexes may be more volatile than others.

Questions

1. The term *securities markets* is widely used.
   a. Distinguish between the capital market and the money market.
   b. Distinguish between the primary market and the secondary market.
2. There is a substantial interrelationship between the various markets. Explain.
3. Generally, a security must have what three characteristics before a viable secondary market will develop?
4. The terms *the nation's wealth* and *capital formation* are often used.
   a. Distinguish between these two terms.
   b. What role do financial intermediaries play in the process of capital formation?
5. There are a number of different types of members on the NYSE. Explain what these are.
6. Security transactions involve a number of different orders and operations that may be used by the investor. Define each of the following:

Marker order	Short selling
Limit order	Initial margin
Stop order	Maintenance margin
Stop-limit order	Undermargined
Discretionary order	Debit balance

7. Suppose that the initial margin is 60 percent at the time when an investor buys 100 shares of stock on margin at $75 a share. These shares have subsequently dropped to $38 per share. Is this account undermargined?

8. An investor sold short 100 shares of stock selling at $65 per share. The initial margin was 50 percent. If the price of the stock goes to $85 per share, is the account undermargined?

9. Contrast the Securities Act of 1933 with the Securities Exchange Act of 1934. What was the purpose of the Maloney Act?

10. Are the capital markets efficient? Explain.

11. Two types of market indexes are the arithmetic mean index and the aggregate index.
   a. Explain the essential difference between these two types of indexes.
   b. What are the major criticisms of the following major market indexes?
      (1) Dow-Jones Industrial Average
      (2) The AMEX Index
      (3) The Standard and Poor's indexes
      (4) The NYSE Index
   c. For purposes of evaluating market conditions, does it matter very much which index is used? Explain.

Selected References

Baumol, William J. *The Stock and Economic Efficiency.* New York: Fordham, 1965.

Cootner, Paul H. "Stock Market Indexes—Fallacies and Illusions." *Commercial and Financial Chronicle,* vol. 204, no. 6616 (Sept. 29, 1966), pp. 18–20.

Dougall, Herbert E. *Capital Markets and Institutions,* 2d ed. Englewood Cliffs, N.J.: Prentice-Hall, 1970. Chapter 1.

Feuerstein, Donald M. "Toward a National System of Securities Exchanges: The Third and Fourth Markets." *Financial Analysts Journal,* vol. 28, no. 4 (July–Aug., 1972), pp. 57–60.

Fisher, Lawrence. "Some New Stock Market Indexes." *Journal of Business,* vol. 39, no. 1, part II (Jan., 1966), pp. 191–225.

Latane, Henry A., and Donald L. Tuttle, *Security Analysis and Portfolio Management.* New York: The Ronald Press, 1970. Chapter 7.

Latane, Henry A., Donald L. Tuttle, and William E. Young. "Market Indexes and their Implications for Portfolio Management." *Financial Analysts Journal,* vol. 27, no. 5 (Sept.–Oct., 1971), pp. 75–86.

Leffler, George L., and Loring C. Farwell. *The Stock Market,* 3d ed. New York: The Ronald Press, 1963.

Lorie, James H., and Mary T. Hamilton. *The Stock Market: Theories and Evidence.* Homewood, Ill.: Richard D. Irwin, 1973. Chapter 3.

Milne, Robert D. "The Dow-Jones Industrial Average Re-examined." *Financial Analysts Journal,* vol. 22, no. 6 (Nov.–Dec., 1966), pp. 83–89.

Molodovsky, Nicholas. "Building a Stock Market Measure—A Case Story." *Financial Analysts Journal,* vol. 23, no. 3 (May–June, 1967), pp. 43–47.

Robbins, Sidney M. *The Securities Markets: Operations and Issues.* New York: The Free Press, 1966.

Schoomer, J. B. Alva. "The American Stock Exchange Index System." *Financial Analysts Journal,* vol. 23, no. 3 (May–June, 1967), pp. 57–62.

Smith, Paul F. *Economics of Financial Institutions and Markets.* Homewood, Ill.: Richard D. Irwin, 1971. Part III.

Walter, James E., and J. Peter Williamson. "Organized Securities Exchanges in Canada." *Journal of Finance,* vol. 15, no. 3 (Sept., 1960), pp. 307–25.

West, Stan, and Norman Miller, "Why the NYSE Common Stock Indexes?" *Financial Analysts Journal,* vol. 23, no. 3 (May–June, 1967), pp. 49–55.

Chapter 3

Role of Economic Analysis

The analysis of economic activity at the national level is an important aspect of investment management. In security analysis, evaluating the level of overall economic growth and the prospects of particular industry groupings is an integral part of determining the prospects of most firms. This approach recognizes the interrelationship between overall economic activity, the performance of particular industries, and the performance of individual firms. Undoubtedly some firms and some industries will outperform other firms and other industries; but there is generally a strong interrelationship among the firm, the industry, and the economy as a whole. Consequently, economic prospects should be evaluated to give an indication of the environment in which firms will be operating.[1] Industry analysis focuses on the prospects of the various industries in order to determine their prospects and to provide a backdrop for the evaluation of individual firms.

This chapter will focus on measures of economic activity and industry analysis. Economic analysis also plays an important role in other areas of investment management. For example, in the selection of bonds for a bond portfolio, forecasts of interest rates can be very useful. Business and economic indicators can be useful when an investor attempts to time his investments to take advantage of turning points in the bond market and the stock market. These applications of economic analysis will be discussed in later chapters.

Common Measures of Economic Activity

There are several measures of national economic output, but the Gross National Product is probably the single best indicator of the level of economic activity. The GNP attempts to measure the total production of goods and services within

[1] For an example of the use of this type of economic analysis, see the *Value Line Investment Survey*. For an explanation of its use, see Arnold Bernhard, *The Evaluation of Common Stock* (New York: Simon & Schuster, 1959), pp. 57–65.

the economy. This total production is normally viewed in terms of four sectors, which are

$$Y = C + I + G + (X - M) \tag{3-1}$$

where C is consumption, I is business investment, G is government spending, X is the amount of exports, and M is the amount of imports. Equation 3–1 is sometimes referred to as the demand side, since this equation focuses on the demand for goods and services. Equation 3-1 may be equivalently written as

$$Y = C + T + S \tag{3-2}$$

where T is taxes paid to government bodies, and S is personal saving. Equation 3-2 may be referred to as the supply side, since this is the source of the aggregate demand.

   Equation 3-1 visualizes a framework in which aggregate demand within the economy comprises the four sectors of households, business firms, government, and the rest of the world. Economic theorists have developed a theoretical underpinning for the behavior of each one of these sectors. In this framework the income of the nation is generated by the process of production and sale of that product. Firms produce the goods and services that are sold to all four sectors. That is, firms sell goods and services to households, governments, other firms, and the rest of the world. Ultimately, the income of the firms may be viewed as accruing to the households. In turn, households have certain options between current consumption and personal saving. Investment is equated to personal savings, since in an ex post sense savings must always equal investment.

   In practice the computation of the GNP follows Equation 3-1 quite closely. Table 3-1 shows the GNP for selected years from 1929 to 1973. The GNP as shown in Table 3-1 consists of personal consumption expenditures, gross private investment, net exports, and government expenditures. Each of these categories has further breakdowns. For example, personal consumption expenditures are broken down into durable goods, nondurable goods, and services. An item at the bottom of Table 3-1 which is of particular importance is the GNP in constant 1958 dollars. All of the GNP components shown are in current dollars. The GNP in constant dollars shows the impact of inflation on the GNP and gives an indication of the rate at which economy is expanding its physical output.

   The GNP is generally accepted to be the best measure of the nation's level of economic output, but it is not the only way to portray the aggregate income of the nation. There are three other measures, and in particular instances these may be more appropriate than the GNP. They are as follows:

   1. Net National Income
   2. Personal Income
   3. Disposable Personal Income

TABLE 3-1 *Gross National Product for Selected Years* (In Billions of Dollars)

Item	1929	1933	1941	1950	1968	1969	1970	1971	1972	1972 I	1972 II	1972 III	1972 IV
Gross national product	103.1	55.6	124.5	284.8	864.2	930.3	976.4	1,050.4	1,151.8	1,109.1	1,139.4	1,164.0	1,194.9
Final purchases	101.4	57.2	120.1	278.0	857.1	922.5	971.5	1,046.7	1,145.9	1,108.6	1,134.4	1,156.0	1,184.6
Personal consumption expenditures	77.2	45.8	80.6	191.0	536.2	579.5	616.8	664.9	721.0	696.1	713.4	728.6	745.7
Durable goods	9.2	3.5	9.6	30.5	84.0	90.8	90.5	103.5	116.1	111.0	113.9	118.6	120.8
Nondurable goods	37.7	22.3	42.9	98.1	230.8	245.9	264.4	278.1	299.5	288.3	297.2	302.0	310.4
Services	30.3	20.1	38.1	62.4	221.3	242.7	261.8	283.3	305.4	296.7	302.4	308.0	314.5
Gross private domestic investment	16.2	1.4	17.9	54.1	126.0	139.0	137.1	152.0	180.4	168.1	177.0	183.2	193.4
Fixed investment	14.5	3.0	13.4	47.3	118.9	131.1	132.2	148.3	174.5	167.7	172.0	175.2	183.1
Nonresidential	10.6	2.4	9.5	27.9	88.8	98.5	100.9	105.8	120.6	116.1	119.2	120.7	126.1
Structures	5.0	0.9	2.9	9.2	30.3	34.2	36.0	38.4	42.2	41.3	42.0	41.8	43.7
Producers' durable equipment	5.6	1.5	6.6	18.7	58.5	64.3	64.9	67.4	78.3	74.8	77.2	79.0	82.3
Residential structures	4.0	0.6	3.9	19.4	30.1	32.6	31.2	42.6	54.0	51.6	52.8	54.4	57.0
Nonfarm	3.8	0.5	3.7	18.6	29.5	32.0	30.7	42.0	53.2	51.0	52.1	53.7	56.1
Change in business inventories	1.7	−1.6	4.5	6.8	7.1	7.8	4.9	3.6	5.9	0.4	5.0	8.0	10.3
Nonfarm	1.8	−1.4	4.0	6.0	6.9	7.7	4.8	2.4	5.6	0.1	4.3	7.9	10.1
Net exports of goods and services	1.1	0.4	1.3	1.8	2.5	1.9	3.6	0.7	−4.2	−4.6	−5.2	−3.4	−3.5
Exports	7.0	2.4	5.9	13.8	50.6	55.5	62.9	66.1	73.7	70.7	70.0	74.4	79.6
Imports	5.9	2.0	4.6	12.0	48.1	53.6	59.3	65.4	77.9	75.3	75.2	77.8	83.1
Government purchases of goods and services	8.5	8.0	24.8	37.9	199.6	210.0	219.0	232.8	254.6	249.4	254.1	255.6	259.3
Federal	1.3	2.0	16.9	18.4	98.8	98.8	96.5	96.8	105.8	105.7	108.1	105.4	104.0
National defense			13.8	14.1	78.3	78.4	75.1	71.4	75.9	76.7	78.6	75.1	73.2
Other			3.1	4.3	20.5	20.4	21.5	26.3	29.9	28.9	29.6	30.2	30.8
State and local	7.2	6.0	7.9	19.5	100.8	111.2	122.5	135.0	148.8	143.7	146.0	150.2	155.2
Gross national product in constant (1958) dollars	203.6	141.5	263.7	355.3	706.6	725.6	722.1	741.7	789.5	766.5	783.9	796.1	811.6

Source: *Federal Reserve Bulletin*, May, 1973, p. A68.
Note: Dept. of Commerce estimates. Quarterly data are seasonally adjusted totals at annual rates. For back data and explanation of series, see the *Survey of Current Business*, July 1968, July 1969, July 1970, July 1971, July 1972, and Supplement, Aug. 1966.

Net National Income is the total of all payments to the factors of production. These include wages, profits, interest, and rent. Table 3-2 shows the determination of the NNI and shows the NNI for the period 1929 to 1973. The basic difference between the NNI and the GNP is that the NNI is a representation of the sources of income, whereas the GNP is demand oriented. Table 3-3 shows an alternative method of deriving the NNI, which subtracts depreciation charges, tax liabilities, and business transfer payments from the GNP. Subsidies less the current surplus of the government are added back. Either calculation will arrive at the same value for the NNI.

Personal Income and Disposable Personal Income are further refinements of the NNI. They focus on the income in the hands of households. These measures are often particularly useful in determining the prospects of certain industries and certain firms. Personal Income is the income that is actually paid out to individuals. For this reason there may be a slight difference between NNI and PI. This difference is evident by comparing the NNI and PI figures in Table 3-3. As with the NNI, the PI can be determined in two ways. Table 3-4 shows the sources of PI based upon actual payments of wages, profits, interest, and rent to individuals. Table 3-3 shows the alternative additions and subtractions that may be made to NNI to arrive at PI. Disposable Personal Income is simply PI less tax and nontax payments. The DPI is also shown in Table 3-3.

An evaluation of the national economy is a necessary backdrop for security analysis. Whenever an analyst is evaluating securities, whether bonds or stocks, his estimates presuppose a hypothesized state of the economy. Generally the postulated state of the economy involves what may be referred to as "most likely" estimates of specific economic variables. These variables are usually anticipated economic growth in either current or real dollars, the level of inflation, the level of unemployment, and monetary conditions. Firms and industries are evaluated in light of these expected economic conditions. Since growth is so important to common stock investment, the level of anticipated economic growth is of particular concern. The other factors are also important, however, since they are closely interrelated. An additional facet of focusing on growth is that industries and firms that are not experiencing a reasonable rate of growth probably are showing a decline in profits and profitability. This results because of the upward pressure on costs.

The national income accounts also provide a useful point of reference for ex post analysis as well as for forecasting. The first step in forecasting is to collect an adequate history of what has transpired. In evaluating this information, particularly with reference to industry data, the level of economic activity plays an important role. For example, when evaluating the growth of sales and earnings of industry groupings, the standard measure of performance is the growth of the GNP. The stability of the firm's earnings stream is generally evaluated over the business cycle, and the performance of the securities markets is also closely tuned to the level of economic activity. Obviously, the level of economic activity plays an important role in investment management. However, no attempt will be made at this point to discuss methods of forecasting the

TABLE 3-2 Components of the National Income (In Billions of Dollars)

Item	1929	1933	1941	1950	1968	1969	1970	1971	1972	1972				1973
										I	II	III	IV	I^p
National income	86.8	40.3	104.2	241.1	711.1	766.0	798.6	855.7	935.6	903.1	922.1	943.0	974.2	—
Compensation of employees	51.1	29.5	64.8	154.6	514.6	566.0	603.8	644.1	705.3	682.7	697.8	710.2	730.3	757.3
Wages and salaries	50.4	29.0	62.1	146.8	464.9	509.7	541.9	573.5	626.5	606.6	620.0	630.6	648.8	668.4
Private	45.5	23.9	51.9	124.4	369.2	405.6	426.8	449.7	491.9	475.8	487.1	494.8	510.0	524.9
Military	0.3	0.3	1.9	5.0	17.9	19.0	19.6	19.4	20.6	20.8	20.5	20.4	20.6	21.8
Government civilian	4.6	4.9	8.3	17.4	77.8	85.1	95.5	104.4	114.0	110.0	112.4	115.4	118.1	121.6
Supplements to wages and salaries	0.7	0.5	2.7	7.8	49.7	56.3	61.9	70.7	78.8	76.1	77.8	79.6	81.5	88.9
Employer contributions for social insurance	0.1	0.1	2.0	4.0	24.3	27.8	29.7	34.1	38.5	37.3	38.0	38.8	39.8	46.2
Other labor income	0.6	0.4	0.7	3.8	25.4	28.4	32.1	36.5	40.3	38.8	39.8	40.8	41.8	42.7
Proprietors' income	15.1	5.9	17.5	37.5	64.2	67.2	66.8	70.0	75.2	73.3	73.2	75.3	79.0	81.2
Business and professional	9.0	3.3	11.1	24.0	49.5	50.5	49.9	52.6	55.6	54.3	54.4	56.2	57.4	58.7
Farm	6.2	2.6	6.4	13.5	14.7	16.7	16.9	17.3	19.6	19.1	18.7	19.1	21.6	22.5
Rental income of persons	5.4	2.0	3.5	9.4	21.2	22.6	23.3	24.5	25.6	25.2	24.2	26.2	26.9	26.5
Corporate profits and inventory valuation adjustment	10.5	-1.2	15.2	37.7	84.3	79.8	69.9	78.6	88.2	81.8	86.1	89.6	95.6	—
Profits before tax	10.0	1.0	17.7	42.6	87.6	84.9	74.3	83.3	94.3	88.2	91.6	95.7	101.5	—
Profits tax liability	1.4	0.5	7.6	17.8	39.9	40.1	34.1	37.3	41.3	38.8	40.1	41.8	44.3	—
Profits after tax	8.6	0.4	10.1	24.9	47.8	44.8	40.2	45.9	53.0	49.5	51.5	53.9	57.2	—
Dividends	5.8	2.0	4.4	8.8	23.6	24.3	24.8	25.4	26.4	26.0	26.2	26.5	26.7	27.2
Undistributed profits	2.8	-1.6	5.7	16.0	24.2	20.5	15.4	20.5	26.6	23.5	25.3	27.3	30.5	—
Inventory valuation adjustment	0.5	-2.1	-2.5	-5.0	-3.3	-5.1	-4.4	-4.7	-6.0	-6.5	-5.5	-6.1	-5.9	-13.3
Net interest	4.7	4.1	3.2	2.0	26.9	30.5	34.8	38.5	41.3	40.1	40.9	41.7	42.5	43.4

Note: Dept. of Commerce estimates. Quarterly data are seasonally adjusted totals at annual rates. See also Note to Table 3-1.
Source: *Federal Reserve Bulletin*, May, 1973, p. A68.

TABLE 3-3 *Measures of the National Income for Selected Years* (In Billions of Dollars)

Item	1929	1933	1941	1950	1968	1969	1970	1971	1972	1972 I	1972 II	1972 III	1972 IV	1973 I
Gross national product	103.1	55.6	124.5	284.8	864.2	930.3	976.4	1,050.4	1,151.8	1,109.1	1,139.4	1,164.0	1,194.9	1,235.5
Less: Capital consumption allowances	7.9	7.0	8.2	18.3	74.5	81.6	86.3	93.8	103.7	99.7	105.3	104.1	105.6	107.2
Indirect business tax and nontax liability	7.0	7.1	11.3	23.3	78.6	85.9	93.4	101.9	110.1	106.7	108.7	111.4	113.7	116.3
Business transfer payments	0.6	0.7	0.5	0.8	3.4	3.8	4.2	4.6	4.9	4.8	4.9	5.0	5.0	5.1
Statistical discrepancy	0.7	0.6	0.4	1.5	-2.7	-6.1	-4.7	-4.8	-0.8	-4.1	-0.1	2.3	-1.5	—
Plus: Subsidies less current surplus of government enterprises	-0.1	—	0.1	0.2	0.7	1.0	1.5	0.9	1.7	1.2	1.6	1.8	2.2	0.7
Equals: National income	86.8	40.3	104.2	241.1	711.1	766.0	798.6	855.7	935.6	903.1	922.1	943.0	974.2	—
Less: Corporate profits and inventory valuation adjustment	10.5	-1.2	15.2	37.7	84.3	79.8	69.9	78.6	88.2	81.8	86.1	89.6	95.6	—
Contributions for social insurance	0.2	0.3	2.8	6.9	47.1	54.2	57.7	65.3	74.0	71.9	73.1	74.6	76.3	88.9
Excess of wage accruals over disbursements	—	—	—	—	—	—	—	0.6	-0.5	-1.4	-0.5	-0.2	0.0	0.0
Plus: Government transfer payments	0.9	1.5	2.6	14.3	56.1	61.9	75.2	89.0	99.1	94.4	95.7	97.7	108.5	109.3
Net interest paid by government and consumers	2.5	1.6	2.2	7.2	26.1	28.7	31.0	31.1	31.6	30.9	31.8	31.7	32.0	32.7
Dividends	5.8	2.0	4.4	8.8	23.6	24.3	24.8	25.4	26.4	26.0	26.2	26.5	26.7	27.2
Business transfer payments	0.6	0.7	0.5	0.8	3.4	3.8	4.2	4.6	4.9	4.8	4.9	5.0	5.0	5.1
Equals: Personal income	85.9	47.0	96.0	227.6	688.9	750.9	806.3	861.4	935.9	907.0	922.1	939.9	974.6	993.9
Less: Personal tax and nontax payments	2.6	1.5	3.3	20.7	97.9	116.5	116.7	117.0	140.8	136.5	139.5	141.1	146.4	143.0
Equals: Disposable personal income	83.3	45.5	92.7	206.9	591.0	634.4	689.5	744.4	795.1	770.5	782.6	798.8	828.2	850.9
Less: Personal outlays	79.1	46.5	81.7	193.9	551.2	596.2	634.7	683.4	740.2	714.9	732.5	748.0	765.5	793.9
Personal consumption expenditures	77.2	45.8	80.6	191.0	536.2	579.5	616.8	664.9	721.0	696.1	713.4	728.6	745.7	773.7
Consumer interest payments	1.5	0.5	0.9	2.4	14.3	15.8	16.9	17.6	18.2	17.8	18.0	18.2	18.6	19.0
Personal transfer payments to foreigners	0.3	0.2	0.2	0.5	0.8	0.9	1.0	1.0	1.1	1.0	1.1	1.2	1.2	1.2
Equals: Personal saving	4.2	-0.9	11.0	13.1	39.8	38.2	54.9	60.9	54.8	55.7	50.1	50.8	62.8	56.9
Disposable personal income in constant (1958) dollars	150.6	112.2	190.3	249.6	499.0	513.6	533.2	554.7	578.5	565.7	571.4	579.6	597.3	605.9

Note: Dept. of Commerce estimates. Quarterly data are seasonally adjusted totals at annual rates. See also Note to Table 3.1.
Source: *Federal Reserve Bulletin*, May, 1973, p. A69.

TABLE 3-4 *Components of Personal Income* (In Billions of Dollars)

Item	1971	1972	1972										1973		
			Mar	Apr.	May	June	July	Aug.	Sept.	Oct.	Nov.	Dec.	Jan.	Feb.	Mar.
Total personal income	861.4	935.9	913.6	919.4	924.0	922.9	932.9	940.0	946.8	964.6	976.2	982.9	986.0	994.5	1,001.2
Wage and salary disbursements	572.9	627.0	612.4	617.6	619.9	624.0	625.7	630.6	636.0	643.0	648.5	654.9	662.7	668.4	674.1
Commodity-producing industries	206.1	224.6	220.1	221.7	222.5	223.5	222.4	225.2	227.8	231.0	233.3	235.8	237.7	240.9	243.2
Manufacturing only	160.3	175.8	171.3	173.3	173.8	175.0	174.5	176.6	178.8	181.5	183.9	186.2	187.0	189.5	191.3
Distributive industries	138.2	151.5	148.0	149.4	149.4	151.4	151.9	152.3	153.0	155.0	156.3	158.0	159.5	160.2	161.4
Service industries	105.0	116.1	112.8	113.9	114.7	115.5	116.9	117.3	118.2	119.3	119.9	121.5	123.0	124.1	125.0
Government	123.5	134.8	131.5	132.5	133.2	133.6	134.5	135.8	137.0	137.7	139.0	139.7	142.5	143.5	144.5
Other labor income	36.5	40.3	39.1	39.5	39.8	40.1	40.5	40.8	41.1	41.4	41.8	42.1	42.4	42.7	43.0
Proprietors' income	69.9	75.2	74.2	74.0	74.0	71.6	74.3	75.4	76.2	77.7	79.5	79.8	80.4	81.2	81.9
Business and professional	52.6	55.6	54.7	54.9	55.3	53.2	55.7	56.3	56.7	57.0	57.4	57.8	58.2	58.7	59.1
Farm	17.3	19.6	19.5	19.1	18.7	18.4	18.6	19.1	19.5	20.7	22.1	22.0	22.2	22.5	22.8
Rental income	24.5	25.6	25.3	25.5	25.6	21.5	25.8	26.3	26.5	27.0	26.7	26.9	26.6	26.6	26.3
Dividends	25.4	26.4	26.0	26.1	26.3	26.3	26.4	26.6	26.5	26.7	26.6	26.8	27.1	27.3	27.1
Personal interest income	69.6	72.9	71.3	72.0	72.7	73.4	73.5	73.4	73.3	73.7	74.5	75.4	75.9	76.2	76.5
Transfer payments	93.6	104.0	100.1	99.7	100.9	101.3	102.2	102.8	103.2	111.6	115.2	113.6	113.3	114.8	115.2
Less: Personal contributions for social insurance	31.2	35.5	34.8	35.0	35.1	35.3	35.5	35.8	36.0	36.4	36.5	36.6	42.4	42.7	43.0
Nonagricultural income	837.2	909.3	887.1	893.4	898.3	897.5	907.3	914.0	920.3	937.1	947.2	953.9	956.6	964.6	971.1
Agricultural income	24.2	26.6	25.5	26.0	25.8	25.4	25.5	25.9	26.5	27.6	29.0	29.0	29.4	29.8	30.1

Note: Dept. of Commerce estimates. Monthly data are seasonally adjusted totals at annual rates. See also Note to Table 3-1.
Source: *Federal Reserve Bulletin*, May, 1973, p. A69.

level of economic activity. There are a number of large GNP forecasting models which can readily make these forecasts, and several of these models will be introduced in later chapters.

Probably the most important area of economic analysis currently used in security analysis is industry analysis. There are several ways in which industry analysis may be undertaken; the following discussion will focus on the important variables that the analysis should bring out. Industry analysis has traditionally focused on historical results. It compares the industry's sales and earnings growth with that of the GNP and perhaps other competing industries. This type of analysis provides a basis for making predictions about the future prospects of particular industries. In addition, this evaluation of the industries provides a backdrop for evaluating the performance and prospects of individual firms within the industry. An additional use for industry analysis is to single out those industries with the best prospects and then evaluate firms in these industries as possible investment candidates.

Life-Cycle Concept

The life-cycle concept is often used in conjunction with industry analysis. This concept hypothesizes that industries go through stages of growth similar to the biological life cycle. Initially, the industry is established as a result of a technological breakthrough. There are many examples of such breakthroughs—the automobile, steel processing, oil producing and refining, and the transistor. According to the life-cycle concept, the industry will go through three different phases of growth once the technological breakthrough occurs. These are the pioneering stage, the expansion stage, and the stabilization stage, and are illustrated in Figure 3-1.

Stages of Growth

The pioneering stage is usually the period in which substantial growth occurs. The industry is in a state of flux. With the technological breakthrough, a number of firms enter the new industry as venture capital flows in. As a result, there may be a large number of small firms competing for the market. With these firms competing for survival, the pattern of the industry is not established. As might be expected, this competition leads to a good many firms dropping out of the industry. Sometimes this occurs as the result of the normal course of events; sometimes it results in conjunction with business conditions. For example, a slowdown in business activity would lead to an industry shakeout whereby the weaker firms would be forced out.

Examples of the pioneering stage are easily found among the various industries in existence today. The experience of the auto industry is probably the best-known example of the life-cycle concept. In the first two decades of the

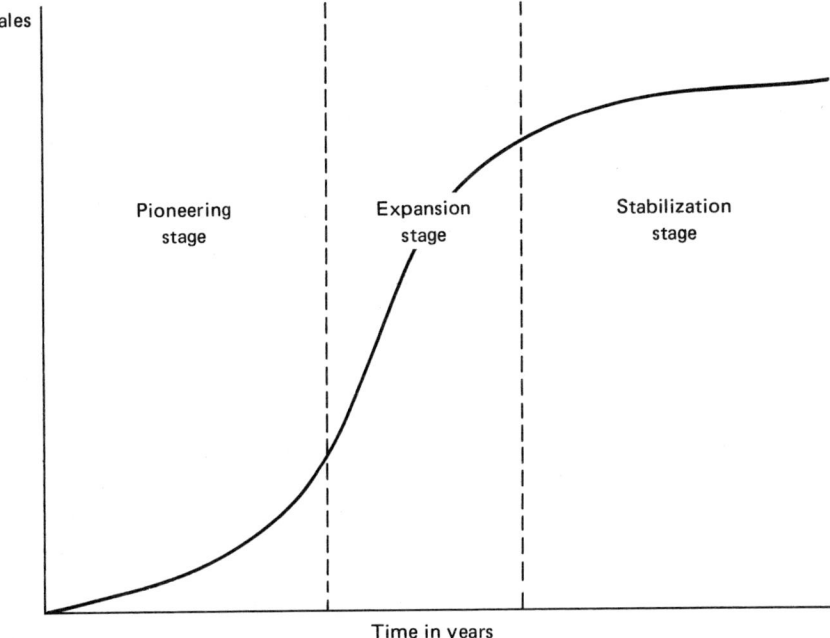

FIGURE 3-1 *The Life-Cycle Concept of Industry Growth*

twentieth century, there were hundreds of auto manufacturers. In fact, one estimate is that as many as 1,500 firms were engaged in the manufacture of automobiles at one time or another.[2] By 1920, probably 10 firms constituted the major segment of the industry, and this number has since declined to 4 firms. The auto industry showed tremendous growth during this period. Thus, while the 1900 census of business did not even mention the auto industry, by 1914 it was the eighth-ranked industry.

The expansion stage is the period of rapid growth that occurs after the pattern of the industry becomes established. The weaker firms have dropped out, and the major firms in the industry are clearly established. During this period there may be some shifting of positions within the industry, and some firms may drop out of the industry, but major movements into and out of the industry do not occur. During this stage the dominant firms in the industry are expected to record substantial growth and profitability. As time passes, however, the growth of the industry tends to slow, and the industry begins moving toward the stabilization stage. An example of this transition is vividly illustrated by the chemical industry. Throughout the 1950s and up to the mid-1960s, the chemical industry was considered a growth industry. In the mid-1960s an oversupply situation developed, mainly as a result of the petroleum industry expanding into chemical production. In the period 1965–72, the chemical industry had a

[2] Donald L. Kemmerer and C. Clyde Jones, *American Economic History* (New York: McGraw-Hill, 1959), p. 325.

number of problems. The net effect is that the chemical industry has probably moved out of the expansion stage into the stabilization stage.

The stabilization stage has been defined in terms ranging from stagnation to slow growth. It is unclear which of these terms should be applied. The important characteristic is that the industry has passed through the rapid growth stage. A number of reasons have been cited for the slowing of the growth rate, but the most important reason probably is that there is more and more competition in the marketplace.

Criticisms

Two major criticisms have been leveled against the life-cycle concept. The first is that not all industries follow the life-cycle concept as protrayed by Figure 3-1. It is argued that not all industries follow the life cycle, since some industries have been formed without a large number of firms entering the industry during its initial stage. Many of the more recent industries have not experienced the influx of new firms and venture capital commonly associated with the pioneering stage. One example is the computer industry. Large computer systems were not possible until the transistor was developed. Pretransistor computers involved a lengthy process of replacing burned-out vacuum tubes every morning before the computer could be used. With the advent of the transistor and the development of the computer, only a relatively small number of firms entered this new industry.

Whether this criticism is valid or not depends largely on how strictly the life-cycle concept is interpreted. If it is interpreted as a general framework that will explain the growth cycle of most industries, then exceptions are expected. If a stricter interpretation is required, exceptions may be viewed as being violations of the framework. It is doubtful that the original intent of the life-cycle concept was that of a universal "law." More likely it should be used as a general framework which applies in many cases.

The second criticism of the life-cycle concept is that the stabilization stage does not adequately describe the growth of a mature firm. First, it is unclear whether the stabilization stage means no growth or below-average growth. Both interpretations have been applied to this stage. Second, it is argued by some that growth during this period may be fairly volatile, with the industry experiencing reasonably good growth for several years and then little or no growth for several years. It may be said, therefore, that the growth of such an industry is anything but stable. Third, it is well known that industries can experience a revival. A recent example is the coal industry. This industry declined during the 1950s and early 1960s but has shown a marked rejuvenation with the advent of the so-called energy crisis. Again, the criticism of the stabilization stage may be a matter of interpretation. If this interpretation is rather liberal, a slow growth rate may be viewed as indicating stabilization. A strict interpretation, on the other hand, would dispute this view.

In summary, there are several criticisms of the life-cycle concept that are worth noting. It is clear that it does not hold in every case, but conceptually it provides a useful framework for viewing growth which may be applied to investment management. If the industry is in the pioneering stage, then the investor is undertaking a risky investment. If the firm he selects for investment becomes successful, the potential gain is great. The chance of loss is also great. What some investors do in this situation to reduce the risk is to invest in several firms in the industry, hoping that one or two will survive. Regardless of the strategy used, the potential rewards are great. For example, some firms specializing in advancing venture capital operate on the premise that one successful venture in 10 will provide a satisfactory return.

If the industry is in the expansion stage, many consider this to be an ideal period for investment. Some of the risk has been reduced, since some of the weaker firms have dropped out of the industry, and it is fairly clear which firms will be the leaders in the industry. Investment in these firms should lead to an above-average return because of the growth potential of the industry. Nevertheless, there is still substantial risk involved in investing in these firms since the growth may not materialize. The chemical industry provides an illustration. Consequently, the potential return is great, but the risk is also substantial.

The strategy in the stabilization stage is somewhat unclear. Some argue that industries in this stage should be avoided because of the lack of growth potential; this is true for the individual who is seeking above-average growth. Besides, a principle of conservatism would advocate avoiding industries whose prospects are clouded. However, for someone requiring dividend income with modest growth, some of these industries may be appropriate. And for the more aggressive investor there is always the possibility of a turnaround or a short-term period of growth.

It appears, therefore, that the life-cycle concept does help explain the growth of industries. It is important to remember that it is not a rigorous model; it is a generalized framework that provides a backdrop for evaluating the growth of a particular industry.

Industry Analysis

The traditional approach to industry analysis focuses on the growth of the industry and its weaknesses. The ultimate objective is to estimate the industry's performance in the future, but this prediction is based largely upon an analysis of how the industry has performed in the past. The growth of the industry is a primary consideration, and the growth of the industry applies not only to the industry sales growth but also to the growth of earnings. It is common to focus on several different characteristics of the industry's growth, as follows:

1. The rate of growth compared with the rate of growth for the economy
2. The growth record during recessions
3. The rate of growth of dollar sales versus the rate of growth of unit output

The concern over the rate of growth focuses on whether the industry is growing at a rate which is less than that of the economy as a whole. The desirable situation is for a growth rate that is greater than that of the economy as a whole, but not all industries can exhibit this growth rate. Therefore, the major concern is with those that are growing at a slower rate. The focus on recessionary periods gives an indication of the impact of recessions on sales and earnings. This impact is markedly different from industry to industry and can have important implications for investment management. Finally, by focusing on the growth of the volume of output, it is possible to isolate the impact of price increases on the growth of sales revenue and the impact of increases in output.

The analysis of the growth of industry's sales and earnings give an indication of its weaknesses, but the important step is to determine the causes of these weaknesses and determine what action is being taken to correct the problems of the industry. For example, from the analysis of the industry's growth rate, it may be clear that its growth has been sluggish. It is then necessary to determine the reason for the sluggish growth; this may be foreign competition, a technological breakthrough in a competing industry, or excessive costs making expansion of the industry uneconomical. Whatever the reason, the probable effect of these problems must be considered. It is at this stage that the industry's strengths and weaknesses become of paramount importance. Finally, of course, the focus on historical growth and the factors affecting growth is to aid in forecasting the risk and return on securities. The focus on historical performance is useful in making future predictions.

An Illustration

To illustrate the type of analysis that may be undertaken, consider the steel industry. The steel industry as a basic industry is very important to the nation's manufacturing industries. Furthermore, the steel industry is considered by many to be a mature industry without substantial growth prospects. Estimates of future growth rates vary, but the consensus appears to be 2 to 3 percent. The industry is very cyclical, with demand and therefore sales and earnings highly affected by business conditions. This factor is further compounded by the large capital investment of the industry, which in effect gives the industry substantial operating leverage. Finally, the industry has been faced with substantial foreign competition and upward cost pressures. As a result, this industry should provide an interesting study.

Basic Industry Analysis   Analysis of growth in sales revenues provides a useful backdrop for the analysis of the industry's growth in earnings. Table 3-5 presents the typical type of analysis of sales growth. Columns 2 through 4 present the GNP, sales revenues of the steel industry, and the total manufacturing segment of the economy converted to indexes, with 1963 set equal to 100. It is useful to include an additional series besides the GNP for comparison. In this

TABLE 3-5 *Growth of the Steel Industry, 1963–73*

Year (1)	GNP (2)	Steel (3)	Total manufact'g (4)	Total prod. (5)	Steel (6)	Total manufact'g (7)	Steel to GNP (in percent) (8)
		Sales indexes			*Federal Reserve's indexes*		
1963	100.0	100.0	100.0	76.5	85.8	75.8	3.2
1964	107.1	114.2	106.6	81.7	98.7	81.2	3.4
1965	116.0	126.4	117.0	89.2	106.2	89.1	3.5
1966	127.0	129.5	128.1	97.9	107.5	98.3	3.3
1967	134.4	120.6	130.5	100.0	100.0	100.0	2.9
1968	146.6	131.4	143.6	105.7	103.6	105.7	2.9
1969	157.5	139.0	153.1	110.7	113.0	110.5	2.8
1970	163.4	135.8	155.4	106.7	105.3	105.2	2.6
1971	177.9	140.7	158.7	106.8	96.6	105.2	2.5
1972	195.1	160.1	178.0	114.4	106.8	113.1	2.6
Rate*	6.9	4.8	6.0	4.1	2.2	4.1	

* Annual compound rate

example total manufacturing was used, but in some cases a closely competing industry may be used just as readily. Columns 5 to 8 give the Federal Reserve Board's production indexes for total production, the steel industry, and total manufacturing. These indexes, which set 1967 equal to 100, are in units of output and therefore are useful in determining the effect of price increases on the growth rate of the sales revenues. The last column in Table 3-5 shows the industry's size relative to the GNP. This statistic is largely descriptive, but it does give an indication of the relative importance of the industry in the economy.

Finally, the rate of growth given at the bottom of the table is a compound rate of growth for the 10-year period 1963–73. This growth rate can be easily found with the use of logarithms. The first step is to find the ratio of the initial value to the terminal value, and then with the aid of logarithms determine the compound rate of growth. Notationally, this may be represented as follows:

$$\log G = 1/n \log \left[\frac{V_{t+n}}{V_o}\right] \qquad (3\text{-}3)$$

where V_{t+n} is the terminal value of the series, and V_o is the initial value.[3] For example, the growth rate for the GNP is found by substituting into Equation 3-3 and taking the antilogarithm. That is,

$$\log G = \tfrac{1}{10} \log 1.951$$

$$= 0.02902$$

[3] Note that distortion may enter into this formulation if either the initial year or the terminal year are not typical. An extreme example would be an initial year that was a recession year and a terminal year that was a boom year. In such cases some of the distortion may be removed by averaging the first three years and the last three years. Alternatively, regression analysis may be used to find the initial value and the terminal value. Jerome B. Cohen and Edward D. Zinbarg report little difference in the two methods for growth rates of less than 10 percent. Regression analysis was found to be better where growth rates were greater than 10 percent. See Jerome B. Cohen and Edward D. Zinbarg, *Investment Analysis and Portfolio Management* (Homewood, Ill.: Richard D. Irwin, 1967), pp. 275–76.

Taking the antilog of 0.02902 gives 1.069. The compound rate of growth is found by subtracting 1 to give 1.069 − 1.0 = 0.069, or 6.9 percent. The compound rate of growth for the GNP in current dollars, therefore, is 6.9 percent. The same method may be applied to the other series in Table 3-5.

Turning now to the actual data contained in Table 3-5, it is clear that the growth of the steel industry and total manufacturing was not equal to that of the GNP. Total manufacturing was fairly close at 6.0 percent, but the steel industry did not grow nearly as fast at 4.8 percent. The Federal Reserve's production indexes indicate that the total production index and the total manufacturing index increased at approximately the same rate. As a result, the greater growth in the GNP came about because of price increases. This result is easily seen by comparing the growth rates. The GNP grew at 6.9 percent, whereas both the Federal Reserve's indexes of total production and total manufacturing grew at a rate of 4.1 percent. The differences of 2.8 and 1.9 percent, respectively, represents price increases. It is clear, therefore, that the only reason that the GNP had a greater growth rate than total manufacturing is that the general price level rose faster than manufacturing prices. In other words, the 0.9 percent of greater growth for the GNP was the result of larger price increases.

The growth of sales for the steel industry is somewhat slower than either of these other two series. Moreover, a substantial portion of this growth is a result of price increases. The rate of growth of the steel industry's sales was 4.8 percent, but the Federal Reserve's production index shows that real output of the steel industry increased by a rate of 2.2 percent. As a result, price increases accounted for more than half the growth in sales revenue, which means the steel industry is growing at a very slow rate measured in terms of physical output. Indeed, the steel industry may be at the stabilization stage in its life cycle.

Finally, the sales revenues of the steel industry as a percent of GNP indicate that the sales of the steel industry are declining in proportion to the GNP. This result must be expected, since the GNP is growing somewhat faster than the sales revenues of the steel industry. It is clear that the steel industry is an important factor in the economy, even though approximately 3 percent of the GNP may appear quite small. For example, the largest industries only amount to approximately 7.0 percent of the GNP.

The second phase of the traditional approach to industry analysis is to determine the growth in earnings for the industry. Following the analysis of industry sales growth with an analysis of earnings growth provides insight into the extent that the growth in sales is being reflected in earnings. Moreover, it also gives insight into other characteristics of the industry such as its stability over the business cycle. The normal way of undertaking this analysis is to use the Standard and Poor's industry indexes for which earnings per share data is readily available in the *Analysts Handbook*. Table 3-6 shows the growth of earnings per share and the earnings margins for the steel industry and Standard and Poor's 425 stock index for the period 1963–73. Table 3-7 presents the

TABLE 3-6 *Earnings Per Share Growth and Earnings Margins for Steel Industry and Standard and Poor's 425 Index*

Year (1)	Index of earnings per share		Operating earnings margin (as a percent)		Net earnings margin (as a percent)	
	S & P's 425 (2)	Steel (3)	S & P's 425 (4)	Steel (5)	S & P's 425 (6)	Steel (7)
1963	100.0	100.0	15.7	17.4	6.2	5.3
1964	113.9	129.0	15.9	17.4	6.6	6.1
1965	130.0	138.7	16.3	16.7	6.8	6.0
1966	138.9	139.4	16.4	16.5	6.6	6.0
1967	121.7	105.3	15.5	14.8	6.1	4.8
1968	145.0	138.0	15.8	14.0	6.1	5.2
1969	145.5	123.0	15.3	12.3	5.7	4.5
1970	128.1	78.3	14.5	9.7	5.0	3.0
1971	142.0	76.7	14.6	10.2	5.0	2.8
1972	161.6	97.2	15.0	11.3	5.3	3.3
Rate*	4.3%	0.0%				

* Annual compound rate

dividend payout ratios and the price-earnings ratios for the steel industry and S & P's 425 stock index.

The indexes of earnings per share *(EPS)* shown in columns 2 and 3 of Table 3-6 illustrate the nature of the steel industry quite vividly. For the years in which business conditions were quite good, the steel industry's growth of earnings per share was relatively good. That is, in the years 1964, 1965, 1966, 1968, and 1972, the *EPS* of the steel industry showed about the same growth as the S & P's 425; but in the years in which business conditions were not so good, the *EPS* of the industry fell considerably more than the *EPS* of the S & P's 425. For example, in 1967 the S & P's 425's *EPS* declined about 17 percent, but the steel

TABLE 3-7 *Dividend Payout Ratios and Price-Earnings Ratios for Steel Industry and Standard and Poor's 425 Index*

Year (1)	Dividend Payout		Price-earnings ratios			
			S & P's 425		Steel	
	S & P's 425 (2)	Steel (3)	High (4)	Low (5)	High (6)	Low (7)
1963	55.7	57.4	18.7	15.4	14.7	11.6
1964	53.2	45.7	18.8	16.4	13.3	11.1
1965	51.3	43.2	17.9	15.7	11.4	9.8
1966	50.2	46.4	17.1	13.1	11.4	7.6
1967	52.9	63.0	18.8	15.1	13.4	11.0
1968	51.3	48.9	19.2	15.5	10.1	8.1
1969	53.0	56.0	19.0	16.0	12.1	8.3
1970	59.2	88.2	19.0	14.0	14.4	10.7
1971	52.9	67.3	19.4	16.6	13.2	10.5
1972	47.1	50.0	19.5	17.4	11.3	9.4

industry's *EPS* declined about 24 percent. This 24 percent decline in *EPS* resulted from an approximately 9 percent decline in sales revenues for the steel industry. During the years 1969, 1970, and 1971, which correspond to the recession of 1970, the *EPS* of S & P's 425 declined about 3 percent, but the *EPS* of the steel industry declined by about 61 percent. During this period sales of the steel industry grew almost 2 percent while sales of total manufacturing grew by about 15 percent. This illustrates the cyclical nature of the steel industry, and particularly the impact of the proportionally large amount of fixed costs on its *EPS* growth.

The source of the decline in the growth of *EPS* is evident from columns 4 through 7 in Table 3-6. These show the earnings margins for the steel industry and S & P's 425 stock index. The operating earnings margin, shown in columns 4 and 5, is defined as the earnings before interest and taxes divided by the net sales; and the net earnings margin, shown in columns 6 and 7, is defined as the income available to the stockholders divided by the net sales. The operating earnings margins for the steel industry have declined from 17.4 percent in 1963 to a low of 9.7 percent in 1970. In 1971 and 1972, some improvement was experienced. The operating earnings margins of S & P's 425, on the other hand, show a slight decline over the same period from 15.7 percent to 14.5 percent. In the years of 1971 and 1972 they also showed some improvement. The net earnings margins for the steel industry declined from a high of 6.1 in 1964 to 2.8 in 1971, while the net earnings margins for the S & P's 425 reached a peak in 1965 of 6.5 percent and declined to 5.0 percent in 1971. The year 1972 was a year of improvement for both the steel industry and S & P's 425.

It appears, therefore, that a major problem facing the steel industry is operating efficiency. This factor has always been a major problem of the steel industry, but the developments of 1963–73 must be somewhat disconcerting to the industry because of the amount of capital that has been invested to improve its efficiency. Moreover, foreign competition is putting greater pressure on the steel industry. It is not clear whether foreign competition is becoming so strong because of the inherent inefficiency in the steel industry or because of genuine cost advantages.

Two other series which may be useful in the analysis of the industry are the dividend payout ratios and the price-earnings ratios. The dividend payout ratios give an indication of the proportion of earnings that are being retained in the business. The normal assumption is that rapidly growing firms will retain a large proportion of their earnings to finance this growth. Viewing the dividend payout ratios once the growth analysis is completed can determine whether this assumption is valid for the industry in question. Furthermore, this may be an important consideration in portfolio composition. Price-earnings ratios purport to indicate the market's sentiments about a particular industry or stock. Table 3-7 shows the dividend payout ratios and the price-earnings ratios for the steel industry and the S & P's 425 for the period 1963–73. The dividend payout ratios for the steel industry were not too different from those of the S & P's 425 stock index. In the years 1967, 1970, and 1971, the dividend payout ratios of the steel industry increased significantly. This does not mean a change in dividend policies, but it does reflect the poor earnings of the industry during this period. Generally, there is a tendency to maintain the level of dividend payments even though profits decline. Consequently, when earnings fell in these years, dividends remained constant, and therefore the dividend payout ratios increased significantly. It would seem that the dividend payout ratios of the earlier period are more representative of the desired policy of the industry.

The *P/E* ratios of the industry have been historically below those of the S & P's 425, indicating that investors are not willing to pay as much for the earnings of the steel industry as they are for industrial firms in general. Undoubtedly the steel industry's lackluster performance has been an important factor in this outcome. The *P/E* ratio is generally used as a method of evaluating the market's view of a particular stock or a particular industry. If the *P/E* ratio is relatively high, the market is optimistic about the prospects of the firm or the industry. On the other hand, if the *P/E* ratio is relatively low, the market is somewhat pessimistic about the prospects of the firm or the industry. It is clear that the market does not view the steel industry's prospects as being as good as manufacturing firms in general. This evaluation coincides with the above analysis.

Industry Weaknesses   From the above analysis, two basic weaknesses are evident. First, the sales growth has been sluggish. The compound rate of growth for the steel industry's sales revenues was 4.8 percent for the period 1963–73, while that for the GNP was 6.9 percent and all manufacturing firms was 6.0 percent. Furthermore, over half the growth in the steel industry's sales revenues was accounted for by price increases. Second, the growth in *EPS* has been very erratic since 1966. There have been several reasons for this. One is that recessionary periods have an extreme impact on the steel industry. During the recessionary period of 1970, the decline in *EPS* was substantially greater than that of all manufacturing firms. A major reason for this result is that the steel industry has a relatively large amount of fixed costs, which accentuates the cyclical nature of the demand for steel products.

Another major reason for the lack of growth in *EPS* has been the decline in the earnings margins of the industry. In 1963, the operating earnings margin was 17.4 percent. By 1970, the operating earnings margin had fallen to 9.7 percent as compared to 14.5 percent for the S & P's 425. In 1971 and 1972, the operating earnings margins improved somewhat. The net earnings margins tend to reflect this trend in the operating earnings margins. Essentially the decline in the earnings margins occurred after 1966, coinciding with the slowing of economic growth in 1966 and the recession of 1970. It is clear that these low earnings margins are a major problem for the steel industry and must be remedied before any significant growth in *EPS* may be expected.

Finally, a factor that is becoming an increasing problem for the industry is foreign competition. Table 3-8 shows apparent United States consumption based on imports, exports, and domestic shipments. It is apparent that net industry shipments have not increased as rapidly as apparent consumption,

TABLE 3-8   *Steel Shipments Including Imports and Exports for Period 1963–73 (Shipments in Thousands of Tons)*

Year (1)	Net industry shipments (2)	Imports (3)	Exports (4)	Apparent consumption (5)	Imports to apparent consumption (in percent) (6)
1963	75555	5446	2224	78777	6.9
1964	84945	6440	3442	87943	7.3
1965	92666	10383	2496	100553	10.3
1966	89995	10753	1724	99024	10.9
1967	83897	11455	1685	93667	12.2
1968	91856	17960	2170	107646	16.7
1969	93877	14034	5229	102682	13.7
1970	90798	13364	7062	97100	13.8
1971	87038	18304	2827	102515	17.9
1972	91805	17681	2873	106613	16.6
Rate*	2.0%	12.5%	0.0%	3.1%	

* Annual compound rate
Source: Standard and Poor's *Industry Surveys.*

although both series are somewhat erratic. An important reason for this is that imports have more than doubled their share of the apparent consumption of steel products in the nation. The growth of the steel industry suffered from this foreign competition; its growth could have been improved if it could have competed more effectively with foreign competition. Nevertheless, it is worth noting again the irregular nature of the growth of demand for steel products.

This analysis is used as a means of evaluating the prospects for an industry such as the steel industry. Once the strengths and weaknesses are determined, this information is used to make forecasts of sales and earnings growth over a time horizon. The common forecast is a sales forecast used to predict sales for individual firms within the industry. There are a number of methods commonly used for making such forecasts, such as trend analysis, regression analysis, and trend adjusted exponential smoothing. These methods are discussed in Chapter 9 and will not be discussed here.

Importance of Industry Analysis

Substantial criticism has been leveled at the use of the industry concept and industry analysis. The performance of the industry has been widely used as a means of measuring the performance of individual firms within the industry. Thus, in ratio analysis, one widely used standard is the particular industry to which the firm belongs. Another use is to analyze industry data as a means of characterizing the firms within the industry. The traditional approach to portfolio composition, for example, which will be discussed in Chapter 13, selects stock to meet various portfolio objectives on the basis of industry characteristics. Regardless of the intended use of industry data, its relevance has been criticized.

The major criticism of industry analysis is that the firms within the industry groupings lack homogeneity, reducing the usefulness of such data for predictive purposes. There have been a number of studies that have questioned the meaningfulness of the concept of the industry for this reason. For example, Gordon Donaldson questioned the use of the industry average as a blanket standard for determining the debt capacity of the firm.[4] He was unwilling to accept the industry average as a guide in determining the debt capacity of a particular firm. Instead, he felt that each firm should be viewed in terms of its particular situation.

Studies by Norman O. Miller and Edwin J. Elton and Martin J. Gruber follow in the same vein.[5] Miller's study was concerned with the evaluation of growth stocks and particularly whether investors should pursue investments in industries whose sales have shown substantial growth. In other words, he was concerned with the use of the industry concept as a screening device to determine growth situations. He found that above-average industry sales growth did not lead to above-average earnings growth, and he concluded that there was a wide divergence in profitability among firms within a given industry. The Elton and Gruber study was concerned with making industry forecasts and the methods of improving these forecasts. Their findings were that the Standard Industrial Classifications developed by the Department of Commerce lack the homogeneity necessary to give reasonably accurate industry sales forecasts. They also point out that many economic forecasting models are extremely sensitive to the sample data to which they are applied. Thus, the lack of homogeneity among firms within an industry grouping takes on additional importance.

Moreover, evidence on the usefulness of historical industry data as a predictor of future industry performance appears to indicate that it is of little value. This problem will emerge again with respect to the forecasting of earnings per share. It has been found that year-to-year changes in earnings per share are virtually random, and much the same phenomenon has been found for changes in industry performance. Milford S. Tysseland tested the hypothesis that past industry performance had little predictive value.[6] Tysseland was concerned with using past industry market performance as a method of forecasting the future return that may be expected. He concluded that past rates of return have little value for predicting future rates of return. In addition, he found a great inconsistency in the returns of industries over time. He concluded that the

---

[4] Gordon Donaldson, "New Framework for Corporate Debt Policy," *Harvard Business Review,* vol. 40, no. 2 (Mar.–Apr., 1962), p. 119.
[5] Norman O. Miller, "Are Growth Stocks Really Profitable?" *Business Horizons,* vol. 1, no. 5 (Winter, 1958–59), pp. 45–50; and Edwin J. Elton and Martin J. Gruber, "Improved Forecasting Through the Design of Homogeneous Groups," *Journal of Business,* vol. 44, no. 4 (Oct., 1971), pp. 432–50.
[6] Milford S. Tysseland, "Further Tests of the Validity of the Industry Approach to Investment Analysis," *Journal of Financial and Quantitative Analysis,* vol. 6, no. 2 (Mar., 1971), pp. 835–49.

industry forecasts available from the various financial services were of little practical value.

The question of the usefulness of industry analysis is unresolved. The industry approach is widely used in business and governmental studies; this seems to imply a general acceptance of the concept. Nevertheless, the number of studies that have questioned the industry approach has increased, giving additional support to this point of view. For example, it is generally accepted that firms within an industry should be analyzed and compared because of the wide divergence of performance among firms within the same industry. This recognizes the lack of homogeneity among firms within an industry grouping. Furthermore, the emergence of a group of firms known as conglomerates and the tendency toward diversification in general reduces the meaningfulness of the industry approach. Consequently, the industry concept presents some difficulties. On the one hand, it is common to attribute certain characteristics to specific industries, yet individual firms within these industries may not exhibit these characteristics. The real test of industry analysis, therefore, will be whether it improves forecasts for individual firms.

Summary

It is common to focus on the prospects of the economy and industry groupings as an aid in evaluating the prospects of individual firms. Economic conditions generally have a direct impact on the various industries in the economy and the firms within the industries. There are wide variations among industries within the economy and among firms within the industries. For this reason, not only is economic analysis conducted, but an analysis of industry and the firm is also required. Economic analysis may be undertaken by simply focusing on the national income accounts, and in particular on the GNP. Such forecasts are useful in the preparation of other forecasts. For example, forecasting industry sales and earnings may begin with a forecast of the GNP.

It is common to focus on the prospects of the industry as a method of characterizing the firms within the industry. For example, industries may be referred to as growth industries, mature industries, or cyclical industries. Since appreciation is an important part of the return to the common stockholder, the life-cycle concept has been used to characterize the growth of an industry. This concept associates the growth of an industry with the biological life cycle; accordingly, firms are believed to go through various stages of growth. These stages are commonly referred to as the pioneering stage, the expansion stage, and the stabilization stage. Critics point out that this concept does not apply in every case, nor does industry growth follow the life cycle strictly in all cases. Nevertheless, this concept does offer a way to conceptualize the growth of an industry.

In the evaluation of industry prospects, the traditional approach has been to evaluate the historical growth of sales and earnings of the industry. This growth is generally compared to that of the GNP. Beyond this, an attempt is made to determine the strengths and weaknesses of the industry and the effect these will have on future growth of the industry. Forecasts of industry sales and earnings may be accomplished by means of some form of linear regression analysis or perhaps exponential smoothing, and will most likely reflect the analyst's evaluation of the firm's prospects based upon its historical performance. These techniques for forecasting will be discussed in more detail in Chapter 9.

Questions

1. Distinguish between the following terms: Gross National Product, Net National Income, Personal Income, Disposable Personal Income.
2. How may economic analysis be used to aid the security analyst?
3. What are the purposes of industry analysis?
4. The life-cycle concept is occasionally used to describe the growth of industries.
    a. What are the major features of this concept?
    b. What are the criticisms of this concept?
    c. Could you apply the life-cycle concept to the aluminum industry? Conduct the necessary research to support your position.
5. The rate of growth of the industry is an important concern in industry analysis.
    a. What are the common characteristics that this analysis should focus on?
    b. What is the purpose of determining the weaknesses of the industry?
6. Research Problem: Undertake a historical analysis of one of the following industry groupings:

    Automobile   Cosmetics
    Motion Pictures   Office and Business Equipment
    Aluminum   Electronics
    Soaps   Air Transport
    Beverages-Brewers   Home Furnishings

7. The usefulness of industry analysis has been questioned. How has this analysis been criticized?

Selected References

Almon, Clopper, Jr. *The American Economy to 1975: An Interindustry Forecast.* New York: Harper & Row, 1966.

Amling, Frederick. *Investments: An Introduction to Analysis and Management,* 2d ed. Englewood Cliffs, N.J.: Prentice-Hall, 1970. Chapter 10.

Berkwitt, George J. "Input-Output: Management's Newest Tool." *Dun's Review*, vol. 97, no. 3 (Mar., 1971), pp. 57–59.

Bonham, Howard B., Jr. "Input-Output in Common Stock Analysis." *Financial Analysts Journal*, vol. 23, no. 1 (Jan.–Feb., 1967), pp. 19–29.

Bourque, Philip J. *Forecasting with Input-Output.* Business Studies No. 5; Seattle: University of Washington Graduate School of Business Administration.

Brigham, Eugene F., and James L. Pappas. "Rates of Return on Common Stock." *Journal of Business*, vol. 42, no. 3 (July, 1969), pp. 302–17.

Cohen, Jerome B., Edward D. Zinbarg, and Arthur Zeikel. *Investment Analysis and Portfolio Management*, rev. ed. Homewood, Ill.: Richard D. Irwin, 1973. Chapter 6.

Elliott-Jones, M. F. "An Introduction to Input-Output Analysis." *Conference Board Record*, vol. 7, no. 1 (Jan., 1971), pp. 16–20.

Elton, Edwin J., and Martin J. Gruber. "Homogeneous Groups and the Testing of Economic Hypotheses." *Journal of Financial and Quantitative Analysis*, vol. 4, no. 5 (Jan., 1970), pp. 581–603.

————. "Improved Forecasting Through the Design of Homogeneous Groups." *Journal of Business*, vol. 44, no. 4 (Oct., 1971), pp. 432–51.

Latane, Henry A., and Donald L. Tuttle. "Framework for Forming Probability Beliefs." *Financial Analysts Journal*, vol. 24, no. 4 (July–Aug., 1968), pp. 51–62.

Miller, Norman O. "Are Growth Stocks Really Profitable?" *Business Horizons*, vol. 1, no. 5 (Winter, 1958–59), pp. 45–50.

Palyi, Melchior, "Input-Output Analysis Examined." *Commercial and Financial Chronicle*, vol. 211, no. 6992 (May 7, 1970), p. 3.

Tysseland, Milford S. "Further Tests of the Validity of the Industry Approach to Investment Analysis." *Journal of Financial and Quantitative Analysis*, vol. 6, no. 2 (Mar., 1971), pp. 835–49.

Chapter 4

Financial Statement Analysis

The starting point in the analysis of the firm is an evaluation of the firm's historical performance. Undertaking this evaluation requires a heavy reliance on its published financial statements. These statements are probably the most important and most controversial source of information on the firm. They are important because they indicate the general condition of the firm; they are controversial because of the variations that exist from year to year and from firm to firm. In other words, since a firm normally can record a transaction in several different ways, there may not be uniform treatment of a transaction by a firm over time, and there may not be uniform treatment of the transaction among firms. As a result, before an evaluation of the firm's performance may be undertaken, the financial statements must be analyzed to determine whether the reported results of the firm truly reflect its operating position. Particular emphasis must be placed upon determining the "true" earnings per share of the firm.

Since the firm has substantial latitude in treating certain items, it is necessary to determine the method of handling these transactions and their impact upon the reported performance of the firm. In particular, this concern focuses on the impact upon the current operating results of the firm and the comparability of these results. Normally the firm's current results are compared with past results and with the performance of other firms in the industry. Before these comparisons may be undertaken, it is necessary to compare the financial data utilized with past data of the firm and with that of other firms in the industry.

Financial Statements

In security analysis, the starting point is to determine the historical performance of the firm. This requires an evaluation of the income generated by the firm and its present position. The income statement provides an estimate of the income that has been generated for specific intervals, while the balance sheet indicates the size and nature of the resources at the firm's disposal. Within the income statement and the balance sheet, there are certain items which generally require perusal. The focus here will be on these items, and the emphasis will be on developing certain specific guidelines for adjusting the reported data.

Income Statement

The net income of the firm is measured by matching the revenues and costs for a specified period of time. Recognizing these costs and revenues must be in accordance with generally accepted accounting principles and procedures. These principles and procedures still permit substantial variations in the reporting of firms. The presentation of the income statement may take various forms, but the consolidated income statement for the hypothetical ABC Corporation shown in Table 4-1 is representative of the form current income statements are taking. Consolidated statements are statements in which the firm has combined its operations with certain of its subsidiaries. The purpose of consolidating the statements is to show the parent and the subsidiaries as one

TABLE 4-1   *Consolidated Income Statement for the ABC Corporation for the Year Ending December 31,197   (In Millions)*

Net sales		$3,300
Deductions		
Cost of goods sold	2,230	
Selling, general, and administrative expenses	350	
Depreciation and depletion	245	2,825
Income from operations		475
Other income	5	
Less: interest on debt	56	51
Income before provision for income taxes		424
Current income taxes	137	
Deferred income taxes	20	157
Income before minority interest and unconsolidated share of companies carried at equity		267
Less: minority stockholders share of income	18	
Plus: unconsolidated share of companies carried at equity	4	14
Income before extraordinary items		253
Extraordinary items		3
Net income		$ 250

economic entity. As a general rule, owning more than 50 percent of the voting stock of a firm is sufficient to classify it as a subsidiary and to include its results in the consolidated statements of the parent. There are additional considerations that may affect the decision, however, such as continuity of control and the degree of existing restrictions. The analyst, therefore, must determine whether or not all of the parent firm's subsidiaries are consolidated. If not, the effect of the consolidation procedure, in particular, whether it leads to an overstatement or understatement of earnings and assets, must be determined.

In Table 4-1 the sales revenues presented are after discounts and returns are deducted. From these sales revenues, the direct and indirect costs of operations are subtracted as indicated under the caption *Deductions*. Within this category there are two items which are widely recognized as being able to affect reported net income. The category entitled the *Cost of goods sold* can be substantially affected by the method of valuing inventories. There are several acceptable methods of valuing inventories, and each has a particular impact on the cost of goods sold and therefore on the net income of the firm. Another category that has a significant effect upon reported net income is *Depreciation and depletion*. There are a number of methods of reporting depreciation and depletion charges. These deductions are subtracted from the net sales revenue to give the *Income from operations*, which represents the profit from operations before the addition of other income and the deduction of financial charges, income taxes, and perhaps extraordinary items. *Other income* represents income earned by the firm from sources other than normal operations. One major source is investments in marketable securities. This other income is netted out against the interest paid on the firm's debt to give *Income before provision for income taxes*. The provision for income taxes may provide for both current and deferred income taxes. The deferred income tax liability reflects the treatment of depreciation charges. If the firm utilizes accelerated depreciation for tax purposes and a different method for financial reporting, it will credit this liability.

Before the net income may be determined, two other items must be considered. First, since the statement is consolidated, subsidiaries that are less than 100 percent owned may be included. Therefore, the *Minority interest* in the income of these subsidiaries must be shown as a reduction in the net income of the ABC Corporation. On the other hand, recent changes in accounting principles by the Accounting Principles Board permit the inclusion of income of affiliates as long as the parent owns 20 percent or more of the affiliate's common stock.[1] The entry *Unconsolidated share of companies carried at equity* represents ABC's interest in earnings of affiliated firms.

Extraordinary items represent either inflows or outflows as a result of nonrecurring transactions. For example, a subsidiary may have been sold at a capital gain. The profit on the transaction after the payment of the necessary income taxes would be shown as an extraordinary item. The recording of these extraordinary items then lead to the *Net income* of the firm. From this net income,

---

[1] Accounting Principles Board, *Opinion 18*, p. 335.

dividends on common and preferred stock may be paid, and the remainder constitutes an addition to the retained earnings of the firm.

In the income statement, there are four entries that should be investigated because of their impact on the earnings and earnings per share of the firm. First, the method of valuing inventories varies from firm to firm and also may affect the reported net income of the firm. Second, methods of reporting depreciation to the Internal Revenue Service and the stockholders may vary. Close attention must be paid to the method used to report to stockholders to make certain net income is not overstated. Third, since extraordinary items represent gains or losses to the firm from transactions other than from operations, adjustments for these items are often required. Finally, all of this analysis is designed to determine a reasonably realistic estimate of the *EPS* for the firm. However, recent changes in accounting principles have introduced additional complexity into the *EPS* calculation by introducing the concepts of primary and fully-diluted *EPS*. It is thus necessary to explore the nature of these calculations.

Balance Sheet

The income statement presents information on the operating results of the firm for a specified period of time, normally on a quarterly and annual basis; the balance sheet presents the financial position of the firm at the end of such periods. In a sense the balance sheet presents a history of the firm up to that point in time. Essentially the balance sheet gives information on three basic items: the assets of the firm, the liabilities, and the stockholders' equity. The typical format for the balance sheet is shown in Table 4-2 for the hypothetical ABC Corporation. The assets are divided into current, or short-term, assets which are relatively liquid, and normally due within one year, and the long-term assets which are somewhat illiquid. Included in current assets are cash, inventories, accounts receivable, marketable securities, and prepaid expenses. Generally the long-term assets are made up largely of fixed assets, but they may also include advances to and equity in affiliated firms, and it is not uncommon to capitalize intangible assets, such as goodwill, patents, and trademarks. These intangible assets are normally recorded under the caption *Other assets*.

Liabilities are basically divided into short-term and long-term liabilities. The current, or short-term, liabilities parallel the current assets and are due within one year. Included in this category are accounts payable, accruals, such as accrued taxes and wages, and other short-term liabilities, such as bank borrowing and sinking fund payments. Long-term liabilities are largely made up of funded debt issues, but also include other liabilities not expected to mature within a year. Finally, the net worth of the firm represents a portion of the firm's financing contributed by the owners. This includes the capital stock recorded at par value, contributed capital in excess of par, if any, and the retained earnings. It may also reflect the purchase of treasury stock, as illustrated by the ABC Corporation, and may also include preferred stock.

TABLE 4-2 *Consolidated Balance Sheet for the ABC Corporation, Year Ending December 31, 197 (In Millions)*

Assets

Current assets	
Cash	$ 100
Accounts receivable	577
Inventories	743
Marketable securities	162
Prepaid expenses	46
Total current assets	1,628
Fixed assets (net)	1,954
Investments and advances	
Companies carried at equity	76
Other	8
Total investments and advances	84
Other assets	52
Total assets	3,718

Liabilities and stockholders' equity

Current liabilities	
Accounts payable	159
Short-term borrowings	69
Payments due within one year on long-term debt	57
Accrued taxes	142
Other accrued liabilities	204
Total current liabilities	631
Deferred credits	117
Long-term debt	901
Minority stockholders' equity in consolidated subsidiaries	135
Stockholders' equity	
Capital stock ($1.00 par value)	323
Retained earnings	1,618
Less: Treasury common stock	7
Total stockholders' equity	1,934
Total liabilities and stockholders' equity	$3,718

There are generally two types of transactions that may affect the balance sheet of the firm. First, mergers and acquisitions may have several effects. The most obvious effect is the discontinuity that results. Moreover, there are two different methods of recording a merger or acquisition, each of which will have a different effect on the balance sheet. In addition to the impact on the balance sheet, the effect of mergers and acquisitions will be reflected on the income statement. Second, leasing poses a particular problem. Certain kinds of leases are really financial transactions in which the lease acts as a method of financing the purchase of particular fixed assets. Therefore, the lease obligations of the firm will be of particular interest. These two considerations will be treated in a section on special problems along with the income tax reconciliation.

Items from the Income Statement

Three major items in the income statement that may affect the reported earnings of the firm are the methods of valuing inventories, the method of reporting depreciation and depletion, and the impact of nonrecurring items. There may be other items, but these are the most common. Some of these are very difficult to handle, in particular, the method of valuing inventories.

Inventory Valuation

The difficulty with inventory valuation, as with the other topics in this section, is that there are several ways of allocating costs between inventory and the costs of goods sold. Some of the more common methods are as follows:

1. Specific cost
2. Average cost
3. Base stock
4. First-in, first-out
5. Last-in, first-out

Specific costing of inventories is feasible in situations in which inventories involve large items. Since these are large dollar items, it is entirely possible to identify the cost of specific items in the inventory.

The average cost method of valuing inventories simply means an average value for the inventory is determined based on either the number of orders placed or the number of items purchased. One method of determining the average cost is simply by summing the unit cost per order and dividing by the number of orders to give a simple average cost per unit. Alternatively, a weighted-average cost may be used, which sums the total cost per order and divides by the number of units purchased. The simple average cost per unit is not usually an acceptable method and is not widely used, whereas the weighted-average method is acceptable and more widely used.

The base stock method assumes that there is a base stock of goods that must be maintained. This basic stock is a constant amount that is not subject to change over time and is normally priced at a very low level to avoid future writedowns. The base stock method is not widely used because it is not acceptable for federal income tax purposes.

Two very common methods of valuing inventories are the first-in, first-out (FIFO) and the last-in, first-out (LIFO) methods. The FIFO method allocates the cost of inventory items to the cost of goods sold on the basis of first-in, first-out. Hence, those items that were purchased first are assumed to be used first. LIFO makes the opposite assumption. Each of these methods has its critics, but security analysts in general tend to prefer LIFO as opposed to FIFO. The criticisms of FIFO are twofold. First, it tends to overstate profits in periods of rising prices. Second, if the prices a firm pays for its goods rise and fall with the business cycle, FIFO tends to accentuate the swings in the firm's profits.

To illustrate, consider the following situation. Suppose the XYZ Corporation makes the following purchases of an inventory item.

Date	Number of units	Price/unit	Total cost
Beginning inventory	200	1.00	$ 200
April 2	800	1.15	920
May 6	600	1.20	720
June 12	400	1.30	520
	2,000		$2,360

Now suppose 500 units are left in inventory. Using FIFO, these 500 units in inventory would be valued at $640. That is

$$\begin{array}{rl} 100 \times \$1.20 = & \$120 \\ 400 \times \quad 1.30 = & \underline{520} \\ \overline{500} & \$640 \end{array}$$

Therefore, the amount charged to the cost of goods sold would be $1,720 ($2,360 − $640).

The effect on the profits of the firm can be illustrated by assuming that the 1,500 units were sold for a total of $2,300. The gross profit from the sale of these units before other expenses would be

Revenue	$2,300
Cost of goods sold	1,720
Gross profit	$ 580

The gross profit is $580.

If LIFO were used, the 500 units in inventory would have the following value:

$$\begin{array}{rl} 200 \times \$1.00 = & \$200 \\ 300 \times \quad 1.15 = & \underline{230} \\ \overline{500} & \$430 \end{array}$$

The amount charged to the cost of goods sold, therefore, would be $1,930 ($2,360 − $430). If these 1,500 units were sold for $2,300 as before, then the gross profit would be

Revenue	$2,300
Cost of goods sold	1,930
Gross profit	$ 370

This gross profit of $370 is somewhat less than the $580 gross profit recorded by FIFO.

FIFO leads to a larger gross profit because the items with the highest unit costs remain in inventory while the lower cost items are reflected in the cost of goods sold. LIFO, on the other hand, leads to a lower gross profit because the items with the lowest unit costs remain in inventory. As a result, in a period of rising prices, FIFO tends to lead to higher profits for the firm, whereas LIFO does not, since the cost of goods sold tends to be higher.

Extending the analysis, it is clear that LIFO tends to smooth out profits if the prices of inventory items tend to accentuate these fluctuations. FIFO tends to overstate profits in periods of rising prices as shown above, but it tends to understate it in periods of declining prices. It understates profits in periods of declining prices because the inventory is valued on the basis of the lowest cost items, the highest cost items being charged into the cost of goods sold. LIFO, on the other hand, avoids this problem because the inventory is based upon the more distant purchases. Consequently, the cost of goods sold reflects the more recent lower prices, and the profits are not understated. LIFO is therefore preferred by security analysts, because it does not tend to overstate profits in periods of rising prices; nor does it tend to accentuate profit fluctuations for those firms whose material prices tend to fluctuate with demand.

Applying the above analysis to the first three methods of valuing inventories, it is clear that the specific cost method can have much the same effect as FIFO, while the base stock method is analogous to LIFO. The average cost method takes a middle ground between FIFO and LIFO. The specific cost method of valuing inventories may be analogous to FIFO if the items in inventory were sold according to their length of time in inventory. The firm, however, would have to follow a conscious policy that is basically first-in, first-out for these large dollar items. Base stock, on the other hand, is similar to LIFO and is used normally in conjunction with LIFO because it maintains a basic inventory at a very low price, which means the cost of goods sold is charged with items near their current costs. Average cost is a middle-ground approach between FIFO and LIFO: its effect is not as extreme as that of FIFO, but the prices used to compute the cost of goods sold may vary somewhat from the current prices depending upon the trend in prices.

Surveys of the practice of firms indicate that approximately 40 percent use FIFO, 18 percent use LIFO, 27 percent use the average cost method, and 15 percent use miscellaneous methods.[2] Since LIFO is not widely used, a ques-

---

[2] AICPA, *Accounting Trends and Techniques*, 26th ed. 1971.

tion arises as to the handling of inventory valuation in the analysis of the financial statements. The desirable approach is to put all firms on the same basis, preferably LIFO, for purposes of comparison. If the same basis is being used, whether FIFO, LIFO, or some other, then the firms are at least comparable. However, when the firms being compared do not use the same basis, then an adjustment should be made to put the firms on a comparative basis. The difficulty arises in making these adjustments. For the analyst to make such adjustments requires estimates of the LIFO/FIFO difference. Making this estimate is extremely difficult for an outside analyst, and a reliable estimate may not be forthcoming. In such cases, all that can be done is to use the knowledge of the impact of the two different methods in a qualitative sense without attempting to quantify the impact.

Depreciation, Depletion, and Amortization

Depreciation, depletion, and amortization are methods of recording the expiration of tangible and intangible assets. Depreciation and depletion are used in connection with tangible assets, while amortization is used to record the expiration of intangible assets. When the firm acquires assets, these assets are expected to generate revenue over their useful lives. The allocation of the initial cost of these assets may be made against revenues to reflect the expiration of the assets' usefulness. This process involves three distinct procedures. First, there is depreciation, which is the periodic allocation of the cost of a fixed asset over its useful life in a systematic and rational manner. For example, plant and equipment are depreciated according to several methods of recording depreciation charges. Second, there is depletion, the periodic allocation of the cost of a natural resource. For example, oil and mineral deposits may be depleted to reflect the using up of the resource base. Finally, amortization applies to the periodic allocation of the cost of an intangible asset. For example, the firm may have goodwill on its books or have capitalized patents or trademarks. The cost of these intangibles may be amortized over a period of years to reflect the decline in their value to the firm.

Depreciation   The expiration of an asset's usefulness results from two basic sources, which are sometimes referred to as physical factors and functional factors. The physical factors include normal wear and tear, deterioration, and decay. The functional factors include inadequacy, supersession, and obsolescence. A distinction is made between accounting depreciation and economic depreciation. In accounting practice it is common to relate depreciation to the cost of the item, and this practice is consistent with the accounting principle of cost. Economic depreciation, however, is based upon market values. That is, depreciation in a capital asset over a period of time is determined by its market price at the beginning of the period and its market price at the end of the period. In this sense, economic depreciation is determined by appealing to the market for goods. Therefore, all the factors involved in determining the value of capital assets—for example, obsolescence, replacement costs, and useful life —are included. Accounting depreciation is determined solely by the initial cost, anticipated useful life span, and expected salvage value at the expiration of the asset's useful life.

The principle of recording depreciation charges based upon market values is not accepted in accounting principles and procedures; therefore, all financial statements record depreciation charges based upon initial cost. In general, recording depreciation charges follows one of four principal methods:

1. Straight line
2. Service hours
3. Productive output
4. Accelerated depreciation

The first three methods rely on either time or output to determine the depreciation charges. Accelerated depreciation is the use of a method of fast write-off principally for tax benefits.

Time or Output Related Methods   Straight-line depreciation simply writes off equal portions of the asset's cost over its expected life span. Notationally, the determination of the amount of straight-line depreciation to be charged off each year may be represented as follows:

$$D_{it} = \frac{C_{io} - S_{in}}{n} \qquad (4\text{-}1)$$

where D_{it} is the amount of depreciation to be written off against the cost of asset i at time t, C_{io} is the cost of asset i initially, S_{in} is the expected salvage value of asset i, and n is the estimated useful life. It is clear from Equation 4-1 that straight-line depreciation writes off an equal portion of its cost over the asset's useful life.

To illustrate, suppose a corporation acquired a machine costing $10,000. Suppose that it is expected to have a useful life of five years and a salvage value at the end of five years of $1,000. Substituting into equation 4-1 gives the annual straight-line depreciation charge of

$$D = \frac{\$10,000 - \$1,000}{5}$$

$$= \$1,800$$

As a result, the straight-line depreciation is $1,800 for each of the five years.

The use of service hours to determine depreciation is very similar to straight-line depreciation, except that the useful life is expressed in expected hours of service instead of in years. Using service hours to determine depreciation may be represented as follows:

$$DR_i = \frac{C_{io} - S_{iH}}{H_i} \qquad (4\text{-}2)$$

where DR_i is the depreciation rate on asset i per hour, C_{io} is the initial cost of asset i, S_{iH} is the salvage value of asset i at the end of its useful life expressed in service hours H, and H_i is the number of service hours which may be expected from asset i. The only difference between this method and the straight-line method is the unit of time used; this difference may result in different computations of the annual depreciation charges under the two methods. This depends on whether the annual usage in service hours varied significantly from year to year.

To illustrate, consider the same machine purchased by the corporation in the above example, but suppose that instead of estimating a useful life of five years, a useful life of 8,000 service hours is estimated for this machine. Substituting into Equation 4-2 gives a depreciation rate per hour of

$$DR = \frac{\$10,000 - \$1,000}{8,000}$$

$$= \$1.125$$

Therefore, the service-hour charge is $1.125. Determining the annual depreciation charge depends upon annual usage. Suppose the machine was used the following number of hours over a five-year period:

Year	Service hours utilized	Depreciation expense	Accumulated depreciation	Book value
0				$10,000
1	2,500	$2,813	$2,813	7,187
2	2,250	2,531	5,344	4,656
3	1,750	1,969	7,313	2,687
4	1,000	1,125	8,438	1,562
5	500	562	9,000	1,000
	8,000	$9,000		

Consequently, the depreciation varied from year to year with usage, but the end result may be the same as for straight-line depreciation.

Finally, the productive output method of determining depreciation charges is similar to the service hours approach, but the useful life of the asset is related to output. Notationally, this method may be represented as follows:

$$DR_i = \frac{C_{io} - S_{io}}{O_i} \tag{4-3}$$

where O_i is the number of units of output that may be processed by asset i, S_{io} is the salvage value of asset i at the end of its useful life O, and the other terms are as previously defined.

Suppose the machine in the above example has a useful life that is expressed in terms of output, say 20,000 units. Substituting into Equation 4-3 gives

$$DR_i = \frac{\$10,000 - \$1,000}{20,000}$$

$$= \$0.45$$

Thus, the depreciation charge per unit of output is $0.45. If the following units are processed over a five-year period, the depreciation will be as follows:

Year	Units of output	Depreciation expense	Accumulated depreciation	Book value
0				$10,000
1	6,000	$2,700	$2,700	7,300
2	5,000	2,250	4,950	5,050
3	4,000	1,800	6,750	3,250
4	3,000	1,350	8,100	1,900
5	2,000	900	9,000	1,000
	20,000	$9,000		

As a result, given the above units of output over a five-year period, the asset is depreciated to the extent of $9,000, and the balance of $1,000 equals the antici-pated salvage value.

Accelerated Depreciation   For tax purposes a firm may use one of several different methods of accelerated depreciation. Firms using accelerated depre-ciation to report to the Internal Revenue Service use one of the above methods of reporting to their stockholders. This dual system of reporting can cause some difficulty. The management of the firm is carrying out its responsibility by reducing its tax burden as much as the Internal Revenue Code permits, and the stockholders would applaud such behavior. However, in reporting such trans-actions to the stockholders, the firm must recognize that the use of accelerated depreciation only defers the income tax liability; it does not eliminate it. Con-sequently, the firm must set up an account to reflect this anticipated tax liabil-ity. If this account—sometimes referred to as a deferred income tax liability —has not been set up, the current net income of the firm has been overstated.

Two common methods of determining accelerated depreciation are the sum-of-the-years' digits (SYD) method and the declining balance method. The SYD method determines the portion of depreciation expense by taking a de-clining fraction of the cost of the asset each year. The fraction is determined by summing the number of years to give the denominator while the numerator is determined by reversing the order of the digits. For example, suppose an asset has a three-year useful life and is to be depreciated by the SYD method. The denominator would be the sum of the years, or digits, $1 + 2 + 3 = 6$, and the numerator for each of the three years is the digits in reverse order, or 3, 2, and 1. Therefore, the fraction in the first year is $\frac{3}{6}$, the second year is $\frac{2}{6}$, and the third year is $\frac{1}{6}$.

Obtaining the denominator may be simplified by applying the following formula:

$$SYD = n\left(\frac{n+1}{2}\right) \tag{4-4}$$

where n is the number of years over which the asset will be depreciated. To illustrate using 10 years, the SYD by Equation 4-4 is

$$SYD = 10\left(\frac{10 + 1}{2}\right)$$

$$= 55$$

Thus the denominator in this example is 55.

Once the fractions are found, it is an easy matter to determine the depreciation expense for each year. To illustrate, suppose a machine is purchased for $10,000 and has an expected useful life of five years and a salvage value of $1,000. The depreciation expense is as follows:

Year		Depreciation expense	Accumulated depreciation	Book value
0				$10,000
1	($\frac{5}{15}$ × $9,000)	$3,000	$3,000	7,000
2	($\frac{4}{15}$ × 9,000)	2,400	5,400	4,600
3	($\frac{3}{15}$ × 9,000)	1,800	7,200	2,800
4	($\frac{2}{15}$ × 9,000)	1,200	8,400	1,600
5	($\frac{1}{15}$ × 9,000)	600	9,000	1,000
		$9,000		

The denominator in this example is 15, and the fractions are $\frac{5}{15}$, $\frac{4}{15}$, and so on, for years 1 through 5. Multiplying $9,000 by these fractions gives the depreciation expense shown in column 2.

The declining balance approaches utilize a fast write-off that is based on a straight-line depreciation rate. Current regulation limits the amount that can be written off to twice the straight-line rate. As a consequence, the amount of depreciation expense for the double declining balance method may be determined by simply multiplying $2(1/n)$ times the value of the asset on the books. Applying this method to the previous example gives the following depreciation expenses for the five-year life of the machine:

Year		Depreciation expense	Accumulated depreciation	Book value
0				$10,000
1	($\frac{2}{5}$ × $10,000)	$4,000	$4,000	6,000
2	($\frac{2}{5}$ × 6,000)	2,400	6,400	3,600
3	($\frac{2}{5}$ × 3,600)	1,440	7,840	2,160
4	($\frac{2}{5}$ × 2,160)	864	8,704	1,296
5		296	9,000	1,000

The amount of depreciation expense in this example is determined by taking $\frac{2}{5}$ of the value of the machine on the books, that is, cost less accumulated depreciation. For example, in year 3 the depreciation expense would be $\frac{2}{5}$ of the value of the machine on the books, or $3,600, and the amount of depreciation would be $\frac{2}{5}$ × $3,600 = $1,440. This procedure is followed in every year except the last. Recall that the salvage value was ignored in determining the annual depreciation expense. However, it is introduced in the last year, and the depreciation expense is the difference between the book value and the salvage value, or $1,296 − $1,000 = $296. If there were no salvage value, the entire amount would be written off in the last year.

Since these accelerated methods of depreciation permit a larger write-off in earlier years and a smaller write-off in later years, income taxes are smaller in earlier years but larger in later years. As a result, income taxes are deferred by these methods of depreciation but not eliminated, and generally accepted accounting principles require the firm to recognize this eventual income tax liability. For the analyst the task is twofold. First, he must determine whether the firm uses accelerated depreciation. This is normally disclosed in the notes accompanying the income statement and the balance sheet. Second, if it is established that the firm uses accelerated depreciation, the next task is to determine whether a deferred income tax liability account has been set up. If it has, the analyst must assume that the amount set aside is sufficient to meet the anticipated liability. If it has not, the analyst must attempt to estimate the amount of this liability and adjust the net income accordingly. Needless to say, this is a difficult task.

Depletion and Amortization   Depletion and amortization represent additional methods of writing off assets as their useful lives expire. Depletion is the writing off of assets that take the form of natural resources. It follows that a natural resource, such as an ore body, may be used up over time. Hence, depletion permits a recovery of the costs of developing the natural resource. In determining the depletion allowances, the methods used are cost depletion and statutory depletion. Cost depletion means recovering the costs of developing a natural resource. The factors involved are:

1. The cost including all development costs
2. Estimated residual value of the property
3. Amount of minerals extracted over the life of the mineral deposit

These factors are similar to those used to determine depreciation expense by the productive output method.

To illustrate, suppose the total cost of developing an oil well is $200,000, and the recoverable crude oil is 500,000 barrels. The unit depletion rate is

$$\text{UDR} = \frac{\$200,000}{500,000}$$

$$= \$0.40 \text{ per barrel}$$

Thus, the depletion rate is $0.40 per barrel for this well, and the annual depletion charge will depend upon the amount of oil sold during the year.

For tax purposes the depletion that may be taken is set out in the Internal Revenue Code and is commonly known as statutory depletion. If this method is used, the amount of the depletion that is charged off is purely a matter of statute. Based on the Internal Revenue Act of 1969, the following are indicative of the rates of depletion permitted:

Oil and gas wells	22 percent
Sulphur, uranium, molybdenum	22
Metal mines	14–15
Coal and asbestos	10
Sand, clay, and gravel	5

These percentages may be applied to the gross income to determine the amount of depletion for tax purposes. The only restriction is that the depletion allowances may not exceed 50 percent of the earnings before depletion and taxes. For example, suppose an oil-producing firm had gross revenue of $20 million from the production and sale of crude oil. The firm's depletion allowances following statutory depletion would be $4.4 million subject to the constraint that this amount did not exceed 50 percent of earnings before depletion and taxes. Moreover, the depletion charged off by this method does not involve costs at all; the amount charged off may therefore substantially exceed the costs involved in developing the natural resource.

Amortization of an intangible asset occurs when potential service declines over time. To be capitalized, an intangible must be generated externally, such as copyrights, patents, trademarks, and goodwill. These intangibles are recorded at cost and then amortized over the anticipated useful life of the asset. The amount amortized should coincide as nearly as possible with the decline in service of the intangible asset. Amortization may be written off by the firm; for tax purposes certain types of amortization are deductible, such as patents and copyrights, while other types, such as goodwill, are not.

Nonrecurrent Items

Nonrecurrent items may be either gains or losses incurred by the firm from transactions not connected with normal operations. For example, the firm may have experienced a capital gain in the sale of an asset. The amount of the gain minus capital gains taxes would be recorded as a nonrecurrent item or, as it is now commonly referred to, an extraordinary item. Sources of these nonrecurrent items are manifold, but the following is a representative list of some of them:

1. Capital gains or losses
2. Back tax payments or refunds
3. Settlement of legal litigations
4. Proceeds of a life insurance policy
5. Write downs or recovery of foreign assets
6. Adjustments to market value

In each case, these items represent transactions that do not result from normal business operations.

There are two methods for reporting these items in the income statement. One is known as the current operating performance concept, and the other is referred to as the all-inclusive concept. The current operating performance concept places primary emphasis on reporting only current operating results. Under this concept, nonrecurrent items do not appear on the income statement, but are charged directly to the retained earnings. In other words, nonrecurrent items do not appear on the income statement at all. The all-inclusive concept, on the other hand, places primary emphasis on reporting all nonrecurring items on the income statement. At one time there was considerable controversy concerning these two approaches. The conflict has largely been settled by the Accounting Principles Board in its Opinion No. 9, in which it essentially adopted the all-inclusive concept. In its Opinion it stated that the income statement should reflect all items that affect the profit and loss of the firm with the exception of certain prior period adjustments. However, extraordinary items should be reported separately.

As a result, nonrecurring items are normally reported in the following way:

Income before extraordinary items	XXX
Extraordinary items	X
Net income	XXX

From the standpoint of the security analyst, the current operating performance concept is preferable, since the analyst is concerned with the operating results of the firm. Since these nonrecurring items do not affect the firm's current operations, they should be eliminated from the net income whenever they appear. However, extraordinary items are reported separately, and therefore it is not a difficult task for the analyst to adjust for these nonrecurring items. For purposes of determining the current net income of the firm, the appropriate figure is the income before extraordinary items. This figure represents the earnings of the firm before it is affected, either positively or negatively, by the nonrecurring items.

Calculating Earnings Per Share

Contrary to what might be expected, calculating the earnings per share *(EPS)* of the firm is no longer straightforward. There are several aspects of the reported *EPS* that must be evaluated. First, recent opinions of the Accounting Principles Board have led to the publication of two *EPS* figures by many firms. One figure is referred to as the primary *EPS* and represents the results of the income available to the common stockholders divided by the average number of common shares and common share equivalents outstanding. The second figure is referred to as the fully-diluted *EPS* and represents the *EPS* giving effect to all potential dilution. This figure includes any factor which may lead to dilution of the *EPS*, and it may differ somewhat from the primary *EPS*.

Primary *EPS* are determined by dividing the net income available to the stockholders by the average number of common shares outstanding and share equivalents. Convertible securities, stock options, and warrants are the most common share equivalents. Stock options and warrants are always considered common stock equivalents; convertible securities are only considered common stock equivalents if their coupon rate at the time of issuance is less than $66\frac{2}{3}$ percent of the prime rate. Fully-diluted *EPS*, on the other hand, include in addition all convertible securities whose yield at time of issuance is greater than $66\frac{2}{3}$ percent.

To illustrate the calculation of primary and fully-diluted *EPS*, consider the following data for a hypothetical corporation. The firm has two convertible issues outstanding, which are classified as follows:

Security	Yield at issuance	Prime interest rate at issuance	Common stock equivalent or senior
Convertible debenture 6s	5.9%	6.0%	Senior security
$1 convertible preferred	3.7%	6.0%	C/S equivalent

The convertible debentures are not considered common stock equivalents for purposes of determining primary *EPS*, but the convertible preferreds are, because their yield at the time of issuance was less than $66\frac{2}{3}$ percent of the prime rate.

Suppose there are 100 convertible debentures outstanding, each convertible into 30 shares of common stock, and 1,000 convertible preferreds outstanding, each convertible into common shares on a one-for-one basis. Suppose there were 20,000 common shares outstanding at the beginning of the year, but an additional 5,000 shares were issued in June of that year. Finally, suppose the net income is as follows:

Income before extraordinary items	$50,000
Extraordinary items	(2,500)
Net income	47,500
Preferred dividends	(1,000)
To retained earnings	$46,500

The calculation of the number of shares outstanding takes two steps in this case. When common shares are sold throughout the year, the normal procedure is to determine the weighted-average number of shares outstanding. For this corporation, the appropriate calculations are as follows:

Inclusive dates	Months	Shares	Months × shares
Jan. 1 to June 30	6	20,000	120,000
July 1 to Dec. 31	6	25,000	150,000
	12		270,000

The weighted average, then, is

$$\frac{270,000}{12} = 22,500$$

However, to this weighted-average number of shares must be added the common stock equivalent for the convertible preferred stock of 1,000 shares, giving a total of 23,500 shares outstanding.

The primary *EPS* for our hypothetical corporation, therefore, is calculated as follows:

Income before extraordinary items	2.13
Extraordinary items	(0.11)
Net income	2.02

The *EPS* based on income before extraordinary items is determined by dividing the $50,000 by 23,500 shares, yielding $2.13. Since the convertible preferred are considered common stock equivalent, the dividends paid on them do not have to be subtracted before determining the primary *EPS*. If they were straight preferreds, or not common stock equivalents, their dividends would have to be subtracted before determining the primary *EPS*. The extraordinary item is also put on a per share basis, or $2,500 ÷ 23,500 = $0.11. Thus, the net income per share is $2.13 − $0.11 = $2.02 or, stated a little differently, $47,500 ÷ 23,500 = $2.02. Since the income for this corporation does include extraordinary items, the analyst considers the *EPS* to be $2.13 for purposes of analysis. This figure reflects the exclusion of nonrecurrent items.

Fully-diluted *EPS* assume that all potential dilution is realized. Therefore, any item that may lead to dilution is included. To illustrate with the data for our hypothetical corporation, the number of shares are as follows:

Average number of common shares	22,500
Conversion of convertible preferreds	1,000
Conversion of convertible debentures	3,000
Total number of shares	26,500

In other words, if the convertible preferreds and convertible debentures are assumed converted, the weighted-average number of shares will be 26,500. The earnings per share on a fully-diluted basis cannot be determined until the after-tax interest on the convertible debentures is added back, however. That is

Income before extraordinary items	$50,000
After-tax interest on convertible 6s	3,120
Total	53,120
Extraordinary item	(2,500)
Net income	$50,620

Calculating the addition to the income, assuming the convertible debenture is converted, $0.52 × $6,000 = $3,120. The interest must be added back, since we are assuming that these convertible debentures have been converted and interest would therefore not be paid on them. Since each convertible debenture has a 6-percent coupon rate, the before-tax interest cost will be $6,000; but since *EPS* are after taxes, this amount is put on an after-tax basis by multiplying by 1 − marginal tax rate, or 1 − 0.48 = 0.52.

Fully-diluted *EPS* for the corporation will be as follows:

Income before extraordinary items	$2.00
Extraordinary items	(0.09)
Net income	$1.91

The income before extraordinary items refers to the figure of $53,120, which reflects the adding back of the after-tax interest payments on the convertible debentures; and income before extraordinary items on a per share basis is $53,120 ÷ 26,500 = $2.00. The extraordinary items are $2,500 ÷ 26,500 = $0.09, and the resulting net income per share is $2.00 − 0.09 = $1.91 or, stated differently, $50,620 ÷ 26,500 = $1.91.

Several comments seem appropriate after the completion of these calculations. First, it is clear that determining the appropriate number of shares to use is rather complicated. In fact, the above calculations have only scratched the surface. Warrants present a very complex situation, particularly with respect to primary *EPS* calculations. Second, no longer does the analyst have to contend with one *EPS* figure; he may have as many as four to contend with. It is important, therefore, to select the proper *EPS* figure to use in determining past growth rates and in projecting future *EPS*. As it stands now, the situation is perplexing, but probably fully-diluted *EPS* are the most representative figure of the *EPS* of the firm. If fully-diluted *EPS* are used for making projections, at least all potential dilution has been considered. This approach has the obvious advantage of being conservative. Of course, these fully-diluted *EPS* are determined subject to the adjustments suggested above for such items as accelerated depreciation, inventory valuation methods, and nonrecurring items.

Specialized Problems

There are a number of transactions that may affect the income statement and balance sheet. Essentially, the analyst must attempt to ferret out any items that may affect the comparability of these statements over time. Two problems that have been particularly difficult are the treatment of mergers and acquisitions, and leases. In the 1960s mergers and acquisitions occurred at an unprecedented rate, raising the question of the appropriate method of recording these business combinations. The problem of handling leases arises because some leases are clearly financing arrangements in the same sense as a bank loan. Yet neither the loan nor the asset appears on the balance sheet of the firm renting the asset. Handling such items in the financial statements has posed a dilemma for the accounting profession and for those using the statements. Finally, a useful check that may be valuable in projecting *EPS* is the income tax reconciliation. It is one of the few tasks that is straightforward, and at times it is quite revealing.

Mergers and Acquisitions

Mergers and acquisitions are terms used to apply to a number of different types of business combinations. Mergers normally refer to combinations in which two or more firms are involved but only one firm survives. The implication is that all the parties to the merger have a continuing interest approximately equal to their previous interest. A consolidation normally refers to the combination of two or more firms in which a new firm emerges. Generally, consolidations are undertaken when the firms involved are attempting to strengthen their positions; consolidations often result when the individual firms have not been particularly profitable. Finally, an acquisition is an outright purchase of one firm by another.

In recording these combinations, two methods are commonly used. One is the pooling-of-interests method, which essentially assumes that the firms have pooled their resources, and the books of the surviving firm are simply determined by adding together assets and liabilities of the individual firms involved. The other method is the purchase method. A purchase treats a business combination in much the same fashion as the purchase of any other asset. The acquisition price is recorded at cost, and any liabilities created as a result of the acquisition are shown on the liability side of the balance sheet.

For a pooling-of-interests approach to be used, there are 12 general criteria that must be met. If they are not met, the combination is treated as a purchase. All these criteria will not be set out here, but the following capture their essence:

1. There must be a continuing interest in the surviving firm by all of the original stockholders that essentially parallels their interest in the firms to the mergers.
2. Payment can only involve an exchange of common stock.
3. The combination must be completed in one year, and part of the assets cannot be spun off for at least two years after the combination.

For firms meeting these criteria, the pooling-of-interests method simply means that their assets and liabilities are added together. Similarly, the net worth of the surviving firm cannot exceed the total net worth of the firms involved in the combination.

A purchase, on the other hand, results when a combination does not meet these criteria for a pooling-of-interests. A purchase follows the accepted principles for acquiring assets. The difficulty arises in that a number of assets are being acquired. The purchase price, therefore, must be allocated over a number of assets; moreover, the price paid normally exceeds the book value of these assets and their fair market value. As a result, goodwill is normally generated from a purchase. The common practice in a purchase is to value the tangible assets on the books of the firm at their fair market value. If the price paid exceeds the fair market value, the difference between this value and the price paid becomes the goodwill. Another difference is that retained earnings are not carried onto the books of the acquiring firm. Only in a purchase are the liabilities created by the combination reflected on the balance sheet.

Substantial criticism has been directed toward the pooling-of-interest method, especially when the method is used in conjunction with convertible preferred stock as a means of payment.[3] Much of the criticism stems from the fact that the surviving firm's books simply result from adding together the book values of the individual firms. The assets of the acquired firms are not taken onto the books of the surviving firm at their fair market value. It is argued that the depreciation expenses are, therefore, understated, and the profits are over-stated. For example, suppose a pooling takes place in which the assets of a firm are acquired in exchange for common stock valued at $10 million. In addition, suppose that the undepreciated value of these assets on the books of the ac-quired firm is $5 million, but the fair market value is $7 million. In the pooling, the assets of this firm are recorded on the books of the surviving firm at $5 million; consequently, the depreciation expense is smaller than if they were recorded at their fair market value. Net income and *EPS* are larger, therefore, under a pooling than under a purchase because of the impact of depreciation charges. Because of this result, some critics suggest that the pooling-of-interests method should be outlawed completely.

This controversy developed during the great merger movement of the 1960s and especially during the development of the conglomerate industry. Many believed that the pooling-of-interest method facilitated the merger movement of the 1960s because it was another means for these firms to generate growth in *EPS* and thus maintain market interest. Now that the dust has settled, it appears that the controversy was not as serious as first thought. Some firms have un-doubtedly attempted to use pooling to improve their earnings stream, but it must be recalled that by using the pooling approach the cash flow of the firm is diminished. However, the greatest difficulty that emerges from business com-binations for the analyst is probably the discontinuity in net income and *EPS*. One solution is the use of pro forma statements in which the results of the surviving firm are estimated for the premerger period. In this fashion compara-ble data may be obtained. Another solution, which is feasible when the combi-nation occurred several years before, is to view the periods before and after the combination as two distinct periods with the period subsequent to the merger or acquisition being used to evaluate the firm.

Financial Leases

A firm may enter into a number of different types of leases; in general they may be categorized as operating leases and financial leases. Operating leases are generally short-term and are cancelable at the option of the lessee. For exam-ple, the rental of a typewriter to meet a temporary increase in workload is an operating lease. Financial leases, on the other hand, give rise to special prop-erty rights, which are in fact purchases. The lease in these situations is being

---

[3] For a discussion of the use of convertible preferreds to finance mergers and acquisitions, see George E. Pinches, "Financing With Convertible Preferred Stock, 1960–1967," *Journal of Finance*, vol. 25, no. 1 (Mar., 1970), pp. 53–64; Jerry J. Weygandt, "A Comment on Financing with Convertible Preferred Stock, 1960–1967," *Journal of Finance*, vol. 26, no. 1 (Mar., 1971), pp. 148–50; and C. Ronald Sprecher, "A Note on Financing Mergers with Convertible Preferred Stock," *Journal of Finance*, vol. 26, no. 3 (June, 1971), pp. 683–86.

used as a method of financing. The most notable example is the sale-and-leaseback arrangement, in which a firm builds a facility to meet its specifications, then sells the facility with the option to lease the property for a specified period of time. Department stores make extensive use of this device to reduce their investment in fixed assets.

The advantages of a financial lease result because the transaction does not appear on the balance sheet. That is, the asset is not recorded, nor is a liability created by this transaction. At the same time, the lease payments are "buried" in the income statement as an operating expense. If the firm had borrowed funds to build the facility, the interest paid on that loan would be reflected in the income statement in the category of interest paid on debt. It then would be explicitly recognized in the interest coverage ratios, and the debt created would affect the firm's debt-to-equity ratio. However, the financial lease may be overlooked because it lacks visibility. It is for this reason that lease arrangements are advocated as a method of "preserving one's borrowing power." The assets and liabilities of firms that utilize financial leases, therefore, are understated, leading to an overstatement of many of the financial ratios of such firms, especially the profitability and interest coverage ratios.

As a result of the distortion that may be introduced by financial leases, it is generally recognized that these financial leases should be capitalized. However, the actual implementation of the capitalization procedure is not generally agreed upon. For example, the Accounting Principles Board's Opinion No. 5 holds that operating leases should be expensed, but only the sale-and-leaseback type of financial leases should be capitalized. Many people both in and out of the accounting profession hold that all financial leases should be capitalized. In addition, a problem emerges in selecting the appropriate rate of discount. There are many alternatives that may be used, but it is not clear which one is the most appropriate. Finally, it is desirable for the lessor and lessee to use the same discount rate in capitalizing an asset; yet this is unlikely to happen.

From the analyst's point of view, it is generally desirable to capitalize all financial leases. In this fashion, a more accurate representation of the firm's position is achieved. The difficulty, however, is in obtaining adequate information. In some cases the notes connected with the financial statements will not adequately describe the firm's financial leases. In other cases the firm will actually capitalize the leases and explicitly show their impact. Whatever the case, the analyst should attempt to determine the firm's situation with respect to leases and then attempt to make any adjustments that may be necessary.

Income Tax Reconciliation

Unlike most of the aspects of financial statement analysis discussed in this chapter, income tax reconciliation is straightforward and possibly quite revealing. The corporate tax rate is currently 22 percent of the first $25,000 of pretax income and 48 percent of pretax income above $25,000. Generally, then, the effective tax rate will have a ceiling of 48 percent of pretax income. The effective income tax rate, including current income taxes and deferred income taxes, will usually be less than the ceiling of 48 percent, however. There are several reasons for this:

1. The first $25,000 of income is taxed at 22 percent.
2. Dividend income is taxed only to the extent of 15 percent of the dividend income received.
3. Losses from previous years' operations must be carried back three years and then forward five years.
4. Depletion allowances for natural resource firms may reduce the taxable income significantly.
5. Investment tax credits effectively reduce the income tax paid.

The income tax reconciliation essentially involves calculating the effective tax rate and comparing this to the ceiling rate of 48 percent. This calculation includes the current income taxes and the deferred income taxes. The effective tax rate is expected to be somewhat below the ceiling level but not too far below. If the effective tax rate is well below the ceiling rate, there is always a possibility of the income tax rate increasing and effectively reducing the net income of the firm. For example, if the effective rate is found to be in a narrow range around 44 percent over the past several years, then in all probability income taxes will not be a major factor adversely affecting the net income of the firm in the future. On the other hand, the situation could parallel that of American Motors in 1972, where that corporation had $43 million in tax benefits from past operating losses to be used up. In such a case, current income taxes may be abnormally low and net income may be unsustainably high. Forecasting *EPS* must recognize the potential effect of income taxes, or else there may be a wide divergence between forecast and realized *EPS*.

In summary, then, the income tax reconciliation is a two-step procedure. The effective income tax rate is determined, then compared to the ceiling rate of 48 percent to determine whether income taxes will constitute a factor that will adversely affect earnings in the future. The second step is initiated if it appears that income taxes may be a factor in the future profits of the firm. In this situation, the cause of the low effective tax rate must be ascertained. For example, if it is tax losses or the investment tax credit, these may expire, having a significant effect on the net income of the firm. On the other hand, if depletion allowances are the cause, then it may continue indefinitely.

Summary

Good information normally leads to better decisions. The financial statements are probably the single most important source of information about a firm. However, the data contained in these statements must be analyzed to determine whether the situation portrayed is really representative. Since the financial statements are largely made up of estimates, there are a number of items that affect the reported results of the firm. Four items in the income statements that should be investigated are the methods of valuing inventories, methods of recording depreciation and depletion, nonrecurrent items, and the calculation of *EPS*. Recent changes in accounting principles have substantially complicated the calculation of *EPS*. It is now common for firms to report two *EPS* figures. One figure is referred to as primary *EPS* and represents earnings available to the outstanding common stock and common stock equivalents. The other *EPS* figure is the fully-diluted *EPS*, which represents *EPS* giving effect to all potential dilution.

In addition to these four items, there are certain specialized problems, particularly mergers and acquisitions, financial leases, and the income tax reconciliation. Mergers and acquisitions present a special situation because they represent a discontinuity in the financial statements. Whenever mergers and acquisitions take place, the subsequent financial statements cannot be related to earlier ones. However, pro forma statements can be used to overcome the problems caused by the discontinuity. Probably the most satisfactory method occurs when there is enough history subsequent to the combination to permit sufficient analysis. Financial leases present difficulty because they represent a form of financing, yet they may not appear on the balance sheet and, as a result, may be overlooked in the analysis. Finally, in contrast to many of the other items discussed in this chapter, the income tax reconciliation is straightforward and provides insight into the potential impact of income taxes on the net income of the firm in the future.

Questions

1. Why is financial statement analysis required? Distinguish between financial statement analysis and financial ratio analysis.
2. Many firms report their operations on a consolidated basis.
    a. What does this mean?
    b. When can a firm include the results of another firm along with its own in the consolidated statements?
    c. Why would a firm exclude the results of a subsidiary from its consolidated statements?
3. What are some of the common methods of valuing inventories? What is the relationship between inventory valuation and the cost of goods sold?
4. Two widely used methods of valuating inventories are FIFO and LIFO.
    a. Contrast these two methods.
    b. Why do security analysts tend to prefer LIFO to FIFO?
5. There are a number of methods for determining depreciation expenses.

a. What is the difference between accounting depreciation and economic depreciation?
b. What are some of the more common methods which do not permit a fast write-off?
c. What are two common methods of accelerated depreciation?
d. When analyzing the methods of reporting depreciation charges, what is the major concern? Where does one obtain the information to make this evaluation?

6. Explain two methods of reporting depletion. Why doesn't the same problem exist with depletion allowances as with the use of accelerated depreciation?

7. A certain corporation has reported the following income figures:

Income before extraordinary items	$222,600,000
Extraordinary items	21,400,000
Net income	$243,000,000

In addition, the following items were disclosed in the financial statements.
(1) Nonconvertible preferred stock dividends paid equalled $3,200,000.
(2) The number of shares of common outstanding during the year was as follows:
(a) On January 1, 40 million shares were outstanding.
(b) On June 30th an additional 5 million shares were issued, and on September 30th, 500,000 more shares were issued.
(3) Finally, three debenture issues are outstanding:

Issue	Number	Yield at issuance	Prime rate at issuance	Conversion ratio
Debenture 5s	20,000	5 10%	4.75%	Nonconvertible
Convertible 4½s	40,000	4.47	5.00	50
Convertible 3s	50,000	3.10	5.25	50

With this data provide the following information:
a. What are the primary and fully-diluted *EPS* for this corporation according to current accounting practices?
b. Which *EPS* figures would an analyst use as a basis for making subsequent forecasts?

8. In connection with business combinations, a number of terms are used. Define each of the following:

Merger	A pooling-of-interest
Consolidation	A purchase
Acquisition	

9. Leases are widely used in business today.
a. Distinguish between an operating lease and a financial lease.
b. Explain how the failure to recognize financial leases in the financial statements may distort the operating results of the firm.

   c. How should financial leases be handled in the financial statements? What do current accounting principles and procedures require?

10. How does the income tax reconciliation enter into the forecasting of *EPS?*

11. Determine the effective tax rate for the following firms over the past five years and then determine the reasons for that rate.

> Atlantic Richfield Company
> Aztec Oil and Gas Company
> Cleveland-Cliffs Iron Company
> Exxon Corporation
> Hudson's Bay Oil and Gas Co. Ltd.
> Northgate Exploration Limited
> Occidental Petroleum
> Pacific Petroleums Limited
> Royal Dutch Petroleum Company
> Texas Gulf Sulphur

Selected References

Accounting Principles Board. *Accounting Principles,* rev. ed., 2 vols. Chicago; Commerce Clearing House.

Axelson, Kenneth S. "Needed: A Generally Accepted Method for Measuring Lease Commitments." *Financial Executive,* vol. 39, no. 7 (July, 1971), pp. 40–47.

Berstein, Leopold A. *Financial Statement Analysis—Theory, Application and Interpretation.* Homewood, Ill.: Richard D. Irwin, 1973.

Bissell, George S. "A Professional Investor Looks at Earnings Forecasts." *Financial Analysts Journal,* vol. 28, no. 3 (May–June, 1972), pp. 73–79.

Briloff, Abraham J. *Unaccountable Accounting.* New York: Harper & Row, 1973.

Gant, Donald R. "A Critical Look at Lease Financing." *The Controller,* vol. 29, no. 6 (June, 1961), pp. 274–78.

Graham, Benjamin. *The Intelligent Investor,* 4th rev. ed. New York: Harper & Row, 1973. Chapter 12.

Graham, Benjamin, David L. Dodd, and Sidney Cottle. *Security Analysis: Principles and Technique,* 4th ed. New York: McGraw-Hill, 1962. Part II.

Griffin, Charles H., Thomas H. Williams, and Kermit D. Larson. *Advanced Accounting,* rev. ed. Homewood, Ill.: Richard D. Irwin, 1971.

Mauriello, Joseph A. *Accounting for the Financial Analyst.* C. F. A. Monograph Series, rev. ed. Homewood, Ill.: Richard D. Irwin, 1971.

Newell, Gale E. "Revisions of Reported Quarterly Earnings." *Journal of Business,* vol. 44, no. 3 (July, 1971), pp. 282–86.

Pinches, George E. "Financing With Convertible Preferred Stock, 1960–1967." *Journal of Finance,* vol. 25, no. 1 (Mar., 1970), pp. 53–64.

Shank, John K. "Case of the Disclosure Debate." *Harvard Business Review,* vol. 50, no. 1 (Jan.–Feb., 1972), pp. 142–58.

Singhvi, Surendra S. "Disclose to Whom? Annual Financial Reports to Stockholders and to the Securities and Exchange Commission." *Journal of Business,* vol. 41, no. 3 (July, 1968), pp. 347–52.

Sprecher, C. Ronald. "A Note on Financing Mergers with Convertible Preferred Stock." *Journal of Finance,* vol. 26, no. 3 (June, 1971), pp. 683–86.

Welsch, Glenn A., Charles T. Zlatkovich, and John Arch White. *Intermediate Accounting,* 3d ed. Richard D. Irwin, 1972.

Weygandt, Jerry J. "Comment on Financing with Convertible Preferred Stock." *Journal of Finance,* vol. 26, no. 1 (Mar., 1971), pp. 148–50.

Whitman, Robert O. "Accounting Issues in the Capitalization of Leases." *Public Utilities Fortnightly,* vol. 88, no. 7 (Sept. 30, 1971), pp. 24–30.

Zises, Alvin, "Disclosure of Long-Term Leases." *Journal of Accountancy,* vol. III, no. 2 (Feb., 1961), pp. 37–48.

II

Security Evaluation—
Common Stock

Chapter 5

Risk in Investment Management

Risk and uncertainty are an integral part of the investment decision.[1] Whenever the investor contemplates making an investment, whether it is short-term or long-term, bonds or stocks, the risk of obtaining an anticipated return must be explicitly considered. The question of risk is really two-sided. We must consider the risk inherent in the security under consideration, and we must also consider the investor's willingness to accept risk. For example, two securities, a stock and high-quality bond, will have different characteristics. The return on the common stock will be somewhat more uncertain than that on the bond; the expected return, on the other hand, may be somewhat higher. The function of the security analyst is to determine the amount of risk inherent in making an investment in a particular security.

This still leaves the question of whether the investor is willing to undertake that amount of risk. The normal response to this question based upon economic theory is that the investor will attempt to invest in those securities that will maximize his expected utility. That is, the investor has some set of utility preferences that will specify the characteristics that acceptable investments must have. Hence, the investor is always assumed to be acting to maximize his expected utility. Obviously this is a conceptual formulation of investor behavior, but it assumes that utility preferences are the final result of a number of constraints that the investor may face. These may be psychological, or they may be imposed by other considerations. Whatever the source, many factors are presumed to play a role in determining the investor's utility preferences.

The important implication for investment management is that the security analyst must attempt to determine the expected amount of risk coincident with individual securities, and the portfolio manager must attempt to determine the

---

[1] Risk is generally defined as applying to situations in which the subjective probabilities can be reasonably estimated for specific outcomes. Uncertainty, on the other hand, is generally defined to apply to situations where these probabilities cannot be estimated. Throughout this text, however, we shall use the terms interchangeably.

amount of risk that the investor should take. Hence, the concept of risk is fundamental to both these functions of investment management. This chapter will introduce the concept of utility as well as several measures of risk. In particular, attention will be devoted to the various attitudes toward risk that individuals may exhibit. At the same time, several common measures of risk will be developed.

An Illustration of the Problem

To illustrate the type of situations the investor may face, consider the investor deciding whether to buy the warrants of a fairly small oil-producing firm. The warrants give the holder the opportunity to buy common stock at $28 per share. The common stock is currently selling for $10 per share and the warrants for $3. The warrants expire in two years. The investor has heard on "good authority" that the firm's extensive exploration program is about to pay off handsomely. Indications are that the firm may be on the verge of a big oil discovery. If this does occur, there is a good chance that the common stock may go as high as $40 per share. This means that the warrants could sell for as much as $12, if not more, depending upon the premium above the theoretical value. But this depends upon many factors, for example, the size of the field, the quality of the crude oil, and the location of the firm's lease parcels.

If the investor had $6,000 to invest, he could buy 2,000 warrants at current market prices, excluding brokerage costs. If the oil discovery materialized, the investor's 2,000 warrants could be worth as much as $24,000. On the other hand, if no oil was discovered, then the investor could very well lose his entire investment of $6,000. After considerable deliberation the investor develops the following probability distribution of possible outcomes:

Probability	Warrant price	Product
0.10	$12	$1.20
0.20	9	1.80
0.40	6	2.40
0.20	3	0.60
0.10	0	0.00
		$6.00

Therefore, the expected warrant price is the product of the probability times the corresponding outcome, meaning that the expected warrant price is $6.00. If the investor purchased 2,000 of these warrants at $3 per warrant, his expected gain would be $6,000 ($12,000 − $6,000). Hence, this investment could be quite profitable.

The fact that the situation promises a considerable return does not necessarily mean that the investor will invest in these warrants, even though there is a possibility of earning a 100 percent return over a two-year period. Actual behavior varies from investor to investor and depends upon each investor's evaluation of whether the expected return compensates for the risk involved. In this example, this tradeoff hinges on whether a possible gain of $6,000 is sufficient to compensate for the possibility of losing up to $6,000. The actual decision by a particular individual will depend upon his attitude toward risk. Some investors are willing to undertake very risky situations while others are not.

Attitudes Toward Risk

Every investment opportunity involves some degree of risk, and the major factor that determines whether a particular investment is suitable for an individual hinges largely on the matching of his preferences for risk and expected return with those of the security in question. It is common, therefore, to refer to the utility of a certain set of outcomes for a particular individual. The concept of utility originates with the classical economists; according to them, utility is measurable in specific units of satisfaction.

The expected utility of various risk situations will vary from person to person, but it is common to classify the attitudes toward risk into three categories of behavior, referred to as risk aversion, risk seeking, and risk neutral. The risk averter dislikes risk and consequently must be compensated for risk by what is referred to as a risk premium. The risk seeker, on the other hand, finds risky situations so much to his liking that he will actually pay a premium to take part in them. The typical gambling situation provides an example of risk-seeking behavior. The gambler participates even though the house takes a percentage off the top, which reduces his potential payoff. In roulette, for example, the payoff is $35 for a $1 bet on a single number, but the odds of winning are 1 in 38. Risk-neutral behavior occurs when the individual is unconcerned about the risk associated with a given payoff. Individuals exhibiting this type of behavior are concerned only with the expected return on a particular investment.

To illustrate these attitudes towards risky situations, consider two individuals in a typical gambling situation. Suppose that individual A approaches individual B on a Friday afternoon before the big Saturday football game against a conference rival and proposes a bet. Individual A wants to bet $10 on the home team. Individual B, in evaluating the possible outcomes, must weigh the utility of winning the $10 bet against the utility of losing $10. The expected value of the bet is simply given by

$$\overline{X} = pX_1 + qX_2 \qquad (5\text{-}1)$$

where p is the probability of losing, q is the probability of winning, X_1 is the value of the loss outcome, and X_2 is the value of the winning outcome. If the probability of each outcome is 0.5, substituting into Equation 5-1 gives

$$\overline{X} = 0.5(\$0) + 0.5(\$20) = \$10$$

This is a fair gamble, since the cost of the gamble to each player is equal to the expected value.

The fact that this is a fair gamble does not indicate whether individual B will enter into the bet. Individual B's actual behavior will depend on the utility of the $10 that may be lost versus the utility of the $10 that may be won. For example, if individual B has only $10 to last until Monday, payday, he may be very reluctant to undertake the bet. The disutility of being hungry all weekend may outweigh the utility of winning the $10. In this instance, the utility of $10 in the hand is much greater than the utility of winning $10, and he would be reluctant to enter into the bet. Individual A, on the other hand, may be eager to bet because he wants to take Mary Lou to a special night spot after the movie on Saturday night but he needs $20 to cover expenses.

In this situation individual B would have to be offered a premium to participate in the game. For example, he may be willing to bet $7 for the opportunity of winning $13. Thus, he is a risk averter. He must be paid a premium to participate in a fair gamble. Individual A, on the other hand, may be a risk seeker if he is willing to accept such a bet. Figure 5-1 contrasts the utility functions of a risk averter and a risk seeker. The outcomes, X_1 and X_2, correspond to those in Equation 5–1. The 45° ray extending from the origin gives the utility of the expected value. It also is the utility function of anyone who is risk neutral. That is, anyone who is indifferent to risk. Finally, X^* is the value of the potential payoffs to the risk averter and the risk seeker, respectively.

Referring to Figure 5-1(a), it is evident that the utility of the expected value of the gamble is somewhat less than $10. This is shown by X^*. Consequently, individual B would be willing to bet something less than the expected value. Conversely, the utility of $10 is somewhat greater than $U(\overline{X})$, and the expected payoff would have to be somewhat greater than the expected value as indicated by $\overline{X}$. The utility of the expected value to the risk seeker, on the other hand, is actually greater than $10, as shown in Figure 5-1(b). This is shown by X^*. Such an individual would actually be willing to pay a premium over the expected value in this bet. Hence, it is common to say that the risk averter requires a premium to accept risk, whereas the risk seeker will actually pay a premium to participate in a risky situation.

Most financial behavior is generally characterized by risk aversion. That is, it is widely accepted that rational behavior in risky situations requires an expected return that adequately compensates for the risk involved. To individual B, a certain $10 had more utility than an uncertain $20. The risk seeker, on the other hand, is willing to pay a premium to enter a risky situation simply because he places more utility on the winning payoff than he does on the losing payoff. For example, individual A appears to place more utility on a big night out with Mary Lou than on losing $10. However, it should be noted that individuals appear to be risk seekers in some situations and risk averters in others. For example, almost everyone has gambled at one time or other; this seems to indicate that individuals who are risk averters may become risk seekers on

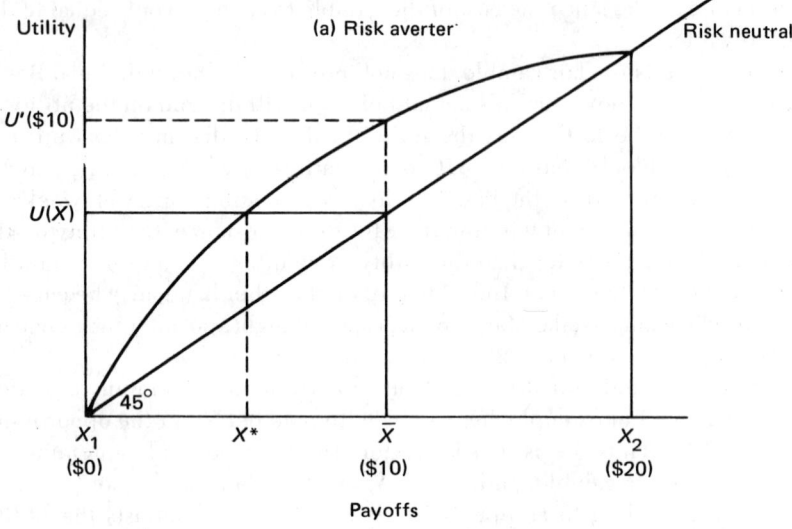

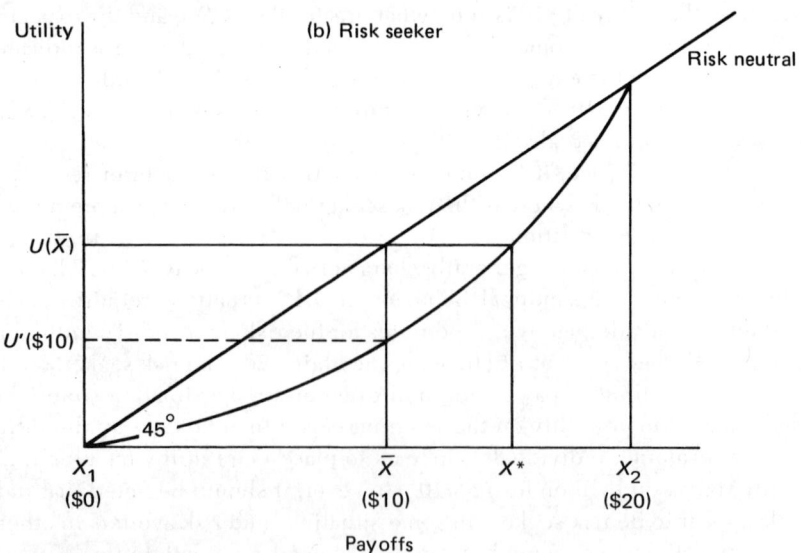

FIGURE 5-1 *The Utility of Risky Situations*

occasion. Milton Friedman and Leonard J. Savage suggest that individuals' utility functions may be concave over certain intervals and convex over other intervals.[2] As a result, individuals may not be exclusively risk seekers or risk averters.

Financial behavior, however, is assumed to be characterized by risk aversion, since this type of behavior is considered to be rational for risky situations. The risk averter, therefore, can be characterized as follows. First, he will not undertake a fair gamble. That is, he is not willing to pay the expected value to undertake a fair gamble, because the utility of the payoff is not sufficient. Second, a risk averter requires a premium to accept risk. If the premium is not sufficient, he may not participate. For example, if individual A had agreed to bet $11 against $9 of individual B, this would not mean that B would participate. The premium may be insufficient to draw him into the bet. Finally, it is generally assumed that the greater the risk, the greater the risk premium that is required to get a risk averter to participate. Thus, if the risk averter were asked to select one security from among three with the same expected return and different levels of risk, he would select the one with the lowest level of risk.

The concepts of risk aversion, risk seeking, and risk neutrality can easily be transformed to a risk-expected return framework as illustrated in Figure 5-2. In Figure 5-2(a) it is evident that the risk averter requires a higher expected return to compensate for additional risk. This assumes diminishing marginal utility. The risk seeker, as illustrated in Figure 5-2(c), will actually accept a lower expected return than the risky situation may offer. This results because the risk seeker attaches more utility to the possibility of exceptional gain, even though the expected return may be lower. The higher risk associated with the chance of exceptional gain does not deter the risk seeker. The risk averter, on the other hand, is concerned with the possibility of exceptional loss. Finally, the risk neutral, as shown in Figure 5-2(b), is indifferent to risk. Such an investor ranks potential investment opportunities purely in terms of their expected return.

FIGURE 5-2 *Risk-Expected Return Indifference Curves*

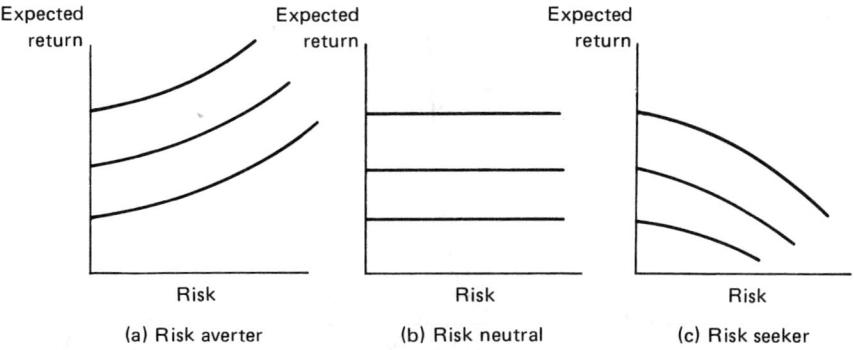

(a) Risk averter   (b) Risk neutral   (c) Risk seeker

[2] Milton Friedman and Leonard J. Savage, "Utility Analysis of Choices Involving Risk," *Journal of Political Economy*, vol. 55, no. 4 (Aug., 1948), pp. 279–304.

Measuring Risk and Return

The discussion of the concepts of risk and return has been quite general up to this point. However, these terms are central to investment management. The investment decision is characterized as a tradeoff between risk and expected return, unless the investor is risk neutral, which many consider unlikely. In addition, there is not one accepted measure of risk and return. It is therefore necessary to begin with some basic definitions and then proceed to their applications.

Expected Return and Variance

The common measures of central tendency and dispersion of probability distributions are the expected value and standard deviation. The expected value and the standard deviation are graphically illustrated in Figure 5-3 for stocks A and B. In each case the expected value is $50. But the dispersion of outcomes for stock B is much greater than that for stock A. In essence, we have a situation in which the expected monetary value is the same, $50 for both stocks, but the dispersion of possible outcomes is quite different. If risk can be associated with dispersion, stock B would be riskier than stock A. If a risk averter and a risk seeker were considering buying these shares, the risk averter would prefer stock A because of the greater certainty of its expected value. A risk seeker may prefer stock B because of the possibility of the stock's price going as high as $100.

The rate of return is generally determined as a percent return on invested capital. For stocks, this includes capital appreciation or loss and dividend income, while for bonds this includes capital appreciation or loss and interest

FIGURE 5-3   *Dispersion of Returns*

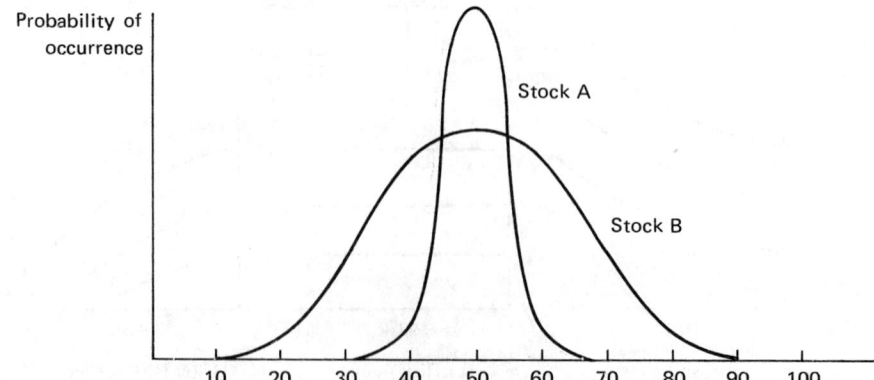

income. The return on a security, therefore, reflects the change in capital value as well as cash inflows in the form of dividends or interest. The return on a common stock for a given year can be determined as follows:[3]

$$R_{it} = \frac{P_{it} + D_{it} - P_{it-1}}{P_{it-1}} \qquad (5\text{-}2)$$

where P_{it} is the price of stock i at time t, D_{it} is the dividends received on stock i during the time t, and P_{it-1} is the price of the stock at time $t - 1$.

To illustrate, suppose that on January 1, 1973, a certain common stock is selling for $60. One year ago it sold for $50, and during 1972 dividends of $3.50 were paid. The return during this one-year period then would be

$$R = \frac{60 + 3.50 - 50}{50}$$

$$= \frac{13.50}{50}$$

$$= 0.27 \text{ or } 27 \text{ percent}$$

The return for this one-year period is 27 percent.

It is convenient to state the return as return relative, which means the return is referenced in terms of one. If the return relative is greater than one, then there has been a positive return. On the other hand, if the return relative is less than one, the return has been negative. Equation 5-2 can be conveniently converted to a return relative as follows:

$$RR_{it} = \frac{P_{it} + D_{it}}{P_{it-1}} \qquad (5\text{-}3)$$

where the terms are as previously defined. To illustrate the derivation of a return relative, RR, the data for our hypothetical common stock can be substituted into Equation 5-3 to give[4]

$$RR = \frac{60 + 3.50}{50} = 1.27$$

Thus, the RR for our common stock is 1.27, which indicates an annual return of 27 percent.

---

[3] For bonds this formulation would be

$$R_{it} = \frac{B_{it} + I_t - B_{it-1}}{B_{it-1}}$$

where B_{it-1} is the price of bond i at time $t-1$, I_t is the interest income received during time t, and B_{it} is the price of bond i at time t. Note that when an investor buys a bond, the expected return is given as the yield to maturity. The above formulation gives the actual return while the yield to maturity gives the anticipated return.

[4] A return relative may also be referred to as a holding period return, HPR. See Henry A. Latane and Donald L. Tuttle, *Security Analysis and Portfolio Management* (New York: The Ronald Press, 1970), Chapter 4.

Return relatives are convenient to use for two reasons. First, as we have seen, the return on a particular security is made up of the change in capital value plus dividends or interest income. A return relative easily reflects these factors and indicates the return that has been realized. Second, and more important, the return on securities over time is a compound return, which means that to determine the average compound return, the geometric mean return, the return for individual periods must be stated in form $1 + R$. Since the return on securities is compounded over time, this feature of the *RR* becomes quite convenient for this calculation. In addition, the wealth-maximization model of portfolio composition discussed in Part IV makes extensive use of the geometric mean return. Thus, the return relative is a useful form for our purposes.

A common measure of return is the expected return. This is simply an arithmetic mean that can be defined as follows:

$$\overline{RR}_i = \frac{1}{n} \sum_{t=1}^{n} RR_{it} \tag{5-4}$$

where the terms are as previously defined. The disperion about this mean is commonly used as a measure of risk. The standard deviation can be used to determine this dispersion and is defined as:

$$\sigma_i = \left[\frac{1}{n-1} \sum_{t=1}^{n} (RR_{it} = \overline{RR}_i)^2 \right]^{\frac{1}{2}} \tag{5-5}$$

To illustrate, suppose we have the following *RR*s for the common stock for a certain corporation:

Period	RR	rr	(rr)²
1	0.96	−0.13	0.0169
2	1.10	0.01	0.0001
3	1.20	0.11	0.0121
4	0.99	−0.10	0.0100
5	1.05	−0.04	0.0016
6	1.10	0.01	0.0001
7	1.20	0.11	0.0121
8	1.60	0.51	0.2601
9	0.90	−0.19	0.0361
10	0.80	−0.29	0.0841
	10.90		0.4332

The mean return relative for this series of *RR*s is found to be

$$\overline{RR} = \tfrac{1}{10} (10.90) = 1.09$$

Similarly, the standard deviation is determined to be

$$\sigma = [\tfrac{1}{9} (0.4332)]^{\frac{1}{2}} = \pm 0.2194$$

Therefore, the $\overline{RR}$ is 1.09 and the standard deviation is 0.219. If risk can be associated with standard deviation, the $\overline{RR}$ is 1.09 ± 0.219. Thus, the smaller the range of the $\pm\ \sigma$ the smaller risk, and the more certain we are of obtaining the $\overline{RR}$.

From the $\overline{RR}_i$ and σ_i it becomes an easy matter to determine the expected return, μ_i, and the standard deviation of that return. The μ_i is simply found by

$$\mu_i = \overline{RR}_i - 1.0 \tag{5-6}$$

where the terms are as previously defined. The dispersion about μ_i is unchanged from that determined by Equation 5-5. Thus, the standard deviation is 0.219 and the expected return is 0.09. Or, stated differently, the expected return is 9.0 percent with a standard deviation of $\pm\ 21.9$ percent.

With the standard deviation and the expected return for a security, a cardinal measure of risk can be determined as follows:

$$CV = \frac{\sigma_i}{\mu_i} \tag{5-7}$$

where CV is the coefficient of variation, and the other variables are as previously defined. For the common stock of firm A, the coefficient of variation is

$$CV = \frac{0.22}{0.09} = 2.44$$

If risk can be associated with the variation in expected return, the larger this ratio the greater the uncertainty of obtaining the expected return.

Geometric Mean Return

The investment decision involves cumulative returns over time. During the holding period, the return to the investor is the change in the market value plus the cash received in the form of dividends or interest. If the holding period is one year, the return relative gives an accurate measure of the return. For longer periods of time, it is evident that we are dealing with a series that is being compounded at some unknown rate. Most of us are familiar with this concept in the form of compound interest. Consequently, the geometric mean return is a more appropriate measure than the arithmetic mean return. The geometric mean may be defined as follows:

$$G_i = \left[\prod_{t=1}^{n} RR_{it} \right]^{1/n} \tag{5-8}$$

where $\prod$ is the product of the RR_{it}s for n years. The geometric mean G then is the nth root of the product of n annual return relatives.

Returning to our previous example, the geometric mean return for the stock is

$$G = [(0.96)\ (1.10)\ (1.20)\ (0.99)\ (1.05) \ldots (0.80)]^{1/10}$$
$$= 1.072$$

The geometric mean return, G, is 1.072, which is slightly less than the arithmetic mean, $\overline{RR}$, of 1.09.[5] The geometric mean, G, is normally less than the arithmetic mean, $\overline{RR}$, and the greater the dispersion of the distribution the greater the spread. This fact is utilized in determining the standard deviation.

To determine the degree of dispersion about the geometric mean, the standard deviation is

$$\sigma_i = [(\overline{RR}_i^2 - G_i^2)]^{1/2} \tag{5-9}$$

where the other variables are as previously defined. Thus, once the arithmetic and geometric means are known, they can be used to determine the standard deviation about the geometric mean. The standard deviation for our hypothetical stock is

$$\sigma = [(1.09)^2 - (1.072)^2]^{1/2}$$
$$= 0.1972$$

As previously indicated, the standard deviation can be utilized to give an indication of the risk associated with obtaining a G of 1.072 by indicating that the investor can be approximately 68 percent certain of a G of 1.072 ± 0.1972. The compound rate of return can then be found in the same fashion as for the expected return. That is, 1 is subtracted from the geometric mean return. In this example the compound rate of return is 7.2 percent with a standard deviation of ± 19.7 percent.

Two Important Utility Functions

Fundamental to the discussion of risk is the utility that the investor assigns to expected outcomes. Earlier in the discussion of attitudes to risk, the utility of various outcomes was used to illustrate the basic attitudes of risk aversion and risk seeking. The following discussion will focus on two utility functions that are commonly referred to in the financial literature and used in portfolio composition theory. In both cases these utility functions make important assumptions about the nature of the decision-makers' preferences for risk and expected return.

Quadratic Utility Functions

It will be recalled from the earlier discussion of attitudes toward risk that the individual's utility function for risky situations may be linear, which means the individual is risk neutral, or nonlinear, which means that he is either a risk

---

[5] There are several ways to determine the geometric mean, but probably the easiest is to determine the product in the brackets of Equation 5-8 and then use logarithms. The geometric mean for the stock in the example is determined as follows:

$$G_i = \tfrac{1}{10} \log \left(\prod_{t=1}^{n} RR_{it} \right)$$
$$= \tfrac{1}{10} \log (2.003)$$
$$= (0.0302)$$
$$= \text{antilog of } (0.0302)$$
$$= 1.072$$

seeker or a risk averter. It is common to represent risk aversion as a concave function as shown in Figure 5-4. Investors with this type of utility function exhibit behavior in which increases in return have diminishing marginal utility. By comparison, individuals with linear utility curves, as represented by the curve $U = R$, have constant utility for increases in return. The concave utility curve is consistent with risk aversion because risk aversion means that the investor requires a risk premium to compensate for additional risk. The linear function $U = R$ does not, however, since each additional unit of return has the same utility as the previous one. This function, therefore, is consistent with risk neutral behavior.

A concave curve can be represented by the simple expression

$$U = a + bR + cR^2 \qquad (5\text{-}10)$$

where U is utility, R is the return, a and b are positive constants, and c is a negative constant. Equation 5-10 is quadratic in R and therefore is a quadratic utility curve. Generally, however, the utility of investing in securities is measured in terms of the expected return, μ, and the standard deviation, σ. Therefore, these terms must be substituted into Equation 5-10, and in particular it should be noted that the term R^2 becomes $(\sigma^2 + \mu^2)$. This is necessary because

FIGURE 5-4 *Concave and Linear Utility Curves*

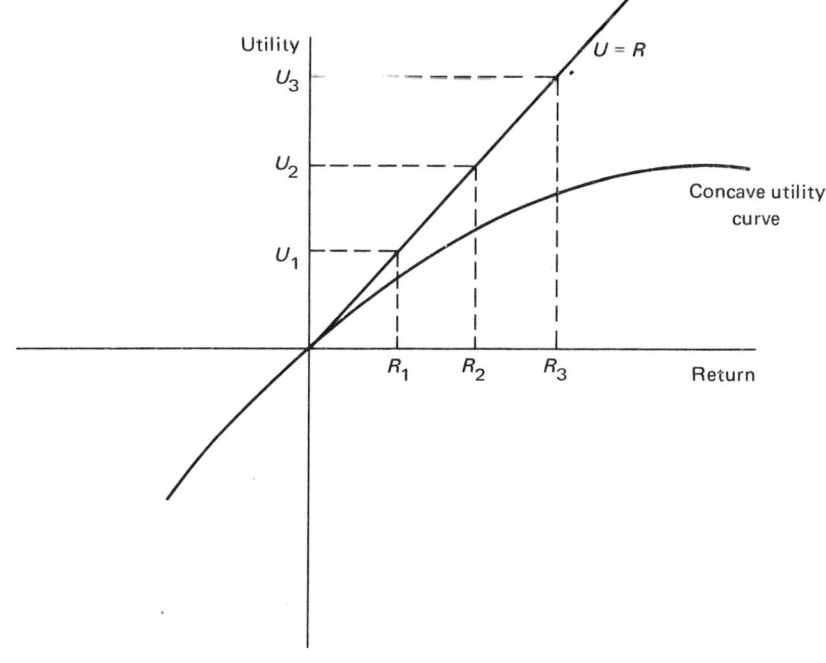

utility is now being determined in terms of μ and σ and not just R. Thus, the expected utility is given by

$$E(U) = a + b\mu + c(\sigma^2 + \mu^2) \tag{5-11}$$

where the terms are as previously defined.

Quadratic indifference curves are commonly used in portfolio analysis because they are relatively simple in their derivation as illustrated above, and also because they incorporate the assumption of risk aversion, which is intuitively appealing. Figure 5-5 illustrates a family of quadratic indifference curves. Each indifference curve represents equal utility, which means the investor would be indifferent to expected return-risk combinations that fall on any of these indifference curves. For example, the investor would be indifferent to the investment opportunities represented by the points a and b. That is, the opportunity represented by point a would be equally as acceptable as the opportunity represented by point b. Moreover, these quadratic indifference curves assume risk aversion. Consider again points a and b. As the risk increases, measured by the standard deviation, the expected return also increases to compensate for the additional risk. Hence, these quadratic indifference curves are consistent with risk averse behavior.

Finally, it is generally assumed that individuals prefer higher levels of satisfaction to lower levels; therefore, it is expected that individuals will tend to move to the highest possible level of satisfaction. Increasing utility is represented by the movement from right to left as indicated by the arrow. Consider

FIGURE 5-5 *Indifference Curves Reflecting Quadratic Utility*

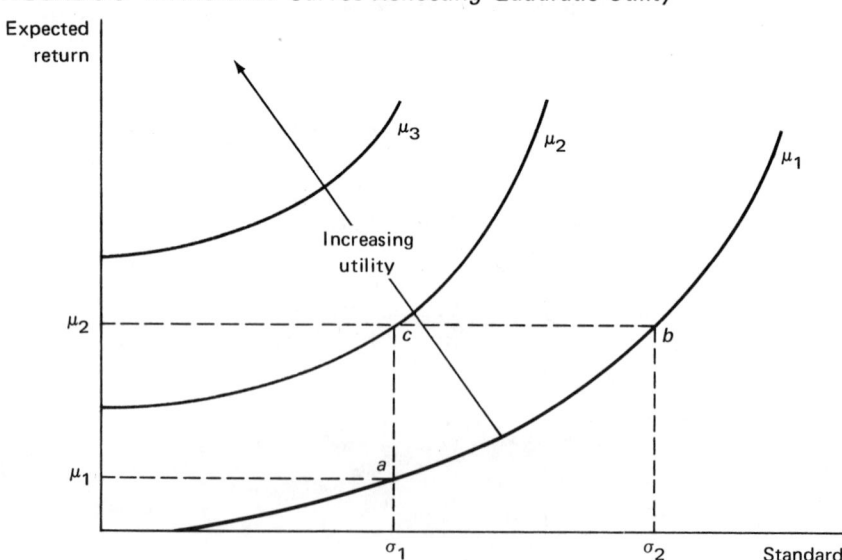

points a and c. It is expected that the typical investor would prefer the investment opportunity represented by point c to that represented by point a. This conclusion follows because the risk associated with the two opportunities is equal, that is, σ_1, but the expected return associated with opportunity c is higher. It is expected, therefore, that opportunity c would be preferred.

In spite of their intuitive appeal, the quadratic utility functions have several weaknesses. First, an examination of Figure 5-6 indicates that quadratic utility functions reach a maximum at some point. Tracing the quadratic utility functions in Figure 5–6, it is evident that the expected utility increases as the expected return increases up to a point and then declines. This maximum occurs at the point given by $\mu = -b/2c$.[6] Logically, it is difficult to justify the utility of a return beyond some point actually falling. Since this does not seem to be rational, it is common to cut off the utility function at this point. This practice raises the question of whether the utility function covers the relevant range. A second weakness of the quadratic utility function is that it utilizes a finite variance. Some empirical studies tend to indicate that the variance of common stock returns is infinite, and that the quadratic utility function is therefore not appropriate. This is a controversial position that does not have wide acceptance.

FIGURE 5-6 *A Hypothetical Safety First Utility Function*

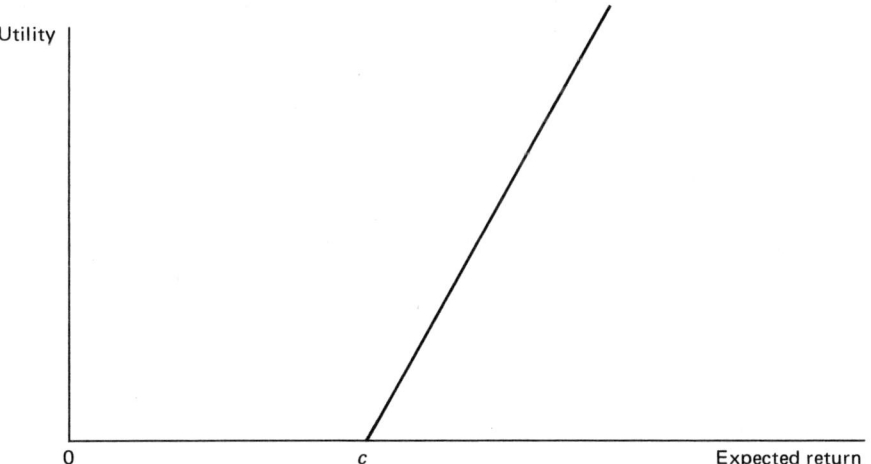

[6] This can be shown as follows:

$$E(U) = a + b_1\mu + c_2(\mu^2 + \sigma^2)$$

$$\frac{\partial E(U)}{\partial \mu} = b + 2c_\mu$$

where $b > 0$ and $c < 0$. Setting the derivative equal to zero indicates that a maximum occurs at $\mu = -b/2c$. For values of $\mu > -b/2c$, the derivative is negative, and it is common to assume that the indifference curve is invalid over this range.

Safety First

An alternative utility function that has much intuitive appeal is one in which the investor requires a minimum acceptable return.[7] For example, the investor may have a constraint that requires a 6 percent return on his investments to maintain a certain standard of living. This investor's minimum acceptable return is 6 percent, and he is concerned with the probabilities of not obtaining it. A more general example is to impute a cost of capital to the investor in the same fashion as is commonly done in managerial finance. This is not an unrealistic approach since it is widely assumed that investors have required returns for various types of securities. Therefore, the investor using a safety first criterion is concerned with the probabilities of not receiving this required return. This type of utility function places the primary emphasis on the probabilities of not attaining some minimum return.

Such a utility function takes the following form:

$$U(\mu) > 0, \mu \geq c$$
$$U(\mu) < 0, \mu < c$$

where c is the minimum acceptable return. This concept is shown in Figure 5-6. It is evident that rates of return above point c have positive utility, and this utility is shown as being linearly related to expected returns above point c.[8] This means that an investment with an expected return of 20 percent is preferred to one with an expected return of 15 percent. Since the safety first criterion places primary emphasis on the probability of not attaining some minimum return, semivariance is used as the measure of risk.

The semivariance can be obtained as follows:

$$SV_i = \frac{1}{n-1} \sum_{t=1}^{n} (RR_{it} - c)^2 \qquad \text{for all } RR_{it} < c \tag{5-12}$$

where SV is the semivariance of stock i, c is a minimum acceptable return, and the remaining terms are as previously defined. The semistandard deviation can be derived from Equation 5-12 in the same fashion as the standard deviation is determined when the variance is known. Therefore, the semistandard deviation is given by

$$\sigma_i^* = (SV_i)^{1/2} \tag{5-13}$$

To illustrate the use of the semivariance as a measure of risk, suppose we have the following RRs for two stocks, X and Y. In addition, suppose that the minimum acceptable return is 10 percent, or an RR of 1.10.

---

[7] A. D. Roy uses this type of utility function. See A. D. Roy, "Safety First and the Holding of Assets," *Econometrica*, vol. 20, no. 3 (July, 1952), pp. 431–49.

[8] An extreme form of the safety first criterion is

$$U(\mu) = 1, \mu \geq c$$
$$U(\mu) = 0, \mu < c$$

This type of function indicates that all returns above c have constant utility. Consequently, the investor with this type of utility function is only concerned with the probability of obtaining a return of c.

Time	Stock X			Stock Y		
	RR	rr*	(rr*)²	RR	rr*	(rr*)²
1	0.90	−0.20	0.0400	0.80	−0.30	0.0900
2	1.05	−0.05	0.0025	0.90	−0.20	0.0400
3	1.20	0.00	0.000	1.05	−0.05	0.0025
4	1.30	0.00	0.000	1.18	0.00	0.0000
5	1.30	0.00	0.000	1.20	0.00	0.0000
	5.90		0.0425	4.93		0.1325

The semivariance for stock X is

$$SV = \tfrac{1}{4}(0.0425) = 0.0106$$

while that for stock Y is

$$SV = \tfrac{1}{4}(0.1325) = 0.0331$$

The semistandard deviation is

$$(0.0106)^{1/2} = 0.1031 \text{ for stock X and}$$
$$(0.0331)^{1/2} = 0.1819 \text{ for stock Y}$$

If the investor wants to minimize the probability of the expected return falling below 10 percent, stock X is preferred to stock Y because its semivariance is smaller. Note that the RRs for both stocks are asymmetrical. If the distributions were symmetrical about c, the semivariance would be one-half the variance. (This is illustrated in Question 6 at the end of this chapter.)

The safety first utility function has several desirable features. First, it assumes risk aversion. That is, the investor is very much concerned about the probabilities of obtaining a return below some minimum level. Second, returns beyond this minimum have increasing utility. This is a definite advantage over the quadratic utility function, which reaches a maximum. The safety first criterion has several disadvantages, however. First, using semistandard deviation as a measure of risk is believed by some to be more difficult to compute. Standard deviation is more familiar to most investment analysts, although the greater familiarity with statistics by most analysts may not make this such an important disadvantage as it once was. Second, empirical studies have shown that semistandard deviation is a poor measure of risk. If this is indeed the case, despite its intuitive appeal the safety first criterion may not be an appropriate measure of risk.

Summary

Fundamental to investment decision-making is the concept of investors' preferences. Some investors are willing and able to take risks, while others are not. Of particular importance is the tradeoff between risk and expected return. Neoclassical economics indicates that the investor attempts to maximize his expected utility for a given investment or portfolio. To analyze this tradeoff between risk and expected return required the simultaneous development of the concepts of expected utility, risk, and expected return. Traditional utility theory was used to illustrate the concept of expected utility. To relate expected utility to investment management required that we develop the concepts of risk and expected return. The concept of an annual return relative will prove useful in subsequent discussion. Dispersion about the expected return was used to determine risk; consequently, the standard deviation was introduced as a measure of risk. Another useful concept is the geometric mean return. Returns in investment management are more adequately described by a geometric mean than an arithmetic mean. Therefore, this measure as well as its standard deviation are useful alternatives to the arithmetic mean, the expected return.

Finally, the concepts of expected utility, risk, and expected return were combined in the discussion of the quadratic utility function and the safety first utility function. The quadratic utility function has the desirable features of simplicity and risk aversion, but it may not cover the range of expected returns. The safety first criterion is intuitively appealing. Expected returns above the minimum acceptable return have increasing utility. Nevertheless, there are practical difficulties with this criterion. Probably the most important disadvantage is the lack of empirical verification of the usefulness of semistandard deviation as a measure of risk.

Questions

1. A major consideration in investment management is determining the risk associated with securities and the investor's ability to accept risk. What are the commonly recognized attitudes toward risk?

2. Stock X and Stock Y have the following prices and dividends for the period 1961–70:

	Stock X Price			Stock Y Price		
Year	January 1	December 31	Dividends	January 1	December 31	Dividends
1961	$20.00	$25.00	$1.00	$33.50	$40.25	$1.20
1962	25.00	18.00	1.00	40.25	45.00	1.20
1963	18.00	25.00	1.00	45.00	46.00	1.20
1964	25.00	35.00	1.20	46.00	28.00	1.00
1965	35.00	42.00	1.30	28.00	25.00	1.00
1966	42.00	48.00	1.30	25.00	20.00	1.10
1967	48.00	30.00	1.40	20.00	28.00	1.20
1968	30.00	40.00	1.40	28.00	32.00	1.20
1969	40.00	30.00	1.50	32.00	34.00	1.20
1970	30.00	35.00	1.50	34.00	42.00	1.20

   a. Determine the arithmetic mean return relatives and standard deviation for the stocks.

   b. What is the expected return for each stock?

c. Using the coefficient of variation as a cardinal measure of risk, which stock is riskier?

d. What is the geometric mean return and the dispersion about the geometric mean return for these two stocks?

3. The arithmetic mean *RR*s and standard deviations have been estimated for the following stocks:

Stock	$\overline{RR}$	σ
A	1.10	0.02
B	1.12	0.12
C	1.08	0.02
D	1.06	0.03
E	1.25	0.12

a. Determine the coefficient of variation for each stock and rank the stocks from least risky to most risky.

b. Which stock or stocks would you purchase? Why?

c. What type of investor would select securities purely on the basis of expected return, ignoring risk?

4. The quadratic utility function presupposes risk aversion on the part of the investor. Explain why this is true.

5. An alternative utility function that is intuitively appealing is one in which the investor minimizes the probability of the expected return on a security falling below a certain level. If the minimum acceptable return is 10 percent, which stock in Question 2 is the better buy?

Selected References

Bernoulli, Daniel. "Exposition of a New Theory on the Measurement of Risk." *Econometrica*, vol. 22, no. 1 (Jan., 1954), pp. 23–36.

Curran, Ward S. *Principles of Financial Management.* New York: McGraw-Hill, 1970. Chapter 7.

Friedman, Milton and Leonard J. Savage. "The Utility Analysis of Choices Involving Risk." *The Journal of Political Economy*, vol. 56, no. 4 (Aug., 1948), pp. 279–304.

Latane, Henry A. "Criteria for Choice Among Risky Ventures." *The Journal of Political Economy*, vol. 67, no. 2 (Apr., 1959), pp. 144–55.

Latane, Henry A. and Donald L. Tuttle. *Security Analysis and Portfolio Management.* New York: The Ronald Press, 1970. Chapter 24.

Mao, James C. T. *Quantitative Analysis of Financial Decisions.* London: MacMillan, 1968. Chapter 2.

———. "Models of Capital Budgeting, E-V vs. E-S. *Journal of Financial and Quantitative Analysis*, vol. 4, no. 5 (Jan., 1970), pp. 657–76.

Markowitz, Harry. *Portfolio Selection: Efficient Diversification of Investments.* New York: John Wiley and Sons, 1959.

Moore, Basil J. *An Introduction to the Theory of Finance: Assetholder Behavior Under Uncertainty.* New York: The Free Press, 1968. Chapter 2.

Roy, A. D. "Safety First and the Holding of Assets." *Econometrica*, vol. 20, no. 3 (July, 1952), pp. 431–49.

Stigler, George J. "The Development of Utility Theory." *The Journal of Political Economy*, vol. 58, nos. 4 and 5 (Aug. and Oct., 1950), pp. 307–27 and pp. 373–96, respectively.

Tobin, J. "Liquidity Preference as Behavior Towards Risk." *The Review of Economic Studies*, vol. 26, no. 1 (Feb., 1958), pp. 65–86.

Von Neuman, John and Oskar Morgenstern. *Theory of Games and Economic Behavior.* Princeton, N.J.: Princeton University Press, 1947.

Chapter 6

A Framework for Analysis

Chapter 5 illustrated that investment management involves decision-making under conditions of uncertainty. We now turn to the problem of estimating returns in such an environment. The return on securities is composed of dividends or interest plus the change in market price over a specific period of time. The function of security analysis is to estimate the size of each of these streams of benefits and the assurance of receiving them. This task is more difficult for common stock than it is for bonds because there is greater uncertainty associated with the returns on common stock. In the evaluation of common stock, a concept known as the intrinsic value is commonly used as a means of estimating the anticipated return. This concept implies that the shares of a firm have some central or intrinsic value that can be estimated from the historical performance of the firm.

For bonds the underlying process is not essentially different, but the nature of the bond instrument makes the analysis much simpler. Bonds are a prior-claim security, and investors buy them because there is greater assurance of receiving principal and interest. Since interest, principal, and maturity are stated explicitly in the bond contract, it becomes an easy matter to ascertain the anticipated yield to maturity. However, there is always the possibility of bankruptcy and default, which may mean a loss of principal as well as interest to the bondholder. As a general rule, the bond analyst attempts to analyze everything that might affect the firm's ability to pay interest and principal. This analysis includes standard ratio analysis to determine the financial performance of the firm, an evaluation of the protective covenants, and an evaluation of any other qualitative factors that may be relevant, such as quality of management and past solvency record. Once all these factors have been analyzed, the bond analyst assigns a rating to the bond, indicating the probabilities of default on interest and principal payments. With these ratings the investor can decide whether to invest in a particular bond issue or not.

Whether the analysis is of a bond or a stock, it has four distinct steps. It appears that the performance of a particular firm is the result of a complex interaction of a number of forces that range from those that are national in scope to those that are peculiar to the individual firm. In some cases these factors are highly dependent; in other cases they are highly independent. The four steps in the process of evaluation are designed to aid in evaluating these linkages as they pertain to a particular firm. The first step is the analysis of economic conditions. Generally, the performance of most industries and most firms is closely related to that of the economy as a whole. The second step is industry analysis, which enables the analyst to determine the relative performance of various industries given a postulated outlook for the economy. This analysis is particularly useful for evaluating the growth prospects for various industries. The third step is the analysis of the performance of the firm within its economic and industrial context. The performance of firms varies, given a particular economic and industry outlook, and firm analysis attempts to determine the relative performance of individual firms. The final step is the analysis of market conditions. In the final analysis, the return that will be earned on a particular security depends largely on market conditions, and therefore market conditions are an important factor in investment management. Some of the factors involved in steps one and two were discussed in Part I. The task that remains is to analyze the firm and then determine the combined effect of these four factors as they affect the expected return and the risk associated with a particular security.

In the past it was commonly assumed that the market performance of the firm's common stock depended solely on its economic performance. For example, if a firm was highly profitable and had rapid growth in earnings, it was assumed that the market would recognize this performance, which would then be reflected in the price of the stock. This is probably a valid assumption in the long-run, but close observation of the stock market indicates that expectations may diverge from current performance. In other words, a stock may show steady upward growth in earnings per share, yet the stock price may actually be falling. Another aspect of market conditions is the amount that investors will pay for each dollar of earnings or dividends. Growth stocks commonly sell at very high price-earnings ratios. A dollar of earnings for these stocks may command anywhere from $25 to $100, depending on conditions. This is somewhat higher than the Dow-Jones Industrial Average, which normally commands $15 to $25. Consequently, a shift in the general level of the price-earnings ratios constitutes a major source of risk to the common stock investor.[1]

Also, market conditions have a significant impact on the value of high-quality bonds and debentures.[2] For example, a 4 percent debenture with 10 years to

---

[1] For an example of the importance of market-related risks as opposed to firm-related risks, see Benjamin F. King, "Market and Industry Factors in Stock Price Behavior," *Journal of Business,* vol. 39, no. 1, part II (Jan., 1966), pp. 139–90.

[2] For an example of the impact of changing interest rates on bond prices, see Harry C. Sauvain, "Changing Interest Rates and the Investment Portfolio," *Journal of Finance,* vol. 14, no. 2 (May, 1959), pp. 230–44.

maturity priced to yield 7.5 percent will sell for $756.80. For the investor who bought this debenture at par, his wealth has declined by $243.20 because of the change in interest rates in the market. This sort of situation is not unusual. For example, in 1965 interest rates on high-quality corporate bonds ranged between 4.5 and 5.0 percent, yet by 1972 interest rates on high-quality corporate bonds had risen to 7.0 percent. As a result, the bond investor faces market-related risks just like the common stock investor. The major difference is that bonds will be redeemed at par upon reaching maturity; they therefore have a fixed value at some point in time. Nevertheless, changes in interest rates can have a severe impact on bond values.

It is convenient, therefore, to reduce the analysis of securities to those factors that affect the firm—firm-related risks—and those that affect market conditions—market-related risks. Obviously such a framework is an oversimplification. The underlying factors are interdependent. General economic conditions and industry factors affect the performance of firms in some fashion, but these same factors will also influence market conditions. Similarly, the performance of the firm is reflected in the market price of its securities. The factors that affect the firm's performance and general market conditions are not independent; they simultaneously influence one another. Nevertheless, for the purpose of evaluating securities, the terms *firm-related* and *market-related* are useful for isolating the major sources of risk.

Firm-Related Risks

The price an investor will pay for a security may be defined as the present value of a future stream of benefits discounted at the appropriate rate. Typically, the stream of benefits can take two distinct forms. One is that of contracting for a constant income stream for a finite period of time. This is normally the case in bond or debenture investment. The bondholder contracts for a definite stream of interest payments for the life of the bond or debenture, at which time the principal amount is repaid. Dividend payments on common stock, however, are neither contractual nor constant. The common stockholder has a claim to dividends only if declared. It is common, however, to assume that dividends will increase at some rate over time. The following discussion will begin with the common approaches to common stock valuation and then turn to the valuation of debt instruments.

Common Stock Valuation

The value of a common share is generally derived from three different sources. These are as follows:

1. Liquidating value
2. Dividends per share
3. Earnings per share

Liquidating value is generally defined to mean the book value per share. This measure generally has little relevancy since it presupposes liquidation, which normally means that the firm has been operating at unprofitable levels. Consequently, when the assets of such firms are sold they may very well be sold at prices considerably less than their value on the books of the firm. A major reason for this is that these assets are highly specialized, and therefore are not in wide demand. The exception to this general rule occurs in cases where the assets are securities and not plant and equipment. In such instances the book value per share has some meaning.[3]

The question of whether investors place the emphasis on dividends or earnings per share cannot be so easily resolved. There has been much discussion of the stream of benefits that investors do capitalize. Cash dividends traditionally were thought to be the stream of benefits that investors purchased.[4] Merton H. Miller and Franco Modigliani in their classic article on dividend policy, however, put forth a very sophisticated argument for the irrelevancy of dividends.[5] This question is unresolved to the satisfaction of all parties, but the consensus appears to be that investors do purchase a stream of cash dividends.[6] The rationale for this point of view can be illustrated simply. Suppose a firm was incorporated, and its charter stated explicitly that the firm would never pay dividends. The advocates of dividends argue that this firm will never be worth anything to the average stockholder because the benefits will never be realized. Even though this firm may be very profitable, its stock will not have any value, because these profits cannot be passed on to the stockholders in the form of dividends.

Admittedly, this is an idealistic situation, but it does illustrate how the profits ultimately must be available to the stockholders at some point in time. Dividends can be deferred while the firm is experiencing above-average growth, but ultimately the purpose for buying stock is believed to be the dividends that will be received. Consequently, the dividend valuation model is used in most theoretical work. For example, in determining the cost of retained earnings in the cost of capital calculation, the dividend valuation model is used. Yet in security analysis it is common practice to use an earnings per share valuation model. The general reasons given for this are: (1) the *EPS* valuation model is simpler and easier to work with, and (2) the *EPS* valuation model provides a method to deal with stocks that do not pay dividends. In the subsequent analysis, aspects of both of these models will be used. In general the rationale of the dividend valuation model will be accepted as the explanation for investors buying common stock. At the same time, the ease of analysis connected with the *EPS* valuation model will be useful for certain calculations.

[3] Liquidating value would be a meaningful measure for such firms as investment companies and some mining companies, whose assets are made up largely of securities or cash.
[4] For a discussion that follows the traditional vein, see Benjamin Graham, David L. Dodd, and Sidney Cottle, *Security Analysis: Principles and Techniques*, 4th ed. (New York: McGraw-Hill, 1962), p. 518.
[5] Merton H. Miller and Franco Modigliani, "Dividend Policy, Growth, and the Valuation of Shares," *Journal of Business*, vol. 34, no. 4 (Oct., 1961), pp. 411–33.
[6] Stephen A. Archer and LeRoy G. Faerber, "Firm Size and the Cost of Externally Secured Equity Capital," *Journal of Finance*, vol. 21, no. 1 (Mar., 1966).

Dividend Valuation Model   The current price of a share may be defined as the present value of expected future dividends discounted at the rate the investor expects to receive. The current price of a share is given by

$$P_{io} = \frac{D_{i1}}{(1+k)} + \frac{D_{i2}}{(1+k)^2} + \frac{D_{i3}}{(1+k)^2} + \cdots + \frac{D_{i\infty}}{(1+k)^\infty} \tag{6-1}$$

where $D_{i1}, D_{i2}, D_{i3}, \ldots D_{i\infty}$ are the dividends paid on stock i at times $1, 2, 3, \ldots,$ ∞, K is the return required by the investor on stock i.

Dividends on common stock, however, are expected to grow over time. Dividends may be reduced during periods of low profits, but there appears to be a reluctance on the part of firms to reduce dividends unless absolutely necessary. Equation 6-1, therefore, can be restated to include the constant growth rate that may be reasonably expected. The current price of a share would then be given by

$$P_{io} = \frac{D_{i1}}{(1+k)} + \frac{D_{i1}(1+g)}{(1+k)^2} + \frac{D_{i1}(1+g)^2}{(1+k)^3} + \cdots + \frac{D_1(1+g)^\infty}{(1+k)^\infty} \tag{6-2}$$

where g is a constant growth rate, and D_{i1} is the dividend paid on stock i at time $t = 1$. Equation 6-2 is an infinite series and therefore can be simplified to[7]

$$P_{io} = \frac{D_{i1}}{k-g} \qquad k > g \tag{6-3}$$

This means simply that the current price an investor is willing to pay for a common share is equal to the dividend at time $= 1, D_1$, capitalized at a rate of $k - g$. For the capitalization rate, $k - g$, to be meaningful, however, $k > g$. Otherwise this model does not give a meaningful result.

To illustrate this model, suppose that a common share is expected to pay a $5 dividend in the coming year, the required return is 10 percent, and its expected dividend growth rate is 5 percent. The price that the investor would be willing to pay for this share is

$$P = \frac{\$5}{.10 - .05}$$

$$= \frac{5}{.05}$$

$$= \$100$$

Therefore, the investor would be willing to pay $100 per share for this common stock. As indicated earlier, the investor's focus is really on the growth of dividends, g, in this model and the return, k, the investor expects from this equity investment. Firm-related risks concern factors that may affect the growth of earnings per share and consequently the growth of dividends. These factors

[7] Equation 6-3 results assuming either discrete or continuous compounding and discounting. See Eugene M. Lerner and Willard T. Carleton, *A Theory of Financial Analysis* (New York: Harcourt, Brace & World, 1966), pp. 108–9.

include the growth of the economy, competition, industry considerations, ability of management, research, and patents. The securities analyst is required to make the estimate of the growth rate and the appropriate capitalization rate.

Earnings Per Share Valuation Model   The EPS valuation model is generally used to estimate the value of a share at a particular point in time. For example, the security analyst may be using a five-year time horizon to make his estimates. As a result, he will be concerned with estimating the value of a particular share five years from now. Therefore, the EPS valuation model can be given by

$$\widehat{P_{it}} = \widehat{EPS}_{it} \times \widehat{P/E}_{it} \qquad (6\text{-}4)$$

where $\widehat{EPS}_{it}$ is the estimated earnings per share of stock i at time t, and $\widehat{P/E}_{it}$ is the estimated price-earnings ratio of stock i at time t. Consequently, the security analyst only needs two estimates to estimate the value of a share at a particular point in time. This is not to say that these estimates are easily obtained, but this approach does provide a relatively simple starting point for comparing the prospective returns on different stocks.

To illustrate, suppose that an analyst estimates the EPS five years from now for a particular stock at $7 per share and the appropriate P/E ratio at 20 times. Then the price of that stock will be estimated to be:

$$P = \$7 \times 20$$

$$= \$140$$

Therefore, this stock is estimated to be selling for about $140 five years from now. If this stock is selling for $70 and is not expected to pay dividends, the anticipated return from this stock is determined to be about 14 percent.

In practice the procedure has been to forecast a price for the particular stock at some point in time and compare that predicted price with the current price as illustrated above to determine whether a stock was a worthwhile investment. Dividends are not generally combined with anticipated appreciation to give an expected return figure. In most cases the dividend yield and potential appreciation are treated separately. For example, the *Value Line Investment Survey* gives the dividend yield and then shows the potential appreciation as a percent of the current market price of the common stock. For example, if the stock was expected to appreciate from $70 per share to $140, potential appreciation would be estimated to be 100 percent. In the approach we will use, however, the potential appreciation over some time horizon is estimated along with the dividend receipts for that period to give an estimate of the expected return. To obtain the forecast at the selected time horizon, the EPS valuation model will be used.

Therefore, determining the return on common stock requires the following estimates. First, the analyst must select some time horizon for the analysis. Once this is done, the growth in earnings per share over this time horizon must be forecast. These EPS forecasts facilitate a forecast of anticipated dividends as well as the price of the stock in the horizon year. This requires an analysis of the many factors that will affect the profitability of the firm and the growth in earnings. Second, an appropriate price-earnings ratio must be selected. This will reflect a number of factors that affect the firm at the time the stock is being evaluated. Third, the firm's performance must be considered, as well as the market's performance in the horizon year. For example, if it happens to be a good market year and a good year for the firm, the return will be substantially higher than if it is a bad market year and a bad year for the firm. However, as we will see, it is only necessary to forecast the price of a share assuming a good or bad market in the horizon year.

Valuation of Debt Instruments

In contrast to common stocks, bonds and debentures represent a contractual agreement specifying the interest for a certain period of time, after which the principal is repaid. The only uncertainty that enters is whether the firm can meet its contractual obligations. As a result of the nature of the instrument, the degree of uncertainty is greatly reduced, but the potential return is also reduced.

The value of a bond or debenture can be expressed as follows:

$$B_{it} = \sum_{t=1}^{n} \frac{\frac{1}{2} I_{it}}{(1 + \iota/2)^{2t}} + \frac{F_{in}}{(1 + \iota/2)^{2n}} \tag{6-5}$$

where $\frac{1}{2} I_{it}$ is the amount of interest received semiannually on bond i, ι is the market rate of interest for bonds of that quality and maturity, and F_{in} is the face value of bond i upon maturity n years from now. Determining the market value of a bond at any point in time is relatively easy since all of the information is readily available. The bond contract spells out the amount of interest to be received, the principal amount to be received, and the duration of the contract. The bond market provides the investor with the market rate of interest, and, the valuation process is therefore relatively straightforward.

To illustrate this valuation process, suppose that a particular debenture has a coupon rate of 6 percent, a term to maturity of 10 years, and the current market rate of interest on securities of the same quality and maturity is 7 percent. The market price of this bond would be

$$B_0 = \left[\sum_{t=1}^{20} \frac{30}{(1 + 0.035)^{2t}} \right] + \frac{1,000}{(1 + 0.035)^{20}}$$

$$= \$928.94$$

Thus, this debenture would sell for $928.94 in the market.[8]

The investment in bonds and debentures is quite secure but not without risk. This risk comes from two sources. One source is the possibility of default on

[8] This formula is used to illustrate the valuation process. In an actual situation, the value could be determined from a bond table. In fact, the more likely situation is that the investor will know the price and will have to determine the yield to maturity, which is synonymous with the market rate of interest.

principal and interest, which is referred to as the quality of the bond. The other source of risk is the possibility of a change in the market rate of interest. If interest rates rise, the market value of bonds will fall. This is illustrated in the above example in which the market rate of interest is 7 percent and the coupon rate is 6 percent. In this example it appears that the market rate of interest rose from approximately 6 percent to 7 percent leading to a decline in the market value of the bond. The effect and importance of changes in interest rates will be discussed in the next section on market-related risks.

In determining the quality of bonds, the accuracy of the Moody's and Standard and Poor's quality ratings over approximately five decades has led most investors to accept these ratings almost without question. These ratings primarily indicate the probability of default on principal and interest. In deriving these estimates, the bond analyst attempts to use every bit of available information. This includes economic and industry analysis, ratio analysis of the firm's past performance, and an evaluation of the protective covenants. The four top rating categories for Moody's and Standard and Poor's are as follows:

Moody's	Aaa	Aa	A	Baa
Standard and Poor's	AAA	AA	A	BBB

Those bonds in the highest rating category, Aaa for Moody's and AAA for Standard and Poor's, have the least likelihood of default. The chance of default increases as we go from the triple A ratings down to the lower ratings. Nevertheless, these top four ratings for each investor service are believed to be relatively high quality. On the other hand, those bonds and debentures with ratings below Baa or BBB are speculative, with a higher probability of default. It is generally believed that the bond ratings by these major investment services have been extremely accurate.[9]

Market-Related Risks

One major source of risk to the investor is the financial performance of the firm—firm-related risks. The investor shares in this performance on the basis of his claim. Bondholders have a contractual right to principal and interest. Stockholders have a residual claim to any profits remaining after all other claims are paid. The final arbiter of the value of these claims, however, is the securities markets. Therefore, it is not sufficient only to analyze the performance of the firm; attention must also be given to current and future market conditions. For the common stockholder, this involves an evaluation of the near-term and long-term prospects for the stock market; for the bond investor this involves an estimate of the near-term and long-term trend of interest rates. Making these

---

[9] W. Braddock Hickman, *Corporate Bond and Investor Experience* (New York: National Bureau of Economic Research, 1958), p. 10.

forecasts is extremely difficult, but recognizing the importance of the effect of market conditions on the investor's return will aid in understanding the investment process.

Market Effect on Common Stock

Investment in common stock is particularly susceptible to the vagaries of the market. The general assumption is that the performance of the stock market reflects the profitability of the corporate sector of the economy. As a general tendency this is true, as indicated in Figure 6-1. Yet there are periods of divergence. For example, in 1962 corporate profits held up fairly well, but the stock market fell precipitously. In the period 1967–69, a divergence took place. During this period, corporate profits actually declined somewhat, but stock prices reached a new high. The investor must therefore be concerned with how these developments will affect his portfolio of stocks. Some stocks will be less affected than others, but it is well established that stocks will be affected in some fashion.[10]

The Problem Illustrated   It is not uncommon for a situation to arise in which the fundamental performance of the firm has not altered substantially, yet the price of the common stock falls dramatically. An example of this type of market behavior is exhibited by General Mills' shares during the period 1966–71, as

FIGURE 6-1   *Standard and Poor's 500 Stock Index and Corporate Profits after Taxes*

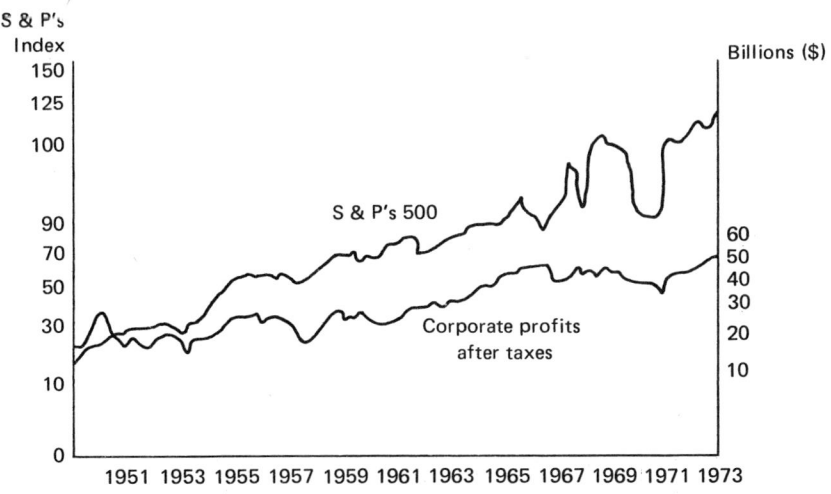

[10] One study indicates that over 30 percent of the variance of return can be attributed to market conditions. See Benjamin F. King, "Market Factors in Stock Price Behavior," *Journal of Business*, vol. 39, no. 1, part II (Jan., 1966), pp. 139–90.

shown in Table 6-1. During this period, earnings and dividends per share increased from year to year. Earnings and dividends per share did not grow spectacularly, but they grew consistently at approximately 3 percent and 2 percent per annum, respectively. Yet the price of the common stock reached a peak in 1968 and has since fallen back to lower levels. The reason for this can be seen in the S & P's 425 stock index, which reached a peak in late 1968 and then declined. As a result, General Mills' common stock fell back from its 1968 high because the market declined, in spite of its growth in earnings and dividends per share.

This illustrates the dilemma that the typical investor faces. Not only must he be concerned with the firm's operating results, but he must also be concerned with market conditions. Good operating results may not be reflected in the market—at least not immediately. Conversely, mediocre operating results may lead to fairly sizable gains under favorable market conditions.

Market Conditions   One method of determining the impact of market conditions on the return of common stock is to use regression analysis to determine the elasticity of a stock's return with respect to that of a market index.[11] This analysis indicates the return that can be expected for a particular stock, given the expected return on a market index, and takes the form $Y = a + bX + u_i$.[12] Therefore, determining the relationship between individual stocks and a market index takes the form

$$RR_i = a_i + b_i(RR_I) + u_i \qquad (6-6)$$

where RR_i is the annual return relative for stock i, a_i is the intercept, b_i is the regression coefficient, RR_I is the annual return relative for a market index, and u_i is a normally distributed error term.

TABLE 6-1   *Performance of General Mills'*
Common Stock 1966–70

Year	Earnings per share	Dividends per share	Price range	Range S & P's 425
1966	1.63	0.70	33¼–26	100.6 –77.89
1967	1.72	0.75	38 –29¼	106.2 –85.31
1968	1.67	0.79	43⅝–34	118.0 –95.05
1969	1.77	0.80	39¼–30	116.2 –97.75
1970	1.88	0.88	38⅝–23⅝	103.75–74.86

[11] The introduction of an index to account for the market behavior of stocks in portfolio selection models was first suggested by Harry M. Markowitz and later elaborated by William F. Sharpe. See Harry M. Markowitz, *Portfolio Selection: Efficient Diversification of Investments* (New York: John Wiley & Sons, 1959), pp. 96–101; and William F. Sharpe, "A Simplified Model for Portfolio Analysis," *Management Science,* vol. 9, no. 2 (Jan., 1963), pp. 277–93.

[12] In the Markowitz-Sharpe portfolio selection model, the index to be used was not specified precisely. It could be a measure of the level of the stock market, a stock market index, or economic activity, the Gross National Product. Keith V. Smith, using ex post data, found that generally better results could be obtained by using one of the three leading stock market indexes, the DJIA, S & P's, or NYSE. See Keith V. Smith, "Stock Prices and Economic Indexes for Generating Efficient Portfolios," *Journal of Business,* vol. 42, no. 3 (July, 1969), p. 336.

To illustrate, suppose we have the following hypothetical return relatives for stocks A and B and a leading stock market index:

Year	Market index RR	Stock A RR	Stock B RR
1	1.10	1.20	1.08
2	0.85	0.80	0.90
3	1.20	1.30	1.22
4	1.35	1.50	1.40
5	1.25	1.60	1.22
6	1.00	1.10	1.00
7	1.12	1.25	1.10
8	1.15	1.26	1.09
9	1.00	0.90	1.00
10	0.80	0.70	0.95

Regressing stocks A and B on the market index gives the following:

Stock	Intercept a	Regression coefficient b
A	−0.589	1.617
B	0.210	0.819

With this information the anticipated return for stocks A and B can be determined, given an expected return for the market index. Suppose that the RR for the market index is expected to be 1.10 for the coming year. The expected return for stock A would be

$$RR_A = -0.589 + 1.617(1.10) = 1.19$$

while the expected return for stock B would be

$$RR_B = 0.210 + 0.819(1.10) = 1.11$$

Thus, the return on stock A would be somewhat higher than for stock B.

The important point for our purposes is the effect of the market on the return of common stock. In a good market, some stocks will fare much better than others. This can be seen by referring to stocks A and B. If the market return was expected to be 1.10, stock A would give a return of 1.19, while stock B would give a return of 1.11. Stock A tends to fare better in good markets than stock B, but stock B will fare better in bad markets. Suppose that the return relative on the market index is expected to be 0.80 in the coming year instead of 1.10. The expected return on stock A would be

$$RR_A = -0.589 + 1.617(0.80) = 0.70$$

while the expected return for stock B would be:

$$RR_B = 0.210 + 0.819(0.80) = 0.87$$

Thus, stock B would fare much better in a bad market than stock A.

The reason for the performance of stock A and B in the two types of markets is the elasticity of the two stocks relative to the market, which is indicated by the regression coefficient, b_1. The regression coefficient measures the elasticity of return on a particular stock with respect to a given change in the market index. The larger the regression coefficient, sometimes referred to as the beta coefficient, the greater will be the effect of the market. In a good market, stocks with large beta coefficients may be expected to perform better than the market; but in a bad market, they may be expected to perform worse than the market. Hence, some stocks are quite volatile and are expected to perform well in good markets, while the more stable stocks are expected to perform better in bad markets.

Market Behavior During 1950–73   The previous discussion focused on the volatility of stocks with respect to the market. It is important, however, not to lose sight of the long-run trends in the market. Table 6-2 presents the earnings per share, the dividends per share, and the price-earnings ratios for the S & P's

TABLE 6-2   *Market Behavior During the Period 1950–73 Standard and Poor's 425 Industrials*

Year	Earnings per share	Dividends per share	Price-earnings ratio	425 index
1950	2.74	1.53	7.51	20.58
1951	2.52	1.45	9.62	24.23
1952	2.63	1.44	10.22	26.89
1953	2.57	1.47	9.68	24.87
1954	3.06	1.57	12.17	37.24
1955	3.83	1.68	12.65	48.44
1956	3.70	1.78	13.54	50.08
1957	3.32	1.84	12.91	42.86
1958	3.33	1.79	17.71	58.97
1959	3.26	1.90	19.79	64.50
1960	3.25	2.00	18.92	61.49
1961	3.67	2.08	20.63	75.72
1962	4.19	2.20	15.75	66.00
1963	4.48	2.38	17.69	79.25
1964	4.78	2.60	18.75	89.62
1965	5.58	2.85	17.65	98.47
1966	5.77	2.98	14.77	85.24
1967	5.91	3.01	17.79	105.11
1968	6.35	3.18	17.80	113.02
1969	5.88	3.27	17.26	101.49
1970	5.43	3.24	17.64	100.90
1971	6.02	3.18	18.72	112.92
1972	6.86	3.22	19.22	131.87

Note: Earnings per share are the fourth quarter seasonally adjusted rate Dividends per share are the 12-month moving total adjusted to the index, and the price-earnings ratios are the fourth quarter ratios. The fourth quarter index was used for the S & P's 425 Industrial Index.

Source: *Standard and Poor's Trade and Securities Statistics: Security Price Index Record.*

425 Industrial Index for 1950–73. Two important conclusions can be drawn from this data. First, dividends and earnings per share have tended to grow consistently at approximately 3 and 4 percent, respectively. This in itself should lead to an increase in the level of the S & P's 425. Second, the price-earnings ratios after 1957 are considerably higher than those of the 1950–57 period. In fact, these ratios are considerably above the 85-year average of 13.5 for the period 1871 to 1955.[13] The high *P/E* ratios of the late 1950s and 1960s are a major reason that S & P's 425 index increased at a rate of over 8 percent per year, approximately twice that of either dividends or earnings per share.

There are a number of possible explanations for the rise in the *P/E* ratios, but three points should be emphasized. First, it is obvious that the *P/E* ratios of the earlier 1950s were low by historical standards. This is attributed by many to the fact that earnings during this period were overstated.[14] Much of the plant and equipment in use was of pre–World War II vintage. Consequently, depreciation allowances were insufficient to provide for replacement of existing equipment. This meant that reported net earnings did not make adequate provision for the replacement of existing facilities, and hence were overstated.

A second possible reason for the rise in the *P/E* ratios concerns the return required on equity investment. This return can be thought of as comprising the risk-free rate of interest, and premiums for various types of risk. Notationally this can be represented as follows:

$$k = \alpha + \beta_1 + \beta_2 + \cdots + \beta_n \tag{6-7}$$

where k is the required rate of return on equity investment, α is the pure rate of interest, and $\beta_1, \beta_2, \ldots, \beta_n$ represent various premiums for risk, such as business risk and financial risk. If equity investors become more certain of earnings and dividends, the required return on equity investment will fall, and the *P/E* ratios will increase. This results because the premiums for business risk and perhaps financial risk fall. A major reason for the increased confidence in the corporate sector has been the growth in confidence that the business cycle can be controlled by monetary and fiscal tools. Hence, the premiums for business and financial risk may have declined, leading to lower ks and higher *P/E* ratios.[15]

A third possible factor is the expected rate of growth for stocks in general:

	Stock X	Stock Y
Dividends per share	$2.00	$2.00
Required return	12%	12%
Expected growth rate	4%	5%

[13] Benjamin Graham, David L. Dodd, and Sidney Cottle, *Security Analysis: Principles and Techniques* (McGraw-Hill, 1962), p. 509.
[14] Paul M. Van Arsdell, *Corporation Finance: Policy, Planning, Administration* (New York: The Ronald Press, 1968), pp. 1183–84.
[15] For an excellent discussion of the differences in business and stock market cycles in the period since World War I, see Benjamin Graham, "Some Investment Aspects of Accumulation Through Equities," *Journal of Finance*, vol. 17, no. 2 (May, 1962), pp. 203–14.

Substituting this information into the dividend valuation model represented by Equation 6-3, the market value of the two firm's shares is

$$\text{Stock X} = \frac{\$2.00}{.12 - .04} = \$25$$

$$\text{Stock Y} = \frac{\$2.00}{.12 - .05} = \$40$$

Thus, because stock Y is expected to grow at a rate of 5 percent, only 1 percent greater than that of stock X, the price of stock Y will be 60 percent greater. Consequently, if investors revise upwards their expectations about growth for stocks in general, *P/E* ratios will be expected to increase.

Needless to say, the trends in *P/E* ratios for stocks in general is an important consideration for the security analyst. Market *P/E* ratios are usually used as a standard for comparing *P/E* ratios of individual stocks. Stocks that sell at *P/E* ratios above the market are generally believed to possess superior characteristics. Most often such stocks are believed to have superior growth potential, but other factors such as size and earnings stability may also be important. Conversely, those stocks whose *P/E* ratios are lower than that of the market are believed to possess less than average characteristics. Regardless of a stock's position relative to the market *P/E* ratio, a general trend has important implications for the valuation of common stock.

Interest Rate Risk

The major source of risk to investors in high-quality bonds is changes in interest rates, commonly referred to as interest-rate risk. Since the price of high-quality bonds is inversely related to interest rates, the market price of such bonds fluctuates as interest rates fluctuate. As Figure 6-2 illustrates, interest rates have fluctuated during the period 1945–73 from very low levels of less than 1 percent for short-term government securities to over 8 percent. Long-term government securities have not fluctuated quite as much, fluctuating within a range of less than 3 percent to almost 8 percent. It is unlikely that interest rates on government securities will ever again be as low as 3 percent. The period following World War II represents artificially low interest rates, as the Federal Reserve attempted to keep the interest costs of war financing to a minimum. The Federal Reserve's intervention was stopped in April of 1951 with the Federal Reserve-Treasury Accord. After this Accord, interest rates were permitted to find their own level. This is evident in Figure 6-2, as interest rates have steadily risen since 1951.

Interest-rate risk affects all investors in high-quality bonds, whether they invest in short-term or long-term bonds. Rising interest rates have the greatest impact on the market value of long-term bonds and hence constitute a source of risk to long-term bond investors, but changes in short-term interest rates also constitute a source of risk to the investor who invests in short-term bonds. The

Percent per annum (monthly average)

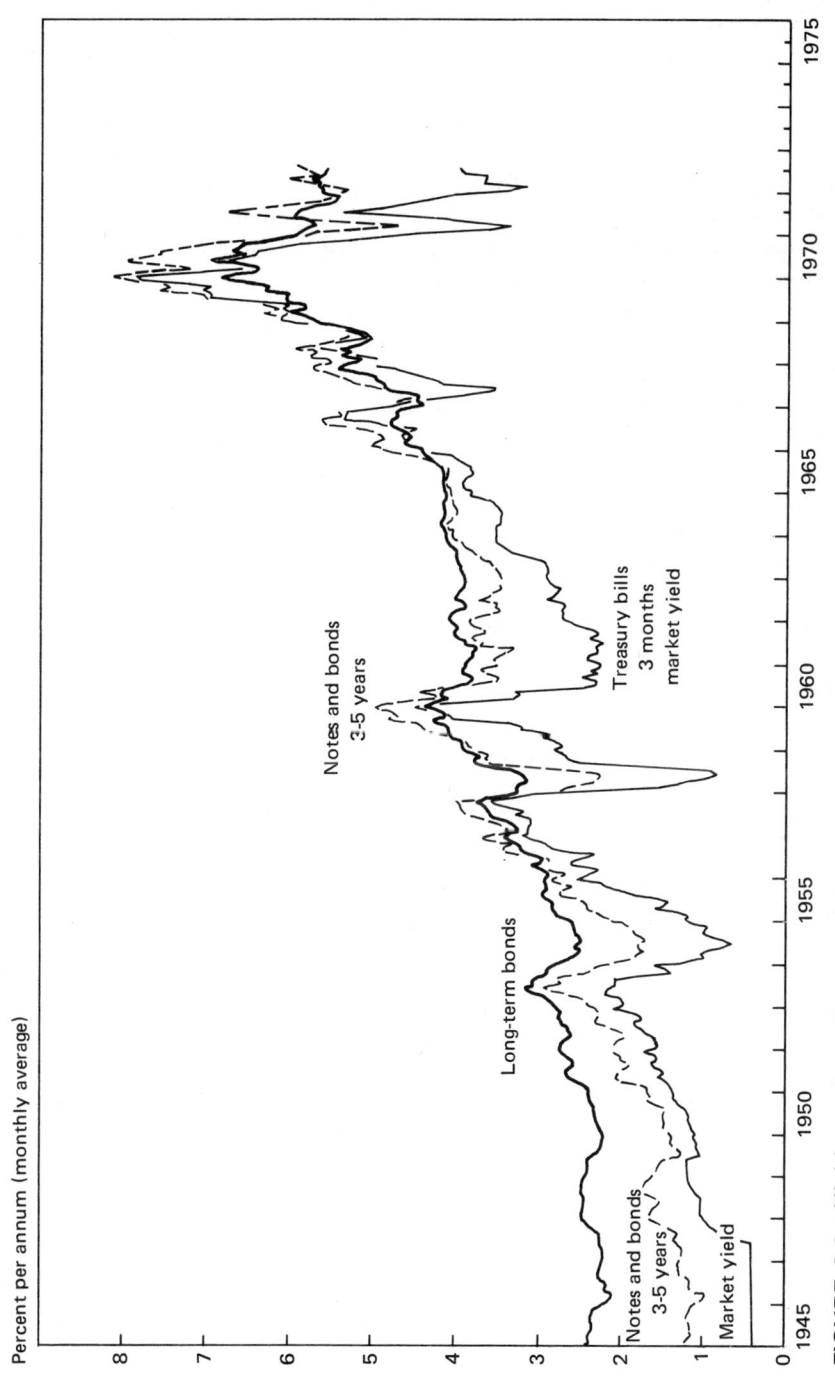

FIGURE 6-2 *Yields on Long-Term and Short-Term Government Securities, 1945–73*

Source: Board of Governors of the Federal Reserve System, *Historical Chart Book*, 1973.

longer the maturities on long-term bond holdings, the greater the impact of an increase in interest rates. Conversely, the investor in short-term bonds is not significantly affected by this increase in interest rates. Thus, whenever the main objective of a portfolio is safety of principal, the normal procedure is to invest in high-quality short-term bonds, such as Treasury bills, bankers' acceptances, and commercial paper.

The investor who invests in short-term bonds to protect the portfolio against the loss of principal value faces interest-rate risk in the form of volatile interest income. Short-term interest rates are much more volatile than long-term rates, as illustrated in Figure 6-2; hence, the income generated by a short-term bond portfolio may fluctuate significantly. Long-term bonds, on the other hand, provide a stable income, but the market value of the bonds fluctuate, at times markedly, with changes in interest rates. As a result, interest-rate risk involves a tradeoff between the stability of the market value and the stability of interest income, and bond investment decisions are based on which of these considerations is more important.

To illustrate the effect of changes in interest rates, consider the market price of various maturities ranging from 1 to 30 years, all having a 5 percent coupon rate. In addition, suppose there is a change of only 1 percent in market rate of interest from the coupon rate, that is, market rates of interest of 4 and 6 percent, respectively. Table 6-3 shows the effect on the market price for the various maturities. It is evident that the greater the length to maturity, the greater the effect of the change in interest rates. For example, a 1-year maturity priced to yield 6 percent declines to 99.04, but a 30-year maturity declines to 86.16.

The investor who attempts to protect himself against this effect by investing in short-term instruments substitutes instability of income for instability of market value. Investors who invest in short-term instruments, such as commercial banks and industrial firms are primarily concerned with liquidity. It is possible that an unforeseen exigency may arise, forcing liquidation of the short-term portfolio. Consequently, these firms want to minimize the possibility of a loss of principal, but by preserving principal they incur instability of

TABLE 6-3   *Prices on Selected Maturities with a 5 Percent Coupon Rate*

Maturity in years	To yield 4 percent	To yield 6 percent
1	100.97	99.04
2	101.90	98.14
3	102.80	97.29
5	104.49	95.73
10	108.18	92.56
15	111.20	90.20
20	113.68	88.44
25	114.95	87.14
30	117.38	86.16

income. Interest-rate risk, therefore, cannot be avoided. In dealing with interest-rate risk, it becomes a question of whether stability of income or stability of market value is more important. Long-term bonds provide a stable income stream but an unstable market value, whereas short-term bonds provide a relatively stable market value but an unstable income stream.

Consequently, the risks associated with bonds can be viewed in terms of market-related risks and firm-related risks, just as was previously outlined for common stocks. In determining the importance of market-related risks for a particular issue, the primary consideration is the quality of the issue. For high-quality issues, the major risk faced is market-related or, as it is more commonly referred to, interest-rate risk. For low-quality issues, the major concern is default, and therefore economic conditions become a major determinant of the prospects for these bonds. For common stock the impact of the firm-related and market-related factors is somewhat more complex. The remainder of Part II will deal with the factors involved in common stock analysis while Part III will deal with the factors involved in bond analysis.

The Evaluation of Common Stock

The previous analysis has attempted to show that the valuation of securities can be decomposed into two parts. On the one hand, there are what we have referred to as firm-related risks. These risks have to do with the financial performance of the firm. For common stock analysis, firm-related risks are the probability of obtaining an adequate return. For bond analysis, the firm-related risks are the probability of not receiving the contractual principal and interest. On the other hand, the return to both the stockholder and the bondholder are affected by market conditions. The stock market may be either good or bad. In addition, the firm may be experiencing either a good or bad year. Similar firm and market conditions do not necessarily coincide. Market conditions can also affect the return on bonds and debentures, particularly high-quality bonds and debentures. Hence, changes in interest rates constitute the market-related risks for bond investors.

The focus of the following analysis will be on forecasting the expected return of common stock and the risk associated with that return. The risk will be decomposed into firm-related and market-related risk; however, most of the discussion will focus on evaluating the firm-related factors. Figure 6-3 outlines the firm-related factors that affect the expected return and the risk associated with obtaining that return. Factors that are vital in determining the return on common stock are the cash dividends received plus appreciation. The appreciation results from growth of earnings per share, which may or may not be reflected in current dividends. Consequently, growth analysis is the focal point of the evaluation of firm-related factors. Determining anticipated growth is necessary to determine the anticipated return that may be expected. Growth

FIGURE 6-3 *Firm-Related Factors Affecting Return on Common Stock*

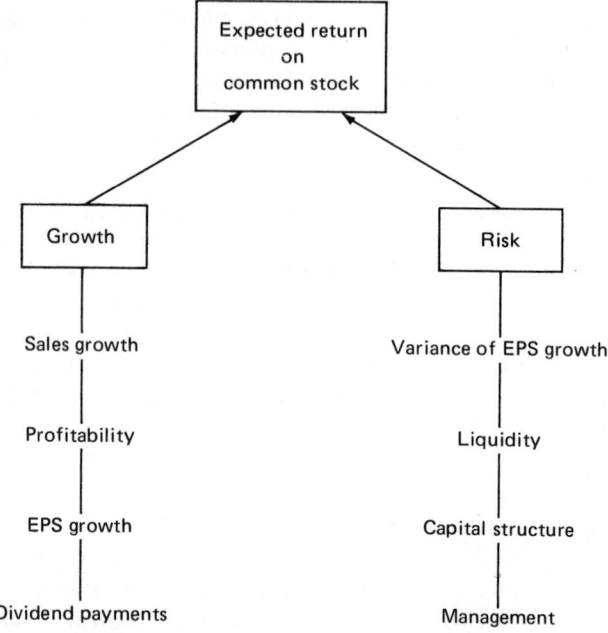

analysis may be viewed in several different ways, but one approach is to begin with the analysis of past sales growth, focusing on the firm's rate of growth relative to its industry and the economy as a whole. The final test of the marketing effort, however, is the profitability of the firm, which can be translated into *EPS* growth and cash dividends payments.

The risk associated with obtaining the expected return on a particular stock involves a number of factors; the variance of *EPS* growth, liquidity, capital structure, and the management of the firm. Each of these factors may or may not be an important factor in assessing the probability of obtaining the expected return on a common stock and therefore must be evaluated separately before a conclusion can be reached. Once all these factors have been evaluated, it is possible to estimate the expected return on a particular stock and the risk of obtaining that return over some time horizon.

The estimating process involves two important features. First, the *EPS* valuation model is used to determine the expected price of the stock—the anticipated appreciation—at the specified time horizon. This appreciation plus the dividends paid out by the firm then constitute the total return on that particular stock. Second, two estimates are made for the horizon year. One assumes that the stock market in the horizon year will be good; the other assumes it will be bad. From these two estimates, it is possible to obtain the range of outcomes. These in turn can be used to give the expected return and the standard deviation about that return. Recall that there are four possible outcomes for a given year, as follows:

1. Good firm year, good market year
2. Bad firm year, good market year
3. Good firm year, bad market year
4. Bad firm year, bad market year

These four outcomes seem to indicate that four different estimates are needed. However, if sufficient diversification is undertaken, good and bad firm years will average out over the portfolio of common stock. Hence, only market conditions remain to be taken into consideration. Chapters 8, 9, and 10 will outline the various approaches to estimating the expected return and the risk of obtaining that return.

Summary

The security analysis function is to evaluate the risk and return associated with securities. Generally this analysis involves four steps: (1) economic analysis, (2) industry analysis, (3) firm analysis, and (4) market analysis. Economic, industry, and market analysis were discussed in Part I. This leaves only firm analysis to be discussed in this section and Part III.

In the common stock valuation process, the investor may value either dividends or earnings. It is generally recognized that the principal source of value for common stock is dividends, but security analysts tend to use an EPS valuation model because it is easier to use. We will follow this convention, but this does not mean that earnings are believed to be a stream of benefits that investors capitalize. The most important aspect of this analysis is growth analysis, which will be discussed in Chapter 7. Growth leads to appreciation, but it also constitutes a source of risk. In addition to growth analysis, the firm's working capital position and the firm's capital structure are analyzed for any sign of deterioration. Finally, an important but somewhat intangible consideration is the quality of the firm's management, which is vital to the firm's success, but difficult to analyze.

For common stock recent research has shown that there is a close correlation between the return on individual stocks and the return on the market. If this is true, the return on common stock portfolios is closely related to that of the market in general, and market conditions consequently constitute a major source of risk to the investor. Market conditions also constitute the major source of risk for high-quality debt instruments. There is no way to avoid this risk. Essentially, it is a tradeoff between instability of principal and instability of income. Those investing in high-quality short-term instruments for liquidity are accepting instability of income to preserve stability of principal. The long-term investor, on the other hand, is accepting instability of principal to obtain a stable income stream.

Questions

1. It is common to follow four basic steps in security analysis. Explain.

2. The security analyst examines factors that are considered either firm-related or market-related, as a matter of convenience. Explain the rationale for this approach. Why is this an oversimplification?

3. There are three possible sources of value for common stock. Explain.

4. A certain stock is expected to pay a $2.50 dividend next year, and it is expected to grow at 7 percent for the foreseeable future. Suppose the investor's required return is 12 percent. What is the value accorded this stock? What is the appropriate price if the expected growth rate is 14 percent?

5. A particular stock currently earns $2.00 per share and sells for $50 per share. In five years the earnings per share are expected to grow to $4.00, but the price-earnings ratio is expected to remain unchanged. What will be the expected price of the stock in five years?

6. What factors are used in determining bond ratings? How accurate are these ratings?

7. The annual *RR*s of the S & P's 500 were regressed on the *RR*s of the stock of a certain corporation for a 15-year period. The intercept was found to be 0 and the regression coefficient 1.0. Suppose the *RR* for the S & P's 500 is expected to be 1.10 for the coming year. What is the expected return on the stock in question? Would you normally expect the regression coefficient to be positive? Why?

8. Any investor who invests in high-quality debt instruments, whether short-term or long-term, faces interest-rate risk. Explain why this is true.

Selected References

Amling, Frederick. *Investments: An Introduction to Analysis and Management,* 2d ed. Englewood Cliffs, N.J.: Prentice-Hall, 1970. Chapter 11.

Archer, Stephen A., and LeRoy G. Faerber. "Firm Size and the Cost of Externally Secured Equity Capital." *Journal of Finance,* vol. 21, no. 1 (Mar., 1966), pp. 69–83.

Fisher, Irving. *The Theory of Interest,* rev. ed. New York: Kelley and Millman, 1954. Chapter 11.

Gibson, William E. "Price-Expectations Effects on Interest Rates." *Journal of Finance,* vol. 25, no. 1 (Mar., 1970), pp. 19–34.

Graham, Benjamin, David L. Dodd, and Sidney Cottle. *Security Analysis: Principles and Technique,* 4th ed. New York: McGraw-Hill, 1962.

Hickman, W. Braddock, *Corporate Bond Quality and Investor Experience.* New York: National Bureau of Economic Research, 1958.

King, Benjamin F. "Market and Industry Factors in Stock Price Behavior." *Journal of Business,* vol. 39, no. 1, part II (Jan., 1966), pp. 139–90.

Lerner, Eugene M., and Willard T. Carleton. *A Theory of Financial Analysis.* New York: Harcourt, Brace, and World, 1966. Chapter 7.

Markowitz, Harry M. *Portfolio Selection: Efficient Diversification of Investments.* New York: John Wiley & Sons, 1959.

Miller, Merton H., and Franco Modigliani. "Dividend Policy, Growth, and the Valuation of Shares." *Journal of Business,* vol. 34, no. 4 (Oct., 1961), pp. 411–33.

Sauvain, Harry C. "Changing Interest Rates and the Investment Portfolio." *Journal of Finance,* vol. 14, no. 2 (May, 1959), pp. 230–44.

Sharpe, William F. "A Simplified Model for Portfolio Analysis." *Management Science,* vol. 9, no. 2 (Jan., 1963), pp. 277–93.

Smith, Keith V. "Stock Price and Economic Indexes for Generating Efficient Portfolios." *Journal of Business,* vol. 42, no. 3 (July, 1969), pp. 326–36.

Soldofsky, Robert M., and James T. Murphy. *Growth Yields on Common Stocks: Theory and Tables.* Iowa City; Bureau of Business and Economic Research, University of Iowa, 1961.

Van Arsdell, Paul M. *Corporation Finance: Policy Planning, Administration.* New York: The Ronald Press, 1969. Chapter 37.

Weil, Roman L. "Realized Interest Rates and Bondholders Returns." *American Economic Review,* vol. 60, no. 3 (June, 1970), pp. 502–11.

Chapter 7

Growth Analysis

In the estimation of risk and return for a particular stock, the general approach is to determine how well the firm has performed within its environment and then estimate future prospects. Initially, this means comparing the firm with other firms within its industry and ultimately comparing a large number of firms in order to select only those with the best prospects. It is conceivable that although a firm has outstanding prospects, these prospects are incorporated into the current price so that anyone purchasing the firm's stock would not receive an adequate return. Such stocks are commonly referred to as being overpriced. In this case, the investor probably should not buy. On the other hand, the investor is always seeking out situations in which the stock is underpriced; these situations promise an above-average return.

The focal point of the analysis, therefore, is predicting the anticipated growth in earnings per share, which may or may not be reflected immediately in cash dividends. It has long been accepted that the growth in earnings is the primary force leading to appreciation.[1] Growth in earnings and *EPS* depends upon the growth in sales and the profitability of the firm. It is common to assume that firms whose sales are growing at an above-average rate will also have above-average growth in profits. More and more this view is being challenged by the recognition that sales growth per se implies little about the growth of profits. In marketing, for example, the view is taking hold that the key indicator of a successful marketing effort is the contribution to profit, not sales. This view will be taken throughout this analysis. Substantial emphasis will be placed upon sales analysis, but the ultimate test of the firm's success will be its profitability.

[1] Victor Niederhoffer and Patrick Regan, "Earnings Changes, Analysts' Forecasts and Stock Prices," *Financial Analysts Journal*, vol. 28, no. 3 (May–June, 1972), pp. 65–71.

Sales Analysis

The sales of firms may follow a multitude of patterns. For example, they may be cyclical, as in the paper and steel industries. Or they may be quite stable over the entire business cycle, as in the supermarket segment of the retailing industry and in the candy manufacturing industry. Or sales may be growing very rapidly, as in the computer and drug industries. Isolating the various characteristics of a firm's sales involves reviewing the following factors:

1. Historical sales record
   a. Rate of growth
   b. Impact of recessionary periods
   c. Impact of price increases versus volume increases on sales revenue
2. End-use analysis

An evaluation of the historical sales record should provide insight into the past performance of the firm's sales and any problems that may exist. End-use analysis, on the other hand, provides information that may be helpful in evaluating future prospects for the firm's sales.

Historical Sales Record

In analyzing the firm's historical sales growth, varying time periods can be used. It has been general practice to use five to seven year's data on the assumption that this period is sufficient to determine any trends that might exist but short enough so that the data is relevant. Probably a more desirable solution may be found by screening the data and determining the appropriate time period on the basis of the characteristics of the data. In the subsequent analysis, 10 years of data will be used on the assumption that this period of time will provide a proper perspective. In addition, it is common to compare the growth of sales of particular firms within an industry grouping with one another and with the industry as a whole. This permits a comparison of the sales performance of the firms being analyzed. In turn, these firms may be compared with the sales growth of the industry to determine where they stand in relation to the entire industry. Finally, the industry's sales growth may be compared with the growth in the GNP to determine whether the industry is growing faster than the economy as a whole.

Most of the important questions concerning the historical growth rate can be answered by comparing three series. They are as follows:

1. Sales of the firms under study
2. Sales of the industry
3. Growth in the industry production index

This data can be used to generate the necessary series so that a complete analysis of the historical growth can be undertaken.

To illustrate the type of analysis that may be used, consider Du Pont Corporation and GAF Corporation. Du Pont is the leading firm in the chemical industry, with a wide product line ranging from various types of fibers to pharmaceutical products. GAF is a small chemical firm that specializes in building products, photographic equipment and supplies, and other specialty chemical products. Table 7–1 shows the relevant data for Du Pont, GAF, and the industry for the period 1963–73. Columns 2 through 4 show the sales data of Du Pont, GAF, and the chemical industry converted to indexes with 1963 as the base year. This approach is the same as that used in Chapter 4. Moreover, the growth rate at the bottom is calculated with logarithms as illustrated in Chapter 4.

Column 5 of Table 7-1 gives the Federal Reserve Board's chemical index. This index gives the output of the chemical industry in units of production. A comparison of the FRB's chemical index with the sales indexes enables one to determine whether the increase in sales revenues results essentially from increases in unit selling prices or unit output. As a general rule, the growth in sales revenue should not result solely from price increases. In other words, increases in the firm's physical output should account for a substantial portion of the firm's increases in sales revenues. It is equally undesirable for the firm's growth in sales revenues to result proportionately more from increases in physical output. In this type of situation, the selling prices of the firm's products are falling; increases in sales revenues thus depend disproportionately on increases in physical output. Falling selling prices do not necessarily spell trouble for the firm because the firm may be increasing its profitability as a result of its increased volume, but whenever this situation occurs it warrants special consideration.

TABLE 7-1   *A Comparison of the Sales Growth of Du Pont and GAF*

Year (1)	Du Pont (2)	GAF (3)	Industry (4)	FRB's chemical index (5)	Du Pont to FRB's chemical index (6)	GAF to FRB's chemical index (7)	Industry to FRB's chemical index (8)	Percent of industry sales — Du Pont (9)	GAF (10)
1963	100.0	100.0	100.0	67.3	1.486	1.486	1.486	8.04	0.56
1964	108.1	108.2	107.8	73.9	1.463	1.464	1.459	8.06	0.56
1965	117.4	121.2	117.9	82.2	1.428	1.474	1.434	8.00	0.64
1966	123.6	164.3	128.3	92.8	1.331	1.770	1.382	7.74	0.71
1967	120.5	295.0	133.3	100.0	1.205	2.950	1.333	7.27	1.23
1968	135.2	322.5	146.2	109.9	1.230	2.934	1.330	7.44	1.23
1969	142.2	343.3	153.2	120.4	1.181	2.851	1.272	7.46	1.24
1970	141.6	330.4	153.5	120.3	1.177	2.746	1.276	7.42	1.20
1971	150.6	387.2	164.2	126.4	1.191	3.063	1.299	7.38	1.31
1972	170.9	435.2	180.3	139.3	1.227	3.124	1.294	7.62	1.34
Rate*	5.5%	15.8%	6.2%	7.5%					

*Annual compound rate of growth

The FRB's chemical index now uses 1967 as the base year; therefore, a direct comparison with the sales indexes is not possible. However, this provides an opportunity to use another technique that may be useful to compare the growth rate of two series. That is, a simple ratio of the two series may be calculated. If one series is growing faster than the other, this will be reflected in the ratio. In Table 7-1, the sales of Du Pont, GAF, and the industry have been used as the numerator, with the FRB's chemical index as the denominator. These ratios are shown in columns 6 through 8. If the ratios increase over time, this means that the sales revenues have been growing faster than the unit output as represented by the FRB's chemical index. Conversely, if the ratios decline, as it does for Du Pont and the industry, this means that the sales revenues are increasing at a slower rate than the unit output.

Finally, the last two columns provide additional information on the sales growth of the firms, giving the percentage of the market held by Du Pont and GAF, respectively. Determining the percentage share of the market is useful for two reasons. First, it indicates whether the firm is maintaining its share of the market. The most desirable situation is for the firm to be increasing its share of the market over time, in which case its sales growth will be increasing at a faster rate than that of the industry. A declining share of the market, of course, is a source of concern. Second, it gives an indication of the importance of the firm within the industry. For example, General Motors is considered a major force in the auto industry since it holds approximately 50 percent of the United States car market. Du Pont, on the other hand, is the leading chemical company, but it does not have the clout within the industry—or outside it, for that matter—that GM does. Hence, the share of the market figures provide additional information at little expense of time and effort.

Turning to the analysis of Du Pont and GAF as shown in Table 7–1, it is evident that there are substantial differences between these two firms. Du Pont's sales growth was somewhat less than that of the industry, growing at a rate of 5.5 percent as opposed to 6.2 percent for the industry. Du Pont's sales began trailing the industry's in 1966 and have not caught up, although in 1972 Du Pont's sales growth was greater than that of the industry. It is thus clear that Du Pont's sales did not perform as well as the industry. GAF, on the other hand, substantially outperformed the industry and Du Pont. The reason for this extraordinary growth was a merger with Ruberoid in 1967. Nevertheless, GAF's sales growth has been somewhat better than that of the industry. In the years 1963–67, GAF's sales increased approximately 64 percent, as compared to approximately 28 percent for the industry. After the merger, year-to-year growth was substantial with the exception of 1970, which experienced a negative growth. This occurred because construction was curtailed sharply in 1970, having a significant effect on the Ruberoid Division. In summary, it appears that GAF sales growth has been markedly better than that of Du Pont.

The data in columns 6 through 8 illustrate one of the basic problems of the chemical industry, that is, continued keen competition from within and without the industry has led to lower selling prices. This becomes particularly apparent by reference to column 8, in which the ratio of industry sales to the FRB's chemical index fell from 1.486 to 1.294, indicating that the industry's sales revenue has not increased as fast as the industry's output. Du Pont's ratio fared even worse than that of the industry, indicating that Du Pont's selling prices fell even more than those of the industry. GAF, on the other hand, has had mixed results. In the period 1963–66, its selling prices fell, paralleling the industry's, but then rose sharply in 1966. Again, after the merger in 1967, its selling prices fell in three successive years but then rose in 1971 and 1972. GAF was thus able to increase its selling prices over the period, whereas Du Pont and the industry both experienced lower selling prices at the end of the period than at the beginning. Whenever a firm or an industry experiences secular declining prices, as experienced by the chemical industry, it may have important implications for the profitability of the firm and the industry.

Columns 9 and 10 show the percent of the market held by Du Pont and GAF. Market share is always an important statistic to be concerned with, particularly whether it is increasing or decreasing. Du Pont's market share has declined somewhat over the period. This confirms what might have been suspected based upon the growth of Du Pont's sales relative to those of the industry. GAF, on the other hand, has markedly increased its market share, mainly because of its merger with Ruberoid. However, in the periods before and after the merger, GAF's market share has increased, despite the difficulties of the industry. Moreover, it appears that the chemical industry is not highly concentrated. If Du Pont is the industry leader with only 8 percent of the market, then the market must be shared by a large number of firms. This situation could make for a very competitive industry.

End-Use Analysis

Since the primary concern is future growth of sales—hence, future growth of earnings—additional information may be obtained by decomposing a firm's sales into its major marketing segments. Ideally, this type of analysis should be based upon the industries to which the firm is selling its products. It would then be possible to analyze the growth of these industries and estimate the impact on the firm. However, the information needed for this type of analysis is not always provided by the firm. An alternative approach is to analyze the sales growth by division. An advantage of this approach is that some firms provide not only sales but also contribution to profits by operating divisions. This information may be useful in pointing out the trouble spots within the firm. Again, of course, this information is not always available to outsiders.

The anlysis involves two steps. First, the current breakdown of sales must be ascertained. This information may be found in either *Standard and Poor's Listed Stock Reports, Moody's Handbook,* or the firm's annual report. Second, an analysis of the growth of its major segments is required. If data is available on the industries to which the firm sells its products, then the analysis attempts to determine the rate of growth of these industries and any problems that might be present. On the other hand, if the data available is given by division, the analysis attempts to determine the rate of growth for these divisions and any problem areas that may be present. Du Pont and GAF present examples of both of these methods. Du Pont gives the proportions of its sales that are sold to various industries and a breakdown of its sales by product line. GAF reports on a divisional basis, giving the sales by division and also the contribution to profit by each division.

The information on Du Pont is presented in Tables 7-2 and 7-3. Table 7-2 shows the proportion of its output sold to various industries in the years 1968 and 1972. It is evident that in 1972, textile mill products and foreign sales constituted 49 percent of Du Pont's sales. Selling in these two markets points up a major dichotomy facing Du Pont. Du Pont's textile mill sales include fibers, dyes, bleaches, finishing and sizing agents, weaving aids, and pigment colors. This is a rapidly growing market, since synthetic fibers are replacing natural fibers. It appears that Du Pont would not only benefit from the normal growth of the textile industry, but it would also be obtaining an increasing share of that market. Generally, this type of situation is considered ideal, but not in this case. A major problem with this group of chemical products is that it is more prone to price fluctuations, and the fluctuations appear to be around a strong downward trend. In 1972, for example, Du Pont's fiber sales increased 29 percent, a remarkable accomplishment, yet it appears that selling prices fell by about 5 percent. In addition, in the 10-year period 1963–73, Du Pont's fibers selling-price index fell more than 40 percent. This can be compared with Du Pont's nonfiber selling price index, which fell about 5 percent over the same time period. It may be concluded that a major portion of Du Pont's sales are subject to substantial selling-price volatility and downward pressure.

Foreign sales are in marked contrast to Du Pont's textile mill products sales. Foreign sales for Du Pont include fibers, synthetic rubber, plastic, petroleum additives, films, and industrial and agricultural chemicals. In recent years foreign sales have shown better growth than domestic sales, and in many cases

TABLE 7-2 *Du Pont's Sales by Industry, 1968 and 1972*

Industry	1968	1972
Textile mill products	32 percent	31 percent
Foreign sales	13	18
Chemical and allied products	8	8
Rubber and plastic	8	8
Transportation	6	6
Machinery-electrical	4	5
Petroleum	5	5
Paper	3	5
Food and related products	4	3
Medical services	0	2
Other	17	9
	100	100

TABLE 7-3 *Du Pont's Sales by Major Product Groups*

Product	1969	1972
Fibers	36 percent	39 percent
Plastics materials and synthetics	22	21
Industrial chemicals	22	19
Other chemicals and products	22	21
	100	100

are more profitable. For example, foreign chemical sales had a 15 percent increase in 1972 over 1971, and it is estimated that foreign sales will continue to grow at about 8 percent per year. Consequently, the large proportion of foreign sales should provide a vigorous stimulus to Du Pont's sales, and to some extent dampen any detrimental effects that may result because of the difficulties in the domestic sales of textile mill products.

The remaining 51 percent of Du Pont's sales are split up among nine industries, which will not be discussed because it does not appear that they will have a major adverse effect on Du Pont's sales. However, it is useful to have the firm's sales broken down by product grouping. Du Pont reports its sales by four product groupings as shown in Table 7–3. This table shows that fibers are Du Pont's major product grouping. It appears that the future success of Du Pont will hinge upon what occurs in the market for fibers. However, since it is not a question of stagnating growth but one of selling prices, the important question emerges as to the impact of these declining selling prices on the profitability of Du Pont. If Du Pont's profitability has declined and its *EPS* growth has slowed, then the fibers segment is largely responsible.

GAF permits an evaluation of another type of reporting. GAF does not report on the basis of end-use; it reports sales and operating profit contribution by division or group. Table 7-4 shows the dollar sales and operating profits, and Table 7-5 shows the proportional breakdown by operating groups. The data in Table 7-5 facilitates an evaluation of the operating groups by showing the contribution to sales and operating profits of each division. First, it should be noted that the sales increased at compound rate of 6.7 percent during this five-year period, but operating profits—profits before general administrative expenses—grew by compound rate of 4.9 percent. It is thus clear that operating profits are not increasing in proportion to sales.

A brief comparison of Tables 7-4 and 7-5 illustrates the major problem areas of GAF's operations. Its best performing groups appear to be building materials and industrial products. These two product groups show growth in operating profits, with the building materials division showing substantial growth. Operating profits for the chemical division have been stagnant. On the other hand, photo products and business systems have not been very profitable. Operating profits have dropped below their 1968 levels in both cases, and the photo products division actually operated at a loss in 1970. These two groups have been real problem areas for GAF, yet they have shown reasonably good

TABLE 7-4 *Sales and Contribution to Operating Profits by GAF's Operating Groups for Period 1968–73*

Net sales	1968	1969	1970	1971	1972
Chemicals	$137.1	$151.1	$142.0	$145.8	$156.3
Photo products	135.4	145.3	137.8	177.8	205.4
Business systems	69.6	74.8	83.9	80.6	89.1
Building materials	168.2	175.7	176.1	233.0	263.5
Industrial products	44.0	45.1	43.7	46.7	54.2
Total net sales	$554.3	$592.0	$583.5	$683.8	$768.5
Direct operating profits					
Chemicals	$ 21.0	$ 24.2	$ 20.9	$ 20.9	$ 20.5
Photo products	13.4	6.8	(3.1)	4.5	8.9
Business systems	4.9	4.4	4.5	2.4	2.3
Building materials	17.9	17.0	18.4	39.3	42.2
Industrial products	8.4	9.2	8.3	8.5	9.8
Total direct operating profit	$ 65.6	$ 61.6	$ 49.0	$ 75.6	$ 83.6

sales growth, as have the other divisions. GAF's real strength has been its building materials group. This group has been essentially responsible for the growth in GAF's operating profits. It may be concluded that the building materials group is GAF's star performer, two groups appear to be having difficulty, and two appear to be just holding their own.

Consequently, GAF's future success hinges on three important factors. First, the two divisions that have performed badly in the period 1968–73 must be turned around. It appear that a turnaround is in progress in the photo products group. If this materializes, it will aid GAF's profitability. On the other hand, there is little evidence of a turnaround in the business systems group, and this group may be a continuing problem. Second, improved results will be needed from the chemical and industrial products groups. It may be speculated that

TABLE 7-5 *Proportional Contribution to Sales and Operating Profits GAF's Operating Groups, 1968–73*

Net sales (in percent)	1968	1969	1970	1971	1972
Chemicals	24.7	26.0	24.3	21.3	20.4
Photo products	24.4	24.5	23.6	26.0	26.7
Business systems	12.6	12.6	14.4	11.8	11.6
Building materials	30.3	29.6	30.2	34.1	34.3
Industrial products	7.9	7.6	7.5	6.8	7.0
Direct operating profits (in percent)					
Chemicals	32.0	39.3	42.7	27.6	24.5
Photo products	20.4	11.0	(6.3)	6.0	10.6
Business systems	7.5	7.2	9.1	3.2	2.7
Building materials	27.3	27.6	37.6	52.0	50.5
Industrial products	12.8	14.9	16.9	11.2	11.7

these two groups will show improved results simply because the conditions of the chemical industry appear to be improving. Finally, this means that much of the future growth depends upon the growth of the building materials divisions. Recall that this is a cyclical industry, with sales dependent on housing starts and construction. Generally, this cycle runs counter to the general business cycle, meaning that sales are highest when general business activity is sluggish and peaks out somewhat before the peak in general business activity. Hence, if the other four divisions could begin to make a substantial contribution to profits growth, GAF would have a good combination for stabilized growth. These other four divisions, however, hold the key to the success of GAF. If they begin performing relatively well, then GAF may well have the key to well-balanced growth.

Conclusion

The rates of growth of the two firms are substantially different. Du Pont's sales grew at a compound rate of 5.5 percent, whereas GAF recorded a growth of 15.8 percent. By comparison, the industry growth rate was 6.2 percent. Du Pont, therefore, lagged behind both the industry and GAF in sales growth. However, much of GAF's sales growth resulted from a merger with Ruberoid in 1967 which increased its size markedly. Nevertheless, GAF's sales were recording substantial increases before and after the merger.

Beyond the comparison on the rates of growth, several other conclusions can be drawn with respect to the sales growth of Du Pont and GAF. First, Du Pont's selling prices have been subject to substantial pressure. This fact is evident by a comparison of the index of sales with the FRB's chemical index, which indicates that Du Pont's selling prices and those of the chemical industry have been under considerable pressure. GAF's selling prices have turned in a mixed performance, but GAF's selling prices appear generally to have run counter to the industry trend. Further, previous analysis shows that the severest price declines occurred in the fibers segment of the industry. This segment happens to constitute Du Pont's major product group, and it appears therefore that events in this segment will be the key to Du Pont's future success.

Second, although GAF's sales performance appears better than that of Du Pont, GAF's size and the mixed performance of its operating groups are definitely factors to be considered. GAF is not a large factor in the chemical industry with approximately 1 percent of the market. Moreover, the market does not appear to be highly concentrated, indicating that it may be fairly competitive. A more important consideration, however, is that only one of its five operating groups made a significant contribution to the growth of operating profits. Two groups turned in mediocre performances and two groups appear to be having difficulty. The future success of GAF appears to hinge upon the continued success of the building materials group, a turnaround in photo products and business systems, and a better performance by the chemicals and industrial products groups.

Profitability Analysis

Although growth in sales is generally necessary for growth in earnings and *EPS*, it is not sufficient. The real test of the performance of the firm is its profitability. Fundamental to this success in most cases is the marketing effort, but profitability goes beyond the marketing function to incorporate all the functions of the firm. Essentially, the question that is being raised is: what is the source of growth in profits and *EPS?* For example, consider the *EPS* data in Table 7-6 for Du Pont, GAF, the chemical industry, and S & P's 425. These *EPS* data present a rather interesting picture. It seems that GAF has turned in a superior performance, and in some respects it has. However, further investigation is needed before substantive conclusions can be drawn about the performance of either firm and about their future prospects.

Generally, the growth in earnings is derived from three sources. These are:

1. Growth in the asset base
2. Increased productivity
3. Some combination of sources 1 and 2

If the growth in profits results solely from the growth in the asset base, this means that the productivity of the firm's assets in aggregate has remained unchanged. Future growth in earnings would be expected to be directly related to additions to the asset base. Increased productivity, on the other hand, occurs when a firm is able to reduce its costs of operation. For example, there may be a technological breakthrough that permits the production of certain products at lower costs. The profits of the firm may be increased from this factor alone.

Finally, the preferred situation, and the one firms strive for, is growth in profits that result from the expansion of the asset base and increased productivity. The subsequent analysis will focus on the productivity of the firm, which is

TABLE 7-6 *Comparative Primary* EPS *for Du Pont, GAF, S & P's Chemical Industry, and the S & P's 425 1963–73*

Year	Du Pont	GAF	S & P's Chemical Industry	S & P's 425
1963	$6.35	$0.59	$2.75	$4.24
1964	7.55	0.78	3.34	4.83
1965	8.35	0.96	3.41	5.51
1966	7.97	1.18	3.50	5.99
1967	6.39	1.19	2.84	5.66
1968	7.60	1.28	3.16	6.16
1969	7.27	0.84	3.17	6.17
1970	6.80	0.53	2.70	5.36
1971	7.28	1.66	2.93	6.02
1972	8.50	1.75	3.58	6.86
Rate*	3.0%	11.5%	2.7%	6.8%

*Annual compound rate of growth

viewed as being synonymous with profitability. By focusing on the profitability of the firm, some conclusions can be reached about the sources of future growth. For example, if the firm's productivity is increasing and if the firm is increasing its asset base, earnings will increase at an increasing rate. Conversely, if the productivity is declining, but the firm is still expanding its asset base, earnings will be expected to increase but at a decreasing rate.

An easy way to determine whether trends in productivity exist and what the level of productivity is, is to calculate the return on total assets. If this rate is fairly constant over time, the firm's growth in earnings will most likely result from expansion of the asset base. However, calculating what is sometimes referred to as the earning power of the firm will help explain whatever trends may exist in the ratios of return in total assets of the firm. Another useful calculation is to determine the return on new investments. The return on total assets and the earning power calculations are aggregate measures, and at times aggregate measures tend to obscure outcomes at the margin. Marginal analysis, however, will overcome this difficulty.

Aggregate Measures

The two sets of aggregate ratios that will be developed below are the earning power and the return on total assets. In form, these ratios are very similar. The major difference between them is that the earning power *(EP)* attempts to measure the profitability of operations before financial charges and income taxes, and the return on total assets *(RTA)* attempts to measure the profitability after all of these outflows. In general, the earning power concept can be expressed notationally as follows:

$$EP_{it} = TAT_{it} \times OEM_{it} \qquad (7\text{-}1)$$

where EP_{it} is the gross return on total assets for firm i at time t, TAT_{it} is the total asset turnover for firm i at time t, and OEM_{it} is the operating earnings margin for firm i at time t. Since there does not exist a set of standard definitions in ratio analysis, *TAT* and *OEM* will be defined more specifically. The *TAT* is the net sales of the firm excluding nonoperating revenue divided by the total assets of the firm. The *OEM* is found by dividing profits of the firm after all operating expenses, but before all financial charges and income taxes, by the net sales.

This formulation divides the *EP* into its constituents so that a more detailed analysis can be undertaken. The approach focuses on operating results and excludes all nonoperating items, such as nonoperating income and financial charges. The *OEM* indicates the spread between sales revenues and operating costs. The greater the spread, the more favorable this is for the firm. However, *OEM* alone does not indicate the *EP* of the firm. The *TAT* must also be considered because the *OEM* may be quite low with a high *EP* if there is sufficient turnover. The operating profit of the firm depends upon both these elements.

A variation of the *EP* formulation can be used to explain the return on total assets. That is

$$RTA_{it} = TAT_{it} \times NEM_{it} \qquad (7\text{-}2)$$

where RTA_{it} is the return on total assets for firm i at time t, and the NEM_{it} is the net earnings margin for firm i at time t. In this formulation, the NEM is the net income available to the common stockholders divided by the net sales of the firm. Equation 7-2 is very similar to Equation 7-1 conceptually, but it is concerned with the profitability of the firm after taxes and after financial charges.

Equations 7-1 and 7-2 can be used to help determine the factors influencing the growth in earnings. Du Pont and GAF can be used to illustrate the use of Equations 7-1 and 7-2, as shown in Table 7-7. Columns 2 to 6 contain the earnings margins, the total asset turnover, the earning power, and the return on total assets as previously defined. In addition, column 7 shows the return on the net worth *(RNW)*. This is a common measure of the return to the owners of the

TABLE 7-7   *Comparative Profitability Ratios for Du Pont Corporation and GAF Corporation 1963–73*

| | Du Pont Corporation (in percent) | | | | | |
Year (1)	Operating earnings margin (2)	Net earnings margin (3)	Total asset turnover (4)	Earning power (5)	Return on total assets (6)	Return on net worth (7)
1963	24.3	11.8	116.5	28.3	13.8	17.5
1964	23.9	13.0	115.9	27.7	15.1	19.7
1965	24.2	13.2	115.9	28.0	15.4	20.4
1966	21.6	12.0	113.7	24.5	13.6	18.2
1967	17.4	9.9	100.0	17.4	9.9	14.0
1968	20.9	10.5	105.0	22.0	11.0	15.7
1969	18.5	9.5	101.8	18.8	9.7	13.6
1970	15.1	8.9	96.7	14.6	8.6	11.9
1971	14.9	9.0	96.2	14.3	8.7	12.0
1972	16.2	9.3	101.9	16.5	9.4	13.3

| | GAF Corporation (in percent) | | | | | |
Year (1)	Operating earnings margin (2)	Net earnings margin (3)	Total asset turnover (4)	Earning power (5)	Return on total assets (6)	Return on net worth (7)
1963	8.3	4.6	87.3	7.2	4.0	5.1
1964	9.3	5.6	88.2	8.2	4.9	7.4
1965	10.3	6.2	93.7	9.6	5.8	7.4
1966	10.1	5.5	92.3	9.3	5.1	8.0
1967	7.1	3.1	110.0	7.8	3.2	6.1
1968	7.9	3.1	106.4	8.4	3.4	6.2
1969	6.3	1.9	105.6	6.6	2.0	4.0
1970	4.9	1.3	104.0	5.0	1.3	2.5
1971	7.4	3.3	116.2	8.6	3.8	7.6
1972	7.6	3.1	125.8	9.5	3.9	7.6

firm and is useful also for indicating the impact of leverage on the return to the owners.

The analysis of the profitability of Du Pont and GAF provides a study in contrasts. Du Pont, of course, is the most profitable firm in the chemical industry, and its EP and RTA ratios illustrate why. GAF, on the other hand, is having difficulty, particularly with its earnings margins. However, there are several interesting trends evident for Du Pont and GAF. In the years 1963–67, Du Pont's OEM and TAT were relatively high, and the EP varied in a range of 26 to 28 percent. Since 1966, the EP has fallen and has been somewhat unstable. The cause has been the combined effect of a decline in the OEM and the TAT. The OEM declined from a high of 24.3 percent in 1963 to a low of 14.9 percent in 1971. It showed some improvement in 1972, increasing to 16.2 percent. Similarly, the TAT has fallen from a high of 116.5 percent in 1963 to a low of 96.2 percent in 1971. The TAT also showed some improvement in 1972, increasing to 101.9 percent. Consequently, Du Pont's profitability has been affected by both a declining OEM and TAT, which reflect the industry's problems.

The RTA reflects the trends evident in the EP. The NEM has declined from a high of 13.2 in 1965 to a low of 9.0 percent in 1971. This decline in the NEM combined with the decline in the TAT has led to a decline in the RTA from 15.4 percent in 1965 to a low of 8.7 percent in 1971. The year 1972 showed some improvement, with RTA increasing to 9.4 percent. Finally, the return on net worth indicates the return on the stockholder's investment and gives an indication of the impact of leverage. Again the RNW has fallen substantially from a high of 20.4 in 1965 to a low of 11.9 percent in 1970. While the actual rate of return must be viewed as quite high, the downward trend indicates that conditions in the industry, and for Du Pont in particular, have changed.

In summary, four conclusions can be drawn about Du Pont's profitability during the period 1963–73. First, 1965 appears to be the turning point in Du Pont's performance. Almost all of the measures of profitability reached a peak in 1965, marking the high point for Du Pont and the industry. Second, Du Pont has since faced declining profitability, as indicated by its earning power, return on total assets, and return on net worth. The cause is both a decline in the earnings margins and the total asset turnover, which reflects the generally held view that the industry suffered from oversupply. Third, the measures for 1972 seem to indicate that the downward trend may have ended, but one year's experience is not sufficient to support this view. Finally, while trends are important, the absolute levels of the profitability measures for Du Pont must not be overlooked. Comparable ratios for the industry are not available for the earning power and return on total assets, but the return on net worth for the chemical industry excluding Du Pont was within a range of 9.0 to 13.4 percent for the period of 1964 to 1973. It is clear that Du Pont is still out performing its industry by a substantial margin and compares favorably with firms in general. Du Pont's profitability is not as high as it once was, but it is still quite profitable.

GAF's situation is markedly different than that of Du Pont, with respect to both the level of its profitability ratios and the general trend. GAF's earnings margins are much lower than those of Du Pont, and its *EP*, *RTA*, and *RNW* are substantially lower. The *OEM* exhibits a pattern similar to that of Du Pont, but the major difference is the upward trend in the *TAT*. In the years 1963 to 1967 the *OEM* was relatively high, within the range of 8.3 to 10.3 percent, but the *OEM* declined in the subsequent years to a low of 4.9 percent in 1970. It is interesting to speculate on GAF's situation without the acquisition of Ruberoid in 1967, since it was shown that the building products division made the major contribution to profits and profit growth in the period 1967–73. Similarly, the *NEM* follows the same pattern as the *OEM*. It reached a peak of 6.2 percent in 1965, and fell to a low of 1.3 percent in 1970. It recovered to a range of 3.1 to 3.3 percent in 1971 and 1972. Nevertheless, this is a very narrow profit margin and a source of concern.

A factor that operated to GAF's advantage and aided in offsetting the impact of the declining earnings margins was the upward trend in the *TAT*. In the period 1963–73, GAF's *TAT* increased more than 50 percent. In fact, the effect was almost sufficient to offset entirely the lower *OEM*. For example, the *EP* in 1972 was as high as in the peak years of 1965 and 1966, yet the *OEM* is substantially lower. However the *RTA* has not benefited from this effect because GAF had financed much of its expansion in the period by additional fixed charge financing. This can be quickly verified by comparing the *RTA* for the years 1963 and 1972 with the *RNW* for the same years. The *RTA* was 4.0 percent in 1963 and 3.9 percent in 1972, yet by comparison the *RNW* in 1963 was 5.1 percent but 7.6 percent in 1972. The substantially higher return on net worth given that *RTA* is approximately equal for the two years means that the expansion in the asset base during that period was the result of the greater use of leverage.

In summary, three basic conclusions can be drawn about GAF's profitability. First, the levels of GAF's ratios are substantially below those of Du Pont and may be considered generally low. This factor constitutes a major source of risk for any potential investor in GAF's stock. Second, one desirable trend is the increase in the *TAT*, which has shown a substantial increase during the period 1963–73. This has had the effect of returning GAF's *EP* to its previous high, and, considering the difficulties of the industry and the recession of 1970, this result is gratifying. However, the *RTA* has not benefited because the firm has tended to use more leverage, but this tactic has improved the *RNW*. Finally, for GAF to attain acceptable levels of profitability, it appears that the key lies in increasing its profit margins. The *TAT* has increased significantly, and it may not be possible to attain further increases, which means that the margins must improve to improve the profitability of the firm.

It appears that Du Pont and GAF are two very different firms not only in their product mix and size but also in their profitability and profitability patterns. Du Pont's profitability appeared to be declining with some possibility of stabilizing in 1972, but its profitability ratios were still quite high and remain relatively high. GAF, on the other hand, is struggling with below-average profitability, but has recently shown some signs of improvement. If the present situation stabilizes at Du Pont, the growth in earnings for Du Pont will come from additions to the asset base, not from improved productivity. Growth in earnings for GAF may very well benefit both from increased productivity and increases in the asset base. The key to the increased productivity appears to be in increasing the profit margins, since the *TAT* has increased sharply and may not permit further increases. If this does occur, it means that GAF will be moving toward more normal profitability.

Marginal Analysis

One of the major difficulties with the aggregate measures of profitability is that they obscure the profitability on new investments. For example, the analysis of Du Pont and GAF may lead to the conclusion that a dollar of assets will make a larger contribution to earnings for Du Pont than for GAF. The truth of this conclusion depends on the rate of return earned on new investments. Marginal analysis enables one to evaluate this question and permits an evaluation of the increase in earnings that may result from an increase in the asset base. Marginal analysis may thus provide vital information in formulating expectations about future growth of the firm's earnings.

One method of conducting this analysis is simply to relate the change in profits to the change in total assets over some time period. Again it is useful to distinguish between operating earnings and net earnings. Looking at both of these measures of profits may illustrate whether there is a dichotomy between the operating profit and the profit available to the common stockholders. Notationally, this formulation may be represented as

$$MR_{i\tau} = \frac{\Delta OE_{i\tau}}{\Delta TA_{i\tau}} \tag{7-3}$$

where $MR_{i\tau}$ is the marginal return for firm i during the period τ, $\Delta OE_{i\tau}$ is the change in operating earnings for firm i during the period τ, and $\Delta TA_{i\tau}$ is the change in total assets for firm i during the period τ. Equation 7-3 indicates the gross return on new investment over some time period and consequently indicates the profitability of new investments disregarding income taxes and financial charges.

Equation 7-3 can be modified to apply to the income available to the common stockholders instead of the operating earnings. Therefore, Equation 7-3 may be revised as follows:

$$M_{i\tau}^* = \frac{\Delta NI_{i\tau}}{\Delta TA_{i\tau}} \tag{7-4}$$

where $\Delta NI_{i\tau}$ is the change in net income for firm i during the period τ, and $\Delta TA_{i\tau}$ is as previously defined.

The only difference between these two equations is that one focuses on operating earnings, while the other focuses on the income available to the common stockholders. Used together these two equations can be particularly useful in determining the anticipated growth in earnings. Equation 7-3 can be used to determine the return at the margin from operations, which can be compared with the *EP* for individual years to determine whether the *MR* is above or below it. This may have important implications for future growth. For example, if the *MR* were somewhat below the *EP* on the average, then one could expect a decline in the rate of growth of earnings. Conversely, if the *MR* were greater than the *EP* on the average, then the growth in earnings could be expected to accelerate. Equation 7-4 provides the same type of information as Equation 7-3 with respect to the net income. Since appreciation results from increases in *EPS* and dividends per share, the marginal impact on the earnings available to the common stockholders is a critical consideration.

To illustrate the use of marginal analysis, we can again refer to Du Pont and GAF. The data are presented in Table 7-8. The results are somewhat different and perhaps surprising when compared to the aggregate analysis previously completed. For Du Pont, the return at the margin is well below that for the firm as a whole. Recall that the range for the *EP* for the period 1963–73 was approximately 14 to 28 percent; yet the return at the margin was a meager 4.2 percent. Similarly, the *RTA* was within a range of approximately 8 to 16 percent; yet the return at the margin was 4.9 percent. Consequently, even though Du Pont made substantial new investments amounting to approximately $2.1 billion, the amount of profit generated was relatively small, amounting to something on the order of $100 million. This explains the decline in the aggregate profitability measures and also has important implications for future growth of earnings. Obviously, this situation cannot continue to exist much longer or Du Pont's position in the industry will be eroded.

GAF illustrated a rather mixed situation. GAF's *EP* fell within a range of approximately 5 to 10 percent, but its *MR* was 10.7 percent, which is substantially above that of Du Pont and also above its own *EP*. Consequently, new

TABLE 7-8 *Marginal Analysis for Du Pont Corporation and GAF Corporation, 1963–73*

Du Pont Corporation ($ millions)			
Year	Total assets	Operating earnings	Net income
1972	4284.7	707.4	404.5
1963	2193.2	620.0	302.2
Difference	2091.5	87.4	102.3
Marginal return (percent)		4.2	4.9

GAF Corporation ($ millions)			
Year	Total assets	Operating earnings	Net income
1972	610.8	58.2	24.1
1963	202.4	14.6	8.1
Difference	408.4	43.6	16.0
Marginal return (percent)		10.7	3.9

investments by GAF are generating a higher return than the existing assets. This should lead one to expect the growth in earnings to accelerate. On the other hand, the *MR**, which shows the relationship of the growth in net income to total assets, was not much different from the *RTA*. The *RTA* for the period fell within a range of approximately 1 to 6 percent, but the *MR** was found to be 3.9 percent. It appears that taxes and financial charges have thus had a significant impact on income available to the common stockholders. Further investigation shows that the expansion by GAF has been financed largely by debt and preferred stock. In 1963 GAF had virtually no debt or preferred stock outstanding; by 1972, debt and preferred stock had climbed to the point where interest expenses were $10.2 million and preferred dividends were $3.8 million. As a result, the *MR** has shown no improvement over the *RTA* as was evident with *MR* and the *EP*.

GAF's situation with respect to the *MR* and *MR** may still be preferred to that of Du Pont's, since at least the *MR* is showing progress. Hence, if GAF can use retained earnings for financing further expansion, then the *MR** may reflect the higher return at the margin. This could very well be the case since much of the debt was issued about the time of the Ruberoid merger during 1965–70. In the years 1970–73, the amount of debt has been reduced.

Summary

Growth analysis is probably the single most important aspect of common stock analysis since the investor expects growth in earnings and *EPS* to lead to appreciation of common stock. It seems clear that investors look to growth in earnings and *EPS* as the source of potential appreciation, even though dividends may be tangible evidence of this growth. The investor is typically faced with the question of whether the existing price in the market is too high or not, and this means that he must ascertain whether the existing price will permit a reasonable rate of return over some time horizon. Growth analysis attempts to determine the growth that can be reasonably expected in earnings and *EPS* so that the potential appreciation and the cash dividends paid may be estimated. The starting point in the analysis is to analyze the growth in net sales. One commonly used assumption is that above-average growth in sales will eventually lead to above-average growth in profits. However, it has become recognized more and more that the key consideration is the impact on profits. In other words, it is reasonable to suppose that sales growth is necessary for the growth in profits, but it is not sufficient for the growth in profits. Consequently, analysis of sales growth must be coupled with analysis of profits growth to give a proper picture of the firm's performance.

The analysis of sales growth involves three separate comparisons. First, it is common to determine the rate of growth of sales relative to some standard of comparison. A firm's sales growth may be compared with that of the economy, the industry, and other firms in the industry. This comparison permits an evaluation of how the firm is doing relative to other segments of the economy.

Second, it is useful to determine the source of sales growth. It may result essentially from increases in the firm's prices, or it may result essentially from increases in physical output. In Du Pont's case, for example, it was found that selling prices declined substantially. This type of situation may put the firm in a difficult position. The most desirable situation occurs when selling prices remain constant or increase slightly. Increases in physical output account for most of the increases in sales revenue, without profit margins being eroded. Third, the increases or decreases in the firm's market share may be useful in evaluating the firm's competitive position. For example, if a firm is increasing its share of the market at a fairly rapid rate, then its growth rate is expected to be greater than that of the industry. More importantly, it gives an indication of the firm's position in the industry.

The ultimate test of the firm's success is its profitability. At this point all the factors relevant to the firm come to bear. The approach taken here was to focus on two groups of measures of profitability. The aggregate indicators included the earning power, return on total assets, and return on net worth. The *EP* and *RTA* can be reduced to their components. These are the operating earnings margin, net earnings margin, and the total asset turnover. The profitability of the firm as measured by either the *EP* or the *RTA* depends on the appropriate earnings margin and the total asset turnover.

The actual analysis involves two steps. First, evidence of trends are looked for. If a trend persists, especially a downward trend, then the earnings margin and the *TAT* will show what the source of the problem is. Second, the levels of the ratios must be considered relative to a standard of comparison. Industry figures normally are used, and this permits an evaluation of how the firm is doing as compared to the industry.

Marginal analysis may be used to supplement aggregate analysis. Many times trends persist at the margin that are obscured by aggregate statistics. Marginal analysis can add valuable information about the return that is being earned on new investments. Generally, the amounts committed to new projects are a small proportion of the assets of the firm. For this reason trends in the return on marginal investments may not be apparent in the aggregate ratios. And more importantly, the magnitude of the discrepancy between the return on new investments and existing assets may not be apparent. The two measures used here involve operating earnings and net income, since these two measures can be quickly related to the *EP* and the *RTA*. It can be determined, therefore, whether additions to the asset base are significantly more or less profitable than existing assets. Such information is valuable in making predictions about future profitability.

Questions

1. A major problem facing the investor is to establish whether the current price of a common stock is too high. Explain why this is true.
2. Suppose a firm's sales are increasing at an above-average rate.

a. Give some reasons for *not* expecting this growth to be reflected in earnings and earnings per share.

b. What is the assumption for expecting earnings and earnings per share to
reflect the above-average sales growth?

3. What characteristics of the firm's sales is the analyst particularly interested
in?

4. Suppose the following indexes have been developed for the GNP, the sales
of firms A and B, the sales of the industry, and the Federal Reserve Board's
index for that industry.

Sales indexes

Year	GNP	Firm A	Firm B	Industry	FRB's index
1	100.0	100.0	100.0	100.0	102.0
2	107.8	107.1	102.6	105.1	104.4
3	112.8	114.6	109.5	109.8	107.3
4	116.2	117.1	111.0	118.2	112.1
5	119.9	119.2	113.1	120.4	117.1

a. How has the industry's growth compared with that of the GNP?

b. How has the firm's growth compared with that of the industry?

c. Have price increases been important factors to either firm A or B or the
industry in general?

d. What has been the compound rate of growth for each index series?

5. Suppose that two firms held the following shares of the market:

Year	Firm C	Firm D
1	27.1 percent	38.6 percent
2	28.2	42.0
3	29.6	40.7
4	30.1	39.9
5	32.1	40.1

a. How would you determine the degree of concentration in this industry?
How would this fact influence your conclusion about the market position
of each firm?

b. How would you characterize the market share of each firm? Could this
affect future sales forecasts for either firm?

6. Suppose the following operating earnings margins, net earnings margins,
and total asset turnover ratios are given for firms X and Y.

Firm X

Year	Operating earnings margin	Net earnings margin	Total asset turnover
1	25.1 percent	13.4 percent	110.0 percent
2	22.6	12.2	111.0
3	23.1	12.4	108.0
4	20.1	9.7	104.0
5	18.4	8.4	102.0

Firm Y

Year	Operating earnings margin	Net earnings margin	Total asset turnover
1	18.2 percent	8.7 percent	100.1 percent
2	18.4	8.6	103.2
3	18.7	8.9	104.1
4	17.9	8.4	107.3
5	19.2	8.9	109.1

a. Calculate the earning power and the return on total assets for each firm.

b. Are there any trends evident? If so, what are the sources?

7. Suppose firm 1 and firm 2 have the following operating earnings, net income, and total assets for the initial and last years of the most recent 10-year period.

Firm 1

	Operating earnings	Net income	Total assets
Initial year	$ 48,000	21,200	$200,000
Tenth year	120,000	51,200	600,000

Firm 2

	Operating earnings	Net income	Total assets
Initial year	$58,000	29,200	$480,000
Tenth year	75,000	38,000	930,000

a. What is the marginal return for both operating earnings and net income?

b. Calculate the earning power and return on total assets for each firm.

c. Suppose the tenth-year figures for the earning power and return on total assets are representative of trends that have occurred. Is the return on new investments for these two firms likely to lead to earnings growth at an increasing rate?

Selected References

Amling, Frederick. *Investments: An Introduction to Analysis and Management.* Englewood Cliffs, N.J.: Prentice-Hall, 1970. Chapters 11 and 12.

Cohen, Jerome B., and Edward D. Zinbarg. *Investment Analysis and Management.* Homewood, Ill.: Richard D. Irwin, 1967. Chapters 7 and 8.

Crisp, Richard D. *Sales Planning and Control.* New York: McGraw-Hill, 1961.

Hayes, Douglas A. "Some Reflections on Techniques for Appraising Growth Rates." *Financial Analysts Journal,* vol. 20, no. 4 (July–Aug., 1964, pp. 96–102.

Helfert, Erich A. *Techniques of Financial Analysis,* 3d ed. Homewood, Ill.: Richard D. Irwin, 1972. Chapters 2 and 6.

Jerome, William Travers, III. *Executive Control—The Catalyst.* New York: John Wiley & Sons, 1961. Chapter 13.

Johnson, Robert W. *Financial Management,* 4th ed. Boston: Allyn & Bacon, 1971. Chapter 3.

Mayer, Robert W. "Business Risk and the Earnings Multiplier." *Financial Analysts Journal,* vol. 21, no. 5 (Sept.–Oct., 1965), pp. 19–22.

Neiderhoffer, Victor, and Patrick Regan. "Earnings Changes, Analysts' Forecasts, and Stock Prices." *Financial Analysts Journal,* vol. 28, no. 3 (May–June, 1972), pp. 65–71.

Vaughn, Donald E. *Survey of Investments.* New York: Holt, Rinehart & Winston, 1967. Chapter 12.

Weston, J. Fred, and Eugene F. Brigham. *Essentials of Managerial Finance.* New York: Holt, Rinehart & Winston, 1971. Chapter 3.

Chapter 8

Working Capital, Financial Structure, and Management

In addition to growth analysis, which was discussed in the previous chapter, the firm's working capital position, its financial structure, and its management may be important considerations in determining its prospects. Working capital is an important consideration because the firm must have enough funds to meet its current obligations, such as the purchase of materials and supplies, additions to plant and equipment, and debt repayment. If sufficient funds are not provided, the firm runs the risk of being forced into involuntary bankruptcy proceedings. In common stock analysis, the important question is the role of the analysis of the firm's working capital position, in particular, the role of working capital management with respect to the profitability of the firm. This will be the focus of the subsequent analysis of the firm's working position.

In financial theory a controversial topic is whether the mix of debt and equity can affect the value of the firm. The traditional view holds that there is an optimum mix of debt and equity for the firm. This view has come under attack by some theorists who hold that an optimum capital structure does not exist. The security analyst, of course, is interested in any factor that may affect the value of the firm; consequently, this controversy must be investigated.

Finally, an important factor is the quality of the firm's management. The firm operates within a dynamic milieu, which means that the management of the firm must be sensitive to ever-changing conditions. Consequently, firms with good management teams are expected to outperform their competition. The difficulty, of course, is evaluating such an intangible as the quality of management. The evaluation becomes even more difficult for an outsider such as a security analyst. However, substantial research has been done in this area, and it should provide some insight into the evaluation of the quality of management.

Working Capital Analysis

The firm's working capital position focuses on the answers to two related questions. First, what is the firm's liquidity position? That is, does the firm appear to have sufficient liquid resources to meet its current obligations? The measurement of the firm's liquidity position has become fairly standardized in recent years, with certain measures emerging as generally accepted indicators of the firm's working capital position. A more important question is under what circumstances the working capital position is a major consideration in common stock analysis. For example, is it a primary consideration in all cases, or is it generally a secondary consideration except in certain specific situations?

Measurement

There are several generally accepted measures of the working capital position. Two measures that are widely used are the current ratio and the acid-test ratio. These ratios measure the overall liquidity position of the firms. More specific measures are the average collection period and the inventory turnover, which measure the liquidity of specific components of the current assets. Each of these measures will be discussed subsequently.

Current Ratio   The current ratio is probably the best known measure of the firm's liquidity. It simply indicates the size of the current assets relative to the current liabilities. Presumably, the firm's working capital position is adequate when the current assets sufficiently exceed the current liabilities. To determine the appropriate level for the firm, either of two methods are usually used, and many times both are used. First, the current ratios for some past period, say 5 to 10 years, are compared to determine whether any trends are present. This approach is sometimes referred to as trend analysis. Second, the current ratios may be compared to the industry average to determine whether the firm is above or below the industry. The current ratio is determined as follows:

$$CR_{it} = \frac{CA_{it}}{CL_{it}} \qquad (8\text{-}1)$$

where CA_{it} is the current assets for firm i at time t, and CL_{it} is the current liabilities for firm i at time t.

To illustrate the use of Equation 8-1, consider the current assets and current liabilities of a hypothetical corporation for a particular year, as shown in Table 8-1. The current ratio for the corporation is:

$$CR = \frac{690}{334}$$

$$= 2.07$$

Thus, the corporation's current ratio is 2.07, meaning that current assets are 2.07 times the current liabilities.

TABLE 8-1 *Current Assets and Current Liabilities for a Hypothetical Corporation*

Current assets (In $ millions)		Current liabilities (In $ millions)	
Cash	30	Accruals	56
Accounts receivable	173	Accounts payable	40
Inventories	436	Notes payable	118
Market securities	51	Bank notes payable	120
Total current assets	690	Total current liabilities	334

The actual ratio—2.07, for example—has little meaning for the analyst until it is compared to some standard. A relatively simple method is to compare the ratios over a past time period. If the ratios remain relatively constant, it may be concluded that the firm's liquidity position is relatively sound. A downward trend, however, is viewed as a source of concern because it may be symptomatic of a deteriorating position. In these situations, an alternative approach of comparing the firm's ratios with those of the industry becomes particularly useful. If the firm's ratios have been greater than those of the industry, the firm's liquidity position may be viewed as sound. However, if the current ratio has recently dropped below that of the industry, this is viewed as a source of concern.

Acid-Test Ratio   A major problem with the current ratio is that it views the various types of current assets as having equal liquidity. Obviously, this is not the case. Cash and marketable securities are much more liquid than inventories and receivables. Receivables are more liquid than inventories. For a typical manufacturing plant, the three types of inventories are raw materials, goods-in-process, and finished goods. Materials and supplies may involve a considerable time period before they are processed and actually reach the market. Hence, some inventory items are quite illiquid. In addition, there is the possibility that some of the inventory items may become obsolete. Receivables are less liquid than cash because they still must be collected, and the possibility exists that the debt may not be collected.

The current ratio treats all these current assets as being equally liquid. The remaining liquidity measures, however, attempt to determine the liquidity of the firm by attempting to isolate the impact of these various current asset items. The acid-test ratio attempts to determine the liquidity of the firm exclusive of inventories. Other techniques attempt to determine the liquidity of the other less liquid current assets. These measures will be discussed later.

The acid-test ratio is calculated in the same manner as the current ratio, except that the inventories are excluded. Inventories are much less liquid than cash, accounts receivable, and marketable securities; the acid-test ratio assumes that these current asset items are more homogeneous. The acid-test ratio may be defined as

$$AT_{it} = \frac{CA_{it} - IN_{it}}{CL_{it}} \tag{8-2}$$

where IN_{it} is the value of the inventories for firm i at time t, and the other terms are as previously defined. For the hypothetical corporation discussed above, the acid-test ratio is

$$AT = \frac{254}{334}$$

$$= 0.76$$

Therefore, this firm's acid-test is 0.76 as compared to a current ratio of 2.07.

This example illustrates the type of situation that might occur. The hypothetical corporation's current assets included a large investment in inventories, which accounted for the significant difference between the current ratio and the acid-test ratio. It is not possible with one-year's data to draw any conclusions about the firm's liquidity position. A series of perhaps the last 5 to 10 years' ratios would probably enable one to determine whether any trends exist. Or, alternatively, these ratios could be compared with the acid-test ratios for the industry to determine whether the firm was above or below the industry's ratios. The same method of evaluation is involved for the acid-test ratio as for the current ratio, and this method may be extended to the inventory turnover ratios and the average collection period.

Inventory Turnover   An alternative method of dealing with inventories is the direct attempt to estimate the liquidity of the inventories. The inventory turnover ratio attempts to do this by determining how many times a firm's inventory turns over in a year. The more often a firm's inventory turns over, the more liquid the inventory may be considered. In other words, the inventory turnover ratio attempts to measure the length of the cycle from the time of manufacture to the time of sale. The shorter this period is, the more liquid the firm's inventory is. The inventory turnover ratio is given by

$$IT_{it} = \frac{CG_{it}}{AI_{it}} \tag{8-3}$$

where CG_{it} is the cost of goods sold for firm i during time t, and AI_{it} is the average inventory for firm i during time t. Generally, the average inventory may be determined by taking the simple average of the beginning and ending inventories. A strong seasonal component, however, may necessitate a weighted average.

To illustrate, suppose that the cost of goods sold for our hypothetical corporation is $841 million during a recent time period and the average inventory for the same time period is $417 million. The inventory turnover ratio, therefore, is

$$IT = \frac{841}{417}$$

$$= 2.02$$

It is not possible to draw any conclusions about this ratio until a series has been calculated to determine whether any trends exist, or until it is compared to the average for the industry to determine how the firm compares.

Average Collection Period A measure that may be used to determine the liquidity of the accounts receivable is to determine the average period required to collect the outstanding debt. Accounts receivable represent sales that have been consummated but remain uncollected. The possibility exists that the receivables will not be collected. The probability of collection really is a question of the quality of the receivables. If the quality is high, the payments for the most part should not be overdue, and this will be reflected in the average collection period. The average collection period may be determined by

$$ACP_{it} = \frac{365\,(AR_{it})}{CS_{it}} \tag{8-4}$$

where AR_{it} is the accounts receivable for firm i during time t, and CS_{it} is the annual credit sales for firm i during time t.

The only real difficulty that may arise with this formulation is determining the annual credit sales. A breakdown of credit sales and cash sales is not usually published by the firm. Under such circumstances, the common assumption is that all of the sales are credit sales. Such an assumption leads to understating the average collection period; this is undesirable but unavoidable. To reach a conclusion about the quality of the receivables also requires information on the firm's credit terms. For example, does the firm use $\frac{2}{10}$, net 30 days, net 60 days as a payment period? This information is needed to judge the quality of the receivables. If the firm uses net 60 days as its payment period, an average collection period of 52 days would be quite satisfactory. On the other hand, an average collection period of 72 days would not be satisfactory. When the terms are not known, the average collection period may be compared for a number of years to determine whether it is stable or displaying a trend. If the average collection period is stable or trending downward, the quality of the receivables may be considered satisfactory.

To illustrate the use of Equation 8-4, consider again the hypothetical corporation discussed above. Suppose the accounts receivable are as given, $173 million, and the annual credit sales are $1,262 million. The average collection period would be

$$ACP = \frac{365(173)}{1,262}$$

$$= 50.0 \text{ days}$$

The average collection period is 50 days. If the credit terms are known, the 50-day average collection period can be compared directly with that. For example, if it is known that the corporation's terms are net 30 days, this indicates that a substantial portion of the receivables are overdue. Alternatively, in cases where the credit terms are not known, trend analysis may be used.

Conclusions

Having reviewed the most common measures of the firm's liquidity position, the question still remains as to how liquidity and the firm's working capital position affect the process of common stock evaluation. Obviously, a weak liquidity position is a source of risk to the investor. The ratios used to measure the firm's liquidity position are designed to point out these weaknesses. The important question that the analyst must face is what role an analysis of the firm's working capital position should play. In traditional financial analysis, the firm's liquidity position was viewed as being independent of its profitability. That is, profitable firms could be illiquid and therefore become technically insolvent. However, a recent empirical study by Edward I. Altman indicates that probably liquidity is dependent upon the firm's profitability. Hence, if a firm is unprofitable, then the liquidity ratios may give an indication of the probability of involuntary bankruptcy.[1]

The firm's liquidity position is not generally a major concern in common stock. The major reason for this is that poor profitability is an indication of difficulty for the firm. The firm may not be an acceptable candidate for this reason. An exception to this might be relatively small firms that are growing very rapidly, or firms that have experienced difficulties and are now turnaround candidates. The analyst needs as much information as possible to evaluate this situation. Investment in either of these types of situations should be made only by individuals who are willing to accept above-average risk; the working capital position is one of these risks.

A second situation in which the working capital position may be an important consideration occurs when a particular stock has been included in the portfolio, but its performance has not been up to expectations. If the firm has not performed well, it is conceivable that this poor performance may be reflected in the firm's liquidity position after a period of time. The liquidity position conceivably could deteriorate to the point where the firm would experience technical insolvency, but generally this outcome would result because the firm was relatively unprofitable. Moreover, the analyst would have sufficient time to decide upon the prospects for the firm and be able to make a recommendation on whether to continue to hold the stock or not.

These remarks are not designed to mean that the firm's working capital position is unimportant in security analysis. There are situations in which the firm's liquidity position will be pivotal, for example, where potential default is a major consideration. In most situations, other considerations will be more important. In particular, the growth in sales that may be expected, the growth in earnings and *EPS,* and the general profitability of the firm are major considerations that dominate the liquidity position of the firm.

Capital Structure

In the financial literature, much consideration has been given to the question of the capital structure of the firm and its impact on the value of the firm. The issue is whether the use of financial leverage will increase the value of the firm in the market. The traditional view, as it is commonly called, holds that the mix of debt and equity in the capital structure does affect the value of the firm and that

---

[1] Edward I. Altman, "Financial Ratios, Discriminant Analysis and the Prediction of Corporate Bankruptcy, *Journal of Finance,* vol. 23, no. 4 (Sept., 1968) pp. 589–610.

there is one mix which will maximize the value of the firm. The dissenting view, whose strongest advocates are probably Franco Modigliani and Merton H. Miller, hold that the capital structure does not make any difference in determining the value of the firm. Obviously, any factor that may affect the value of the firm is of practical importance to the security analyst.

The question is whether the use of low cost debt funds can increase the value of the firm. The benefit that accrues to the firm is that the funds generated by the issuance of debt can be invested at rate greater than their cost. For example, if funds can be borrowed at 6.5 percent and invested to earn 12 percent, the difference of 5.5 percent before taxes accrues to the benefit of the common stockholders. The disadvantage, however, is that the issuance of debt constitutes a source of risk to the firm. Therefore, if investors are risk averters, they will raise their discount rates to account for this additional amount of risk, commonly referred to as financial risk.[2] The question becomes whether the increase in the discount rate offsets any benefits that may accrue from the increased earnings.

To illustrate the issue, consider the two firms Y and Z. Suppose each firm has net operating earnings of $1,000, but while firm Y has $5,000 worth of debt outstanding with a coupon rate of 6 percent, firm Z has no debt at all. In addition, suppose that in every other respect the firms are equal and there are no taxes. If the market does follow the traditional view and if firm Z does not have too much debt, firm Y will have a higher value than Z. This can be shown as follows:

	Firm Y	Firm Z
Net operating income	$ 1,000	$ 1,000
Interest	300	0
Net income	700	1,000
Market capitalization rate	0.13	0.10
Market value of the stock	5,384	10,000
Market value of the bonds	5,000	0
Market value of the firm	$10,384	$10,000

Consequently, firm Y has a value in the market that is higher by $384; the reason for this is that the additional risk created by the debt in the capital structure is not sufficient to raise the discount rate to a level that would offset the benefits of leverage to the stockholders.

The dissenting view holds that the discount rate would increase sufficiently to offset any benefits that might result from the use of low-cost debt. If this were the case, the values of firm Y and Z would be equal. This can be illustrated as follows:

	Firm Y	Firm Z
Net operating income	$ 1,000	$ 1,000
Interest (6 percent of $5,000)	300	0
Net income	700	1,000
Market capitalization rate	0.14	0.10
Market value of stock	5,000	10,000
Market value of bonds	5,000	0
Market value of the firm	$10,000	$10,000

[2] Financial risk is normally defined as the risk resulting from the way the firm is financed.

If this is the case, the reason is that debt in the capital structure has the effect of increasing the capitalization rate on the common stock to the point where the value of the firm is unchanged. The difference in the two results for firm Y is simply that the market capitalization rate was 13 percent in the first case and 14 percent in the second, and what becomes important is how the market values a leveraged earnings stream versus an unleveraged earnings stream.

Most of the controversy has been viewed in a highly idealized environment, and the real controversy only applies in a highly unrealistic environment that includes no income taxes. To set the stage for the subsequent discussion, the general setting of the controversy must be presented. First, the term *capital structure* normally applies only to long-term sources of financing. This includes long-term debt, such as mortgage bonds and debentures, preferred stock, and common equity. This definition is generally used because it is assumed that the accruals and accounts payable will be a source of permanent financing, whereas short-term borrowing is temporary and will be paid off within the year.

The common assumptions that are used are as follows:

1. There are no income taxes. As we shall see later, this is a crucial assumption in the controversy.
2. The capital markets are perfect. This means that all current information is readily available at no cost, and all investors interpret it in the same fashion. In addition, there are no transaction costs, and all investors are rational.
3. Changes in the capital structure are instantaneous.
4. Firms can be put into risk categories in which all the firms in that category have the same risk characteristics.
5. No growth is anticipated.

These assumptions will be used in the intial discussion of the net operating income approach, the traditional approach, and the Modigliani and Miller modification to the net operating income approach. The impact of relaxing each of these will be discussed subsequently.

Net Operating Income Approach

The net operating income approach (NOI) to the capital structure may be summarized as follows.[3] The NOI approach holds that the overall cost of capital to the firm is unaffected by the capital structure. In other words, the market value is unaffected by the proportions of debt and equity used by the firm. According to the NOI approach, the overall cost of capital to the firm, k_0, remains unchanged because the cost of equity capital, k_e, is a linear function of the amount

---

[3] David Durand, "Costs of Debt and Equity Funds for Business: Trends and Problems of Measurement," *Conference on Research in Business Finance* (New York: National Bureau of Economic Research, 1952), pp. 215–48.

of leverage used by the firm. Therefore, irrespective of the amount of debt used, the overall cost of capital remains unchanged and the market value of the firm remains unchanged. Figure 8-1 illustrates the NOI approach.

In Figure 8-1 the terms k_e, k_0, and k_i refer to the cost of equity, the overall cost of capital, and the cost of debt, respectively. The leverage measure used is the debt-to-equity ratio (D/E ratio). Since the cost of capital normally only includes permanent sources of financing, the debt only includes long-term debt. Also, the use of preferred stock is ignored to simplify the analysis. Further, market values are normally used in estimating the various costs, and therefore the leverage of the firm is measured in terms of the market value of the common stock and the debt. That is, the value of the debt and equity in the debt-to-equity ratio are based upon their respective market values.

In Figure 8-1, the k_e is a linear function of the D/E ratio. This means that anytime there is a change in the mix of debt and equity, the change will have a proportional effect on the k_e. If the firm added proportionally more debt to its capital structure, the market would instantaneously decrease the price of the stock, which is another way of saying that the k_e would increase. The net effect would be that the k_0 would be unchanged. The NOI approach, therefore, holds that the capital structure is immaterial. The mix of debt and equity will not affect the value of the firm.

FIGURE 8-1 *The Net Operating Income Approach*

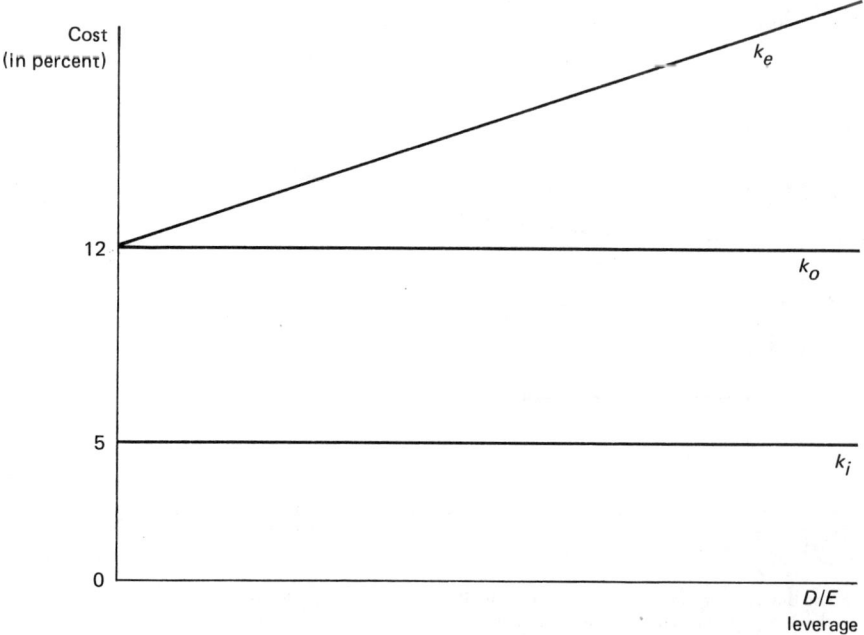

The Traditional View   The traditional view is so named because it has long been the prevailing view. Only in the last 15 years has it come under any serious attack at all. It maintains that the mix of debt and equity does affect the value of the firm, and there is one mix which is optimal. In other words, by seeking the optimal mix of debt and equity the firm can reduce its k_0 to a minimum. Recall that the NOI approach holds that an optimal does not exist. These two viewpoints are in direct conflict.

Figure 8-2 illustrates the traditional view. The terms are the same as before. The key relationship is the market's reaction to the increase in the D/E ratio. The traditional approach does not accept the premise that there is a linear relationship between the k_e and the D/E ratio. Advocates of the traditional view accept the premise that investors are risk averters, but they do not accept the premise that the relationship between k_e and the D/E ratio is linear. For example, at low levels of the D/E ratio, the traditionalists hold that additions to the debt of the firm have little effect on the k_e, since the substitution of debt for equity at these levels would have little effect on the risk of the firm. At the other extreme both the k_e and the k_i would increase substantially, with an increase in the D/E ratio for extremely high levels of the D/E ratio. At these levels, investors would demand a substantial premium to compensate for the substantial amount of financial risk. These concepts are apparent by reference to Figure 8-2. The k_e slopes gently upwards for low levels of the D/E ratio but rises steeply for high levels. The k_i is relatively flat for low levels of D/E, but it rises steeply for high levels of D/E.[4] The slope of both of these reflect the financial

FIGURE 8-2   *The Traditional Approach*

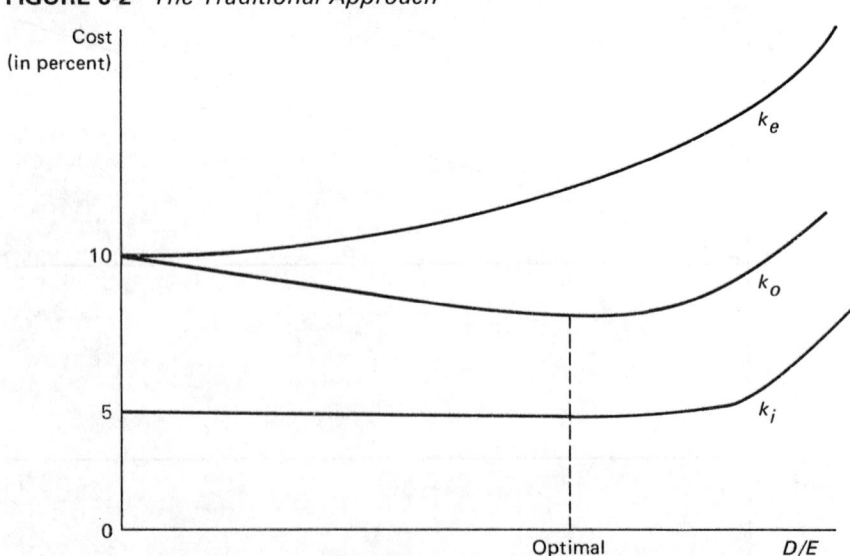

[4] Some theorists portray the k_i as rising gradually from the outset reflecting increments of risk. This is another unresolved issue in capital structure theory.

risk of the firm as represented by the D/E ratio. Finally, the combined effect of the k_e and the k_i is a downsloping k_0 to some minimum point, which would be the optimal capital structure since the k_0 would be the lowest at this point.

The implications for the firm are clear. If the firm wants to maximize the wealth of the owners, it should attempt to determine the optimal mix of debt to equity. At this point, the k_0 would be at a minimum, and the value of the firm would be at a maximum. The major difference between these two points of view is, therefore, the extent to which the market reacts to the substitution of debt for equity in the capital structure. Both approaches assume that the investor is a risk averter, but the NOI approach postulates a linear relationship between the D/E ratio and k_e, which the traditional view does not.

Modigliani and Miller Hypothesis   Highly sophisticated support for the NOI approach was provided by the studies of Franco Modigliani and Merton H. Miller.[5] The M & M hypothesis is that the cost of capital to the firm is independent of the capital structure. In other words, the capital structure does not affect the value of the firm. The major contribution of Modigliani and Miller came about from their development of the arbitrage model. The arbitrage model was developed to explain why the k_0 would remain unchanged irrespective of the mix of debt and equity in the capital structure. Arbitrage occurs in the capital markets whenever perfect substitutes sell at different prices. Arbitragers bring about equilibrium by buying one and selling the other, thus equalizing the two prices. In the M & M formulation, risk classifications are used to categorize the firms, and the arbitrage model is the mechanism by which firms in the same risk classification have the same overall cost of capital irrespective of their capital structures.

The arbitrage model is formulated on two premises. First, the shares of firms in the same risk category are perfect substitutes. This assumption implies that the firms are identical in every way, except perhaps for their capital structure. Therefore, if the shares of one of these firms were selling to give a higher yield than the shares of the other firms in this risk category, arbitrage would take place. Second, arbitrage brings about equilibrium for firms that are in the same risk class and differ only in their capital structure. This equilibrium results because arbitragers substitute personal leverage for corporate leverage and thus nullify any of the benefits of the latter. That is, suppose the return on one firm's shares in a particular risk classification were yielding more than another as a result of the more extensive use of leverage. The M & M hypothesis holds that arbitragers could leverage themselves in the same proportions as the firm and at the same rate of interest, and undo the benefits of leverage that might otherwise accrue to that firm.

To illustrate the effect of this "homemade" leverage, consider firms A and B. Both firms are in the same risk class, but firm A has no debt while firm B utilizes debt costing 5 percent. If the situation postulated initially was consistent with

[5] Franco Modigliani and Merton H. Miller, "The Cost of Capital, Corporation Finance and the Theory of Investment," *American Economic Review*, vol. 48, no. 3 (June, 1958), pp. 261–98.

the traditional approach, firm B would have a higher market value and conversely a lower k_0. This is shown below.

	Firm A	Firm B
Total market value *(V)*	$10,000	$12,000
Market value of debt *(D)*	0	6,000
Market value of stock *(E)*	10,000	6,000
Net operating income *(NOI)*	1,000	1,000
Interest (at 5%) *(k_iD)*	0	300
Net income *(NI)*	1,000	700
k_e *(NI/E)*	10%	11.7%
k_0 *(NOI/V)*	10%	8.33%
Proportion of debt *(D/V)*	0	$\frac{1}{2}$
Proportion of equity *(E/V)*	1	$\frac{1}{2}$

It is evident that firm B has a lower k_0 and therefore is benefiting from the use of leverage.

The M & M hypothesis holds that this condition cannot persist because arbitragers can leverage themselves in the same proportions as firm B and undo the leverage of firm B. In the above example, the arbitrager could sell his shares of firm B and borrow funds at 5 percent equal to his investment in firm B. The total amount—that is, his original investment in shares of firm B plus the amount borrowed—could be invested in the shares of firm A. By doing this he would make an arbitrage profit. At the same time, the use of arbitrage would bring the value of the two firms into equilibrium. To illustrate the arbitrage model, suppose an arbitrager has $1,000 worth of stock in firm B. He could sell these shares, and borrow $1000 at 5 percent, and invest the total amount, $2,000, in firm A. The benefits of this action would be a $13 arbitrage profit.

Return on investment in firm A	$200
Return on investment in firm B	117
Gross profit	63
Interest cost (0.05 × $1000)	50
Net arbitrage profit	$ 13

From the standpoint of the firm, the arbitrage opportunity leads to a final equilibrium in which the overall cost of capital is the same for both firms. This equilibrium may be shown as follows for firms A and B:

	Firm A	Firm B
Total market value *(V)*	$11,000	$11,000
Market value of the debt *(D)*	0	6,000
Market value of the stock *(E)*	11,000	5,000
Net operating income *(NOI)*	1,000	1,000
Interest (at 5%) *(k_iD)*	0	300
Net income *(NI)*	1,000	700
k_e *(NI/E)*	9.09%	14.00%
k_0 *(NOI/V)*	9.09%	9.09%
Proportion of debt *(D/V)*	0	$\frac{6}{11}$
Proportion of equity *(E/V)*	1	$\frac{5}{11}$

The final equilibrium results because arbitragers can sell shares of firm B and, with the use of personal leverage, buy shares of firm A and realize an arbitrage profit. This action would drive the price of firm B's shares downward while driving firm A's shares upward until the arbitrage profit was eliminated.

The controversy between the traditionalists and the advocates of the M & M position concerns the market's reaction to the use of leverage in a very idealized situation. Even under these conditions, the traditionalists argue that the discrete use of debt will lead to an increase in the value of the firm. The M & M hypothesis takes issue with this and builds a strong case for the capital structure being immaterial in determining the value of the firm. However, as we shall show in the following section, once the assumptions are relaxed, the differences between the two views is not as pronounced, and the two positions move close together. The major reason for this is the introduction of income taxes.

Relaxation of the Assumptions

Criticism of the M & M hypothesis normally is directed at two areas. First, the arbitrage model is attacked because when the assumptions are relaxed, arbitrage may not be as feasible as it would be under the highly idealized set of conditions. Second, the impact of income taxes is an important consideration, which Modigliani and Miller recognize.

There are a number of reasons to believe that the arbitrage process, as visualized by the M & M hypothesis, would be impeded in the real world. First, some argue that the individual would be reluctant to borrow in the same proportions as the firm because of the risk involved. Moreover, the amount of borrowing is controlled by law, which may effectively eliminate this possibility. The response is that this may be true for some investors, but arbitragers are used to taking risks and would not be adverse to borrowing in the same proportions as the firm. These two arguments appear to be at a standoff, and little more of value can be added. Second, an argument which is probably more telling is that it is unlikely that the individual can borrow at the same rate as the firm. It is argued that it is more likely that the individual will have to pay more for borrowed funds than the firm will. Therefore, the arbitrager cannot fully undo the firm's leverage. Third, transactions costs would impede the arbitrage process, since some of the arbitrage profits would be used to pay them. These transaction costs could reduce the profitability of the process to the point where it would not be worthwhile.

Although the above factors probably would have an effect on the arbitrage process, it is unclear just how significant the effect would be. The impact of income taxes, on the other hand, is recognized by both the traditionalists and Modigliani and Miller, who agree that the income taxes make the use of debt in the capital structure beneficial to the firm. Modigliani and Miller show how the introduction of income taxes reduces the k_0. They show that with the introduction of income taxes, debt reduces the k_0, as shown in Figure 8-3, but they still contend that there is not an optimal structure. In their formulation the k_0 continues to decline for increases in debt to the capital structure. Consequently, it

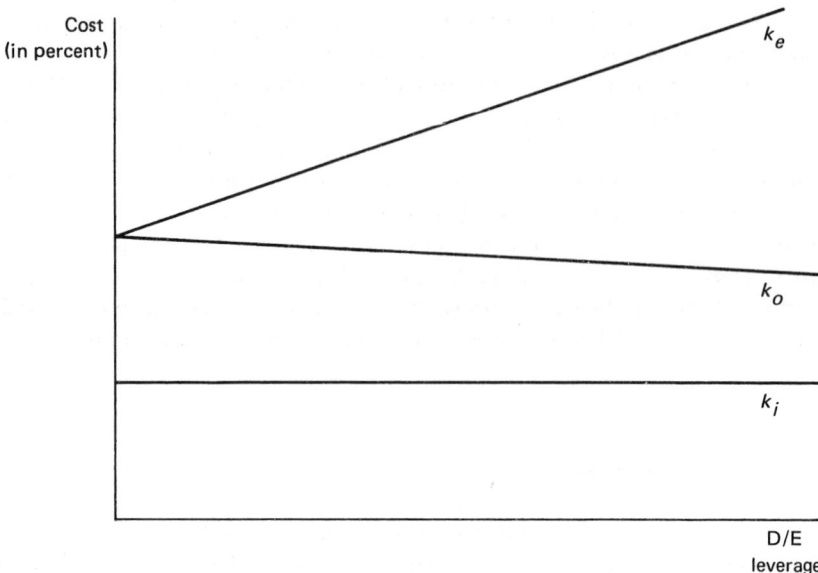

FIGURE 8-3 *The M & M Hypothesis Giving Effect to Income Taxes*

appears that for the case involving income taxes, both the M & M hypothesis and the traditionalists agree to the extent that income taxes make debt desirable and beneficial to the firm.

From the standpoint of security analysis, the issue has been greatly simplified. It is clear that debt is beneficial to the firm—at least as long as we face the prospect of income taxes—and therefore it becomes a question of the appropriate amount of debt. Since it is unclear whether there is such a thing as an optimal capital structure, probably the most appropriate approach is to determine whether the firm's debt increased significantly recently. Standard approaches for determining whether or not the firm is using too much debt have involved reviewing the debt-to-equity ratios over time along with the interest coverage ratios. These will be discussed in more depth in Chapter 10. It appears that the major concern should be whether the firm can service its debt. If it can, the debt in the capital must be viewed as beneficial to the firm.

Management

The previous aspects of the analysis of the firm and the firm-related risks have focused on factors that are quantifiable. Evaluating the management of the firm, however, requires estimating the effectiveness of an intangible factor. There is little question that the quality of management is very difficult to evaluate, since the analyst is an outsider without access to much vital information. Although evaluating the management function can be a problem, substantial research has been completed in this area that presents a systematic method for evaluation.

Business Operations

Business operations may be viewed as a process in which inputs are converted into outputs, the transformation process being the key to the success of the firm. To succeed and prosper, the firm must have some comparative advantage. Figure 8-4 illustrates the nature of this process. It is evident that the firm is competing in a number of markets. On the one hand, it is a buyer of inputs, such as labor and materials; on the other hand, it is a seller of its goods and services. The process by which the firm combines all its inputs to generate its output is the process of business operations. From the standpoint of evaluating management, the central focus is how effectively the firm accomplishes this task. If we

FIGURE 8-4 *A Model of Business Operations*

Source: Reprinted by permission from IBM Data Processing Techniques—Study—Basic System Study Guide © International Business Machines Corporation 1963.

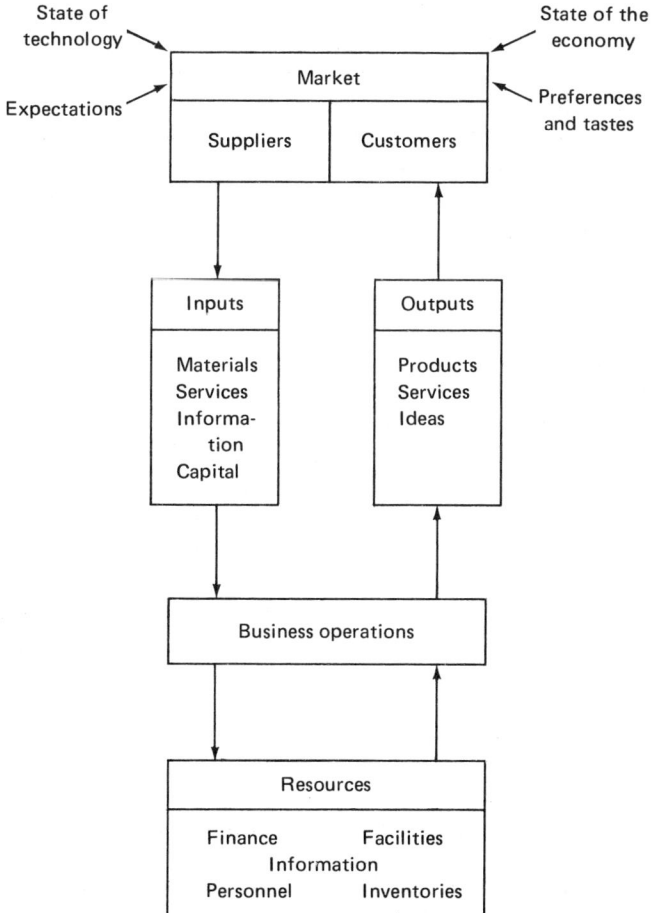

take a systems approach and view the firm as a system, as shown in Figure 8-4, the firm's operations may be viewed as including four basic decisions:[6]

1. Systems determination
2. Design and creation
3. Operation and control
4. Review and evaluation

Systems determination means simply the initial decision to start a particular type of business, and is important because of the obvious restriction it imposes on subsequent decisions. Once the initial field of operation is decided upon, a number of decisions must be made in connection with getting the firm under way—the location of the facilities, size of the operation, and the method of financing are a few of these decisions. All these decisions constitute the design and creation and are vital to the success of the enterprise. Once they have been made, the operations of the firm and controlling its operations become of paramount importance. The firm will produce some product or service, which must meet certain standards. The control function means measuring the output and comparing the results with the standards. If the standards are not met, changes in the operations are made. In this sense, there is a feedback mechanism which constantly evaluates the performance of the firm's operations and makes adjustments. Finally, review and evaluation of the system refers to the system as a whole. This final step determines how effectively the firm has performed within its environment. In this regard the firm should have some general goals to compare its performance against. The performance with respect to these goals will determine what future action the firm takes. If the firm is not satisfied with its performance, the design of the system and its operation may be changed.

This review and evaluation step is of utmost importance in the process of evaluating the management of the firm. The firm's environment is dynamic, meaning that the management group must be constantly disseminating information about the firm's environment, interpreting it in terms of the firm's operations, and then taking the necessary steps to maintain or improve the firm's comparative position. Consequently, it is management's function to translate the information it receives from outside the firm along with the knowledge it has on its own operations into methods of competing effectively. This means that managament must be sensitive to current trends and be able to anticipate coming changes so that the firm will be prepared for their eventuality. Good management, therefore, is crucial to the success of the firm, and management's focus must always be on the design of the system, and its operation and control.

The Management Function

The management function is portrayed as involving a number of elements. These vary among writers in the field, but generally the following are included:

[6] The approach taken here follows that of Richard A. Johnson, William T. Newell, and Roger C. Vergin, *Operations Management: A. Systems Concept* (Boston: Houghton Mifflin, 1972), pp. 8–9.

1. Planning
2. Organizing
3. Staffing
4. Directing
5. Controlling

The planning function includes setting objectives and formulating procedures, policies, and programs. Without this function, no organization could survive. This function has an impact on the design and operation of the system. Organizing is an important part of the process of designing the system. Part of the process of organizing is delegating authority, determining the span of control, and developing the interrelationship between the line and staff groups within the organization.

Staffing refers to developing a pool of human resources that the firm can draw upon. It is widely recognized that the capital available to a firm takes two forms. One form is capital goods. The other is human capital, so called because there is a great deal of time, effort, and cost involved in achieving the level of training required for today's business. Directing is the actual supervision of the various tasks within the firm and the use of authority to achieve some set of objectives. This function involves communicating ideas and motivating people to achieve a set of objectives. Finally, controlling involves setting performance standards, evaluating performance, and taking the necessary corrective action. These functions of management are useful to describe what management should be doing; it remains to be determined whether management is performing these functions effectively. What is needed is a methodology for evaluating how well these functions are being performed throughout the organization in relation to the firm's particular situation.

A second observation must be made about the functions of management. All five functions take place at all levels of the organization. For example, the shop foreman is performing all five of these functions; so is the executive vice president. The distinction between them is the impact that their respective decisions have on the firm. Since decisions made by top management have more impact than those made at lower levels within the firm, it is common to conduct a management audit at two levels—for the firm as a whole, and for each department within the firm. From the standpoint of common stock analysis, the focus should probably be on the quality of management for the firm as a whole, because decisions by top management are so vital to the success of the firm.

Management Audit

The American Institute of Management has conducted substantial research into the question of evaluating the management of the firm by means of auditing. The principal part of the audit is a questionnaire to be completed by various officers within the firm.[7] There are special versions of the questionnaire for manufacturing firms, financial institutions, advertising agencies, public utilities, government facilities, and universities and colleges. It is an extensive process, also involving follow-up interviews. From this, the AIM publishes its lists of excellently managed firms.[8] The AIM research presents an illustration of the method that might be employed in analyzing the management of the firm. This is particularly useful as a point of reference when evaluating the management of a firm. In addition, in those cases where AIM has analyzed the management of the firm, the AIM research simplifies the task of the security analyst.

The procedure used by AIM involves the use of three different types of questionnaires. One form is used in a screening process to identify potentially well-managed firms. This questionnaire is short, consisting of only 12 questions. A second variation of the questionnaire consists of 71 questions and is used by those firms that are well-known to the Institute and those firms about which information is readily available from public sources. The information collected in this questionnaire simply supplements existing data. The fact that the Institute can reach conclusions about some firms largely by using generally available data should be of interest to most analysts. The third variation is known as "The Management Audit Questionnaire," which consists of 301 questions and is the principal information-gathering vehicle used by the Institute. It is used for all firms for which an extensive analysis is to be made. Finally, before a firm is admitted to the Institute's list of excellently managed firms, an interview is used.

The questionnaires are designed to give information on 10 characteristics that the Institute has found to be indicative of good management. These are shown in Table 8-2 along with the weighting scheme for each characteristic and the minimum number of points required to be rated an excellently managed firm. In the *Optimum rating* column, the weight given to each characteristic is shown. For example, the economic function is given a maximum weighting of 1,000 points, or 10 percent of the total of 10,000 points. The *Minimum rating for excellence* column shows the minimum number of points that must be obtained to be considered an excellently managed firm. In each case the minimum is 75 percent of the optimum number of points available.

Some of these characteristics—the economic function, directorate analysis, fiscal policies, and executive evaluation—require explanation, which should give some insight into the methodology that is used. The economic function is a category that serves to determine the importance of the firm with respect to the national economy. To obtain a high rating in this category requires that the firm is important to the national economy, has survived the business cycles, has successfully competed with other firms, and has earned its reputation with the

[7] For an example of the questionnaire, the technique, and an illustration of how these may be used, see *Management Audit Questionnaire* (New York: American Institute of Management Incorporated, 1961). In addition, the methodology is constantly being changed and improved. Reference should be made to a recent copy of *Manual of Excellent Managements* (New York: American Institute of Management).
[8] This publication has been published sporadically since 1952. The 11th edition came out in 1970. See *Manual of Excellent Managements*, 11th ed. (New York: American Institute of Management, 1970).

TABLE 8-2   *The Management Rating Scheme*

	Optimum rating	Minimum rating for excellence
Economic function	1,000	750
Corporate structure	500	375
Health of Earnings	600	450
Service to stockowners	700	525
Research and development	800	600
Directorate analysis	800	600
Fiscal policies	1,000	750
Production efficiency	1,100	825
Sales vigor	1,300	975
Executive evaluation	2,200	1,650
Total	10,000	7,500

Source: *Manual of Excellent Managements,* op. cit., p. 69.

general public. Directorate analysis is of interest because directors can play an important role in the success of the firm. This characteristic is viewed as having three dimensions, described in terms of the following questions:

1. What is the quality of each director and his contribution to the Board of Directors?
2. Does the Board work well together?
3. Do the directors carry out their trusteeship?

Of these questions, the second one is the most important because of the impact of the Board's actions on the firm.

Fiscal policies refer to acquisition and disposition of funds and to the financial policies of the firm. Important considerations are:

1. Capital structure
2. Mechanism for developing financial policies and controls
3. Application of financial policies

Executive evaluation is a general category that attempts to evaluate the quality of the management team directly, in terms of ability, industry, and integrity.

In using the AIM's *Manual of Excellent Managements,* it must be remembered that the primary purpose of the Institute's management audit is to identify excellently managed firms. Although AIM's first list appeared in 1952, conducting the management audits involves a great deal of time, as does updating the existing audits. Consequently, the fact that a firm does not appear on the list does not mean it is not a well-managed firm; it can mean simply that it has not been evaluated. This problem would be resolved if the Institute published a list of all firms evaluated. Note also that the publication of the manual is rather sporadic, and that the evaluations may not be completely current. Firms appearing in the list of excellently managed firms may not have been evaluated just prior to publication. Nevertheless, this publication and the research leading up to its publication represent one of the most extensive efforts to evaluate the performance of the management group available to the general public. For this reason, it provides an illustration of the factors that may be used to evaluate the management group. The fact that important variables have been isolated is an important step forward, providing a framework by which an analyst may begin his own analysis.

Summary

Growth analysis is important in common stock analysis, but several other factors must also be considered, such as the firm's working capital position, capital structure, and the quality of its management. The firm's management has been found to be the most important of these factors. Much attention was given here to the question of the firm's capital structure, but a review of the prevailing views on capital structure showed that the primary concern is whether the firm can service its debt. If it appears that it can, even in adverse circumstances, the debt in its capital structure is probably beneficial to the firm. The firm's working capital position, therefore, may be quite important to meet all cash outflows. Yet the working capital position of the firm does not normally play a large role in common stock analysis. The firm's liquidity position usually comes to the forefront where bankruptcy is a possibility.

Management is a factor that is vital to the growth of the firm, yet its intangible nature leads analysts to a tendency to ignore it. The management function may be viewed as being responsive to the needs of the segment of the general public served by the firm, and at the same time having a keen understanding of the firm's operation and its potential. The firm operates in a dynamic environment, meaning that the management team must be aware of changes and be willing to adjust to these changes. Evaluating the management function has been greatly simplified by the work of AIM. In a project that dates back to the 1930s, AIM has continually evaluated the management function. In 1952, AIM finally set forth its list of 10 characteristics used to determine well-managed firms. Besides making available the names of approximately 500 excellently managed firms, the methodology involved is particularly useful to analysts concerned with evaluating the quality of management for particular firms.

Questions

1. Why is it necessary to analyze the working capital position of the firm, its capital structure, and its management?
2. Common measures of the firm's working capital position are the current ratio, acid-test ratio, inventory turnover ratio, and average collection period.
    a. Define each of these ratios.
    b. What is the reason for having a number of ratios to measure the firm's liquidity? How do these ratios accomplish that objective?
3. Consider the current assets and current liabilities of a certain corporation, as follows:

Current assets ($ millions)		Current liabilities ($ millions)	
Cash	80	Accruals	53
Accounts receivable	130	Accounts payable	75
Inventories	210	Bank note payable	82
Marketable securities	25		210
	445		

a. Suppose that the inventory a year earlier was $242 million and the cost of goods sold during this most recent period was $348 million. What is the inventory turnover ratio?

b. Suppose the annual credit sales for the corporation are $627 million. What is the average collection period?

c. What is the current ratio and acid-test ratio for this corporation?

d. How would you determine whether or not the working capital position of the corporation is sound?

4. Contrast the net operating income approach to capital structure with the traditional approach.

5. What important contribution did Modigliani and Miller make to the theory of the capital structure?

6. Following the Modigliani and Miller line of reasoning, suppose the following disequilibrium situation exists in the market value of firms A and B. These firms are in the same risk classification and are identical in every way, except firm B is using $80,000 of debt costing 6 percent.

	Firm A	Firm B
Total market value *(V)*	$200,000	$240,000
Market value of debt *(D)*	0	120,000
Market value of stock *(E)*	200,000	120,000
Net operating income *(NOI)*	25,000	25,000
Interest (at 6%) $(k_i D)$	0	7,200
Net Income *(NI)*	25,000	17,800
k_e *(NI/E)*	12.5%	14.8%
k_0 *(NOI/V)*	12.5%	10.4%
Proportion of debt *(D/V)*	0	$\frac{1}{2}$
Proportion of equity *(D/V)*	1	$\frac{1}{2}$

a. Suppose an arbitrager owned $4,000 worth of stock in firm B. What could he do to earn an arbitrage profit from this situation? How much profit could he make?

b. According to the M & M hypothesis, this situation could not persist. How would arbitrage as undertaken by a number of arbitragers bring about equilibrium in the firm A-firm B situation?

7. A number of simplifying assumptions were made in connection with the various hypotheses on the capital structure.

a. What were some of these?

b. If the assumptions are relaxed, what is the impact on the M & M hypothesis?

c. In a real world situation, what is the appropriate approach to the question of the capital structure?

8. Business operations may be viewed as a system. Explain why this is true.

9. The management function is portrayed as involving a number of functions.
   a. What are these functions?
   b. The American Institute of Management has done extensive research into the question of evaluating the management of firms. How may this information be used?

10. In this chapter, the working capital position, the capital structure, and the management of the firm were discussed.
    a. Assuming that all other things are equal, how would you rank these three items in terms of importance for common stock analysis?
    b. Cite examples where this ranking scheme would not hold true.

Selected References

Barges, Alexander. *The Effect of Capital Structure on the Cost of Capital.* Englewood Cliffs, N.J.: Prentice-Hall, 1963.

Donaldson, Gordon. "New Framework for Corporate Debt Policy." *Harvard Business Review,* vol. 40, no. 2 (Mar.–Apr., 1962), pp. 117–31.

Durand, David. "Costs of Debt and Equity Funds for Business: Trends and Problems of Measurement." *Conference on Research in Business Finance.* New York: National Bureau of Economic Research, 1952, pp. 215–48.

Greenwood, Frank. *Casebook for Management and Business Policy: A Systems Approach.* Scranton, Pa.: International Textbook Company, 1968, pp. 4–9.

Greenwood, William T. *Business Policy: A Management Audit Approach.* New York: McMillan, 1967. Part I.

Management Audit Questionnaire. American Institute of Management, 1961.

Manual of Excellent Managements, 11th ed. New York: American Institute of Management, 1970.

Mao, Tames C. T. *Quantitative Analysis of Financial Decisions.* London: Collier-MacMillan, 1969. Chapter 11.

Martindell, Jackson. *The Scientific Appraisal of Management: A Study of Well-Managed Companies.* New York: Harper & Brothers, 1950.

———. *The Appraisal of Management: For Executives and Investors.* New York: Harper & Brothers, 1962.

Modigliani, Franco, and Merton H. Miller. "The Cost of Capital, Corporation Finance and the Theory of Investment." *American Economic Review,* vol. 48, no. 3 (June, 1958), pp. 261–98.

———. "Some Estimates of the Cost of Capital to the Electric Utility Industry." *American Economic Review,* vol. 56, no. 3 (June, 1966), pp. 333–92.

Schwartz, Eli. "Theory of the Capital Structure of the Firm." *Journal of Finance,* vol. 14, no. 1 (Mar., 1959), pp. 18–39.

Solomon, Ezra. *The Theory of Financial Management.* New York: Columbia University Press, 1963. Chapter 8.

———. "Leverage and the Cost of Capital." *Journal of Finance,* vol. 18, no. 2 (May, 1963), pp. 273–79.

Van Horne, James C. *Financial Policy and Management,* 2d ed. Englewood Cliffs, N.J.: Prentice-Hall, 1971. Chapter 7.

Weston, J. Fred. "A Test of Cost of Capital Propositions." *Southern Economic Journal,* vol. 30, no. 2 (Oct., 1963), pp. 105–13.

Chapter 9

Estimating Risk and Return

The objective of common stock analysis is to predict the expected return on common stock and the risk associated with obtaining that return. The return on any security is made up of capital appreciation (depreciation) and cash income received. For common stock capital appreciation is the major source of return to the investor, since cash dividends on most common stock are relatively small. As a result, forecasting appreciation is the major focus of common stock analysis, but the expected risk and return include both expected appreciation and expected dividends. The factors involved are divided into what has been referred to as firm-related factors and market-related factors. The firm-related factors were discussed in Chapters 7 and 8. All these factors must be combined to provide estimates of potential dividends and appreciation. Forecasting the potential appreciation requires three separate estimates. First, a time horizon must be selected. In actual practice, the time horizon used varies from one year to approximately five years, depending upon the preference of the analyst. In the analysis below, a five-year time horizon will be used, but this time horizon was selected principally for purposes of illustration. Second, following the earnings-per-share valuation model, the earnings per share and price-earnings ratio for the time horizon year must be predicted. These will be used to estimate the price of individual stocks at the time horizon year. Finally, the range of the individual stock's price must be estimated. This range will be used to forecast the risk associated with a particular stock.

The earnings-per-share valuation model will be used to make three forecasts of the price of the stock at the selected time horizon. These will be a forecast for a good market year and a bad market year. In other words, it will be assumed that the return in the horizon year will be a function solely of market conditions. This assumes that an investor has a well-diversified portfolio of common stock. In a well-diversified portfolio, it may be assumed that half the firms in the portfolio will have good years and half will have bad years. As a result, the good and bad firm-years will average out. The only source of concern, therefore, is the state of the market. This approach is consistent with the premises of the capital-market theory, which were introduced briefly in Chapter 6 and will be introduced in more detail in Chapter 15.

A good market forecast is given by

$$\widehat{P_{iG}} = \widehat{EPS_i} \times \widehat{P/E_{iG}} \tag{9-1}$$

where $\widehat{P_{iG}}$ is the predicted price of stock i in the horizon year assuming a good market year, $\widehat{EPS_i}$ is the predicted earnings per share of stock i in the horizon year, and the $\widehat{P/E_{iG}}$ is the predicted price-earnings ratio for stock i in the horizon year assuming a good market year.

For a bad market year, the formulation is essentially the same as in Equation 9-1, except that the P/E ratio reflects the state of the market. Therefore, for a bad market the predicted price for a particular stock is given by

$$\widehat{P_{iB}} = \widehat{EPS_i} \times \widehat{P/E_{iB}} \tag{9-2}$$

where $\widehat{P/E_{iB}}$ is the predicted price-earnings ratio for stock i assuming a bad market year. The prices for the stock as predicted by Equations 9-1 and 9-2 can be averaged to give the expected price for the stock in the horizon year. These three price forecasts can be used, therefore, to give a predicted return in a good market year, a predicted return in a bad market year, and an expected return for a particular stock.

Several observations may be made about Equations 9-1 and 9-2. First, they indicate that three forecasts are required. Two predicted P/E ratios are used to indicate the state of the market. These P/E ratios are assumed to capture existing market conditions in the horizon year. On the other hand, only one EPS estimate is required because EPS forecasting errors are assumed to average out in a well-diversified common stock portfolio. Also, once these estimates have been made, an important step has been completed in estimating the risk and return on common stock. The broader the range, the greater the risk for a particular stock; conversely, the narrower the range the smaller the risk. Finally, these data along with the forecasted cash dividends received are used to predict the risk and return that may be expected on a particular stock.

In the following analysis, four methods of forecasting EPS will be presented. These methods are relatively simple and appear to be in widespread use. There is evidence that these methods are relatively accurate. Next, methods for predicting P/E ratios will be presented. Accurate methods of forecasting P/E ratios have not yet been developed, but the state of the art as it is will be explored. Finally, all this data will be combined to predict potential appreciation. The potential appreciation combined with anticipated cash dividends may be used to give estimates of expected return and the risk associated with that return.

Predicting Earnings Per Share

There are a number of methods for predicting EPS, but four methods appear to have a wide following. These methods vary in the degree of complexity, but are all straightforward. These are:

1. Projecting a trend line
2. Regressing *EPS* on sales
3. Net earnings margin approach
4. Trend-adjusted exponential smoothing approach

Each of these methods appear to be fairly accurate. There is evidence that changes in *EPS* appear to be approximately random, generally around a trend. Therefore, the analyst should not use a method of forecasting that is quite costly because of the difficulty in making accurate forecasts. These mechanical methods of forecasting meet this requirement as well.

Projecting a Trend Line

One approach, which is sometimes referred to as a form of the naive model, is to project the past trend in *EPS* into the future. This approach has been referred to as a naive approach because it assumes that past trends will continue over the time horizon selected. Even though it is widely recognized that the past may not be a good indicator of the future, trend projection is a major method of forecasting *EPS*. Notationally, projecting a trend line may be represented as follows:

$$\widehat{EPS}_{it+k} = a_i + b_i \, (\text{Time}) + u_i \tag{9-3}$$

where a_i and b_i are regression constants, and u_i is a normally distributed error term.

To illustrate this approach, consider the fully-diluted *EPS* of the Burroughs Corporation for the period 1960–73.

Year	EPS	Year	EPS
1960	0.45	1967	1.69
1961	0.51	1968	2.13
1962	0.46	1969	2.93
1963	0.41	1970	3.52
1964	0.50	1971	3.88
1965	0.85	1972	4.53
1966	1.50		

Graphically, the actual *EPS* for the Burroughs Corporation are shown in Figure 9-1 along with the trend projection to the year 1978.

It is clear from Figure 9-1 that the *EPS* of Burroughs have a strong upward trend. Using Equation 9-3 to project a trend line gives an estimated *EPS* for 1977 of \$5.74. That is, substituting the Burroughs data into Equation 9-3 gives the following results:

$$\widehat{EPS} = -702.829 + 0.35841 \, (\text{Time})$$

Therefore, the projected *EPS* for Burroughs in 1977 is

$$\widehat{EPS}_{77} = -702.829 + 0.35841 \, (1977)$$

$$= 5.74$$

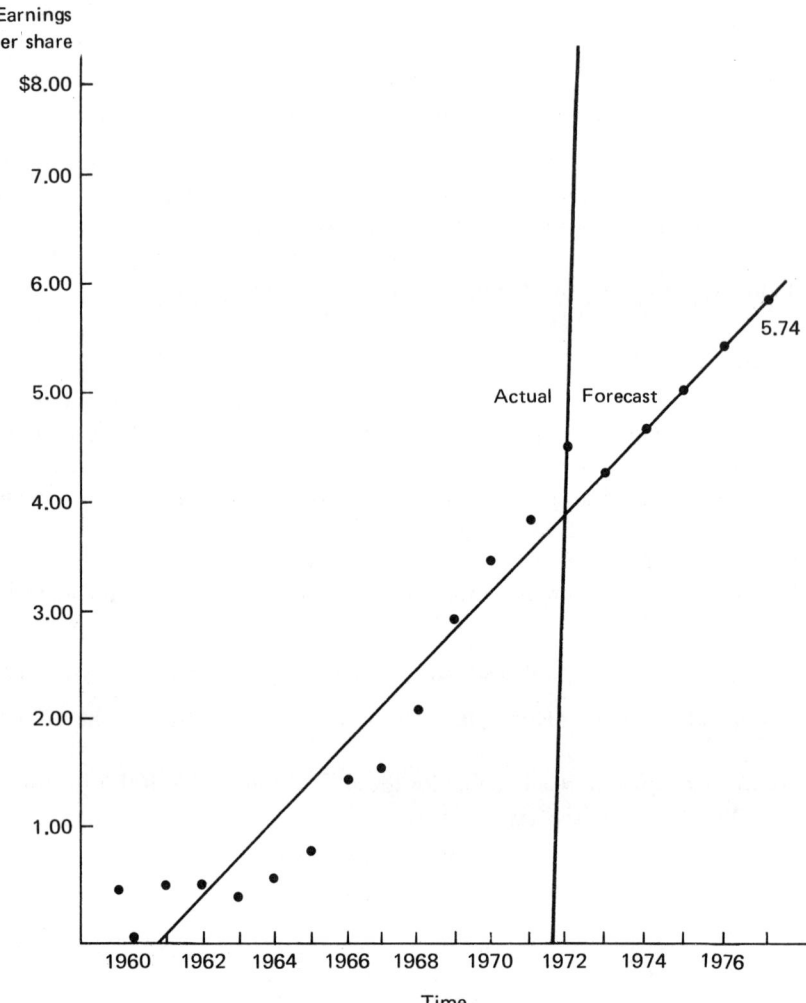

FIGURE 9-1   *Projected* EPS *for Burroughs Corporation*

Extending the trend line as illustrated in Figure 9-1 gives a trend projection of the *EPS* for each year from 1972 to 1978.

It is evident from the above illustration that projecting the historical trend is a relatively straightforward method of predicting *EPS*. The essential question that the analyst must answer to his own satisfaction is whether the past is a good indicator of the future. If it is highly probable that the future will be significantly different from the past, projecting the historical trend will not be appropriate. Moreover, trend projection also raises the problem of selecting the appropriate time period so that the trend is clearly reflected in the data. For example, in the Burroughs data, it is apparent that the current growth in *EPS* began after 1964. If the observations for 1960, 1961, 1962, 1963, and 1964 were not included, the upward trend would be much steeper. As a result, the trend approach may not be appropriate in every case, and if it is used it may require selecting the appropriate time period so that the projected trend line reflects what appears to be the most recent trend.

Regressing EPS on Sales

An alternative method of forecasting *EPS* is to regress *EPS* on sales revenues. In form this approach is the same as projecting a trend line. The only difference is that the independent variable is sales revenues instead of time. Beyond this these two methods are both applications of regression analysis. Notationally, this can be represented as follows:

$$\widehat{EPS}_{it+k} = a_i + b_i \widehat{S}_{it+k} + u_i \tag{9-4}$$

where $\widehat{S}_{it+k}$ is the projected sales for firm i at time $t + k$, a_i and b_i are regression constants, and u_i is a normally distributed error term. This approach assumes *EPS* are solely a function of sales. Consequently, a sales forecast is used as a basis for making an *EPS* forecast.

To illustrate, consider the following data for Burroughs Corporations for the period 1960–73:[1]

Year	FPS	Sales (in $ millions)	Year	FPS	Sales (in $ millions)
1960	0.45	387	1967	1.69	551
1961	0.51	399	1968	2.13	651
1962	0.46	423	1969	2.93	752
1963	0.41	387	1970	3.52	885
1964	0.50	390	1971	3.88	933
1965	0.85	457	1972	4.53	1,040
1966	1.50	490			

Graphically, these data are shown in Figure 9-2 along with a projection up to the year 1978. All *EPS* figures are not shown because of overlap.

Regressing the sales on *EPS* gives the following:

$$\widehat{EPS} = -1.94524 + 0.00628 \, \widehat{S}_{t+k}$$

Forecasting *EPS* for 1977 depends upon the sales forecast for the year 1977. For example, suppose that sales in 1977 are predicted to be $1.8 billion. The predicted *EPS* would be

$$\widehat{EPS} = -1.945 + 0.00628 \, (1,800)$$

$$= 9.36$$

[1] One difficulty that develops with this approach is the "scaling" problem. That is, *EPS* are such a small number relative to sales that the regression coefficient may become very small. A way to handle this problem is to round off the sales revenue numbers to the nearest millionth as we have done in this example.

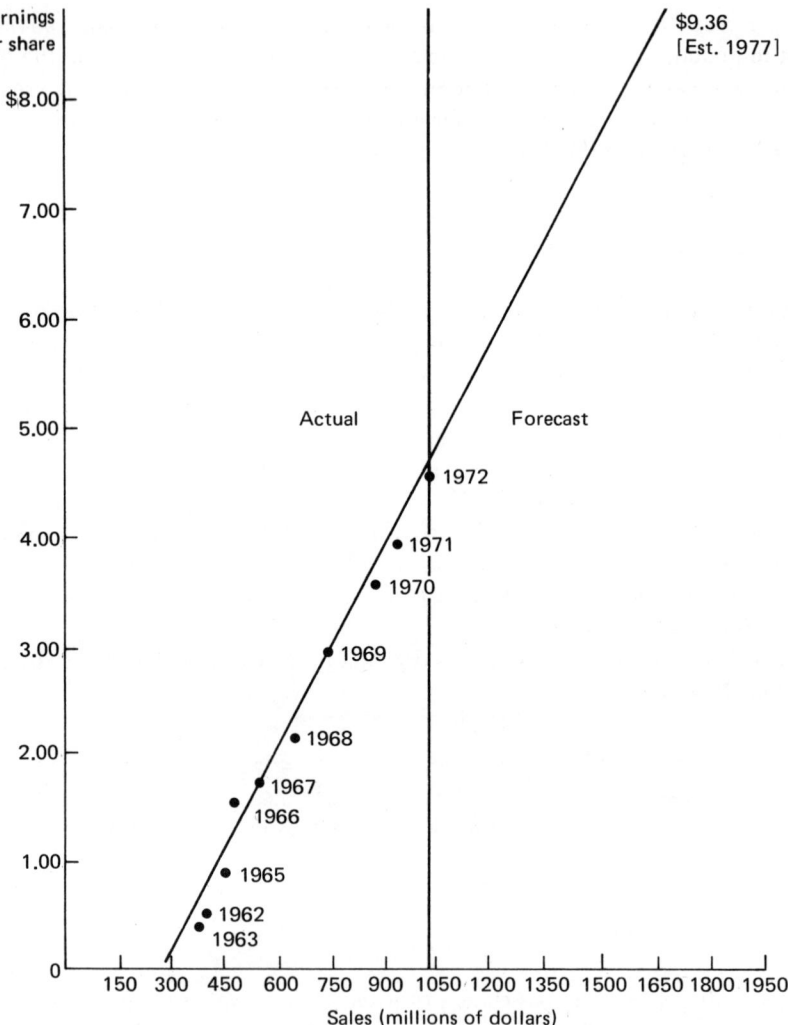

FIGURE 9-2   *Sales as a Predictor of* EPS *for Burroughs Corporation*

Thus, the forecasted *EPS* given a sales forecast of $1.8 billion for 1977 is $9.36. This is illustrated in Figure 9-2.

In summary, regressing *EPS* on sales is an application of simple linear regression analysis, which is very similar to projecting a trend line. The major difference between the two approaches is that projecting a trend line assumes the past trend will continue into the future, whereas regressing *EPS* on sales assumes that *EPS* are solely dependent upon sales. Therefore, the predicted *EPS* are dependent upon the predicted sales at the selected time horizon, which means the accuracy of this method depends upon two factors. First, a primary consideration is the stability of the relationship between *EPS* and sales. If this relationship is unstable, the forecasts are not going to be particularly accurate. Second, the sales forecast must be reasonably accurate. Even if the relationship between *EPS* and sales is fairly stable over time, poor sales estimates will still lead to inaccurate forecasts. As a result, either of these sources of error may lead to inaccurate estimates of *EPS*.

Net Earnings Margin Approach

The net earnings margin approach is substantially different from the two previous methods, which were applications of simple linear regression. The NEM approach makes a forecast of *EPS* based upon the anticipated earnings of the firm at the horizon year, which in turn may be converted into an *EPS* estimate. Obtaining the anticipated earnings of the firm is accomplished by forecasting the sales of the firm at the horizon year and then estimating the net earnings margin of the firm. As a result, the *NEM* approach requires three specific estimates for a particular time horizon. These are as follows:

1. A sales forecast
2. An expected net earnings margin
3. A predicted number of common shares and share equivalents outstanding

Notationally, the predicted earnings for the firm at the selected time horizon are

$$\widehat{NI}_{it+k} = \widehat{NEM}_{it+k} \times \widehat{S}_{it+k} \qquad (9\text{-}5)$$

where $\widehat{NI}_{it+k}$ is the predicted earnings of firm i at time $t + k$, $\widehat{NEM}_{it+k}$ is the predicted net earnings margin for firm i at time $t + k$, and S_{it+k} is the predicted sales of firm i at time $t + k$.

Once the predicted earnings of the firm are determined, predicting the *EPS* requires only a forecast of the number of shares expected to be outstanding at the time horizon. Therefore, the predicted *EPS* are found as follows:

$$\widehat{EPS}_{it+k} = \frac{\widehat{NI}_{it+k}}{\widehat{N}_{it+k}} \qquad (9\text{-}6)$$

where $\widehat{N}_{it+k}$ is the number of common shares and share equivalents of firm i expected to be outstanding at time $t + k$, and the other terms are as previously defined. The term $\widehat{N}_{it+k}$ may include only anticipated common shares and share equivalents outstanding, or it may include all anticipated items that will lead to dilution of the *EPS*, depending upon whether primary or fully-diluted *EPS* are being forecasted.

To illustrate, suppose the Burroughs Corporation's figures are used again. Suppose that the following forecasts were made for the year 1977:

$$\widehat{S} = \$1{,}800{,}000{,}000$$

$$\widehat{NEM} = 0.083$$

$$\widehat{N} = 20{,}600{,}000$$

Substituting into Equation 9-5 gives

$$\widehat{NI} = 0.083\,(\$1{,}800{,}000{,}000)$$

$$= \$149{,}400{,}000$$

Thus, the earnings of Burroughs for 1977 are estimated to be $149 million. This result assumes that Burroughs sales revenues will approach $1.8 billion, and that Burroughs will earn 8 percent on these sales after all expenses of operation including financial charges and taxes.

The *EPS* for the year 1977 then would be given by substituting into Equation 9-6. That is

$$EPS = \frac{\$149{,}400{,}000}{20{,}600{,}000}$$

$$= \$7.25$$

Based on these estimates, the predicted *EPS* for 1977 would be $7.25.

As with the two previous methods, the *NEM* approach is relatively simple and is fairly widely used. Its simplicity is due to the fact that the net earnings may be forecast without explicit reference to the various cost items, such as the cost of goods sold, selling, general, and administrative expenses, and so forth. Moreover, the estimates of sales and net earnings margins may be made for some firms with relative certainty. One difficulty that arises on occasion is predicting the approximate number of shares at the time horizon year. It may seem that the number of shares to be used would be the easiest of the variables to forecast, but this is not always the case. This results because of the difficulty in forecasting the number of shares that will be issued or their equivalent.

Trend-Adjusted Exponential Smoothing

Exponential smoothing is a technique which has been used in recent years for routine forecasting situations. This technique is similar to calculating a moving average, but it has the very desirable feature that a large amount of information need not be kept on file as with a moving average. Therefore, the calculations are greatly simplified. More importantly, this approach has been found to be the most accurate of a number of mechanical methods of forecasting *EPS*.[2]

[2] Edwin J. Elton and Martin J. Gruber, "Earnings Estimates and the Accuracy of Expectional Data," *Management Science*, vol. 18, no. 8 (Apr., 1972), p. B-409–B-424.

Exponential smoothing is admittedly more complex than the previous techniques, but it is included because it has been found to be a relatively accurate method of forecasting *EPS*. As with a moving average, exponential smoothing may be adjusted to reflect a trend component. For forecasting *EPS*, trend-adjusting exponential smoothing appears to be the most reasonable method to use. However, we will begin with a review of direct exponential smoothing before we discuss trend-adjusted exponential smoothing.

Exponential smoothing estimates of *EPS* may be defined as follows:[3]

$$\overline{EPS}_{it} = \omega(EPS_{it}) + (1 - \omega)\,(\overline{EPS}_{it-1}) \qquad (9\text{-}7)$$

where $\overline{EPS}_{it}$ is an exponentially weighted average of past *EPS* of firm i at time t, and ω is the weight placed upon current *EPS* versus more distant *EPS*. In other words, the three bits of information necessary to make forecasts of *EPS* are the current *EPS*, the weights to be placed on current *EPS* relative to past *EPS*, and the exponentially weighted average of *EPS* at time $t - 1$. Once this information is available, forecasts are made by simply determining the time horizon for the forecasts, $t + k$. This forecast is

$$\widehat{EPS}_{it+k} = \overline{EPS}_{it} \qquad (9\text{-}8)$$

where the terms are as previously defined.

To illustrate, suppose exponential smoothing is used to forecast the *EPS* of the Burroughs Corporation. In addition, suppose a weight, ω, of 0.5 is placed upon current *EPS* and a weight of 0.5 $(1 - 0.5)$ is placed upon past *EPS*. Assume a time horizon of five years as was previously used. Table 9-1 illustrates these forecasts. Column 2, captioned *EPS_t*, gives the actual *EPS* of the Burroughs Corporation. Column 3, captioned 0.5 *EPS_t*, is determined by taking 0.5 of the value in column 2 for that particular year. Column 4, captioned $0.5\ \overline{EPS}_{t-1}$, is determined by taking 0.5 of the value in column 5 for one year prior to the year being used in column 4. Note that there will not be a value in columns 3 and 4 in 1960 because in the initial year a naive forecast is used. For example, in 1960 there would not be forecasts in columns 3 and 4, but the value in column 5 is taken directly from column 2. This is necessary to get the forecasts under way. In subsequent years, the values in column 5, captioned $\overline{EPS}_t$, are determined by adding the values of columns 3 and 4. For example, the value of $\overline{EPS}$ in column 5 for 1961 is

$$\overline{EPS}_{61} = 0.5\ (\$0.51) + 0.5\ (0.45) = \$0.49$$

Similarly, the value for 1962 is

$$\overline{EPS}_{62} = 0.5\ (\$0.46) + 0.5\ (\$0.49) = \$0.48$$

[3] For an excellent discussion of direct exponential smoothing and trend-adjusted exponential smoothing, see G. Hadley, *Introduction to Business Statistics* (San Francisco; Holden-Day, 1968), pp. 401–24.

TABLE 9-1 *An Exponential Smoothing Forecast for the EPS of Burroughs Corporation*

Year (1)	EPS$_t$ (2)	0.5 EPS$_t$ (3)	0.5 $\overline{EPS}_{t-1}$ (4)	$\overline{EPS}_t$ (5)	EPS$_{t+k}$ (6)
1960	$0.45			0.45	
1961	0.51	0.26	0.23	0.49	
1962	0.46	0.23	0.25	0.48	
1963	0.41	0.21	0.24	0.45	
1964	0.50	0.25	0.23	0.4ε	
1965	0.85	0.43	0.24	0.67	0.45
1966	1.50	0.75	0.34	1.09	0.49
1967	1.69	0.85	0.55	1.40	0.48
1968	2.13	1.07	0.70	1.77	0.45
1969	2.93	1.47	0.89	2.36	0.48
1970	3.52	1.76	1.18	2.94	0.67
1971	3.88	1.94	1.47	3.41	1.09
1972	4.53	2.27	1.71	3.98	1.40
1973					1.77
1974					2.36
1975					2.94
1976					3.41
1977					3.98

All of the other entries in the $\overline{EPS}_t$ column were determined in the same fashion.

The $\overline{EPS}_t$ column then is used to forecast for $t + k$ years into the future. Therefore, given a five-year forecasting time horizon, the forecasts, $\overline{EPS}$, found in column 6 is simply the value found in column 5 for the time $t - 5$. For example, the value $0.45 found in column 6 for 1965 is simply the value in column 5 for 1960. Similarly, the value in column 6 for 1966 is simply the value in column 5 for the year 1961. All of the subsequent forecasts in column 6 were obtained in the same fashion.

One important point stands out in Table 9-1; the predictions appear to be very poor. This conclusion becomes evident simply by comparing columns 6 and 2. The predicted *EPS* for 1977 is $3.98, compared to $4.53 for 1972. It seems unlikely in light of the strong upward trend in the Burroughs *EPS* that the *EPS* in 1977 would be only $3.98. This result always occurs whenever direct exponential smoothing is applied to a series with a strong upward trend. Direct exponential smoothing is only useful for forecasting where a strong upward trend does not exist in the series. One method of making an adjustment for the trend component is to add a trend factor to the direct exponential smoothing results. This method of forecasting can be represented notationally as follows:

$$\overline{EPS}_{it} = \omega(EPS_{it}) + (1 - \omega)(\overline{EPS}_{it-1}) \qquad (9\text{-}9)$$

Equation 9-9 is identical to Equation 9-8, with the addition of a trend correction to make the forecasts. This trend correction requires an initial estimate of the trend component:

$$T_{it} = \omega(\overline{EPS}_{it} - \overline{EPS}_{it-1}) + (1 - \omega)T_{it-1} \qquad (9\text{-}10)$$

where T_{it} is the value of the initial trend correction for the EPS of firm i at time t, and the other terms are as previously defined. The forecasted EPS are then given by adding the EPS_t and the T_{it}. That is

$$\widehat{EPS}_{it+k} = \overline{EPS}_{it} + T_{it}\left(k + \frac{1 - \omega}{\omega}\right) \qquad (9\text{-}11)$$

where the terms are as previously defined.

To illustrate the use of trend-adjusted exponential smoothing, the Burroughs data will be used. An immediate problem is initiating the trend-adjusted approach. Recall that in direct exponential smoothing the first term for the $\overline{EPS}_{it}$ was the EPS_{it}. However, when a trend is present it is desirable to incorporate it immediately. The trend component may be incorporated as follows:

$$T_{i1} = (1 - \omega)\left[2\left(\sum_{t=1}^{n} EPS_{it}\right) - (EPS_{it+n-1} + 2EPS_{it+n-2} + 3EPS_{it+n-3}\right.$$
$$\left. + 4EPS_{it+n-4})\right] \qquad (9\text{-}12)$$

Equation 9-12 establishes the weighted-trend component for the next five years. The value of T_{i1} is then subtracted from the average of the EPS_t for that same time period. That is

$$\overline{EPS}_{i1} - 1/n \sum_{t=1}^{n} EPS_{it} - T_{i1}\left(\frac{n-1}{2} + \frac{1-\omega}{\omega}\right) \qquad (9\text{-}13)$$

Equation 9-13 then permits an estimate of EPS at time $t = 1$, which will reflect the trend for the next five years.

Table 9-2 shows a trend-adjusted exponential forecast for the EPS of the Burroughs Corporation. Equations 9-12 and 9-13 were used to obtain the 1960 estimate of the $\overline{EPS}$ shown in column 3 and T in column 6. Substituting into Equation 9-12 gives

$$T_{60} = 0.5[2(2.33) - (0.41 + 0.92 + 1.53 + 1.80)]$$

$$= 0.5[4.66 - 4.66] = 0$$

Hence T_{60} equals zero. The reason for this result is that a trend was not apparent in the first five years of data for the Burroughs EPS. Determining the EPS for 1960 then is accomplished by substituting into Equation 9-13:

$$\overline{EPS}_{60} = \frac{2.33}{5} = \$0.466$$

TABLE 9-2 *An Exponential Smoothing Forecast with Trend Adjustment for the EPS of Burroughs Corporation*

Year (1)	EPS (2)	$\overline{EPS}$ (3)	$0.5\,(\overline{EPS}_t - EPS_{t-1})$ (4)	0.5T (5)	T (6)	6T (7)	EPS_{t+k} (8)
1960	$0.45	$0.47			0.00		
1961	0.51	0.49	0.01	0.00	0.01		
1962	0.46	0.48	−0.01	0.01	0.00		
1963	0.41	0.45	−0.02	0.00	−0.02		
1964	0.50	0.48	0.02	−0.01	0.01	0.06	
1965	0.85	0.67	0.10	0.02	0.12	0.72	
1966	1.50	1.09	0.21	0.06	0.27	1.02	
1967	1.69	1.40	0.16	0.09	0.25	1.50	
1968	2.13	1.77	0.19	0.13	0.32	1.92	
1969	2.93	2.36	0.27	0.16	0.43	2.58	0.54
1970	3.52	2.94	0.29	0.22	0.51	3.06	1.39
1971	3.88	3.41	0.24	0.26	0.50	3.00	2.11
1972	4.53	3.98	0.29	0.25	0.54	3.24	2.90
1973							3.69
1974							4.94
1975							6.00
1976							6.41
1977							7.22

Therefore, the $\overline{EPS}$ for 1960 are $0.47 as shown in column 3 of Table 9-2.

Once the trend-adjusted exponential smoothing technique is initiated, it is a relatively simple matter to make the forecasts using Equations 9-10 and 9-11. Again, the weight of 0.5 will be used for current *EPS* and (1 − 0.5) will be used for past *EPS*. Column 2 gives the actual *EPS* for the years 1960–73, and column 3 gives the exponentially smoothed *EPS*, $\overline{EPS}$, from Table 9-2. Columns 4 and 5 give the two components of Equation 9-10. Column 4 gives the value of $\omega(\overline{EPS}_t - \overline{EPS}_{t-1})$ for the Burroughs Corporation. Column 5 gives the other segment of Equation 9-10, namely, $(1 - \omega)T_{t-1}$. Column 6 then is the sum of these two values in columns 4 and 5. Column 7 gives the $T_{it}[k + (1 - \omega/\omega)]$ portion of Equation 9-11. To illustrate, consider the data for 1961.

$$T_{61} = 0.5(0.49 - 0.47) + (1 - 0.5)(0.0)$$

$$= (0.01 + 0.0)$$

$$= 0.01$$

Therefore, the value of T for the Burroughs' data for the year 1961 is $0.01. Similarly, for the year 1962 the value of T is

$$T_{62} = 0.5(0.48 - 0.49) + (1 - 0.5)(0.01)$$

$$= (-0.05 + 0.05)$$

$$= 0.0$$

The value of the T for 1962, therefore, is 0.0. This results because of the lack of a trend in the initial data. The remaining values for T as shown in Table 9-2 can be found in the same fashion.

The actual forecast values can now be determined by substituting into Equation 9-11. Using a five-year forecasting time horizon, the trend-adjustment component will appear in 1964 and the first forecast in 1969. The trend-adjustment component of Equation 9-11 is shown in Table 9-2, and the forecasts are shown in column 8 of Table 9-2. The forecast for 1969 is

$$EPS_{69} = \$0.48 + \$0.01\left[5 + \left(\frac{1 - 0.5}{0.5}\right)\right]$$

$$= 0.48 + 0.01(6)$$

$$= \$0.54$$

Similarly, the forecast for 1970 is

$$EPS_{70} = \$0.67 + \$0.12(6)$$

$$= 0.67 + 0.72$$

$$= \$1.39$$

The subsequent forecasts were derived in the same fashion with the forecast *EPS* for 1977 equaling $7.22.

As previously noted, all these mechanical methods of forecasting are reasonably accurate and are quite simple, two commendable attributes. Since it has been established that the changes in *EPS* are approximately random, the cost of forecasting *EPS* should be minimized because of the difficulty of obtaining accurate forecasts. Extensive tests of these simple methods of forecasting *EPS* are not available, but the available evidence seems to indicate that all these methods are quite accurate. Trend-adjusted exponential smoothing appears to be the most accurate of these. This seems to indicate that trend-adjusted exponential smoothing is the preferable technique; however, additional tests of accuracy are necessary. At this point, a suitable alternative may be to analyze the data and determine which technique appears to give the most reasonable estimate.

Predicting *P/E* Ratios

Once the *EPS* have been predicted over the time horizon, the appropriate *P/E* ratios and the cash dividends to be received must be predicted. However, *P/E* ratios by definition encompass all the factors involved in valuing common stock. That is, the numerator, which is the price of a common share, reflects all the factors that affect the value of a share, such as growth prospects for the *EPS*, dividend policy, risk, and so forth, but the problem is that the role of the factors that affect the value of common stock has not been clearly determined. For this reason, P/E ratios are used instead of all these factors. If a reliable common stock valuation model could be developed, then there would be no further need for P/E ratios in valuing common stock, but such valuation models have not yet been developed. To illustrate the factors that might affect the P/E ratios, or more correctly the value of a share, a study by Volkert S. Whitbeck and Manown Kisor, Jr. will be discussed. Alternative methods of forecasting P/E ratios will then be presented.

The Whitbeck-Kisor Study

One of the major problems in developing a model to explain common stock prices is that the parameters of the model are unstable. There is little difficulty in developing a model with a high degree of explanatory power, but the parameters shift from year to year. As a result, the model has little predictive value. An example of this problem is an early stock valuation model developed by J. W. Meader during the 1930s.[4] Meader used a cross-section multiple regression model to explain common stock prices, using samples of stocks listed on the New York Stock Exchange during the period 1930–40. In 1930 the relationship was found to be

$$\widehat{P} = 22.86 + 0.16B + 0.20W + 15.45EPS - 7.05D$$

where B is the book value per share, W is the net working capital, EPS is the earnings per share, and D is the dividends per share. Applying these same variables for subsequent years, Meader found that the parameters shifted from year to year. In 1931, for example, the parameters of Meader's formulation were:

$$\widehat{P} = 8.21 + 0.10B + 0.18W + 8.84EPS + 3.23D$$

Finally, for the year 1939, the parameters were

$$\widehat{P} = 1.04 + 0.07B + 0.44W + 3.21EPS + 11.71D$$

The predictive value of this model is unreliable since the parameters tended to shift from year to year, even though the correlation coefficient was high in the range of 0.85 to 0.94 for the period 1930–40.

This problem tends to exist for most stock valuation models developed in later years.[5] However, a P/E estimating formulation by Whitbeck and Kisor has short-run usefulness in determining those stocks that are currently undervalued.[6] Their approach was to determine the influence of various explanatory variables for the P/E ratios of a sample of representative stocks using

[4] J. W. Meader, "Stock Price Estimating Formulas, 1930–1939," *The Annalist*, vol. 55, no. 1432 (June 27, 1940), p. 890.

[5] For an example of one of these models, see Dorothy H. Bower and Richard S. Bower, "Test of a Stock Valuation Model," *Journal of Finance*, vol. 25, no. 2 (May, 1970), pp. 483–93. The discussion by Edwin J. Elton on pp. 500–503 is very interesting.

[6] Volkert S. Whitbeck and Manown Kisor Jr., "A New Tool in Investment Decision Making," *Financial Analysts Journal*, vol. 19, no. 3 (May–June, 1963), pp. 55–62.

multiple regression analysis. Once the parameters for this sample of stocks were found, they could be used to estimate theoretical P/E ratios for individual stocks. The theoretical P/E ratio could then be compared with the existing P/E ratio to determine whether the stock was overvalued or undervalued. For example, if the existing P/E ratio were 20 and the theoretical P/E was found to be 30, this stock would be considered undervalued under current market conditions. Presumably the investor should invest in the undervalued stocks, since if they are really undervalued they can be expected to appreciate as they move toward an equilibrium level.

To illustrate, suppose we refer to the parameter values for a sample of 135 stocks for the year June 8, 1961 to June 8, 1962 used by Whitbeck and Kisor in their study. For this sample, they derived the following equation:

$$\widehat{P/E} = 8.2 + 1.5g + 6.7D - 0.2\sigma$$

where $\widehat{P/E}$ is the theoretical P/E ratio, g is the estimated growth rate of EPS stated in percent, D is the dividend payout ratio stated as a decimal, and σ is the standard deviation of the rate of EPS growth. Whitbeck and Kisor were able to use this formulation as a screening device by determining overvalued and undervalued stocks. For example, consider the stock of a hypothetical corporation, whose $g = 7.5$, $D = 0.5$, and $\sigma = 7.5$. Substituting into the above equation gives the following theoretical P/E ratio:

$$\widehat{P/E} = 8.2 + 1.5(7.5) + 6.7(0.5) - 0.2(7.5)$$

$$= 8.2 + 11.25 + 3.35 - 1.5$$

$$= 21.3$$

Therefore, based upon current conditions, the appropriate, or theoretical, P/E ratio is determined to be 21.3.

Once the theoretical P/E ratio is determined, it becomes a matter of comparing it with the existing P/E ratio. For example, if the current P/E ratio for the hypothetical stock were 28.7, then the stock would be considered overvalued. On the other hand, if the existing P/E ratio were 15.1, then the stock would be considered undervalued.

Whitbeck and Kisor's approach is particularly useful for two reasons. First, there is the obvious screening function for which it was developed. This approach is feasible because it may be expected that investor sentiment will change only slowly over the short run. It is not appropriate for predicting the theoretical P/E ratios for a firm's stock far into the future. As Meader's study illustrated, the parameters of these regression models are unstable over time. The Whitbeck-Kisor approach, therefore, cannot be used for predicting P/E ratios for a time horizon of one, two, or five years. Second, and more importantly, the Whitbeck-Kisor formulation gives an indication of the type of factors that affect the P/E ratio of a firm. These are the growth in EPS, the variation in that growth, and dividend policy. Each of these factors influence the P/E ratio because they affect the price of the firm's stock.

Forecasting P/E Ratios

There are a number of ways of forecasting *P/E* ratios, but two methods have gained some measure of acceptance. One simply involves extrapolating the past experience into the future. That is, it assumes that the market's sentiment toward a particular stock will not change significantly from the past, that is, that the market will take a consistent view of an earnings stream. An alternative formulation is a qualitative judgment based on the number of years the current growth in *EPS* is expected to continue. This approach simply determines the number of years the current growth is expected, as indicated by the level of the *P/E* ratio.

Extrapolation   The extrapolation approach assumes that the past relationship of price to earnings will continue into the future over some time horizon. In essence, the assumption is that the market's sentiment will not change significantly from the past, and thus implies that the firm's performance will not be very different than it has been in the past period. The normal methods for determining the *P/E* ratio using extrapolation are to take the mean or median of past *P/E* ratios. The period of time used may vary, but in any case the period chosen should be representative. It is common to relate the *P/E* ratio of the firm with that of the firm's industry and that of a common stock index, such as Standard and Poor's 500 or the Dow-Jones Industrial Average. These comparisons provide a point of reference for the *P/E* ratios of the firm.

To illustrate the determination of *P/E* ratios by extrapolating past results, consider the Burroughs Corporation again. Burroughs' high and low *P/E* ratios for the 13-year period beginning in 1960 are as follows:

Year	High	Low	Year	High	Low
1960	29	19	1967	45	19
1961	28	17	1968	48	30
1962	38	17	1969	50	33
1963	30	19	1970	45	21
1964	21	16	1971	40	26
1965	22	11	1972	49	31
1966	25	13			

The arithmetic mean *P/E* ratio for Burroughs is 28.5 and may be rounded to 29. Hence, the average *P/E* ratio for Burroughs may be considered to be 29. If a median is used instead of an arithmetic mean, it is found to be 27.

The Burroughs data illustrate two important points. First, this data illustrate just how unstable the *P/E* ratios can be. In the 13-year period studied, Burroughs' *P/E* fell within a range of 11 to 50. This stock appears to be very volatile, which raises a question about the usefulness of the mean or a median as a meaningful predictor. Second, there appears to be an upward trend in Burroughs' *P/E* ratios, which undoubtedly reflects the growth in *EPS* that has occurred since 1965. In this case, it may not be reasonable to use *P/E* data prior to 1967, since there appears to be a major break in the data.

Introducing industry *P/E* ratios for a major common stock index may shed additional light on this question. Table 9–3 shows the *P/E* ratios for Burroughs, the office equipment industry, and the Standard and Poor's 425 stock index for the period 1963–73. It is clear that in the period 1960–67, Burroughs' *P/E* ratios were somewhat lower than those of the office equipment industry. During this period Burroughs' *EPS* did not show a particularly strong growth trend. At the same time, however, Burroughs' *P/E* ratios were somewhat higher than those of S & P's 425 stock index. After 1966, Burroughs' *P/E* ratios have essentially paralleled those of the industry. Both Burroughs and the office equipment industry's *P/E* ratios were considerably above those of the S & P's 425 stock, reflecting the superior growth prospects of the industry and Burroughs in particular.

P/E Ratios for Growth Firms   A particularly difficult situation involves predicting the *P/E* ratios for growth firms, as evidenced by the Burroughs example. Extrapolating past *P/E* ratios for firms that have had average growth in the past is probably acceptable, since the *P/E* ratios for these firms will be moderate— —probably fairly close to those of the leading stock indexes. However, extrapolating high *P/E* ratios for growth stocks introduces two potential sources of error. First, there is always the possibility that the high growth rate for the firm will slow down. It may be expected that as time passes more competition will enter the growth industry bringing about a decline in the profitability of that industry. Consequently, when the analyst uses a high *P/E* ratio to predict what the price of the stock will be, say, five years from now, he is assuming that the

TABLE 9-3   P/E *Ratios for Burroughs Corporation, the Office Equipment Industry, and the S & P's 425 for the Period 1960–73*

Year	Burroughs High	Burroughs Low	Office equipment industry High	Office equipment industry Low	S & P's 425 Industrials High	S & P's 425 Industrials Low
1960	29	19	57	40	19	16
1961	28	17	73	48	23	20
1962	38	17	62	35	20	14
1963	30	19	39	30	19	15
1964	21	16	39	33	19	16
1965	22	11	41	30	19	16
1966	25	13	40	32	17	13
1967	45	19	54	31	19	15
1968	48	30	48	38	19	15
1969	50	33	44	36	19	16
1970	45	21	44	26	19	14
1971	40	26	39	32	20	18
1972	49	31	42	36	19	17
Mean	29		41		18	
Median	27		39		18	

past growth will not slow. Moreover, it will be recalled that the *EPS* for the time horizon also include anticipated growth. Therefore, when a high *P/E* is used to predict the price of a stock at a time horizon, it is implicitly assumed that the high growth of the firm will exist not just up to the selected time horizon, but much beyond the time horizon. In other words, a *P/E* ratio at a point in time reflects anticipated growth, which means that a predicted *P/E* ratio for a future point in time presumably reflects anticipated growth from that point forward over another time horizon. As a result, predicting *P/E* ratios, not just *P/E* ratios for growth firms, really encompasses forecasts for two time horizons, not one. This results because *P/E* ratios reflect expectations, not past results.

The second source of error is the possibility of a shift in the manner in which investors value various income streams. In the period since 1950, there appear to be two such shifts, as discussed previously in Chapter 6. Recall that *P/E* ratios were relatively low in the early 1950s. This situation changed in the late 1950s and 1960s with *P/E* ratios in general increasing to somewhat higher levels. In 1973, however, there appears to have been another shift, with *P/E* ratios retreating from their previous levels. It is difficult to determine at this time whether the 1973 shift is temporary or not.

There is not yet a reliable technique that can be used by the analyst to predict the *P/E* ratios for growth stocks. However, several mechanical approaches have been developed, which may be of assistance to the analyst in estimating these *P/E* ratios. A technique first introduced by Charles C. Holt and subsequently adapted by Robert M. Baylis and Suresh L. Bhirud can be most useful.[7] This approach essentially attempts to determine the number of years before the *P/E* ratio of the growth stock is expected to decline to that of stocks in general. This approach gives an indication of the length of time the current *P/E* ratio antici- pates the above-average growth rate to continue. With this information it is possible for the analyst to determine whether this estimate is realistic.

Determining the period of time that the growth is being expected can be accomplished by applying the following formula:

$$\frac{P/E_i}{P/E_I} = \left(\frac{1 + g_i}{1 + g_I}\right)^n \tag{9–14}$$

where P/E_i is the price-earnings ratio of the growth firm i, P/E_I is the price- earnings ratio of a leading market index I, g_i is the expected growth for firm i, g_I is the expected growth of the market index I, and n is the number of years necessary to bring about the equality. In Equation 9-13, n is the unknown and important variable, since it indicates the number of years the above-average growth rate is expected to continue. Consequently, once n has been deter- mined, the analyst is in a position to determine whether the period is too long and whether the *P/E* ratio is too high.

To illustrate, suppose the *P/E* on a leading growth stock is 54 and the firm's past growth for the last six years has been 16 percent. Further, suppose the

[7] Charles C. Holt, "The Influence of Growth Duration on Share Prices," *Journal of Finance*, vol. 17, no. 4 (Sept., 1963), pp. 465–76; and Robert M. Baylis and Suresh L. Bhirud, "Growth Stock Analysis: A New Approach," *Financial Analysts Journal*, vol. 29, no. 4 (July–Aug., 1973), pp. 63–71.

growth in the *EPS* on the Standard and Poor's 425 has been 5 percent and its *P/E* ratio is 18. Substituting this data into Equation 9–14 gives

$$\frac{54}{18} = \left(\frac{1 + 0.16}{1 + 0.05}\right)^n$$

Solving this formulation can be easily handled by converting to logarithms. That is

$$\log\left(\frac{54}{18}\right) = n \log\left(\frac{1.16}{1.05}\right)$$

$$\log(3.0) = n \log(1.105)$$

$$0.4771 = n (0.0433)$$

$$n = 11.02$$

Therefore, the current *P/E* ratio of the corporation anticipates that the growth rate of 16 percent will continue for approximately 11 years. It is now possible for the analyst to make a judgment about the current *P/E* ratio of the corporation's stock. In particular, he is faced with the question of whether the 16 percent growth rate can be reasonably expected to persist for 11 years. If it can, then the *P/E* ratio of 54 is not too high. If it cannot, then a lower, more reasonable *P/E* ratio should be used to coincide with the expected time span that the growth is expected to last.

It is clear that the above analysis does not provide a panacea, but it does provide a method to determine the period over which the anticipated growth is expected to last. This concept is sometimes referred to as the period over which the anticipated growth has already been discounted.

The Ultimate Prediction

Ultimately the analyst must make a prediction of the expected return on a security and the assurance of obtaining that return. The expected return on securities, whether bonds or common shares, is made up of price appreciation (depreciation) plus interest or dividend income. For common stock a greater portion of the return normally takes the form of appreciation, whereas interest income makes up the greater portion of the return on bonds and debentures. Risk in common stock investment results from errors in forecasting the performance of the firm and from market conditions. These risks have been referred to as firm-related and market-related risks. By diversifying, we can ignore the firm-related risks, because with sufficient diversification errors in forecasting firm performance should cancel out. This means that errors in forecasting the expected return on a stock will depend upon the conditions of the market. Moreover, it means that the expected return in a good market and a bad market must be predicted.

This approach varies somewhat from earlier approaches in that it attempts to quantify risk, but its approach to estimating the expected return is similar to earlier approaches. In many of the earlier approaches, the assumption was that the firm was having neither a good nor a bad year and that the market was neither bad nor good.[8] In other words, the approach taken here and earlier approaches both forecast the expected return for a particular stock; and given the same initial estimates, both approaches arrive at the same estimate of the expected return for a particular stock. The essential difference then is that the approach taken here attempts to quantify risk and explicitly recognize the factors that may lead to errors in forecasting the expected return.

Thus, three separate bits of information are required. First, the potential appreciation must be established. This can be determined by means of the *EPS* valuation model. Second, anticipated dividends must be estimated. The general procedure is to apply an anticipated payout ratio to the estimated *EPS*. This approach assumes that firms have a tendency to pay out a certain proportion of their earnings in dividends, as evidenced by past experience. Finally, the risk associated with this return is assumed to depend on the realized appreciation, in particular, on the state of the market in the horizon year. The actual forecast may be a judgment based on an analysis of the firm's past results and anticipated economic and industry conditions, or it may be largely an extrapolation of past results. Regardless of the approach taken, a high and low *P/E* ratio can be used to indicate the impact of good and bad market conditions.

As a result, this data can be used to give the expected appreciation and the expected dividends that will give the annual expected return on a particular stock. At the same time, forecasting the expected return for good and bad market conditions will give the risk associated with obtaining that return. To illustrate, suppose we attempt to determine the expected return on Burroughs common stock. Suppose the *EPS* forecasts derived by the trend-adjusted exponential smoothing are used and a dividend payout of 25 percent is assumed. Finally, suppose that the *P/E* ratio for Burroughs in a good market is assumed to be 45 and in a bad market, 30. These two *P/E* ratios presumably were derived after evaluating the data on Burroughs' and the industry's *P/E* ratios shown earlier in Table 9-3. With these basic predictions, it is possible to proceed to predicting the expected return on Burroughs' common stock. Table 9-4 shows the cash dividend estimates and the potential price range in 1977. The estimated dividends shown in column 3 are derived by taking 0.25 of the predicted *EPS* shown in column 2. The price of the stock in a good market and a bad market for 1977 is derived by multiplying the 1977 *EPS* by the *P/E* ratios for 1977 of 45 and 30, respectively. This gives estimates of a price of $325 in a good market and $217 in a bad market for 1977.

As a result, the expected price in 1977 is the average of these two, or $271. If the current price is $200, the expected appreciation is $71, but it may be as high

---

[8] For example, see Jerome B. Cohen and Edward D. Zinbarg, *Investment Analysis and Portfolio Management* (Homewood, Ill.: Richard D. Irwin, 1967), pp. 219–20.

TABLE 9-4 *Predicted Risk and Return for Burroughs Common Stock for Period up to 1977*

Year	EPS	DPS	State of the market	
			Good	Bad
1973	$3.69	$0.80		
1974	4.94	1.24		
1975	6.00	1.50		
1976	6.41	1.60		
1977	7.22	1.81	$325.00	$217.00
		$6.95		

Current price = $200.00

as $125 or as low as $17. To obtain the annual expected return requires determining the average appreciation and the average dividend income. The annual appreciation is expected to be $14.20, but it may be as high as $25 or as low as $3.40. The average dividend income for the five years is $1.39. Therefore, the return relative if the market in the horizon year is good is

$$RR_G = \frac{\$225 + \$1.39}{\$200} = 1.132$$

On the other hand, if the market in the horizon year is bad, the RR_B is

$$RR_B = \frac{\$203.40 + \$1.39}{\$200} = 1.024$$

Finally, the expected return as given by $\overline{RR}$ is

$$\overline{RR} = \frac{\$214.20 + \$1.39}{\$200} = 1.078$$

Thus, the return could be within a range of a high of 13.2 percent, to a low of 2.4 percent, with an expected return of 7.8 percent. The expected return on Burroughs' stock would be 7.8 percent ± 5.4 percent. At this point the analyst's job is essentially finished.

Before closing this chapter, it may be useful to reconcile the approach used above with the present value approaches widely used today. Recall from Chapter 6 that the geometric mean return can be determined as follows:

$$G_i = [(\overline{RR}_i + \sigma_i)(\overline{RR}_i - \sigma_i)]^{\frac{1}{2}} \tag{9-15}$$

Substituting Burroughs' data into Equation 9–15 gives

$$G = [(1.078 + 0.054)(1.078 - 0.054)]^{\frac{1}{2}}$$
$$= [(1.132)(1.024)]^{\frac{1}{2}}$$
$$= 1.077$$

As a result, the geometric mean is 1.077 and the compound rate of return that can be expected on this stock is 7.7 percent.

On the other hand, if present values had been used, the mean return would have been somewhat less than 7.7 percent. The explanation is that the above calculations assume that the appreciation is earned in equal increments over the time horizon used. This assumption is consistent with the concept of growth occurring over time. Note, however, that some calculate the return by discounting dividends received plus the value of the stock in the horizon year to give the compound rate of return that may be expected. This approach tends to give a more accurate compound rate of return, but the approach shown above gives a reasonably accurate estimate.

Summary

The ultimate task in the evaluation of common stock is to determine the expected return and the risk of obtaining that return so that a portfolio of common stock may be selected that will provide the investor with a reasonable return. This estimate involves a number of individual predictions, including assumptions about the performance of the economy, the performance of particular industries, the state of the market, and, finally, the performance of the firm within its environment. Ultimately these factors were segregated into firm-related and market-related factors, and much attention was focused on firm-related factors. As a result, most of these estimates and predictions were used to forecast *EPS* and dividends, and little attention was given to predicting market conditions. The reason for this is that in a sufficiently diversified portfolio of common stock errors in predicting *EPS* and dividend growth will average out. On the other hand, market conditions may be either bad or good, and each of these possibilities is equally likely. Consequently, forecasts assuming good and bad market conditions must be made.

In the actual forecasting of *EPS*, four different methods were presented. Each method was quite straightforward. These methods are not only simple, but they are also fairly accurate. It has been shown that *EPS* tend to change from year to year in a rather random fashion. Therefore, predicting *EPS* is difficult. These methods appear to do a reasonably good forecasting job and are not particularly costly. Forecasting the appropriate *P/E* ratio is a more hazardous task. For stocks whose *P/E* ratios are not much different from the normal stock's, extrapolating the past *P/E* ratios may not be too hazardous. However, for growth stocks with high *P/E* ratios, extrapolating past *P/E* ratios may be hazardous, since the high growth may decline and with it the *P/E* ratios. An aid in such situations is a device that indicates the number of years the above-average growth is expected to continue. With this knowledge the analyst is able to make a judgment about the current level of the *P/E* ratio.

Questions

1. In forecasting the risk resulting from market-related factors, why is it necessary to make a forecast for a good market year and a bad market year? Why is it not necessary to make forecasts for good and bad firm years?

2. In forecasting the risk and return on common stock, what do you feel is the appropriate time horizon?

3. Consider the following data for a certain corporation.

Year	Sales ($ million)	EPS
1	210	2.00
2	200	1.60
3	205	1.69
4	211	1.86
5	215	1.91
6	236	2.20
7	239	2.29
8	251	2.40
9	271	2.51
10	269	2.45

 a. Using a trend line projection and regressing EPS on sales, forecast EPS five years hence. (Use a sales forecast of $325 million.)

 b. What are the weaknesses of these two methods of forecasting?

4. Consider the following data for a certain corporation for the most recent seven-year period.

Year	NEM	EPS
1	0.05%	0.01
2	1.00	0.10
3	2.00	0.20
4	3.00	0.38
5	1.00	0.11
6	2.50	0.45
7	3.00	0.49

 In addition, suppose sales for five years hence are expected to be $400 million, and the number of shares is expected to be 22 million. Using the NEM approach, forecast the EPS five years from now.

5. Using the data in question 3, forecast EPS for the next three-year period using trend-adjusted exponential smoothing. (Use the weights you feel are appropriate.)

6. Attempts have been made to develop stock price forecasting models. What has been the major disadvantage of these models?

7. Regression analysis has been used to forecast P/E ratios for individual stocks.

a. Explain why these forecasting models are only reliable in the short run.

b. Suppose a P/E forecasting model was developed with the following parameters:

$$P/E = 8.2 + 1.9g + 8.2D - 0.5\sigma$$

where g = growth of EPS

D = dividend payout stated as a percent

σ = standard deviation of EPS growth

With this model forecast the theoretical P/E ratio for a corporation that has $g = 21\%$, $D = 0.1$, and $\sigma = 9.5\%$. How would you use this theoretical P/E ratio?

8. Extrapolation may be used as a method of forecasting P/E ratios. Under what circumstances may the extrapolation method be reasonably reliable?

9. A security analyst and a portfolio manager have been discussing certain growth firms to determine which ones should be included in a growth portfolio. The portfolio manager thought that the current prices discounted all future growth. Since the security analyst had no quantitative data on this question, the meeting was adjourned with the analyst agreeing to supply some quantitative data for further discussion. The P/E ratios and expected growth rates for these firms and the S & P's 425 are as follows:

	Current P/E Ratio	EPS Growth
Corporation A	64	20 percent
Corporation B	48	10
Corporation C	80	40
Corporation D	48	15
Corporation E	32	10
S & P's 425	16	5

Determine the number of years that these growth rates are anticipated in the P/E ratios of these growth firms.

10. Suppose the following EPS and DPS forecasts have been made:

Year	Corporation X		Corporation Y	
	EPS	DPS	EPS	DPS
1	1.00	0.30	2.25	1.12
2	1.15	0.40	2.32	1.12
3	1.26	0.40	2.38	1.20
4	1.37	0.48	2.46	1.20
5	1.55	0.52	2.60	1.30

Suppose the P/E ratio is expected to be 18 in a good market, and 14 in a bad market for Corporation X, while for Corporation Y the P/E ratio in a good market is expected to be 15, and 12 in a bad market. Finally, X's stock is currently selling at $13 per share, and Y's stock is currently selling for $19.

a. Which stock promises the higher expected return?
b. Do you feel that either of these stocks merit consideration as a potential investment?
c. What compound rate of return may be expected on these two stocks?

Selected References

Baylis, Robert M., and Suresh L. Bhirud. "Growth Stock Analysis: A New Approach." *Financial Analysts Journal*, vol. 29, no. 4 (July–Aug., 1973), pp. 63–71.

Bower, Dorothy H., and Richard S. Bower. "Test of a Stock Valuation Model." *Journal of Finance*, vol. 25, no. 2 (May, 1970), pp. 483–93.

Brown, Philip, and Victor Niederhoffer. "The Predictive Content of Quarterly Earnings." *Journal of Business*, vol. 41, no. 4 (Oct., 1968), pp. 488–502.

Cragg, J. G., and Burton G. Malkiel. "The Concensus and Accuracy of Some Predictions of the Growth of Corporate Earnings." *Journal of Finance*, vol. 23, no. 1 (Mar., 1968), pp. 67–85.

Elton, Edwin J., and Martin J. Gruber. "Earnings Estimates and the Accuracy of Expectational Data." *Management Science*, vol. 18, no. 8 (Apr. 1972), p. B-423.

Graham, Benjamin. *The Intelligent Investor*, 4th rev. ed. New York: Harper & Row, 1973. Chapter 11.

Graham, Benjamin, David L. Dodd, and Sidney Cottle. *Security Analysis: Principles and Technique*, 4th ed. New York: McGraw-Hill, 1962. Part IV.

Holt, Charles C. "The Influence of Growth Duration on Share Prices." *Journal of Finance*, vol. 17, no. 4 (Sept., 1963), pp. 465–76.

Latane, Henry, and Donald L. Tuttle. "An Analysis of Common Stock Price Ratios." *Southern Economic Journal*, vol. 33, no. 3 (Jan., 1967), pp. 343–55.

———. *Security Analysis and Portfolio Management*. New York: The Ronald Press, 1970. Chapters 10 and 21.

Little, I. M. D., and A. C. Raynor. *Higgledy Piggledy Again*. New York; Augustus M. Kelley, 1966.

Niederhoffer, Victor, and Patrick Regan. "Earnings Changes, Analysts' Forecasts, and Stock Prices." *Financial Analysts Journal*, vol. 28, no. 3 (May–June, 1972), pp. 65–72.

Whitbeck, Volkert S., and Manown Kisor, Jr. "A New Tool in Investment Management Decision Making." *Financial Analysts Journal*, vol. 19, no. 3 (May–June, 1963), pp. 55–62.

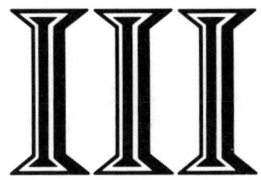

Security Evaluation–
Bonds, Debentures,
and Preferred Stock

Chapter 10

Determining Bond Quality

Bonds and debentures, unless convertible into common stock, derive their value from the promise to pay a stated interest over the life of the instrument and to repay the face value upon maturity. Nonconvertible preferred stock derive their value from the promise to pay a stated dividend perpetually. If the firm prospers, holders of these claims do not benefit in any way. However, if the firm does not fare well and goes into bankruptcy, then these holders will in all probability share in the losses incurred along with the common stockholders. It should be recognized, therefore, that the bond form is an inherently disadvantageous type of investment because while the benefits are limited by contract, the potential loss may equal the entire amount of the investment. This asymmetrical situation means that bond quality is the major concern to investors. In fact, it is a generally accepted rule among bond investors that only *quality* instruments be considered for investment. Some experts recommend that preferred stocks be avoided completely because of the nature of their claim. In other words, since preferred stocks have no legal recourse to enforce their claim, this form is highly disadvantageous and should be avoided.

Determining the quality of bonds is an important function because bond quality is the only assurance the investor has that he will receive the contractual interest and principal.[1] Determining the quality of an issue involves both quantitative analysis and qualitative analysis. The quantitative analysis normally involves the use of financial ratios. This analysis attempts to determine how well the firm has performed in general, but specifically it focuses on the firm's potential ability to service its debt. The qualitative analysis focuses on variables that are not easily quantifiable, such as the protective covenants of the issue, the size of the issuer, and the nature of the industry.

---

[1] In the remaining discussion, the focus will be on bonds, since they are the most important form of fixed-income security. Most of the important bond considerations will apply to preferred stocks. In situations where preferred stocks do vary significantly from bonds, the differences will be noted.

The quality of a bond issue may be referred to as the firm-related risk of the issue. In addition to the quality of the issue, there is what may be referred to as the market-related risk. This risk is commonly referred to as the interest-rate risk. Since interest-rate risk constitutes the most important source of risk to high-quality bondholders, it follows that the outlook for interest rates is very important. The motives for purchasing bonds varies from investor to investor, but whatever the motive, a knowledge of the outlook for interest rates is useful. For example, a knowledge of the long-run trends in interest rates and the short-run outlook is valuable information in arriving at the appropriate means for accomplishing an investment objective. In addition, the study of the term structure of interest rates may provide valuable insight into the process by which changes in interest rates are transmitted from short-term to long-term interest rates. In addition to the determinants of the quality of a bond issue that will be discussed in this chapter, the term structure of interest rates and the various means of forecasting interest rates in the short run are also important. These factors will be discussed in Chapter 11.

Finally, many firms attach "sweeteners" to fixed-income securities to improve their marketability. These normally take the form of including either a conversion feature or attaching warrants. When these features are present, the nature of fixed-income securities changes substantially. This is particularly true of the conversion feature, which gives the convertible security many of the attributes of the common stock. Warrants, on the other hand, may be detachable, which means that the warrant and the bond trade separately. In this case the warrant only affects the initial selling price of the bond issue. After this the warrant trades in the secondary market in relation to the common stock. These speculative features will be discussed in Chapter 12.

Nature of Senior Securities

Senior securities are generally divided into the broad categories of bonds and preferred stock. These two categories are used because of the substantial difference between the nature of the claims of these two types of securities. Bonds are creditorship instruments, which can bring about involuntary bankruptcy in the event that interest and principal are not paid as prescribed in the bond covenants. Preferred stocks, however, are viewed as a special class of common stock and as such do not have any means to force payment of unpaid dividends. The only compulsion on the firm to pay preferred dividends is the desire to pay common stock dividends. If the firm decides to pay dividends on its common stock, it must pay dividends on the preferred and also pay all preferred dividend arrearages before it can initiate dividends on the common stock. If arrearages do exist, the common practice is for the firm to reach an accommodation with the preferred stockholders whereby a lump-sum payment is made, which usually is less than the amount of dividends in arrears. This further illustrates the undesirable nature of preferred stocks.

It is common to see reference to four different types of bonds. The nature of the claim of each of these varies to some extent, but in general bonds may be classified as either secured or unsecured. Secured bonds have specific collateral pledged to afford a certain amount of protection to the bondholder in the event that default occurs. The unsecured bonds, on the other hand, do not have specific collateral pledged for the protection of their claims. These issues rely on the financial position of the firm for their assurance of payment of principal and interest.

Secured Issues

The collateral for secured issues may be either real assets or financial assets. Mortgage bonds and equipment trust certificates have claims against fixed assets. Mortgage bonds have either liens on specific fixed assets or blanket liens against all the fixed assets of the firm. Equipment trust certificates are a special form of claim peculiar to railroad financing, in which the rolling stock of the railroad is used as collateral for the loan. The collateral may also take the form of financial assets. Bonds with other securities pledged as collateral are commonly known as collateral trust bonds.

Mortgage Bonds   With a mortgage bond issue, specific property or all of the property of the firm may be subject to the lien. Generally the size of the mortgage bond issue is somewhat less than the fair market value of the property being used as collateral. For example, if the fair market value of the property being used as collateral for a mortgage bond issue is $100 million, the bond issue might be limited to $75 million. The difference of $25 million provides a margin of safety for the mortgage bondholders. However, the property may be used as collateral for more than one loan. If the firm uses the property as collateral for another mortgage lien of, say, $10 million, this property would be subject to a first mortgage lien of $75 million and a second mortgage lien of $10 million. The distinction between a first mortgage and a second mortgage results from the time at which the lien is registered—the first mortgage registered becomes the first mortgage. There is no legal limit on the number of mortgages that can be placed on a piece of property. From a practical point of view, however, the limit becomes the willingness of lenders to accept the property as collateral. There have been cases in which as many as five mortgages have been placed on a piece of property.

In addition to the priority of the lien, there are several other features of mortgage bonds that should be noted. The mortgage may be open-end or closed-end. Open-end mortgages permit the issuance of additonal bonds under the lien. They usually include an after-acquired clause, which means that fixed assets acquired subsequent to the mortgage lien are also subject to it. This clause has the advantage of permitting the firm to issue additional series of the mortgage bond issue without preparing a new issue. There are, of course, certain restrictions on the issuance of new series of mortgage bond under an existing lien, such as a limit on the maximum percentage that the mortgage bonds can be of the market value of the assets subject to the lien. The major advantage of the after-acquired clause is that for firms that issue substantial amounts of debt—for example, public utilities—this provision simplifies the firm's financing. Closed-end mortgage liens, on the other hand, do not permit the issuance of additional bonds under the existing lien. The firm must use new properties as collateral for a new mortgage issue, with the effect that each mortgage lien will apply only to certain property. For firms using a substantial amount of debt financing, this feature can lead to a very complex capital structure.

Collateral Trust Bonds These bonds have securities pledged as collateral instead of fixed assets. Otherwise they are similar to mortgage bonds in that in the event of default the trustee has the right to foreclose and use the proceeds to pay off the claims of the bondholders. The security provided by the collateral trust bond depends upon the quality of the securities pledged. Both the collateral trust bond and the mortgage bond suffer from the same basic weakness: there is an essential difficulty in determining the market value of the collateral should liquidiation be necessary. With mortgage bonds, the bondholders seldom obtain 100 cents on each dollar claimed. With collateral trust bonds, the value of the collateral lies in the quality of the issues used as collateral. Therefore, high-quality bonds are suitable collateral, but low-quality bonds represent weak security. Secured bonds were once fairly widely used, but the experience of the 1930s showed that security results not from the collateral pledged, but from the earning power of the firm. This realization has led to a decline in the use of secured instruments, particularly collateral trust bonds.

Equipment Trust Certificates Technically, equipment trust certificates represent a form of leasing, but they are a form of investment that has a wide following. Railroads contract with suppliers for the manufacture of "rolling stock," but the railroad arranges with a trustee to purchase the "rolling stock" and lease it to the railroad. When delivery of the equipment is made, the trustee issues equipment trust certificates which are used to purchase the equipment along with railroad's downpayment. The trustee holds title to the equipment, and the lease payments are sufficient to pay a fixed interest to the holder and amortize the certificates over their lifetime. Thus, when the lease period expires, the equipment trust certificates will have been amortized and the title to the equipment passes to the railroad.

These certificates are widely accepted among investors because the "rolling stock" makes excellent collateral. There is a sufficiently wide market for "rolling stock," such that if default occurs the collateral can be quickly leased or sold to another railroad. Equipment trust certificates, therefore, have a ready market, particularly among financial institutions, and the railroads have enjoyed substantial success with this type of financing.

Unsecured Issues

Where secured bond issues have specific assets pledged as collateral for the claims of the bondholders, unsecured issues only have a general creditorship claim. In other words, the unsecured bondholders are considered to be general creditors of the firm and share equally with other general creditors in liquidation. The implication is that the only security for these issues is the earning power of the firm. If the firm is profitable, these claims will be relatively secure; however, if the firm is unprofitable, the claim may very well be in jeopardy. The three different types of unsecured bonds are debentures, subordinated debentures, and income bonds. The distinctions among these result from differences in the claim to either assets or interest income. Since debentures are similar to mortgage bonds except for the pledge of collateral, only subordinated debentures and income bonds will be discussed below.

Subordinated Debentures   Debentures represent a general creditorship claim. Subordinated debentures, however, have a claim that ranks behind that of other debt instruments in the capital structure. For example, they may be defined as being subordinated to a straight debenture issue. This means that the subordinated debentures holders will only receive payment in liquidation once the debenture holders receive full payment of their claims. To illustrate, suppose that a firm's assets were liquidated for $5 million, and it had $4 million of claims by the straight debenture holders, $2 million of claims by the subordinated debenture holders, and claims of $4 million by general creditors. It might be expected that the debentures holders and the general creditors would share equally in proceeds of liquidation. This is not the case, however, since the subordinated debenture holders' share goes to the debenture holders. As a result, the debenture holders will receive 60 percent of the proceeds, or $3 million, and the general creditors would receive the remainder, or $2 million. Subordinated debentures thus tend to augment the claims of the senior securities.

Note that the subordinated debentures share in the proceeds of liquidation ahead of the preferred stockholders, but it is nevertheless a highly disadvantageous form of investment. As a result, the coupon rate on subordinated debentures is higher than that on straight debentures to compensate for the additional risk.

Income Bonds   Income bonds are probably the least attractive of all the bond instruments. They require that interest be paid only when earned. Therefore, if the firm does not operate at a profit, it is not obligated to pay interest on the bonds. When the interest is earned, however, it must be paid. The advantage to the firm is obvious. Whenever interest is paid, it is a taxable expense that reduces the effective cost of these securities. Yet the risk associated with these securities is minimal. Essentially, income bonds have the same risk characteristics as preferred stock, with the tax features of bonds. The firm is obligated to pay cumulative interest if there are arrearages, but the cumulative obligation is for a short period of time, usually three years. Note that these securities do have priority in liquidation over subordinated debentures and preferred stock. These obligations clearly are highly advantageous to the firm, but have few advantages for the investor. For this reason, they have not received wide investor acceptance.

Some Concluding Comments

Although it is common to associate quality with the nature of the security's claim to assets, the primary determinant of quality is the ability of the firm to service its debt. It is true that the nature of the claim to assets is important, particularly with mortgage bonds, but generally the only assurance the bondholder has of receiving principal and interest is the earning power of the firm. In other words, secured and unsecured bonds alike will probably suffer a loss in bankruptcy and liquidation.

An important reason for this is that the value of the assets of a firm in liquidation will be somewhat less than that for a going concern. This results because the assets of a firm are highly specialized; selling these assets can only occur at bargain basement prices. As a consequence, the recovery in liquidation is a good deal less than might be expected.[2] For example, for the fiscal year ending June 30, 1966, the claims paid amounted to slightly more than 16 percent of the amount claimed under the Bankruptcy Act. Specifically, the amounts paid to the various claimants were[3]

Nature of claim	Amount of claim	Payment	Percent of claim paid
Priority	$ 40,811,855	$14,789,084	36.2
Secured	51,780,278	32,427,785	62.6
Unsecured	347,803,029	24,194,351	6.9
Total	$440,395,139	$71,411,220	16.2

It is clear that the secured claimants fared much better than either the priority claimants or the unsecured claimants. Still, they received only about 62 percent of their claims.

Another factor that is often overlooked is the time involved in settling a bankruptcy case. There are extreme examples in which it took more than 10 years to settle the various claims of the security holders. Graham, Dodd, and Cottle report several instances of receivership which involved substantial delays.[4] For example, the Seaboard-All Florida Railway went into bankruptcy in 1931, but the first mortgage bondholders did not receive settlement until 1946–47 at approximately 20 cents on the dollar. Thus, not only did the bondholders have a long wait before the settlement, but they also took a severe loss.

[2] For an excellent discussion of bankruptcy, see Paul M. Van Arsdell, *Corporation Finance: Policy, Planning, Administration* (New York: The Ronald Press, 1968), Part IX.
[3] Ibid., p. 1,503.
[4] Benjamin Graham, David L. Dodd, and Sidney Cottle, *Security Analysis: Principles and Technique,* 4th ed. (McGraw-Hill, 1962), pp. 311–12.

It is difficult to say whether such delays would exist today, but it is safe to say that settlement would not be forthcoming within a year or two. If nothing else, one has lost one or two year's interest.

All of this leads to one indisputable rule of thumb: the bond purchaser should buy only high-quality bonds. Regardless of the lien, receivership is a costly and disheartening experience. This supports the view that the bond form is inherently disadvantageous. At best, one can only expect to receive the contracted principal and interest. At worst, one may suffer a severe loss. It follows, therefore, that the appropriate course of action is to pursue safety in bond investment. Obtaining this safety is accomplished primarily by emphasizing the earning power of the firm. The lien will affect the amount collected in liquidation, but nevertheless a loss will most likely occur. As a result, the only real assurance of obtaining principal and interest the investor has lies with the earning power of the firm.

Quality Ratings

Determining the quality of bonds has a history dating back to 1909 when John Moody published his *Analysis of Railroad Investments.*[5] Since that time, other services, in particular Standard and Poor's and Fitches', have prepared bond ratings, and these ratings have generally been valuable to investors. They are designed to indicate the probability of default on the issue. The bond analyst utilizes all of the data available to arrive at a rating for a particular issue. However, certain factors play a more important role in determining bond ratings than others. These variables will be discussed later. The section that follows will present a brief discussion of the Standard and Poor's and Moody's ratings, their meaning, and their accuracy.

Leading Ratings Services

In Table 10-1 the explanation for the ratings of Standard and Poor's and Moody's are presented. Both rating services are very similar for the first six rating categories. Ratings below these categories vary somewhat. Normally, the first four rating categories are considered to represent investment-grade bonds. Bonds rated below the first four categories have some speculative elements, which means that the chance of default is greatly increased. The speculative element referred to in Table 10-1 generally means that the probabilities of receiving interest during periods of economic slowdown are relatively low. Bonds rated in either of the lower B ratings are currently meeting their interest requirement, but there is a grave question about whether these payments would continue in an economic slowdown. Once the ratings drop below the B range, their meaning varies according to the services. However, the prospects

[5] Thomas F. Pogue and Robert M. Soldofsky, "What's in a Bond Rating," *Journal of Financial and Quantitative Analysis,* vol. 4, no. 2 (June, 1969), p. 203.

TABLE 10-1 *Moody's and Standard and Poor's Corporate Bond Quality Ratings*

Moody's	Standard and Poor's	
Aaa	AAA	Highest grade obligations. They possess the maximum degree of protection for principal and interest.
Aa	AA	High quality obligations differing from AAA or Aaa only to a small degree. These issues along with the "triple A" issues are generally known as high-grade bonds.
A	A	These are regarded as upper-medium-grade bonds. They are of fairly good quality, but factors are present that may lead to impairment.
Baa	BBB	These are considered medium-grade obligations. They provide sufficient safety, but elements are present which make them susceptible to changing business and economic conditions. They have investment characteristics, but certain speculative characteristics also exist.
Ba	BB	Lower-medium-grade obligations. They have speculative elements that jeopardize their investment quality.
B	B	Speculative. Interest payments are not assured under difficult economic conditions.
	CCC-C	Outright speculations, but interest is being paid. In difficult economic conditions, continuation is unlikely.
Caa		Poor standing. May be in default.
	C	Income bonds with no interest being paid.
Ca		Highly speculative. Often in default.
	DDD-D	In default, with DDD, DD, D indicating relative salvage value.
C		Lowest ranking. Bonds with this ranking have very poor prospects.

for bonds in any of these categories are not too promising, while the probabilities of suffering a loss are great.

Standard and Poor's also rate preferred stocks. These ratings are designed to fulfill the same function as the bond ratings. Although preferred stock is technically considered an equity instrument, the principal source of return from these instruments is the dividends received. Since the preferred stockholders have no means to force the firm to pay dividends, these ratings become even more valuable. The ratings are as follows:

AAA	Prime	BB	Lower grade
AA	High grade	B	Speculative
A	Sound	C	Submarginal
BBB	Medium grade		

S & P's preferred stock ratings follow the same format as the bond ratings and basically have the same meanings and symbols. Although the preferred stock is evaluated independently of the bonds the firm may have outstanding, many of the factors affecting the rating of the bonds will also affect the rating of the stock. This is particularly true of any factors connected with the earning power of the firm.

It is generally believed that the bond ratings of the various services have been very accurate. A study by W. Braddock Hickman evaluated the default record of issues for the period 1900–43.[6] The default record for this period shows a remarkable record of accuracy.[7]

Rating category	Default rate
1	6 percent
2	6
3	13
4	19
5–9	42

Default in the highest two ratings categories was approximately 6 percent for each category, and it increases in categories 3 and 4 to 13 and 19 percent, respectively. The remaining categories showed a substantial percentage of defaults. It thus appears that the ratings categories do meet their purported objective of indicating the probability of default. The highest categories consistently had the smallest percentage of defaults, while the lower ratings had the largest percentage of defaults. Moreover, the investment grade bonds represented by the first four rating categories had a substantially smaller percentage of defaults than the bonds rated as speculative. This record must be considered the "acid test" for bond ratings. When ratings can be this accurate through a period that included a serious depression, they must be considered quite accurate.[8]

Determinants of Bond Ratings

Although the raters attempt to evaluate all available information in arriving at their ratings, certain factors are given more emphasis than others. Empirical studies of bond ratings appear to point to several factors as being pivotal in the bond rating process.[9] First, as may be expected, profitability is central in determining the quality of the issue. Profitability is important because bond investment is a long-term commitment, and the only assurance the bond investor has of obtaining principal and interest is the profitability of the firm. This is in contrast to some short-term loans that are made to unprofitable firms because the cash flow of these firms is sufficient to service the debt. In evaluating the

[6] W. Braddock Hickman, *Corporate Bond Quality and Investor Experience* (New York: National Bureau of Economic Research, 1958).
[7] Ibid., p. 10.
[8] Note that a study was conducted for the post-World War II period to update the Braddock study. See Thomas R. Atkinson, *Trends in Corporate Bond Quality* (New York: National Bureau of Economic Research, 1967). However, there have not been enough bankruptcies in the post-World War II period to obtain meaningful statistics on the quality of bond ratings (see Atkinson, page 2).
[9] George E. Pinches and Kent A. Mingo, "A Multivariate Analysis of Industrial Bond Ratings," *Journal of Finance*, vol. 28, no. 1 (Mar., 1973), pp. 1–19.

profitability of the firm, it appears that two dimensions of profitability are considered. On the one hand, the rate of return on investment is an important determinant of profitability. On the other hand, the stability of that earnings stream is important. Therefore, the bond raters not only consider the level of return on investment, but they also view an unstable income stream as being an indication of risk.

Second, in addition to the profitability of the firm, the method of financing the firm is an important consideration. It is common to segregate the types of risks that the firm faces into two major types, which are referred to as business risk and financial risk. Business risk is the probability of unexpected variations in net operating earnings and therefore the probability of not earning an adequate return on investment. Financial risk is concerned with the way in which the firm is financed, that is, the mix of debt and equity in the capital structure. A firm can increase its total risk by using debt to finance its assets. Consequently, business risk and financial risk are additive. The firm without any debt financing faces a certain amount of risk; if debt is introduced into the capital structure, the risk faced by the firm is increased. As a result, the extent to which debt financing is used by the firm must be evaluated. Normally, the evaluation of the firm's profitability will determine its business risk. An evaluation of the firm's use of financial leverage will determine its financial risk.

Third, it has been found that working capital measures are particularly important determinants of default. Recall that adequate working capital did not play a very important role in the evaluation of common stock. Empirical studies of investment-grade bonds have found that working capital considerations are not an important determinant of these bond ratings. On the other hand, empirical studies of financial ratios as indicators of potential default have found that working capital measures are important indicators of potential default. These two findings are probably consistent. For the investment grade bonds, working capital considerations are not important because the liquidity of these firms is adequate. However, once firms start failing, the liquidity position becomes impaired. Working capital considerations thus may be important only in situations in which default is a possibility. They will be discussed in this vein.

Finally, other factors have been found to be important besides these major considerations. Among these are a number of qualitative considerations, such as the type of industry, size of the firm, and the nature of the bond covenants. These factors are difficult to quantify, but they nevertheless play an important role in determining bond ratings.

Financial Ratios

Since certain financial ratios have been shown to play an important role in the assignment of bond quality ratings, the focus in the following discussion will be on describing them. In particular, it appears that the profitability and leverage ratios play a vital role in the assignment of bond ratings. Studies on the use of financial ratios to predict default have found that working capital measures are quite important. Consequently, these will also be included.

Profitability

Measuring the profitability of the firm is an important aspect of common stock analysis, and the various methods involved were discussed in detail in Chapter 7. The three measures utilized were the earning power, the return on total assets, and the return on net worth. The earning power was based on earnings before interest and taxes, whereas the return on total assets utilized the net income. These two measures permit an evaluation of the impact of taxes and financial charges on the profitability of the firm. In this sense these measures permit an evaluation of the firm's operating efficiency and the impact of financial charges and income taxes on the firm's profitability. The return on net worth gives an indication of the impact of leverage on the return to the stockholders.

Both the earning power and the return on total assets can be decomposed into their components. That is

$$EP_{it} = TAT_{it} \times OEM_{it} \tag{10-1}$$

where TAT_{it} is the total asset turnover ratio for firm i at time t, and OEM_{it} is the operating earnings margin for firm i at time t. Similarly, the return on total assets can be decomposed as follows:

$$RTA_{it} = TAT_{it} \times NEM_{it} \tag{10-2}$$

where NEM_{it} is the net earnings margin for firm i at time t.

The decomposition of these two ratios is particularly useful because it permits a more refined analysis of the causes of any trends that may exist in either the earning power or the return on total assets. For example, the earning power for a particular firm may show a downward trend. Decomposing the earning power of this firm according to Equation 10-1 may determine whether lower operating earnings margins or total asset turnover is the cause. The same type of analysis may be undertaken for the return on total assets. The result of the analysis is that any difficulties the firm may be facing can be pinpointed a little more precisely. In contrast, the return on net worth gives an indication of the impact of leverage on the return to the stockholders and, along with the earning power and return on total assets, should give a fairly good indication of the firm's profitability, any trends that may be present, and their causes.

Another common measure of profitability that is widely used by the financial community is the return on invested capital. This ratio measures the return in relation to the total amount of long-term permanent financing. That is

$$ROI_{it} = \frac{NI_{it}}{LTF_{it}} \tag{10-3}$$

where NI_{it} is the net income of firm i at time t, and LTF_{it} is the total long-term financing of firm i at time t.

Total long-term financing is used on the premise that the net income should only be related to that portion of its assets represented by permanent long-term financing. The sources of this financing are debt issues, common stock issues, retained earnings, and other forms of long-term financing. Short-term financing in the form of accounts payable and accruals are ignored because these sources are spontaneous and do not require recourse to the money markets, while short-term loans and commercial paper are viewed as temporary financing. The return on total assets, on the other hand, assumes that the net income of the firm should be related to the total assets of the firm, since these assets represent the total resources at the disposal of the firm. Advocates of the return on invested capital argue that the return should be measured in terms of funds acquired with permanent forms of financing.

Clearly, there is not an obviously superior measure. The earning power and the return on total assets are used because they can be readily decomposed. This does not mean that the return on invested capital would not be an effective measure. What we are witnessing is a phenomena that occurs quite often in financial ratio analysis, in which a number of different ratios are used to measure a particular characteristic of the firm. In most cases all these ratios will do a reasonably good job of measuring the characteristic in question. Therefore, the user will normally settle on a group of ratios that meet his needs and preferences.

Financial Leverage

Since the inclusion of debt in the capital structure constitutes a source of risk, it is necessary to determine the extent of this risk. This evaluation usually involves two different aspects. First, it is common to determine the proportion of debt used by the firm in its financing. Determining whether too much debt is being used by the firm is normally accomplished by comparing the firm's debt ratios with standards that have been developed, or by comparing the existing ratios with the past experience of the firm. Either of these methods may give an indication of the financial risk associated with the firm. Second, the ability of the firm's income stream to service the debt is vital to avoid default. This aspect is by far the more important of the two. For example, it is conceivable that a firm may be able to meet the standard set for debt ratios and still not be able to service its debt. Thus, the coverage ratios which measure this ability are of paramount importance in evaluating the financial risk of the firm.

Debt Ratios   Debt ratios take several different forms. One commonly used debt ratio may be referred to as the total debt ratio, which is

$$TDR_{it} = \frac{TD_{it}}{TA_{it}} \tag{10-4}$$

where TD_{it} is the total debt of firm i at time t, and TA_{it} is the total assets of firm i at time t. An alternative formulation that is widely used is the debt-to-equity ratio, given by

$$D/E_{it} = \frac{LTD_{it}}{NW_{it}} \tag{10-5}$$

where LTD_{it} is the long-term debt of firm i at time t, and NW_{it} is the net worth of firm i at time t. The debt-to-equity is also calculated by some analysts by utilizing total debt instead of just long-term debt.

The actual calculation of these two ratios is straightforward and will not be illustrated, but they effectively measure the amount of debt used by the firm. The important consideration is whether the firm has the appropriate amount of debt in its capital structure. There are two ways of determining this. One method is to use trend analysis. A comparison of the debt ratios for a period of time will give an indication of whether any trends are apparent, particularly an upward trend in the amount of debt used. If an upward trend is apparent, then the impact of this occurrence must be determined. On the other hand, if the level of the debt ratio is fairly stable, it may be assumed that this level of debt is optimal or near optimal for this firm. This assumption may not always be justified, but it appears to be a reasonable starting point that can be modified by viewing other indicators.

Another method is to use industry standards as a basis for comparison. These standards are normally determined from industry data and attempt to indicate the appropriate margin of safety in light of industry characteristics. For example, a table of normal ratios such as the following may be used:[10]

Industry	Normal total debt ratio
Manufacturing	30 percent
Public Utilities	65
Railroads	30
Airlines	40
Mining	20

These ratios are presented only as illustrations, but a standard similar to them is generally used. If the firm being analyzed has more debt than the standard would indicate is appropriate, this is indicative of too much debt. The actual impact depends on the interest coverage ratios as well as other factors. These standards normally are not absolute measures in the sense that the standard debt ratio must be met, but rather indicators of possible weakness.

In many cases trend analysis and the standards are used together. The standards are considered as a target that the firm should meet, but any trends that may exist may be introduced as qualitative factors. That is, the firm's debt ratios should be within the range specified by the standard, but any conclusions

---

[10] These ratios were derived from financial norms developed by Paul M. Van Arsdell. See Paul M. Van Arsdell, *Corporation Finance: Policy, Planning, Administration* (The Ronald Press, 1968), pp. 583, 651, 721, 751, and 770.

drawn may be qualified by any trends present in the debt ratios. For example, a manufacturing firm may have a total debt ratio of 33 percent, which is slightly more than the maximum permitted of 30 percent, but this ratio might have dropped from 40 percent down to the current 33 percent over the last five years. In such a case, the trend would be considered a positive factor. However, it would be only one factor; the interest coverage ratio would still need to be determined.

Interest Coverage Ratios   The most important test of the firm's debt capacity is the interest coverage ratios. These ratios measure the margin of safety between the income stream and the financial charges. This ratio is normally determined as follows:

$$ICR_{it} = \frac{EBIT_{it}}{I_{it}} \tag{10-6}$$

where $EBIT_{it}$ is the earnings before interest and taxes for firm i at time t, and I_{it} is the total interest expense of firm i at time t. Earnings before interest and taxes are normally used in this calculation on the premise that they represent the earnings available to pay interest. Generally, all interest is used in the denominator on the assumption that the firm must be able to service all of its debt. If it cannot, then all the creditors will be adversely affected. However, there are four variations of the interest coverage ratio. These are:

1. Overall method
2. Cumulative-deductions method
3. Prior-deductions method
4. Preferred dividends coverage

To illustrate these methods, consider a corporation that has *EBIT* of $10 million. Suppose also that the corporation has three debt issues outstanding as follows:

Mortgage bond 6s	$20,000,000
Debenture 7s	10,000,000
Subordinated debenture 8s	5,000,000

The total interest paid on these issues is $2.3 million. The interest coverage ratios for these three issues would be determined as follows:

Issue	Overall	Cumulative deductions	Prior deductions
Mortgage bond 6s		8.33	8.33
Debenture 7s		5.26	12.57
Subordinated		4.35	20.25
	4.35		

The overall method corresponds to Equation 10-6. That is, the ratio is determined by using all of the interest costs in the denominator without consideration to the priority of claims. In other words, the overall interest coverage ratio for the corporation is $10,000,000 ÷ $2,300,000 = 4.35.

The cumulative-deductions method, on the other hand, does consider the priority of claims. That is, the cumulative-deductions method assumes that since certain bondholders have priority over other bondholders, these will have a prior claim to earnings and consequently more assurance of receiving principal and interest. The coverage ratios, therefore, are calculated for each class of claim by determining the claims on the available earnings. For example, the mortgage bond 6s have a coverage of $10,000,000 ÷ $1,200,000 = 8.33. However, for the debenture 7s, the coverage ratio is somewhat less than that for the mortgage bonds, $10,000,000 ÷ $1,900,000 = 5.26. Finally, the coverage for the subordinated debentures is the same as the overall coverage ratio. Therefore, these two methods ultimately give the same answer. It remains questionable whether the premise on which the cumulative-deductions method is based is valid. The assumption that certain bondholders may be adequately secured while others may not be appears tenuous. Since all bondholders are affected by default, it seems reasonable that all bond claims should be adequately covered. This assumption is the basis for the overall method. However, since the cumulative-deductions method eventually gives the same answer as the overall method, it is probably acceptable.

The prior-deductions method gives a completely misleading indication of the margin of safety for a particular class of claim. Whereas the cumulative-deductions method adds the interest of each claim, the prior-deductions method subtracts the interest required to meet prior claims and divides the remainder by the required interest. For example, the interest coverage for the mortgage bonds is the same as for the cumulative-deductions method. However, the debenture 7s has a coverage of 12.57. The earnings figure is $10 million minus $1.2 million which equals $8.8 million, and the coverage is $8,800,000 ÷ $700,000 = 12.57. Similarly the coverage for the subordinated debenture 8s is $8,100,000 ÷ $400,000 = 20.25. The problem with this approach is that it implies that the junior issues have greater protection than the senior issues. This implication is obviously misleading. For this reason the prior-deductions method has been severely criticized and is not in widespread use.

Preferred stocks present a special case when it comes to determining the coverage ratios. Preferred dividends are paid out of after-tax income; therefore, to determine the coverage of preferred dividends, the dividends must be converted to a before-tax amount. This is accomplished simply by dividing the amount of dividends by 1 minus the effective tax rate. For example, suppose our hypothetical corporation has $5 million of 6 percent preferred stock outstanding, and the effective tax rate is 40 percent. The before-tax amount of preferred dividends is $300,000 ÷ (1 − 0.4) = $500,000. The total amount of fixed charges now is $2.8 million, and the overall coverage ratio is $10,000,000 ÷ $2,800,000 = 3.57. It is common to refer to this ratio as the preferred coverage ratio.

In evaluating coverage ratios, the same approach is used as that for the debt ratios. Tables of standards are generally used, and it is with the coverage ratios that standards have their widest application. These tables may vary, but Table 10-2, developed by Graham, Dodd, and Cottle, illustrates the form that these tables may take. This table utilizes general industry classifications to differentiate among the various types of firms in the economy, and it utilizes two alternative standards that may be applied. These standards are determined by the overall method and are calculated by using earnings before interest and taxes. One set of standards is the minimum average overall coverage ratio for the last seven years. Alternatively, the poorest-year coverage ratio can also be used. Normally this poorest-year ratio should be a coverage ratio in a recession year. For preferred stocks Graham advocates a minimum ratio of two.[11] As with debt ratios, trends may be introduced as a qualitative factor, but generally these minimums are quite inflexible. In other words, if a bond does not meet these standards, it is not accorded investment-grade status.

Working Capital Ratios

Measures of working capital are not important factors in determining the ratings of investment-grade bonds. However, these measures are important in determining the firm's ability to meet its current obligations. The major role of these working capital ratios is in predicting the probabilities of involuntary bankruptcy. As a result, the working capital ratios, such as the current ratio, the acid-test ratio, and so forth, will be discussed below in connection with using financial ratios to predict bankruptcy.

Predictive Value of Financial Ratios

Recent empirical studies have established that financial ratios have substantial predictive value in forecasting bankruptcy.[12] This has been found to apply to both small and large business firms. These findings are particularly important

TABLE 10-2 *Minimum Coverage for Bonds*

Type of industry	Overall coverage before interest and taxes	
	Average of past 7 years	Alternative: poorest year
Public Utility	4.0	3.0
Railroad	5.0	4.0
Industrial	7.0	5.0
Retailers	5.0	4.0

Source: Abridged and adapted Table 11-1 (page 148) from *The Intelligent Investor,* Fourth Revised Edition by Benjamin Graham (Harper & Row, 1973).

[11] Benjamin Graham, *The Intelligent Investor,* 4th rev. ed. (New York: Harper & Row, 1973), p. 148.
[12] See Edward I. Altman, "Financial Ratios, Discriminant Analysis and Prediction of Corporate Bankruptcy," *Journal of Finance,* vol. 23, no. 4 (Sept., 1968), pp. 589–610; William H. Beaver, "Financial Ratios as Predictors of Failure," *Empirical Research in Accounting: Selected Studies* (Chicago: University of Chicago, 1967), pp. 71–111; and Robert O. Edmister, "An Empirical Test of Financial Ratio Analysis for Small Business Failure Prediction," *Journal of Financial and Quantitative Analysis,* vol. 7, no. 2 (Mar., 1972), pp. 1477–94.

because financial ratios have been widely criticized. The major criticism that has been raised is: What do they mean? Part of the problem appears to be that there were a large number of ratios in use and a solid theoretical base did not exist. However, recent empirical research has reaffirmed the usefulness of financial ratios, and the major consideration appears to be the objective of the analysis. For example, certain ratios are useful in evaluating the credit worthiness of a potential short-term borrower, while other ratios are useful for determining the quality of long-term bonds. This was also found to be the case with predicting bankruptcy.

Generally, it was found that the profitability, liquidity, and leverage measures had predictive content. The actual ratios used varied from study to study, but all studies attempted to measure the firm's position in these three major areas. Out of these studies, three basic conclusions can be drawn. First, as previously noted, the liquidity, or working capital, ratios were good predictors of bankruptcy. It appears, therefore, that the liquidity ratios have their most important application to deteriorating situations. This implies that the liquidity ratios become important once a firm starts failing because at this point survival depends upon being able to meet all current obligations. Second, these studies generally used multiple discriminant analysis, which segregates observations into bankrupt and nonbankrupt sample groupings and simultaneously evaluates the predictor variables. This approach implies that these ratios must be viewed in the aggregate to determine potential bankruptcy. This conclusion is not surprising, since the various financial ratios are designed to evaluate specific areas of consideration; it follows that an overall evaluation of the firm's position would require a balancing of its financial strengths and weaknesses. Thus, a simultaneous evaluation would be needed.

Finally, an important consideration is the time horizon over which accurate forecasts can be reasonably expected. Edward I. Altman found that the financial ratios made accurate forecasts up to two years. Beyond two years the predictive accuracy dropped significantly. The implication of this finding is that continuous review of bond ratings is needed to assure the accuracy of the bond quality ratings. If this review is conducted on a regular basis, a fairly accurate prediction may be made sufficiently in advance of default to warn the investor adequately. All in all, it appears that financial ratios are a useful means of evaluating bonds and deserve some of the credit for the accuracy of past ratings.

Qualitative Considerations

In rating bonds certain qualitative considerations play an important role. The major difficulty with these variables is identifying their impact; nevertheless, it is generally accepted that these factors do play a role in the assignment of quality ratings. A number of these could be included, but the following discussion will focus on factors that relate to the issuer of the bonds and to the protective covenants of the issue.

Issuer-Related Factors

Three important qualitative considerations are the type of industry the issuer is in, the size of the issuer, and the issuer's solvency and dividend record. Little needs to be said about the influence of the industry on bond ratings. Industry groupings are generally associated with certain characteristics. For example, public utilities are considered to be more stable than manufacturing firms. Cyclical stability is an important consideration to the bond investor because the investor's major concern is how the firm performs in an economic slowdown. Cyclical firms would be more seriously affected by an economic slowdown, and hence these firms must provide an additional margin of safety. In addition, there is evidence that the yields on public utility bonds have been slightly higher recently than those on manufacturing bonds. The explanation appears to be that in periods of rapidly rising prices public utilities are severely affected, since the rate commissions have been reluctant to give rate increases to compensate for changes in the general price level. As a result, inflation tends to work a hardship on public utilities.

Size of the Issuer   There is ample evidence that the size of the issuer is an important factor in the default on bonds.[13] W. Braddock Hickman's bond study illustrates the impact of the size of the issuer on the default of industrial issues.[14]

Asset size of issuer	Percent of offerings defaulted
Under $5 million	38.0 percent
$5–99 million	25.3
100–199 million	17.2
200 and over	3.4

It appears clear that the size of the issuer had an important effect on whether or not default occurred among industrial firms. However, it should be noted that the impact of size was not as clearly evident in other industry categories. It is not clear what the reason for this is, but it may have occurred because other factors dominated the size factor. Alternatively, it may be, as Graham, Dodd, and Cottle contend, that firm size is more important for industrial firms.[15]

A major difficulty of attempting to introduce firm size into the bond evaluation process is determining the appropriate minimum size that will separate investment-quality bonds from noninvestment-quality bonds. Graham, Dodd, and Cottle have advocated quantitative guides, as follows:[16]

[13] For example, see Thomas F. Pogue and Robert M. Soldofsky, "What's in a Bond Rating?" *Journal of Financial and Quantitative Analysis*, vol. 4, no. 2 (June 1969), p. 212; and W. Braddock Hickman, *Corporate Bond Quality and Investor Experience* (Princeton, N.J.: Princeton University Press, 1958), p. 495.
[14] Hickman, p. 495.
[15] Benjamin Graham, David L. Dodd, and Sidney Cottle, *Security Analysis: Principles and Technique*, 4th ed. (New York: McGraw-Hill, 1962), p. 329.
[16] Ibid. Used with permission of McGraw-Hill Book Company.

Issuer	Minimum requirement for size
Public Utilities	$ 4 million
Railroads	5 million
Industrials	15 million

These minimum size requirements were stated in terms of revenues rather than assets. For public utilities and railroads, the minimum size was stated in terms of operating revenues, while for industrial firms size was stated in terms of sales revenues. Whether these figures are appropriate is difficult to judge, but it is widely recognized that small firms have a larger probability of default than large firms. Hence, the size of the issuer should be considered in rating bonds, especially with industrial firms.

Solvency and Dividend Record   These two variables are used as an indicator of the period of successful operation of the firm. Generally, it is desirable for the firm to have a long record of successful operation because this is an indication that the firm has been able to adapt to changing conditions. The solvency record indicates the period of time that the firm has been carrying on successful business operations. The dividend record is a refinement of this general criterion. A long record of continuous dividend payments can be viewed as an indicator of successful operations, particularly if the dividends have not been reduced. These two indicators mean that new firms and firms that have emerged from a period of financial difficulty should not be considered to be investment-grade.

The solvency and dividend record criteria are only indicators of past successful operations. They do not necessarily mean that the future operations will be as successful as the past. However, such criteria do give an indication that the firm has been able to adapt to changing conditions.

Bond Provisions

The provisions of the bond agreement spell out the rights of the bondholders and the obligations of the firm. In addition to the most obvious provisions, such as the amount of interest to be paid and the maturity date of the issue, there are a number of other provisions designed to preserve and protect the claim of the bondholders. In general these are referred to as the protective covenants of the bond issue. These protective covenants are included to limit the actions of the firm in order to prevent the firm from eroding the claim of the bondholders, and they enable the bondholders to exert some control over the firm whenever its actions may affect them adversely. It is the function of the trustee to enforce the protective covenants and act on behalf of the bondholders. These protective covenants usually concern five different features of a bond:

1. Retirement provisions
2. Call provisions
3. Equity cushion
4. Position in the capital structure
5. Working capital position

The covenants normally apply to bonds; they vary in their application to preferred stocks. The protective covenants of preferred stocks will be discussed separately.

Retirement Provisions   Periodic retirement provisions have become fairly standard in bond issues, mainly as a result of the large number of defaults in the 1930s. Prior to the 1930s, many firms did not make provision for retiring their debt. During the 1930s many firms had bond issues mature that could not be paid off, which resulted in a substantial number of defaults. This experience led to almost universal inclusion of retirement provisions, generally in the form of a sinking-fund provision. Another method which accomplishes the same end is the use of serial bonds. Whatever the approach used, the reason for including a retirement provision is to avoid a large lump-sum payment at maturity and all of the uncertainty that goes with it. The features of the sinking fund tend to vary, but in recent years the tendency has been to delay institution of the sinking fund for five or six years. After this period the firm will begin retiring the issue. Normally this is accomplished by one of three methods:

1. Purchase in the market
2. Advertising an offer to purchase in the financial news sources
3. Exercise of the call privilege for sinking-fund purposes

Regardless of the type of retirement provision, it appears that retirement provisions are widely regarded as a desirable feature. However, sinking fund provisions do not mean that the firm is committed to retiring a specified amount of the issue each year. Sinking-fund provisions may be optional, conditional, or obligatory. Clearly, an optional sinking-fund provision provides little protection to the bondholders. The conditional and obligatory sinking funds provide more protection. The conditional provision normally means that the sinking-fund payments only become a requirement once a certain level of profit is earned. When this level is reached, the firm is obligated to make the stipulated sinking-fund payments. The fact that the sinking fund is conditional weakens the provision to a certain extent, but it nevertheless provides a certain amount of protection. The obligatory sinking fund provides the greatest assurance that the sinking-fund payments will be made, since failure to do so may be considered default. Hence, there is no question of the sinking-fund requirements being met.

Call Provision   Although the call provision facilitates the sinking-fund provision, it is not included for the benefit of the bondholders. Actually, this provision is more for the benefit of the firm. The call provision permits the firm to call all or part of the issue at a specified price. This price includes what is known as a call premium. This provision becomes particularly useful in periods when interest rates decline below the level currently being paid. Under these circumstances it may be economical to call the issue and replace it with a new issue at a lower coupon rate. When this occurs, the bondholder must give up an asset that is earning a relatively high return. Consequently the call provision actually constitutes a threat to the bondholder.

There are two ways in which the bondholders may seek protection. One method is to prohibit calling an issue for purposes of replacing it with another issue for a stated number of years. Many issues, for example, include a deferral period in which the issue cannot be called for three to five years. This assures bondholders of a minimum period in which the bond issue will not be called. Another method is to include two call-price schedules. One schedule is for sinking-fund purposes, and the other is for refunding purposes. The schedule for sinking-fund purposes is lower than the one for refunding. In this sense the two call-price schedules are designed to deter refunding the issue.

Equity Cushion   Another set of protective covenants may attempt to maintain a minimum level of equity capital. The stockholders' equity is commonly viewed as a buffer for creditors' claims. Generally, the greater the proportion of total financing provided by the stockholders, the greater the protection for the creditors. Protective covenants may be included in the bond provisions in order to attempt to provide assurance that the equity cushion will not be eroded away. The actual provisions will vary, but commonly they restrict the level of dividends that may be paid and the repurchase of the firm's common stock. The limit on dividends may be that cash dividends cannot exceed the net income. Occasionally, the objective is to build up the equity cushion; then the dividends may be restricted to the amount above a certain figure. For example, a firm may be restricted in its dividend policy by a covenant that does not permit the payment of a dividend until net income is $5 million, and dividends can only equal the amount of net income above this figure. Therefore, if the firm earned $7 million, dividends could not exceed $2 million. A variation of this type of covenant is to restrict dividends to a certain proportion of net income. Stock repurchases by the firm reduce the number of shares outstanding and therefore can erode the creditors' buffer in the same fashion. Consequently, stock repurchases may be either limited or completely forbidden.

Working Capital Position   Another way in which the bondholders' claims may be eroded is for the firm to use excessive amounts of short-term financing. These short-term creditors may have either an equal claim or a prior claim, which will dilute the claims of the bondholders. To protect the bondholders, a covenant may be included requiring a certain amount of working capital. In some cases the requirement may simply be that a minimum current ratio must be maintained. For example, the minimum current ratio may be stated as 225 percent. In other cases the minimum amount of net working capital may be a stated amount. In any event, the purpose is to protect the bondholders against the excessive use of short-term debt. The criticism that is leveled against this provision is that it may force the firm to keep too much cash on hand and thus reduce the profitability of the firm. It is difficult to evaluate the merits of such an argument. The answer probably lies in whose point of view is being taken. If the bondholders' point of view is taken, it may be a worthwhile provision.

Position in the Capital Structure   In addition to the bondholders' claims being eroded by the use of excessive short-term debt, particular issues may find their position eroded by the introduction of additional equivalent or senior issues. One way this may occur is for the firm to issue senior bonds. For example, the firm could issue mortgage bonds that would have a senior claim to the existing debentures. Or the firm could issue additional bonds of an already outstanding issue or issue new bonds with the same status as existing bonds. As a general rule, existing bondholders want at the very minimum the right to vote on whether a new issue should be sold by the firm. Moreover, it is desirable for debenture holders to have a voice in the issuance of senior bond issues. In this fashion the debenture holders can preserve their position in the capital structure. Therefore, it is desirable for debenture issues to be closed-end and to have an "equally and ratably" provision. The closed-end provision prevents the issuance of additional debentures of the same series. The "equally and ratably" provision means that if mortgage bonds are subsequently issued the debentures become secured equally and ratably with the mortgage bonds. In this fashion the debentures are secured by the same assets as the mortgage bonds, and they have an equivalent claim with the mortgage bonds.

Open-end mortgage bonds constitute an exception to the general rule that additional securities of the same issue should be restricted. However, the reason that this provision is acceptable is that these mortgage bonds have an after-acquired clause, which means there are additional assets to act as collateral for the new mortgage bonds of the existing series. Consequently, the margin of safety is still present for the bondholders.

Preferred Stock   As previously indicated, the preferred stock form is inherently disadvantageous because it has all of the disadvantages of the common stock without the advantages. As a result, the claim of the preferred stockholders is inherently weak. The protective covenants of preferred stock generally parallel those of bonds. This results probably because firms tend to view preferred stock as an alternative for debt. However, there are some differences. For example, only about 50 percent of the preferred stock issues have sinking-fund provisions. It is probably desirable to include a sinking-fund provision because of the weak position of the preferred stock. Additionally, it is common not to give the preferred stockholders any control over the issuance of additional debenture issues, but there may be restrictions on the issuance of prior-claim preferred stock and mortgage bonds. These two provisions have some value, but the lack of control over debenture issues greatly reduces their importance.

Finally, the preferred stockholders are normally given the right to vote in the event of failure to pay preferred dividends. In some cases it may mean that the preferred stockholders can vote along with the common stockholders. In other cases the preferred stockholders can elect several directors. Although these provisions may appear to offer suitable protection to the preferred stockholders, they seldom do. In practice the preferred stockholders normally constitute a small percentage of the total number of common shares; therefore, being able to vote offers little protection to the preferred stockholders. Being able to elect several directors is an improvement, but it still may not be adequate.

Summary

Determining bond quality requires that three different aspects of the problem be recognized. First, the bond form is inherently disadvantageous. In particular, the potential return is limited to the anticipated yield to maturity. If the firm is highly successful, the bondholders will receive the contracted principal and interest. If the firm is not successful, the bondholders will in all likelihood share in the losses along with the common stockholders. Once this aspect of bonds is recognized, the importance of quality and quality ratings becomes clear.

Second, it appears that the major rating services, such as Moody's and Standard and Poor's, have done an excellent job of rating bonds. Based on the pre–World War II experience, it appear that investment-grade bonds have had a low default rate, particularly the first two ratings categories, while the speculative bonds have shown a high level of default.

Third, the actual ratings appear to result from the combined evaluation of two types of variables. One group of variables include the financial ratios, which can be used to measure the profitability and leverage of the firm. Measures of working capital were not found to be important determinants in the rating of investment-grade bonds, but they appear to be quite important in determining whether a firm will go into bankruptcy. A second group of variables included a number of qualitative variables. Included in this group were size of the issuer, the issuer's record of solvency and dividends, the type of industry, and the protective covenants of the issue. The bond raters evidently view all of these factors—profitability, leverage, and qualitative factors—and arrive at an estimate of the quality rating of a particular bond issue.

Questions

1. Why is bond quality such an important consideration to the investor?
2. A number of terms are commonly associated with bonds and debentures.

Define each of the following:

Open-end clause	Collateral trust bonds
Closed-end clause	Equipment trust certificates
After-acquired clause	Subordinated debentures
Trustee	
Debentures	

3. Secured bonds have not been used as much in recent years as they were in earlier years.
   a. Why has this occurred?
   b. Why are equipment trust certificates so popular?
4. A corporation has gone into bankruptcy. Its assets have been liquidated for $10 million. Against this amount there are the following claims:

1st mortgage bonds 6s	$4,000,000
Debentures 6½s	$4,000,000
General creditor claims	$6,000,000
Subordinated debentures 6¾s	$4,000,000

The subordinated debentures are subordinated to the mortgage bonds and the debentures. The mortgage bonds have a blanket mortgage lien on all fixed assets. What will be the proceeds of liquidation for each class of claim?

5. The important factors in determining bond-quality ratings may be categorized as quantitative and qualitative factors.
   a. What are the important quantitative factors?
   b. What do these quantitative variables measure?
6. Both the debt ratios and the interest coverage ratios are used in estimating the financial risk of the firm. How are they used?
7. A corporation has three debt issues outstanding and a preferred issue. The firm's *EBIT* for last year is $86 million, and the face value of each issue is as follows:

Mortgage bonds 5s	$40,000,000
Debentures 6s	$20,000,000
Subordinated debentures 7s	$10,000,000
Preferred stock 4s (par $100)	$10,000,000

   a. What is the interest coverage ratios for this firm, using the overall method, the cumulative-deductions method, and the prior-deductions method?
   b. Which measure is the more meaningful?
   c. Determine the preferred stock coverage ratio (assume an effective tax rate of 50 percent).
8. Liquidity ratios apparently have their most important use in determining firms with deteriorating financial positions.
   a. What explanation can be given for this?

b. Given that liquidity ratios are most useful in ascertaining potential bankruptcy, how would they be of use to the bond analyst?

9. Qualitative factors are introduced into the determination of bond quality.
    a. What are some of the qualitative factors that may be considered?
    b. How are these used?

10. What protective covenants do investors generally seek to have included in the bond agreement?

Selected References

Altman, Edward I. "Financial Ratios, Discriminant Analysis and Prediction of Corporate Bankruptcy." *Journal of Finance*, vol. 23, no. 4 (Sept., 1968), pp. 589–610.

Atkinson, Thomas R. *Trends in Corporate Bond Quality*. New York: National Bureau of Economic Research, 1967.

Beaver, William H. "Financial Ratios as Predictors of Failure." *Empirical Research in Accounting: Selected Studies*. Chicago: University of Chicago, 1967, pp. 71–111.

Cohen, Jerome B., Edward D. Zinbarg, and Arthur Zeikel. *Investment Analysis and Portfolio Management*, rev. ed. Homewood, Ill.: Richard D. Irwin, 1973. Chapter 9.

Edmister, Robert O. "An Empirical Test of Financial Ratio Analysis for Small Business Failure Prediction." *Journal of Financial and Quantitative Analysis*, vol. 7, no. 2 (Mar. 1972), pp. 1477–94.

Graham, Benjamin. *The Intelligent Investor*, 4th rev. ed. New York: Harper & Row, 1973. Chapter 11.

Graham, Benjamin, David L. Dodd, and Sidney Cottle. *Security Analysis: Principles and Technique*, 4th ed. New York: McGraw-Hill, 1962. Part III.

Hickman, W. Braddock. *Corporate Bond Quality and Investor Experience*. New York: National Bureau of Economic Research, 1958.

Horrigan, James O. "Some Empirical Bases of Financial Ratio Analysis." *Accounting Review*, vol. 60, no. 3 (July, 1965), pp. 558–69.

———. "The Determination of Long-Term Credit Standing With Financial Ratios." *Empirical Research in Accounting: Selected Studies*. Supplement to *Journal of Accounting Research*, vol. 4. (1966), pp. 44–63.

Pinches, George E., and Kent A. Mingo. "A Multivariate Analysis of Industrial Bond Ratings." *Journal of Finance*, vol. 28, no. 1 (Mar., 1973), pp. 1–19.

Pogue, Thomas F., and Robert M. Soldofsky. "What's in a Bond Rating?" *Journal of Financial and Quantitative Analysis*, vol. 4, no. 2 (June, 1969), pp. 201–29.

Stiglitz, Joseph E. "Some Aspects of the Pure Theory of Corporate Finance: Bankruptcies and Take-Overs." *Bell Journal of Economics and Management Science*, vol. 3, no. 2 (Autumn, 1972) pp. 458–81.

"The Men Who Make Treasurers Tremble." *Forbes*, vol. 106, no. 5 (Sept., 1970), pp. 19–21.

Williams, W. H., and M. L. Goodman. "A Statistical Grouping of Corporations by Their Financial Characteristics." *Journal of Financial and Quantitative Analysis*, vol. 6, no. 4 (Sept., 1971), pp. 1095–1105.

Van Arsdell, Paul M. *Corporation Finance: Policy, Planning, Administration*. New York: The Ronald Press, 1968. Parts III and IX.

Vaughn, Donald E. *Survey of Investments*. New York: Holt, Rinehart & Winston, 1967. Chapter 2.

Chapter 11

Interest Rates

At the time of the purchase of a bond, the market rate of interest determines the yield the investor will obtain on it. This market rate of interest is the yield that is currently available on debt instruments and represents the collective forces that determine interest yields. For the individual investor, these forces are an important consideration in the decision to invest in bonds. They also represent an important consideration in the decision to invest in short-term or long-term bonds, particularly since changes in the market rate of interest are the major cause of changes in the market value of high-quality bonds. Bond investment is by its nature defensive, and the concern is therefore whether interest rates will rise and cause the market value of bonds to fall. This risk is a particular problem for long-term bonds, which are affected more by changes in interest rates. Consequently, for high-quality bonds interest rates determine not only the yield on a particular bond investment when it is purchased, but also the subsequent risk that may be associated with a particular bond.

In the following discussion of interest rates, the focus will be on the forecasting of interest rates and the transmission process among the interest rates on various maturities. It is common to refer to a market rate of interest; realistically, however, a number of interest rates exist simultaneously. Forecasting interest rates thus normally focuses on forecasting the general direction of interest rates. The impact of the factors affecting changes in interest rates will vary with the quality and the maturity, and normally the higher the quality of a bond the more closely its price changes will be related to interest rate changes. The transmission process of changes in interest rates among various maturities is less straightforward. Changes in interest rates are generally believed to occur with short-term interest rates initially and then are transmitted to long-term interest rates. The mechanism for facilitating changes in interest rates is commonly referred to as the term structure of interest rates. However, the manner

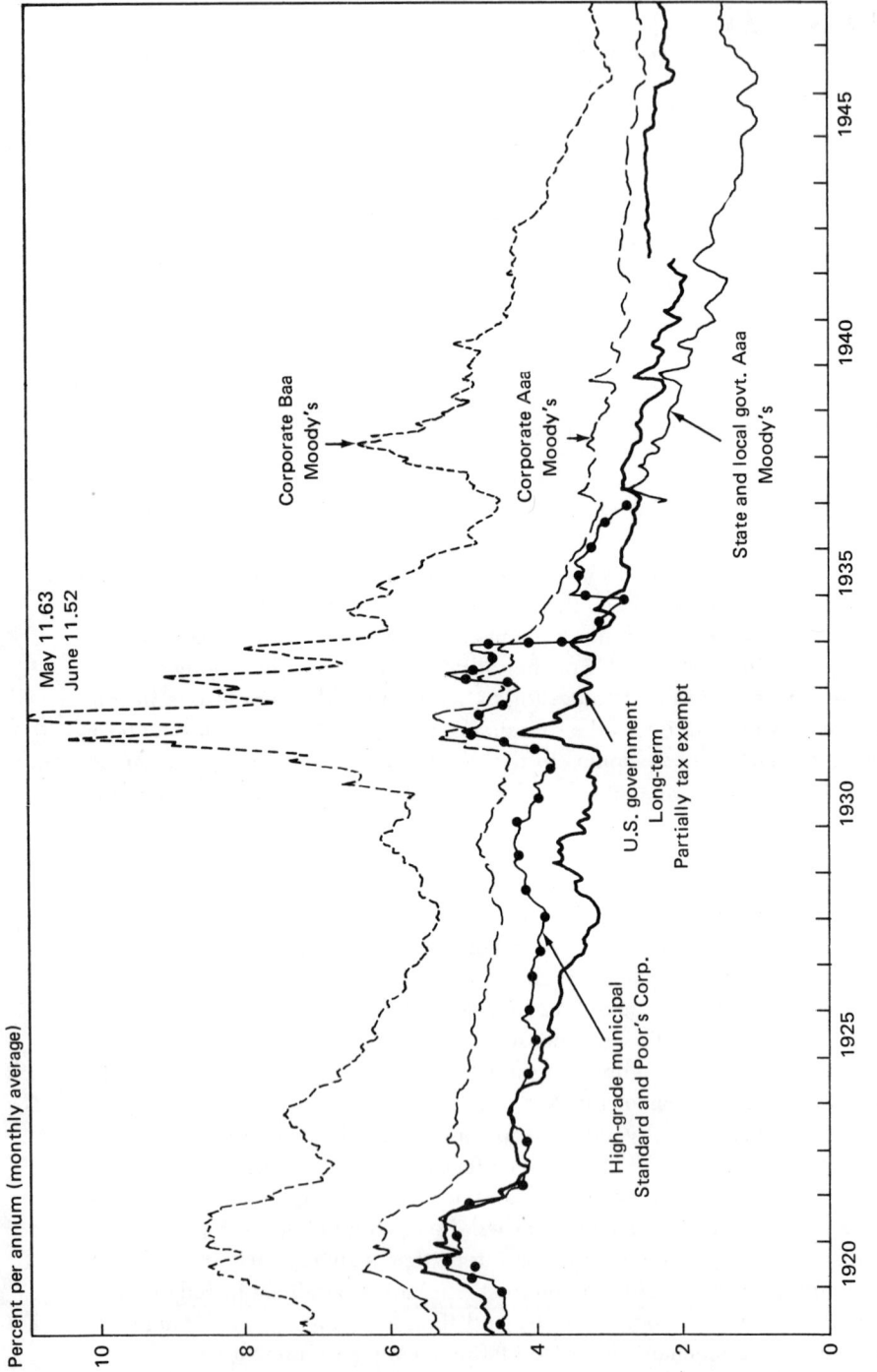

Percent per annum (monthly average)

May 11.63
June 11.52

Corporate Baa
Moody's

Corporate Aaa
Moody's

State and local govt. Aaa
Moody's

U.S. government
Long-term
Partially tax exempt

High-grade municipal
Standard and Poor's Corp.

1920   1925   1930   1935   1940   1945

FIGURE 11-1   *Interest Rates on Long-Term Bonds, 1919–73*

Source: Board of Governors of the Federal Reserve System, *Historical Chart Book,* 1973.

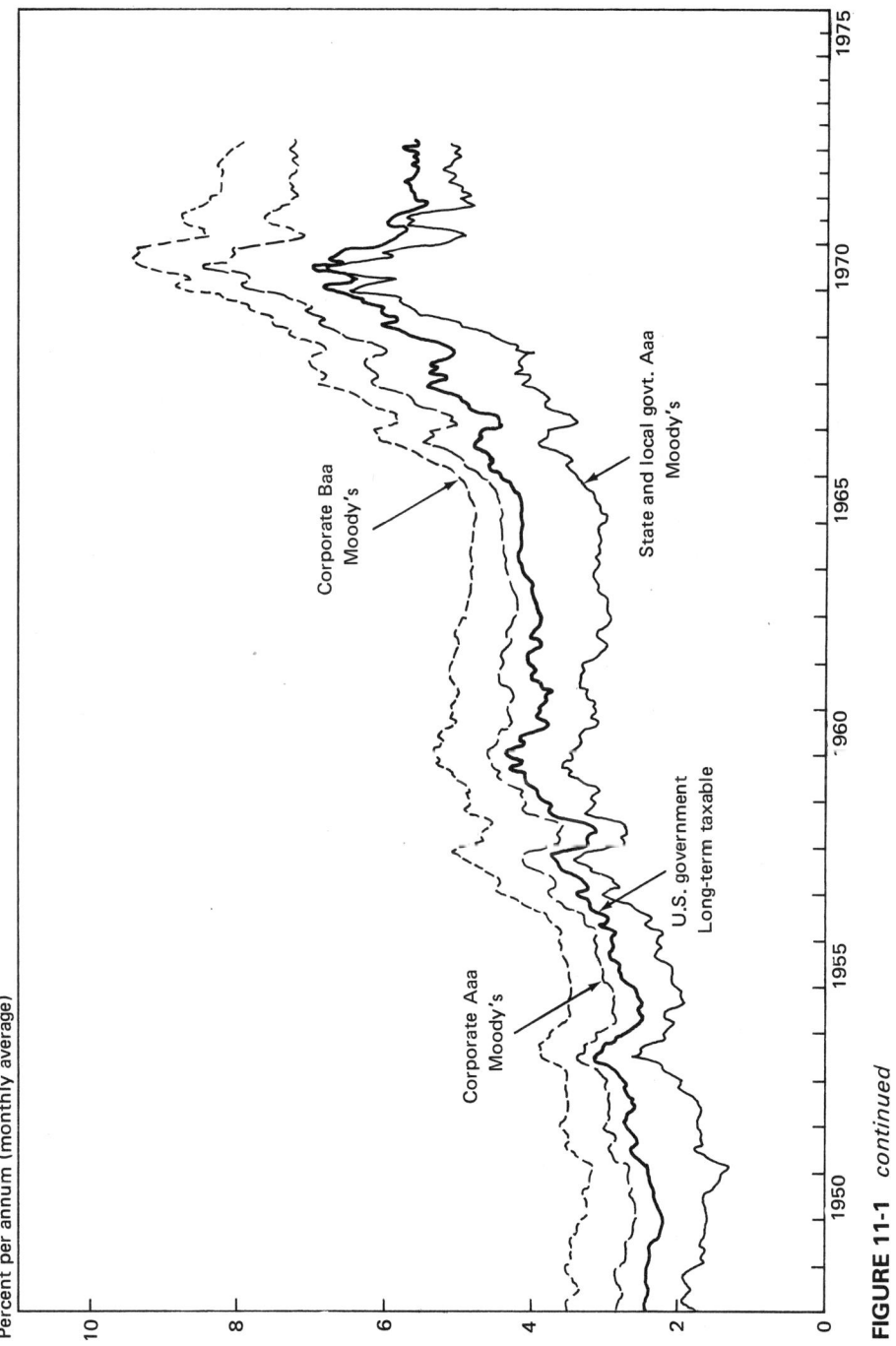

Percent per annum (monthly average)

Corporate Baa
Moody's

State and local govt. Aaa
Moody's

U.S. government
Long-term taxable

Corporate Aaa
Moody's

1950   1955   1960   1965   1970   1975

FIGURE 11-1 *continued*

in which changes in interest rates are transmitted is unclear, and several theories have been advanced to explain the term structure of interest rates.

Interest Rates in Perspective

There are several reasons for the large number of interest rates in the market. Interest rates vary with the quality of the instrument, its length to maturity, and the various economic factors that determine the level of interest rates at a point in time. A major distinction in bonds and bond interest rates emerges between federal government and corporate and municipal issues. Federal government issues are considered to be the highest quality issues because of the government's unlimited powers of taxation. Thus, the payment of interest and principal is virtually assured. Corporate and municipal bonds, however, do not provide such assurance. Their quality may vary from triple A to those selling in default, and the quality has a definite affect on their yield. This difference in yield for long-term government bonds and long-term corporate and municipal issues is shown in Figure 11-1.

As a general rule, the poorer the quality of the bond issue, the higher the yield. This relationship reflects risk aversion on the part of investors. It does not, however, explain the lower yield on municipal bonds. Interest paid on state and local government issues are tax-exempt; therefore, the yield on these issues will be somewhat lower than that on other long-term issues. Municipal bonds, however, will still vary in quality from triple A to D, with the quality having an inverse relationship with the yield. Moreover, federal bond issues were fully or partially tax-exempt during the period from 1919 to 1942. Consequently, the low yield on these issues is also explained by this feature. Since 1942, however, these issues are fully taxable and their yields have increased correspondingly.

It is clear that corporate bonds have always sold to yield more than federal government issues. The difference in yield, or risk premium, varies with the quality of the corporate bond issues and, to some extent, with the economic outlook, which plays a role in determining the optimism or pessimism of investors. When the outlook is good, the spread will narrow because investors are more willing to undertake riskier investments. However, when the outlook becomes somewhat clouded, investors begin acquiring higher quality bonds, and the spread widens. For example, consider the years 1969 and 1970. In 1970 the spread between government and corporate bonds widened considerably. The explanation is that a recession occurred in 1970, which led to a switching into higher quality issues.

In addition to the effect of quality on the yields of bonds, the length to maturity also has an effect. As Figures 11-2 and 11-3 show, the nature of this relationship has varied from time to time. Figure 11-2 presents the short- and long-term interest rates on federal government issues for the period since 1942. It is clear from Figure 11-2 that during most of the period long-term interest rates were higher than short-term interest rates. At certain times, however,

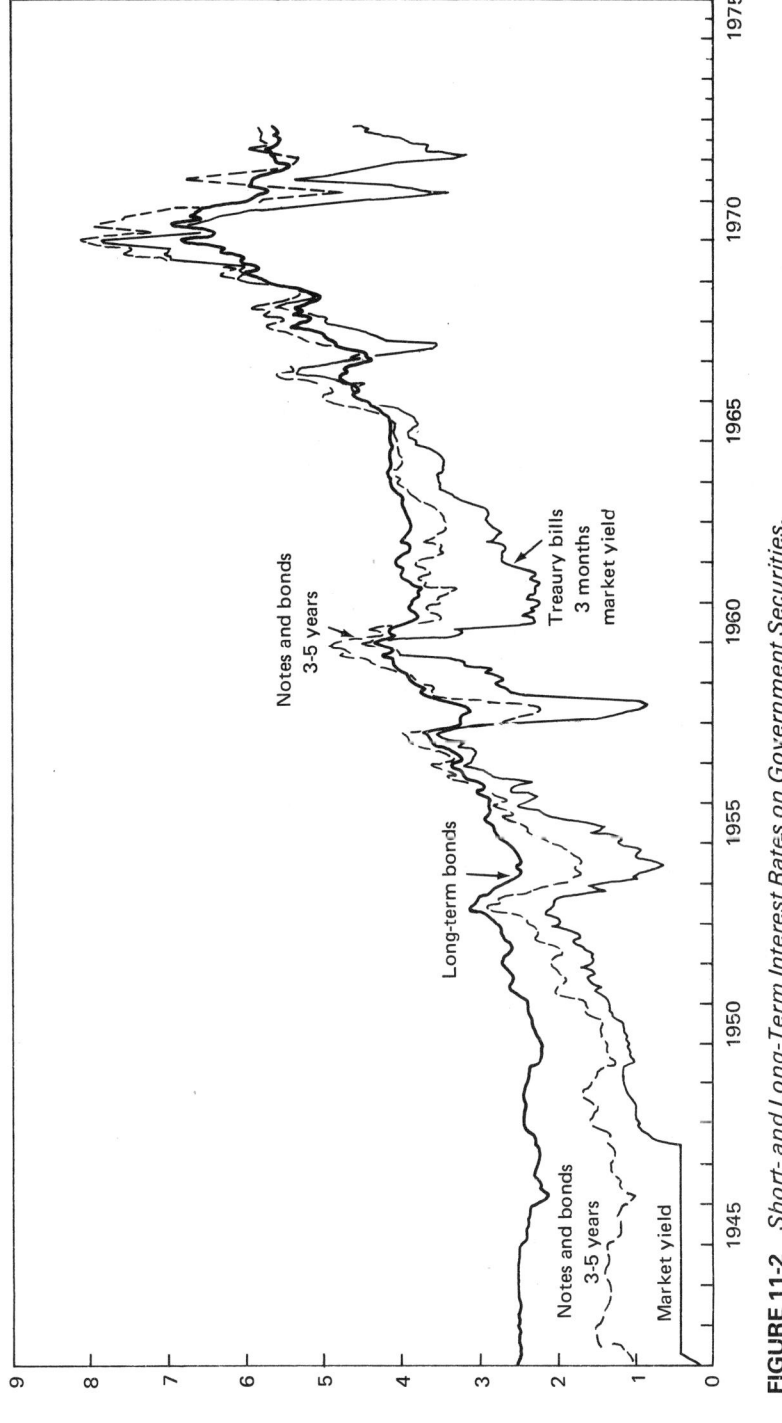

Percent per annum

FIGURE 11-2 *Short- and Long-Term Interest Rates on Government Securities, 1942–73*

Source: Board of Governors of the Federal Reserve System, *Historical Chart Book*, 1973.

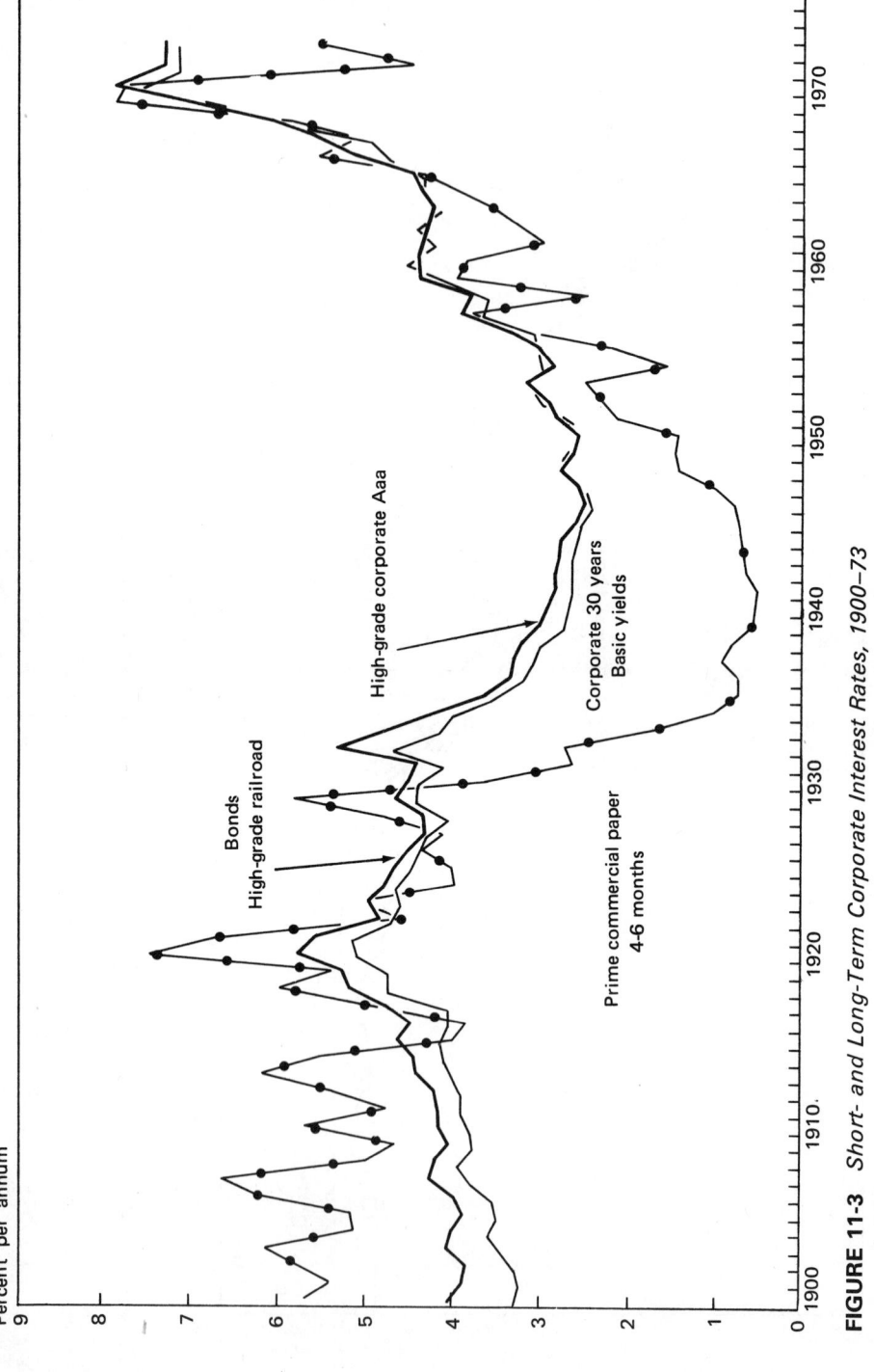

FIGURE 11-3   *Short- and Long-Term Corporate Interest Rates, 1900–73*

Source: Board of Governors of the Federal Reserve System, *Historical Chart Book,* 1973.

short-term interest rates were higher than long-term interest rates. In the period 1940–56, long-term interest rates were consistently higher than short-term interest rates. This relationship also predominated from 1959 to 1965. During these two periods, an upsloping yield curve prevailed, with long-term interest rates higher than short-term rates. This type of yield curve is often referred to as a normal yield curve. In the other periods, such as 1956–59 and 1965–71, the short-term and intermediate-term interest rates were often higher than long-term interest rates. This type of yield curve is often referred to as a humped-back yield curve and is normally associated with high levels of economic activity.

Developing an explanation for the term structure of interest rates involves formulating a rationale for the shape of the yield curve at any point in time. The importance of developing this rationale is that it is generally believed that changes in the supply and demand for funds initially affect short-term interest rates. This effect in turn is imparted to long-term interest rates via the term structure of interest rates. Consequently, the rationale for the term structure of interest rates is quite important.

Just as the relationship of interest rates among federal government securities has varied considerably over time, the relationship between short-term and long-term corporate securities has also varied. These relationships are shown in Figure 11-3, which shows the interest rates for high-quality corporate bonds and four- to six-month prime commercial paper during the period 1900–73. It is clear that during 1900–22 prime commercial paper generally had a higher interest rate than long-term bonds. The explanation appears to be that certain firms and industries tended to rely heavily on commercial paper for financing. For example, the textile industry relied heavily on this form of financing. During the 1920s this form of financing declined in importance, with the result that the interest rates on commercial paper dropped and were generally below those on long-term corporate bonds. This relationship continued until 1965. After 1965 the interest rates on commercial paper rose above those on long-term bonds on several occasions. Consequently, it appears that the relationship between long- and short-term corporate interest rates now parallels that for government bonds.

An additional factor that should be noted is the downward trend in interest rates that began in the 1930s and culminated in the 1950s. Between 1930 and 1952, interest rates were historically low. During the 1930s the explanation was the lack of demand for long-term financing. There was a substantial demand for the high-quality bonds outstanding with the resultant low interest rates. During the period 1940–52, the Treasury wanted to keep the interest cost on its debt to a minimum. This called for the Federal Reserve to stand ready to purchase all government bonds presented to it. This action kept government interest rates low, but it minimized the Federal Reserve's powers to pursue other policies. However, the Accord between the Treasury and the Federal Reserve in April of 1951 meant that the Federal Reserve would not intervene as it had in the past. After 1951 interest rates began to rise to more normal levels.

This review of interest rates indicates that there are three important factors that affect the level of interest rates. First, the quality of a bond will affect its yield, the yield being inversely related to the quality. The determination of the quality of a bond issue was discussed in the previous chapter. Second, the outlook for interest rates is an important consideration in the investment decision. Forecasting interest rates involves an evaluation of all the factors that affect interest rates and therefore is quite involved. Nevertheless, such forecasts can be quite useful in investment management. Third, knowledge of the mechanism for transmitting changes among the interest rates of various maturities, commonly referred to as the term structure of interest rates, will be useful.

Forecasting Interest Rates

There are several different methods of forecasting interest rates. One of the simplest methods is to extrapolate past trends. Extrapolation is a widely used method of forecasting, but it is not particularly useful for forecasting interest rates. Interest rates generally have two components, if not three. They tend to be rather cyclical around a general trend component. When business activity is slow, interest rates tend to be relatively low, but when the economy is operating near capacity, interest rates are relatively high. As a result, interest rates have a cycle that parallels the business cycle. Extrapolating past interest rates into the future, therefore, could lead to major errors.

The long-term trend component in interest rates has been downward from the mid-1920s up to the mid-1950s. In fact, some argue that it has been downward since after the Civil War. However, since the mid-1950s the trend in interest rates has been upward, and in the early 1970s the level of interest rates is unprecedented in the twentieth century. As a result, extrapolation does not appear to be a particularly appropriate method of forecasting interest rates. There are, however, two methods of forecasting interest rates that have been fairly successful. One of these is the flow of funds, and the other is an outgrowth of the development of the complex GNP forecasting models. The flow of funds approach makes use of the flows of funds between suppliers and users to predict the direction of interest rates. The GNP models predict interest rates because these models include a fairly extensive financial sector.

Flow of Funds Forecasts

Conceptually, the flow of funds is a large source and uses of funds statement.[1] The Federal Reserve publishes a flow of funds statement which accounts for the flows of funds among users and suppliers. A summary flow of funds state-

---

[1] Two important works in the use of the flow of funds analysis are William C. Freund, "An Appraisal of the Sources and Uses of Funds Approach to the Analysis of Financial Markets," *Journal of Finance*, vol. 13, no. 2 (May, 1958), pp. 275–94; and William C. Freund and Edward D. Zinbarg, "Application of Flow of Funds to Interest-Rate Forecasting," *Journal of Finance*, vol. 18, no. 2 (May, 1963), pp. 231–48.

ment for 1972 is shown in Table 11-1. This table of sources (S) and uses (U) of funds is available on a quarterly basis, and the data is seasonally adjusted so that normal seasonal aberrations are accounted for in the data. The table shows all sources and all uses of funds by type of supplier or user and by type of security. For example, it is possible to determine what financial institutions supplied mortgage money, what proportion of these funds were used in commercial development, and what proportion in residential development. The same is also true of any other use of funds. The data used in the Federal Reserve's sources and uses of funds may be used to develop a flow of funds statement. However, it should be noted that the data contained in the Federal Reserve's table may be too general for the development of a sources and uses statement such as that illustrated in Table 11-2. For example, the nonbank financial sector may be too broad for practical use. This problem can be solved quite readily since there is sufficient supplementary information available to provide the necessary detail.

The actual construction of a sources and uses statement is shown in Table 11-2. This particular table has been constructed by the Bankers Trust Company and is available at the beginning of the year in the Bankers Trust Company's publication *The Investment Outlook*. In the construction of a sources and uses table, several points must be made. First, only incremental supply and demand are included in the table. That is, only new funds are included in the statements. For example, if a firm refunded a security issue, only the difference between the old and new issue would appear in the statement. Similarly, if a financial institution supplied $10 million in new financing during a particular year, but if $5 million of this was the result of previous loan repayments, only $5 million would be recorded in the statement. As a result, the sources and uses of funds statements represent only net new funds.

Second, intermediate transactions are netted out. In other words, to avoid "double counting," only "final" supply and demand are recorded. This means that the transactions recorded represent a flow of funds exclusive of the intermediate stops in the intermediation process. For example, suppose that an individual deposits a sum of $10,000 in a commercial bank. Suppose the commercial bank uses those funds to make a loan to a business firm. In the sources and uses statement, only the $10,000 loan by the commercial bank would be recorded. Otherwise the $10,000 would be counted twice, and the statements would be misleading.

Forecasting with the flow of funds statements is undertaken by disaggregating the data and forecasting by the type of source and use. The first step normally involves a forecast of the level of business activity because this factor has such an important impact on the level of interest rates. For example, if business activity is sluggish, interest rates may be expected to be relatively low because of the slack demand for funds. On the other hand, if business activity is brisk, interest rates may be expected to be relatively high because of the high demand for funds. The second step normally involves a prediction of the Federal Reserve's monetary policies. Is the Federal Reserve expected to follow a "tight" monetary policy or an "easy" monetary policy? For example, if the

TABLE 11-1   *A Summary of the Flow of Funds for 1972 (Seasonally Adjusted Annual Rates—In billions of dollars)*

Transaction category	Private domestic nonfinancial sectors								Rest of the world		U.S. Govt.	
	House-holds		Busi-ness		State and local govts.		Total					
	U	S	U	S	U	S	U	S	U	S	U	S
1 Gross saving		191.2		102.3		5.9		299.4		8.4		−19.1
2 Capital consumption		105.9		87.6				193.4				
3 Net saving (1 − 2)		85.3		14.8		5.9		105.9		8.4		−19.1
4 Gross investment (5 + 10)	206.4		87.4		−1.8		291.9		11.4		−20.1	
5 Private capital expenditures	157.8		133.3				291.1					
6 Consumer durables	117.4						117.4					
7 Residential construction	34.3		19.3				53.6					
8 Plant and equipment	6.1		108.0				114.0					
9 Inventory change			6.0				6.0					
10 Net financial investment (11 − 12)	48.6		−46.0		−1.8		.8		11.4		−20.1	
11 Financial uses	117.5		33.2		11.0		161.7		19.4		.9	
12 Financial sources		68.9		79.1		12.9		160.9		7.9		21.0
13 Gold, SDR's, and official fgn. exchange									.6	−.2	−.3	
14 Treasury currency and SDR ctfs.												.5
15 Demand deposits and currency	12.8		.2		1.8		14.8		1.5		−1.0	
16 Private domestic	12.8		.2		1.8		14.8					
17 U.S. Government											−1.0	
18 Foreign									1.5			*
19 Time and savings accounts	75.8		3.1		6.8		85.7		2.6		.1	
20 At commercial banks	29.8		3.1		6.8		39.7		2.6		.1	
21 At savings institutions	46.0						46.0					
22 Life insurance reserves	7.3						7.3					.1
23 Pension fund reserves	20.7						20.7					3.2
24 Interbank items												
25 Corporate shares	−5.0			10.4			−5.9	10.4	2.3	−.4		
26 Credit market instruments	8.9	63.2	4.6	59.5	2.0	12.3	15.4	135.0	8.4	3.8	2.3	17.3
27 U.S. Goverment securities	4.4		−2.4		2.1		4.1		8.4		*	17.4
28 State and local obligations	1.3		1.0		−.2	11.9	2.1	11.9				
29 Corporate and foreign bonds	4.9			12.2			4.9	12.2	*	1.0		
30 Home mortgages	−2.2	38.4		1.2	*		−2.2	39.7			−.6	−.1
31 Other mortgages	.2	1.4		26.2			.2	27.6			.4	
32 Consumer credit		19.2	2.6				2.6	19.2				
33 Bank loans n.e.c.		2.9		16.5				19.4	2.4			
34 Other loans	.4	1.3	3.3	3.4		.3	3.7	5.0	−.1	.4	2.6	
35 Security credit	.1	4.7					.1	4.7	.1	.1		
36 To brokers and dealers	.1						.1		.1			
37 To others		4.7						4.7		.1		
38 Taxes payable				.6	.5		.5	.6				.5
39 Trade credit		.5	19.8	13.4		.6	19.8	14.5	.8	.6	−.8	−.1
40 Equity in noncorporate business	−5.0			−5.0			−5.0	−5.0				
41 Miscellaneous claims	2.7	.5	5.6	.2			8.2	.7	3.1	4.0	.1	*
42 Sector discrepancies (1 − 4)	15.2		15.0		7.7		7.4		−3.1		1.0	

Source: *Federal Reserve Bulletin*, September, 1973, p. A 70.

Federal Reserve is expected to follow an "easy" monetary policy, the supply of loanable funds would be expected to increase at a rapid pace. Conversely, if the Federal Reserve is expected to tighten up monetary conditions, then the reduced credit availability must be introduced into the estimates. These two factors, therefore, represent important considerations in the forecasting of the demand for and the supply of funds.

Once these conditions are forecasted, a trial-and-error method may be used to obtain the estimates of the sources and uses of funds. Estimates of the uses of

		Financial sectors												
Total		Sponsored credit agencies		Mone- tary auth.		Coml. banking		Pvt. nonbank finance		*All sectors*		Discrep- ancy	*Natl. savings and invest- ment*	
U	S	U	S	U	S	U	S	U	S	U	S	U		
	9.1		.1		.1		3.7		5.2		297.7		289.3	1
	2.7						1.3		1.4		196.1		196.1	2
	6.4		.1		.1		2.4		3.8		101.5		93.2	3
11.4		.1		.1		5.1		6.0		294.6		3.0	284.3	4
4.6						2.5		2.1		295.7		2.0	295.7	5
										117.4			117.4	6
.4								.4		54.0			54.0	7
4.2						2.5		1.7		118.2			118.2	8
										6.0			6.0	9
6.8		.1		.1		2.6		3.9		−1.1		1.1	−11.4	10
191.4		6.6		2.1		78.3		104.5		373.4		1.1	7.9	11
	184.6		6.5		2.0		75.6		100.6		374.5		19.4	12
−.4				−.4						−.2	−.2			13
.7				.7						.7	.5	−.2		14
1.9	20.4	*			4.0	.2	16.4	1.8		17.2	20.4	3.1		15
1.9	18.4	*			4.4	.2	14.0	1.8		16.7	18.4	1.7		16
	.4				−.3		.7			−1.0	.4	1.4		17
	1.5				−.1		1.6			1.5	1.5			18
.3	88.7						42.3	.3	40.4	88.7	88.7			19
−.1	42.3						42.3	−.1		42.3	42.3			20
.4	46.4							.4	46.4	46.4	46.4			21
	7.2								7.2	7.3	7.3			22
	17.6								17.6	20.7	20.7			23
2.0	2.0			1.6	−1.0	.4	3.0			2.0	2.0			24
15.6	2.0					.1	.5	15.4	1.5	12.0	12.0			25
156.4	20.4	0.0	0.2	.2		69.7	4.3	80.5	15.9	182.5	182.5			26
11.1	6.2	−1.4	6.2	.3		6.5		5.7		23.6	23.6			27
9.8						6.3		3.5		11.9	11.9			28
15.2	6.9					1.7	1.1	13.5	5.8	20.1	20.1			29
43.5	1.2	4.3				9.0		30.2	1.2	40.7	40.7			30
27.6	.5	2.4				7.0		17.4	.5	28.1	28.1			31
16.5						10.1		6.4		19.2	19.2			32
28.5	6.8					28.5	.8		5.9	28.5	28.5			33
4.2	4.9	.8			−.2	−.2	2.4	3.8	2.5	10.4	10.4			34
8.7	4.1					4.8		3.9	4.1	8.9	8.9			35
3.9	4.1					3.9			4.1	4.1	4.1			36
4.8						.8		3.9		4.8	4.8			37
	.1				*		−.2		.3	1.0	.7	−.3		38
.3									.3	20.0	14.9	−5.1		39
										−5.0	−5.0			40
6.0	16.2	.6	.3		−1.0	3.1	9.3	2.3	7.6	17.5	20.9	3.5		41
−2.3		−.1				−1.5		−.8		3.0		3.0	5.1	42

funds will depend to some extent upon the forecast of business activity. For example, if the economy is expanding rapidly and capital expenditures are expected to be high, the analyst will need to forecast the impact on new bond issues. The resulting forecast will be based on these expectations. This procedure is followed for each use. Predicting the sources begins with a prediction of the Federal Reserve's monetary policies. Once this assumption is made, the impact of these conditions is combined with the expected level of business activity to make a forecast for each source of funds.

TABLE 11-2   Sources and Uses of Funds Forecast for the Period 1965–74 (In billions of dollars)

	1965	1966	1967	1968	1969	1970	1971	1972 (est.)	1973 (proj.)
USES (FUNDS RAISED)									
Investment funds	44.3	42.2	52.3	55.5	59.0	69.7	104.1	109.9	107.0
Short-term funds	22.7	21.6	18.0	31.3	35.9	21.4	23.0	46.0	48.8
U.S. Government and budget agency securities, privately held	−1.9	.4	7.7	8.7	−8.8	6.9	16.7	15.5	12.3
Total uses	65.1	64.2	78.0	95.5	86.1	98.0	143.8	171.4	168.1
SOURCES (FUNDS SUPPLIED)									
Contractual-type savings institutions									
Life insurance companies	8.3	8.1	8.5	8.7	8.7	9.0	11.9	12.9	14.0
Private noninsured pension funds	5.2	5.9	5.5	6.0	6.3	6.9	7.3	6.6	7.0
State and local government retirement funds	3.3	3.7	3.6	4.5	5.1	6.4	6.9	7.6	8.6
Fire and casualty insurance companies	1.4	2.2	2.2	2.5	2.3	4.0	6.2	6.2	5.9
Total	18.2	19.8	19.8	21.7	22.3	26.3	32.3	33.3	35.5
Deposit-type savings institutions									
Savings and loan associations	9.6	4.2	9.3	10.2	9.5	11.5	28.3	36.1	30.6
Mutual savings banks	3.9	2.6	5.2	4.4	2.7	3.9	9.3	10.0	9.1
Credit unions	1.1	1.0	.8	1.5	1.8	1.6	2.5	3.1	2.9
Total	14.6	7.8	15.2	16.0	14.1	17.1	40.2	49.2	42.6
Mutual funds	1.9	2.5	1.0	2.4	3.4	1.6	−.1	−1.9	.3
Total savings institutions	34.7	30.1	36.0	40.2	39.8	45.1	72.4	80.6	78.4

Commercial banks	26.6	19.0	39.0	37.9	15.8	33.1	48.7	64.5	58.5
Nonfinancial corporations	2.0	-.1	3.2	9.7	5.0	1.7	7.1	6.2	8.8
Financial corporations	5.1	2.4	.6	5.3	8.4	3.7	5.7	8.6	9.0
Government									
U.S. Government	.2	1.4	1.1	1.4	1.4	.4	.7	.3	.4
Non-budget agencies	1.5	3.9	2.5	2.3	4.7	8.3	3.2	4.5	4.3
State and local general funds	2.3	1.4	.7	1.9	2.9	.2	.7	5.5	7.0
Federal Reserve banks	.1	—	—	-.1	—	—	.2	-.2	—
Total	4.1	6.7	4.3	5.5	9.0	8.9	4.8	10.1	11.7
Other investor groups									
Noncorporate business	.4	.5	.4	.5	.5	.6	.6	.6	.5
Foreign investors	.3	-2.0	2.0	1.5	.1	11.0	27.1	10.2	7.7
Total	.7	-1.5	2.4	2.0	.6	11.6	27.7	10.8	8.2
Residual: Individuals and others	-2.6	15.5	-4.9	1.6	29.5	4.2	-15.6	1.0	4.7
Total gross sources	70.7	72.1	80.7	102.3	108.0	108.2	150.8	181.8	179.3
Less: Funds raised by financial intermediaries									
Investment funds	2.6	.9	1.3	1.1	2.6	3.6	5.9	5.9	4.5
Short-term funds	1.0	3.4	1.8	2.5	9.0	-1.7	.5	1.6	2.4
Non-budget agency securities, privately held	2.0	3.6	-.5	3.1	10.4	8.3	.6	2.9	4.3
Total	5.6	7.9	2.6	6.7	22.0	10.2	7.0	10.4	11.2
Total net sources	65.1	64.2	78.0	95.5	86.1	98.0	143.8	171.4	168.1

Source: Bankers Trust Company, *The Investment Outlook*, 1973, p. 11.

After all the individual sources and uses of funds have been predicted, the total sources and uses must be compared. Total sources of funds must equal total uses of funds; on the first round of estimation, however, it is unlikely that they will be in balance. At this point the analyst must decide what to do to bring about equilibrium. For example, if the uses of funds exceed the sources of funds, the analyst may decide that equilibrium will result because interest rates will be forced up. By this trial-and-error procedure, the analyst can arrive at an equilibrium between the sources and uses. In addition, this procedure also gives the analyst a "feel" for the pressures that might exist in the capital markets.

In predicting interest rates by means of the flow of funds approach, the first consideration is the current level of interest rates. In general, the analyst is attempting to predict the short-term direction of interest rates, and this may be accomplished simply by experience. An alternative approach that has been particularly useful is to focus on the *Residual, individuals and others* line, which represents the funds supplied by individuals, foreign investors, and various forms of nonfinancial organizations. This category appears to be very interest-sensitive; consequently, focusing on this category gives an indication of the direction of interest rates. For example, if the demand for funds exceeds the sources, the interest rates must rise to draw out the additional funds necessary to meet the demand. This line on the sources and uses table thus can be very useful. To illustrate, in Table 11-2 the *Residual* line was very large in the years 1966 and 1969, and was fairly large in 1970. Each of these years was subject to substantial upward pressure on interest rates.

One problem in the construction of the sources and uses table that causes a great deal of consternation is the interrelationship between interest rates, on the one hand, and the supply and demand for funds, on the other. For example, neo-Keynesian economic theory places a great deal of emphasis on interest rates as a determinant of the level of capital investment. As a result, the level of interest rates is believed to affect the level of investment, which in turn affects the demand for funds. This circularity is a problem, but it may be overcome by the successive approximations of the trial-and-error method.

GNP Forecasting Models

It is beyond the scope of this text to provide an extensive discussion of large GNP forecasting models. There are currently a number of these in operation. One of the better known is the Brookings–Social Science Research model; others are the Federal Reserve Board–MIT model, the University of Michigan model, the University of Pennsylvania model, and the Duke University model. All these models are divided into the real and financial sectors. The real sector represents the production of goods and services of the nation, while the financial sector represents the exchange of financial assets.

The particular model presented here to illustrate the use of these GNP fore-casting models to forecast interest rates is the Federal Reserve–MIT model.[2] This model is designed to quantify the impact of monetary policy. Like all these GNP forecasting models, the model is developed into major segments, or blocks. This model is comprised of three large blocks: (1) a financial block, (2) an investment block, and (3) a consumption-inventory block. No effort will be made to discuss the makeup of any of these segments, but the financial segment is particularly useful to anyone interested in forecasting interest rates.

Tables 11-3 and 11-4 illustrate the type of information available from the financial block of this model. The monetary statistics shown in the bottom portion of Table 11-3 may not be of interest to the average investor, but the interest rates are of particular interest. This is especially true because both short-term and long-term interest rates are forecasted. As a result, not only is there a forecast of the general direction of interest rates, but the term structure of interest rates is also predicted. In addition, it appears that the predictions were fairly accurate for the seven quarters beginning in the third quarter of 1965. Table 11-4 shows the predictions of the entire model for the six quarters begin-

TABLE 11-3 *Predictions of the Financial Block*

Item	1965		1966				1967
	QIII	QIV	QI	QII	QIII	QIV	QI
	(In percent)						
Treasury bill rate:							
Actual	3.86	4.16	4.60	4.58	5.03	5.20	4.52
Predicted	3.40	4.24	4.51	4.98	5.21	5.13	4.48
Corporate Aaa bond rate:							
Actual	4.50	4.61	4.81	5.00	5.32	5.38	5.12
Predicted	4.60	4.82	5.02	5.20	5.35	5.42	5.35
Mortgage Rate:							
Actual	5.76	5.78	5.85	6.03	6.17	6.39	6.34
Predicted	5.74	5.82	5.97	6.14	6.30	6.42	6.46
	(In billions of dollars)						
Demand deposits:							
Actual	128.9	131.1	133.3	132.8	132.2	131.6	133.5
Predicted	129.3	131.0	132.1	132.6	133.0	134.1	135.8
Time deposits							
Actual	142.6	147.5	150.5	155.5	158.1	160.4	167.4
Predicted	141.7	145.8	140.2	143.7	156.9	160.4	164.7
Free reserves:							
Actual	−0.15	−0.02	−0.26	−0.36	−0.40	−0.09	+0.21
Predicted	−0.17	+0.04	−0.10	−0.27	−0.46	−0.40	+0.02

Source: de Leeuw and Gramlich, op. cit., p. 15.

[2] The discussion that follows draws heavily on the discussion of this model by Frank de Leeuw and Edward Gramlich, "The Federal Reserve–MIT Econometric Model," *Federal Reserve Bulletin,* vol. 54, no. 1 (Jan., 1968), pp. 11–41.

TABLE 11-4   *Predictions of the Three Major Blocks of the Federal Reserve Board–MIT Model*

Item	1965 QIII	1965 QIV	1966 QI	1966 QII	1966 QIII	1966 QIV
	(In billions of dollars)					
GNP level:						
Actual	690.0	708.4	725.9	736.7	748.8	762.1
Calculated	690.7	709.4	725.4	736.1	745.6	753.1
GHP changes:						
Actual	14.6	18.4	17.5	10.8	12.1	13.3
Calculated	15.3	18.7	16.0	10.7	9.5	7.4
Consumer expenditures:						
Actual	436.4	447.8	458.2	461.6	470.1	473.8
Calculated	441.1	450.3	460.1	466.7	473.8	479.7
Residential construction:						
Actual	26.4	26.2	26.5	25.3	23.2	20.4
Calculated	26.6	26.3	25.7	25.1	24.2	23.3
Producers' equipment and nonresidential structures:						
Actual	71.9	75.8	78.3	78.7	81.3	82.8
Calculated	71.2	74.2	76.3	77.1	76.9	76.4
Inventory investment:						
Actual	7.9	8.7	9.6	14.4	12.0	19.0
Calculated	5.4	9.8	10.4	10.6	7.0	6.6
Demand deposits:						
Actual	128.9	131.1	133.3	132.8	132.2	131.6
Calculated	129.1	130.8	132.2	132.3	132.5	132.8
	(In percent)					
Corporate bond yield:						
Actual	4.50	4.61	4.81	5.00	5.32	5.38
Calculated	4.65	4.84	4.95	5.29	5.39	5.51
Treasury bill rate:						
Actual	3.86	4.16	4.60	4.58	5.03	5.20
Calculated	3.60	4.26	4.22	5.42	5.16	5.47

Source: de Leeuw and Gramlich, op. cit., p. 26.

ning in the third quarter of 1965. These predictions are for the major blocks of the model.

It is clear from even this brief discussion of GNP forecasting models that they offer a great potential for anyone interested in the direction of interest rates. Not only do these models forecast the direction of interest rates, which is essentially all the flow of funds forecasts do, but they also give an actual estimate of long-term and short-term interest rates. This capacity enables the potential investor to evaluate a little more precisely the pressures in the money and bond markets. As a result, these models give an indication of not only the direction but also the magnitudes of changes over some time horizon.

Term Structure of Interest Rates

The term structure of interest rates refers to the relationship of interest rates for bonds of different maturities. As noted earlier in this chapter, there have been occasions when short-term interest rates have been higher than long-term rates, lower than long-term rates, and equal to long-term rates. It is common to note two relationships that are commonly referred to as the normal yield curve and the humped-back yield curve. These two yield curves are illustrated in Figure 11-4. The humped-back yield curve reaches a maximum in the intermediate-term range, normally around three to five years, and this type of yield curve is normally associated with periods of economic strain, such as that which occurs during a period of economic expansion. The Federal Reserve attempts to slow the boom period and the resultant inflationary pressures by restricting the flow of short-term credit, thus forcing these short-term rates, and all rates to some extent, upwards. The normal yield curve has come to be associated with more normal times in which longer-term rates are higher than short-term rates.

FIGURE 11-4 *Normal and Humped-Back Yield Curves*

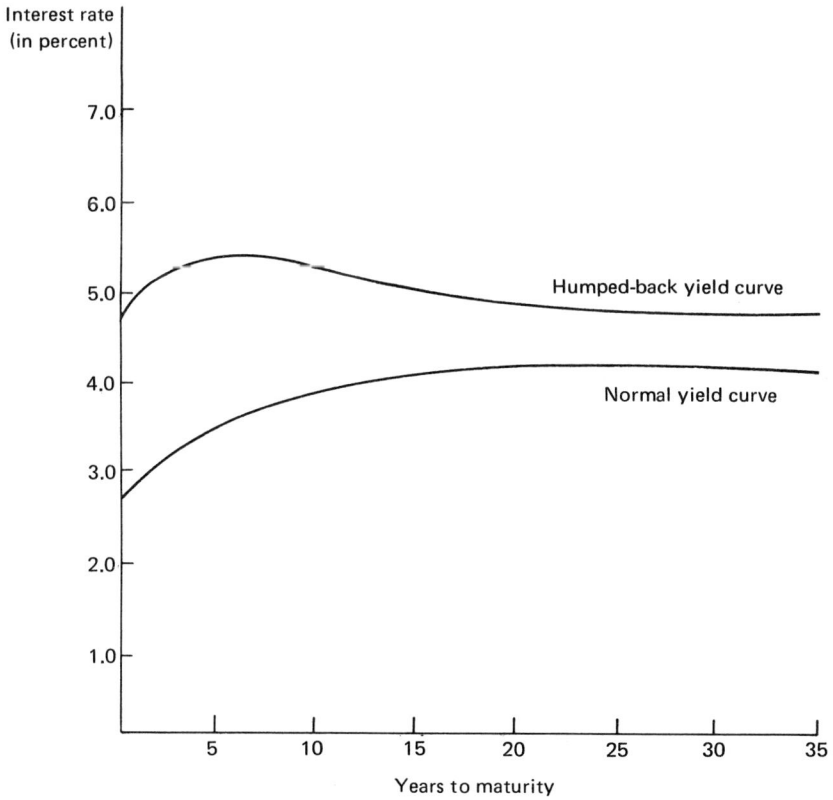

Explaining the term structure of interest rates is important because changes in the underlying economic conditions are believed to be reflected first in short-term interest rates and then transmitted to long-term rates via the term structure. Several explanations have been advanced, with the result that there has been some debate about the nature of the term structure of interest rates. The three common explanations are the expectations hypothesis, the liquidity-preference hypothesis, and the segmented markets hypothesis.

Expectations Hypothesis

The expectations hypothesis is formulated on the premise that the term structure of interest rates reflects investors' expectations of future short-term rates. In other words, the shape of the yield curve at a particular point in time reflects the level of short-term interest rates that is anticipated for the future. For example, if the yield curve is upsloping, short-term interest rates will be expected to rise. If the yield curve is downsloping, short-term rates will be expected to fall.

The derivation of this hypothesis involves the following simplifying assumptions about the environment in which decisions affecting interest rates are made:

1. Investors are profit maximizers.
2. There are no transactions costs.
3. All securities are riskless with respect to default on principal and interest.
4. Investors have uniformly accurate short-term forecasts.

Given this set of assumptions, the yield curve could conceivably represent the expectations of investors. That is, with uniformly accurate short-term forecasts, arbitrage would occur whenever an interest rate for a particular maturity got out of line. For example, consider a flat yield curve in which all maturities yielded 4 percent, except the five-year maturity, which yielded 6 percent. This situation could not prevail because arbitragers would be able to sell other maturities, forcing their yield up, and buy the five-year maturity, forcing its yield down. The net effect would be an equilibrium interest rate for all maturities. Moreover, the absence of transactions costs would make this a costless operation.

The net effect would be that an investor would be indifferent to holding short-term or long-term bonds, since his yield would be the same irrespective of the maturities held. To illustrate this, consider the following interest rates for one-, two-, and three-year maturities.

Maturity	Interest Yield
1-year	4 percent
2-year	6
3-year	7

This term structure indicates that the one-year rate is 4 percent and the two-year rate is 6 percent, but it also indicates that the one-year rate one year from now will be substantially above today's rate. The one-year rate one year from now will be

$$(1.06)^2 = (1.04)\,(1.0 + i)$$

$$(1.0 + i) = (1.06)^2/(1.04)$$

$$= 1.08$$

Thus, the one-year rate one year from now is expected to be approximately 8 percent, and investors who bought successive one-year securities would receive 4 percent in the first year and 8 percent in the second year for an average of 6 percent. This return is identical to the 6 percent that could be earned by purchasing a two-year maturity.

From this example it is clear that long-term interest rates are simply a geometric mean of the current rate and the short-term interest rates that are expected to exist in subsequent periods. For example, suppose we are concerned with the interest rate on 20-year bonds. The prevailing yield on these bonds would be a geometric mean of the current short-term rate and all intervening short-term rates. This implies that the length to maturity in itself will not affect the interest rate on a bond. This conclusion is markedly different than that drawn by the liquidity-preference hypothesis discussed subsequently, and it follows from the initial assumptions.

With these rather idealized assumptions, it may be assumed that the expectations hypothesis will not provide a realistic explanation of the term structure under conditions of uncertainty, but expectations may be a major factor if investors treat long-term and short-term instruments as perfect substitutes. Under these circumstances the apparent violations of the assumptions may not be as serious as might be supposed. This is an empirical question, however, and the discussion of the empirical findings will not be presented until after the discussion of the liquidity-preference hypothesis and the segmented markets hypothesis.

Liquidity-Preference Hypothesis

A criticism of the expectations hypothesis is that its assumptions violate real world conditions; in particular, the assumption of perfect foresight means that the expectations hypothesis is not a realistic explanation. Under conditions of uncertainty, it is argued that short-term and long-term bonds would not be perfect substitutes. In addition, the other factors that were assumed away in the expectations hypothesis may affect the yield curve under conditions of uncertainty. For example, the introduction of transactions costs may affect the arbitrage mechanism that would tend to equalize long-term and short-term rates. The liquidity-preference hypothesis, however, does not argue that expectations are unimportant; it holds that expectations are an important determinant of the term structure. However, it is argued that under conditions of uncertainty there is a tendency to prefer short-term bonds to long-term bonds, since investors are risk averse. Long-term bonds would involve more risk because there is a greater uncertainty about interest and principal payments at more distant points in time. As a result, long-term issues would be required to pay a premium because of the illiquidity that would attach to them. On the demand side, the liquidity-preference hypothesis assumes that borrowing firms prefer to use long-term issues to assure themselves of the required funds. As a result, the demand for long-term funds would be such that the liquidity premium would be expected to exist.

The liquidity-preference hypothesis, therefore, assumes an upsloping yield curve similar to the normal yield curve illustrated in Figure 11-4. The higher interest rates on longer maturities would compensate the investor for the lack of liquidity. The liquidity-preference hypothesis is intuitively appealing. Risk premiums for longer maturities appear to be consistent with risk aversion. Empirical evidence seems to support this hypothesis, since the yield curves in the post–World War II period have been upsloping for the most part. However, the liquidity-preference hypothesis cannot explain the existence of the humped-back yield curve that exists at certain times. This inability led to the emergence of the expectations hypothesis and the segmented markets hypothesis.

Segmented Markets Hypothesis

The above discussion of the liquidity-preference hypothesis may lead to the conclusion that investors prefer short-term bonds to long-term bonds. However, long-term bonds have the advantage of generally promising a higher contractual rate of interest than short-term bonds, although there is greater uncertainty connected with prospective interest and principal payments. In addition, long-term bonds do promise a stated interest for a specific number of years, which can be relied upon with some assurance. In contrast, if the investor invested in short-term bonds, there would be greater certainty about the principal value, but the level of income received would vary with short-term interest rates. Therefore, while these short-term instruments do promise greater certainty against impairment of principal, the rate of return will be quite unstable, or uncertain. Long-term bonds, on the other hand, would promise a stable return for the life of the long-term bond. Advocates of the segmented markets hypothesis argue that certain financial institutions, notably life insurance companies, private pension plans, and investment companies, are more concerned with a stable income than a stable principal value.

This preference for long-term bonds by certain financial institutions is the basis for the segmented markets hypothesis. This hypothesis states that the market for securities is highly segmented. The short-term market is purportedly dominated by the industrial corporations and commercial banks. The industrial corporations invest in short-term bonds to earn a return on excess funds that are currently on hand. Because these funds may be needed on short notice by the firm, they must be invested in highly liquid instruments, which are high-quality, short-term instruments, such as Treasury bills, bankers' acceptances, and commercial paper. Commercial banks also invest in short-term bonds to earn a return on funds not currently needed but which may be needed on short notice. Liquidity is the primary objective of these industrial firms and commercial banks. The long-term market, on the other hand, is purportedly dominated by financial institutions, such as life insurance companies, private pension plans, and investment companies, which are more concerned with the stability of income than with the stability of principal. These firms, therefore, acquire long-term bonds without being concerned with the possibility of forced liquidation leading to a capital loss. It is argued, then, that two separate markets exist, and there is little substitution between these markets.

This hypothesis is appealing because it appears to conform closely to what can be observed in the real world. Moreover, the segmented markets hypothesis can explain the existence of the normal yield curve and the humped-back yield curve. The shape of the yield curve simply reflects the supply and demand conditions in the two markets. The flow of funds into the two markets determine the relative demand for long- and short-term bonds. For example, the humped-back yield, curve which exists in periods of restrictive monetary policies and rapid business expansion, may be explained as the result of business firms and commercial banks being net sellers of short-term instruments. Commercial banks may be selling short-term bonds and perhaps intermediate-term bonds to meet increased loan demand and reserve losses, while firms may be selling short-term bonds to meet the increased needs for fixed assets, current assets, and other operating requirements. In more normal times there is less pressure on industrial firms and commercial banks to liquidate their portfolios of short-term bonds. Hence, the normal yield curve prevails during these periods.

In spite of its appeal, the segmented markets hypothesis does not have a wide following. The major criticism of it has resulted from empirical studies that have determined that there is a fair amount of substitution between the short-term and long-term markets. The markets are not as segmented as this hypothesis has envisioned. Leading empirical studies indicate that a combination of the expectations hypothesis and the liquidity-preference hypothesis appears to give the best explanation of the term structure of interest rates.[3]

Summary

The level of interest rates is of major concern to investors because of its impact on all investment decisions. Interest rates represent the return that can be earned on debt instruments, and although it is common to speak of the

[3] Burton Malkiel, *The Term Structure of Interest Rates* (Princeton, N.J.: Princeton University Press, 1966), p. 39.

"interest rate," realistically the investor is faced with a vast array of interest rates. Interest rates tend to vary with the quality of the bond and its length to maturity, as well as other institutional factors. In the post–World War II period, interest rates were at artificially low levels. With the Federal Reserve-Treasury Accord in 1951, interest rates proceeded up to more normal levels by the mid-1960s. However, since the mid-1960s interest rates have proceeded to substantially higher ground as a result of the higher levels of inflation.

The outlook for interest rates can be particularly useful in the selection of bonds. Two methods of forecasting interest rates are the flow of funds and the complex econometric forecasting models, such as the Federal Reserve Board–MIT model. The flow of funds method is a trial-and-error approach that attempts to forecast the sources and uses of funds within the economy. The starting point is a forecast of business activity and the Federal Reserve's monetary policies in the coming year. Once these two forecasts are made, it becomes a matter of balancing the sources and uses of funds, which in turn provides the basis for the subsequent short-run interest-rate forecast. The complex GNP forecasting models can be useful because they make forecasts for the financial sector as well as the real sector, and these forecasts include predictions of short-term and long-term interest rates.

The term structure of interest rates is generally believed to be the mechanism by which changes in interest rates are transmitted. Historically, short-term interest rates have been quite volatile, reflecting the basic supply and demand conditions in the securities markets. The effect of these changes is believed to be transmitted from the short-term interest rates to the long-term interest rates by means of the term structure of interest rates. However, the nature of the interrelationship among interest rates on various maturities has been somewhat controversial. As a result, three theories have been advanced to explain the term structure of interest rates. It appears that the combination of the expectations hypothesis and the liquidity-preference hypothesis has provided the best explanation. The segmented markets hypothesis does not appear to have a wide following. This hypothesis postulates that there is little substitution between the short-term and long-term bond markets. Empirical studies, however, have found that there is more substitution than would be expected by the segmented markets hypothesis.

Questions

1. Both the quality of an instrument and its length to maturity are generally believed to affect its interest yield. Explain.
2. In the period since World War II, short-term interest rates have been higher than long-term rates on several occasions.
   a. What is meant by a normal yield curve?
   b. What is meant by a humped-back yield curve?
   c. What role does the term structure of interest rates play in determining the level of rates?

3. In the flow of funds approach to interest-rates forecasting, it is necessary to forecast business activity and the Federal Reserve's monetary policies.
   a. Why is this necessary?
   b. Once these forecasts are made, how is the direction of interest rates forecast?
4. The large GNP forecasting models have a real sector and financial sector. What is meant by this?
5. After reviewing the flow of funds method and the GNP forecasting model, which method do you prefer in the forecasting of interest rates?
6. The expectations hypothesis has recently emerged as a leading explanation of the term structure of interest rates.
   a. What assumptions are made in developing the hypothesis?
   b. Given the following interest rates, are short-term interest rates expected to rise or fall?

Maturity	Interest Yield
1-year	7.5 percent
2-year	7.0
3-year	6.0

   c. What will be the one-year rate one year from now?
7. Both the liquidity-preference hypothesis and the segmented markets hypothesis differ somewhat from the expectations hypothesis.
   a. Explain the major differences.
   b. What is the major weakness of the liquidity preference hypothesis?
   c. What is the major weakness of the segmented markets hypothesis?
   d. Which hypothesis appears to be the most appropriate in explaining the term structure? Why?

Selected References

Culbertson, John M. "The Term Structure of Interest Rates." *Quarterly Journal of Economics,* vol. 71, no. 4 (Nov., 1957), pp. 485–518.

Dauten, Carl A., and Lloyd M. Valentine. *Business Cycles and Forecasting,* 3d ed., Cincinnati; South-Western, 1968. Chapter 9.

de Leeuw, Frank, and Edward Gramlich. "The Federal Reserve MIT–Econometric Model." *Federal Reserve Bulletin,* vol. 54, no. 1 (Jan., 1968), pp. 11–41.

Durand, David. *Basic Yields of Corporate Bonds, 1900–42.* Technical Paper No. 3. New York: National Bureau of Economic Research, 1942.

Fisher, Lawrence. "Determinants of Risk Premiums on Corporate Bonds." *Journal of Political Economy,* vol. 67, no. 3 (June, 1967), pp. 217–38.

Fisher, Lawrence, and Roman L. Weil. "Coping with the Risk of Interest-Rate Fluctuations: Return to Bondholders from Naive and Optimal Strategies." *Journal of Business,* vol. 44, no. 4 (Oct., 1971), pp. 408–32.

Fraser, William J. *The Demand for Money.* New York: World, 1967. Chapter 4.

Friedman, Milton. "Factors Affecting the Level of Interest Rates." *Proceedings of the Conference on Savings and Residential Financing.* U.S. Savings and Loan League, 1968, pp. 11-27.

————. *A Theoretical Framework for Monetary Analysis*. Occasional Paper no. 112. New York: National Bureau of Economic Research, 1971.

Friedman, Milton, and Anna Jacobson Schwartz. *Monetary Statistics of the United States: Estimates, Sources, Methods*. New York: National Bureau of Economic Research, 1970.

Freund, William C. "An Appraisal of the Sources and Uses of Funds Approach to the Analysis of Financial Markets." *Journal of Finance*, vol. 13, no. 2 (May, 1958), pp. 275–94.

Freund, William C., and Edward D. Zinbarg. "Application of Flow of Funds to Interest-Rate Forecasting." *Journal of Finance*, vol. 18, no. 2 (May, 1963), pp. 231–48.

Gibson, William E. "Price Expectations Effects on Interest Rates." *Journal of Finance*, vol. 25, no. 1 (Mar., 1970), pp. 19–35.

Granger, C.W.J., and H.J.B. Rees. "Spectral Analysis of the Term Structure of Interest Rates." *Review of Economic Studies*, vol. 25, no. 101 (Jan., 1968), pp. 66–77.

Hendershott, Patrick H. "Recent Developments of the Financial Sector of Econometric Models." *Journal of Finance*, vol. 23, no. 1 (Mar., 1968), pp. 41–67.

Homer, Sidney. *A History of Interest Rates*. New Brunswick, N.J.: Rutgers University Press, 1963.

Keran, Michael W. "Expectations, Money, and the Stock Market." *Review—Federal Reserve Bank of St. Louis*, vol. 57, no. 1 (Jan., 1971), pp. 16–31.

————. "A Structural Model of the Stock Market." *Business Economics*, vol. 6, no. 4 (Sept., 1971), pp. 23–29.

Latane, Henry A. "Cash Balances and the Interest Rate—A Pragmatic Approach." *Review of Economics and Statistics*, vol. 36, no. 4 (Nov., 1954), pp. 456–61.

————. "Income Velocity and Interest Rates: A Pragmatic Approach." *Review of Economics and Statistics*, vol. 42, no. 4 (Nov., 1960), pp. 445–50.

Malkiel, Burton G. *The Term Structure of Interest Rates*. Princeton, N.J.: Princeton University Press, 1966.

Meisel, David. *The Term Structure of Interest Rates*. Englewood Cliffs, N.J.: Prentice Hall, 1962.

Mellon, Giles W. "Financial Econometric Model Building." In *Financial Institutions and Markets*, ed. Murray F. Polakoff, pp. 485–96. Boston: Houghton Mifflin, 1970.

Renwick, Fred B. Introduction to Investments and Finance: Theory and Analysis. New York: Macmillan, 1971. Chapter 9.

Shapiro, Eli, Ezra Solomon, and William L. White. *Money and Banking*, 5th ed. New York: Holt, Rinehart & Winston, 1968. Chapter 21.

Sprinkel, Beryl Wayne. *Money and Markets: A Monetarist View*. Homewood, Ill.: Richard D. Irwin, 1971. Chapter 8.

Suits, Daniel B. "Forecasting and Analysis with an Econometric Model." *American Economic Review*, vol. 52, no. 1 (Mar., 1962), pp. 104–33.

Zarnowitz, Victor. *An Appraisal of Short-Term Economic Forecasts*. New York: National Bureau of Economic Research, 1967.

Chapter 12

Convertible Securities and Warrants

In Chapters 10 and 11, the focus was on the evaluation of nonconvertible bonds or, as they are sometimes referred to, straight bonds. However, some bonds have speculative features in the form of a conversion feature or the attachment of warrants. These features enhance the marketability of these bonds, but they also mean that additional analysis is required. Convertible bonds and preferred stocks permit the holder to convert into common stock according to a stated formula. Hence, analysis of these securities involves combining bond analysis and common stock analysis in order to evaluate their investment merits. In this sense the analysis of convertible securities acts as a capstone for bond and common stock analysis. Warrants, on the other hand, are options to purchase common stock at a specified price. The specified price is normally substantially above the market price of the common stock at the time the warrants are issued. These securities are highly speculative, because the purchaser is speculating on the possibility that the price of the common stock will rise above the option price. Once this point is reached, the warrant will have a definite value, that is, the difference between the option price and the market price of the common stock.

Convertible securities and warrants derive their value, at least to a certain extent, from the underlying common stock, yet the nature of these securities is very different. Convertible securities are considered to be conservative investments, since they normally do not have as much risk as common stock. This results because convertible securities promise to pay a stated interest, or dividends, and convertible bonds promise to repay principal upon maturity. In this sense they are fixed-income securities. Warrants, on the other hand, are highly speculative because of the uncertainty that the price of the common stock will rise above the option price within a certain time period.

Convertible Securities in Perspective

Convertible securities have a long history of usage in the form of both convertible debentures and convertible preferred stock. The data that will be presented in this section will focus on the more recent experience, but convertible securities have been in use for most of the twentieth century. The focus will be on two factors. One is the extent of use of convertible securities, particularly convertible debentures in the latter part of the 1960s and early 1970s. This will provide some perspective on their historical use and may provide some insight into their future use. The other factor is quality. As will be shown, most convertible debentures are not investment-grade securities. This aspect of convertible debentures is an important factor in the investment decision.

Table 12-1 shows the market value of convertible debentures offerings, total corporate bond offerings, and the proportion of convertible debenture offerings to corporate bond offerings for the period 1960–73. The use of convertible and nonconvertible bonds by corporations has increased significantly. The increased use of debt reflects the tendency of firms to use relatively more debt financing in recent years. It appears, however, that the use of convertible debentures has varied from year to year. During the period 1960–66, convertible debentures were a relatively unimportant form of financing. However, the period 1966–70 witnessed an abrupt reversal. During 1967–70 in particular, the offerings of convertible debentures reached approximately 20 percent of the total bond offerings. The use of convertible bonds and debentures increased by approximately three times during this period. In the early 1970s, convertible debenture offerings declined to much lower levels, but not to the levels of 1960–66. It appears that during the period 1967–70, financing with convertible debentures reached its peak.

TABLE 12-1 *Convertible Bond Issues During 1960–73*

Year	Market value of convertible bond issues (in $ millions)	Market value of corporate bond issues (in $ millions)	Convertible bonds as a percent of corporate bond issues
1960	462	8,081	5.7
1961	710	9,420	7.5
1962	445	8,969	5.0
1963	357	10,856	3.3
1964	425	10,865	3.9
1965	1,264	13,720	9.2
1966	1,872	15,561	12.0
1967	4,475	21,954	20.4
1968	3,281	17,383	18.9
1969	4,041	18,348	22.0
1970	2,656	30,315	8.8
1971	3,644	32,129	11.3
1972	2,286	28,896	7.9

Source: Compiled from the SEC's *Statistical Bulletin,* vol. 32, no. 11, p. 379, and the *Survey of Current Business.*

The reasons for the sharp increase in the years 1966–70 are unclear, but there are three possible reasons. First, it is clear that the demand for debt financing increased markedly, and interest rates increased sharply during the period after 1965, which may have led firms to include the conversion feature as a means of reducing the interest cost. An important advantage of convertible debentures to the issuing firm is the reduced interest that must be paid compared to a straight-debt issuance. A second reason may have been that firms felt that their common shares were selling at unrealistically low prices, and therefore they did not want to sell common stock directly. However, this explanation seems unlikely, since stock prices were historically high during this period. Finally, there may have been an unusually strong demand for these securities resulting from the rising level of inflation. Since convertible debentures offer potential appreciation, they may be viewed as a means to hedge against inflation. This fact may be important in explaining their relative popularity in the late 1960s.

Another important facet of convertible debentures is the quality of these issues. They have a fixed claim on the income of the firm; if the firm cannot meet the interest payments, this failure can bring about involuntary bankruptcy. As a result, the holder of a debenture wants to be assured of the firm's ability to meet interest and principal payments. The quality of the issue is thus important. A more general consideration is reflected by a study by Robert M. Soldofsky, indicating that investors have experienced a combination of low yield and high risk.[1] Specifically, this study found that the yield on convertible debentures and preferred stock was about the same as that for nonconvertible debentures and preferred stocks. If this situation persists, the amount of risk associated with convertible debentures is particularly important.

The data in Table 12-2 gives the quality ratings for a sample of industrial convertible debentures reported in *Moody's Industrial Manual*. This sample presumably represents all the convertible debentures of firms Moody's report on in their industrial manuals. It is clear from this sample that convertible

TABLE 12-2 *Quality Ratings of Selected Industrial Convertible Bonds Outstanding at the End of 1972*

Ranking category	Number	Percentage
Aaa	0	0.0
Aa	2	0.5
A	4	1.0
Baa	40	10.5
Ba	192	50.3
B	140	36.6
Caa and below	4	1.1
Total	382	100.0

Source: Compiled from *Moody's Industrial Manual,* 1973, vol. 1, pp. a202–a207.

[1] Robert M. Soldofsky, "Yield-Risk Performance of Convertible Securities," *Financial Analysts Journal,* vol. 27, no. 2 (Mar.–Apr., 1971), p. 79.

debentures for the most part are not of investment quality. Only 12 percent of the sample was in the first four rating categories, and the majority of these were in the Baa category. On the other hand, about 87 percent were in the Ba and B rating categories, and about 1 percent were in the Caa rating categories or below. It appears, therefore, that the average convertible debenture is not of particularly good quality.

The importance of this finding will become clearer as the discussion progresses, but several implications may be pointed out briefly. First, it is clear that most of these firms are quite risky which raises some question about their prospects. Second, the downside protection provided by the straight-debt value of the issue, which will be discussed in more detail later, may not be as important a protection as one may be led to believe. Finally, a general consideration that emerges is that convertible debentures must be scrutinized very closely to make certain that the prospective return compensates for the risk involved. If indeed convertible securities promise a return that is little different from that of nonconvertible securities, there is little advantage in considering these securities as prospective investment candidates.

The use of preferred stock, whether convertible or nonconvertible, has not been as prevalent as bonds. For example, in 1972 new preferred stock issues constituted about 8 percent of total corporate financing, while common stock constituted about 23 percent, and bonds about 69 percent. Furthermore, during the period 1950–66, the number of preferred stock issues listed on the New York Stock Exchange declined from 433 issues to 373. The number of issues has subsequently increased to 525. This increase is largely the result of the use of convertible preferred stocks to finance mergers and acquisitions. Convertible preferred stocks have certain characteristics that are particularly amenable to the financing of mergers and acquisitions.[2] The reasons for the use of convertible preferred stocks in corporate financing are thus different from the reasons for using convertible bonds. Since preferred stocks are not a popular financing device and convertible preferred stock is used largely in mergers and acquisitions, the following discussion will focus on convertible debentures. Basically, the principles that apply to convertible bonds will also apply to convertible preferred stock. Where significant differences do exist, they will be noted.

Features of Convertible Securities

Convertible securities are normally viewed as hedge securities because they combine the features of bonds and common stock. In this sense these securities may be viewed as having the advantages of bonds and common stocks combined. On the one hand, convertible securities can appreciate in value as the underlying common stock appreciates. On the other hand, convertible securities promise a fixed interest income until they are converted or until they

[2] For a discussion of these factors, see C. Ronald Sprecher, "A Note on Financing Mergers with Convertible Preferred Stock," *Journal of Finance*, vol. 26, no. 3 (June, 1971), pp. 683–87.

mature. Therefore, they have the potential safety commonly associated with fixed-income securities. Since convertible securities have the attributes of both common stocks and bonds, the value of these attributes must be evaluated before determining their investment worth. For example, consider Occidental Petroleum's 7½s due in 1996, which are convertible into common stock at $20 per share. These convertible debentures offer an interest income of $75 per bond plus the opportunity to share in any appreciation that may occur. The immediate question is whether these securities are a worthwhile investment. If the investor is really interested in common stock investment, why not invest directly in the common stock?

The problem of evaluating convertible securities is further complicated by the fact that the market price of the convertibles normally includes a premium. This premium simply means that the current market price is greater than either the conversion value of the convertible or its straight-debt value. Consequently, the size of the premium must be incorporated into the analysis. In the following discussion, the focus will be on the straight-debt value and the conversion value of the convertible security. These will be used to lay the groundwork for evaluating convertible securities. However, before this analysis is undertaken, the discussion will return to the premium that normally exists and its causes.

Conversion Feature

The conversion feature simply provides for the conversion of the security into common stock. This feature may be stated as either a conversion ratio or a conversion price. A conversion ratio indicates how many shares of stock can be obtained for each bond or preferred stock. For convertible debentures, the conversion ratio is based upon the number of shares that can be obtained for each $1,000 of face value. For example, if a corporation's debenture 4¾s due in 1996 have a conversion ratio of 40, this means that each debenture can be converted into 40 shares. For convertible preferreds the conversion ratio has the same meaning, but since preferred stock has a lower par value than debentures, a preferred stock may be convertible into one or two shares of stock. For convertible debentures, the conversion ratio can be easily transformed into a conversion price by dividing the face value by the conversion ratio. For example, a corporation's debenture 4¾s have a conversion price of $1,000 ÷ 40 = $25 per share. The conversion price has little meaning to the investor except in determining the conversion ratio. Generally, the more important consideration is the effective price that is being paid for the stock. However, the terms of many convertible debentures are stated as a conversion price, which means it must be used to obtain a conversion ratio. This is accomplished by dividing the face value of the convertible debenture by the conversion price.

Determining the conversion value of a security involves multiplying the current market price of the stock by the conversion ratio. For example, suppose a corporation's debenture 6s were convertible into 40 shares of common stock that is currently selling at $27 per share. The conversion value would be $1,080 (40 × $27). That is, if the holder of this security decided to convert immediately, the value of the common stock received would by $1,080. However, this convertible debenture probably would be selling at a higher price than $1,080. For example, it may be selling at $1,150. The difference of $70 represents the premium of the market price over the conversion value. For an investor contemplating the purchase of this convertible debenture, the effective price paid for this stock would be $28.75 per share. Consequently, the existence of the premium affects the return that may be earned on the convertible security.

Conversion features vary from issue to issue, but it is fairly common to include an acceleration clause that reduces the conversion ratio. For example, the conversion ratio may be set at 40 for a particular issue for the first five years the issue is outstanding and then decrease to 35 shares for the next five years. The effect of such a clause is to encourage conversion to avoid a loss of value, and firms include such clauses to encourage holders of the issue to convert into common stock. This action reduces the interest expense of the firm and in some cases is needed to improve the firm's debt-to-equity ratio.

Straight-Debt Value

Convertible debentures promise to pay interest periodically and principal upon maturity. These securities therefore have a value as a fixed-income security apart from their conversion value. Notationally, the straight-debt value of a convertible debenture is given by

$$B_{i0} = \sum_{t=1}^{n} \frac{I_{i/m}}{(1 + \iota/m)^{mt}} + \frac{FV_{in}}{(1 + \iota/m)^{mn}} \tag{12-1}$$

where B_{i0} is the current market value of convertible debenture i, I_i is the interest paid by debenture i with a maturity of n years, ι is market rate of interest for a nonconvertible debenture of the same quality and maturity, and FV_{in} is the face value of bond i upon maturity. The m represents the number of times interest is paid during the year. Since convertible debentures pay interest semiannually, this term equals 2. Equation 12-1 is purely definitional, but represents the methodology used in the bond tables to arrive at the appropriate value.

For convertible preferred stocks, the straight-preferred value is straightforward. Since preferred stocks are a perpetuity, the value of a nonconvertible preferred stock is given by

$$P_{i0} = \frac{D_i}{\pi} \tag{12-2}$$

where P_{i0} is the current market price of preferred stock i, D_i is the dividend paid by preferred stock i, and π is the market yield for preferred stocks of that quality.

The market values given by Equations 12-1 and 12-2 represent the values that convertible securities would sell for as nonconvertible debentures or preferred stock. That is, if the conversion feature were completely worthless, these securities would still have a value equal to their straight-debt or straight-preferred values. As a consequence, the straight-debt or straight-preferred value is referred to as the "floor," or minimum value for a convertible security. To illustrate, consider a 20-year 6-percent debenture, which is convertible into 25 shares of common stock. Suppose the market rate of interest for straight debentures of the same maturity and quality is 7.5 percent. The straight-debt value for this issue would be 89.32. Now suppose the current market price of the common stock is $20 per share. The conversion value would be $500, but the market value would not drop below $893.20. In other words, the straight-debt value would be the floor for this convertible debenture issue, and its market price would not fall below this level even though the conversion value was somewhat below the straight-debt value. The same effect also holds for convertible preferred stocks.

The straight-debt value of convertible securities provides the hedge element of these securities. The conversion value provides capital appreciation potential, but the straight-debt value removes some of the loss potential that would be associated with the common stock. Therefore, convertible securities have the upside potential of the common stock, but the downside risk is reduced by the bond characteristics. For this reason convertible securities may be thought of as hedge securities.

Convertible Premiums

As previously noted the market value of convertible securities is generally above the straight-debt value and the conversion value. Normally, the three reasons cited for the existence of the premium are: (1) the potential for appreciation through conversion into common stock, (2) the downside protection provided by the straight-debt value, and (3) substantial demand by financial institutions.

The conversion features introduce a speculative element that is not available from straight-debt instruments. It follows, therefore, that investors may be willing to pay a premium for this potential appreciation. However, several other conditions are necessary for this premium to exist. First of all, the conversion feature must have some value before the investor will be willing to pay a premium for the conversion privilege. That is, there must be a reasonable probability that the price of the stock will appreciate above the effective price paid for the common stock. For example, consider the value of the conversion feature for a bond whose current price is $800 and is convertible into 10 shares of stock which are currently selling for $10. Moreover, suppose the probabilities of this security reaching $80 per share were estimated to be one in a thousand. It is unlikely that the conversion feature of this security would have any value. Consequently, for the conversion value to have any value, the spread between the effective price paid for the associated common stock and the current market price of the common stock must not be too great. If it is, the probabilities of benefiting from the conversion feature are greatly reduced.

Realistically, however, the appreciation potential of convertible securities is not sufficient in itself to command a premium, because greater appreciation potential normally exists from purchasing the common stock directly. The other factor that is necessary is the downside protection provided by the straight-debt value. The major advantage of convertibles is that they commonly afford the investor downside protection in the event of a sudden drop in the price of the stock. The extent of this downside protection varies with the spread between the straight-debt value and the market value of the convertible security, but in general this downside protection combined with the potential appreciation of the underlying common stock have been cited as the major reasons for the existence of the premium. A study by Roman L. Weil, Jr., Joel E. Segall, and David Green, Jr. concluded that the floor was not an important reason for the existence of premiums in convertible debentures.[3] Others, however, have taken serious issue with the results of this study.[4] The importance of the "floor effect" is the subject of some controversy, but traditionally it has been given great weight, especially when the "floor" is not too far below the market value.

A third factor affecting the existence of a premium is the demand for convertible debentures by financial institutions. Certain financial institutions are subject to regulatory restrictions that sharply limit their commitments in common stock. For insurance companies, for example, these restrictions may take the form of limiting the acceptable investments to a small percentage of common and preferred stock with the remainder of the portfolio being invested in investment-grade bonds. Convertible debentures enable these firms to meet the regulatory requirements and to have an equity interest as well. As a result of their dual role, convertible debentures are believed to have a substantial demand from financial institutions, which in turn has an effect on the premium. The exact importance of this effect is unclear. As K. L. Broman shows for the period 1949–59, most convertible debentures were not of investment grade and therefore would not be eligible for the portfolios of financing institutions.[5] Moreover, it will be recalled that of the convertible debentures outstanding in 1972, only 12 percent were of investment grade. The effect of institutional demand on the premium of convertible debentures therefore may not be that significant.

---

[3] Roman L. Weil, Jr., Joel E. Segall and David Green, Jr., "Premiums on Convertible Bonds," *Journal of Finance*, vol. 23, no. 3 (June, 1968), pp. 460–61.
[4] For a discussion of the Weil, Segall, and Green article, see the following articles: Paul D. Cretien, Jr., "Premiums on Convertible Bonds: Comment"; David Tell Duvel, "Comment"; G. A. Mumey, "Comment"; and a reply by Weil, Segall, and Green in the *Journal of Finance*, vol. 25, no. 4 (Sept., 1970), pp. 917–34.
[5] Keith L. Broman, "The Use of Convertible Subordinated Debenture by Industrial Firms, 1949–1959," *Quarterly Review of Economics and Business*, vol. 3, no. 1, (Spring, 1963), pp. 65–76.

Reasons for Issuing Convertibles

The reasons for firms issuing convertible securities can shed additional light on the decision to purchase convertible securities. In general, the two reasons cited for the use of convertible securities are: (1) to issue common stock indirectly, and (2) to reduce the interest costs. Before C. James Pilcher's 1955 study, many believed the primary reason firms used convertible securities was to reduce the interest costs.[6] This effect is referred to as a sweetener to improve the marketability of the issue. In any event, the inclusion of a conversion feature normally permits the firm to use a lower coupon rate on the issue than would normally be used on a straight-debt issue. For example, consider the Carrier Corporation's subordinated debenture $5\frac{1}{2}$s due in 1989, issued in June of 1969. These convertible debentures had a yield to maturity of $5\frac{1}{8}$ percent, while nonconvertible debentures of the same quality and maturity had a yield to maturity of approximately $7\frac{3}{4}$ percent.

Pilcher's study found that not only was reducing interest costs an important reason for using convertibles, but the need to issue common stock indirectly was also important.[7] His study found that the need to issue common stock indirectly was the more important of the two. In other words, firms were found to issue convertible debentures as a method of assuring themselves of equity financing over the longer run. Presumably the firms needed equity financing, but it was not a good time to issue common stock because the market price of their stock was depressed. Selling common stock directly would mean that a large number of common shares would have to be sold with the substantial dilution of earnings per share that would follow. The use of convertible debentures meant that fewer share equivalents were required, because the conversion price was somewhat above the current market price. In effect, the common stock is being sold today at tomorrow's higher price.

A study conducted by Eugene F. Brigham in the early 1960s confirmed Pilcher's findings.[8] Brigham's study revealed that management indeed used convertible debentures as a form of indirect common stock issuance, as well as a method of reducing the interest costs.[9] In many cases, the firm wanted to issue common stock, but felt that convertibles would be better than issuing the common stock directly. It appears that the primary reason for issuing convertible securities is to obtain additional equity at some future point in time.

This finding has important implications for the investor. It implies that the firm anticipates that the common stock will appreciate, making conversion possible. It implies that this should be anticipated in the not-too-distant future. This period generally may be expected to be three to five years. Confirming

---

[6] C. James Pilcher, *Raising Capital With Convertible Securities* (Michigan Business Studies, vol. 12, no. 2 (Ann Arbor: University of Michigan Press, 1955).
[7] Ibid., p. 95.
[8] Eugene F. Brigham, "An Analysis of Convertible Debentures: Theory and Some Empirical Evidence," *Journal of Finance,* vol. 21, no. 1 (Mar., 1966), pp. 35–55.
[9] Ibid., p. 51.

this, Otto H. Poensgen concluded that if the price of the associated common stock does not reach the conversion price within a few years, there was a good chance that it would never do so.[10] This period, therefore, could be viewed as the expected life of a convertible security, and the investor's decisions could be gauged accordingly. That is, when a convertible debenture is initially issued, its anticipated life span may be viewed to range between three to five years, and it may be expected that the common stock will appreciate to the point where the firm may be expected to force conversion by calling the issue. The point at which forced conversion may be expected varies with the issue and various conditions that may prevail, but one rule of thumb that may be followed is that the firm may be expected to force conversion once the conversion value exceeds the call price by 20 percent.[11] Consequently, the holding period for a convertible security may be relatively short.

Evaluating Convertible Securities

The selection of a convertible security involves a tradeoff between the downside protection provided and the potential appreciation. Admittedly the investor may obtain a larger return by investing directly in the common stock, but the risk may be greater than that associated with convertible debentures. The result is that the expected return should be somewhat less than that on the common stock, since the risk is not expected to be as great, but it still should be somewhat above that on a comparable nonconvertible debenture. The analysis, therefore, involves evaluating the convertible security both as a fixed-income security and as a common stock to determine whether there is reasonable assurance of obtaining a return commensurate with the risk involved. These two aspects of the decision require an analysis of the quality of the issue, the extent of the premium being paid, and the anticipated return on the convertible security.

Factors Involved in the Evaluation

Convertible securities are fairly complex because they involve all of the facets of the analysis of bonds and stocks. The analysis, therefore, must focus on the following factors:

1. The quality of the issue
2. The current price of the convertible security relative to its conversion value and its straight-debt value
3. The potential appreciation of the associated common stock

[10] Otto H. Poensgen, "The Valuation of Convertible Bonds," *Industrial Management Review*, vol. 7, no. 2, part II (Spring, 1966), p. 95.
[11] Brigham's study indicated that it was fairly common for firms to force conversion once the conversion value exceeded the call price by 20 percent. See Brigham, op. cit., p. 52.

The quality of the issue is important since the convertible security has a fixed claim on earnings until it is converted. Morever, if there is a possibility of default on the interest on the convertible debentures, this eventuality has important implications for the value of the associated common stock and the conversion feature. The quality of the convertible as a fixed-income security should not be overlooked; specifically, convertible debentures should be of investment grade.

The current market price of the convertible security will probably be above either its conversion value or its straight-debt value. This fact raises certain questions about the appropriate relationship among these three values for the convertible security. First, the straight-debt value provides a floor that will reduce the downside risk of the issue. The floor must not be too far below the market price, or it will be of little value in reducing the downside risk. For example, consider a convertible debenture that is convertible into 20 shares of common stock currently selling for $75 per share, and suppose its market price is $1,660 and its straight-debt value is $980. The straight-debt value in this case would not provide a great deal of protection, because the market price of the stock would have to fall over 33 percent before the floor would become a factor. As a rule of thumb, some believe that the floor should not be more than 15 percent below the market price of convertible debenture. In such instances, the straight-debt value offers some downside protection.

The above requirement is consistent with the premise that the purchase of a convertible security represents a method to reduce the risk while attempting to obtain a return that is greater than that expected on a nonconvertible debenture. The other side of the coin is that the potential appreciation of the associated common stock must be somewhat above the effective price paid for the stock. In the previous example, the convertible debenture was convertible into 20 shares of common stock selling for $75 per share, and the convertible debenture's current price was $1,660. In effect, a purchaser of this security was paying $83 per share for the associated common stock. If the investor believed that its potential price three to five years from now would be about $80, there would not be much justification for buying this convertible. For that matter, there would not be much justification for buying the common stock. Consequently, the associated common stock should have substantial appreciation potential beyond its current level to assure the investor of an appropriate return. A rule of thumb that is sometimes used is that the stock should be reasonably expected to appreciate 25 percent above the effective price paid for the common stock.

Finally, the market price of the convertible security should not incorporate too large a premium over the conversion value. A guideline that may be used is that the effective price per share should not be more than 20 percent above the market price per share. For example, a convertible debenture that is convertible into 20 shares of common stock currently selling at $50 per share and is selling for $1,220 has a premium that is too large. Even if the common stock is expected to appreciate to $75 per share, a substantial premium has been paid for the stock, which would undoubtedly reduce the potential return on this convertible debenture. For example, it is entirely possible that as the associated stock price increases to $60 per share, the convertible security would only increase slightly to $1,230. This could result because investors believe that the firm will call the issue once the conversion value reaches a range of $1,200 to $1,250. Thus, the premium could largely disappear as the market anticipated forced conversion of the issue. The size of the premium, therefore, is an important factor affecting the potential return on convertible securities.

Estimating the Return on Convertibles

Estimating the return on a convertible security requires certain assumptions that follow from the empirical studies discussed earlier. From the investor's point of view, it is assumed that the purchase of the convertible security represents a hedge investment in which the investor is seeking the protection offered by the floor effect of the convertible debenture and a certain amount of appreciation offered by the conversion feature. From the firm's point of view, it is assumed that the firm has issued the convertible debenture as a method of obtaining equity financing indirectly. This means that the firm anticipates that the convertible debentures will be converted in the not-too-distant future. It also probably means that once the convertible debenture's conversion value reaches a range of approximately 20 percent above its call price the issue will be called. It may be assumed that convertible securities will not remain outstanding for a very long period of time.

In estimating the return on a convertible debenture, these assumptions will be useful. Two estimates that will be needed are an estimate of the conversion value and the point in time when forced conversion may be expected. Since empirical research seems to indicate that forced conversion can be expected once the conversion value is 20 percent above the call price, the course of action that may be taken, therefore, is to estimate an approximate price at which forced conversion may be expected and then estimate the period of time that will be required to reach this level. For example, suppose the current conversion value is $920 and forced conversion is expected when the conversion value reaches $1,260. If the analyst expects that the stock will appreciate at 6 percent per year, it would take five years before the conversion value reached the point where forced conversion would be expected. This can be determined by reference to Table B-1 of the Appendix, which gives the future value of $1 in period n.

Once the period of time before forced conversion occurs and the conversion value at that time are estimated, determining the return that may be expected can be accomplished by finding the internal rate of return that equates the initial cost of the convertible debenture with the present value of the inflows in the form of interest receipts and the conversion value upon forced conversion. That is, we solve the following equation:

$$B_{j0} = \sum_{t=1}^{n} \frac{I_j/2}{(I + r/2)^{2t}} + \frac{\widehat{TV_{jn}}}{(1 + r/2)^{2\hat{n}}} \qquad (12\text{-}3)$$

where B_{j0} is the current market price of the convertible debenture j, $I_j/2$ is semiannual interest receipts from convertible debenture j, and $\widehat{TV_{jn}}$ is the estimated terminal value convertible debenture j upon conversion.

To illustrate, suppose that a 6.5 percent convertible debenture of a corporation can be purchased for $1,000. Suppose it is estimated that the convertible debenture will be converted once it reaches $1,260, and that it will reach this level in three years. The conversion value of the security is currently $920. Substituting into Equation 13-3 gives

$$1,000 = \sum_{t=1}^{3} \frac{32.50}{(1 + r/2)^{2t}} + \frac{1,260}{(1 + r/2)^{6}}$$

Solving for r, we obtain $r \cong 14$ percent. In this particular example, the convertible debenture promises a return of approximately 14 percent for three years.

The real difficulty in determining the rate of return expected on a convertible debenture involves estimating the point at which conversion may be expected. Fortunately, there are several empirical studies to draw on to aid in making these estimates. Since it can be assumed that forced conversion will occur once the conversion value is 20 percent or more above the call price, it only remains to estimate the period of time it will take the conversion value to reach this level. Once this is accomplished, the anticipated yield on a convertible debenture may be determined by solving for r in Equation 12-3. Note that this technique can also be used for convertible preferred stock.

In summary, several factors are involved in evaluating a convertible debenture. First, several factors can be used as screening devices. One of these is the quality ranking of the issue. Generally, these securities should be of investment quality. Otherwise protection against the downside risk may not be particularly strong. Second, the market price of the convertible debenture should not be too far above the straight-debt value, because (1) the floor provided by the straight-debt value will not be of much value, and (2) when the market price of the convertible debenture is quite high—say, in a range of $1,500 to $2,000—the probabilities of forced conversion are high, and the probabilities of further appreciation are greatly reduced. Third, the final test of the acceptability of a particular convertible debenture is its expected return. It must promise a return that will compensate for the risk incurred.

Warrants

Warrants are options to purchase common stock at a specified price, normally for a specified period of time. They are usually attached to bonds to improve their marketability. Warrants act as a method of reducing the interest cost on the bonds in much the same fashion as the conversion feature normally reduces the interest cost on convertible debentures. At the time of the issuance of the warrants, the option price is usually somewhat higher than the current market price of the common stock. For example, Chrysler warrants were issued during May of 1971 with an option price of $34; they expire on May 15, 1976. The market price of Chrysler's common stock ranged from $28 to $31 per share during May, 1971. The more valuable type of warrant, from purely a speculative point of view, is detachable from the senior security and therefore can be traded on organized exchanges. Nondetachable warrants must be exercised by the holder of the senior securities. This type of warrant, of course, reduces the speculative gains that may be obtained by the investor because a market for these warrants does not develop.

The risk-return characteristics of warrants offer an unusual opportunity for the investor who is willing to accept a substantial amount of risk. First, the value of the warrant hinges on the value of the associated common stock. The warrant, therefore, derives its value from the expected appreciation of the common stock, and the fact that the option price of the warrant is somewhat higher than the current market price of the stock when it is issued means the investor must focus on the potential return of the common stock. Second, the risk characteristics of warrants are further complicated by the limited duration of the warrants. Generally, the shorter the duration of the warrants, the greater the risk, because the stock must appreciate above the option price before the warrant expires. Otherwise the warrant is worthless. Third, a commitment in the warrants entails a smaller cash outlay than a direct investment in the common stock. For example, the Chrysler warrants that have an option to buy the common stock at $34 closed at 12¾ on August 31, 1971. The stock, however, closed at 26⅜, which means the purchase of 100 shares of common stock would involve a cash outlay of $2,637.50 plus transactions costs, while 100 warrants could be purchased for $1,275 plus transactions costs. Consequently, one could have a commitment in the common stock at a smaller cash outlay.

Although warrants and convertible securities have speculative features, warrants involve much more risk. In the spectrum of risk associated with securities, warrants are considered very risky, while convertible securities in general are considered to fall somewhere between bonds and common stock. Consequently, these securities require careful analysis and should only be considered by those who are able to accept the above-average risk.

Range of Value

In most cases the investor faces a situation in which its market price includes a premium over its theoretical value. The first consideration in evaluating warrants is the nature of the premium for the typical warrant over its life span. This range is shown in Figure 12-1. The vertical axis shows the market price of the warrant i at time t, W_{it}, and the horizontal axis shows the market price of the associated common stock i at time t, P_{it}. Point O_i represents the option price of the warrant i. Once the common stock reaches this point, the warrant will have

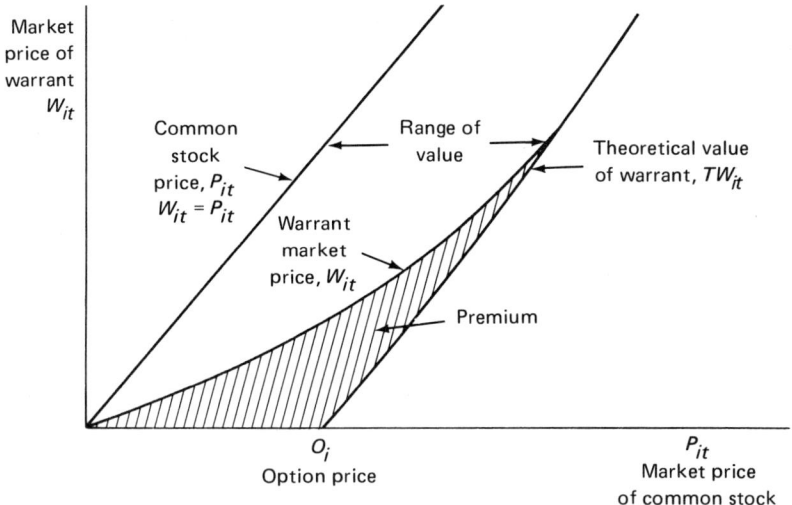

FIGURE 12-1 *Range of Plausible Values for a Typical Warrant*

a theoretical value which is represented by the line TW_{it}. The range of plausible value is given by the area between the curves represented by $W_{it} = P_{it}$ and TW_{it}. Therefore, the market price of the warrant will be within this range, and typically it will sell at a premium as represented by the shaded area. We will first discuss the reasons for warrants being expected to trade within a range of $W_{it} = P_{it}$ and TW_{it}. Then the reasons for the existence of a premium will be explored.

The theoretical value of a warrant, TW_{it}, can be determined by solving:

$$TW_{it} = N_i(P_{io} - O_i) \qquad (12\text{-}4)$$

where N_i is the number of shares of firm i that can be purchased by the warrant, P_{io} is the current market price of stock i, and O_i is the option price at which stock i may be purchased.

To illustrate, consider Uris Building warrants, which permit the holder to purchase two shares of common stock at $12.50 per share. On April 15, 1971, for example, the common stock closed at 21⅜. The theoretical value of these warrants is

$$TW = 2(21.38 - 12.50) = \$17.76$$

The theoretical value of the warrants is the lowest level at which the warrants would be expected to trade simply because arbitrage would assure that the market price would not fall below this level. For example, if the Uris Building warrants sold for $15.00, an arbitrage profit could be obtained by buying the warrants in the market, exercising them, and reselling the common shares. Ignoring transactions costs for the moment, this transaction would promise the arbitrager a profit of $2.76 per warrant. Even on a small operation in which 100 warrants were purchased, the profit would be $276 before transactions costs, and the risk involved would be very low. Consequently, the warrants would never be expected to trade below their theoretical value.

Similarly, arbitrage can be used to explain why the market price of the warrant, W_{it}, would not exceed the price of the common stock, P_{it}. This is represented in Figure 12-1 by the line $W_{it} = P_{it}$. If the warrant should sell for the same price as the common stock, the holder of the warrants would be wiser to sell the warrants and purchase the common stock. This course of action would be the least costly. For example, consider the Uris Building warrants, and suppose the warrants were selling for $42.76 and two shares of common stock sold for $42.76. In this situation, the total cost connected with purchasing the warrants and exercising the option would be $42.76 plus an additional $25.00, or $67.76, ignoring transactions costs. It would be wiser to sell the warrants for $42.76 and purchase the common stock directly for $42.76. This would reduce the cash outlay of the investor by $25.00 per warrant minus transactions costs. For this reason it would be expected that warrant prices would not exceed $W_{it} = P_{it}$, and it would be expected that warrants would sell within the range shown in Figure 12-1. Empirical studies have confirmed this range. J. P. Shelton, for example, in a study of warrants during the period 1959–62, found that warrants seldom exceeded 75 percent of the market price of common stock.[12]

Reasons for the Premium

Warrants generally sell at a premium above their theoretical value, and the reasons for the existence of the premium depend on several factors. The premium usually is attributed to leverage, but there are other factors that affect the amount of the premium. Each of these will be discussed below.

Leverage   Leverage probably is the most important reason for the existence of the premium. The leverage occurs as a result of the greater proportional increase in the warrant for a given change in the price of the common stock. To illustrate, suppose a corporation's warrants permit the purchase of one share of stock at $40 per share, and initially the stock sells at $50 per share. Suppose also that after nine time periods the price of the stock has risen to $120 per share, and by the tenth time period the price of the common stock has risen to $130 per share. The effects of leverage are as follows:

Time	Price of common stock P_t	Percent change	Option price O	Theoretical value of the warrant W_t	Percent change
0	$ 50	—	$40	$10	—
1	60	20.00	40	20	100.00
⋮	⋮	⋮	⋮	⋮	⋮
9	120	—	40	80	—
10	130	8.33	40	90	12.50

[12] J. P. Shelton, "Relation of the Price of a Warrant to the Price of Its Associated Stock, Part I," *Financial Analysts Journal*, vol. 23, no. 3 (May–June, 1967), p. 146.

When the theoretical value of the warrant is low, a change in the stock price will have a significant effect on the theoretical value of the warrants. This effect is evident in this example by comparing time periods 0 and 1 with 9 and 10. When the theoretical value of the warrant is relatively low at $10 per share in year 0, and the stock increases 20 percent to $60, the effect on the theoretical value of the warrant is substantial. In particular, a 20 percent increase in the market price of the common stock leads to a 100-percent increase in the theoretical value of the warrant. This illustrates the effects of leverage on the value of the warrant. However, the advantage of leverage disappears when the theoretical value of the warrant rises to fairly high levels. For the warrants in the example, once the theoretical value reached $80 in time period nine, the leverage effect was greatly reduced. In particular, in time period 10 the stock rose $10 per share to $130, or 8.33 percent, but the theoretical value increased by only 12.5 percent. Thus, the leverage effect is greatest when the theoretical value of the warrant is relatively low. As the theoretical value of the warrant increases, the benefits of leverage are reduced. The premium for leverage would be expected to decline as the price of the stock rose to higher levels.

Several researchers have investigated this phenomenon and concluded that once the price of the stock reaches four times the option price, the premium will all but disappear.[13] In the above example, this would mean that the premium for the warrants would virtually disappear once the stock price reached $160 per share, since at this level the benefits of leverage would be minimal.

Other Factors   Leverage is generally considered to be the most important factor affecting the premium. Other factors that play a role are: (1) the length of time before the warrant expires, (2) the volatility of the associated common stock, and (3) the opportunity costs connected with lost dividends and funds invested. The length of time that the warrant will remain in existence has an important impact on the premium incorporated into the warrants price. The premium is usually directly related to the remaining life of the warrant. Warrants that do not expire for a substantial period of time give the holder a greater opportunity to profit from the investment, since there is a greater opportunity for the common stock to appreciate to the point where the warrant has a theoretical value. On the other hand, if the warrant will expire within a short period of time, the appreciation potential is greatly reduced, and with it the premium that will be paid for the warrants. This effect is illustrated in Figure 12-2. In the figure, each dark line represents the path of the market price of the warrant over its life span, and the longer the remaining life of the warrant the greater will be the premium. Conversely, as the warrant approaches expiration, the market price of the warrant tends to converge with the theoretical value.

Another factor that affects the market price of the warrant, and consequently its premium, is the volatility of the associated common stock. Volatility refers to the range of possible prices for a particular common stock. A so-called volatile stock would be expected to fluctuate over a wide range in a given period of

[13] Both J. P. Shelton and Paul H. Samuelson have investigated this phenomenon. See J. P. Shelton, op. cit., p. 144; and Paul A. Samuelson, "Rational Theory of Warrant Pricing," *Industrial Management Review*, vol. 6, no. 2 (Spring, 1965), p. 29.

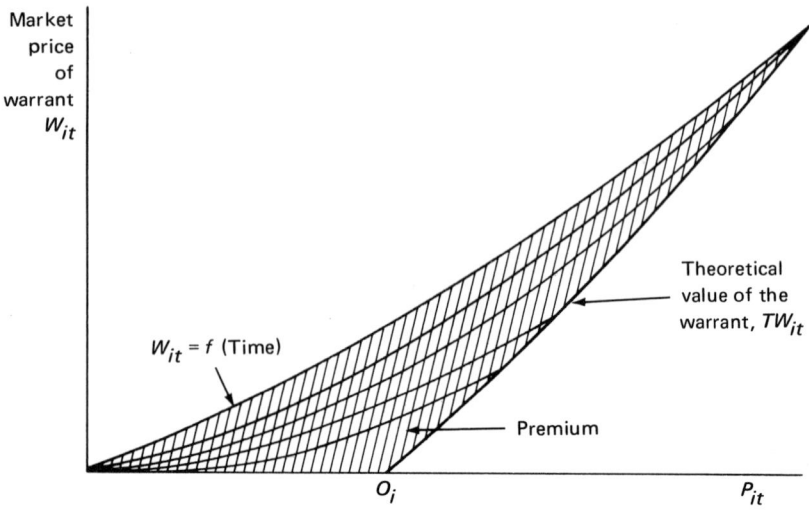

FIGURE 12-2   *Warrant Price as a Function of Remaining Life*

time. A stable stock, on the other hand, would not fluctuate over such a wide range. Volatility, therefore, refers to the probability distribution of possible outcomes and particularly to the dispersion of those outcomes. The volatility of the stock directly affects the market price of the warrants. In particular, the more volatile the common stock, the greater the value of the warrants. This effect results because there is a greater chance of the warrants achieving a theoretical value. Thus, the premium on warrants is directly related to the volatility of the associated common stock.

To illustrate, suppose we consider a corporation's warrants that permit the purchase of one share of common stock at $40 per share. Suppose investors in general have the following subjective probability distribution of possible outcomes for the corporation's common stock for the next year:

| | Market | |
Probability	price	Product
0.10	$20	$ 2
0.20	30	6
0.40	40	16
0.20	50	10
0.10	60	6
1.00		$40

Therefore, the expected price of the common stock would be $40 in the next year, and these warrants would not be expected to have a theoretical value during the next year.

However, warrant prices are not symmetrical in the sense that they may have negative prices as well as positive prices. Only those common stock prices above the option prices influence the market price of the warrants. Thus, the expected market value of the warrant during next year would be

$$E(W) = 0.10(0) + 0.20(0) + 0.40(0) + .20 \, (50 - 40) + 0.10 \, (60 - 40)$$

$$= 2.00 + 2.00 = \$4.00$$

These warrants would be expected to have an expected market value of $4.00, even though they do not have a theoretical value. The greater the volatility of the associated common stock, the greater will be the premium on a warrant, other factors being held constant.

A final factor that may affect the premium is opportunity costs, which may take two forms. Since warrants, unlike the associated common stock, will not pay a dividend, this lack of dividends may be a factor that would reduce the demand for the warrants. Empirical studies, however, have found that this factor has little effect on the market value of the warrants.[14] Another form of opportunity cost is value associated with funds. This factor has been found to be important.[15] To illustrate, suppose that the cost of acquiring the common stock of a hypothetical corporation is $50 per share, but the cost of the warrants is $10, with warrant providing the option to acquire one share of stock at $60 per share. If the investor expects the shares to increase in value in the coming year, he has the option of buying 100 shares costing $5,000 or 100 warrants costing $1,000. The more valuable funds are to the investor the more likely he is to favor the warrants, since the initial cash outlay would be reduced by $4,000. At the same time, he still has a commitment in the corporation's common stock.

Summary

In this chapter we have attempted to round out the discussion of fixed-income securities. It is fairly common to include a conversion feature or to attach warrants. The inclusion of a conversion feature gives a fixed-income security the attributes of both a bond and stock. Consequently, when a convertible security is analyzed, it must be analyzed from both standpoints to determine its investment merit. The analysis as a bond is concerned with determining the merits of the security as a debt instrument. It must be remembered that convertible securities promise to pay a fixed interest or dividend until the security is converted or matures. The investor must be concerned with the assurance of receiving the contracted amount of interest or dividends. If the firm does default on these payments, the appreciation potential of the convertible security will be virtually eliminated. The common stock analysis is necessary to determine whether the conversion feature has any value. If it has, the investor may be willing to trade off some of the interest or dividend yield for potential

[14] James C. Van Horne, "Warrant Valuation in Relation to Volatility and Opportunity Costs," *Industrial Management Review*, vol. 10, no. 3 (Spring, 1969), pp. 25–26.
[15] Ibid., p. 28.

appreciation. Otherwise the convertible security will require a yield similar to that of comparable nonconvertible securities.

Warrants are different from convertible securities in their risk characteristics. The investor in warrants is speculating that the price of the common stock will appreciate above the option price, with the result that the warrant will have a theoretical value. An important factor in the market price of the warrant is the premium above its theoretical value. Important factors in determining this premium appear to be: (1) the period of time before the warrant expires, (2) the amount of leverage that may be obtained, (3) the volatility of the price of the associated common stock, and (4) the opportunity costs of funds to the investors.

Questions

1. Convertible debentures have normally constituted a small portion of total bond financing.
   a. What are some possible explanations for this?
   b. What may be some of the reasons for the increased use during 1967–70?
2. Generally, convertible debentures are not high-quality instruments. How do you account for this?
3. Why do firms use convertible securities as a means of financing?
4. What particular features of convertible securities may appeal to investors?
5. For convertible debentures it is common to refer to a call price, a par value, a straight-debt value, a conversion value, and a market value.
   a. What is the role of the call price? Is it an important function?
   b. Why would the market price normally be greater than the straight-debt value or the conversion value?
6. A corporation's subordinated debenture $7\frac{1}{2}$s of '96 are convertible into common stock at $40 per share. The market price of the common stock is currently $41 per share, and several reliable investment services expect the stock to go as high as $60 per share. The subordinated convertible debenture currently is selling for 125 and is rated as Ba. Similar nonconvertible debentures are yielding 9 percent. Would this convertible debenture be a worthwhile investment to consider?
7. A corporation's debenture 7s are convertible into common stock at $20 per share and are currently selling for $108. The associated common stock does not pay a dividend and is currently selling for $17 per share. The prospects for the stock seem good with some investment services predicting a price in the neighborhood of $50 in three to five years. However, forced conversion may be expected long before the stock reaches this value. Suppose forced conversion is anticipated when its conversion value reaches $1,400, which is expected to occur in about three years. Would the stock provide a higher return over that three-year period than the convertible?

8. Warrants, like convertible debentures, normally sell at a premium over their theoretical value.
   a. What reasons are normally cited to explain the existence of the premium in warrants?
   b. Why are warrants normally expected to trade in a range bounded by the theoretical value and the price of the stock?
9. A corporation is anticipating issuing debentures with warrants that will expire in five years. The warrants permit the purchase of common stock at $8 per share. The common stock currently is selling for $4 per share.
   a. What price must the common stock attain before the warrants have a theoretical value?
   b. The corporation's common stock is quite volatile. The following is a probability distribution of possible prices for the stock for the next year.

Probability	Market price/share
0.10	$ 1
0.25	4
0.30	8
0.25	12
0.10	15

   Given this probability distribution, what is the expected market price of the warrants, all else being equal?
10. Leverage is generally accepted to be a major factor contributing to the premium in warrant prices. Using the data for the corporation in question 9, illustrate the effects of leverage on the return to the warrant holder.

Selected References

Baumol, William J., Burton G. Malkiel, and Richard E. Quandt. "The Valuation of Convertible Securities." *Quarterly Journal of Economics*, vol. 80, no. 1 (Feb., 1966), pp. 48–60.

Brigham, Eugene F. "An Analysis of Convertible Debentures: Theory and Some Empirical Evidence." *Journal of Finance*, vol. 21, no. 1 (Mar., 1966), pp. 35–55.

Broman, Keith L. "The Use of Convertible Subordinated Debentures by Industrial Firms, 1949–1959." *Quarterly Review of Economics and Business*, vol. 3, no. 1 (Spring, 1963), pp. 55–76.

Cohen, Jerome B., Edward D. Zinbarg, and Arthur Zeikel. *Investment Analysis and Portfolio Management*, rev. ed., Homewood, Ill.: Richard D. Irwin, 1973, Chapter 11.

Cretien, Paul D., Jr. "Premiums on Convertible Bonds: Comment." *Journal of Finance*, vol. 25, no. 4 (Sept., 1970), pp. 917–23.

Duvel, David Tell. "Premiums on Convertible Bonds: Comment." *Journal of Finance*, vol. 25, no. 4 (Sept., 1970), pp. 923–28.

Lindsay, J. Robert, and Arnold W. Sametz. *Financial Management: An Analytical Tool*, rev. ed., Homewood, Ill.: Richard D. Irwin, 1967. Chapter 24.

Mumey, G. A. "Premiums on Convertible Bonds: Comment." *Journal of Finance*, vol. 25, no. 4 (Sept., 1970), pp. 928–31.

Pilcher, C. James. *Raising Capital with Convertible Securities.* Michigan Business Studies, vol. 12, no. 2. Ann Arbor: University of Michigan Press, 1955.

Pinches, George E. "Financing with Convertible Preferred Stock, 1960–1967." *Journal of Finance,* vol. 25, no. 1 (Mar., 1970), pp. 53–65.

Poensgen, Otto H. "The Valuation of Convertible Bonds," Parts I and II. *Industrial Management Review,* vols. 6 and 7, nos. 1 and 2 (Fall, 1965, and Spring, 1966), pp. 77–93 and 83–99.

Samuelson, Paul A. "Rational Theory of Warrant Pricing." *Industrial Management Review,* vol. 6, no. 1 (Spring, 1965), pp. 13–32.

Shelton, John P. "The Relation of the Price of a Warrant to the Price of its Associated Stock," Parts I and II. *Financial Analysts Journal,* vol. 23, Nos. 3 and 4 (May–June, 1967, and July–Aug., 1967), pp. 143–52 and 88–100.

Sprecher, C. Ronald. "A Note on Financing Mergers with Convertible Preferred Stock." *Journal of Finance,* vol. 26, no. 3 (June, 1971), pp. 683–86.

Sprenkle, Case. "Warrant Prices as Indicators of Expectations." *Yale Economic Essays,* vol. 1 (1961), pp. 179–233.

Van Horne, James C. "Warrant Valuation in Relation to Volatility and Opportunity Costs." *Industrial Management Review,* vol. 10, no. 3 (Spring, 1969), pp. 19–33.

Walter, James E., and Agustin V. Que. "The Valuation of Convertible Bonds." *Journal of Finance,* vol. 28, no. 3 (June, 1973), pp. 713–33.

Weil, Roman L., Joel E. Segall, and David Green, Jr. "Premiums on Convertible Bonds." *Journal of Finance,* vol. 23, no. 3 (June, 1968), pp. 445–64.

IV

Portfolio Composition

Chapter 13

The Traditional Approach

Portfolio composition is the ultimate decision since the investor must decide what securities to include in his portfolio. Arriving at this decision involves evaluating many factors that combine to form the universe of risk and return possibilities available from securities. As Chapter 6 pointed out, it is generally assumed that the investor will select the portfolio whose risk and expected return will maximize his expected utility. This presupposes risk and uncertainty, since portfolio composition would not be necessary under conditions of certainty. In a world of risk and uncertainty, portfolio composition is used as a means of diversifying and therefore reducing the risk that is incurred. By diversifying among a number of securities, the investor can reduce the amount of risk in his portfolio because errors will tend to average out over the portfolio. Some securities will perform as expected, others will not. By diversifying, the effect of those that do not perform up to expectations is offset to some extent by those that do. The principles of diversification will be discussed in more detail in Chapter 14.

Security analysis is concerned with ascertaining the risk and expected return associated with securities. Portfolio composition must combine these expectations with the investor's preferences and needs. The traditional approach places substantial emphasis on the problem of determining the constraints on the investor. However, the analysis is largely qualitative. More recent portfolio composition models involve the quantification of the risk and return variables, and, in the case of mean-variance models, mathematical programming techniques are used to derive the actual portfolios. These techniques will be discussed in Chapter 15. In the traditional approach, risk is a qualitative variable, and the actual portfolios are derived intuitively.

Steps in Traditional Approach

The traditional approach typically involves two major decisions. These are determining the appropriate portfolio objective and actually selecting the securities to be included in the portfolio. The process normally involves four to six steps, as illustrated in Figure 13-1. The principal objective of the traditional approach is to maximize the expected utility of the investor. That is, the portfolio selected is supposed to maximize the investor's utility preferences for risk and return in the same fashion as the consumer is expected to select the goods that will maximize his utility. This is taken to mean that the investor will attempt to maximize his expected return subject to the level of risk involved. This assumption also is the basis for the Markowitz formulation discussed in Chapter 15, and a major point of departure in the wealth-maximization model, which will be discussed in Chapter 16.

The first step is to obtain the pertinent facts about the individual. This information aids the portfolio manager in determining the constraints on the portfolio and hence aids in determining the most appropriate portfolio objective. In

FIGURE 13-1   *Steps in the Traditional Approach*

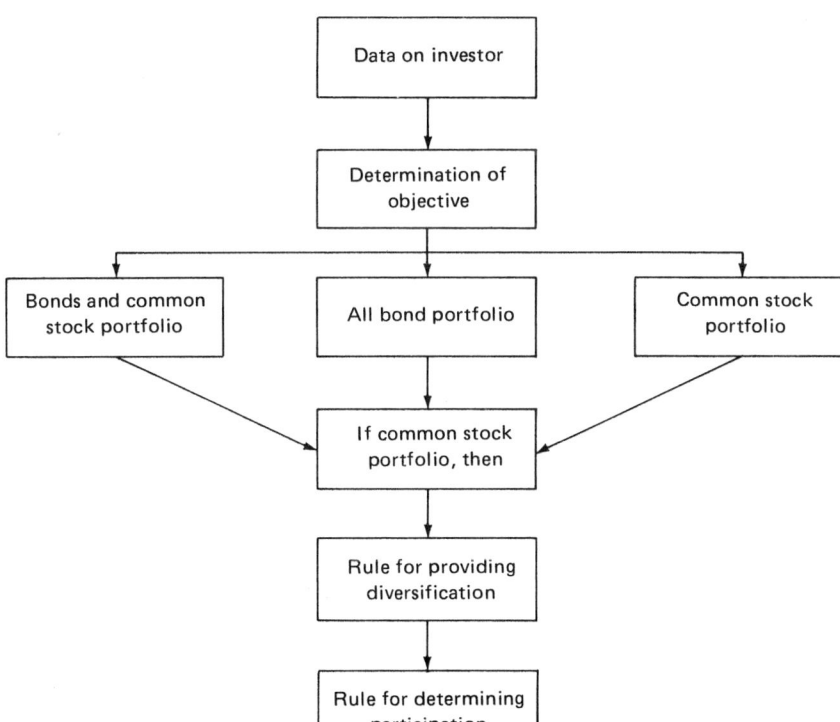

general terms the issue is whether the portfolio should be invested in bonds or common stocks. High-quality bonds have substantially less risk than common stock, but of course the return is not as high as that on a well-diversified portfolio of common stock. Generally, the fundamental question that the portfolio manager attempts to answer is whether the investor is able to accept the greater risk that accompanies the ownership of common stock. If he can, a strong case can be made for investing in common stock because of the substantially higher expected return.

In attempting to establish a portfolio objective, the traditional approach goes beyond simply specifying whether stocks or bonds should be included. For bond portfolios the concern is whether the portfolio should be invested in short-term or long-term securities. This decision is concerned with determining whether the essential purpose of the portfolio is income or safety of principal. If the major objective is income, the portfolio will be made up of high-quality long-term bonds. Long-term interest rates are normally higher than short-term rates, and the fact that the bonds are long-term assures a stable income stream for a long period of time. If safety of principal is the objective, the portfolio will be made up of high-quality short-term debt instruments. Such a portfolio will have a relatively unstable income stream since short-term interest rates are quite volatile, but it will provide safety of principal in the event of forced liquidation.

Objectives for common stock portfolios are more complex and range from income to rapid appreciation. The objectives for common stocks portfolios have been variously conceived, but the following is a typical representation:

1. Income
2. Income and appreciation
3. Appreciation and income
4. Appreciation

These four objectives represent different degrees of emphasis on appreciation. Those portfolios that stress income as opposed to appreciation tend to be quite conservative. Stocks that meet this objective tend to have a high dividend payout ratio. A notable example is the stocks of public utilities, but any firm that pays a relatively large proportion of its earnings in dividends may be an income stock. While these stocks provide a relatively high dividend yield, their appreciation is expected to be quite modest. Nevertheless, they are expected to provide some appreciated that will partially offset the effects of inflation.

At the opposite extreme is the objective of appreciation. Investors pursuing this objective presumably are seeking an above-average return and invest in stocks that have wide appreciation potential—usually stocks of firms that are growing very rapidly and, consequently, retaining a large percent of their earnings for expansion purposes. Since these firms are growing so rapidly, the potential return to the investor is substantial, but not everyone is able to invest in these stocks. The obvious constraint is that some investors may need a level of income that these stocks do not provide. Further, growth stocks involve substantial risk in the form of both market-related and firm-related risks. The potential rewards are great, but so is the risk of failing to attain the anticipated return.

Although there is substantial motivation to invest in growth stocks to achieve an above-average return, many investors may prefer to pursue a less aggressive investment policy. For these investors the two other objectives—income and appreciation, and appreciation and income—may be more suitable. The objective of income and appreciation simply places more emphasis on income and less on appreciation. An investor pursuing this objective would not require as high a dividend yield as would be obtained from income stocks, but the dividend yield would be fairly high with only moderate appreciation potential. On the other hand, the objective of appreciation and income places the emphasis on appreciation, and the portfolio would be made up of stocks with relatively good appreciation potential but only a moderate dividend yield. Hence, the objectives in the traditional approach range from the conservative income objective to the aggressive appreciation approach.

Once the objective of the portfolio has been determined, the next step is to select the securities to make up the portfolio. A corollary consideration is the amount to be invested in each security to be included in the portfolio. Selecting a bond portfolio is relatively easy, since the bonds are high quality and the risk is relatively low. Therefore, some diversification may be desirable, but the number of bonds in the portfolio may be small. Ten issues from different industries should provide the desired diversification, and at the same time transactions costs can also be minimized. Equal allocation among the issues in the portfolio is probably desirable, since the risk associated with each issue is approximately equal. With common stock portfolios, this problem is more complex because stocks must be selected to meet the objective of the portfolio. A screening mechanism is used to categorize common stocks according to the various common stock objectives. This generally is accomplished by associating industries with the common stock portfolio objectives. For example, industries that meet the objective of appreciation might be the business machine and drug industries. Hence, if the portfolio manager had a portfolio with an objective of appreciation, several stocks from each of these industries might be included. This application of the industry concept further explains the widespread emphasis on industry analysis in security analysis and portfolio composition.

The questions of the number of securities to be included in common stock portfolios and the participation of each are not so clear in the traditional approach. These questions presumably are left to the discretion of the portfolio manager and hinge to some extent on his estimation of the amount of risk that can be assumed. If the risk is to be minimized, fairly broad diversification would be in order. On the other hand, if more risk can be assumed, the portfolio can be concentrated. Similarly, the allocation of each security in the portfolio is somewhat unclear, but the amount allocated to one stock could be directly proportional to the number of stocks to be included in the portfolio or could be inversely related to the amount of risk associated with each stock to be included.

Collecting the Basic Data

The basic data is collected to aid in determining the appropriate objective for the portfolio. Generally, savings are used for investments, which implies that the funds for securities portfolios are residual funds after a number of other expenditures. Every family has its own priority of expenditures, but experts generally agree that the following priority listing of expenditures is appropriate for most families:

1. Food, clothing, and housing
2. Life insurance
3. Pension plan
4. Savings equal to about six months of disposable income
5. Investment

This list of priorities indicates that the household budget must first take care of basic necessities, such as food, clothing, medicine, and shelter. Once these are taken care of, any funds left over can be devoted to life insurance needs and providing a retirement fund. Finally, most experts agree that savings equal to about six months of disposable income should be available for emergencies. It is only after these basic family needs are taken care of that investment in securities can be considered.

The type of data that may be collected includes a number of items. A partial list of these is as follows:

1. Stated purpose for the portfolio
2. Age
3. Health
4. Marital status and responsibilities
5. Occupation
6. Approximate income, sources, and expected duration
7. Saving habits
8. Property ownership

A fundamental consideration is whether the items of food, clothing, and housing, life insurance, pension plan, and savings have been taken care of. If they have, this removes possible constraints on the portfolio manager, and permits him greater freedom to pursue a more aggressive policy. An example of the type of questionnaire that may be used is illustrated by Merrill Lynch's Confidential Inventory for Investors, shown in Figure 13-2.

If it is evident that these higher priority items have not been adequately provided for, or if improper estate plans have been laid, it may be the duty of the portfolio manager to correct these deficiencies before proceeding to the

Code 30R—1/71
Printed in U.S.A.

MERRILL LYNCH, PIERCE, FENNER & SMITH INC

CONFIDENTIAL INVENTORY FOR INVESTORS

FOR:_____
(Please Print Full Name)

_____
(Address)

_____
(City and State)   (Zip Code)

Acct. No._____ ☐ Prospect

Portfolio Reviewed Last On:_____

From: _____ Date: _____
(Office)

Service: ☐ WRITTEN PORTFOLIO ANALYSIS
Mail original reply to: ☐ Customer   ☐ AE

☐ TELEPHONE CONSULTATION

Acct. Exec.: _____ No.: _____

Approved by: _____
(Manager)

AN IMPORTANT WORD ABOUT THESE INVESTMENT OBJECTIVES

If SAFETY is of prime importance, it MUST BE RELATED to a secondary objective. When INCOME is the primary objective, the safety of interest or dividends should be just as important as the level of the yield. When the INCOME DESIRED IS UNUSUALLY HIGH and cannot be achieved from dividends or interest income alone, we will assume it is to be derived from a combination of income and appreciation. INTERMEDIATE TERM refers to a period of up to 12 months. LONG TERM refers to a period of more than 12 months. GOOD QUALITY and SPECULATIVE QUALITY classifications indicate the difference between a corporation's relative industry position, its financial strength, its capital structure, and its record of earnings and dividends. GROWTH characterizes industries with better long term potential than the economy as a whole.

INVESTMENT OBJECTIVES: *(If more than **one,** please indicate order of importance)*

☐ Relative safety of capital

☐ Income of about_____ %

Intermediate term appreciation_____ good quality ☐
                                       speculative ☐

Long term growth_____ good quality ☐
                                  speculative ☐

PERSONAL AND FINANCIAL INFORMATION:

Sex
☐ Male
☐ Female

Marital Status
☐ Single
☐ Married
☐ Widowed

Age
☐ 21—40
☐ 41—50
☐ 51—60

☐ 61—65
☐ over 65

Cash for investment_____

Cash savings (excluding
cash now available)_____

Approximate top
federal income tax bracket_____ %
Annual income (excluding
income from securities)_____

Occupation or profession_____
Number and age
of dependents_____

Life insurance_____

Real estate_____

Other resources_____

Fixed obligations_____

ADDITIONAL PERTINENT INFORMATION:

Please name companies in the portfolio with which there is an association and give reasons for large concentrations of capital. Give complete details for trusts and estates and indicate bank approval where appropriate. For institutions, indicate liquidity requirements etc.

_____

_____

_____

_____

_____

_____

_____

FIGURE 13-2 *Merrill Lynch's Confidential Inventory for Investors*

construction of a portfolio of securities. This entire area of investment management is sometimes referred to as estate planning. Generally, estate planning may be thought of as the disposition of an estate by a wealthy person. However, estate planning may also be defined as the accumulation and disposition of wealth. Typically, a married man has to consider the purchase of a house, life insurance, medical insurance, adequate disability insurance, and a pension plan. Generally, medical insurance, disability insurance, and the pension plan are part of the fringe benefits provided by firms. Nevertheless, a deficiency in any of these areas can jeopardize the results from the best laid portfolio plans, since any of these items could lead to forced liquidation of the portfolio at an inopportune time.

To illustrate, consider the following example. Suppose an investor had begun purchasing securities rather than providing for these other needs of the household. As the family increases in size and maturity, it may become necessary to purchase a home. This need may lead to liquidating the securities portfolio at an undesirable time in favor of the new home. A perfect example would be the market conditions of the 1968–70 period. Standard and Poor's 500 reached a high late in November, 1968, of 108.4, from which it plunged to a low of about 69.3 in May of 1970. Subsequently, it began to rise, and closed at approximately 90.1 in December of 1970. Liquidation of a portfolio of common stock during this period could have led to a sizable loss.

Another aspect of estate planning concerns the disposition of the portfolio upon the death of the investor. This can be complex because there is usually a will describing the division of the assets of the deceased. This fact may place a constraint upon the construction of the portfolio. It may also be desirable to minimize gift and estate taxes, which may place another constraint on the portfolio. In summary, then, there are a number of factors that may affect the construction of the portfolio, and the portfolio manager undoubtedly will require as much information as possible to determine the appropriate course of action for a given portfolio.

Formulating the Portfolio Objective

Determining the portfolio objective requires ascertaining the constraints on a portfolio. The greater the number of constraints and the more binding these constraints, the more conservative the portfolio must be. Recall that the objectives in the traditional approach range from income, on the one hand, to appreciation, on the other. There are normally six possible portfolio constraints to be evaluated to determine the appropriate objective. These are:

1. Need for income in current dollars. Some portfolios will have to supply enough funds to meet all or part of the living expenses of the investor.
2. Need for income in constant dollars. Inflation will reduce the purchasing power of a constant stream of income; consequently, the investor may wish to offset this effect as much as possible.

3. Need for safety of principal in current dollars. Some portfolios may have to be liquidated on short notice; for these portfolios, safety of principal is a major consideration.

4. Need for safety of principal in constant dollars. Inflation may reduce the purchasing power of a portfolio of securities and hence the investor may want to reduce this effect to a minimum.

5. Need for tax-exemption. Individuals in high tax brackets may require tax-sheltered investments.

6. Temperament. Although a higher return may be expected from a well-diversified portfolio of common stock than from a portfolio of bonds, some individuals may not be willing to accept the greater risk associated with common stock.

Need for Income

In formulating the objectives for a portfolio, the starting point is normally establishing the amount of income the portfolio must generate. This involves two steps. First, the amount of income required from the investment portfolio must be determined in current dollars. Second, the effect of a rising price level on the purchasing power of this income must be established. Establishing the income that the portfolio must generate can be derived as follows:

$$E_t = (1 + \alpha)^t H_o - O_t \qquad (13\text{-}1)$$

where E_t is the amount of income that the portfolio must generate during time t, H_o is the total amount of income required for the household budget stated in terms of the purchasing power when the portfolio is established, $(1 + \alpha)^t$ is a coefficient reflecting the expected change in the general price level during period up to time t, and O_t is the income from other sources during time t.

To illustrate, suppose that Mr. Fox is a successful businessman, aged 60, who has $500,000 available to invest. He was a plant manager of a medium-sized manufacturing firm in the Midwest until his recent retirement. He plans to retire to the family home in a medium-sized Illinois city. Estimates of the family budget indicate that about $10,000 annually is required so that he and

	Time Period						
	1	2	3	4	5		20
Budget, H	10,000	10,000	10,000	10,000	10,000	...	10,000
(1 + α)	1.02	1.040	1.061	1.082	1.104	...	1,486
Adj. budget	10,200	10,400	10,610	10,820	11,040	...	14,860
Other income, O	9,400	9,400	9,400	9,400	9,400	...	11,960
Needed income, E	600	1,000	1,210	1,420	1,640	...	2,900

his wife can live comfortably. Income from other sources include social security at age 65 of $213 per month, and a corporate pension plan of $10,000 annually. For purpose of illustration, we will consider a 20-year period but only show the calculations for the first five years and the twentieth year. The rate of inflation is optimistically assumed to be 2 percent. Although this rate may be low, the effect over a 20-year period is still substantial. Also, taxes on one-half of the corporate pension are estimated to be $600. As a consequence, there is an immediate income requirement of $600. This will gradually increase until Mr. Fox reaches age 65, at which time he and his wife will begin collecting social security benefits of approximately $213 per month. After age 65, other sources of income will exceed the budget requirements, and this fortunate state of affairs will continue until he is 75 years old.

It is evident that the need for current income is not a serious constraint on Mr. Fox's portfolio. The importance of the income constraint essentially determines whether the portfolio should be invested in bonds or common stock. If the income constraint is relatively unimportant, then the portfolio can be invested in common stock. Mr. Fox could obtain a higher return since historically portfolios of common stocks have had substantially higher returns than portfolios of bonds. The focus, then, is whether the investor is able to accept the lower dividend yield to achieve the higher overall return on his portfolio. Furthermore, common stock dividends are expected to grow over time and probably will keep abreast of price increases. Consequently, the concern is whether the investor is able to take advantage of the benefits offered by common stock investment. Even among common stock portfolios, however, the income constraint can be important, since the dividend yields on common stocks can range from fairly high levels of approximately 6 percent or more to no dividends at all for some growth stocks and some speculative stocks. This explains the portfolio objectives of common stock portfolios, ranging from income on the one hand to appreciation on the other. In Mr. Fox's case, if the portfolio yielded 1 percent, this would be more than adequate. Consequently, the need for income does not impose a serious constraint at all.

Mr. Fox's case is relatively straightforward. The difficult case emerges when the portfolio must generate as much income as possible to meet current needs. This situation occurs many times when retirement age is reached but an adequate pension does not exist. In such cases the proper course of action becomes difficult because by investing entirely in bonds it is obvious that the purchasing power of the income generated slowly will be eroded, yet a common stock portfolio which may provide some protection against increases in the general price level will not provide an adequate amount of current income. In such circumstances, the proper course of action cannot be generalized, and the proper solution depends to a large extent on the circumstances surrounding each individual case.

A variation of this problem emerges in cases where a will makes provision for a life tenant with the disposition of the portfolio passing to a remainderman upon the death of the life tenant. This situation can arise when a head of the family leaves a portfolio of securities to a son or daughter, but the income of the portfolio is to be used to support his wife until her death. In such circumstances, the wife may want as much income as possible from the portfolio, meaning that it should be invested in bonds. If the trustee does this, however, he is subject to criticism from the remainderman, because the purchasing power of the portfolio may be seriously eroded by such a policy. This is a difficult position for the portfolio manager.

Safety of Principal

Another factor that can impose a serious constraint on the portfolio is the need for safety of principal. This means that the portfolio must maintain its principal in the event of forced liquidation. Obviously, the investor does not want to accept a loss of principal, particularly when it can be avoided. There are three important considerations involved in determining the need for safety of principal: (1) tenure of ownership, (2) collateral value, and (3) the effect of inflation.

Tenure of ownership is probably the most important consideration. Weak tenure of ownership means that there is a high probability that the portfolio will be liquidated to meet some contingency. Examples of portfolios with weak tenure of ownership are the secondary reserves of commercial banks and many industrial firms. The funds tied up in these secondary reserves may be required at any time for some operating purpose. As a result, the secondary reserves may be liquidated at any time. These reserves could not be invested in either long-term bonds or common stocks since there is a strong probability that forced liquidation may lead to a loss of principal. Stock prices are quite volatile, and the time to liquidate a common stock portfolio should be at the discretion of the investor, not dictated by unforeseen events. Much the same is true of long-term bond investment. Prices of high-quality bonds fluctuate with interest rates, and the longer the maturity of the bonds, the greater the effect of a change in interest rates. Forced liquidation subsequent to a rise in interest rates can lead to a substantial loss of principal. These secondary reserves, therefore, should be invested in high-quality short-term debt instruments, such as Treasury bills, banker's acceptances, and commercial paper in order to minimize the loss of principal.

Another strategy involves using an investment portfolio as potential collateral. This occurs from time to time with small businessmen. Many small businessmen put their savings into securities portfolios, but the portfolios may be used as collateral for loans when needed. For example, suppose the initial amount of the portfolio is $100,000. Suppose also that a bank will lend up to 75 percent of the market value of bonds and up to 40 percent of the market value of common stocks. These loan requirements alone tend to favor bond portfolios, but the major consideration is the maximum size of the potential loan. If the potential loan is in the range of $80,000 to $100,000, neither a bond nor common stock portfolio can be used as collateral for the full amount. If the maximum loan requirement is $50,000, this may favor investing in a bond portfolio. However, since interest rates appear to be fairly volatile, it follows that the collateral value of a bond portfolio may be rather limited. Nevertheless, investing in bonds simply to provide collateral for loans may be an appropriate approach in some cases.

As a result, the more pressing the need for safety of principal, the more conservative the investment policy. This constraint appears to be either a serious constraint or not a constraint at all. There do not appear to be the intermediate tradeoffs as with the need for income. This results because changes in long-term interest rates have a substantial impact on the prices of long-term bonds. For example, suppose long-term interest rates on high-quality bonds increased from 7 percent to 8 percent. Twenty-year bonds with 7-percent coupon rates would then fall from par to 90.10, a drop of about 10 percent. Hence, an increase of 1 percent in the market rate of interest would have an impact on the market value of the bond portfolio that is substantial. The need for safety of principal, therefore, may be most appropriately viewed as an "either/or" decision. That is, either it is an important constraint or it is not. This conclusion may be modified by the long-term outlook for interest rates. If it appears that interest rates are at a cyclical high, the chances of suffering a loss of principal value through increasing interest rates would seem to be reduced. The difficulty here is that some unforeseen events may lead to an incorrect forecast. In 1966, for example, long-term interest rates were at an all-time post–World War II high, at approximately 5 percent. Yet the subsequent inflation prompted by the Vietnam War forced interest rates substantially above 1966 levels to approximately 8.5 percent during mid-1970. The outlook for the 1970s appears to be that there is little chance of interest rates retreating to the 1966 levels. This prediction, of course, is subject to error.

The third consideration is the effect of a rising price level on the principal invested initially in the portfolio. This is particularly important for bond portfolios held for long periods of time. To illustrate, consider a bond portfolio of $500,000 held for a period of 20 years under conditions of "creeping inflation" of 2 percent per year. Under these conditions, the purchasing power of this principal would be reduced by 32.7 percent in 20 years, or the portfolio would have purchasing power equivalent to $336,500. For this reason, most portfolio managers attempt to hedge against inflation by including at least a portion of the portfolio in common stock. Since World War II, common stock in general has provided a return of approximately 12.0 percent, and corporate profits have tended to increase at approximately the same rate as the economy as a whole.[1] Consequently, a portfolio of common stock is believed to protect the purchas-

---

[1] This rate of return is taken from a study by Lawrence Fisher and James H. Lorie. It assumes tax exemption and reinvestment of dividends. See Lawrence Fisher and James H. Lorie, "Rates of Return on Investments in Common Stock: The Year-By-Year Record, 1926–65," *The Journal of Business*, vol. 41, no. 3 (July, 1968), pp. 291–316.

ing power of the principal value of the portfolio. This fact has led to the greater emphasis on common stock for most portfolios.[2]

A second situation that can occur concerns the end-use of the funds involved in the portfolio. If the end-use involves the purchase of goods and services, the investor may be more concerned with a rising price level. If, on the other hand, the investor is only committed to turn over a specified number of dollars to a third party, he can pass the risk of a rising price level on to the third party. The insurance industry vividly illustrates these two situations. Property and casualty insurance companies provide insurance against property damage and personal mishap. As the general price level increases, the costs of repair and bodily injury also increase, yet the premiums are based on historical experience. In addition, the premiums may be paid for several years in advance. Conceivably, the premiums may not cover the actual losses if prices increase sharply. As a result, property and casualty insurance companies are concerned with purchasing power risk and attempt to offset it to some extent by investing in common stock.

Life insurance companies, on the other hand, are really unconcerned with a rising price level because they have contracted to pay a stipulated number of dollars if a specified event occurs. As a consequence, the loss of purchasing power is passed along to the holder of the policy. In some respects this is a unique situation. It is seldom indeed that the investor is able to pass the risk of inflation on to a third party, and this probably explains the relatively slow growth of the life insurance industry in the post–World War II period.

Common Stock Portfolios

The rising price level has led to an increasing emphasis on common stock investment since it is generally believed that firms can increase the selling prices of their products to keep abreast of inflation. Hence, the stockholder is protected against the ravages of inflation. The return on common stocks has been generally higher than that on bonds over much of the period 1926–70, and this is especially true of the period 1950–70. A study by Lawrence Fisher and James H. Lorie provides some evidence of the returns that could have been earned by investing in a portfolio of all of the common stock listed on the New York Stock Exchange between 1945 and 1965.[3] Tables 13-1 and 13-2 reproduce

[2] Note that this hypothesis has come under attack in recent years. See Donald A. Nichols, "A Note on Inflation and Common Stock Values," *Journal of Finance*, vol. 23, no. 4 (Sept., 1968), pp. 655–58; and Frank K. Reilly, Glenn L. Johnson, and Ralph E. Smith, "Inflation, Inflation Hedges, and Common Stocks," *Financial Analysts' Journal*, vol. 26, no. 1 (Jan.–Feb., 1970), pp. 104–10. Furthermore, it has been long recognized that public utilities have not been able to obtain rate increases sufficient to compensate for changes in the general price level in some states. Consequently, the purchasing power of dividends has tended to lag behind price increases during most of the post-World War II period. For an excellent discussion of inflation and public utility rate making, see Paul M. Van Arsdell, *Corporation Finance: Policy, Planning, Administration* (New York: The Ronald Press, 1968), pp. 600–607.

[3] Lawrence Fisher and James H. Lorie, "Rates of Return on Investments in Common Stock: The Year-By-Year Record, 1926–65," *Journal of Business*, vol. 41, no. 3 (July, 1968), pp. 291–316.

TABLE 13-1 Return on New York Stock Exchange Shares With Reinvestment of Dividends, 1945–65 (Compounded Annually)

(a) Cash-to-portfolio, tax exempt

From:

	12/45	12/46	12/47	12/48	12/49	12/50	12/51	12/52	12/53	12/54	12/55	12/56	12/57	12/58	12/59	12/60	12/61	12/62	12/63	12/64
1946	-9.9																			
1947	-4.4	-0.5																		
1948	-3.5	-1.0	-2.9																	
1949	1.9	5.4	8.2	19.3																
1950	7.8	12.4	16.6	27.0	35.8															
1951	9.4	13.3	16.4	23.1	25.2	14.9														
1952	9.4	12.9	15.2	19.7	19.8	12.4	8.9													
1953	7.9	10.5	12.1	15.0	13.7	7.5	3.5	-3.1												
1954	12.5	15.5	17.7	21.3	21.6	17.9	18.5	22.8	54.8											
1955	13.4	16.2	18.2	21.4	21.7	18.5	19.1	22.2	37.2	19.0										
1956	13.3	15.6	17.2	19.8	20.0	17.0	16.9	18.6	26.7	13.3	6.5									
1957	10.5	12.3	13.5	15.3	14.8	12.0	11.1	11.1	14.5	11.1	-3.7	-12.9								
1958	13.2	15.2	16.7	18.7	18.6	16.5	16.5	17.5	21.9	14.5	13.0	17.4	57.9							
1959	13.3	15.3	16.6	18.6	18.6	16.6	16.6	17.6	21.2	15.0	14.0	17.6	36.0	14.4						
1960	12.2	14.0	15.2	16.8	16.5	14.9	14.8	15.3	17.8	12.4	11.2	13.1	21.9	6.4	-1.9					
1961	13.2	14.9	16.0	17.5	17.3	16.0	16.0	16.6	19.0	14.6	13.9	16.1	23.7	13.6	12.9	27.6				
1962	11.3	12.8	13.7	14.9	14.5	13.1	12.8	13.0	14.7	10.5	9.4	10.4	15.1	6.3	3.8	5.9	-13.3			
1963	11.8	13.2	14.0	15.2	14.9	13.5	13.3	13.5	15.0	11.3	10.4	11.5	15.7	8.7	7.4	10.4	2.0	17.7		
1964	12.1	13.4	14.2	15.3	15.0	13.7	13.5	13.8	15.3	11.9	11.2	12.3	16.2	10.4	9.7	12.8	7.6	18.5	16.3	
1965	12.6	14.1	14.9	15.9	15.8	14.5	14.3	14.7	16.2	13.1	12.5	13.6	17.7	12.7	12.4	15.9	12.9	22.6	23.4	28.3

(b) Cash-to-cash, tax exempt

From:

	12/45	12/46	12/47	12/48	12/49	12/50	12/51	12/52	12/53	12/54	12/55	12/56	12/57	12/58	12/59	12/60	12/61	12/62	12/63	12/64
1946	10.6																			
1947	124.9	-1.5																		
1948	123.8	-1.5	-4.0																	
1949	1.6	-5.1	7.6	18.0																
1950	7.6	12.1	16.2	26.4	34.5															
1951	9.2	13.1	16.1	22.8	24.6	13.8														
1952	9.3	12.7	15.0	19.5	19.4	11.9	7.8													
1953	7.7	10.3	11.9	14.8	13.4	7.1	2.9	-4.3												
1954	12.4	15.4	17.6	21.1	21.4	17.6	18.1	22.2	53.2											
1955	13.3	16.1	18.1	21.2	21.6	18.3	18.8	21.8	36.5	17.8										
1956	13.2	15.5	17.1	19.7	19.8	16.8	16.7	18.3	26.3	12.8	5.4									
1957	10.5	12.2	13.4	15.2	14.6	11.8	10.9	10.9	14.2	3.0	-4.2	-13.9								
1958	13.2	15.1	16.6	18.6	18.5	16.4	16.3	17.3	21.6	14.2	12.6	16.8	56.1							
1959	13.2	15.2	16.6	18.5	18.5	16.4	16.5	17.4	20.9	14.8	13.7	17.2	35.2	13.2						
1960	12.2	13.9	15.1	16.7	16.4	14.7	14.7	15.2	17.6	12.2	11.0	12.8	21.4	5.8	-3.1					
1961	13.1	14.8	16.0	17.4	17.2	15.9	15.9	16.5	18.8	14.4	13.7	15.9	23.3	13.2	12.3	26.2				
1962	11.3	12.7	13.6	14.8	14.4	13.0	12.7	12.7	14.5	10.3	9.2	10.2	14.8	6.0	3.4	5.2	-14.4			
1963	11.7	13.2	14.0	15.1	14.8	13.4	13.2	13.4	14.9	11.2	10.3	11.3	15.5	8.5	7.1	10.0	1.4	16.3		
1964	12.0	13.4	14.1	15.0	15.0	13.6	13.4	13.7	15.2	11.8	11.1	12.2	16.0	10.2	9.4	12.5	7.2	17.8	15.0	
1965	12.6	14.1	14.8	15.9	15.7	14.4	14.3	14.6	16.2	13.0	12.4	13.5	17.5	12.5	12.3	15.7	12.6	22.2	22.7	26.9

Source: Fisher and Lorie, op. cit., p. 296.

TABLE 13-2 Return on New York Stock Exchange Shares Without Reinvestment of Dividends (Compounded Annually)

(a) Cash-to-portfolio, tax exempt

From:	12/45	12/46	12/47	12/48	12/49	12/50	12/51	12/52	12/53	12/54	12/55	12/56	12/57	12/58	12/59	12/60	12/61	12/62	12/63	12/64
1946	-9.8																			
1947	-4.6	-0.7																		
1948	-3.6	-1.0	-2.8																	
1949	1.2	4.9	7.7	18.9																
1950	6.6	11.4	15.7	26.5	35.7															
1951	8.1	12.4	15.8	23.1	25.6	15.0														
1952	8.3	12.1	14.8	20.0	20.3	12.5	8.8													
1953	7.2	10.2	12.2	15.8	14.6	7.9	3.6	-3.2												
1954	10.9	14.4	16.9	21.1	21.5	17.3	17.8	22.1	54.8											
1955	11.8	15.0	17.4	21.2	21.6	18.0	18.5	21.8	37.7	19.0										
1956	11.7	14.6	16.5	19.8	20.1	16.6	16.6	18.5	27.4	13.5	6.6									
1957	9.8	12.2	13.7	16.3	15.7	12.2	11.6	11.8	15.9	4.0	-3.3	-12.7								
1958	11.9	14.4	16.2	18.8	18.8	16.2	16.2	17.4	22.5	14.3	12.6	16.9	58.1							
1959	12.0	14.4	16.2	18.8	18.8	16.3	16.4	17.5	21.8	14.9	13.7	17.3	36.5	14.6						
1960	11.3	13.6	15.2	17.4	17.2	15.0	14.9	15.6	18.7	12.5	11.1	13.1	22.6	6.6	-2.1					
1961	12.0	14.2	15.8	17.9	17.7	15.8	15.8	16.6	19.7	14.4	13.6	15.9	24.2	13.5	12.7	27.9				
1962	10.7	12.7	14.0	15.8	15.5	13.4	13.1	13.5	15.8	10.7	9.4	10.6	15.9	6.5	3.8	6.1	-13.5			
1963	11.0	13.0	14.3	16.0	15.7	13.7	13.5	13.8	16.0	11.4	10.4	11.6	16.5	8.8	7.2	10.6	1.8	18.0		
1964	11.3	13.2	14.4	16.1	15.8	13.9	13.7	14.1	16.2	11.9	11.0	12.3	16.7	10.3	9.4	12.8	7.3	18.6	16.4	
1965	11.7	13.7	14.9	16.5	16.3	14.5	14.3	14.8	18.7	13.0	12.2	13.5	18.1	12.4	12.1	15.8	12.5	22.7	23.4	28.3

(b) Cash-to-cash, tax exempt

From:	12/45	12/46	12/47	12/48	12/49	12/50	12/51	12/52	12/53	12/54	12/55	12/56	12/57	12/58	12/59	12/60	12/61	12/62	12/63	12/64
1946	-10.5																			
1947	-5.0	-1.7																		
1948	-3.9	-1.5	-3.8																	
1949	1.0	4.6	7.2	17.7																
1950	6.4	11.1	15.4	25.9	34.4															
1951	8.0	12.2	15.6	22.7	25.0	13.9														
1952	8.2	12.0	14.6	19.7	20.0	12.0	7.7													
1953	7.1	10.1	12.0	15.6	14.3	7.5	3.0	-4.3												
1954	10.9	14.3	16.8	20.9	21.3	17.1	17.4	21.5	53.3											
1955	11.7	14.9	17.3	21.0	21.5	17.8	18.3	21.4	37.0	17.9										
1956	11.6	14.5	16.4	19.7	19.9	16.5	16.4	18.2	27.0	13.0	5.5									
1957	9.7	12.1	13.7	16.2	15.6	12.3	11.4	11.6	15.6	3.7	-3.8	-13.7								
1958	11.8	14.3	16.1	18.8	18.7	16.1	16.0	17.2	22.2	14.0	12.2	16.3	56.3							
1959	11.9	14.4	16.1	18.7	18.7	16.2	16.3	17.4	21.6	14.7	13.4	16.9	35.8	13.3						
1960	11.2	13.5	15.1	17.3	17.1	14.9	14.8	15.5	18.6	12.4	10.9	12.8	22.2	6.0	-3.2					
1961	11.9	14.2	15.7	17.8	17.6	15.7	15.7	16.5	19.5	14.3	13.5	15.7	23.9	13.1	12.1	26.5				
1962	10.6	12.7	14.0	15.8	15.4	13.1	13.1	13.4	15.7	10.6	9.3	10.4	15.7	6.2	3.4	5.5	-14.6			
1963	11.0	13.0	14.2	16.0	15.6	13.4	13.4	13.7	15.9	11.3	10.2	11.4	16.3	8.5	7.0	10.2	1.2	16.6		
1964	11.2	13.1	14.3	16.0	15.7	13.7	13.6	14.0	16.1	11.8	10.9	12.1	16.6	10.1	9.2	12.5	6.9	18.0	15.1	
1965	11.6	13.6	14.8	16.5	16.3	14.4	14.3	14.7	16.8	12.9	12.1	13.4	17.9	12.3	11.9	15.6	12.2	22.3	22.8	27.0

Source: Fisher and Lorie, op. cit., p. 314.

some of these results for that period. Table 13-1 assumes that all cash dividends are reinvested excluding tax considerations, while Table 13-2 assumes that dividends are not reinvested. The assumption of dividend reinvestment leads to a larger return, but not everyone reinvests dividends, so Table 13-2 becomes relevant to those investors who consume some of their dividend income. Further, these returns apply to portfolios made up of equal participation in every common stock listed on the New York Stock Exchange, and consequently these returns seem fairly indicative of the return on stocks in general. Individual portfolios may not show the same performance for a number of reasons. Finally, cash-to-portfolio and cash-to-cash simply refer to the transaction at the end of the period. Cash-to-portfolio means that the portfolio is assumed to be held in securities, whereas cash-to-cash assumes that the portfolio has been liquidated at the end of the period and transactions costs have been included.

Regardless of whether one assumes reinvestment of dividends, it is evident from Tables 13-1 and 13-2 that the return on common stocks during this period has been relatively high. For the entire period, 12 percent appears to be a fairly realistic estimate of the return on common stock for this period. Reinvestment of dividends would have led to a return of about 12.6 percent, while not reinvesting dividends would have led to a return of approximately 1 percent less. Regardless of the treatment of dividends, the return is more than double that on high-quality bonds at any point during the period. These conclusions probably hold true for the period up to 1970. Since 1970, however, the return on common stocks has not been nearly as high as in the period 1950–70. Consequently, common stocks have not provided the protection against inflation that they did in the previous years, raising the question of whether common stocks are indeed the hedge against inflation that they once were.

Taxation

Tax-exempt securities offer an unusual opportunity for those investors in high income-tax brackets to combine a high effective yield with relatively low risk. For example, an investor in the 50-percent marginal tax bracket could receive an effective yield of 8 percent on a 4 percent tax-exempt security. This does not compare too favorably with the return on common stock of approximately 12 percent earned in the post–World War II period. However, when the risk of the two types of securities is compared, the tax-exempt security has much less risk, and it compares more favorably when this risk is considered. This is particularly true when one recalls that the past may not be a good indicator of the future. Consequently, for those who qualify, tax-exempt securities may constitute a very worthwhile investment.

It is often argued that the wealthier investor can readily accept risk because if a loss does occur it will not lead to ruin. This line of reasoning was raised in Chapter 5 in connection with warrants. This does not necessarily follow. If an investor is comfortably well off, why accept extraordinary risks? The utility of the potential gain may be very small; hence, there is very little incentive to accept such risks. This really comes down to a question of utility preference. But wealth may very well make the investor more conservative rather than more willing to accept high degrees of risk. If this is true, there may be strong incentive for many investors in the high tax brackets to invest in tax-exempt municipal securities rather than common stock.

Temperament

In many cases, the most important constraint on the formulation of portfolio objectives is the willingness of the investor to accept risk. Some investors are able to accept considerable risk, while others can accept only a minimum of risk. This has important ramifications for common stock investment. Common stock prices are particularly volatile. It is not uncommon for stocks selling in a price range between $20 to $50 to fluctuate $10 to $15 in a year. If the investor finds this volatility disturbing, particularly when stock prices are falling, he may not have the temperament for common stock investment. This fact may be the overriding constraint in arriving at an appropriate portfolio policy for the investor.

Because of the importance of temperament, some attempt must be made to determine the investor's disposition toward risky situations. There is an obvious similarity here between attempting to determine temperament and utility analysis discussed in Chapter 5. In the traditional approach, however, no attempt is made to quantify this factor. It is ranked on a qualitative scale representing perhaps high, low, or moderate tolerance for risky situations.

Weighing Constraints

The final step in determining portfolio policies is to establish the constraints on the portfolio. This means weighing each constraint individually and determining its importance through the introduction of a ranking scale. This may be undertaken in many different ways.[4] We use a ranking scale of one to five for each constraint as follows:

Need for income in current dollars	1 2 3 4 5
Need for income in constant dollars	1 2 3 4 5
Need for safety of principal in current dollars	1 2 3 4 5
Need for safety of principal in constant dollars	1 2 3 4 5
Taxability	1 2 3 4 5
Temperament	1 2 3 4 5

[4] For an alternative approach, see Harry Sauvain, *Investment Management*, 3d ed. (Englewood Cliffs, N.J.: Prentice-Hall, 1967), Chapter 10.

A low ranking, say a one or a two, would mean that the particular constraint was not that important, whereas a high ranking would mean that the constraint was quite important. Once the checklist is completed, it becomes a matter of weighing the tradeoff among the various constraints to determine the appropriate portfolio objective.

To illustrate, suppose the following constraints have been established for a certain investor:

Need for income in current dollars	① 2 3 4 5
Need for income in constant dollars	1 2 3 4 ⑤
Need for safety of principal in current dollars	① 2 3 4 5
Need for safety of principal in constant dollars	1 2 3 4 ⑤
Taxability	① 2 3 4 5
Temperament	1 2 ③ 4 5

Tax-exempt securities can be immediately eliminated as an investment vehicle for this investor. The major concern of this portfolio appears to be preservation of purchasing power. There is not a strong current income need nor is there a strong need to maintain the principal value of the portfolio in current dollars. Evidently the income requirements on the portfolio are modest with respect to the size of the portfolio. As a result, a bond portfolio is not required to meet current income requirements. In addition, since the tenure of ownership is strong, the portfolio can be invested in long-term instruments. Finally, the evaluation of temperament indicates that this investor is willing to accept a moderate level of risk. These factors taken together seem to indicate that a portfolio of high-quality common stock is appropriate.

The Traditional Approach: A Case Study

Suppose that Mr. Brown is attempting to find an investment outlet for the $500,000 that he received through an inheritance. Mr. Brown is 42 years old, married, with two teen-age children, and in good health. Currently he is sales manager for a small midwestern distributing firm. He has worked with this firm for 10 years. His current salary is $20,000. Although Mr. Brown has never taken a great interest in the stock market, he is accustomed to the uncertainty connected with forecasting future events. An evaluation of Mr. Brown's pension plans and insurance indicate that he has made adequate preparations. He has a company pension plan as well as social security, and he has been careful in providing adequate life insurance to meet his family's needs for the foreseeable future. The family is also covered by a company-sponsored health insurance program. Finally, an examination of other possible contingencies indicates that there is little evidence that an unforeseen occurrence will require sudden liquidation of all or part of the portfolio.

The starting point in the traditional approach is to determine the income requirement of the portfolio. It is evident that the portfolio will not be required to supply some minimum amount of current income, so this is not a serious constraint. Nor does safety of principal in current dollars seem to be a serious constraint. Purchasing power risk, however, may be an important consideration. For example, if the general price level rose at a rate of 2 percent for the next 23 years, the $500,000 portfolio would have to increase to $788,450 to preserve its purchasing power, or an increase of approximately 58 percent. In Mr. Brown's case, there does not appear to be a need for current income, nor does there appear to be a need to preserve the principal value of the portfolio in current dollars. Consequently, these two constraints do not preclude the use of common stock in this portfolio.

Another possibility for Mr. Brown's portfolio is tax-exempt securities. The appropriate marginal tax rate on income of between $16,000 to $20,000 is 28 percent. However, if the portfolio were invested in securities, the marginal tax rate would increase to a range between 39 to 50 percent, depending upon the type of investment. Hence, if we use an effective tax rate of 39 percent, the effective yield on municipal bonds yielding 5 percent is

$$Y_M = \frac{5.0}{1.0 - 0.39} = 7.57\%$$

This return compares favorably with that on corporate bonds that currently yield 7 percent, but is still somewhat below that on common stock. Obviously, municipals may be advantageous to Mr. Brown.

The final factor is the temperament of the investor. Mr. Brown's work familiarized him with various aspects of risk and uncertainty. The uncertainty of the stock market is, of course, somewhat greater than that connected with distribution, although there is considerable risk connected with the distribution of new product lines. A further consideration is that Mr. Brown has never owned common stock. Under the circumstances it may be well to indicate to Mr. Brown that neither bonds nor common stock promise stability of principal. Depending on the outlook for interest rates, high-quality bonds promise more stability than common stock but not by a substantial margin. Hence, it seems fair to conclude that Mr. Brown's temperament may permit some risk-taking but not a great deal.

In summary, the importance of each constraint can be ranked in the following manner:

Need for income in current dollars	① 2 3 4 5
Need for income in constant dollars	① 2 3 4 5
Need for safety of principal in current dollars	① 2 3 4 5
Need for safety of principal in constant dollars	1 2 3 ④ 5
Taxability	4 2 ③ 4 5
Temperament	1 2 ③ 4 5

It is evident that the investment strategies open to Mr. Brown are not greatly restricted. Certainly if common stock is selected as the investment vehicle, it will have to be high-quality common stock. This is dictated by our evaluation of Mr. Brown's temperament. He probably would not be too disturbed by a moderate decline in principal value in the short run, but he may be unwilling to accept a major decline. Municipals pose another alternative, since the yield is somewhat greater than the yield that might be expected on high-quality bonds. The decision hinges to some extent on the temperament of Mr. Brown. Nevertheless, since there are so few constraints, and since his age, health, and future prospects are good, a strong case can be made for investing the entire portfolio in common stock. If this is found not to be appropriate, then a mixed portfolio of high-quality common stocks and municipal bonds would be appropriate.

Selecting the Securities

Once the objective of the portfolio has been determined, the securities to be included in the portfolio must be selected. For bond portfolios, this is not a particularly difficult task. Normally the portfolio is selected from a list of high-quality bonds that the portfolio manager has at hand. These bond portfolios are normally made up of high-quality bonds, since the essential purpose for investing in bonds is safety of principal and interest. Common stock portfolios, however, are somewhat more complex, since the objective may range from income only to pure appreciation. Presumably, common stocks can be found that will meet these needs. A study by Geoffrey P. Clarkson and Allan H. Meltzer enables us to have a first-hand look at how the securities may be selected for portfolios of common stock.[5]

The Clarkson and Meltzer study presents an opportunity to observe the type of rules used by a traditionalist in actually developing a portfolio of common stock. The purpose of the study was to attempt to simulate by computer the actual portfolio building behavior of a trust officer. To do this the computer had to be programmed to make the same decisions that the trust officer would make. For our purposes, it is useful to follow the procedure used by the trust officer to illustrate the traditional approach.

The starting point was the objective of the account. The trust officer followed a procedure similar to that described above to arrive at an appropriate goal for the account. The goals for common stock investment were: (1) pure growth, (2) growth with some income, (3) income with some growth, and (4) income only. Once the goal had been selected, the procedure was as follows:

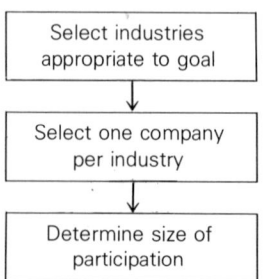

Select industries appropriate to goal

↓

Select one company per industry

↓

Determine size of participation

---

[5] Geoffrey P. Clarkson and Allan H. Meltzer, "Portfolio Selection: A Heuristic Approach," *Journal of Finance*, vol. 15, no. 4 (Dec., 1960), pp. 465–80. Reprinted in Richard E. Ball, ed., *Readings in Investment* (Boston: Allyn & Bacon, 1965), pp. 167–84.

The trust officer associated specific industries with particular investment goals. Admittedly, there is considerable overlap among industries, but in this case each industry was considered to correspond to a specific investment goal. The next step was to select one company from within each industry. In addition to certain qualitative considerations, the decision was based on criteria such as: (1) current uncertainty, (2) growth, (3) yield, (4) expected earnings, (5) past earnings, (6) expected dividends, (7) expected price-earnings ratio, (8) past price-earnings ratio, and (9) the amount spent on expansion and/or research and development. These are all standard variables that are available from the security analysts. Selecting the company with the best prospects is an approach that is widely followed by security analysts and portfolio managers.[6]

The final step in the process was to determine the number of shares of each stock to purchase. The process involved determining the number of different stocks that were required to give adequate diversification. If the size of the portfolio permitted, an equal amount was invested in each stock adjusted to round lots. That is, round lots of each stock in the portfolio were purchased, and consequently the amount invested in each portfolio would not be strictly equal. This procedure was designed to minimize transactions costs. However, if the size of the portfolio was small, and the amount to be invested was below $\frac{3}{8}K$, where K is a constant amount used to determine which procedure to use, then the following was used:

1. Given the amount to be invested and the number of different stocks to be purchased, the average amount to be invested in each stock was found.

2. The average amount was then divided by the current price of the stock to give the number to be purchased. These were generally rounded to the nearest multiple of five.

The approach for small portfolios parallels that for large portfolios, except odd-lots of each stock were purchased. For both small and large portfolios, the starting point was to determine the number of stocks needed to give adequate diversification.

It is obvious that this approach is largely intuitive. However, Clarkson and Meltzer showed that a computer could be programmed to simulate the portfolio-building habits of the trust officer. This study illustrates the traditional approach to selecting stocks for portfolios. In the next three chapters, we will examine some of the more recently developed approaches to portfolio composition.

Summary

Portfolio composition is the ultimate decision and represents the convergence of all the factors involved in investment management. On the one hand, there are the various predictions of the security analysts as to anticipated rates of

---

[6] Frederick Amling, *Investments: An Introduction to Analysis and Management*, 2d ed. (Englewood Cliffs, N.J.: Prentice-Hall, 1970), p. 344.

return and the risk associated obtaining that return. On the other hand, there are the various factors that affect the investor's ability and willingness to accept the risk associated with obtaining the higher return on riskier securities. The traditional approach attempts to provide a framework for making this decision, and the underlying assumption is that an investor wants to maximize his expected utility. This assumption may seem somewhat obvious, but it will be the center of controversy in the wealth-maximization model discussed in Chapter 16. The major decision areas of the traditional approach are: (1) to determine the appropriate portfolio objective, (2) to select the securities to enter the portfolio, and (3) to determine the participation of each security in the portfolio. Each step must be followed in sequence to ultimately develop the portfolio.

Much attention is given to formulating the appropriate objective. The normal procedure is to weigh the constraints placed on the portfolio. The constraints placed on a portfolio can be determined by evaluating six different areas:

1. Need for income in current dollars
2. Need for income in constant dollars
3. Need for safety of principal in current dollars
4. Need for safety of principal in constant dollars
5. Taxability
6. Temperament

The principal concern is the degree of risk that the investor can assume. If the constraints on the investor permit, a portfolio of common stock can be expected to yield a higher return than bond portfolios. There seems to be little question that stocks have outperformed bonds in most of the past 100 years. Consequently, the key consideration is whether the investor is willing and able to accept the risk associated with common stock investment.

Questions

1. Ben Richardson, your next-door neighbor and close friend, asks your advice on investing some savings. Ben is 27 years old and has been married three years, has one child, and has been employed as an accountant with his current employer for four years. Through his employment he has adequate medical insurance and a pension plan, although his retirement needs are a distant concern. His life insurance requirements appear to be adequately taken care of. The family purchased their home two years ago. Ben has accumulated $1,800, which he would like to invest in stocks. He feels that he is now in a position to invest in stocks, although the amount available for future investment will be rather small because of a number of demands on the income of a young family. What is your advice to Ben?

2. Mr. Jack Lathrop has worked for a medium-sized integrated oil company for 15 years. He is now 42 years old and was recently promoted to the position of Manager of the Transportation Department at a salary of $32,000 per year. He has two children, one 14, the other 11 years of age. It appears that his

health insurance, life insurance, and pension plan are adequate. Since Mr. Lathrop recently sold some income property, he now has $28,000 to invest. Through conversation with Mr. Lathrop, it becomes evident that he does not believe in taking risks. However, the extent of this risk aversion is not clear and will require further discussion. What do you feel is the most suitable portfolio objective for Mr. Lathrop, irrespective of his willingness to accept risk?

3. Mr. Art Rasmussen has worked as a truck driver for an interstate mover for 40 years. Next year he is due to retire with a small company pension of $125 per month and social security benefits of $213 per month. The family home is paid for and comfortably meets their needs. The midwestern city in which Mr. Rasmussen and his wife live has been their home since their childhood. The Rasmussens have been thrifty with their modest income and currently own several small rental properties valued at $37,000. They also have $7,500 in a savings account. It has been estimated that the Rasmussens will require about $5,000 to cover all living expenses and provide for the little extras that they deem necessary in their retirement. Mr. Rasmussen is considering selling his rental properties and investing the funds in securities. What advice would you give him for investing these funds?

4. Mr. R. Goodrich has received $110,000 from an insurance company settlement of an automobile accident. The accident left Mr. Goodrich confined to a wheelchair. He is 33 years old and married, with two children aged 6 and 8. The Goodriches purchased their home when they were first married, ten years ago. At that time the house cost considerably less than its current value of $27,000. In 10 more years it will be paid for; monthly payments for principal, interest, and taxes are currently $150. Maintenance is normally $300 per year. Aside from the equity in the home, the Goodriches have little savings. In addition to the housing expense, it is estimated that an additional $4,000 is needed to meet the family's needs. Mrs. Goodrich has not worked since she was married. However, the family disaster has prompted her to consider returning to her previous employment as a stenographer, which should pay about $125 per week. Retraining, however, will require approximately 6 months. Mr. Goodrich will be seeking rehabilitation once he has sufficiently recovered from his injuries. How would you invest these funds for Mr. Goodrich?

5. Mrs. Connie Rosenbloom inherited $150,000 from her late husband, Benjamin. His will provided that the estate should be used to provide for Mrs. Rosenbloom during her lifetime, and then be divided equally between their two children, Eric and Rosemary. Mrs. Rosenbloom is 62 and in good health. The family home is paid for. Mrs. Rosenbloom's living expenses are not expected to exceed $8,000 per year. What recommendations would you make for investing these funds?

6. As a research project, utilize all the sources of information available to determine the industries that would qualify for each of the following common stock portfolio objectives:

Income only
Income and some appreciation
Appreciation with some income
Appreciation only

7. In the Clarkson-Meltzer study, the method of determining the participation normally meant purchasing approximately equal dollar amounts of each stock to be selected for the portfolio. What are the implications of this policy with respect to the firm-related risks of each stock in the portfolio?

Selected References

Clarkson, Geoffrey P., and Allan H. Meltzer. "Portfolio Selection: A Heuristic Approach." *Journal of Finance*, vol. 15, no. 4 (Dec., 1960), pp. 465–80.

Fisher, Lawrence, and James H. Lorie. "Rates of Return on Investments in Common Stock: The Year-By-Year Record, 1926–1965," *Journal of Business*, vol. 41, no. 3 (July, 1968), pp. 291–316.

Gibson, William E. "Price-Expectations Effects on Interest Rates," *Journal of Finance*, vol. 25, no. 1 (Mar., 1970), pp. 19–35.

Latane, Henry A., and Donald L. Tuttle. *Security Analysis and Portfolio Management*. New York: The Ronald Press, 1970. Chapter 24.

Nichols, Donald A. "A Note on Inflation and Common Stock Values." *Journal of Finance*, vol. 23, no. 4 (Sept., 1968), pp. 655–57.

Reilly, Frank K., Glenn L. Johnson, and Ralph E. Smith. "Inflation, Inflation Hedges, and Common Stocks." *Financial Analysts' Journal*, vol. 26, no. 1 (Jan.–Feb., 1970) pp. 104–10.

Sauvain, Harry C. "Changing Interest Rates and the Investment Portfolio." *Journal of Finance*, vol. 14. no. 2 (May, 1959), pp. 230–44.

———. *Investment Management*, 3d ed., Englewood Cliffs, N.J.:Prentice-Hall, 1967.

Weil, Roman. "Realized Interest Rates and Bondholders' Return," *American Economic Review*, vol. 60, no. 3 (June, 1970), pp. 502–12.

Chapter 14

Principles of Diversification

Diversification has long been an integral part of investment management. As the traditional approach illustrated, the benefits of diversification are often taken for granted. One of the benefits of the Markowitz portfolio model was the development of a more rigorous way of investigating the benefits of diversification.[1] That is, with the quantification of risk, it was also possible to set forth the conditions necessary for diversification to reduce the risk of a portfolio of securities. Risk reduction, however, will only result when there are offsetting effects within the portfolio. For example, if the returns of all the securities in a portfolio are highly correlated, the benefits of diversification should be minimal. On the other hand, if the returns on some securities in the portfolio rise while others fall, diversification should be more beneficial. Statements such as these, however, are vague and do not illuminate the process. Quantitative analysis of the process of diversification can provide valuable insight for the portfolio manager in evaluating the tradeoff between risk and expected return.

Aside from the question of the theoretically necessary conditions for diversification to reduce risk, it is necessary to know what conditions actually exist. For example, is it possible to diversify among various types of securities and eliminate all possible risk? If this is not possible, how much risk can be diversified away? The answer to this question varies with the type of portfolio. Diversification in high-quality bonds will help reduce the risk of loss due to default, but in general this risk is relatively low and diversification will not reduce it significantly. On the other hand, diversification in common stocks may reduce the risk substantially, although the remaining risk may still be significant. A related question is the number of securities required to achieve the maximum benefits of diversification. For high-quality bond portfolios,

[1] Harry M. Markowitz, *Portfolio Selection: Efficient Diversification of Investments* (New York: John Wiley & Sons, 1959).

probably a small number of bonds representing various industries, perhaps 10 to 15, provide the maximum benefits, and in general the number of issues in a portfolio is not a major consideration because of the relatively low risk. For common stock portfolios, this becomes a much more important consideration because diversification cannot only reduce the potential risk, but it can also reduce the potential return on a portfolio. Hence, the number of securities required to obtain the maximum benefits of diversification is an important consideration for common stock portfolios.

Rationale for Diversification

Diversification is an example of the tradeoff between risk and return. Whenever the investor considers diversification, he must recognize that the decision involves reducing the risk of not attaining some expected return and also accepting a somewhat lower anticipated return. To illustrate this, consider a portfolio of 10 stocks with expected returns ranging from 20 percent down to 10 percent, with varying amounts of risk. If the investor is indifferent to risk, he will invest the entire proceeds of the portfolio in the stock expected to yield 20 percent. In concentrating the portfolio in one stock, however, there is considerable risk that the anticipated 20-percent return may not materialize. By diversifying the investor is more assured of obtaining 15 percent. A policy of concentration is the appropriate policy for the investor who wants to make a "killing" in the market, whereas diversification provides greater assurance of obtaining a more moderate return.

Basic Relationships

The return on a portfolio of securities is the weighted average of the return of the securities in the portfolio. If we consider this in an ex ante sense, the return can be expressed as

$$E(R) = \sum_{i=1}^{n} X_i \mu_i \qquad (14\text{-}1)$$

where $E(R)$ is the expected return on the portfolio, X_i is the proportion invested in security i, and μ_i is the expected return of security i. This formulation assumes that the X_i will sum to 1, which means that the portfolio is made up entirely of securities.

Generally the risk of the portfolio is given by the standard deviation, but the standard deviation is not only affected by the variance of the securities in the portfolio, but also by the covariance. That is, the risk of the portfolio will be affected to the extent that the securities in the portfolio are correlated. As a result, the variance of return for the portfolio must include the covariance among securities within the portfolio as follows:

$$V(R) = \sum_{i=1}^{n} X_i^2 \sigma_i^2 + 2 \sum_{i=1}^{n} \sum_{j=1}^{n} X_i X_j \sigma_{ij} \qquad i \neq j \qquad (14\text{-}2)$$

where $V(R)$ is the variance of the portfolio return, the σ_i^2 is the variance of return for security i, X_j is the proportion invested in security j, and σ_{ij} is the covariance between securities i and j.[2] The covariance between securities i and j is given by

$$\sigma_{ij} = \rho_{ij} \sigma_i \sigma_j \qquad (14\text{-}3)$$

where ρ_{ij} is the correlation between securities i and j, and σ_i and σ_j are the standard deviation of return on securities i and j, respectively. Once the variance is found using Equation 14-2, the standard deviation is given by taking the square root as follows:

$$S = V(R)^{\frac{1}{2}} \qquad (14\text{-}4)$$

where the terms are as previously defined.

To illustrate the use of Equations 14-1 and 14-2, consider a portfolio of four stocks, with the proportions, expected returns, and standard deviations as follows:

Security	Proportion	Expected return	Standard deviation
1	0.20	10 percent	4 percent
2	0.30	12	6
3	0.40	14	8
4	0.10	16	10

This information is sufficient to determine the expected return on the portfolio, but the correlation between securities in the portfolio is necessary to give the variance, and therefore the risk of the portfolio. Suppose the correlation between the securities is as follows:

	1	2	3	4
1	+1.0	+0.8	−0.2	+0.6
2	—	+1.0	−0.2	+0.6
3	—	—	+1.0	−0.4
4	—	—	—	+1.0

The expected return of the portfolio is given by substituting into Equation 14-1 as follows:

$$E(R) = 0.2(10.0) + 0.3(12.0) + 0.4(14.0) + 0.1(16.0) = 12.8 \text{ percent}$$

[2] Equation 14-2 can also be shown as follows:

$$V(R) = X_1^2 \sigma_1^2 + X_2^2 \sigma_2^2 + \ldots + X_n^2 \sigma_n^2$$
$$+ 2X_1 X_2 \sigma_{12} + \ldots + 2X_1 X_n \sigma_{1n}$$
$$+ 2X_2 X_3 \sigma_{23} + \ldots + 2X_2 X_n \sigma_{2n}$$
$$= \sum_{i=1}^{n} \sum_{j=1}^{n} X_i X_j \sigma_{ij}$$

This is simply the weighted average of the expected return of each stock in the portfolio. Obtaining the variance, the standard deviation, is somewhat more complex. The process can be simplified, however, by first forming a variance-covariance matrix for the four stocks as follows:[3]

	1	2	3	4
1	0.00160	0.00192	−0.00064	0.0024
2	0.00192	0.00360	−0.00096	0.0036
3	−0.00064	−0.00096	0.00640	−0.0032
4	0.00240	0.00360	−0.00320	0.0100

The diagonal of the variance-covariance matrix shows variance for each security. For example, the variance of security 1 as a decimal is $(0.04)^2 = 0.0016$, the variance of security 2 is $(0.06)^2 = 0.0036$, and so on. All of the locations off the diagonal represent the covariances among the securities in the portfolio. For example, the covariance between securities 1 and 2 can be determined by substituting into Equation 14-3 to give $(0.8) (0.04) (0.06) = 0.00192$. Note that the variance-covariance matrix is symmetrical about the diagonal.

With the construction of the variance-covariance matrix, the standard deviation of the portfolio can be determined as follows:

$$
\begin{aligned}
V(R) = {}& 0.2 \, [0.2(0.0016) + 0.3(0.00192) + 0.4(-0.00064) + 0.1(0.0024)] \\
& +0.3 \, [0.2(0.00192) + 0.3(0.0036) + 0.4(-0.00096 + 0.1(0.0036)] \\
& +0.4 \, [0.2(-0.00064) + 0.3(-0.00096) + 0.4(0.0064) + 0.1(-0.0032)] \\
& +0.1 \, [0.2(0.0024) + 0.3(0.0036) + 0.4(-0.0032) + 0.1(0.0100)] \\
= {}& 0.001466
\end{aligned}
$$

The variance of the entire portfolio, therefore, is 0.001466. The standard deviation thus becomes

$$ S = (0.001466)^{\frac{1}{2}} = 0.0383, \text{ or } 3.83 \text{ percent} $$

It is important to note that the standard deviation of the entire portfolio is smaller than the lowest standard deviation of any stock in the portfolio. The reason for this is based on two factors. One is the correlation between pairs of stocks. In this example we had the happy circumstance of a negative correlation between security 3 and the other securities in the portfolio. This significantly reduced the standard deviation of the entire portfolio. Second, the proportion of each stock in the portfolio can further affect the standard deviation of the portfolio. In this example, stock 3 constituted 40 percent of the portfolio and was the largest single holding. Its negative correlation with the other stocks in the portfolio plus its large proportion significantly reduced the risk of the portfolio. In summary, the risk of a portfolio will depend on three factors: (1) the risk of the individual securities in the portfolio, (2) the correlation between pairs of securities in the portfolio, and (3) the proportion of each in the portfolio.

[3] It is worth noting that determining the variance of portfolios can be accomplished by directly substituting into Equation 14-2 without forming a variance-covariance matrix.

Security Correlation

The above example points out the importance of the correlation of securities in the portfolio. Conceivably securities could range from perfect negative correlation, $\rho = -1$, to perfect positive correlation, $\rho = +1$. In the real world it is uncommon to find securities at either of these extremes. Generally, stocks are partially correlated and positively correlated. To illustrate the effect of different degrees of positive and negative correlation, the simple two-stock case will be used to show the effects of perfect negative correlation, zero correlation, and perfect positive correlation. It should be noted that the subsequent discussion will focus on reducing risk. This overlooks the risk-return tradeoff, in which the investor selects the portfolio with the risk-return characteristics that meet his utility preferences.

Positive correlation is a situation in which those securities that are positively correlated can be expected to behave in a similar fashion. The greater the positive correlation, the greater the assurance that the positively correlated securities will behave in the same fashion. Perfect positive correlation is an extreme correlation, in which those securities that are perfectly positively correlated can be expected to behave in exactly the same manner. For example, if we consider two securities, say, securities 5 and 6, that are perfectly positively correlated, and if for some reason the return on security 6 is expected to fall short of expectations, we can be assured that the return on security 5 will also fall short of expectations. For this reason, the greater the positive correlation between securities in a portfolio, the greater will be the risk of the portfolio.

To illustrate the effect of the correlation among securities, suppose that security 5 is perfectly positively correlated with security 6 as postulated above, and suppose their standard deviations are 2 percent and 4 percent, respectively. If funds are committed equally to securities 5 and 6, the variance of the two-security portfolio as given by Equation 14-2 is

$$V(R) = X_5^2 \sigma_5^2 + X_6^2 \sigma_6^2 + 2X_5 X_6 \sigma_{56}$$

$$= (0.25)(0.04) + (0.25)(0.0016) + 2(0.5)(0.5)(0.0008)$$

$$= 0.0009$$

The variance then, is 0.009, and the standard deviation is

$$S = (0.0009)^{\frac{1}{2}} = 0.03, \text{ or } 3 \text{ percent}$$

This result illustrates a very important point with respect to diversification among perfectly positively correlated assets. A re-examination of the standard deviations of securities 5 and 6 and the proportions invested in each shows that the standard deviation of the portfolio is midway between those of securities 5 and 6 because we arbitrarily invested 50 percent of the portfolio in each security. However, as will be shown in Appendix A, when the securities in a portfolio are perfectly positively correlated, the risk of the portfolio is a linear function of the standard deviation of the individual securities in the portfolio. The risk of the portfolio will be bounded by the least risky and most risky securities in the portfolio. Figure 14-1 illustrates this linear relationship.

In Figure 14-1 it has been assumed that the expected return on stocks 5 and 6 is 8 and 12 percent, respectively. Since the expected return on a portfolio is the weighted average of the expected returns of the individual securities in the portfolio, the expected return of this portfolio is 10 percent. However, the risk of the portfolio is also a weighted average of the standard deviations of the individual securities in the portfolio. Consequently, if an investor is considering two perfectly positively correlated securities for inclusion in a portfolio, diversifying will only bring about a proportional reduction in risk. Diversification will not be able to reduce the risk of the portfolio below that of the least risky security in the portfolio as was the case in the previous four security portfolios illustrated above. The investor, therefore, should not expect any benefits of diversification when securities are perfectly positively correlated. In this situation he probably should select the security with the highest expected return or lowest risk as his preferences dictate. Note also that the risk is only a weighted average of the standard deviation of the individual securities in the portfolio only in the special case of perfect positive correlation.

In contrast to the above example, suppose that security 5 is not correlated with security 7. That is, there is zero correlation with security 7. Suppose also

FIGURE 14-1 *Effect of Perfect Positive Correlation on the Risk of a Portfolio*

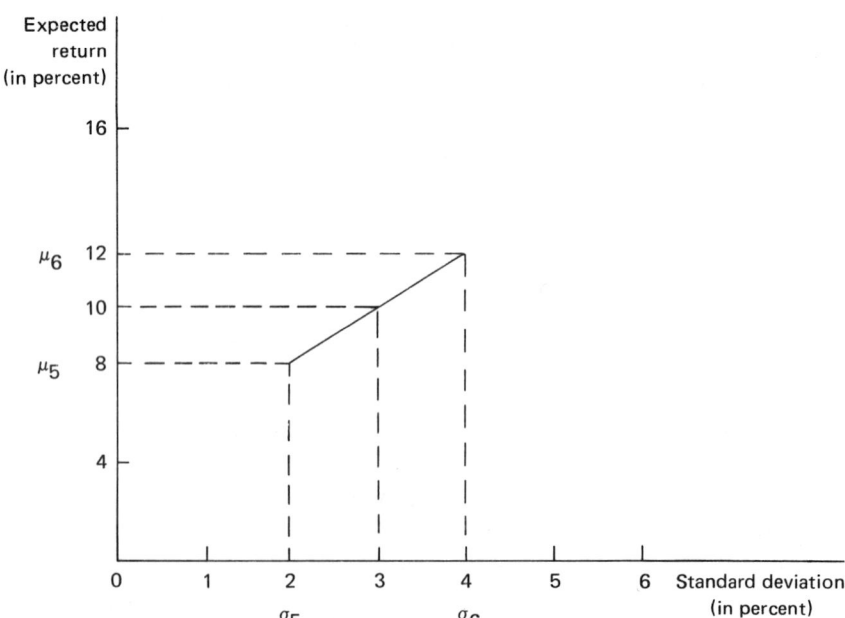

that the standard deviation of the security 7 is 4 percent. The risk of the port-folio, then, is the sum of the variances of the individual securities in the port-folio. Consequently, a two-security portfolio made up of securities 5 and 7 has a variance of

$$V(R) = (0.25)\,(0.0004) + (0.25)\,(0.0016) = 0.0005$$

Since there is no covariance between securities 5 and 7, the variance of the portfolio has been reduced to 0.0005, and the standard deviation is reduced to

$$S = (0.0005)^{\frac{1}{2}} \approx 0.0224, \text{ or } 2.24 \text{ percent}$$

Hence, the risk of a portfolio can be reduced when the securities in it are not correlated. Note that this is not the minimum. The risk can be further reduced by changing the proportions. Equation 14-20A in Appendix A gives these opti-mal proportions.

Finally, if the securities in a portfolio are negatively correlated, the risk can be greatly reduced, and if the securities happen to be perfectly negatively correlated, the risk of a two-security portfolio can be eliminated. Perfect nega-tive correlation means that if the return on one security is expected to fall short of expectations, one can be assured of the other security meeting expectations. In this fashion, perfectly negatively correlated securities significantly reduce the risk of a portfolio since these securities enable the investor to hedge, assur-ing that expectations will be met no matter what is the eventual outcome. To illustrate, suppose that security 8 is perfectly negatively correlated with se-curity 5, and suppose also that the standard deviation of security 8 is 4 percent. The variance of a two-security portfolio made up of securities 5 and 8 would be

$$V(R) = (0.25)\,(0.0004) + (0.25)\,(0.0016) + 2(0.5)\,(0.5)\,(-1.0)\,(0.02)\,(0.04)$$

$$= 0.0001 + 0.0004 - 0.0004$$

$$= 0.0001$$

The variance has thus been reduced to 0.0001, and the standard deviation is 0.01 or 1.0 percent. Again, as with zero correlation, this combination of se-curities 5 and 8 is not optimal. The proportions could be determined with the aid of Equation 14-14A in Appendix A, which would reduce the variance, the risk, of the portfolio to zero. These proportions are 0.67 and 0.33 for securities 5 and 8, respectively.

The cases of perfect positive correlation, perfect negative correlation, and zero correlation illustrates the impact of correlation between securities on the variance of a portfolio. In the real world, however, the extreme cases of perfect positive and perfect negative correlation are rarely found. Partial correlation is generally the case in the real world, and similar types of securities are usually partially positively correlated. This comes as no surprise for high-quality and low-quality bonds. Generally, the return on these bonds is highly positively correlated. In fact, the return on high-quality bonds may be the closest to perfect positive correlation that is available. However, common stocks are also positively correlated. An empirical study by Marshall Blume, for example, found only 7 stocks out of 4,357 were negatively correlated.[4] Consequently, risk reduction for a portfolio of bonds or portfolio of stocks is generally restricted to the narrow range of partial positive correlation. To obtain the benefits of negative or zero correlation normally requires diversifying among various types of securities, such as bonds and stocks, and perhaps even real estate. Even following this policy, obtaining assets that are negatively correlated may not be easy.

The major concern is thus obtaining securities that are partially positively correlated, but the correlation should be sufficiently low so that the variance of the portfolio is reduced. As Equations 14-20A to 14-23A of Appendix A show, if

$$\rho_{ij} > \frac{\sigma_i}{\sigma_j} \qquad \sigma_i < \sigma_j \tag{14-5}$$

diversification between securities i and j will not reduce the risk of the portfolio. As a result, the security with the largest expected return or the lowest risk should be selected for the portfolio.

Diversifiable and Nondiversifiable Risk

The concepts of diversifiable and nondiversifiable risk are particularly important to the common stock investor since they are the outgrowth of much research into the nature of the capital markets, particularly the stock market. In the section above, we discussed the conditions necessary to obtain the benefits of diversification. This information is valuable whenever the investor is contemplating diversifying to reduce the risk associated with security investments. However, such investment decisions will be tempered by the risk-return parameters that exist in the securities markets. Empirical research has found that stocks in general are partially positively correlated, which means that the returns on common stocks tend to follow a fairly similar pattern. As a result, the returns on individual stocks normally are fairly highly correlated to the returns of stocks in general. Since the covariance between securities in a portfolio is a major determinant of the risk of the portfolio, this seems to imply that diversification is of some benefit, but only to a limited extent.

In essence the concepts of diversifiable and nondiversifiable risk hold that a certain amount of risk can be diversified away, and the remainder cannot. These concepts are an outgrowth of capital market theory, which will be discussed in more depth in Chapter 15, and it is assumed that the return on a particular stock is a function of the return on stocks in general. To develop these concepts, suppose the return on common stocks is a function of some stock market index, such as Standard and Poor's 500 stock index. The return on stock i can be given by

$$RR_{it} = a_i + b_i(RR_{It}) + u_{it} \tag{14-6}$$

---

[4] Marshall E. Blume, "On the Assessment of Risk," *Journal of Finance*, vol. 26, no. 1 (Mar., 1971), p. 6.

where RR_{It} is the return relative for a market index at time t, a_i and b_i are constants, and u_{it} is a normally distributed error term. In this formulation, the regression coefficient, b_i is the focus of attention, since it is a measure of the elasticity of the return for stock i with respect to the market index.[5]

As a result, the expected RR, and hence the expected return, μ, for stock i can be given by

$$\overline{RR}_i = a_i + b_i\overline{RR}_I \qquad (14\text{-}7)$$

where the terms are as previously defined. In other words, if we had forecast the return for the stock market index, we could also forecast the return for a particular stock. Just as the return depends on the return of a market index, the risk of not obtaining that return also depends on the variance of return of the market index. As a result, the variance for a particular stock is given by

$$\sigma_i^2 = b_i^2\sigma_I^2 + \sigma_{ui}^2 \qquad (14\text{-}8)$$

where σ_I^2 is the variance of a stock market index, and σ_{ui}^2 is a normally distributed error term. Equation 14-8, therefore, indicates that the risk associated with stock i is a function of the variance of the market index plus a random component. It follows that the risk that results from the common stock index cannot be diversified away since the risk of individual stocks is directly related to it. This is the so-called nondiversifiable risk. It results from the common source, the stock market index. The risk represented by the error term, σ_{ui}^2, can be diversified away, however. This source of risk results from random events, and sufficient diversification will eliminate it. Diversifiable risk thus may be viewed as resulting from errors in forecasting the results for individual securities; but since these errors are assumed to be normally distributed errors of over- and under-estimation, they may be expected to cancel one another out and be eliminated in a well-diversified portfolio of common stock.

In summary, if the return on common stock is assumed to be related to that of a market index, a portion of the risk can be diversified away and a portion cannot. The nondiversifiable, or market-related, risk is associated with the risk of a market index. The diversifiable, or firm-related, risk is assumed to be random. In other words, the risk that can be diversified away can be assumed to be related to errors in predicting the performance of individual firms. For example, the market may be rising and be expected to continue rising, yet not all firms will have increased profits and earnings per share. Similarly, in a poor market some firms may be having relatively good years. These may be considered random occurrences, which can be diversified away.

The single-index approach to estimating diversifiable and nondiversifiable risk utilizes simple linear regression. As already indicated, the regression coefficient indicates the elasticity of the return on a particular stock with respect to the market index, and therefore aids in determining the nondiversifiable risk. The diversifiable risk is given by the standard error of the

---

[5] The b_i is commonly referred to in the finance literature as the beta coefficient and was previously discussed in Chapter 6 in connection with market-related risk.

regression estimate, and the estimate of the market index's standard error, or standard deviation, enables one to estimate the nondiversifiable risk for a particular stock.

To illustrate this approach, consider the following RRs for stocks 9 and 10 and a market index.

Year	Market index RRs	Stock 9 RRs	Stock 10 RRs
1	1.01	1.05	1.00
2	1.10	1.15	1.05
3	0.90	0.85	0.95
4	1.18	1.30	1.15
5	1.10	1.15	1.05
6	1.22	1.30	1.10
7	1.30	1.50	1.20
8	1.20	1.40	1.10
9	0.80	0.60	0.95
10	1.05	1.25	1.08
Mean	1.09	1.16	1.06

By applying Equation 14-6, we obtain the following relationship between the market index and stock 9:

$$RR_9 = -0.684 + 1.694RR_I$$

The coefficient of determination is 0.935, and the standard error of the estimate is 0.072. Since the regression coefficient is quite large, this stock is considered fairly volatile. For example, suppose the RR for the market index is expected to be 1.50 for the next year. The return on stock 9, then, is expected to be

$$RR_9 = -0.684 + 1.694(1.50) = 1.859$$

This is somewhat greater than the expected RR for the market of 1.50. On the other hand, suppose that the RR on the market is expected to fall to 0.80. The RR on stock 9 is somewhat less than that of the market. Thus

$$RR_9 = -0.684 + 1.694(0.80) = 0.671$$

As a result, this stock is considered quite volatile, since it can be expected to do better than the market when the market is rising and worse than the market when it is falling.

By comparison, stock 10 is much less volatile. The relationship between stock 10 and the market is found to be

$$RR_{10} = 0.525 + 0.496RR_I$$

The coefficient of determination is 0.869, and the standard error of the estimate is 0.031. Since the regression coefficient is 0.496, stock 10 is much more stable than stock 9. For example, if the market RR is expected to be 1.50 at the end of next year, the RR for stock 10 is

$$RR_{10} = 0.525 + 0.496(1.50) = 1.268$$

This is somewhat less than the expected RR for the market of 1.50. On the other hand, if the RR on the market index is expected to be 0.80, the RR on stock 10 is

$$RR_{10} = 0.525 + 0.496(1.50) = 0.92$$

Consequently, stock 10 is not expected to perform as well as the market when the market rises, but it will perform better than the market when the market is expected to fall. Stock 10, therefore, is much more defensive than stock 9.

The total risk for a stock is given by the sum of the diversifiable and the nondiversifiable risk, as shown in Equation 14-8. Diversifiable risk is given by the standard error of the regression estimate. For stock 9, it is 0.72; for stock 10, it is 0.031. This gives the range of possible error for each stock given an estimate of the RR for the market index. For example, suppose that the RR on the market index is expected to be 1.50. For stock 9, the expected RR is 1.859 ± 0.072, or a range of 1.79 to 1.93. For stock 10, this range is 1.268 ± 0.031, or 1.24 to 1.30. One can be approximately 68 percent certain of the actual RR falling within these ranges. Nondiversifiable risk can also be derived from Equation 14-8. Suppose the variance of the RR for the market index is 0.0225. The nondiversifiable risk for stock 9, then, is

$$\sigma_{N9}^2 = (1.694)^2 (0.0225) = 0.0381$$

Taking the square root, we find that the standard deviation is

$$\sigma_{N9} = (0.0381)^{\frac{1}{2}} = 0.195$$

Consequently, the standard deviation of return for stock 9, which results because of the volatility of the market index, is 0.195. If σ_{Di} and σ_{Ni} are used to denote diversifiable and nondiversifiable risk for stock i, the total risk is given by Equation 14-8, which can be rewritten as

$$\sigma_i = \sigma_{Ni} + \sigma_{Di} \tag{14-9}$$

For stock 9, this is

$$\sigma_9 = 0.195 + 0.072 = 0.267$$

This means that for any given yearly forecast the realized return can vary within a range of ±0.267. Consequently, this stock is quite risky.

Stock 10, on the other hand, is not nearly as risky. The nondiversifiable risk is

$$\sigma_{N10}^2 = (0.496)^2 (0.0225) = 0.0055$$

Taking the square root gives

$$\sigma_{N10} = (0.0055)^{\frac{1}{2}} = 0.074$$

Therefore, the total risk is given by Equation 14-9. Thus

$$\sigma_{10} = 0.074 + 0.031 = 0.105$$

The expected return on stock 10, therefore, is normally expected to be within a range of ±0.105 of the predicted return. Hence, the risk associated with stock 10 is substantially less than that of stock 9.

In summary, the development of the concepts of diversifiable and nondiversifiable risk have led to some valuable insights into the management of common stock portfolios. Recall that the basis for these concepts is that the risk and return for individual stocks can be adequately described by simple linear regression analysis and, in particular, depends largely on the magnitude of the regression coefficient, b_i. Too much reliance should not be placed on this formulation since it presupposes that the regression coefficients derived for individual stocks are stable predictors. An empirical study by Marshall E. Blume has shown that they are not stable over time. That is, the regression coefficients for individual stocks tend to shift over time. When stocks are combined in portfolios, however, the regression coefficients are relatively stable.

Blume's study covered a period of 42 years, beginning in 1926 and ending in 1968. To test for the stability of the b_i's, the 42-year period was divided into six equal periods, and the b_i's for samples of stocks ranging from 415 to 890 stocks were used. In each period, the stocks in the sample were regressed against a market index to obtain their b_i's. The estimated b_i's are summarized in Table 14-1. It is evident that the distribution is reasonably symmetrical, with b_i's of approximately 1 constituting the mean and the median. In addition, about 80 percent of the b_i's fell within the range of approximately 0.45 to 1.60.

The b_i's for each of the six periods were compared to determine their stationarity. This was accomplished by comparing the b_i's for portfolios of sizes varying from 1 to 100. The portfolios were selected by beginning with the smallest b_i's, then selecting successive portfolios of the appropriate size. It was found that for individual securities, the b_i's tended to shift over time. However, for portfolios with reasonable diversification, the b_i's were good predictors of the risk. Specifically, for portfolios of 10 stocks or more, the b_i's were quite stable. This means that the b_i's are not reliable indicators of the risk for individual stocks, but the b_i's for portfolios with reasonable diversification are accurate predictors of the risk for these portfolios. Consequently, the b_i's are really only useful in the construction of common stock portfolios; not too much confidence should be placed in them taken individually.

TABLE 14-1 *Estimated b_is for Period 1926–68*

Period	Number of companies	Fractiles				
		0.10	*0.25*	*0.50*	*0.75*	*0.90*
7/26–6/33	415	0.498	0.711	1.023	1.352	1.616
7/33–6/40	604	0.436	0.701	1.015	1.349	1.581
7/40–6/47	731	0.500	0.643	0.872	1.186	1.606
7/47–6/54	870	0.473	0.727	0.996	1.263	1.565
7/54–6/61	890	0.458	0.678	0.984	1.250	1.558
7/61–6/68	847	0.475	0.681	0.934	1.199	1.491

Source: Blume, op. cit., p. 5.

Sufficient Diversification

As indicated above, portfolio risk may be segregated into diversifiable and nondiversifiable risk, and diversifiable risk can be eliminated through sufficient diversification. This means that given sufficient diversification a portfolio's risk depends solely on that of the market portfolio. The question then becomes, what is the sufficient number of stocks to hold in a portfolio to obtain most of the benefits of diversification?[6] Two recent studies investigating this question were conducted by John L. Evans and Stephen H. Archer, and Henry A. Latane and William E. Young.[7] The Evans-Archer study attempted to determine the number of stocks required to sufficiently eliminate diversifiable risk by simulating 40 portfolios using semiannual data from January 1958 to July 1967. The 40 portfolios were selected at random from 470 securities included in S & P's 500 Composite Index. Portfolios ranged in size from 1 to 40 stocks and were selected by sampling with replacement with 60 portfolios being selected of each size.

These portfolios were examined to determine whether the following relationship existed:

$$S_{nj} = a + b(1/X_n) \qquad j = 1, 2, 3, \ldots, 60$$

$$n = 1, 2, 3, \ldots, 40$$

(14-10)

where S_{nj} is the standard deviation of the jth portfolio of size n, a and b are constants, and X_n is the size of the portfolio. This formulation basically indicates that the standard deviation of the portfolio's return is an inverse function of the size of the portfolio. The constant a in this formulation is the nondiversifiable risk of the portfolio. This portion of the portfolio risk is related to the market and cannot be diversified away. The constant b, on the other hand, corresponds to the diversifiable risk that can be reduced, if not eliminated, by increasing the size of the portfolio.

The results of the Evans-Archer study are reproduced in Figure 14-2. The estimating equation was found to be:

$$S_n = 0.1191 + 0.08625(1/X_n)$$

The fit was very good with a coefficient of determination of 0.9863. As Figure 14-2 illustrates, the risk of the portfolio drops off sharply as the number of stocks in the portfolio increases. Further, an examination of the curve indicates that most of the benefits of diversification can be obtained with relatively small portfolios of between 8 to 16 stocks. The study by Latane and Young confirmed the findings of Evans and Archer. The methodology of Latane and Young was

[6] One of the first to examine this question was Harry M. Markowitz, *Portfolio Selection: Efficient Diversification of Investments* (New York: John Wiley & Sons, 1959), p. 112.
[7] John L. Evans and Stephen H. Archer, "Diversification and the Reduction of Dispersion: An Empirical Analysis," *Journal of Finance*, vol. 23, no. 5 (Dec., 1968), pp. 761–67; and Henry A. Latane and William E. Young, "Test of Portfolio Building Rules," *Journal of Finance*, vol. 24, no. 4 (Sept., 1969), pp. 595–612.

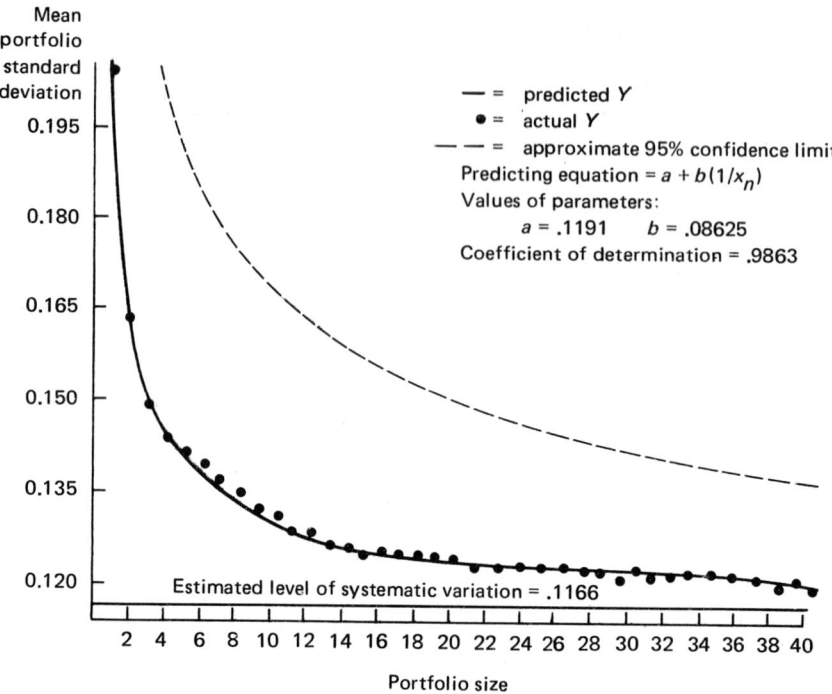

FIGURE 14-2   *Portfolio Size and Sufficient Diversification*

Source: Evans and Archer, op. cit., p. 765.

slightly different, but the findings were that most of the benefits of diversification could be obtained with portfolios of 8 to 16 stocks.[8]

The findings of these two studies have important implications for the investor in general and particularly for those performance-minded portfolio managers. For the portfolio manager who is under no compulsion to diversify extensively, these results tend to indicate that broad diversification would not greatly reduce the diversifiable risk of the portfolio; yet if broad diversification is undertaken, the performance of the portfolio may not be much different from that of the market. That is, broad diversification may not markedly reduce the risk of the portfolio, but the chances of an above-average return on the portfolio are greatly reduced because of the number of securities in it. The aggressive portfolio manager, therefore, could concentrate his portfolio in a relatively small number of stocks that promise above-average returns and in this fashion attempt to do better than market. At the same time this policy would eliminate most of the diversifiable risk.

For the investor in general, these results mean that a relatively small portfolio that is sufficiently diversified can reduce the diversifiable risk to almost

[8] Latane and Young, op. cit., p. 607.

zero. At the same time, this can be undertaken with a relatively small sum. If the portfolio is made up of relatively high-quality stocks, say, from the Dow-Jones 30 industrial list of blue chip stocks, the investor can expect a return not markedly different from that of the market as a whole; and just as importantly, the risk will not be markedly different. If past market performance is any indication of the future, it seems that the investor can expect perhaps a 10 to 12 percent return over a period of perhaps 10 years. For those who have followed the vagaries of the stock market, the fact that the risk may not be much greater than that of the market in general may be little consolation. However, it must be remembered that common stock investment presupposes risk, and if the investor does as well as the market in terms of both risk and return, he has done a creditable job.

Summary

Diversification as a method of reducing risk raises a number of questions. It may be supposed that simply buying a number of different stocks will give the benefits of diversification, but actually the benefits of diversification depend upon the correlation among the securities in the portfolio. If they are highly positively correlated, there will be little risk reduction as a result of diversification. On the other hand, if several of the securities in the portfolio are negatively correlated with the remaining securities in the portfolio, the risk of the portfolio can be greatly reduced. Realistically, however, few stocks have been found to be negatively correlated. It is far more common for stocks to be partially positively correlated. As a result, the benefits of diversification can be realized to a certain extent when the stocks in the portfolio are only slightly correlated. If by some chance one should discover a stock that is negatively correlated to other stocks, this stock should be included in the portfolio.

Recent empirical research on the stock market has developed the concepts of diversifiable and nondiversifiable risk. These concepts have developed since the risk and return on stocks in general seem to be directly related to that of the market. Diversifiable risk arises out of random events that affect the firm. These factors are sometimes referred to as firm-related risk, and can be almost eliminated by sufficient diversification. Simulation studies indicate that sufficient diversification can be obtained with relatively small portfolios of perhaps 8 to 16 stocks. At the same time, there is not much benefit to be derived by broader diversification. The reduction or elimination of diversifiable risk does not eliminate the risk of the portfolio. There still remains the nondiversifiable risk, or market-related risk, which cannot be diversified away. However, it varies with different types of stocks in the portfolio. Some are more volatile than others, and therefore some stocks will be more affected than others by the market. Nevertheless, the major source of risk is that associated with the market.

Appendix A: Formulas for Minimizing Risk

If we are concerned with reducing the risk to a minimum, we must determine the proportions of each security in the portfolio so that the overall risk of the portfolio is at a minimum. The methodology involved can be illustrated by assuming a two-security portfolio whose variance is given by the following:

$$V(R) = X_i^2 \sigma_i^2 + (1 - X_i)^2 \sigma_j^2 + 2X_i (1 - X_i) \sigma_{ij} \qquad (14\text{-}11\text{A})$$

where the terms are as previously defined. Equation 14-11A simply indicates that the variance of the portfolio is the combined variance and covariance of the two securities in the portfolio.

If we want to reduce the variance to a minimum, the proportions that reduce $V(R)$ for the portfolio to a minimun are preferred. These may be obtained by using calculus and taking the first partial derivative of $V(R)$ with respect to X_i^2. That is

$$\frac{\partial V(R)}{\partial X_i} = 2 X_i \sigma_i^2 - 2(1 - X_i) \sigma_j^2 + (2 - 4X_i) \sigma_{ij} \qquad (14\text{-}12\text{A})$$

Setting Equation 14-12A equal to zero yields

$$2 X_i \sigma_i^2 + 2 X_i \sigma_j^2 - 4 X_i \sigma_{ij} = 2 \sigma_j^2 - 2 \sigma_{ij} \qquad (14\text{-}13\text{A})$$

Solving for X_i gives

$$X_i = \frac{\sigma_j^2 - \sigma_{ij}}{\sigma_i^2 + \sigma_j^2 - 2\sigma_{ij}} \qquad (14\text{-}14\text{A})$$

Equation 14-14A is quite general and can be used to solve for any X_i to minimize the variance of the portfolio irrespective of the correlation between the stocks in the portfolio. To illustrate, suppose two securities, i and j, are partially negatively correlated. The optimal proportions are given by substituting into Equation 14-14A as follows:

$$X_i = \frac{\sigma_j^2 + \sigma_{ij}}{\sigma_i + \sigma_j^2 + 2 \sigma_{ij}} \qquad (14\text{-}15\text{A})$$

Equation 14-16A can be further simplified for the special case of perfect negative correlation. This simplification results because $\rho = -1$, and therefore all that changes in Equation 14-14A is the sign of σ_{ij}. Equation 14-15A can be rewritten as follows:

$$X_i = \frac{\sigma_j (\sigma_j + \sigma_i)}{(\sigma_i + \sigma_j) (\sigma_i + \sigma_j)} \qquad (14\text{-}16\text{A})$$

$$= \frac{\sigma_j}{\sigma_i + \sigma_j}$$

Hence, risk minimization for perfectly negatively correlated securities becomes a linear function of the standard deviation of securities i and j. The risk of a two-security portfolio in which the securities i and j are perfectly negatively correlated is inversely related to the risk of each security.

When securities are perfectly negatively correlated, the risk can be eliminated. This can be graphically illustrated by considering securities 5 and 8. Suppose that the standard deviation for securities 5 and 8 are 2 and 4 percent, respectively. Suppose also that the expected return for securities 5 and 8 is 8 and 14 percent, respectively. Applying Equation 14-16A gives the proportion of security 5 that will reduce the risk to a minimum. That is

$$X_5 = \frac{4}{2+4}$$

$$= 0.667$$

As a result, 0.667 should be invested in security 5, and 0.333 should be invested in security 8.

Figure 14-3A illustrates the functional relationship for securities 5 and 8. Based on the proportions for minimization of risk, the expected return of the portfolio is 9.998 percent, but the risk is reduced to zero. Thus, the investor in this two-stock portfolio can expect a return of approximately 10 percent with absolute certainty. This illustrates the ideal situation in which risk is eliminated, and a situation which is unlikely to occur in the real world.

FIGURE 14-3A *Effect of Perfect Negative Correlation on the Risk of a Portfolio*

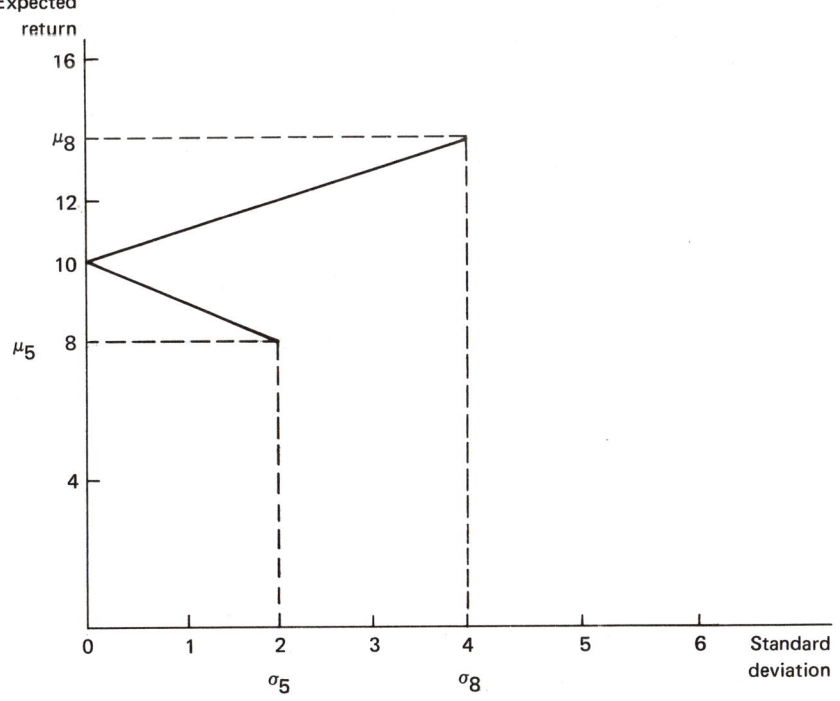

On the other hand, if there is zero correlation between two securities i and j, Equation 14-14A reduces to

$$X_i = \frac{\sigma_j^2}{\sigma_i^2 + \sigma_j^2} \tag{14-17A}$$

Finally, if there is positive correlation between securities i and j, Equation 14-14A can be used. That is

$$X_i = \frac{\sigma_i^2 - \sigma_{ij}}{\sigma_i^2 + \sigma_j^2 - 2\sigma_{ij}} \tag{14-18A}$$

For the special case of perfect positive correlation, Equation 14-18A simplifies to

$$X_i = \frac{\sigma_j(\sigma_j - \sigma_i)}{(\sigma_j - \sigma_i)(\sigma_j - \sigma_i)} \tag{14-19A}$$

Equation 14-19A will only give a meaningful solution when $\sigma_i > \sigma_j$; and under these conditions, Equation 14-19A implies that the entire investment should be placed in security j.

Since investment in perfectly positively correlated securities necessarily means selecting the security with the lowest standard deviation (recall that we are attempting to minimize risk) and investing the entire amount in that security, for partially positively correlated securities, a cutoff point must exist after which diversification will not reduce risk. For example, if two securities have a 0.80 correlation, will diversification reduce the risk? Suppose that all the investment is made in security j since the $\sigma_j > \sigma_i$. That is, $X_j = 1$ and $X_j = 0$. Therefore, rearranging Equation 14-14A gives

$$\sigma_i^2 + \sigma_j^2 - 2\sigma_{ij} = \sigma_j^2 - \sigma_{ij} \tag{14-20A}$$

If $X_i = 1$, Equation 14-20A simplifies to

$$\sigma_i^2 = \sigma_{ij} \tag{14-21A}$$

TABLE 14-2A *Formulas for Determining X_i Given the Correlation*

Correlation	Proportion invested in X_i
$\rho_{ij} = -1$	$X_i = \dfrac{\sigma_j}{\sigma_i + \sigma_j}$
$-1 < \rho_{ij} < 0$	$X_i = \dfrac{\sigma_j^2 - \sigma_{ij}}{\sigma_i^2 + \sigma_j^2 - 2\sigma_{ij}}$
$\rho_{ij} = 0$	$X_i = \dfrac{\sigma_j^2}{\sigma_i^2 + \sigma_j^2}$
$0 < \rho_{ij} < \dfrac{\sigma_i}{\sigma_j}$	$X_i = \dfrac{\sigma^2 - \sigma_{ij}}{\sigma_i^2 + \sigma_j^2 - 2\sigma_{ij}}$
$\rho_{ij} > \dfrac{\sigma_i}{\sigma_j}$	$X_i = 1$

The equality of Equation 14-21A holds if

$$\sigma_i = 0 \qquad \text{(14-22A)}$$

or if

$$\rho_{ij} = \frac{\sigma_i}{\sigma_j} \qquad \text{(14-23A)}$$

Consequently, any time $\rho_{ij} \geq \sigma_i/\sigma_j$, risk cannot be reduced by diversification, and the entire investment should be made in the security with the lowest standard deviation, assuming an objective of risk reduction.

Questions

1. Diversification entails a tradeoff between risk and expected return. Explain.
2. What is the major advantage of diversification?
3. What factors determine the risk of a portfolio measured in terms of standard deviation?
4. John Brown holds a portfolio of four stocks. The expected return, standard deviation, correlation, and proportions of these stocks are as follows:

Stocks	Expected return	Standard deviation	Proportions
1	11 percent	12 percent	20 percent
2	13	14	20
3	15	19	40
4	19	24	20

Correlation among four stocks

	1	2	3	4
1	1.0	-0.3	-0.4	-0.4
2		1.0	0.7	0.4
3			1.0	0.8
4				1.0

Determine the expected return and standard deviation for the above portfolio.

5. The following matrix indicates the degree of correlation between pairs of stocks. Note that the standard deviations of stocks 7 and 8 are 8 and 10 percent, respectively. Complete the matrix, indicating the effect on the risk of the portfolio given that the following pairs of stock were included.

Stocks	Correlation coefficient	Effect on risk
1 and 2	-1.0	
3 and 4	0	
5 and 6	1.0	
7 and 8	0.75	

6. Diversifiable and nondiversifiable risks are important concepts in portfolio management.
   a. What condition is necessary for these concepts to be meaningful?
   b. What are the implications of these concepts for the investor?
7. The following *RRs* have been established for stocks 1 and 2 and a market index.

Year	Market index RRs	Stock 1 RRs	Stock 2 RRs
1	1.06	1.12	1.08
2	0.93	0.86	0.98
3	1.10	1.14	1.09
4	1.25	1.40	1.18
5	1.01	1.10	1.04
6	0.90	0.80	0.96
7	1.03	0.85	0.99
8	1.16	1.26	1.12
9	1.12	1.25	1.08
10	1.06	1.10	1.07

   a. Determine the susceptibility of stocks 1 and 2 to changes in return for the market index, that is, the regression coefficient for stocks 1 and 2.
   b. What are the implications of your findings for the risk and return of each stock?
8. In the context of the recent empirical studies, what constitutes sufficient diversification? What type of risk is reduced?
9. What are the implications for portfolio performance of the empirical findings concerning sufficient diversification?

Selected References

Baumol, William J. "An Expected Gain-Confidence Limit Criterion for Portfolio Selection." *Management Science,* vol. 10, no. 1 (Oct., 1963), pp. 174–82.

Bierman, Harold, Jr., and Seymour Smidt. *The Capital Budgeting Decision,* 3d ed., New York: MacMillan, 1971. Chapter 20.

Blume, Marshall E. "Portfolio Theory: A Step Toward Its Practical Application." *Journal of Business,* vol. 43, no. 2 (Apr., 1970), pp. 152–74.

———. "On the Assessment of Risk." *Journal of Finance,* vol. 26, no. 1 (Mar., 1971), pp. 1–11.

Cohen, Kalman J., and Jerry A. Pogue. "An Empirical Evaluation of Alternative Portfolio Selection Models." *Journal of Business,* vol. 40, no. 2 (Apr., 1967), pp. 166–94.

Evans, John L., and Stephen H. Archer. "Diversification and the Reduction of Dispersion: An Empirical Analysis." *Journal of Finance,* vol. 23, no. 5 (Dec., 1968), pp. 761–68.

Fama, Eugene F. "Risk, Return, and Equilibrium: Some Clarifying Comments." *Journal of Finance,* vol. 23, no. 1 (Mar., 1968), pp. 29–41.

Friend, Irwin, and Marshall Blume. "Measurement of Portfolio Performance Under Uncertainty." American Economic Review, vol. 50, no. 4 (Sept., 1970), pp. 561–76.

Gentry, James, and John Pike. "An Empirical Study of the Risk-Return Hypothesis Using Common Stock Portfolios of Life Insurance Companies." *Journal of Financial and Quantitative Analysis*, vol. 5, no. 2 (June, 1970), pp. 179–87.

Haugen, Robert A. "Expected Growth, Required Return, and the Variability of Stock Prices." *Journal of Financial and Quantitative Analysis*, vol. 5, no. 3 (Sept., 1970), pp. 297–309.

Jensen, Michael C. "Risk, the Pricing of Capital Assets, and the Evaluation of Investment Portfolios." *Journal of Business*, vol. 42, no. 2 (Apr., 1969), pp. 167–247.

Latane, Henry A., and Donald L. Tuttle. "Criteria for Portfolio Building." *Journal of Finance*, vol. 22, no. 3 (Sept., 1967), pp. 359–74.

———. *Security Analysis and Portfolio Management*. New York: The Ronald Press, 1970. Chapter 23.

Latane, Henry A., and William E. Young. "Test of Portfolio Building Rules." *Journal of Finance*, vol. 24, no. 4 (Sept., 1969), pp. 595–613.

Lintner, John. "The Valuation of Risk Assets and the Selection of Risky Investments in Stock Portfolios and Capital Budgets." *Review of Economics and Statistics*, vol. 47, no. 1 (Feb., 1965), pp. 13–37.

———. "Security Prices, Risk and Maximal Gains from Diversification." *Journal of Finance*, vol. 20, no. 5 (Dec., 1965), pp. 587–615.

Mao, James C. T. "Essentials of Portfolio Diversification Strategy." *Journal of Finance*, vol. 25, no. 5 (Dec., 1970), pp. 1109–24.

Markowitz, Harry. "Portfolio Selection." *Journal of Finance*, vol. 7, no. 1, (Mar., 1952), pp. 77–91.

———. *Portfolio Selection: Efficient Diversification of Investments*. New York: John Wiley and Sons, 1959.

Mossin, Jan. "Security Pricing and Investment Criteria in Competitive Markets." *American Economic Review*, vol. 59, no. 5 (Dec., 1969), pp. 749–56.

Renwick, Fred B. *Introduction to Investments and Finance*. New York: MacMillan, 1971. Chapter 13.

Samuelson, Paul A. "A General Proof That Diversification Pays." *Journal of Financial and Quantitative Analysis*, vol. 2, no. 1 (Mar., 1967), pp. 1–14.

Sharpe, William F. "A Simplified Model for Portfolio Analysis." *Management Science*, vol. 9, no. 2 (Jan., 1963, pp. 277–94.

———. "Capital Asset Prices: A Theory of Market Equilibrium Under Conditions of Risk." *Journal of Finance*, vol. 19, no. 3 (Sept., 1964), pp. 425–42.

———. "Risk Aversion in the Stock Market: Some Empirical Evidence." *Journal of Finance*, vol. 20, no. 3, (Sept., 1965), pp. 416–22.

———. "Mutual Fund Performance." *Journal of Business*, vol. 39, no. 1, part II (Jan., 1966), pp. 119–39.

———. "A Linear Programming Algorithm for Mutual Fund Portfolio Selection." *Management Science*, vol. 13, no. 7 (Mar., 1967), pp. 499–511.

———. *Portfolio Theory and Capital Markets*. New York: McGraw-Hill, 1970.

Smith, Keith V. "Stock Price and Economic Indexes for Generating Efficient Portfolios." *Journal of Business*, vol. 42, no. 3 (July, 1969), pp. 326–37.

Tobin, James. "Liquidity Preference as Behavior Towards Risk." *Review of Economic Studies*, vol. 26, no. 1 (Feb., 1958), pp. 65–86.

Chapter 15

Mean-Variance Portfolio
Composition Models

If the investor decides to diversify his portfolio, the problem of portfolio composition emerges. The traditional approach is largely qualitative, with very little quantification of the relevant variables. The mean-variance models, on the other hand, attempt to quantify the relevant variables and put the process of portfolio composition into a standard optimization framework. This requires quantifying the risk associated with each individual security as well as the anticipated return. As a result of the initial work done in portfolio theory, much progress has been made toward quantifying risk. Since portfolio composition is viewed as an optimization problem, an objective function must be derived that captures the manner in which investors view the investment process.

The classic study in portfolio composition was conducted by Harry M. Markowitz in his famous *Portfolio Selection: Efficient Diversification of Investments*.[1] In this study he advocated determining efficient portfolios in terms of the expected return and the variance of that return. This has become the foundation for most contemporary portfolio theory. William F. Sharpe introduced a simplified version of the Markowitz formulation, now commonly referred to as the diagonal model, or single-index model.[2] This model assumes that the return on individual stocks is correlated solely to a market index. This formulation greatly simplifies the determination of efficient portfolios. It can be expanded to incorporate not only a general market index, but also an industry index.[3] Finally, the development of the single-index model led to the formulation of a capital market theory, that is, a theory of investor behavior in the capital markets.

[1] Harry M. Markowitz, *Portfolio Selection: Efficient Diversification of Investments* (New York: John Wiley & Sons, 1959).
[2] William F. Sharpe, "A Simplified Model of Portfolio Analysis," *Management Science*, vol. 9, no. 2 (Jan., 1963), pp. 277–93.
[3] Kalman J. Cohen and Jerry A. Pogue, "An Empirical Evaluation of Alternative Portfolio Selection Models," *Journal of Business*, vol. 40, no. 2 (Apr., 1967), pp. 166–93.

Markowitz's E-V Formulation

Markowitz attempted to determine how the investor should select an efficient portfolio from the universe of possible alternatives. On the New York Stock Exchange alone, there are over 1,700 securities listed. When the securities from the other exchanges and the over-the-counter markets are included, the possibilities become overwhelming.[4] To solve such a problem requires the development of an efficiency criterion. Markowitz, therefore, assumed that the investor is risk averse. Accordingly, the investor attempts to maximize the expected return of the portfolio and minimize the variance of that return. For a given level of risk, the investor prefers the portfolio with the highest expected return. It is also assumed that there is one portfolio from among all available portfolios that is preferred in terms of risk and return.

Basic Formulation

To determine the efficient portfolio for the investor requires that the expected return and the risk of the portfolio be defined. The expected return of the portfolio is simply the weighted average of the expected return of each security in the portfolio. Therefore, the expected return of the portfolio is given by

$$E(R) = \sum_{i=1}^{n} X_i \mu_i \qquad i = 1, 2, 3, \ldots, n \tag{15-1}$$

where $E(R)$ is the expected return of the portfolio, X_i is the proportion of security i in the portfolio, and μ_i is the expected return of security i.

The variance of this return is determined by considering the variance of each security in the portfolio and the covariance of all the securities in the portfolio. Therefore, the variance of the portfolio becomes the familiar formulation

$$V(R) = \sum_{i=1}^{n} X_i^2 \sigma_i^2 + 2 \sum_{i=1}^{n} \sum_{j=1}^{n} X_i X_j \sigma_{ij} \qquad i \neq j \tag{15-2}$$

$$= \sum_{i=1}^{n} \sum_{j=1}^{n} X_i X_j \sigma_{ij}$$

where $V(R)$ is the variance of the portfolio, X_i is the proportion of security i in the portfolio, X_j is the proportion of security j in the portfolio, σ_i^2 is the variance of return of security i, and σ_{ij} is the covariance of return between securities i and j. Thus, the risk in the Markowitz formulation is determined by the variance and covariance of return of all the securities in the portfolio. Equations 15-1 and 15-2 were discussed in Chapter 14.

The Markowitz formulation does not determine a unique optimal portfolio. It determines a series of efficient portfolios. Each portfolio gives the maximum

---

[4] Generally, the universe of securities is screened and the final portfolio selected from a list of possibly 100 securities. Even selecting an efficient portfolio from 100 securities is a formidable task, as we shall see.

expected return for a specified level of risk. As with any optimizing techniques, this means maximizing or minimizing an objective function subject to certain constraints. The portfolio problem only has two constraints. The first of these is that

$$X_i \geq 0 \qquad (15\text{-}3)$$

This means that selling short is not a feasible alternative in this model. In addition, all of the funds must be invested such that

$$\sum_{i=1}^{n} X_i = 1 \qquad (15\text{-}4)$$

This is not a formidable constraint. It simply means that the portfolio will be made up of n securities.

Determining the efficient set of portfolios means satisfying the constraints of Equations 15-3 and 15-4 and at the same time maximizing the objective function. The objective function is formulated to reflect the tradeoff between risk and return and is given by

$$\text{Minimize } f = -A[E(R)] + V(R) \text{ for all } A \qquad 0 \leq A \leq \infty \qquad (15\text{-}5)$$

where $E(R)$ and $V(R)$ are as previously defined Equations 15-1 and 15-2, respectively, and A is a risk aversion index that can take any value from zero to infinity. If the index is zero, the program will select the portfolio with the lowest $V(R)$. Normally, this will be a one-security portfolio because the $E(R)$ will be ignored in selecting this portfolio. On the other hand, if A is very large, the optimal portfolio will be one with a very large $E(R)$. Generally a range of between 1 and 10,000 is quite suitable for A. Solving this problem is accomplished with quadratic programming, since the objective function is nonlinear while the constraints are linear.

Graphically, the solution to this problem can be represented by an efficient frontier as shown in Figure 15-1.[5] This results because the quadratic programming solution will give a number of efficient portfolios, one for each risk-aversion index. The shaded area represents all attainable portfolios. The arc $A\ B$ $C\ D$ represents all possible efficient portfolios. This is commonly referred to as the "efficient frontier." Any point on the efficient frontier dominates any point to the right of it.

To illustrate, consider the pairs of points, B and F, and C and E, in Figure 15-1. These four points represent four different portfolios. The points on the efficient frontier dominate those on the interior since these portfolios promise a certain expected return with less risk than any point on the interior promising the same expected return. Portfolio B dominates portfolio F because it promises the

---

[5] In Figures 15-1 and 15-2 the standard deviation has been used in place of the variance. It is common practice to use $V(R)$ and S interchangeably. Standard deviation is widely used because it facilitates other analysis. For example, an expected return on a hypothetical portfolio may be discussed in terms of an estimated return plus or minus a certain standard deviation, $E(R) \pm S$.

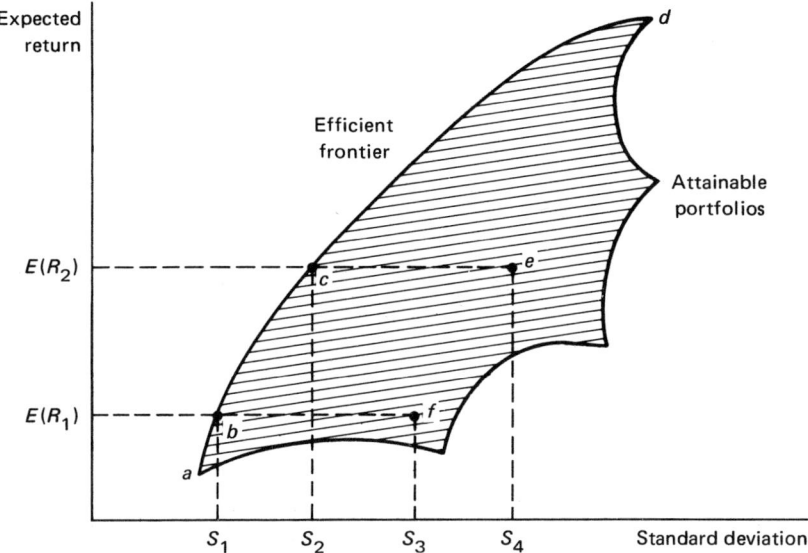

FIGURE 15-1 *Markowitz Efficient Frontier*

Harry M. Markowitz, *Portfolio Selection: Efficient Diversification of Investments,* Cowles Monograph 16, originally published by John Wiley & Sons (1959), Yale University Press (1971).

expected return $E(R_1)$ with S_1, as compared with portfolio F, which also promises $E(R_1)$, but the risk is substantially greater at S_3. The same is true of any other interior portfolio promising an expected return $E(R_1)$. Another is portfolios E and C. Portfolio C dominates portfolio E since it promises an expected return $E(R_2)$, but its risk is substantially lower at S_2, as opposed to S_4 for portfolio E. Hence, investors are expected to prefer portfolios on the efficient frontier as opposed to interior portfolios if they are averse to risk.

The final aspect of the Markowitz formulation is selecting the appropriate portfolio for the investor from all those represented by the efficient frontier. The Markowitz formulation does not select one unique portfolio; it selects a large number of efficient portfolios. Of this number the investor must select the one that best meets his preferences for risk and return. Fundamental to the Markowitz formulation is the assumption that investors are risk averters, and, as shown in Chapter 5, quadratic utility functions imply this type of risk behavior. Investors are thus assumed to have quadratic utility functions, and the optimal portfolio is the one at the point of tangency between the efficient frontier and the investor's utility curves. A family of utility preference curves is shown in Figure 15-2 to illustrate this process.

In Figure 15-2, the quadratic utility preference curves U_1, U_2, and U_3 are shown representing the utility function of a hypothetical investor. The investor selects that portfolio that coincides with his utility preference function, which is point C. At point C the investor's utility function coincides with portfolio C

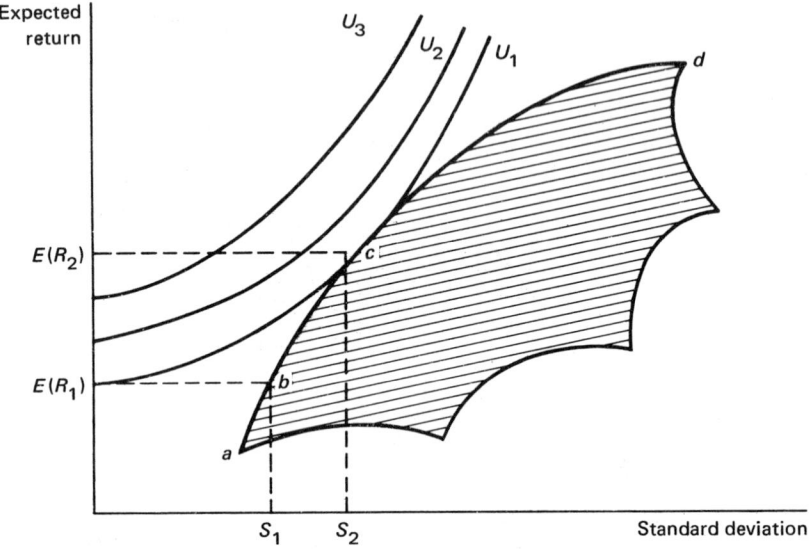

FIGURE 15-2 *Selecting the Optimal Portfolio*

on the efficient frontier, which means that portfolio C maximizes the utility of this investor.

Criticisms of Markowitz Formulation

There have been a number of criticisms of the Markowitz formulation. Normally the focal point of criticism for a model is the assumptions incorporated into it; the Markowitz approach is no exception.

Baumol's Modification Baumol pointed out that the Markowitz efficiency criterion can lead to a paradoxical situation. To illustrate, suppose there are two hypothetical portfolios, A and B, which have the following expected returns and standard deviations:

	A	*B*
E(R)	9 percent	16 percent
S	1	2
E(R) + S	10	18
E(R) − S	8	14

The range of expected returns is given by adding and subtracting one standard deviation.

Neither portfolio dominates the other, since they have different standard deviations and expected returns. That is, we cannot say in general that A is preferable to B, or vice versa. According to the Markowitz efficiency criterion, one portfolio dominates another only when two portfolio have identical expected returns or standard deviations. Following the Markowitz criterion, it may be concluded that the investor will select portfolio A over portfolio B because it has a smaller standard deviation, and therefore less risk. This follows from the assumption that investors are risk averters. However, the conclusion is questionable. If the actual return on portfolio B fell short of the expected return by one standard deviation—and we can be 68 percent certain that it will be within one standard deviation of the expected return—the realized return would still be 14 percent. On the other hand, if the actual return on portfolio A were the expected return plus one standard deviation, it would still give a realized return of 10 percent, which is still less than that on portfolio B. Therefore, given the probable outcomes for portfolios A and B, rational behavior dictates that the investor select portfolio B, even though it has a larger standard deviation and thus more risk.

Baumol suggested an alternative efficiency criterion based upon a lower confidence limit. Rather than maximizing the expected return for a given level of risk, Baumol suggested an efficient frontier made up solely of lower confidence limits. The lower confidence limit would be determined by

$$L = E(R) - k(S) \qquad (15\text{-}6)$$

where L is the lower confidence interval, k is a constant representing the extent of risk aversion, and the other terms are as previously defined. The term k determines how certain the investor wants to be of obtaining a specific return. For example, if $k = 1$, the investor could be approximately 68 percent certain of obtaining a specific return. If $k = 2$, the investor would want to be approximately 95 percent certain of obtaining a specific return.

To illustrate assume in the previous example that the investor wants to be 95 percent certain of receiving a specific return. The range of returns for portfolios A and B is as follows:

	A	B
E(R)	9 percent	16 percent
S	1	2
E(R) + 2(S)	11	20
E(R) − 2(S)	7	12

For portfolio A there is only a 2.5 percent chance that the realized return will exceed 11 percent, while for portfolio B there is only a 2.5 percent chance that the realized return will fall below 12 percent. Therefore, even though portfolio B is riskier than A, the higher return more than compensates for this risk. Thus it is evident that Baumol's criterion results in an efficient set, which is a subset of Markowitz's efficient frontier.

Other Objections In addition to the paradox cited by Baumol, a number of other objections have been raised to the Markowitz formulation. Two of these focus on the way investors perceive risk. In the Markowitz formulation, investors are assumed to be risk averters; it is assumed that risk can be measured by the standard deviation. Both these assumptions have been questioned. A third criticism, which may be the most important of all, is that a large number of computations are required to generate the efficient set of portfolios represented by the efficient frontier.

Those who question the assumption that investors are risk averters argue that it is not necessarily rational for the investor to be concerned about earning some minimum return. To illustrate this argument against risk aversion, consider two portfolios, C and D, with the following $E(R)$ and S.

Portfolio	E(R)	S	Expected range of returns at 2 standard deviations: Minimum	Maximum
C	12 percent	5 percent	2 percent	22 percent
D	12	6	0	24

According to the Markowitz formulation, portfolio C is preferable over D because it has a lower amount of risk for an expected level of return. Critics question whether it is more rational to select portfolio C over D. They argue that it is just as rational to select D because its maximum return is greater than C's. Rather than being concerned with the minimum return of 2 percent for C and zero for D, they emphasize the upper range of 24 percent for D as opposed to 22 percent for C. This argument is recognized, however, as postulating that investors are risk seekers, not risk averters. Traditionally, financial and economic analysis has been couched in terms of risk aversion. In fact, as late as 1965, financial textbooks made no mention of risk-neutral or risk-seeking behavior. Consequently, this criticism is really an argument for risk-seeking behavior, which does not appear to be the type of behavior most investors exhibit.

A second criticism concerns the way risk should be measured. Many connected with finance and economics have argued that the investor is more concerned with minimizing the probability of not obtaining a target return. For example, the investor may want to minimize the probability of not obtaining 15 percent. He will therefore only be concerned with the probabilities associated with those expected returns below 15 percent, since these constitute the source of risk. Consequently, the semivariance, which was discussed in Chapter 5, is a more appropriate measure of risk than the standard deviation.[6] Markowitz considered this measure but discarded it because it was not familiar to most security analysts.

Finally, the computations connected with the Markowitz approach are very large. For example, if the list comprises 100 stocks from which the efficient portfolios are to be selected, 5,150 bits of information are required from the security analysts. This consists of 100 expected returns, 100 standard deviations, and 4,950 pairs of correlation coefficients.[7] Obviously, a substantial amount of data is requred to generate Markowitz E-V portfolios even for a

---

[6] For a discussion of a semivariance as the more appropriate measure of risk, see James C. T. Mao, "Models for Capital Budgeting, E-V vs. E-S," *Journal of Financial Quantitative Analysis*, vol. 4, no. 5, (Jan., 1970), pp. 657–76.

[7] The correlation coefficients required can be determined by applying the formula $n(n-1)/2$. Or, the amount of information required can be viewed in terms of the variance-covariance matrix. Therefore, the formula is $\frac{1}{2}(n^2 + n)$. In the above example, $\frac{1}{2}(10,000 + 100) = 5,050$. To this would have to be added the 100 expected returns, for a total of 5,150.

relatively small universe of securities. This problem led to the single-index model, which will de discussed in the next section.

Conclusion

Although the Markowitz model has its critics, the study was a pioneering work. More than any other work in portfolio management, it laid the groundwork for the subsequent developments. Furthermore, it has been the basis for a great deal of the empirical and theoretical studies in asset management. For these reasons it remains a classic. Its major weakness is probably its lack of practical acceptance. Some evidence of this is given in a footnote of an article by Nils H. Hakansson, which describes the dilemma of a computer service company that had gone to considerable expense to develop a packaged program to be sold to its customers, and failed to find one customer.[8] The explanation for this lack of acceptance was probably the complexity involved in arriving at the necessary estimates.

Single-Index Model

The single-index model developed by William F. Sharpe reduces the number of computations needed to generate efficient portfolios.[9] The model was designed to simplify the process of evaluating efficient portfolios, reducing the number of estimates required from 5,150 to 302 for a universe of 100 securities. However, as Cohen and Pogue have shown, this model is quite accurate.[10]

The fundamental assumptions of the single-index model have been discussed previously in Chapters 6 and 14 in connection with related topics. Nevertheless, we shall review these here in the interest of completeness, and it should be noted that the purpose here is to show how the single-index model can be used to find efficient portfolios in the Markowitz mean-variance sense. The basic premise of the single-index model is that the return on common stocks depends solely on some market index, such as the Standard and Poor's 500 stock index, the Dow-Jones Industrial Average, or the New York Stock Exchange index. Notationally, this relationship is given by

$$\mu_{it} = a_i + b_i E(R_{It}) + u_{it} \qquad (15\text{-}7)$$

where μ_{it} and $E(R_{It})$ are the expected returns on stock i and a market index I, respectively, at time t, a_i and b_i are regression constants, and u_{it} is a normally distributed error term. The variance of return for stocks results from two sources. One is market-related, which means this source results from the firm's elasticity with respect to changes in the market index. This was previously referred to as nondiversifiable risk. On the other hand, there is the second

[8] See Nils H. Hakansson, "Capital Growth and the Mean-Variance Approach to Portfolio Selection," *Journal of Finance and Quantitative Analysis,* vol. 6, no. 1 (Jan., 1971), p. 554.

[9] Sharpe, op. cit.

[10] Kalman J. Cohen and Jerry A. Pogue, "An Empirical Evaluation of Alternative Portfolio-Selection Models," *Journal of Business,* vol. 40, no. 2 (Apr., 1967), p. 180.

source of risk represented by the error term in Equation 15-7. This is some-times referred to as firm-related, since it may be presumed to result from events that occur at the firm level. For example, poor profits as a result of a strike would be expected to be reflected in the firm's stock price for the year in which the strike occurred. Events of this nature are captured in the error term.

The variance return for common stocks is given by

$$\sigma_i^2 = b_i^2 \sigma_I^2 + \sigma_{ui}^2 \tag{15-8}$$

where σ_{ui}^2 is the variance of the normally distributed error term. Since the error term is assumed to be normally distributed, sufficient diversification eliminates this source of risk.

Hence, the expected return on a particular common stock can be predicted given a prediction on a market index by substituting into Equation 15-7. The expected returns for stocks 1, 2, and 3 in the coming year are given by

$$\mu_1 = a_i + b_1 E(R_I)$$

$$\mu_2 = a_2 + b_2 E(R_I) \tag{15-9}$$

$$\mu_3 = a_3 + b_3 E(R_I)$$

If these three stocks were to make up a common stock portfolio, the portfolio would be subject to the following constraint:

$$\sum_{i=1}^{3} X_i = 1 \tag{15-10}$$

To reduce the calculations, another term X_{n+1} is normally introduced. This is done since part of the return can be attributed to the return on the market index. Hence a new b can be developed which is the weighted average of the b_i's of the stock in the portfolio. That is

$$b_p = \sum_{i=1}^{n} b_i X_i \tag{15-11}$$

Now the new term is

$$X_{n+1} = b_p E(R_I) \tag{15-12}$$

The usefulness of the term X_{n+1} can be illustrated by considering the ex-pected return on the three-stock portfolio given by

$$E(R) = X_i[a_i + b_i E(R_I)] + X_2[a_2 + b_2 E(R_I)] + \tag{15-13}$$

$$X_3[a_3 + b_3 E(R_I)] = a_1 X_1 + a_2 X_2 + a_3 X_3 + E(R_I) \sum_{i=1}^{3} X_i b_1$$

And since $E(R_I) \sum_{i=1}^{n} X_i b_i = X_{n+1}$, Equation 15-13 can be simply written as:

$$E(R) = a_1 X_1 + a_2 X_2 + a_3 X_3 + X_4 \tag{15-14}$$

Predicting the risk for a particular stock involves forecasting a market-related source and a random source as indicated in Equation 15-8. Consequently, the risk for the three stock portfolio is given by

$$V(R) = \sum_{i=1}^{3} X_i^2 b_i^2 \sigma_I^2 + \sum_{i=1}^{3} X_i^2 \sigma_{ui}^2 \qquad (15\text{-}15)$$

Just as Equation 15-13 was simplified with a new term, Equation 15-15 can be simplified by adding the term σ_{n+1}^2, which is defined as

$$\sigma_{n+1}^2 = \sum_{i=1}^{3} X_i^2 b_i^2 \sigma_I^2 \qquad (15\text{-}16)$$

Consequently, Equation 15-15 can be simplified to the same form as Equation 15-14 as follows:

$$V(R) = X_1^2 \sigma_{u1}^2 + X_2^2 \sigma_{u2}^2 + X_3^2 \sigma_{u3}^2 + \sigma_4^2 \qquad (15\text{-}17)$$

The major simplification that the single-index model introduces is that there are only $n + 1$ elements along the diagonal of the variance-covariance matrix. This results since the essential assumption of this model is that each stock in the universe is only related to a market index. Hence, there is zero covariance between stocks i and j, and the elements off the diagonal of the variance-covariance matrix is zero. The variance-covariance matrix in the single-index formulation takes the following form:

$$\Omega = \begin{bmatrix} \sigma_{u1}^2 & \sigma_{u2}^2 & & \\ & & \sigma_{u3}^2 & \\ & & & \sigma_{u4}^2 \end{bmatrix}$$

Determining the portfolios that make up the efficient frontier follows the same format as that for the Markowitz formulation. It is a quadratic programming problem, and the objective function is

$$\text{Minimize } f = -A \left[\sum_{i=1}^{n+1} X_i \mu_i \right] + \sum_{i=1}^{n+1} X_i^2 \sigma_i^2 \qquad (15\text{-}18)$$

This is subject to the constraints that

$$X_i \geq 0 \qquad (15\text{-}19)$$

$$\sum_{i=1}^{n} X_i = 1 \quad \text{and} \qquad (15\text{-}20)$$

$$\sum_{i=1}^{n} b_i X_i = b_p \qquad (15\text{-}21)$$

Capital Market Theory

Sharpe's development of the single-index model made an extremely important contribution to the theory of investment management. It is the basis for developing a concept of diversifiable and nondiversifiable risk that was discussed in Chapter 14. A further extension of the single-index model led to the development of what is referred to as the capital market theory, or the capital-asset pricing model. It has its foundation firmly set in the mean-variance efficient portfolio models. At the same time, it is a theoretical construct based upon certain simplifying assumptions, which presents a framework that attempts to explain investor behavior.

A number of assumptions are used in the development of capital market theory. These are enumerated below. Later on, these assumptions will be relaxed to determine the effect of more realistic assumptions on the initial construct.

1. Investors visualize risk and return as set forth in the Markowitz portfolio model. That is, they make their decisions based on only two parameters of the distribution, the expected return and standard deviation.
2. Investors can lend and borrow as desired at the same rate of interest. The rate is considered to be that on a riskless security, or the pure rate of interest. The nearest analogy for this type of security in the real world is perhaps time deposits or Treasury bills.
3. Investors have homogeneous expectations about future outcomes. That is, all investors have the same expectations. This can be extended to include a time horizon. Therefore, investors have the same expectations over the same time horizon.
4. The capital markets are in equilibrium.
5. Institutional considerations are assumed away. Such things as income taxes, transaction costs, inflation, and other market imperfections are not considered to exist.

The capital market theory that will be developed includes two parts. One aspect involves the development of a capital market line. The second is the development of the security market line. Fundamental to both these concepts is the development of the concept of a market portfolio.

Capital Market Line

The capital market line basically indicates that the investor has three alternative courses of action. First, it is assumed that the investor can invest in a riskless asset yielding the pure rate of interest. This is the price the investor demands for giving up immediate consumption. It is also assumed that the investor can borrow at this rate. Second, and fundamental to capital market theory, the investor can invest in a market portfolio. Finally, the investor can invest in the market portfolio and either lend or borrow as he desires. The ultimate portfolio, whatever its composition, is located on the capital market line denoted CML in Figure 15-3.

In Figure 15-3, point L represents the rate that the investor will obtain by lending at the pure rate of interest. Point M represents the market portfolio. The expected return and standard deviation of that return are given by $E(R_m)$

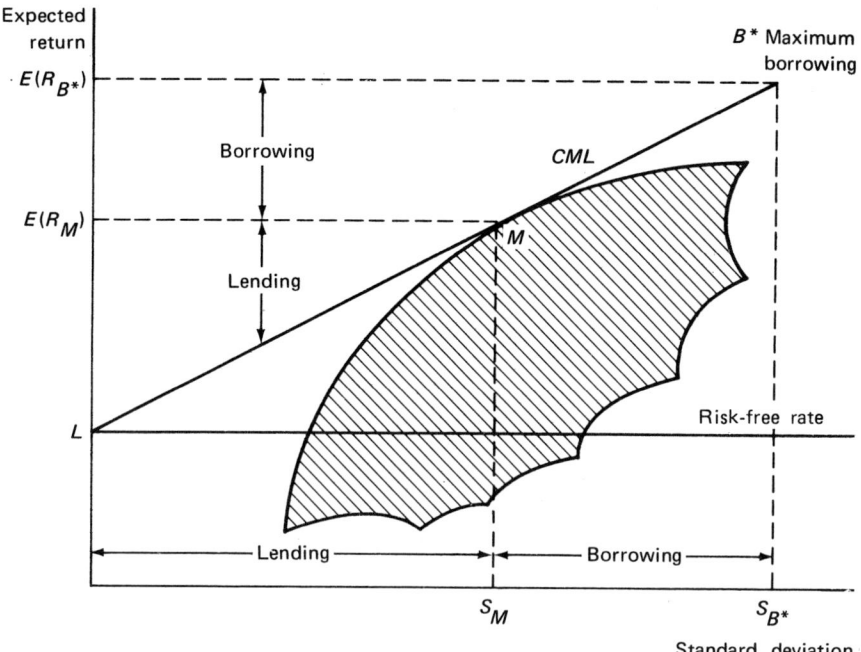

FIGURE 15-3 *The Capital Market Line*

and S_m, respectively. This can be interpreted as the ideal risk-return relationship for a portfolio of all stocks as viewed by the entire investing community. The market portfolio is pivotal because the investor can lend a certain proportion of his portfolio and invest the remainder in the market portfolio. This type of portfolio is the equivalent of a mixed bond and stock portfolio. Conversely, the investor may borrow and invest these proceeds plus his own funds. This action is the equivalent of buying stocks on margin, which is widely practiced in the security markets. In Figure 15-3 these activities are denoted as lending and borrowing, and the $E(R)$ and S of these activities vary with the composition of the portfolio. Consequently, any combination of lending, borrowing, and the market portfolio will be on the capital market line.

The rationale for all investors viewing the market in terms of a single market portfolio follows from two basic assumptions. First, it was assumed that all investors have the same expectations over the same investment horizon. Consequently, investors have the same information and interpret it the same way. All stocks, then, can be combined to form an efficient frontier, as shown in Figure 15-3. Second, it was assumed that the capital market is in equilibrium. Therefore, there is no excess demand for any stock. This results because of the premise of unanimous agreement that M is the most desirable combination of risk and return. At the same time this means that the market portfolio is a combination of the stock universe. Each stock in the market portfolio is included in the desired proportion. Hence, there is no tendency change.

In addition to the concept of the market portfolio, several other aspects of the CML need explanation. In particular, these are

1. Proving that indeed the capital market line is linear
2. Determining the slope of the capital market line
3. Indicating that all portfolios will not be identical

These will be discussed in turn below.

Showing that the *CML* is linear may be accomplished in a straightforward manner. The expected return of a portfolio made up of a riskless security and the market portfolio is the weighted average of the return expected from each segment of the portfolio. Therefore, the expected return for such a portfolio, say, portfolio A, is

$$E(R_A) = L X_L + E(R_M) (1 - X_L)$$ (15-22)

where the $E(R_A)$ is the expected return on portfolio A, L is the return that can be earned from investing in the riskless security, $E(R_M)$ is the expected return that can be earned from investing in the market portfolio, and X_L is the proportion of the portfolio invested in the riskless asset.

The variance of this return is given by the familiar formula for determining the variance of the resulting portfolio A. Thus

$$V(R_A) = V(L) X_L^2 + V(R)_M (1 - X_L)^2 + 2X_L (1 - X_L) \text{Cov}_{LM}$$ (15-23)

where Cov_{LM} is the covariance between the return of the riskless security and that of the market portfolio M. Since lending at the risk-free rate by definition means this asset will have no risk associated with it, its variance, $V(L)$, and covariance, Cov_{LM}, will be zero. Therefore, Equation 15-24 can be simplified to the following:

$$V(R_A) = V(R)_M (1 - X_L)^2$$ (15-24)

Taking the square root to obtain the standard deviation gives

$$S_A = S_M (1 - X_L)$$ (15-25)

Equation 15-25 is obviously linear, indicating that for any two security portfolios in which one is a riskless asset, the relationship will be linear.

The slope of the *CML* represents the reward for taking risk, or as it is commonly called, the reward-to-variability ratio. If the investor's portfolio consists solely of the riskless security, the investor obtains the pure rate of interest with certainty. If the investor decides to accept some risk, whatever the amount, the reward for accepting this risk is given by the slope of the *CML*. The greater the slope of the *CML*, the greater the reward for accepting risk. The slope can be given by

$$SL_M = \frac{E(R_M) - L}{S_M}$$ (15-26)

where SL_M is the slope of the *CML*, and the other terms are as previously defined.

To illustrate, suppose $E(R_M)$ = 20 percent, L = 5 percent, and S_M = 20 percent. Substituting into Equation 15-26 gives

$$SL_M = \frac{15.0 - 5.0}{20.0} = 0.75$$

It can be concluded for this hypothetical example that for each additional unit of risk assumed, the reward will be 0.75 units of expected return.

This is an important concept because it provides an explanation of investor behavior at given points in time. The slope of the *CML* does not need to remain constant over time. It can change to reflect changes in expectations. It must be remembered that portfolio theory is primarily concerned with uncertainty—it is ex ante. Thus, expectations about the expected market return will be reflected in the *CML*. This can explain optimism and pessimism in the stock market and shifts between stocks and bonds. In particular, if the reward for accepting risk is not sufficient, there will be a shift away from stocks to riskless assets. Conversely, when the expected return on common stock is anticipated to be relatively high, there will be shifting away from bonds into common stock. Both these activities are observed in the real world as expectations about the business outlook change.

Finally, simply because there is a unique market portfolio M does not mean that all investors will hold identical portfolios. The investor can still vary his portfolio to the extent that it incorporates lending or borrowing and the market portfolio. In essence the investor can select the preferred point on the *CML*. As shown in Figure 15-4, this can be represented by indifference curves for three hypothetical investors designated as a conservative investor, a common stock investor, and an aggressive investor. The conservative investor, for example, emphasizes safety and would incorporate a larger proportion of the risk-free asset. At the other extreme, the aggressive investor would borrow at the risk-free rate and use these funds to invest in the market portfolio. Finally, the so-called common stock investor would invest in the market portfolio. Realistically, there would be an infinite number of combinations along the *CML*.

Security Market Line

To consider the relationship of individual securities to the market portfolio M, recall that when lending or borrowing at the pure rate of interest plus investing in the market portfolio, all combinations plotted along the *CML* were permitted. This resulted because points on the *CML* gave the greatest expected return for a given level of risk. But it can be shown that this does not hold for individual securities or inefficient portfolios. Consider a stock i and the market portfolio M as shown in Figure 15-5. If stock i and M were combined in a

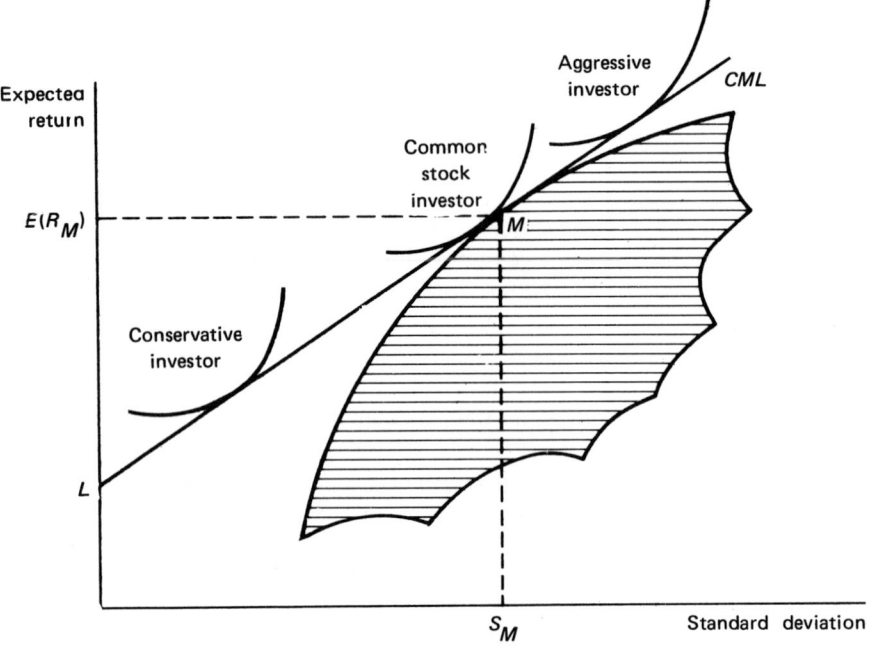

FIGURE 15-4 *Preferred Portfolios for Three Hypothetical Investors*

portfolio, the risk of the resulting portfolio would be given by the familiar formulation

$$V(R) = X_i^2\sigma_i^2 + X_M^2 V(R_M) + 2X_i X_M \text{Cov}_{iM} \qquad (15\text{-}27)$$

where Cov_{iM} is the covariance between stock i and portfolio M. The expected return on the resulting portfolio is

$$E(R) = X_i\mu_i + X_M E(R_M) \qquad (15\text{-}28)$$

The relationship between i and M is shown in Figure 15-6. The slope of the curve iM depends on the correlation between i and M. Furthermore, the curve iM at M must be tangent to CML.[11] In other words, the tradeoff between changes in risk and return for stock i must equal that for M. The slope of the curve iM at point M is given by

$$SL_{iM} = \frac{[\mu_i - E(R_M)]}{\text{Cov}_{iM} - V(R_M)} S_M \qquad (15\text{-}29)$$

And since the slope of CML and the curve iM must be equal at M

$$\frac{[\mu_i - E(R_M)]S_M}{\text{Cov}_{iM} - V(R_M)} = \frac{E(R_M) - L}{S_M} \qquad (15\text{-}30)$$

[11] For a proof of this see William F. Sharpe, *Portfolio Theory and Capitol Markets* (New York: McGraw-Hill, 1970), p. 87.

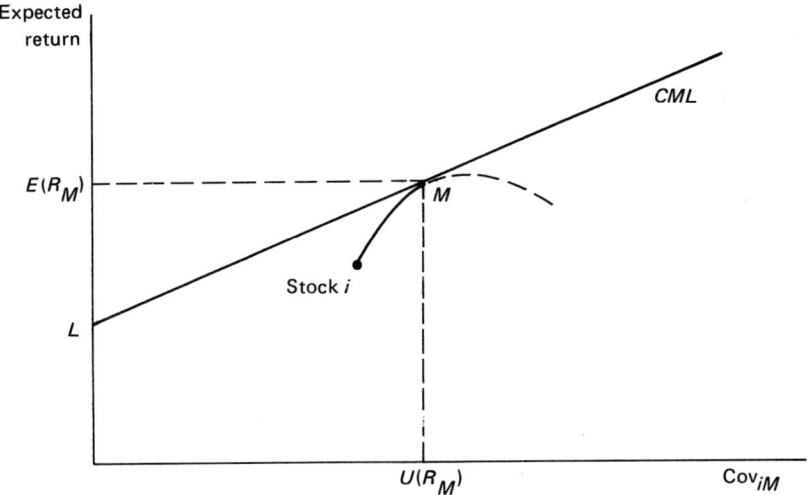

FIGURE 15-5 *Tradeoff Between Stock* i *and the Market Portfolio* M

Simplifying and rearranging Equation 15-29 leads to

$$\mu_i - L = \left(\frac{E(R_M) - L}{V(R_M)}\right) \mathrm{Cov}_{iM} \qquad (15\text{-}31)$$

The left side of Equation 15-31 indicates the premium for accepting risk, while the right side of the Equation indicates that this premium is a function of its slope coefficient multiplied by its covariance with M. The slope coefficient represented by $[E(R_M) - L/V(R_M)]$ is a constant. As a consequence, in equilibrium all stocks plot along a straight line, the security market line, as shown in Figure 15-6 as SML. The slope of the SML is given by Equation 15-31.

FIGURE 15-6 *The Security Market Line*

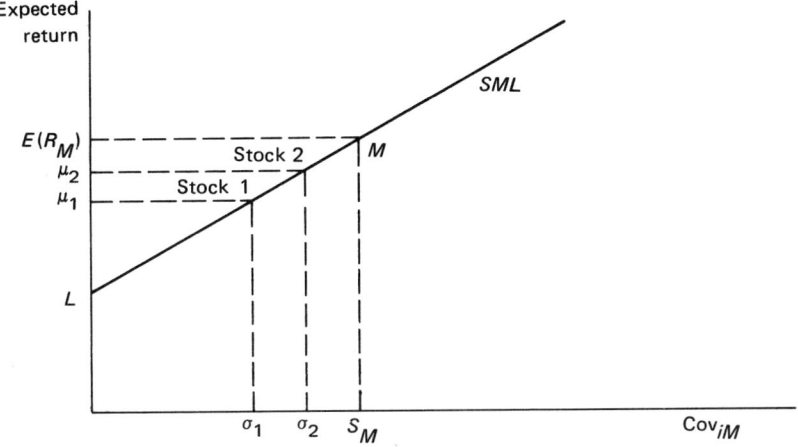

This formulation basically says that the expected return on a risky asset in equilibrium depends on the security's covariance with the market portfolio. In equilibrium, those stocks with high covariance experience low demand and low prices. Conversely, such stocks command a high expected return. Those stocks with low covariance have high demand and high prices. Or, conversely, their expected return is relatively low. The expected return and variance of the market portfolio is the standard of comparison. Those securities that have zero or negative covariance with the market are sought after because of their effect of reducing risk. Their prices are high because of high demand; hence, their expected return is low.

The rationale for *SML* will now be recognized as the basis for diversifiable and nondiversifiable risk discussed in the previous chapter. The concept of diversifiable and nondiversifiable is somewhat more convenient to use than covariance with the market portfolio, although the two concepts are equivalent.

Assumptions Relaxed

At the outset, capital market theory was developed under a specified set of assumptions. This permitted the formulation of the capital market line and the security market line. Now, however, these assumptions will be relaxed to determine the effect of more realistic assumptions. This should enable us to determine how far capital market theory goes in explaining what happens in the real world. The discussion that follows will focus on the three assumptions that have the most important implications for capital market theory.

Different Lending and Borrowing Rates   It is highly improbable for an investor to be able to borrow and lend at the same rate. This is especially true because the security used in this analysis is a risk-free security. If the investor cannot lend and borrow at the same rate, a unique market portfolio no longer exists. This is shown in Figure 15-7. From Figure 15-7, it is evident that two market portfolios exist, and hence two *CMLs*—one for a lending portfolio and the other for a borrowing portfolio. Similarly there is no longer a unique *CML*, since different lending and borrowing rates mean that two *CMLs* emerge with different slopes and covariances. For a borrowing portfolio, as with a lending portfolio, the slope is derived by rearranging Equation 15-30 and substituting B for L to give the expected return for stock i. Thus

$$\mu_i = . \quad + [E(R_{MB}) - B]\left(\frac{\text{Cov}_{iMB}}{V(R_{MB})}\right) \tag{15-32}$$

where the terms are as previously defined.

Furthermore, the covariances between individual securities and the market portfolio differ. This results because the point of tangency is different for the two portfolios, and hence the slope of the curve iM differs. As a consequence, all that can be specified when there are different lending and borrowing rates is a range of expected returns. This is shown in Figure 15-8. It is evident that by

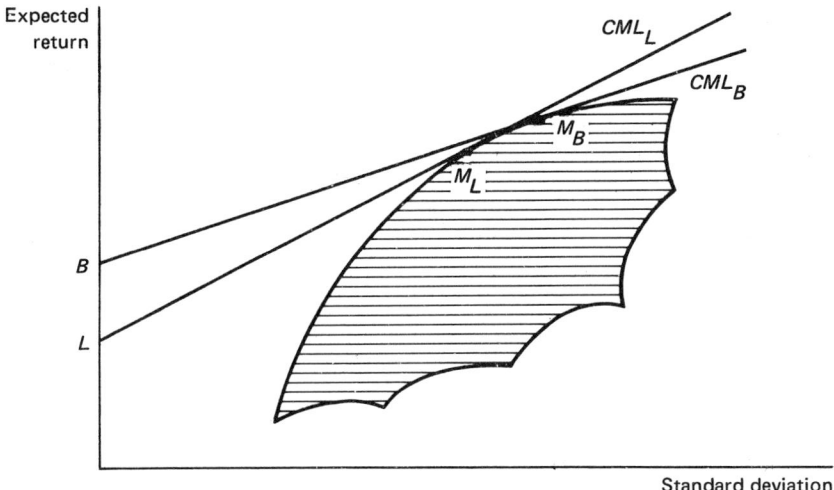

FIGURE 15-7 *Different Lending and Borrowing Rates*

introducing different lending and borrowing rates the explanatory power of the theory is reduced.

Generalized Uncertainty Generalized uncertainty, in contrast to idealized uncertainty, is a much broader concept. Idealized uncertainty generally means that all investors have the same expectations. This assumption was essential to the development of the market portfolio since there was unanimous agreement on the efficiency of this portfolio. This could only come about with homogeneous expectations. Generalized uncertainty is normally defined to mean that individuals have different expectations. For example, some investors may be optimistic about a particular stock's prospects, while others may not. If generalized uncertainty is postulated, the concept of a market portfolio breaks down. No longer will investors have the same expectations, and no longer will there be unanimous agreement on the market portfolio. This result holds even if investors have the same information. That is, two investors may interpret the same information differently. Consequently, the relaxation of the assumption of idealized uncertainty has a significant effect on the theory. It not only introduces a grey area, but it also raises serious questions about the relevance of capital market theory. This assumption, as a result, is fundamental to capital market theory.

Equilibrium Equilibrium was assumed to exist in the market. Realistically, however, the capital markets, as with other markets, can be said to be in a constant state of disequilibrium. This means that there is continuous changing and shifting within the market. There are a number of reasons for this. One of the most important is changing expectations which result from new information. Another reason is the interpretation of new information. One investor may

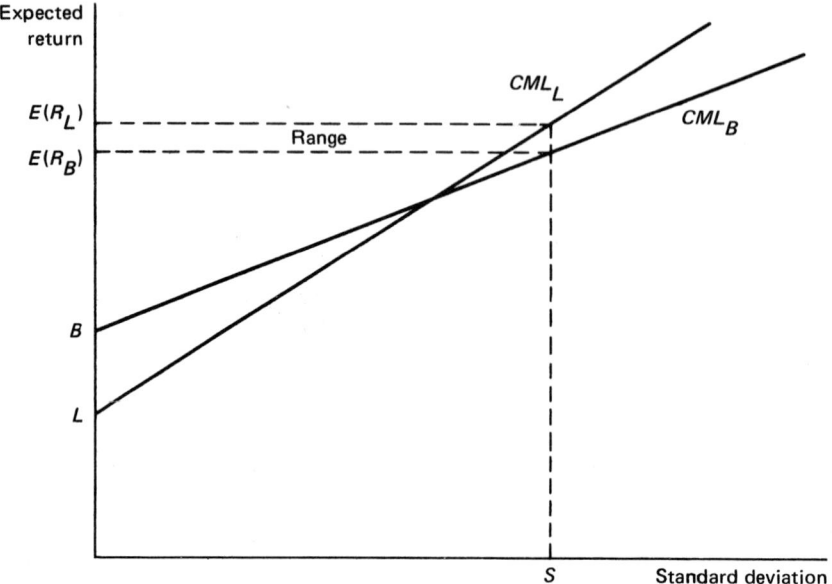

FIGURE 15-8   CMLs *With Different Lending and Borrowing Rates*

feel optimistic about a particular stock while another is pessimistic. This is an everyday occurrence in the stock markets and the capital markets in general. A third reason is the effect of taxation. The tax laws are constructed in such a way that they cause disequilibrium. Ordinary income is taxed at progressively higher rates, and capital gains are taxed at preferential rates. Therefore, every investor views the market slightly differently, and there cannot be a unique *CML* or *SML*.

Relaxing this assumption again greatly affects the results of the theory. Without general equilibrium in a static sense, the *CML* and *SML* could not be developed. This is not an unexpected result. Equilibrium conditions are an important part of economic analysis. The result here is not essentially different than that in other aspects of economic analysis.

At this point some concluding comments are in order. Relaxing these assumptions undoubtedly raises some question about the validity of the capital market theory. However, it should be pointed out that this does not necessarily invalidate the theory. It may be that investors do think as postulated by the capital market theory, in which case the theory captures the real world situation relatively well. In particular, capital market theory captures reality reasonably well if investors tend to view the expected risk and return on individual securities as a linear function of the expected risk and return on a market portfolio. Several empirical tests have been directed at this question, and a study by Sharpe on mutual funds seems to indicate that the capital market model gives a fairly good explanation of the market's behavior.[12] Consequently, the theory may be a reasonably good explanation of investor behavior, and it may only remain to fill in the gaps that exist.

Summary

In the last two decades, mathematical programming models for portfolio selection have received increasing attention. Surprisingly, however, their reception by the practicing portfolio manager has been less than enthusiastic. It has only been in the late 1960s that much attention has been given to computer-augmented techniques of security analysis and investment management. The explanation is probably that only recently has sufficient progress been made toward practical application of these techniques. This chapter attempted to outline briefly the Markowitz E-V formulation. This formulation is the forerunner of recent developments in portfolio theory; it certainly played an important role in the development of the capital market theory. Probably as important as its influence on investment management are its effect on other areas of finance and economics. The Markowitz formulation has been widely used in managerial finance, real estate, and in the development of financial theory. An important corollary result of the theory was the quantification of risk. Controversy still surrounds the use of standard deviation as a measure of risk, but by its use Markowitz gave impetus to efforts to quantify risk.

The single-index model represents a refinement of the Markowitz formulation to meet the practical demands of security analysis and investment management. The essential advantage of this model is its relative simplicity, since the number of inputs is greatly reduced. At the same time, much of the explanatory power of the Markowitz formulation is retained. The single-index model also led to the development of capital market theory. Two important aspects of this theory are the market portfolio and the *CML* and *SML*. Given a certain set of assumptions, it is possible to develop a portfolio from among the entire universe of risky securities that is unanimously preferred by all investors. It involves specific proportions of all risky securities in the universe. In addition to investing in this market portfolio, lending and borrowing at the pure rate of interest may be introduced. These combinations of lending and borrowing lie on a straight line known as the *CML*. Consequently, there are a number of possible portfolios combining lending, borrowing, and the market portfolio. The position on the *CML*, or the portion of each of these three assets, is determined by the investor's preferences for risk and expected return.

Finally, the analysis was extended to include the relationship of individual securities or even inefficient portfolios to the market portfolio. This was the *SML*. This formulation indicates that in equilibrium, the expected return on a

[12] William F. Sharpe, "Mutual Fund Performance," *Journal of Business*, vol. 39, no. 1, part II (Jan., 1966), pp. 119–39.

risky security is a linear function of the pure rate of interest and that security's covariance with the market portfolio.

Questions

1. The Markowitz E-V formulation assumes that the investor is a risk averter. Explain.
2. In the Markowitz formulation, it is assumed that investors view returns in terms of the first two moments of a distribution. Explain.
3. What is the efficient frontier in the Markowitz formulation?
4. How does the investor select the appropriate portfolio from the efficient set?
5. What are the criticisms of the Markowitz formulation?
6. How does the diagonal formulation differ from the Markowitz formulation?
7. An important extension of the single-index portfolio model is capital market theory.
   a. What assumptions are necessary for the development of this theory?
   b. What is the rationale for the market portfolio?
   c. Prove that *CML* is linear.
   d. How do you determine the slope of the *CML*? What does it mean?
   e. Explain why all investors do not have identical portfolios under the theory. How do they determine their portfolios?
8. The *CML* can be extended to the *SML*.
   a. Prove that the *SML* is linear in equilibrium.
   b. What happens to capital market theory if the basic assumptions are relaxed?

Selected References

(See references for Chapter 14.)

Chapter 16

Wealth-Maximization Model

An important aspect of portfolio theory is establishing the type of function investors attempt to maximize. To this point we have accepted the general premise that investors attempt to maximize their expected utility. This approach is taken in both the traditional approach and the Markowitz approach to portfolio construction. An alternative objective that can be used is to strive for wealth maximization. That is, the assumption is made that the investor prefers more wealth to less wealth, and the investor seeks to make investments that will achieve this goal. Such an objective seems rather obvious, but none of the other approaches has focused on this goal. As we will see, this approach has certain features that are highly desirable to all types of investors.

The major advocate of the wealth-maximization model (W-M) has been Henry A. Latane.[1] The major distinction between this model and the Markowitz formulation is that the W-M holds that the investor can achieve wealth maximization by making investments that promise the largest geometric mean return. The major advantage of the geometric mean return is that it takes risk into consideration. Recall from Chapter 5 that the geometric mean return is given by

$$G_i = (\mu_i^2 - \sigma_i^2)^{\frac{1}{2}} \tag{16-1}$$

where μ_i and σ_i are the expected return and standard deviation of return on stock i, respectively. Equation 16-1 shows that the geometric mean takes risk into account, since the larger the σ_i the smaller the geometric mean return, G_i. It is this aspect of the geometric mean criterion that is particularly desirable.

In addition to introducing an alternative objective, the wealth-maximization

---

[1] For example, see Henry A. Latane, "Criteria for Choice Among Risky Ventures," *Journal of Political Economy*, vol. 67, no. 2 (Apr., 1959), pp. 144–55; Henry A. Latane and Donald L. Tuttle, *Security Analysis and Portfolio Management* (New York: The Ronald Press, 1970), pp. 628–38; and Nils H. Hakansson, "Multi-Period Mean Variance Analysis: Toward a General Theory of Portfolio Choice," *Journal of Finance*, vol. 26, no. 4 (Sept., 1971), pp. 857–84.

model presents an opportunity to show the practical application of the theoretical developments on the nature of securities markets. In particular, it will be seen that aside from the use of the geometric mean as the means of maximizing the investor's wealth, the W-M model makes extensive use of the concepts developed in connection with the capital market theory. For example, it makes use of the concepts of diversifiable and nondiversifiable risk, it assumes lending and borrowing at the risk-free rate, and it selects securities on the basis of their reward for taking risk. This last concept is given by the slope of the capital market line and the security market line.

Geometric Mean and Risk—An Illustration

Before discussing the features of the W-M model, it is useful to show how the geometric mean can maximize the wealth of the investor while taking risk into consideration. Suppose we have a situation in which an investor can invest $100,000 in a highly speculative common stock. Suppose also that in a good year the investment could be expected to appreciate to $400,000, but if it is a bad year the security would become virtually worthless. Good and bad years are equally likely. Given these circumstances, the question becomes, what is the proportion of the investor's wealth that should be committed to this speculative stock to maximize his wealth. Two criteria may be used to answer this question. One criterion, which has received a great deal of attention, is that the investor attempts to maximize his expected utility. This criterion uses the expected value, but the expected value is not particularly useful when used in conjunction with wealth maximization, since the expected value is a linear function of the amount of funds committed. Therefore, the expected value does not supply an answer to the question of the appropriate amount of investment to maximize the wealth of the investor. As a result, a second criterion has been advanced, which holds that the investor should attempt to maximize his geometric mean return. This criterion does give a unique solution.

Determining the proportion of the investor's net worth that should be committed to this speculative stock depends upon the possible outcomes. Suppose q is the proportion that is invested in the risky stock. The return for a good year would be given by

$$(4q + 1 - q) = 3q + 1 \tag{16-2}$$

and the return for a bad year would be given by

$$(1 - q) \tag{16-3}$$

Essentially, Equation 16-2 indicates that in a good year the investor's wealth will increase by three times the proportion invested, but in a bad year the investor's wealth will decrease by the amount invested. For example, if 25 percent of the investor's wealth were committed to this stock, in a good year the investor's wealth would increase by 75 percent. On the other hand, in a bad market the investor's wealth would be reduced 25 percent. The geometric mean would indicate the proportion that would maximize the investor's wealth, since it would show the proportion that would provide the highest return to the investor.

Since the geometric mean reaches a maximum, calculus can be used to find the q that will maximize the wealth of the investor. Trial and error can also be used, as shown in Table 16-1. Since good years and bad years are equally likely, the geometric mean return can be determined as follows:

$$G^2 = (3q + 1) (1 - q) \qquad (16\text{-}4)$$

and

$$G = [(3q + 1) (1 - q)]^{\frac{1}{2}} \qquad (16\text{-}5)$$

The $(3q + 1)$ portion of Equation 16-4 is the investor's wealth in a good year and the $(1 - q)$ is the investor's wealth in a bad year. Hence, the geometric mean return is given by taking the products of these two outcomes and taking the square root.

Table 16-1 shows the expected returns using the expected value criterion and the geometric mean criterion. Columns 1 and 2 show the possible outcomes for different investment strategies ranging from zero investment up to committing the investor's entire wealth to this particular stock. Columns 3 and 4 give the return that can be expected using an expected value criterion and the geometric mean criterion. Column 3 is simply an arithmetic average of columns 1 and 2, since the probabilities of good and bad years are equally likely.

A strategy of investing 25 percent in this stock would give a geometric mean return of:

$$G^2 = (3 \times 0.25 + 1) (1 - 0.25)$$

$$= [(1.75) (0.75)]^{\frac{1}{2}}$$

$$G = 1.146$$

The geometric mean return relative for each proportion shown in Table 16-1 was calculated in this fashion. It appears that the investor's wealth would be maximized by investing 33 percent of his wealth in this stock. Differentiating

TABLE 16-1 *A Comparison of the Geometric Mean and the Expected Return for a Risky Situation*

Strategy	Market State		$\overline{RR}$	G
	Good	Bad		
Invest 100 percent	4.00	0.00	2.00	0.000
Invest 75 percent	3.25	0.25	1.75	0.901
Invest 50 percent	2.50	0.50	1.50	1.118
Invest 33 percent	2.00	0.67	1.33	1.155
Invest 25 percent	1.75	0.75	1.25	1.146
Do not invest	1.00	1.00	1.00	1.000
Probability of occurrence	0.5	0.5		

this function confirms that the maximum actually occurs at 33 percent.[2] Table 16-1 illustrates, therefore, that there is an optimal amount of one's wealth that should be committed to the investment in a particular risky situation. If the investor commits more than the optimal level, he risks a possible loss. For example, if the investor committed 75 percent of his wealth to the risky stock shown in Table 16-1 he could actually expect to suffer a loss. Conversely, if less than 33 percent of the investor's wealth were committed to this investment, he would not be taking full advantage of this investment opportunity. For example, if only 25 percent of the investor's wealth were committed to this investment, he would not be maximizing his end-of-period wealth. In contrast the mean does not take risk into consideration. In other words, the mean RR increases as the amount of funds committed to this investment increases.

Consequently, the W-M model makes the assumption that the investor attempts to maximize his end-of-period wealth. If the investor selects stocks with the largest anticipated geometric mean return, he will have the greatest chance of maximizing his end-of-period wealth. This follows since the geometric mean takes risk into consideration, and therefore stocks that promise the largest geometric mean will maximize the wealth of the investor.

Features of the W-M Model

The W-M model, except for its emphasis on the geometric mean as a method of achieving wealth-maximization, may be viewed as an application of the concepts developed in connection with the capital market theory. In this sense it may be viewed as an outgrowth of the capital market theory. It views the risk associated with particular stocks as a function of the risk associated with stocks in general, plus a certain amount of risk that cannot be explained by the risk associated with the market—diversifiable and nondiversifiable risk. In addition, lending and borrowing are introduced at the risk-free rate. Finally, the actual portfolios are constructed by determining the reward for accepting risk. In a practical sense, this is measured by the same formula as the one for determining the slope of the capital market line.

Assumptions of the W-M Model

Basically, four assumptions are made. The first, which needs the least discussion, is that the model's main focus is on risky securities, that is, common stock. As shown in Chapter 13, the construction of bond portfolios does not require complex portfolio models, since the risk can be fairly accurately estimated. The

---

[2] Differentiating Equation 16-5 and setting it equal to zero will give the maximum q. Differentiating Equation 16-5 gives the following:

$$\frac{d}{dq} = [(3q + 1)(1 - q)]^{\frac{1}{4}}$$

$$= \frac{1 - 3q}{(2q - 3q^2 + 1)^{\frac{3}{4}}}$$

Setting this equal to zero shows that a maximum is attained when $q = 0.33$.

sources of concern are changes in interest rates and possible changes in quality that may occur over time. Generally, the major source of concern for a high-quality bond portfolio is changes in interest rates, since these may be fairly volatile.

Second, the W-M model considers portfolio composition as involving three different decision areas, each of which requires a definite decision by the portfolio manager. These are as follows:

1. What stocks should be selected for the portfolio? There is a universe of thousands of stocks from which the portfolio manager may select a portfolio. This decision requires the derivation of some selection criteria. Further, in the Markowitz formulation, the computer output determines what stocks are to be included in the portfolio and their proportions.

2. What amounts should be purchased of each stock? Recall from Chapter 14 that the proportions of each stock in the portfolio can greatly affect the risk and expected return of the portfolio. Hence, this aspect of the portfolio composition problem must be considered.

3. Should leverage be utilized? Lending and borrowing have long been associated with investment management. Consequently, a comprehensive portfolio theory should include these aspects. However, the W-M model assumes that lending and borrowing can occur at the pure rate of interest. This is the same assumption utilized in capital market theory. The implications of that assumption were discussed in Chapter 15. This assumption posed a problem for capital market theory, and therefore it is also a difficulty of the W-M model.

The third assumption is that the investor attempts to maximize his end-of-period wealth. What is unusual about this assumption is the use of the geometric mean return rather than the expected value as the appropriate criterion for attaining this objective. The rationale for using the geometric mean return has already been discussed.

The fourth assumption, like the third assumption, needs no extensive discussion. In the W-M model, it is assumed that the returns on common stocks are normally distributed. This means that the distribution of returns can be fully described by the mean and standard deviation. Needless to say, this assumption greatly simplifies the portfolio-building process. However, recent empirical studies have shown that the distribution of returns on common stocks is not normally distributed. It is unclear which type of distribution does adequately describe the return on common stocks.[3]

Data for the Model

As in the Markowitz formulation, the W-M model begins with a universe, or list, of perhaps 100 to 150 stocks. In the Markowitz formulation, the expected return, variance, and covariance for these stocks were needed to obtain the

[3] See Eugene F. Fama, "The Behavior of Stock-Market Prices, *Journal of Business* vol. 38, no. 1 (Jan., 1965), pp. 34–105; and C. M. Sprenkle, "Warrant Prices as Indicators of Expectations and Preferences," *Yale Economic Essays*, vol. 1 (1961), pp. 178–231.

efficient set of portfolios. For the W-M model, the basic information required to construct portfolios is as follows:

1. The expected return for each stock in a good market year
2. The expected return for each stock in a bad market year
3. The diversifiable and nondiversifiable risk for each stock (The nondiversifiable risk is not really necessary unless it is to be used to determine the proportion of each stock in the portfolio.)

These estimates are based on the premise that the return on a particular stock depends upon the firm's performance and the market's performance. That is, the return on a particular stock is assumed to be made up of two separate components, firm-related factors and market-related factors. Each of these will play a role in determining the return on a particular stock. Therefore, the analyst must make forecasts assuming the following conditions exist:

1. Good firm-year, good market year
2. Bad firm-year, good market year
3. Good firm-year, bad market year
4. Bad firm-year, bad market year

The type of forecast the analyst might make would resemble the forecasts in Table 16-2. Columns 2 and 3 show the RRs for a good market year. If the firm has a good year, and it is also a good market year, the return on individual stocks will be considerable, as shown in column 2. On the other hand, if the firm has a bad year while the market has a good year, this will influence the return on these stocks, which will not be as good as when combined with a good firm-year. Column 4 shows the RRs for a good firm-year and a bad market year, while column 5 shows the case where the firm turns in a bad performance and the market also has a bad year. This situation might occur during recession periods.

In Table 16-2, if in the coming year stock 1's earnings increase substantially and the market is good, we will expect a RR of 1.70. If the firm does badly and market conditions are poor, the RR will be 0.76, a substantial decline in value. Between these two extremes are two other possibilities, a bad firm-year and a good market year, and a good firm-year and a bad market year. If the former

TABLE 16-2 *Hypothetical RRs for Various States of the Firm and the Market*

Stock	Good market		Bad market	
	Good–good	Bad–good	Good–bad	Bad–bad
1	1.70	1.30	1.16	0.76
2	2.10	1.50	1.20	0.60
3	1.60	1.30	1.10	0.80
4	1.90	1.30	1.20	0.60
5	1.65	1.23	1.13	0.71
6	2.16	1.40	1.20	0.44
7	2.00	1.30	1.20	0.50
8	1.47	1.25	1.05	0.83

occurs, we will expect a *RR* of 1.30; if the latter occurs, we will expect a *RR* of 1.16.

Table 16-2 can be simplified to give estimates of the return in good and bad market years on the assumption that good and bad firm years are equally likely. Hence, the $RR_{G/G}$ and $RR_{B/G}$ can be averaged to give the expected return in a good market year. Similarly, the return anticipated in a bad market year is given by averaging the $RR_{G/B}$ and $RR_{B/B}$. For example, the *RR* for stock 1 in a good market year is

$$RR_{G/B} = (1.70 \times 0.50) + (1.30 \times 0.50) = 1.50$$

Similarly, the return in a bad market for stock 1 is

$$RR_{B/B} = (1.16 \times 0.50) + (0.76 \times 0.50) = 0.96$$

The expected *RR* in a good market year for stock 1 is 1.50, and in a bad market year, 0.96. In this fashion, the expected *RRs* were determined for all of the stocks in Table 16-2. These are shown in the first two columns of Table 16-3.

These two estimates permit an estimate of the diversifiable and nondiversifiable risk. The diversifiable risk is simply an estimate of the impact of the state of the firm on the return that may be expected. For example, for stock 1 the *RR* of 1.50 in a good market was an average of $RR_{G/G}$ of 1.70 and $RR_{B/G}$ of 1.30. Therefore, the standard deviation of return brought about by the state of the firm is ± 0.20, and the diversifiable risk for stock 1 is ± 0.20. Note that this standard deviation also applies in a bad market year. The diversifiable risk for the stocks in Table 16-2 are shown in Table 16-3 under the heading σ_{Di}.

The nondiversifiable risk, on the other hand, can be determined from Table 16-3 by simply averaging the *RR* in a good market year and a bad market year This gives the $\overline{RR}_i$ for each stock. Using stock 1 as an example, this is

$$(1.50 \times 0.50) + (0.96 \times 0.50) = 1.23$$

TABLE 16-3 *RRs in Good and Bad Market Years, Diversifiable and Nondiversifiable Risk for Eight Hypothetical Stocks*

	Market State				
Stock	Good	Bad	$\overline{RR}_i$	σ_{Ni}	σ_{Di}
1	1.50	0.96	1.23	0.27	0.20
2	1.80	0.90	1.35	0.45	0.30
3	1.45	0.95	1.20	0.25	0.15
4	1.60	0.90	1.25	0.35	0.30
5	1.44	0.92	1.18	0.25	0.21
6	1.78	0.82	1.30	0.48	0.38
7	1.65	0.85	1.25	0.40	0.35
8	1.36	0.94	1.15	0.21	0.11
Portfolio	1.57	0.91	1.24	0.33	0.00

Source: Table 16-2.

With the aid of $\overline{RR}_i$, it is now possible to calculate the standard deviation. This can be obtained by subtracting 1.23 from 1.50 to give 0.27. Or conversely, it can be obtained by subtracting 0.96 from 1.23 to give 0.27. Hence, the standard deviation, or nondiversifiable risk, is ± 0.27. Table 16-3 shows this calculation for the eight stocks under the heading of σ_{Ni}.

Selecting the Unique Portfolio

The data shown in Table 16-3 permit the determination of a unique portfolio. Note that the W-M model does not select a set of efficient portfolios from a universe of stocks; it selects only one unique portfolio. There are three basic steps involved in determining the optimal portfolio, which answer three important questions of portfolio development. First, how many stocks should be included in the portfolio? Second, which stocks from the universe of stocks should be included in the portfolio? Third, what proportion of the portfolio should each stock constitute?

Portfolio Size   The initial step in the W-M model is to determine the number of stocks to be included in the portfolio. This does not generally have to be a large number, since empirical evidence shows that much of the advantage of diversification can be obtained with approximately 8 to 16 stocks. (See Chapter 15.) A portfolio with a small number of stocks has most of the benefits of diversification inherent in portfolios with many more stocks.

More important is the potential performance of such portfolios. Studies have shown that large managed stock portfolios have not performed significantly better than the market. In fact, studies of mutual fund performance have been consistent in showing that mutual funds have difficulty performing as well as the market as a whole.[4] After expenses were included the funds generally performed worse than the market. This is considered to result because many mutual fund portfolios include more than 50 stocks. Such broad diversification, therefore, leads to performance that is not significantly different than that of the market. For example, if the portfolio manager ranked 100 stocks according to their anticipated performance, and if he were correct, it would follow that the portfolio would have a better performance if it included only the top 10 candidates rather than the top 20, 30, or 40 candidates. At the same time, such a portfolio would have effective diversification.

Stocks to Enter Portfolio   The essential assumption is that a sufficient number of stocks will be included so that diversifiable risk is eliminated. This follows from the initial decision on the size of the portfolio. It is assumed that the portfolio will include enough stocks so that it will only be subject to

[4] See, for example, Michael C. Jensen, "The Performance of Mutual Funds in the Period 1945–1964," *Journal of Finance*, vol. 33, no. 2 (May, 1968), pp. 389–416; William F. Sharpe, "Mutual Fund Performance," *Journal of Business*, vol. 39, no. 1, part II (Jan., 1966), pp. 119–38; and Jack L. Treynor and Kay K. Mazuy, "Can Mutual Funds Outguess the Market," *Harvard Business Review*, vol. 44, no. 4, (July–Aug., 1966), pp. 131–37.

nondiversifiable risk. The W-M model approaches the question of entry candidates in two steps. Initially, there is a screening process that eliminates obviously inferior stocks from consideration. The second step determines those securities to enter the portfolio.

The initial screening process eliminates stocks that would not potentially benefit the portfolio in either a good market year or a bad market year. The method can be illustrated using the eight stocks shown in Table 16-4. Initially, the stock with the lowest RR in a good market is determined. Next, the bad market RR for this stock is compared to that of the remaining candidates. If it is the lowest, it is eliminated from consideration. In Table 16-4, the first candidate for exclusion is stock 2. Its RR in a good market is the lowest, and its RR in a bad market is also the lowest. It is evident, then, that this stock can add nothing either in a good market or a bad market that could not be obtained more effectively from the remaining candidates. This process can be repeated as long as there are a number of obviously inferior candidates in the list.

The next candidate for exclusion in Table 16-4 is stock 8, which illustrates a slight variation in the screening process. The RR for stock 8 in a good market year is the lowest of the remaining stocks, but its RR in a bad market year is not. However, comparing it with stock 5 which has the next lowest good market year RR, we see that the RR in a bad market year for stock 5 is substantially greater than that for stock 8. Stock 8, therefore, can be eliminated because it does not benefit the portfolio as much as stock 5, which makes a greater contribution to the portfolio in both good and bad market years. In this fashion the initial list is narrowed down until all the obvious candidates for exclusion have been removed.

The second part of the selection process requires the determination of what is referred to as the pure-risk yield. This is calculated as follows:

$$\lambda_i = \frac{\overline{RR_i} - L}{\sigma_{Ni}} \tag{16-6}$$

where λ_i is the pure-risk yield for stock i, $\overline{RR_i}$ is the mean RR in good and bad market conditions for stock i, L is the pure rate of interest stated as a return

TABLE 16-4 *RRs for Eight Hypothetical Stocks in Good and Bad Markets*

	Market State	
Stock	Good	Bad
1	1.50	0.50
2	1.20	0.50
3	1.50	0.72
4	1.36	0.80
5	1.35	0.85
6	1.70	0.60
7	1.52	0.75
8	1.33	0.65

relative, and σ_{Ni} is the nondiversifiable risk associated with stock i. This formulation is the one for determining the slope of the capital market line that was discussed in Chapter 15. The λ_i's are commonly referred to the reward-to-variability ratio in Sharpe's terminology, or the price of risk in Lintner's formulation. This ratio is based on the premise that risk must be compensated by a return over and above the pure rate of interest. If the investor puts off consumption and invests his savings, he can earn this pure rate of interest, say 4.0 percent, with certainty. Investments involving risk, therefore, should compensate the investor for the amount of risk involved. The degree of this compensation is measured by the reward-to-variability ratio, or pure-risk yield of Equation 16-6.

To illustrate the use of Equation 16-6, consider stock 1 of Table 16-3. Recall that the $\overline{RR}$ is 1.23, and σ_N is 0.27. Further, suppose the pure rate of interest is 4.0 percent. Substituting these values into Equation 16-6 gives

$$\lambda_1 = \frac{1.23 - 1.04}{0.27}$$

$$= 0.70$$

Hence, the pure-risk yield is 0.70 for stock 1 of Table 16-3. What this pure-risk yield measures is the amount of compensation the investor receives for accepting risk. In this example stock 1 provides 0.70 units of compensation for each unit of risk. This ratio essentially measures the reward for accepting risk.

To illustrate the use of the pure-risk yield, λ_i, in the construction of portfolios, consider the following 16 stocks in 12 industries:

Industry	λ_i	Industry	λ_i
1. Chemical	0.50	9. Property insurance	0.25
2. Automobile	0.46	10. Bank	0.24
3. Automobile	0.42	11. Life insurance	0.22
4. Furniture	0.40	12. Public utility	0.20
5. Food processing	0.36	13. Public utility	0.19
6. Food processing	0.30	14. Paper products	0.17
7. Retailing	0.28	15. Tire and rubber	0.11
8. Retailing	0.27	16. Petroleum	0.10

The industry is listed instead of the company because the portfolio manager can obtain diversification and thus eliminate diversifiable risk by purchasing stocks from different industries. The λ_i's, on the other hand, indicate the reward for undertaking nondiversifiable risk. The risk-averse investor, therefore, prefers stocks with large λ_i's to small λ_i's, but this must be qualified to the extent that diversification is desired. To illustrate, in the above example two automobile stocks are under consideration. The portfolio manager selects stock 2 because it has a higher λ_i than stock 3. The assumption is that stock 3 cannot add anything to the portfolio that cannot be obtained from stock 2. Therefore, stocks with the largest λ_i's are selected for the portfolio subject to the constraint that there is sufficient diversification among industries.

With these basic premises, it is now possible to select a portfolio from the above list of stocks. Assume that 10 stocks are to be included in the portfolio. The following stocks would be selected for inclusion:

Stock 1	Stock 9
Stock 2	Stock 10
Stock 4	Stock 11
Stock 5	Stock 12
Stock 7	Stock 14

Stocks 3, 6, 8, and 13 were not included because other stocks in the same industry promised a higher λ_i. The rule for selecting stocks for the portfolio, then, is to include those stocks with the highest λ_i's, except where there are two or more stocks from the same industry, in which case the stock with the highest λ_i is included.

Allocation Per Stock   The third step in completing the portfolio of stocks involves determining the proportion of the portfolio invested in each stock. The Markowitz-Sharpe formulation determined not only the securities to be included in the portfolios of the efficient set, but also the proportions of each. The W-M model provides two methods of determining the proportions. One method simply provides for an equal allocation among the securities selected for inclusion in the portfolio. This can be represented by

$$X_i = 1/n \qquad (16\text{-}7)$$

where X_i is the relative proportion invested in each of the n stocks in the portfolio. For example, if the investor anticipated investing in 10 stocks, then 10 percent of the portfolio would be invested in each stock. The dollar amount of this commitment, however, could not be determined until leverage has been evaluated. Justification for this approach may be viewed in two different ways. First, it is simple and convenient. It gives a simple rule for allocating among the stocks in the portfolio. Second, from an empirical point of view, it appears to give reasonably good results when compared to the more complex formulation given in Equation 16-8.[5] Thus, there is strong reason to favor Equation 16-7.

Another allocation rule that can be applied attempts explicitly to minimize the diversifiable risk of the portfolio. This method of allocation makes participation in the portfolio inversely related to the sum of the diversifiable risk of all stocks in the portfolio. This allocation rule can be represented as follows:

$$X_i = \frac{1/\sigma_{Di}}{\sum\limits_{i=1}^{n} 1/\sigma_{Di}} \qquad (16\text{-}8)$$

where the terms are as previously defined. Consequently, the proportions of the stocks in the portfolio are inversely related to the diversifiable risk of each stock in the portfolio.

[5] Latane and Young, op. cit., p. 608.

Justification for this alternative allocation rule is the assumption that the diversifiable risk of each stock is independent of every other stock in the portfolio. This follows from the assumption of the diagonal model that each stock under consideration is correlated only with a market index, such as the S & P's 500 index. Therefore, all stocks selected for the portfolio can be assumed to be independent of each other. Furthermore, it is diversifiable risk which the portfolio manager attempts to diversify away. Hence, this allocation rule reinforces the basic premise of the W-M model that the portfolio is subject only to nondiversifiable risk.

Once the initial portfolio has been decided on, the pure-risk yield for the portfolio and the geometric mean return can be obtained. The pure-risk yield for the portfolio is found in exactly the same fashion as the λ_i for individual stocks. That is

$$\lambda_p = \frac{\overline{RR_p} - L}{NS} \tag{16-9}$$

where λ_p is the pure-risk yield for the portfolio, $\overline{RR_p}$ is the mean return relative for the portfolio, L is the pure-rate of interest stated as a return relative, and NS is the nondiversifiable risk of the portfolio. The geometric mean return for the portfolio can be determined by applying the same formulation as that discussed in Chapter 5. That is

$$G_p = (\overline{RR_p^2} - NS^2)^{\frac{1}{2}} \tag{16-10}$$

where the terms are as previously defined.

To illustrate the calculations connected with Equations 16-9 and 16-10, let us again use the data presented in Table 16-3. If these eight stocks were going to make up a portfolio, the pure-risk yield for the portfolio would be

$$\lambda_p = \frac{1.24 - 1.04}{0.33}$$

$$= 0.61$$

Consequently, the compensation for risk provided by this portfolio is 0.61. At the same time, the return on this portfolio would be

$$G^2 = (1.24)^2 - (0.33)^2$$

$$= 1.429$$

Taking the square root gives

$$G = 1.195$$

Thus the geometric mean return relative would be 1.195, indicating that the investor could expect a compound rate of return of approximately 20 percent by investing in this portfolio.

Lending and Borrowing

A final decision facing the investor is whether lending or borrowing should be introduced. This question must be answered before the investment process can be finalized. For example, if lending is found to be desirable, the common stock portfolio will be reduced by the amount of lending undertaken. Similarly, if borrowing is found to be desirable, the portfolio of common stock will be increased by the amount of borrowing. Lending and borrowing are both very familiar processes in investment management. Borrowing is simply the purchase of securities on margin; lending is a mixed portfolio of bonds and stocks.

The introduction of these two alternatives into the portfolio decision is of major importance. It permits an integrated quantifiable approach to these important questions: Should the investor invest only in stocks? Should the investor use leverage; if so what is the appropriate proportion? If the investor lends, what is the appropriate proportion? The optimum mix of stocks, lending, and borrowing can be determined by

$$q = \frac{\lambda_{pL}}{NS(1 - \lambda_p^2)} \qquad (16\text{-}11)$$

where q is the proportion of the investor's funds available for investment in stocks, and the other terms are as previously defined.

These variables require some discussion. The proportion of investment funds invested in stocks can be defined in several different ways. For example, it is common to use the debt-to-equity ratio or the ratio of total debt to total assets as a measure of leverage. However, q is defined as the amount of stocks per dollar of funds available for common stock investment. That is, the ratio q can be equal to, greater than, or less than one. If q is one, all of the investor's funds should be invested in the common stock portfolio. This means no lending or borrowing. On the other hand, if q is greater than one, the investor should borrow and invest these funds in the portfolio of common stock. This is referred to as positive leverage. As a practical matter, the amount of borrowing is limited by the margin requirements set by the Federal Reserve Board. If q is less than one, the investor should become a lender, lending at the pure rate of interest. This is referred to as negative leverage. The pure rate of interest is assumed to prevail for both lending and borrowing.

This leverage measure is based upon the assumption that the investor wants to maximize his terminal wealth. Hence, the investor lends or borrows in such a fashion as to maximize his geometric mean return. The actual derivation of Equation 16-11 involves calculus and is shown in Appendix A. The gist of the formulation is that given equally likely good and bad year returns, Equation 16-11 will give the degree of leverage that should be used in connection with a particular portfolio. If borrowing is used in conjunction with a portfolio of common stock, the expected return on the combined portfolio will be greater, but so will the risk. If lending is undertaken, the expected return and risk will be somewhat lower. The risk associated with lending and borrowing can be adequately determined by

$$\Lambda = qNS \tag{16-12}$$

where Λ is the total risk the investor faces.

In addition to determining the risk facing the investor, the expected return can also be determined. The net expected return under conditions of lending and borrowing is given by

$$\overline{RR}_p^* = q\overline{RR}_p - (q - 1)L \tag{16-13}$$

where $\overline{RR}_p^*$ is the net mean RR of the portfolio, and the other terms are as previously defined.

To illustrate these concepts, suppose we have a common stock portfolio with $\lambda_p = 0.40, L = 1.04$, and $NS = 0.45$. Substituting these into Equation 16-11 we obtain

$$q = \frac{0.40(1.04)}{0.45(1.0 - 0.16)} = \frac{0.416}{0.378} \approx 1.10$$

Borrowing, or positive leverage, thus would be appropriate in this case. That is, the market value of the portfolio at the time of purchase would be greater than the amount of the investor's funds.

Once the appropriate amount of leverage is determined, the net expected return of the portfolio can be obtained using Equation 16-13. If the $\overline{RR} = 1.18, q = 1.10$, and the $L = 1.04$, the $\overline{RR}_p^*$ the investor can expect is

$$\overline{RR}_p^* = 1.10(1.18) - (1.10 - 1.0)1.04$$

$$= 1.298 - 0.104$$

$$= 1.194$$

Therefore, after payment of the costs of borrowing, the $\overline{RR}_p^*$ is 1.194. Stated in terms of expected return, the net expected return is 19.4 percent. This return is somewhat higher than the 18 percent the investor could expect by investing only in the common stock portfolio. Finally, the amount of risk that the investor faces can be determined by applying Equation 16-12. This portfolio, which includes borrowing, has more risk than the common stock portfolio as follows:

$$\Lambda = 1.10(0.45) = 0.495$$

Since this portfolio requires borrowing to maximize the return, it is expected that the risk is greater than that for the common stock portfolio.

A Numerical Example

In this example we will attempt to apply the W-M model to a specific situation. A number of simplifications will be required. Since space prevents the evaluation of a large number of securities, it will be assumed that most of the initial steps have already been completed. The focal point, therefore, will be on the actual stocks entering the portfolio, their proportions, and whether leverage should be used.

An initial step in the W-M model is to determine the number of stocks that enter the portfolio. Since only a small number of stocks are required to eliminate nondiversifiable risk, the possibility of receiving a return above that of the market is greatly improved because the portfolio can be concentrated. At the same time, the portfolio may have effective diversification. For purposes of this example, let us assume that the investor wants a fairly concentrated portfolio of only eight stocks. The next step involves selecting a portfolio from the nondominated stocks. Initially, the portfolio manager may begin with a list of 100 or 150 possible candidates for the portfolio. The screening process can be used to reduce the number of candidates, but there will still remain a number of nondominated candidates for the portfolio. The portfolio is eventually determined on the basis of industry diversification and the pure-risk yield, λ_i, for each nondominated stock. Industry diversification is designed to eliminate diversifiable risk. The pure-risk yield is a measure of the reward for undertaking risk as indicated by the λ's. Thus, stocks entering the portfolio will have the largest λs subject to the limitation that there must be sufficient industry diversification. This requires selecting the stock, or perhaps two stocks, with the highest λ in each industry category. The stocks shown in Table 16-5 represent the culmination of this process. These eight stocks, then, constitute the portfolio.

It is evident that this portfolio has a $\overline{RR}_p$ of 1.13. In other words, the investor can expect a return of 13 percent. This is not the geometric mean return, however. Since it has been assumed that all diversifiable risk has been eliminated, the investor only faces nondiversifiable risk. The average nondiversifiable risk of the portfolio is 0.29. In a good market year, therefore, the portfolio return can be expected to be 1.41, and in a bad market year the portfolio return will be 0.85. Finally, λ_p, which is 0.31, gives the compensation for assuming the risk provided by the portfolio. This provides a measure of the reward for accepting

TABLE 16-5 *Hypothetical Portfolio of Eight Stocks*

| Stock | Market State | | $\overline{RR}_i$ | σ_{Ni} | σ_{Di} | λ_i |
	Good	Bad				
1	1.53	0.90	1.21	0.32	0.24	0.53
2	1.60	0.80	1.20	0.40	0.30	0.40
3	1.49	0.83	1.16	0.30	0.23	0.36
4	1.36	0.88	1.12	0.24	0.15	0.33
5	1.42	0.84	1.13	0.29	0.16	0.31
6	1.33	0.84	1.09	0.24	0.15	0.20
7	1.30	0.86	1.08	0.22	0.12	0.18
8	1.28	0.88	1.08	0.30	0.12	0.13
Portfolio	1.41	0.85	1.13	0.29	0.00	0.31

the risk associated with the portfolio of common stock and is found in the same manner as for individual stocks.[6]

Only two decisions remain to make the portfolio-building process complete. One concerns the participation of each stock in the portfolio. The other concerns lending and borrowing. Two approaches are available for determining the proportion of each stock in the portfolio. The simplest is to invest equal amounts in each stock in the portfolio. For this portfolio, it would mean investing $\frac{1}{8}$ of the portfolio in each stock. Alternatively, we can invest to minimize diversifiable risk, those stocks with the largest diversifiable risk making up a proportionately smaller proportion of the portfolio. Therefore, the participation of each stock in the portfolio can be inversely proportional to its diversifiable risk:

$$X_i = \frac{1/\sigma_{Di}}{\sum\limits_{i=1}^{n} 1/\sigma_{Di}} \tag{16-8}$$

The proportion invested in stock 1 would be

$$X_i = \frac{4.17}{48.10} = 0.087$$

As a result, 8.7 percent would be invested in stock 1 as opposed to 12.5 percent under the equal allocation rule.

The proportions of each stock in the portfolio can be determined in the same manner. The proportions of each stock in the portfolio would be as follows:

Stock 1	0.087	Stock 5	0.130
Stock 2	0.069	Stock 6	0.139
Stock 3	0.090	Stock 7	0.173
Stock 4	0.139	Stock 8	0.173

The total, of course, will be 1.00.

In the W-M model either approach is acceptable, but Latane and Tuttle favor the equal allocation rule. They indicate that the effect on nondiversifiable risk is minimal, and, as a result, its greater simplicity tends to favor its use. It should

---

[6] Once the $\overline{RR}_p$ and NS have been calculated, the pure-risk yield for the portfolio is calculated in the same fashion as for individual stocks as indicated by Equation 16-9:

$$\lambda_p = \frac{\overline{RR}_p - L}{NS}$$

where the terms are as previously defined. This formulation can be alternatively stated as

$$\lambda_p = \frac{\left(\sum\limits_{i=1}^{n} X_i \overline{RR}_i\right) - L}{\sum\limits_{i=1}^{n} X_i \sigma_{Ni}}$$

For this portfolio, λ_p is

$$\lambda_p = \frac{1.13 - 1.04}{0.29}$$

$$= 0.31$$

be pointed out that the dollar amount of the participation of each stock cannot be determined at this point. Only after the decision on leverage is finalized will the dollar size of the portfolio be determined. For example, if it is determined that lending is desirable, the amount available for common stock investment will be reduced. Conversely, if borrowing is desirable, the amount available for common stock investment is correspondingly increased.

Finally, to determine whether lending and borrowing should be used in addition to investing in common stock, Equation 16-11 is used.

$$q = \frac{\lambda_{pL}}{NS(1 - \lambda_p^2)} \qquad (16\text{-}11)$$

For the above portfolio, this is

$$q = \frac{0.31(1.04)}{0.29(1 - 0.096)} = \frac{0.32}{0.26} = 1.23$$

This means that the portfolio should be leveraged, and it should involve borrowing to the extent of 23 percent of the investor's funds available for investment. For example, if the investor had $100,000 to invest in securities, following Equation 16-11 he would borrow $23,000 and have a total portfolio of $123,000, all of which would be invested in the portfolio of eight common stocks.

The final step is to determine the return that can be expected once leverage had been undertaken. In this case let us assume that the investor decided to utilize borrowing to the extent of 23 percent. Equation 16-13 is used to determine the net return after lending or borrowing.

$$\overline{RR}_p^* = q\overline{RR}_p - (q - 1)L \qquad (16\text{-}13)$$

Substituting in Equation 16-11 gives

$$\overline{RR}_p^* = 1.23(1.13) - (1.23 - 1)1.04 = 1.15$$

The geometric mean, however, can be approximated by

$$G = \left(\frac{L^2}{1 - \lambda_p^2}\right)^{\frac{1}{2}} \qquad (16\text{-}14)$$

Substituting in Equation 16-14 gives

$$G = \left(\frac{1.04^2}{1.0 - 0.096}\right)^{\frac{1}{2}} = 1.09$$

This indicates that the investor can expect a compound rate of return of approximately 9 percent on this portfolio.

This portfolio was based upon the initial assumption that the investor only required a sufficient number of stocks to reduce diversifiable risk to a very low level. These stocks were selected, after the initial screening process, by their pure-risk yield and their industry. The proportions committed to each stock could have followed either an equal allocation rule or allocation according to the diversifiable risk of each stock. Since the difference in results is generally minor, the equal allocation rule was used. Finally, it was found that this portfolio could advantageously make use of leverage; we saw that borrowing should equal 23 percent of the common stock portfolio. Consequently, the total portfolio equaled $123,000, and approximately $15,375 was committed to each of the eight stocks assuming equal allocation.

Summary

Latane and Tuttle's wealth-maximization model incorporates most of the recent developments in portfolio theory. Like Markowitz's formulation, the W-M model is a mean-variance formulation. The mean, however, is not an arithmetic mean but a geometric mean. This is a major point of departure for the W-M model over previous portfolio models which have relied essentially on the arithmetic mean, or expected value. Recent theoretical work on the characteristics of the geometric mean and the arithmetic mean have found the geometric mean to have a number of desirable characteristics. This aspect of the W-M model is particularly advantageous.

The actual construction of a portfolio utilizes many of the theoretical developments connected with capital market theory, along with innovations of its own. The concept of a good market–bad market return is a noteworthy innovation. It gives explicit recognition to the force of the market as being distinct from the firm's performance. The relationship of the market and the performance of the firm was previously very vague, and many times the effect of market conditions was ignored and the performance of the firm was emphasized. Presumably, good profitability and earnings growth would be rewarded by dividend growth and price appreciation. Adhering to this approach often led to the situation in which the financial performance continued admirably but the price of the stock dropped precipitously. The Latane and Tuttle approach as an outgrowth of the capital market theory clarifies an aspect of security analysis that was only vaguely prescribed in the more qualitative approaches.

The derivation of a unique portfolio and the use of λ_i to select the common stock portfolio are clearly examples of the application of capital market theory. Capital market theory holds that in equilibrium there will be one best portfolio made up of all stocks available. In a practical sense, to say that there is one best portfolio is an overstatement; but to say that there is a unique portfolio selected from a universe of stocks, perhaps 100 or 150, is not so unacceptable. The λ_i's represent the slope of a straight line between the pure rate of interest and the risk-return paramenters on a particular stock. It is assumed, as Markowitz does, that the investor is a risk averter; consequently, the greater the slope of the line represented by the λ_i, the greater the compensation for risk. Under these conditions an investor attempts to maximize his compensation for risk by selecting the stocks with the highest λ_i subject to sufficient industry diversification.

Finally, the W-M model is a complete model for the acquisition of securities. The question always emerges as to the proper allocation of funds to stocks and fixed-income securities. The investor also considers borrowing to invest in common stocks. This aspect of the W-M model recognizes that the investor normally tends to hold his wealth in a number of real and financial assets. Hence, the allocation process in reality not only involves securities but also real assets. When the W-M model attempts to provide a means of determining whether lending or borrowing should be undertaken, it is attempting to provide an answer to this allocational question, but in the very limited sense of the allocation among securities.

The major drawback of the W-M model is generating the inputs. A major problem of the Markowitz formulation was to gain support of the security analysts. These analysts, it is claimed, are unaccustomed to thinking in terms of probabilities; consequently, little support was generated for the Markowitz formulation. Unquestionably, the W-M model makes even greater use of probabilities, and there may be difficulty in gaining the acceptance of security analysts. This difficulty should not be as formidable as when the Markowitz formulation first appeared, however, because most of the younger analysts are more familiar with the quantitative methods used in business analysis. Nevertheless, this factor will undoubtedly lead to a slowing of the acceptance on a wide scale among major financial institutions. For the enterprising individual, obtaining the inputs is much more formidable. At this time, no financial service publishes the type data required for the W-M model, and the small investor certainly has not the time or the resources to generate the inputs himself.

In spite of these input problems, the W-M model has much to recommend it. Its objective function, which attempts to maximize the wealth of the owner, is gaining increasing recognition for its desirable characteristics. Further, it incorporates much of the more recent developments in portfolio theory. It probably represents the most viable approach to portfolio composition, and it should draw greater attention in the coming years.

Appendix A: Derivation of the Optimum Leverage Measure

The return on a leveraged portfolio is given by the following:

$$\overline{RR}_p^* = q\overline{RR}_p - (q - 1)L \qquad (16\text{-}15A)$$

where the terms are as previously defined. Equation 16-15A can be rearranged as follows:

$$RR_p^* - L = q(\overline{RR}_p - L) \qquad (16\text{-}16A)$$

Equation 16-16A can now be substituted into Equation 16-9, which gives λ_p to give

$$\overline{RR}_p^* - L = qNS\lambda_p \qquad (16\text{-}17A)$$

where the terms are as previously defined. Hence, the left-hand side of Equation 16-16A indicates the effect of leverage on the return to the investor, while the right-hand side gives the effect on risk. If leverage is used, the anticipated return should be higher, but so is the risk. The left-hand side of Equation 16-17A shows the return on the leveraged portfolio, minus interest on the borrowed portion; the right side shows the impact on the risk of the portfolio.

To determine optimum leverage, consider the return for a portfolio, $\overline{RR}_p \pm NS$. The geometric mean return for this stock can be given for the portfolio by using Equation 16-10. Thus

$$G_p^2 = (\overline{RR}_p + NS)(\overline{RR}_p - NS) \tag{16-18A}$$

$$= \overline{RR}_p^2 - NS^2$$

Substituting into Equation 16-17A gives

$$G_p^2 = (L + qNS\lambda_p)^2 - q^2NS^2 \tag{16-19A}$$

Differentiating Equation 16-19A to determine the q that will provide a maximum G gives

$$\frac{d(G_p^2)}{dq} = 2L\lambda_p NS + 2qNS^2b^2 - 2qNS^2 \tag{16-20A}$$

Taking the second derivative confirms that this function will provide a maximum G. Thus

$$\frac{d(G_p^2)^2}{d^2q} = 2NS^2\lambda_p^2 - 2NS^2 \tag{16-21A}$$

For Equation 16-19A to be a maximum, the second derivative given in Equation 16-21A must be negative, and this only occurs when $0 \leq \lambda_p < 1$. Thus, in the W-M model the λ_p is limited by the restriction that $0 \leq \lambda_p < 1$.

Setting Equation 16-19A equal to zero and solving for q gives

$$q = \frac{\lambda_p L}{NS(1 - \lambda_p^2)} \tag{16-22A}$$

which is the measure of the optimum amount of leverage to be used and the result presented in Equation 16-11.

Questions

1. The W-M model is a mean-variance model like the Markowitz formulation. Explain why this true.
2. The W-M model makes the same assumption as the Markowitz formulation with respect to investor preferences for risk and return, but it utilizes a different utility function. Explain.

3. The W-M model focuses on risky securities. We generally take this to mean common stocks. How is the portfolio composition problem conceptualized by the W-M model?

4. Determine the pure-risk yield for the following stocks, assuming the pure rate of interest is 4 percent.

Stock	$\overline{RR}_i$	σ_{Ni}
1	1.20	0.32
2	1.30	0.38
3	1.15	0.33
4	1.19	0.32
5	1.18	0.42

Of the five stocks, which one provides the largest reward for accepting risk?

5. Suppose the pure-risk yields have been determined for the following stocks in the industries shown. Suppose you wanted to select a portfolio of 10 stocks from these. Which ones would you select, following the method advocated by Latane and Tuttle?

Industry	λ_i	Industry	λ_i
Air Transport	0.66	Telecommunications	0.42
Air Transport	0.64	Telecommunications	0.41
Tire and Rubber	0.56	Electrical Equipment	0.39
Tire and Rubber	0.52	Household Products	0.38
Recreation	0.50	Office Equipment	0.38
Recreation	0.47	Textile	0.36
Agricultural Equipment	0.46	Toys and School Supplies	0.35
Drug	0.45	Chemical	0.34
Mobile Home	0.42	Precision Equipment	0.31
Mobile Home	0.40	Precision Equipment	0.30

6. In the W-M model, security analysts must supply forecasts for different states of the market. These estimates are given for the following 10 stocks.

Stock	Good Market		Bad Market	
	Good-good	Bad-good	Good-bad	Bad-bad
1	2.00	1.38	1.24	0.62
2	1.56	1.13	1.06	0.63
3	1.48	1.22	1.08	0.82
4	1.82	1.23	1.14	0.55
5	1.54	1.21	1.09	0.76
6	1.58	1.24	1.12	0.78
7	1.92	1.36	1.18	0.62
8	1.86	1.28	1.18	0.68
9	1.48	1.12	1.03	0.67
10	1.39	1.09	1.06	0.76

a. Simplify the above estimates to reflect different states of the market.
b. Determine the diversifiable and nondiversifiable risk for each stock.
c. Eliminate those stocks which are obviously dominated.
d. Rank the remaining stocks according to their pure-risk yields (use a pure rate of interest of 4 percent).

7. Using the nondominated stocks in question 6, complete the following aspects of the portfolio process:
   a. Assuming that only 6 stocks will be included in a portfolio, select the stocks for this portfolio.
   b. For the portfolio you have selected, should lending or borrowing be undertaken?
   c. If the investor had $100,000 for investment purposes, how much will be invested in each stock?

Selected References

Cheng, Pao L., and M. King Deets. "Test of Portfolio Building Rules: Comment." *Journal of Finance,* vol. 26, no. 4 (Sept., 1971, pp. 965–72.

Hakansson, Nils H. "Multi-Period Mean Variance Analysis: Toward a General Theory of Portfolio Choice." *Journal of Finance,* vol. 26, no. 4 (Sept., 1971), pp. 857–84.

Jones, Irwin E. "Test of Portfolio Building Rules: Comment." *Journal of Finance,* vol. 26, no. 4 (Sept., 1971), pp. 973–75.

———. "Capital Growth and the Mean Variance Approach to Portfolio Selection." *Journal of Quantitative and Financial Analysis,* vol. 6, no. 1 (Jan., 1971), pp. 517–57.

Latane Henry A., "Criteria for Choice Among Risky Ventures." *Journal of Political Economy,* vol. 67, no. 2 (Apr., 1959), pp. 144–55.

———. "Investment Criteria: A Three Asset Portfolio Balance Model." *Review of Economics and Statistics,* vol. 45, no. 4 (Nov., 1963), pp. 427–30.

Latane, Henry A., and Donald L. Tuttle. "Criteria for Portfolio Building." *Journal of Finance,* vol. 22, no. 4 (Sept., 1967) pp. 359–73.

———. *Security Analysis and Portfolio Management.* New York: The Ronald Press, 1970. Chapters 25, 26, and 27.

Latane, Henry A., and William E. Young. "Test of Portfolio Building Rules." *Journal of Finance,* vol. 24, no. 4 (Sept., 1969), pp. 595–612.

Young, William E. and Robert H. Trent, "Geometric Mean Approximations of Individual Security and Portfolio Performance," *Journal of Quantitative and Financial Analysis,* vol. 4, no. 2 (June, 1969) pp. 179–201.

Chapter 17

Evaluating Portfolio Performance

The task of the portfolio manager does not end once the portfolio is constructed. The portfolio's performance must be evaluated periodically to determine whether any of the issues in the portfolio should be replaced. Even though the portfolio manager attempts to select only those securities with the best prospects, errors will occur and certain issues may need to be replaced. This activity is commonly referred to as portfolio revision and will be discussed in Chapter 18. Another purpose of the periodic review is to evaluate the performance of the portfolio manager. In investment management, as in any business, past decisions must be reviewed to determine their wisdom. A great deal of emphasis is placed on performance in investment management, since investors are anxious to maximize their return from their portfolios of securities.

Evaluating portfolio performance involves two distinct aspects. First, there is simply the question of estimating the realized return on a portfolio of securities. Most portfolios have both inflows and outflows that must be considered in determining the actual return on the portfolio. Inflows may result from new funds that are committed to the portfolio; for example, dividends and interest earned, realized capital gains, and new funds for investment in securities. A pension fund, for example, would experience periodic inflows from the employer's and employees' contributions as well as from dividend and interest receipts and realized capital gains. Outflows result from withdrawals from the portfolio. For example, some of the dividend or interest income may be withdrawn to meet living expenses or some other need. There also may be realized capital gains, which require the payment of capital gains taxes. Both inflows and outflows, therefore, must be considered in determining the actual return on a portfolio of securities.

The second aspect of evaluating a portfolio's performance is to determine the effectiveness of past portfolio decisions. This consideration is particularly important for common stock portfolios. For bond portfolios the normal measure of performance is whether the actual yield was approximately equal to the anticipated yield. In most cases the realized yield on high-quality bond portfolios will not be significantly different from the anticipated yield. With common stock portfolios, however, the return on the portfolio is generally compared to some aggregate measure of common stock performance. The performance of an individual portfolio is generally compared with that of a market index. One method simply compares the return of a portfolio with that of a market index. An alternative method not only compares the return on the portfolio with that on a market index but also the risk of the portfolio with that of a market index.

Measuring Portfolio Performance

The easiest situation to measure involves the establishment of a portfolio without subsequent contributions or withdrawals. In such a situation, all dividends or interest received are reinvested. Measuring the return becomes a relatively straightforward task. For a single year a return relative can be used. For example, suppose that an investor invests $100,000 at the beginning of the year in a portfolio of stocks with all dividends received reinvested, but there are no other additions during the year. If at the end of the year the portfolio market value is $112,525, then the investor's return is 12.5 percent for the year. This can be determined as follows:

$$RR_p = \frac{\$112,525}{100,000} = 1.125$$

The return relative for the portfolio is 1.125, and the realized return is 12.5 percent.

If the time period is longer than a year, the process of determining the realized return is only slightly more complicated. The return may be found by determining the ratio of the terminal value of the portfolio to the initial value and converting this ratio to logarithms and dividing by the number of years. Notationally, that is

$$\log G_p = 1/n \, \log \left(\frac{V_{pn}}{V_{po}} \right) \tag{17-1}$$

where V_{pn} is the value of the portfolio at time n, and V_{po} is the value of the portfolio initially. Suppose in the above example that the portfolio has a value of $252,750 at the end of five years. Applying Equation 17-1 gives

$$\log G_p = \tfrac{1}{5} \log(2.5275)$$

$$= 0.08048$$

Taking the antilog gives

$$G_p = 1.204$$

Therefore, the geometric mean RR_p is 1.204, and the compound rate of return is 20.4 percent.

The rate of return for a number of years can be obtained from the annual return relatives in those cases where the RR_ps have been calculated on an annual basis. The methodology is identical with that used in Chapter 5 to obtain the geometric mean return. This procedure is particularly useful for estimating the return on a portfolio when additions and withdrawals occur. Suppose that the following RR_ps have been calculated for a particular portfolio:

Year	RR
1	1.080
2	1.172
3	1.043
4	1.094
5	1.106

Applying the formula for determining the geometric mean return will give the average compound return. That is

$$\log G_p = 1/n \log \prod_{t=1}^{n} RR_{pt} \qquad (17\text{-}2)$$

where the terms are as previously defined. Substituting in Equation 17-2 gives

$$\log G_p = \tfrac{1}{5} \log(1.080 \times 1.172 \times 1.043 \times 1.094 \times 1.106)$$

$$= \tfrac{1}{5} \log(1.597)$$

$$= 0.04068$$

Taking the antilog gives

$$G_p = 1.098$$

As a result, the geometric mean RR_p for this portfolio is 1.098, and the compound rate of return is 9.8 percent.

Determining the return on a portfolio becomes more complex when there are additions and withdrawals. This is the more common case, however, and its importance stems from attempting to isolate the effects of additions and withdrawals from those of performance. For example, a portfolio may have a value of $100,000 at the beginning of the year and $150,000 at the end of the year, leading to the conclusion that the return was 50 percent during the year when in reality there was a $50,000 addition to the portfolio and the return was actually zero. Withdrawals may lead to the opposite error, that is, concluding that the portfolio's performance was worse than it really was. For example, a portfolio may have a value of $100,000 at the beginning of the year and a value of $100,000 at the end of the year, leading to the conclusion that the return was zero. However, if a withdrawal of $25,000 was made, it becomes clear that the portfolio actually had a return of 25 percent. These withdrawals and additions can be taken into account by applying the following equation:

$$RR_{pt} = \frac{V_{pt} - W_{pt}}{V_{pt-1} + A_{pt}} \qquad (17\text{-}3)$$

where V_{pt} is the value of the portfolio at time t, W_{pt} is the withdrawals from the portfolio during time t, and A_{pt} is the additions made during time t.

To illustrate, consider the additions and withdrawals for the following common stock portfolio:

Year	Additions	Withdrawals	Portfolio value
0	$100,000		$100,000
1			110,000
2	100,000		221,000
3		25,000	221,000
4	100,000		303,000
5		25,000	354,000

This portfolio was begun with a $100,000 investment. There were additions of $100,000 in years 2 and 4 and withdrawals of $25,000 in years 3 and 5. It is assumed that all the dividends received are reinvested.

Using Equation 17-3, the *RR*s for this portfolio are as follows:

Year	RR
1	1.100
2	1.052
3	1.113
4	0.944
5	1.251

The use of Equation 17-3 can be illustrated by considering year 3. The *RR* for year 3 is

$$RR_3 = \frac{221,000 + 25,000}{221,000}$$

$$= 1.113$$

In this fashion, the annual *RR*s were calculated for all five years. The average return for the entire period can be estimated by applying Equation 17-2. That is

$$\log G = \tfrac{1}{5} \log(1.521)$$

$$= 0.0364$$

Taking the antilog gives

$$G = 1.087$$

Thus, the geometric mean *RR* is 1.087 and the compound rate of return on the portfolio is 8.7 percent.

Note that by taking additions and withdrawals into consideration, one is able to obtain a more accurate picture of the performance of the portfolio. For example, consider years 1 and 2. If only the change in the portfolio is considered, one can conclude that the portfolio turned in a satisfactory performance in year

1 but a record performance in year 2. That is not the case, however. The large increase in the portfolio was due to a $100,000 addition to the portfolio; consequently, year 2 turned in a poorer performance than year 1. Similarly, consider year 3. On the basis of terminal values it appears that the portfolio had a zero return during year 3. Yet once withdrawals are considered it is apparent that the portfolio had a respectable 11 percent return in year 3. Consequently, additions and withdrawals must be considered to determine the true performance of a portfolio.

A Single-Parameter Measure

Once the rate of return on a portfolio has been determined, the task facing the portfolio manager is to establish whether the performance of the portfolio has been satisfactory. For common stock portfolios, the standard for comparison is normally the market, and one method of using this standard is to compare the return obtained on a portfolio with that of a leading market index. This method is relatively simple and straightforward, but it does not provide very much information about the quality of inputs obtained from security analysts. Recall that security analysts tend to specialize in particular industries; consequently, an aggregate measure of performance does not permit an evaluation of the individual inputs. However, a disaggregated approach can be used in conjunction with the aggregate market index to refine the evaluation of the performance of common stock portfolios.

A leading example of such an approach is the Mobil Oil Corporation computer program, which evaluates the performance of the investments for its pension fund. A description of the Mobil Oil approach was given by Edward A. Fox.[1] Mobil Oil, like many firms, has set up a pension plan for its employees and has entrusted the actual investment of funds to six financial institutions. These institutions are given discretionary authority to maximize the yield on the portfolios under their control. This means that there is no limitation on the amount of common stock that can be included in these portfolios, but, of course, other securities can also be included as the trustees deem appropriate.

For evaluating the performance of these trustees, Mobil then developed a method that is not only concerned with the rate of return on these portfolios but also attempts to evaluate the security selection decision and the timing decision. Its format appears to follow an approach developed by Peter O. Dietz.[2] Performance is particularly important to the firm because the better the performance of the pension fund, the smaller the direct contributions made by the firm. As a result, the performance of the pension fund takes on considerable

[1] Edward A. Fox, "Comparing Performance of Equity Pension Trusts," *Financial Analysts Journal,* vol. 24, no. 5 (Sept.–Oct., 1968), pp. 121–30. The discussion here of the Mobil Oil method of evaluating portfolio performance is based on this article.
[2] Peter O. Dietz, *Pension Funds: Measuring Investment Performance* (New York: A Joint Publication of the Graduate School of Business, Columbia University, and The Free Press, 1966).

importance. Developing a method of measuring performance of the pension fund raises the difficult question of whether to emphasize the performance of the aggregate portfolio under the control of each trustee or to further refine this procedure to scrutinize each security selection decision. Mobil chose to analyze the decision that resulted in each security being included in the various portfolios. This involved answering three basic questions. Was the right industry selected? Was the stock of the right firm from within that industry selected? Were commitments timed appropriately?

Basic Format

The Mobil Oil approach to evaluate the performance of its pension fund trustees is predicated on the assumption that the principal investment vehicle will be common stock. It attempts to evaluate the portfolio composition process at each juncture of the selection process. The objectives of the Mobil Oil pension fund are twofold. Fundamentally, Mobil is seeking growth and the emphasis is on investments in growth companies. The second objective reflects Mobil's emphasis on investment timing, that is, the investment in defensive securities that are truly defensive. This implies switching to maintain the value of the portfolio at critical turns in the stock market. As a result, the trustees are faced with the dual objectives of growth plus the preservation of the principal value of the portfolio. This is a difficult assignment for any portfolio manager. In undertaking the objectives of the pension fund, the trustees have full discretion as to the actual securities that may be included in the portfolio. This also applies to the commitments of contributions received by the trustees. For example, these funds may be invested following a dollar averaging approach. As long as the particular stock follows a secular uptrend, dollar averaging will always show a positive return. However, the trustee may hold funds anticipating a downturn in the market. As a result, substantial demands are made on the trustees by Mobil Oil, but at the same time substantial latitude is given them so that the objectives may be attained.

   The Mobil Oil method evaluates the trustees' decisions from two different viewpoints. The first of these deals with the timing decision. This includes not only the decision as to the type of security needed to meet market conditions, but also the appropriate decision with respect to the performance of individual securities and industry groupings. As a result, the timing decision focuses on determining those industry groupings and firms with the best potential. This is the other side of the coin with respect to selecting defensive securities. The second decision concerns the actual security selection process. One aspect of this decision is selecting the proper industry groupings. This is referred to as the strategic decision. The other aspect is selecting the stock of the firm in each industry grouping that will do better than the industry grouping as a whole. This is referred to as the tactical decision. The Mobil Oil approach then evaluates whether the trustee selected the industries with the best prospects and the firms within those industries which turned in the best market performance. To obtain the best performance, the trustee must select those industry groupings with the best prospects. It is not uncommon to select the right industry but the wrong firm from within that industry. Hence, the Mobil Oil approach focuses on both of these problems. A major advantage is the benefits that result from evaluating past decisions.

Mechanics of Mobil Oil's Approach

Standard and Poor's composite and industry indexes are used as the standards for comparison. S & P's 500 stock index is used as the basis for determining the performance of the market. The S & P's industry indexes are used as standards to evaluate the performance of various industry groupings. To determine the overall performance of the stock market, hypothetical units of the S & P's 500 stock index equal to the contributions of the pension fund are purchased every two weeks. This coincides with the inflows to the actual pension fund that the trustees have to invest. Further, to make the index more comparable, brokerage costs of $\frac{6}{10}$ of 1 percent are subtracted from the initial investments in the S & P's 500 index. If this were not done, the performance standards would be biased against the trustees. Finally, the dividends received on the S & P's 500 index are assumed to be reinvested in the index on a monthly basis.

In addition, 33 S & P's industry indexes are utilized. As with the S & P's 500 index, contributions are assumed invested in the appropriate industry index, and the appropriate brokerage costs, $\frac{6}{10}$ of 1 percent, are reflected. It is unclear how the dividends on these industry indexes are treated, but presumably they are reinvested monthly like the S & P's 500 index. These industry indexes permit an evaluation of the strategic and tactical decisions—investment decisions of the trustee. These indexes are compared with the S & P's 500 and the appropriate industry indexes to determine whether the right industry was selected and whether the right firm from within the industry was selected.

Another aspect of the Mobil Oil approach is the time horizon for evaluating performance. Reports and analysis are conducted on a quarterly basis. This information is useful to the portfolio manager as well as to Mobil Oil, but the evaluation of the performance of a particular trustee is based on a longer term, perhaps one to three years. This longer period of time permits a fair evaluation of the trustee's abilities to meet Mobil Oil's demanding requirements. In addition, when determining the returns on the various securities in the portfolios, the rate of return is determined from the time the particular security is purchased. The rate of return, then, is an internal rate of return for the period in question. Dividends received, however, need not be reinvested in the securities that paid them out. The portfolio manager has discretion over these receipts and may invest them as he deems appropriate. This can lead to bias in the measurement of performance of individual stocks when compared to the market. But this does not appear to be the case with the Mobil Oil approach because hypothetical investments in the industry indexes are equal to the investment in stocks in those industries. Hence, the performance of the indexes are comparable to that of the individual stocks.

Table 17-1 illustrates the type of information that is available. Column 1 gives the actual return on the stock for the entire holding period. This is a compound rate of return for the entire period that the stock has been included in the portfolio. Columns 3 and 5 give a rate of return for a comparable investment in the appropriate S & P's industry index and the S & P's 500 index, respectively. Columns 2, 4, and 6 give the actual dollar amounts earned on the investment in particular stocks, the S & P's industry index, and the S & P's 500 index, respectively. These columns permit a comparison of the actual dollar amounts that were earned in a particular stock versus what could have been earned had the investment been made in either of the indexes. This adds meaning to the rates of return. Columns 1 through 6 enable the evaluation of the portfolio to obtain a reasonably good impression of whether or not a particular stock was a wise selection.

Columns 7 through 9 translate the data in columns 1 through 6 into dollar amounts of gain or loss from a particular investment. These columns attempt to answer the question of whether the investment was made in the right industry and the right firm within that industry. Column 7 indicates whether the right firm was selected from within the industry. This can be determined by comparing the rates of return in columns 1 and 3 for a particular stock. Column 7, however, translates this information into dollar amounts. This is simply the difference between columns 2 and 4. Column 8 compares the performance of the industry selected with the S & P's 500 index. This permits an evaluation of whether the right industry was selected. If the right industry was selected, the dollar amount in column 8 will be positive reflecting the amount of this benefit. A comparison of columns 3 and 5 also answer this question, but column 8 translates this to actual dollar amounts of gain or loss on the amounts invested, the difference between columns 4 and 6. Finally, column 9 summarizes the return on the stock with that of the market alternative. This can be obtained by the difference between columns 6 and 2. The last two columns of Table 17-1 provide additional information on the portfolio. Column 10 gives the average investment in a particular stock. Column 11 gives the proportion of a particular stock in the total common stock portfolio. Column 12, on the other hand, gives the proportion of the particular stock in the total portfolio. Columns 11 and 12, therefore, give an indication of the proportion of the portfolio committed to a particular stock.

To illustrate the type of analysis that would take place, let us refer to two stocks shown in Table 17-1, Ford and Sundstrand Corporation. For Ford the actual return was 7.9 percent as compared to the return on the industry alternative of 32.6 percent and a return of 11.6 percent on the market alternative. These figures are found in columns 1, 3, and 5. At this point several conclusions

TABLE 17-1 An Example of the Mobil Oil Approach of Evaluating Portfolio Performance

	Actual		Rates of return				Analysis				Memo data	
			S & P industry alternative		S & P 500 alternative		Tactical actual vs. industry $-000	Strat indus vs. 500 $-000	Total actual vs. 500 $-000	Average dollars invested $-000	as of total	
	%	$	%	$	%	$					stk	port
Ford Motor Co.	7.9	10,177	32.6	39,345	11.6	14,833	29–	24–	04–	44	0.5	0.4
General Motors Corp.	0.0	1,553–	0.7	6,499	7.1	68,854	08–	62–	70–	310	3.2	2.6
Tot. Automotive	0.8	8,625	4.4	45,844	7.6	83,688	37–	37–	75–	355	3.6	3.0
Corning Glass Works	13.8	45,066	55.9	130,761	24.2	78,500	135–	102–	33–	129	1.3	1.1
McDermott J. Ray Co.	64.7	37,833	47.4	28,943	18.0	12,017	08	16	25	23	0.2	0.2
Tot. Building	22.2	82,899	54.3	209,704	23.0	90,517	126–	119	07–	153	1.6	1.3
Chicago Pneumatic Tool	13.8	52,535	15.1	58,076	7.0	25,781	05–	32	26	130	1.3	1.1
Sundstrand Corp.	112.1	62,429	35.4	23,381	23.6	16,116	39	07	46	28	0.3	0.2
Tot. Machinery	26.2	114,964	18.1	81,457	9.5	41,898	33	39	73	158	1.6	1.3
Alum. Co. of America	5.7	21,681	8.0	30,560	6.4	24,056	08–	06–	02–	142	1.4	1.2
Kennecott Copper Corp.	28.3	244,817	8.6	70,418	9.5	77,557	174	07–	167	332	3.4	2.8
Phelps Dodge Corp.	44.6	8,682	10.0–	2,421–	13.6	2,970	11	05–	05	05	0.1	0.0
Reynolds Metals Co.	7.0–	22,091–	6.2–	19,326–	9.8	31,154	02–	50–	53–	103	1.0	0.9
St. Joseph Lead Co.	6.4–	8,711–	33.0	46,507	1.9	2,756	55–	43	11–	49	0.5	0.4
Scovill Manufacturing	4.0	13,126	6.8–	21,528–	9.2	29,521	34	51–	16–	115	1.2	1.0
Tot. Non-ferrous Metals	12.6	257,504	5.4	104,210	8.4	168,014	153	63–	89	748	7.6	6.3
Freeport Sulphur Co.	179.7	187,163	35.8	97,919	19.9	24,597	89	73	162	67	0.7	0.6
Texas Gulf Sulphur	42.9	253,461	50.8	308,101	8.6	41,563	54–	266	211	251	2.6	2.1
Tot. Mining	65.8	440,624	56.8	406,020	10.9	66,160	34	339	374	319	3.2	2.7
Vanity Fair Mills	16.6	50,000	7.7	22,956	7.3	21,658	27	01	28	98	1.0	0.8
Burlington Industries	3.1	12,438	9.1	35,832	9.4	37,207	23–	01–	24–	122	1.2	1.0
Tot. Misc. Manufact.	9.0	62,438	8.5	58,787	8.6	58,865	03	00	03	220	2.2	1.6
Pennsylvania RR	4.0	16,344	0.5–	2,712–	5.9	24,357	19	27–	08–	142	1.5	1.2
Tot. Rail/Other Trans.	4.0	16,344	0.5–	2,712–	5.9	24,357	19	27–	08–	142	1.5	1.2
Tot. Cyclical Stocks	17.5	983,397	16.0	903,310	9.4	533,499	80	369	449	2,098	21.3	17.6

Source: Fox, op. cit., p. 124.

can be drawn. First, the selection of the automotive industry was the right decision. This is evident because the return on the automotive industry is substantially greater than that on the market. However, the selection of Ford stock was the wrong decision since its return is less than that on the industry. This decision would have had one redeeming aspect if the return on Ford stock had exceeded the market alternative, but this did not occur. As a result, this selection decision represents a case where the right industry was selected, but the wrong firm from within that industry grouping was selected.

This information is summarized in columns 7 through 9. The return as specified in absolute dollar amounts indicates the amounts gained or lost on an investment relative to the industry and market alternatives. Using Ford as an example, column 7, entitled *tactical*, indicates a $29,000 loss by investing in Ford's stocks and not the automative industry index. The pension fund, therefore, lost money on this decision. However, the selection of the industry was appropriate. Column 8, entitled *strategic*, indicates that the industry alternative outperformed the market alternative to the extent of $24,000. Clearly the industry alternative outperformed the market alternative. Finally, column 9, entitled *total*, illustrates that the Ford stock did not perform as well as the market alternative, indicating a loss of $4,000. Thus, the investment in Ford stock represents a bad selection, even though its industry turned in superior results.

Sundstrand Corporation permits an illustration of the ideal outcome from the portfolio manager's point of view. Sundstrand's return was 112.1 percent as compared with 35.4 percent for the industry alternative and 23.6 percent for the market alternative. Sundstrand's performance illustrates the objective of all portfolio managers. The industry selected for investment outperformed the market. Even more importantly, the stock selected from within the industry grouping outperformed the industry as a whole. Column 8 indicates that the industry alternative outperformed the market alternative by $7,000. Sundstrand's stock, however, outperformed the industry alternative by $39,000. This is shown in column 7. A portfolio manager would prefer this result on every investment made, but this fortunate state of events occurs only infrequently. In fact, portfolio managers argue that it does not occur nearly often enough.

The Mobil Oil approach to evaluating portfolio performance is exceptional, but one major criticism of the approach is that risk is not considered at any point in the analysis. Whenever an investment is made in common stock, there is always a question of the amount of risk that the investor had to undertake to obtain the realized return. Mobil's approach appears to imply that risk is not an important consideration. Intuitively, one would expect that an above-average return should be obtained if substantial risk is undertaken, but unless some measure of risk is incorporated it is not known whether the realized return compensated for the risk undertaken. Recall that both the Markowitz approach and the W-M model assumed that investors were risk averse. Hence, efficient portfolios were determined in terms of both risk and return. The Mobil Oil approach, however, only evaluates the performance of a portfolio in terms of one dimension, that is, the realized return. The trustees may turn in superior results only because they are willing to take exceptional risks, and this system of evaluation appears to encourage this. The stress on investment timing becomes clearer now because Mobil Oil's objectives seem to imply the acceptance of above-average risk in pursuit of an above-average return. Consequently, the switching to a more defensive portfolio becomes critical to protect the appreciation realized by accepting substantial risk. The Mobil approach does not indicate whether the realized return compensated for the risk assumed.

A Two-Parameter Aggregate Measure

The Mobil Oil approach is a comprehensive method of evaluating portfolio performance, and its similarity to the traditional approach of portfolio composition is evident. Contemporary portfolio composition puts a great emphasis on the amount of risk assumed by the portfolio manager. The two-parameter aggregate measures attempt to introduce risk into the question of evaluating the performance of portfolios and follows from the development of the capital-market model. The reward-to-variability ratio (*R/V* ratio) is a measure that attempts to take risk into consideration. In other words, portfolios have varying degrees of risk, and the risk assumed is introduced into the evaluation of portfolio performance. For example, portfolios A and B may have returns of 10 and 12 percent per annum, respectively. On the basis of return, portfolio B appears superior; yet to evaluate the performance of these portfolios solely on the basis of return overlooks the risks of the respective portfolios. If portfolio A is considerably less risky than B, its performance may have been superior to B. The *R/V* ratio attempts to introduce this consideration into the evaluation process.

Concept of R/V ratio

The *R/V* ratio is an outgrowth of capital market theory. In the W-M model, common stocks enter the portfolio on the basis of their pure-risk yield. This was the anticipated reward for undertaking risk. This was an ex ante concept because the portfolio manager attempted to select a portfolio of common stock on the basis of the pure-risk yield. The *R/V* ratio, on the other hand, is ex post. It attempts to determine the realized reward for accepting risk. The *R/V* ratio is given by

$$R/V_p = \frac{\overline{RR_p} - L}{S_p} \qquad (17\text{-}4)$$

where RR_p is the average realized return relative on the portfolio over some past period, L is the return relative for a riskless asset, S_p is the standard deviation of the return on the portfolio.

To illustrate the use of R/V ratio, suppose we have the following information about portfolios A and B, and a market index. The market index may be any leading index, such as Standard and Poor's 500.

	Portfolio		
	A	B	Market
$\overline{RR}$	1.15	1.19	1.14
S	0.25	0.30	0.18
L	1.04	1.04	1.04

Applying Equation 17-4 we obtain the following R/V ratios for the three portfolios. For portfolio A, the R/V ratio is

$$R/V_A = \frac{1.15 - 1.04}{0.25} = 0.44$$

For portfolio B, the R/V ratio is

$$R/V_B = \frac{1.19 - 1.04}{0.30} = 0.50$$

And for the market portfolio, the R/V ratio is

$$R/V_M = \frac{1.14 - 1.04}{0.18} = 0.56$$

It is evident that neither portfolio performed as well as the market portfolio, since portfolios A and B provided less reward for undertaking risk than did the market portfolio. This may seem somewhat surprising since both portfolios provided a larger return than the market portfolio. Both portfolios A and B, however, have a larger standard deviation than that of the market. Consequently, the additional return was not sufficient to compensate for the additional risk.

The R/V ratios for the three portfolios are illustrated graphically in Figure 17-1. From capital market theory we know that the greater the slope of the ray connecting the risk-free rate, L, with the intersection of $\overline{RR}_p$ and S_p, the greater the reward for taking risk. In an ex ante sense, the W-M model attempts to select that portfolio which promises the greatest slope for this ray. In evaluating portfolio performance, we are concerned with determining the reward versus the risk accepted to obtain that return ex post. Figure 17-1 indicates that neither portfolio A or B performed as well as the market portfolio because the slopes of the rays extending from risk-free rate of return for portfolios A and B is less than that for the market portfolio. The slope of the ray extending from the risk-free rate is given by the R/V ratio. This was shown earlier in Chapter 15 as the basis for developing the formula for the capital market line and the pure-risk yield in Chapter 16.

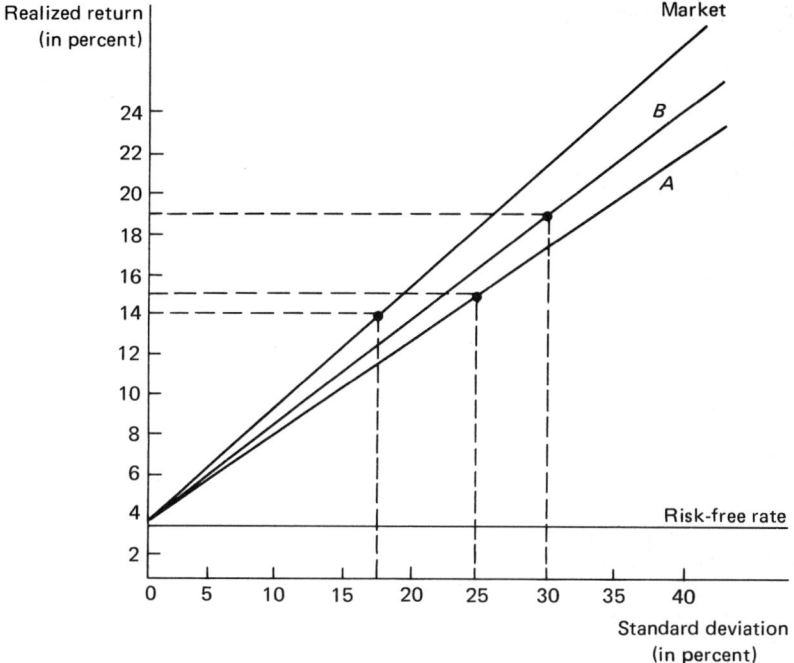

FIGURE 17-1 *Realized Return and Standard Deviation for Two Hypothetical Portfolios and a Market Portfolio*

An Application of R/V Ratio

An example of the application of the R/V ratio is provided by William F. Sharpe in a study of the performance of mutual funds.[3] There have been several studies that have used variation of the R/V ratio to evaluate the performance of mutual funds. Sharpe's study was prompted by the earlier development of the capital market theory. A total of 34 mutual funds was used in the study for the period 1954–63. The mutual fund returns were determined by including dividend payments, capital gains distributions, and changes in the net asset value. Since administrative expenses were deducted, the return was net of administrative expenses.

The R/V ratios for these portfolios are shown in Table 17-2. The risk-free rate used was 3 percent, not 4 percent as was used in the hypothetical example above. The R/V ratios range from a low of 0.43116 to a high of 0.7782. As with the Mobil Oil approach, it is customary to compare the performance of mutual funds with that of the market. A fund that has turned in a superior performance has done so because it has outperformed the market. In Sharpe's study, the

[3] William F. Sharpe, "Mutual Fund Performance," *Journal of Business*, vol. 39, no. 1, part II (Jan., 1966), pp. 119–39.

TABLE 17-2   *Performance of 34 Mutual Funds, 1954–63*

Mutual fund	Average annual return (percent)	Variability of annual return (percent)	Reward-to-variability ratio(R/V)*
Affiliated Fund	14.6	15.3	0.75896
American Business Share.	10.0	9.2	0.75876
Axe-Houghton, Fund A	10.5	13.5	0.55551
Axe-Houghton, Fund B	12.0	16.3	0.55183
Axe-Houghton, Stock Fund	11.9	15.6	0.56991
Boston Fund	12.4	12.1	0.77842
Broad Street Investing	14.8	16.8	0.70329
Bullock Fund	15.7	19.3	0.65845
Commonwealth Investment Company	10.9	13.7	0.57841
Delaware Fund	14.4	21.4	0.53253
Dividend Shares	14.4	15.9	0.71807
Eaton and Howard, Balanced Fund	11.0	11.9	0.67399
Eaton and Howard, Stock Fund	15.2	19.2	0.63486
Equity Fund	14.6	18.7	0.61902
Fidelity Fund	16.4	23.5	0.57020
Financial Industrial Fund	14.5	23.0	0.49971
Fundamental Investors	16.0	21.7	0.59894
Group Securities, Common Stock Fund	15.1	19.1	0.63316
Group Securities, Fully Administered Fund	11.4	14.1	0.59490
Incorporated Investors	14.0	25.5	0.43116
Investment Company of America	17.4·	21.8	0.66169
Investors Mutual	11.3	12.5	0.66451
Loomis-Sales Mutual Fund	10.0	10.4	0.67358
Massachusetts Investors Trust	16.2	20.8	0.63398
Massachusetts Investors—Growth Stock	18.6	22.7	0.68687
National Investors Corporation	18.3	19.9	0.76798
National Securities—Income Series	12.4	17.8	0.52950
New England Fund	10.4	10.2	0.72703
Putnam Fund of Boston	13.1	16.0	0.63222
Scudder, Stevens & Clark Balanced Fund	10.7	13.3	0.57893
Selected American Shares	14.4	19.4	0.58788
United Funds—Income Fund	16.1	20.9	0.62698
Wellington Fund	11.3	12.0	0.69057
Wisconsin Fund	13.8	16.9	0.64091

* R/V ratio = (average return − 3.0 percent)/variability. The ratios shown were computed from original data and thus differ slightly from the ratios obtained from the rounded data shown in the table.
Source: Sharpe, op. cit., p. 125.

Dow-Jones Industrial Average was used as the market index. In the period under study, its average return was 16.3 percent and the standard deviation of return was 19.94 percent. This gave a R/V ratio for the market of 0.667.

It should be noted that the returns for both the DJIA and the mutual funds are overstated. The return on the DJIA is overstated because transaction costs, such as brokerage fees, management costs, and transfer costs were not considered. Therefore, the typical investor could not have achieved 16.3 percent by investing in the DJIA over this period of time. At the same time, the return on the mutual funds is also overstated because the return excludes the loading

charge of the mutual funds, which is the salesman's commission.[4] The performance of the funds, however, is based upon funds available for investment,
and, therefore, the investor could not expect to obtain the returns cited in Table
17-2 by investing in either the DJIA or any of the funds.

Figure 17-2 shows a plotting of the returns and standard deviations of the 34
funds and the DJIA. Figure 17-2 has the axes reversed from those in Figure
17-1. This means that those portfolios with the best performance are farthest to
the right, which is just the opposite of Figure 17-1. In Figure 17-2 the triangular

FIGURE 17-2 *Realized Return and Standard Deviation on 34 Mutual Funds,
1954–63*

Source: Sharpe, op. cit., pp. 124 and 137.

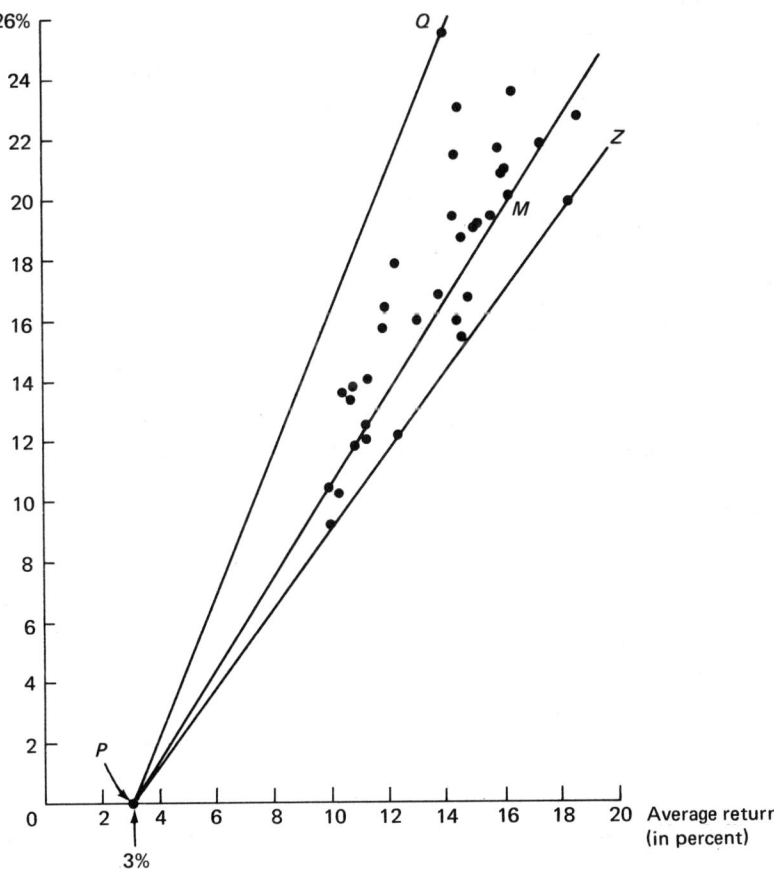

[4] The loading charge varies from approximately 6 to 9 percent. For example, if the investor purchases
$10,000 worth of shares of a particular fund with a loading charge of 8.5 percent, his participation in
the mutual fund would be $9,150. The effective cost is not 8.5 percent but 9.29 percent. Recently
no-load funds have become popular. These have no salesmen and hence no loading charge.

area QPZ represents the area that the funds fell into. Point P is the risk-free rate and the radian PM links the risk-free rate with the point represented by the DJIA. Portfolios above this curve did not perform as well as the DJIA. Those below it performed better than the DJIA. Only 11 funds outperformed the DJIA, and it is evident that the mutual funds did not perform as well as the DJIA. This finding is consistent with previous studies, but the major difference is that previous studies did not include a measure of risk.

From the investor's point of view, the results of this study raise some interesting, if not embarrassing, questions about investing in mutual funds. Both the returns on the DJIA and the mutual funds are overstated, and had the investor invested in any or all of these alternatives he would not have realized the returns cited in this study. We, of course, are interested in the measurement of portfolio performance, and the conclusions of Sharpe's study are probably a worthwhile digression. The main conclusion of this study is that the investor should select a mutual fund, at least to some extent, on the basis of its expense ratio, and the investor should not expect a rate of return greatly in excess of the popular market averages. This follows since the mutual funds must diversify very extensively. Therefore, the investor's best opportunity to improve his return is to minimize the costs of administering the fund.

Criticisms of the R/V Ratio

Capital market theory provided the rationale for using the R/V ratio as a method of evaluating portfolio performance. Its theoretical foundations, therefore, are the same as that of the capital market theory discussed in Chapter 15. If the underlying assumptions of capital market theory are incorrect, this measure will also be inadequate. There could of course be other reasons for the R/V ratio not being appropriate, such as measurement errors and perhaps differences in ex post and ex ante return distributions. The major concern, however, is whether the capital market theory adequately captures reality. If the R/V ratio adequately measures portfolio performance, it provides a measure that has adjusted the return for the risk incurred. It follows, then, that the R/V ratios measuring ex post portfolio performance should be independent of the risk incurred. Therefore, to test the independence of the R/V ratio and portfolio risk, a simple regression can be used:

$$R/V_k = a + b\beta_k + u_k \tag{17-5}$$

where β_k is the risk for portfolio k, a and b are regression constants, and u_k is a normally distributed error term. The risk measure, β_k, can be defined as the nondiversible risk of the portfolio, or as the standard deviation of the portfolio's return over some time period.

If the R/V ratio is an unbiased estimate of the portfolio's performance, the regression coefficient in Equation 17-5 should be nonsignificant. Irwin Friend and Marshall Blume tested this relationship and found that regression coefficient in Equation 17-5, *b*, was highly significant.[5] Further, the *b*'s were consistently negative. This means that the portfolio's performance measures not only eliminate risk but actually reverse its effect. As a result, it was concluded that the *R/V* ratios are biased against risky portfolios. This not only raises some questions about the *R/V* ratio as a measure of portfolio performance, but it also raises some questions about the appropriateness of the capital market theory.

There is little additional evidence on this question, and the usefulness of the *R/V* ratio is thus still subject to review. If the findings of Friend and Blume are correct, this probably means that one or more of the assumptions upon which capital market theory is based are incorrect. Friend and Blume speculated that the assumption of lending and borrowing at the risk-free rate may not be valid. If indeed the capital market theory is found wanting, then it and the W-M model may need to be reformulated. Nevertheless, portfolio management will have benefited from the research and discussion generated.

Summary

Evaluating a portfolio involves a number of considerations. At the most elementary level, the problem of determining the rate of return can be difficult. If a portfolio is purchased without subsequent withdrawals or additions, the questions of measuring portfolio performance can be handled easily. However, if there are additions and withdrawals, special care must be taken in determining the rate of return. This is the more common case for several reasons. In some cases the investor may be setting aside additional savings that can be invested. In other cases the investor may have set up the portfolio to provide a source of income, which necessitates withdrawals from the portfolio. Whatever the case, measuring portfolio performance requires a methodology that is sufficiently general to adapt to either situation.

The second problem is using an appropriate standard of measurement. The general method is to compare the performance of a portfolio with that of a market index. Superior portfolio performance occurs whenever the portfolio outperforms the market as a whole. The Mobil Oil approach refined this approach by introducing industry indexes. This permitted an evaluation of ex post decisions involving specific securities. As a result, not only did the Mobil Oil approach evaluate the performance of the portfolio relative to the market, but it also determined whether the right industries and the right securities were selected. The Mobil Oil approach, therefore, provided for a rather complex evaluation of the performance of a portfolio, since it not only gave a method of

[5] Irwin Friend and Marshall Blume, "Measurement of Portfolio Performance Under Uncertainty," *American Economic Review*, vol. 60, no. 4 (Sept., 1970), pp. 561–76.

evaluating the trustees of its pension funds but it also provided valuable information by which the portfolio managers could improve their performance.

An alternative method of evaluating the performance of a portfolio is to utilize a two-parameter aggregate approach. The Mobil Oil approach evaluated performance in terms of realized return only. For common stock portfolios, an important aspect is risk. This approach could also be extended to bond portfolios. The reward-to-variability ratio utilizes not only realized return but also the risk associated with obtaining that return. Using this approach the investor attempts to determine the compensation he is realizing for accepting risk. Once this has been determined for a portfolio, the normal basis for comparison is a market index. If the R/V ratio for a particular portfolio is greater than that for the market index, the portfolio is considered to have outperformed the market because the investor has received compensation greater than that for the market as a whole. The R/V ratio, like the W-M model, is subject to continued testing. There is some evidence that raises doubts about the theoretical foundations of the capital market theory, and the R/V ratio may be an inappropriate measure of portfolio performance. At this point, this question is unresolved.

Questions

1. An investor invested $200,000 in a portfolio of common stock. Dividends received were reinvested and there were no withdrawals. The portfolio had the following values at the end of each of the previous five years:

Year	Portfolio value
0	$200,000
1	190,000
2	205,000
3	250,000
4	230,000
5	270,000

   a. What rate of return did the investor realize in each of the five years?
   b. What rate of return did he realize over this five-year time span?

2. An investor invests $500,000 initially in a portfolio of common stock. The portfolio has the following pattern of additions and withdrawals:

Year	Additions	Withdrawals	Portfolio value
0	$500,000		$500,000
1	60,000		390,000
2	60,000		460,000
3			530,000
4		$30,000	550,000
5		30,000	560,000

What rate of return did the investor realize on the portfolio over the five-year period?

3. The Mobil Oil approach of evaluating portfolio performance is particularly innovative.
   a. What are the major features of this approach?
   b. Is it predicated on the traditional approach to portfolio composition? Explain.
   c. What benefits from this approach do you foresee?
4. Below is an abbreviated presentation of the Mobil Oil approach.

Firm	Actual		S & P's Industry		S & P's 500	
	Percent	Dollar	Percent	Dollar	Percent	Dollar
A	6.0	7,200	8.0	9,600	6.0	7,200
B	4.5	11,040	8.5	21,264	9.5	23,880
C	1.5	5,484	-10.0	-29,844	13.0	53,148
Total	3.0	23,724	0.0	1,020	10.5	84,228
D	7.5	28,008	7.0	26,082	7.0	26,082
E	12.0	108,324	14.0	124,020	10.5	88,362
Total	11.3	136,332	12.3	150,100	9.6	114,444
F	40.0	90,000	12.5	28,125	7.0	15,750
G	38.5	206,595	14.5	69,975	8.0	37,440
H	26.5	230,467	21.0	173,610	9.0	66,375
Total	33.5	527,062	18.5	271,710	8.5	119,565

   a. Which investments were good "strategic" investments and which were good "tactical" investments?
   b. Does a good strategic decision necessarily mean a good tactical decision? Illustrate with an example from the above table.
   c. What is the major criticism of the Mobil Oil approach?
5. A certain company has decided that it would rather use a measure of investment performance that incorporates risk. The following annual returns were realized by six of its portfolios and a leading market index for the last five years.

	Portfolios						Market
Year	A	B	C	D	E	F	index
1	10%	12%	14%	8%	11%	9%	9%
2	-1	-2	-8	-3	-7	1	-2
3	14	7	6	15	9	12	10
4	3	6	2	9	8	2	4
5	12	18	22	26	19	17	14

   a. With this information generate the inputs for the reward-to-variability ratio. (Use a risk-free rate of 4 percent.)
   b. Rank these six portfolios according to their performance. Did any of these portfolios outperform the market index?
6. What is the criticism of the reward-to-variability ratio cited by Friend and Blume? Explain.
7. After studying the Mobil approach and the reward-to-variability ratio, do you prefer one to the other? Why? If you assume that the criticism in question 6 is not valid, would this affect your conclusions?

Selected References

Arditti, Fred D. "Another look at Mutual Fund Performance." *Journal of Financial and Quantitative Analysis,* vol. 6, no. 3 (June, 1971), pp. 909–13.

Bower, Richard S., and Donald F. Wippern. "Risk-Return Measurement in Portfolio Selection and Performance Appraisal Models: Progress Report." *Journal of Financial and Quantitative Analysis,* vol. 4, no. 4 (Dec., 1969), pp. 417–47.

Committee on Interstate and Foreign Commerce. *A Study of Mutual Funds Prepared for Securities and Exchange Commission by the Wharton School of Finance and Commerce.* Washington, D.C.: U.S. Government Printing Office, 1962. See especially pp. 17–18.

Dietz, Peter O. *Pension Funds: Measuring Investment Performance.* New York: The Free Press, 1966.

Fisher, Lawrence. "Measuring Rates of Return." In *Measuring of Investment Performance of Pension Funds for the Purpose of Inter-Fund Comparison,* ed. James H. Lorie et al. Park Ridge, Ill.: Bank Administration Institute, 1968. Chapter 2.

Fox, Edward A. "Comparing Performance of Equity Pension Trusts." *Financial Analysts Journal,* vol. 24, no. 5 (Sept.–Oct., 1968), pp. 121–30.

Friend, Irwin, and Marshall Blume. "Measurement of Portfolio Performance Under Uncertainty." *American Economic Review,* vol. 60, no. 4 (Sept., 1970), pp. 561–76.

Friend, Irwin, and Douglas Vickers. "Portfolio Selection and Investment Performance." *Journal of Finance,* vol. 20, no. 3 (Sept., 1965), pp. 391–416.

Gray, Kenneth B., Jr., and Robert B. K. Dewar. "Axiomatic Characterization of the Time-Weighted Rate of Return." *Management Science,* vol. 18, no. 2 (Oct., 1971), pp. B-32–B-36.

Jensen, Michael C. "The Performance of Mutual Funds in the Period 1945–1964," *Journal of Finance,* vol. 23, no. 2 (May, 1968), pp. 389–416.

Sharpe, William F. "Mutual Fund Performance." *Journal of Business,* vol. 39, no. 1, part II (Jan., 1966), pp. 119–39.

Treynor, Jack L. "How to Rate Management of Investment Funds." *Harvard Business Review,* vol. 43, no. 1 (Jan.–Feb., 1965), pp. 63–76.

Treynor, Jack L., and Kay K. Mazuy. "Can Mutual Funds Outguess the Market?" *Harvard Business Review,* vol. 44, no. 4 (July–Aug., 1966), pp. 131–36.

Voorheis, Frank L. "Bank Trustees and Pension Fund Performance." *Financial Analysts Journal,* vol. 28, no. 4 (July–Aug., 1972), pp. 60–65.

V

Investment Timing

Chapter 18

Defensive Approaches to Investment Timing

The final decision area facing the investor is the approach that should be taken toward investment timing. Investment timing has many aspects. Policy decisions normally fall within the bounds of a trading policy at the one extreme and a buy-and-hold policy at the other. A trading strategy often used in conjunction with technical analysis involves the trading of securities for short-term gains. Normally, this type of operation has a small profit margin, but there is high turnover. For example, a trader may only require a one-point increase in a $25 stock to be a profitable trade because he intends to invest $25,000. On this one operation, his net profit would be more than $500. If he could trade this successfully once a week for the entire year, his profit would be approximately equal to his initial capital.

An alternative strategy is the so-called buy-and-hold policy. An investor following this strategy ignores timing consideration completely. The rationale for this approach is twofold. First, this strategy puts the primary emphasis on the fundamentals of the stocks selected for the portfolio. The earning power of the firm presumably will be recognized by the investing public, and therefore the investor will receive a fair return. This approach is concerned with the long-run prospects of the firm to the exclusion of market-related factors. Second, the proponents of this approach argue that the market cannot be predicted with any accuracy. For the investor to attempt to forecast the future market levels, turning points, and so forth, is too difficult to be practical. The investor should thus concern himself with stocks that have good long-run prospects and not worry about the market.

Portfolio managers can follow either of these two approaches. Some portfolio managers have been known to say that every security in their portfolios is a candidate for sale on any given day. This is slightly different from the trader's approach, but it is nevertheless a trading philosophy. An extreme example of the buy-and-hold policy occurred in the early 1930s as a reaction to the "managed" investment companies of the 1920s. Fixed trusts were set up with a designated investment in specific securities, and no revisions were made over the life of the trust. Investors following a buy-and-hold policy may not adhere to it this closely; but buying and selling in anticipation of the market is not a regular part of the portfolio strategy. Within these two extremes, several different approaches to the question of investment timing exist. An investor may recognize the importance of investment timing but decide that it is not possible to predict these turning points in the market. In this case he may decide to use one of the defensive approaches, such as dollar-cost averaging or formula timing plans, which do not involve forecasting market conditions. Another approach is to attempt to forecast major turning points in the market and to buy and sell accordingly. This approach is not as aggressive as trading on short-term swings in the market, but it is nonetheless a fairly aggressive strategy.

In this chapter we will deal with portfolio revision and the defensive approaches to investment timing. The major difference between aggressive and defensive policies is whether the investor attempts to forecast market conditions. Defensive approaches do not attempt to forecast market conditions. Typical of these approaches are the formula timing plans, dollar-cost averaging, and the most defensive of all, the buy-and-hold policy. It may seem unusual to include portfolio revision policies that are not related to timing policies, but it is important to identify those revisions that are related to investment timing and those that are not. An aggressive policy involves attempting to forecast market conditions by using either business and economic statistics or market statistics. Business and economic statistics are widely used in forecasting major turning points in the securities markets. Market securities are generally used by technicians to predict intermediate swings in the stock market as well as major turning points in the market. Chapters 19 and 20 will discuss the use of business and economic statistics and market statistics for forecasting security prices. Chapter 21 will discuss the nature of the stock market and provide some insight into the difficulties associated with forecasting future stock market conditions.

Portfolio Revision

Two approaches to portfolio revision may be undertaken. One approach involves reviewing the portfolio and eliminating any securities whose prospects do not meet original expectations. This is commonly referred to as portfolio upgrading and appears to have merit, since new information may change the investor's expectations. Another approach, which has its basis in simulation studies, involves reallocation within the existing portfolio. Following a policy of reallocation means selling off a portion of those securities that have performed better than the portfolio in general and reinvesting the proceeds in those stocks in the portfolio which have not performed as well. In this sense a portfolio does not become dominated by a few stocks. These two approaches are followed for different reasons. Portfolio upgrading is designed to improve the quality of the portfolio, while portfolio reallocation revises proportions invested in each security.

Transactions Costs and Taxes

Whenever a security is bought or sold, there are brokerage fees, transfer costs, and in some cases capital gains taxes. The capital gains tax rate is one-half the rate on ordinary income with a maximum rate set at $32\frac{1}{2}$ percent. Rates above 25 percent only apply when the amount of the capital gain is greater than $50,000. That is, the maximum capital gains rate is 25 percent on amounts of capital gains of less than $50,000. Capital gains taxes on amounts above $50,000 involve rather complex calculations.

Capital gains taxes may involve substantial amounts and may become an important consideration in portfolio upgrading. Consider a situation in which an investor has a security with a substantial capital gain, but the outlook for that security is not particularly good. The investor now is faced with a dilemma. If he sells, he will have a substantial capital gains tax liability. If he holds the security, his return on investment will be relatively low. In this situation there does not appear to be a generally accepted approach. Brokerage houses appear to favor switching, while many investors appear reluctant to do so. An approach that the investor may take is to determine the minimum return required to make switching worthwhile.[1]

The minimum return necessary to make switching worthwhile is a rate equal to that being earned on the stock currently in the portfolio and that also compensates for capital gains taxes to be paid on the stock that is sold. For example, suppose a security in a portfolio promises a return of only 5 percent, yet there will be a capital gains tax of 20 percent if the stock is sold. There is conceivably some rate of return that will provide a minimum return of 5 percent and at the same time compensate for the capital gains taxes incurred. This rate depends to a large extent on the investor's time horizon. If the time horizon is indefinite, the rate of return on the incoming candidate can be determined by the following formulation:

$$g_m = \frac{g_j}{(1 - \tau)} \qquad (18\text{-}1)$$

where g_m is the minimum compound rate of return required on a stock to replace stock j, g_j is the anticipated compound rate of return on stock j, and τ is the capital gains tax rates.

To illustrate, consider an investor who owns a common stock currently selling for $100, which pays a $5 dividend. The investor has a tidy capital gain since the stock was purchased at $10 per share, but the future is somewhat

---

[1] See Charles C. Holt and John P. Shelton, "The Implications of the Capital Gains Tax for Investment Decisions," *Journal of Finance*, vol. 16, no. 4 (Dec., 1961), pp. 559–80.

uncertain. Over the next few years, the stock is not expected to appreciate, and therefore the anticipated return is not likely to exceed 5 percent. If the investor switches he will have a capital gains tax liability of approximately 20 percent. If the investor is willing to recover the capital gains tax over an indefinite time horizon, Equation 18-1 will give the required return on the incoming candidate as follows:

$$g_m = \frac{0.05}{(1 - 0.2)}$$

$$= 0.0625$$

Therefore, any stock that promises a return of 6.25 percent or better will provide the same return as the stock in question, as well as permitting the recapture of the capital gains taxes that result from switching. Equation 18-1 thus determines the minimum return that is required to make switching worthwhile, including the recapture of the capital gains taxes.

Equation 18-1 indicates the return required on a candidate for inclusion in the portfolio if an indefinite holding period is contemplated. In many cases, however, the investor has a definite time horizon that is relatively short. This increases the certainty of recovering the capital gains tax, but it also means a larger return is necessary. This problem can be handled by revising Equation 18-1 to take the time horizon into consideration. To determine the required return on the replacement candidate, estimates of the time horizon and the compound rate of return on the security to be replaced are needed. Notationally, the rate on the candidate for inclusion can be determined as follows:

$$P_o (1 - \tau) (1 + \eta)^t = P_o (1 + g)^t \qquad (18\text{-}2)$$

where P_o is the current price of the stock, τ is the capital gains tax rate, η is the rate required on the incoming candidate, and g is the compound rate of return anticipated on the stock to be replaced over time horizon n. In Equation 18-2 the only unknown is η, and this is what is solved for.

If the investor who was considering switching out of the stock in the above example wanted to recapture the capital gains over some specified time horizon, the return on the incoming candidate would have to be somewhat higher than when an indefinite time horizon is used. For example, if the investor wanted to recover the capital gains tax in one year, the minimum rate on the incoming candidates would have to be quite high. In the following years, the realized return could fall off significantly, but the immediate outlook must be for substantial appreciation and hence a high return. Substituting in Equation 18-2 shows that the following return is needed:

$$100(1 - 0.20) (1 + \eta)^1 = 100(1 + 0.05)^1$$

$$80(1 + \eta) = 105$$

and therefore η equals 0.312. That is, the incoming candidate should promise a 31.2 percent return in the next year, and thereafter a return of greater than 5 percent would improve upon the investor's current situation. Realistically, however, a return somewhat greater than 5 percent may be required in subsequent years to compensate for the risk involved, but any stock that promised a return greater than 5 percent would improve the investor's position.

If the investor selected a longer time horizon, the minimum acceptable return would be lower. The rates of return required for time horizons of one to five years and an indefinite time horizon are as follows:

	Time horizon					
	1	2	3	4	5	Indefinite
Required return (percent)	31.2	17.4	13.1	11.1	9.8	6.25

Thus, assuming that the investor uses a four-year time horizon, a minimum return of 11.1 percent would be required on the incoming candidate. This would promise a recapture of the capital gains tax plus a return equivalent to that on the common stock in the above example over a time horizon of four years. A promised return of 11.1 percent would mean that the investor would be equally well off by selling his stock and buying a replacement that is expected to yield 11.1 percent. However, whether the investor would do so depends on his willingness to accept risk. Nevertheless, it is clear that capital gains taxes could greatly affect the decision.

Portfolio Reallocation

One policy that appears to have empirical support is reallocation of the securities within an existing portfolio. Portfolio reallocation is the process of selling off a portion of those securities that have performed better than the portfolio in general and reinvesting the proceeds in those that have not performed as well. A major study of portfolio reallocation was undertaken by Henry A. Latane and William E. Young.[2] The Latane-Young study used an equal allocation rule, so that at the end of each year there was an equal allocation among all the stocks in the portfolio.

Generally, some stocks will appreciate faster than others, and reallocation means that some of these are sold and the proceeds reinvested in those that had not. The rationale for this approach is based upon the principle of convergence. That is, how long does it take for a given stock to reach its intrinsic value? Some will reach this level faster than others. Once these stocks attain their intrinsic value, further appreciation is somewhat limited. Moreover, without reallocation the portfolio may become concentrated in those securities that have already realized most of their anticipated appreciation. The performance of the portfolio, therefore, will be severely limited.

To illustrate how Latane and Young utilized this approach, consider the following three stock portfolio for two time periods, t and $t + 1$:

[2] Henry A. Latane and William E. Young, "Test of Portfolio Building Rules," *Journal of Finance*, vol. 24, no. 4 (Sept., 1969), pp. 595–613.

	Time *t*			Time *t* + 1	
Stock	Amount invested	Proportion	Stock	Market value	Proportion
1	$10,000	0.333	1	$20,000	0.444
2	10,000	0.333	2	12,000	0.289
3	10,000	0.333	3	13,000	0.267

It is evident that all the stocks in this portfolio have shown remarkable appreciation, but following a reallocation policy would mean that a portion of stock 1 would be sold and the proceeds reallocated to stocks 2 and 3. If an equal allocation rule were used, the proportions after reallocation would be as follows:

Stock	Amount invested	Proportion
1	$15,000	0.333
2	15,000	0.333
3	15,000	0.333

Latane and Young's test of this reallocation policy was conducted on portfolios varying in size from 4 to 32 stocks. The portfolios were selected from a universe of 224 stocks. Four different selection criteria were used in the construction of 420 portfolios (105 portfolios for each criterion). These criteria were as follows:

1. Random selection of portfolios
2. The pure-risk yield used in the wealth-maximization model
3. Market elasticity (this is the regression coefficient, b_i, which indicates elasticity of the yield on a particular stock with respect to the yield on a market index)
4. Expected value

Criteria 2, 3, and 4 were used to select portfolios by going from the largest to the smallest in each case.

Table 18-1 presents the results of the Latane and Young tests. For the 420 portfolios of varying size, the buy-and-hold policy outperformed the reallocation policy in 107 instances. This led Latane and Young to conclude that the

TABLE 18-1 *Numbers of Portfolios with Greater Buy-and-Hold Returns than Reallocation*

Portfolio size	Number of portfolios	Random	Pure-risk yield	Market elasticity	Expected value
4	56	24	6	23	0
8	28	9	4	16	0
16	14	6	2	7	0
32	7	4	1	5	0
Total	105	43	13	51	0

Source: Latane and Young, op. cit., p. 603.

reallocation policy was a viable policy. The only situations in which the buy-and-hold policy performed well were when the portfolios were randomly selected or selected on the basis of market elasticity. Even then it was among the very small and very large portfolios that the buy-and-hold policy appeared to perform the best. Proportionally the best performance for the buy-and-hold policy was obtained among the 32 stock portfolios. The reason for this is open to conjecture, but it appears that the method of selecting portfolios is very important. This probably means that if either of these two criteria are used to select portfolios, reallocation may not be beneficial. However, reallocation is consistent with the pure-risk yield used in the wealth-maximization model.

Reallocation appears to add another dimension to portfolio composition; in the tests of the wealth-maximization model, reallocation appears to provide an additional point return. However, no consideration was given in this study to brokerage fees or transfer costs, and consequently the net return of such a policy is unclear. Since the additional return seems to be about one point, the benefits of reallocation may be eroded by these transactions costs.[3] Latane and Young's study does point up the benefits of time diversification, that is, the benefits of making commitments in the various securities over time. Dollar-cost averaging, which will be discussed in a subsequent section, is an example of a technique using time diversification. However, the benefits of a reallocation policy appear to be in doubt once transactions costs are considered.

Portfolio Upgrading

We have seen that portfolio reallocation may not be a useful concept once transactions costs are introduced. Portfolio upgrading, however, is a concept that appears to have the general blessing of the investment community. The Wall Street maxim is, "let your profits run and cut your losses short." Either aspect of this maxim implies trends. "Cutting your losses short" implies that those stocks that have done badly will continue to do so. Similarly, "letting your profits run" implies that stocks that have performed well will continue to do so. This maxim has its foundation deeply imbedded in technical analysis. On purely intuitive grounds, it is difficult to find fault with an approach that culls out those stocks that are doing badly and retains those that are performing well. Robert A. Levy conducted a study to determine whether this was a viable approach for the investor to undertake, and he found surprisingly little evidence to support portfolio upgrading.[4] The sample used in his study included 200 stocks listed on the New York Stock Exchange for the 260-week period of October 24, 1960 to October 15, 1965. Weekly data were used in the tests. Levy applied a technique known as the relative strength criterion, which will be discussed in some detail in Chapter 20. Generally, the relative strength criter-

---

[3] Ibid., p. 604.
[4] Robert A. Levy, "The Principle of Portfolio Upgrading," *Industrial Management Review*, vol. 9, no. 2 (Fall, 1967), pp. 82–96.

ion attempts to determine which stocks have performed the best in the immediate past, since it is believed that these will continue to perform well in the future.

The method of testing involved setting up cast-out ranks. The stock with the highest ratio, that is, the one that had the best market performance, was given the rank 000, and the stock with the lowest ratio was given a rank of 199. These rankings were used to formulate portfolios. For example, if the cast-out rank were 50, then all stocks ranked 000 to 49 would be included in the portfolio. The cast-out ranks actually used, as illustrated in Table 18-2, ranged from 20 to 195. Once these cast-out ranks were determined and the stocks ranked according to their initial 26-week relative strength ranking, a hypothetical investment of $200,000 was made in the qualifying stocks. Therefore, if the cast-out rank were 50, $4,000 would be invested in these 50 stocks in the twenty-seventh week of the test period. This became the initial portfolio. In the twenty-eighth week and every week thereafter, stocks whose cast-out rank equaled or exceeded 50 were sold and replaced by a stock whose rank did qualify. This procedure was used for all of the cast-out ranks shown in Table 18-2.

The results of Levy's study, as shown in Table 18-2, illustrate that rigorous upgrading does not provide a significant return. The basis for comparison is the geometric average, which is a weekly geometric average return of the 200

TABLE 18-2 *Gross and Net Results of Six Cast-Out Ranks Used in Levy's Study*

	Cast-out ranks						Geometric average
	020	050	100	150	180	195	
Gross results (percent)							
233-week percentage gain	21.3	39.6	60.6	60.2	65.2	70.4	57.2
Rate of return, compounded annually	4.4	7.7	11.2	11.1	11.9	12.9	10.6
Average of four-week rates of return	0.38	0.61	0.86	0.86	0.92	0.97	0.83
Variance of four-week rates of return	17.23	12.65	11.52	11.41	11.87	12.17	12.40
Net results (percent)							
233-week percentage gain	−63.5	−40.0	−3.0	21.8	46.3	64.5	57.2
Rate of return, compounded annually	−20.2	−10.8	−0.7	4.5	8.9	11.8	10.6
Average of four-week rates of return	−1.67	−0.84	−0.01	0.38	0.71	0.91	0.83
Variance of four-week rates of return	16.77	12.58	11.35	11.24	11.85	12.16	12.40

Source: Levy, op. cit., p. 85.

stocks in the sample. Reference to Table 18-2 indicates that, excluding broker-age fees and transfer costs, the cast-out ranks above 100 outperformed the sample geometric mean return. For cast-out ranks of 20 and 50, the rate of return compounded annually is 4.4 and 7.7 percent, respectively. Only at a cast-out rank of 100 does this return exceed the geometric mean return for the entire sample. However, once transactions costs are introduced, only the cast-out rank number 195 outperforms the sample as a whole. This study thus indicates that the policy of portfolio upgrading may be of questionable value.

In summary, the results of the two studies conducted by Latane and Young and Levy have led to the same conclusions but by different routes. Reallocation appears to be a particularly useful policy in connection with the wealth-maximization model as long as transactions costs are not introduced. If transactions costs are introduced, the benefits of portfolio reallocation may not provide a significant increase in portfolio return. A policy of portfolio upgrading, on the other hand, appears to be a costly policy to the investor. Before transactions costs are introduced, extensive upgrading does not appear to improve the portfolio return; consequently, after transactions costs are introduced, this policy would be quite costly.

Formula Timing Plans

Many people in the investment community have argued that it is impossible to predict future market conditions, and it is argued that the investor should therefore follow a defensive policy. As previously noted the buy-and-hold policy is the most conservative policy. This policy does not attempt to benefit from the timing of purchases and sales. Other defensive policies recognize the benefits that can be derived from investment timing but hold that predicting market conditions is difficult if not impossible. Therefore, some mechanical means that does not depend upon forecasting is required to help the investor make these timing decisions. Formula timing plans are designed to fulfill this requirement.

Dollar-Cost Averaging

The simplest and most effective formula timing plan is dollar-cost averaging. In a strict sense, dollar-cost averaging involves only two steps. First, stocks are selected with good long-term prospects. Stocks that have a good long-term growth trend and are fairly volatile provide the maximum benefits from dollar-cost averaging. Second, a regular commitment to purchase a specified amount of a stock at regular intervals is required. For example, a plan may provide a commitment of $1,000 quarterly to purchase a particular stock. In this case the $1,000 would be used quarterly to purchase the stock, regardless of its price or the firm's economic prospects in general.

By following dollar-cost averaging religiously, the investor is in effect varying the number of shares purchased at various points in the stock market cycle. This is sometimes referred to as time diversification. When prices are high, fewer shares are purchased. On the other hand, more shares are purchased when prices are low. For example, if the investor decides to purchase $1,000 worth of a particular stock quarterly, the following gives the transactions for four quarters in one particular year, ignoring transactions costs:

Quarter	Market price	Shares purchased	Cumulative investment	Market value	Unrealized profit (or loss)	Average cost/ share	Average market price share
1	$100	10	$1,000	$1,000	$ 0	$100.00	$100.00
2	90	11	1,990	1,890	(100)	94.76	95.00
3	100	10	2,990	3,100	110	96.45	96.67
4	110	9	3,980	4,400	420	99.50	100.00

In this particular example, the stock fell rather sharply in the second quarter but then recovered. In the second quarter, therefore, the investor purchased more shares than in the subsequent quarters. The benefits of this policy can be viewed by comparing the last two columns. It should be noted that after the second quarter the average cost per share is lower than the average market price per share. Herein lies the benefits of dollar-cost averaging. When prices were low, more stocks, 11, were purchased, while fewer were purchased when prices were higher. Thus, in the third quarter there was an unrealized profit, even though the stock only went back to its initial price of $100. In the long run there is a general tendency for dollar-cost averaging to generate a profit. This will not occur, of course, if the stock being purchased is in a secular downtrend.

It was pointed out previously that strong growth is particularly advantageous, but dollar-cost averaging may be profitable even in a no growth situation if there is substantial volatility. Growth and volatility are desirable, but volatility alone will be sufficient to make dollar-cost averaging profitable. Three examples will be used to illustrate the effect of these two characteristics.

Low Volatility, No Growth To illustrate the situation of low volatility and no growth, suppose that an investor decided to invest $1,000 quarterly in a particular stock. The following are the results of five quarterly transactions:

Quarter	Market price	Shares purchased	Cumulative investment	Market value	Unrealized profit (or loss)	Average cost/ share	Average market price/ share
1	$50	20	$1,000	$1,000	$ 0	$50.00	$50.00
2	45	22	1,990	1,890	(100)	47.38	47.50
3	50	20	2,990	3,100	110	48.23	48.33
4	55	18	3,980	4,400	420	49.75	50.00
5	50	20	4,980	5,000	20	49.80	50.00

When there is no growth and the stock price is not very volatile, it is evident that there is little benefit to be gained from dollar-cost averaging. This is evident by viewing the last two columns. The reason for this is that there is little divergence from the average market price; when prices fall, one is not purchasing significantly more than on the average. In this example, 22 shares were purchased when the price fell to $45. Consequently little benefit is derived, as indicated by the unrealized profit of $20.

High Volatility, No Growth   To illustrate the importance of volatility, consider the following situation. Suppose the investor decides to invest $1,000 quarterly in a common stock that is volatile but has not exhibited a significant long-term uptrend. The following are the results of five quarterly investments:

Quarter	Market price	Shares purchased	Cumulative investment	Market value	Unrealized profit (or loss)	Average cost/ share	Average market price/ share
1	$50	$20.0	$1,000	$1,000	$ 0	$50.00	$50.00
2	40	25.0	2,000	1,800	(200)	44.44	45.00
3	30	33.0	2,990	2,340	(650)	38.33	40.00
4	40	25.0	3,990	4,120	130	38.74	40.00
5	50	20.0	4,990	6,150	1,160	40.57	42.00

The importance of volatility can be seen by simply viewing the effect of dollar-cost averaging in the fourth quarter. In the previous two quarters the price of the stock plummeted 40 percent, yet on a rise of $10 to $40 per share in the third quarter the investor has a small profit. As the stock returns to its initial level in the fifth quarter, the investor's profit increases even further. Reference to the last two columns illustrates the reason for this. There is a fairly wide gap between the average cost and the average market price per share. Consequently, dollar averaging can be useful to the investor even when there is no growth in the price of a stock as long as it is fairly volatile. This in itself is a valuable feature.

High Volatility, High Growth   The ideal stock investment is one that involves high volatility and high growth. Volatility alone is sufficient for dollar-cost averaging to be profitable, but both growth and volatility will lead to substantial profits. The benefits that may be derived are illustrated in the following table:

Quarter	Market price	Shares purchased	Cumulative investment	Market value	Unrealized profit (or loss)	Average cost/ share	Average market price/ share
1	$50	20.0	$1,000	$1,000	$ 0	$50.00	$50.00
2	60	16.0	1,960	2,160	200	54.44	55.00
3	40	25.0	2,960	2,440	(520)	48.52	55.00
4	60	16.0	3,920	4,620	700	50.91	52.50
5	80	12.0	4,880	7,120	2,240	54.83	58.00

It is clear that volatility and high growth can lead to a substantial profit. Ideally the investor using dollar-cost averaging would be interested in stocks that have a high growth rate as well as being quite volatile. As a practical matter, these two factors normally go together. Stocks that have high growth normally are quite volatile because of the high growth rate.

In summary, dollar-cost averaging is a useful approach toward investment timing as long as the stocks invested in are volatile. Ideally, however, dollar-cost averaging obtains the best results when there is also high growth. Needless to say, growth will always lead to a profit with dollar-cost averaging even if the stock is not highly volatile. Generally, it appear that stocks are quite volatile. Even some of the so-called defensive stocks become quite volatile at times, but growth stocks almost certainly turn in good performances because they combine the ideal ingredients of growth and volatility. In any event, the investor who follows dollar-cost averaging has a better than even chance of coming out ahead. Dollar-cost averaging does have some potential weaknesses. First, it requires a large amount of funds to carry it on successfully. The investor typically requires a diversified portfolio initially to minimize or eliminate the diversifiable risk. The investor who follows dollar-cost averaging then needs funds at regular intervals to diversify over time. The funds required are substantial. From a practical standpoint, therefore, it becomes a useful policy only for the wealthy or for financial institutions. Second, dollar-cost averaging requires discipline. Regardless of stock prices or economic outlook, the plan should be followed. This is sometimes difficult. Finally, dollar-cost averaging has little chance for success if stock prices are in a secular downtrend. Nevertheless, when used in the proper context, dollar-cost averaging greatly improves the investor's chances of success.

Constant Dollar Plan

We now turn to what many consider to be the true formula timing plans. This section will discuss the constant dollar plan, and the following sections will examine the constant ratio and variable ratio plans. These plans are considered true formula timing plans because they are designed to force the investor to sell stock as prices rise and to buy as prices fall. The investor is forced to take his profits as stock prices rise and to buy as prices fall. At the same time, forecasts are not required as guides to buying and selling, since following the action prescribed by the formula timing plan automatically enables the investor to take advantage of fluctuations in stock prices.

A major characteristic of these plans is that the portfolio is divided into two portions, a defensive portion and an aggressive portion. The defensive portion is generally high-quality bonds, while the aggressive portion is made up of common stock. The proportions of each in a particular portfolio are arbitrary, but the function of each is specific. The high-quality bond portion is to provide stability. For example, in a falling stock market, the stock portion of the portfolio would be shrinking in value, but the bond portion would be stable if not rising slightly. Conversely, in a rising stock market, the stock portion of the portfolio would be appreciating, but the bond portion would be stable if not falling slightly. It is this portfolio mix which facilitates the automatic buying and selling of securities.

The constant dollar plan facilitates the shift from bonds to stocks and vice versa by maintaining a constant amount invested in the stock portion. As a result, when the stock portion appreciates above this level, some stocks are sold and the proceeds invested in bonds. When stock prices fall and the stock portion falls below this level, bonds are sold and the proceeds are used to buy common stock. For example, a $400,000 portfolio may consist of $200,000 invested in bonds and $200,000 in stocks. If stock prices rose, there would be an automatic sale of stock as the stock portion rose in value. The proceeds of the stock sale would be reinvested in bonds. This would reduce the stock portion to $200,000, but the bond portion would increase reflecting these proceeds. In a falling stock market, a portion of the bond portfolio would be sold and reinvested in stocks.

Instituting a constant dollar plan requires two important decisions. First, there is the formation of the stock and bond portions. This is essentially a matter of preference and to some extent a question of the investor's attitude toward risk. Normally, however, plans are fairly well balanced with ratios of 60-40, 50-50, 40-60 being normally used. Second, a more difficult question concerns when adjustments should take place. Here a guideline is needed that will obtain maximum benefits while minimizing costs. Such a rule might be that adjustments will take place quarterly if the stock or bond portions have appreciated or fallen by 10 percent. This percentage should not be so small that the realized appreciation is greatly reduced through excessive transactions costs. On the other hand, it should not be so large so that the appreciation is not realized.

To illustrate, suppose an investor has $200,000 to invest and decides that the initial division between bonds and stocks should be $100,000 in each segment. Further, suppose that the portfolio adjustment rule is that adjustments will take place every six months if the stock portion has appreciated 20 percent or fallen 10 percent. The results of this hypothetical portfolio are shown in Table 18-3 for a three-year period. In period 1 the stock portion appreciated 25 percent. This initiated an adjustment whereby the stock portion was reduced by $25,000 and the bond portion was increased by the same amount. In period 2 the stock portion decreased by 10 percent, but the bond portion appreciated by 4 percent. This can result because bond yields can fall as stock prices fall. Therefore, $10,000 worth of bonds will be sold and reinvested in common stock. Period 3 was a repeat of period 2 with basically the same transactions occurring. Period 4, however, marked a change in conditions as the stock portion appreciated 23 percent, but the bond portion declined over 4 percent reflecting an increase in bond yields. Finally, period 5 was a continuation of period 4; the stock portion appreciated by 22 percent, but the bond portion continued the previous decline

TABLE 18-3 *A Hypothetical Example of a Constant Dollar Plan*

Semiannual period	Stock portion	Bond portion	Adjustments to stock portion	Total portfolio
0	$100,000	$100,000		$200,000
1	125,000	100,000		225,000
	100,000	125,000	(25,000)	225,000
2	90,000	130,000		220,000
	100,000	120,000	10,000	220,000
3	90,000	125,000		215,000
	100,000	115,000	10,000	215,000
4	123,000	110,000		233,000
	100,000	133,000	(23,000)	233,000
5	122,000	130,000		252,000
	100,000	152,000	(22,000)	252,000

by falling slightly less than 3 percent. Consequently, $23,000 worth of common stock would be sold and reinvested in bonds in period 4, and $22,000 worth of common stock would be sold and reinvested in bonds in period 5. Over the entire $2\frac{1}{2}$ year period, the portfolio appreciated approximately 26 percent, which is a fairly good performance, especially when dividends and interest are yet to be considered. In addition, the entire amount of appreciation is captured in the bond portfolio.

The major advantage of the constant dollar plan, as with all formula timing plans, is that purchases and sales are determined automatically. Consequently, the plan forces the investor to take some of his capital gains as prices rise and to buy stocks as prices fall. This is generally recognized as the proper course of action for the investor to take regardless of whether he is using a formula timing plan. By maintaining a constant dollar amount invested in common stock, the constant dollar plan achieves this end. As stock prices rise, the constant dollar plan forces the investor to sell some of the stock portfolio and capture the appreciation that has taken place. Otherwise the paper profits may never be realized. On the other hand, when stock prices fall, funds are shifted from the bond portion into common stock.

For the plan to operate most effectively, it should not be started when stock prices are either at their peak or extremely depressed. If the plan is started at one of the extremes, there is a possibility of having too small or too large a stock fund. For example, referring back to the previous example, the effect of sustained appreciation of the stock portion would mean that the bond portion would become quite large. To prevent this from occurring requires some forecasting, which runs counter to the philosophy of formula timing plans. Second, this plan does not work well in periods of generally uptrending stock prices. The constant dollar plan and the constant ratio plan, which will be discussed next, were both designed for a stock market cycle which did not include a strong upward trend. Indeed, these plans have performed well in the period 1926–50. However, in the secularly rising market of the past two decades, these plans have not performed very well.

Constant Ratio Plan

The constant ratio plan is similar to the constant dollar plan. The major difference is that the constant ratio plan attempts to maintain a constant ratio between the bond and stock portions. It attempts to overcome a major disadvantage of the constant dollar plan by maintaining proportionate investment in the
bond and stock portions of the portfolio. The ratio is somewhat arbitrary, but it
presumably reflects the risk preferences of the investor. The ratio plan permits
essentially the same operations as the constant dollar plan except a smaller
portion of the appreciation is captured. The constant dollar plan attempts to
capture all of the appreciation of the common stock portion, while the constant
ratio plan attempts to capture only a portion of it. Consequently, the common
stock portion is larger, permitting more appreciation or depreciation.

Two decisions must be made by the investor. First, there is the question of
the ratio of common stock and bonds in the portfolio. This ratio might be 60-40,
50-50, or 40-60. Many investors tend toward a balanced ratio, but the actual
ratio used depends upon the preferences of the investor. Second, the guideline
for adjusting the portfolio may take several forms. It may be a stipulated percentage increase or decrease in the stock portion over a certain period of time. This
parallels the constant dollar plan. An alternative approach is to base adjustments on the changes in a market index, such as the Dow-Jones Industrial
Average. In either case adjustments take place after reviewing the portfolio's
performance for a regular interval of time.

Table 18-4 illustrates how one of these constant ratio plans may be formulated. In this particular plan, the adjustment rule is that the portfolio will be
reviewed every six months, and adjustments will be made once the stock portion has risen or fallen by at least 10 percent. In addition, the ratio used is 50-50.
Initially, there is $100,000 invested in the stock portion and $100,000 in the
bond portion. Note that in almost every respect the constant ratio plan parallels
the constant dollar plan, except that the stock portfolio keeps step with the

TABLE 18-4 *A Hypothetical Example of a Constant
Dollar Ratio Plan*

Period	Stock portion	Bond portion	Adjustment to stock portion	Total portfolio
0	$100,000	$100,000		$200,000
1	125,000	100,000		225,000
	112,500	112,500	(12,500)	225,000
2	100,000	117,000		217,000
	108,500	108,500	8,500	217,000
3	95,000	113,000		208,000
	104,000	104,000	9,000	208,000
4	123,000	100,000		223,000
	111,500	111,500	(11,500)	223,000
5	138,000	111,500		249,500
	124,750	124,750	(13,250)	249,500

bond portfolio. In period 1 the stock portfolio appreciates by 25 percent. One-half of this appreciation is reinvested in the bond portfolio. In period 2 the stock portfolio falls in value, but the bond portfolio rises slightly. The two changes offset each other to some extent, but the bond portfolio is further reduced by $8,500, which is reinvested in common stock. The final three periods witness a reversal in trend. Period 3 is a continuation of the second period with stock prices falling, and part of the bond portion is reallocated to the stock portion. Periods 4 and 5 indicate a turnaround in stock prices. In both periods there is substantial appreciation, which is partially allocated into the bond portion. It is evident from this example that the constant dollar plan and the constant ratio plan are very similar. The major advantage of the constant ratio plan is that it gives more emphasis to the stock portion. As a result, in a period of a general uptrend in stock prices this approach would lead to better performance, since the stock portion would always be a constant proportion of the portfolio. This proportion would not continually diminsh as with a constant dollar plan.

Variable Ratio Plan

Variable ratio plans attempt to achieve the same objectives as the constant dollar and the constant ratio plans by consciously increasing or decreasing the stock portion according to a predetermined set of guidelines. Unlike the other formula timing plans, formulating this plan requires forecasting the expected levels of stock prices. The strong uptrend in stock prices since World War II forced a revision in the constant dollar and constant ratio plans, leading to the development of the variable ratio plan. The key to the success of this plan depends on whether the guidelines are properly conceived.

The variable ratio plan depends heavily on the concept of normal stock prices. The user of the plan makes a forecast of the possible range of stock prices over a given time horizon. He then divides this range into different zones which represent different degrees of over- or undervaluation. Presumably there is a normal range of value, but as the market moves away from this in either direction, it is moving progressively toward over- or undervaluation. Once these value zones are determined, a ratio of stocks and bonds must be determined for each zone. For example, when prices are within the normal range, a 50-50 division may be used. When stock prices move progressively higher, perhaps through three zones above the normal range, the stock portion may be reduced to 40, 30, and 20 percent, respectively. Conversely, the stock portion is increased as stock prices drop below the normal zone. For example, the stock portion may be increased to 60, 70, and 80 percent as stock prices move through three zones below the normal range. Plotting the zones is extremely difficult, but two methods that have been used are regression analysis and an intrinsic value approach. One of the simplest approaches is to fit trend lines by means of linear regression. This approach establishes the general trend and the standard deviation about the trend. From this information the zones can be established. The major assumption of this technique is that a linear relationship exists. This weakness can be overcome by using semilogarithmic paper to capture any nonlinearity.

The major difficulty of using trend analysis is that it assumes that the future can be adequately described by the past. This approach makes no provision for changing conditions. For example, the model does not provide for changes in household saving rates or international trade restrictions. Further, it is well known that investors' expectations changed dramatically in the mid-1950s and again in the early 1970s, leading to dramatic effects on stock values. The extrapolation of past trends may lead to some dangerous errors in judgment. A moving average can be used to overcome this difficulty, but the major problem with a moving average is selecting the proper length. A moving average can be sensitive to basic changes in the stock price series, but a moving average that is too long will be basically the same as the trend projection. On the other hand, a moving average that is too short will simply trace out short-term events.

An alternative approach to projecting the market's trend is to use an intrinsic value approach. This approach simply applies traditional fundamental analysis to the question of determining the normal market value. The first step is to estimate the earnings per share for a market index, such as the Dow-Jones Industrial Average. A price-earnings ratio is then applied to this estimate to derive the anticipated normal level. A high and a low anticipated market value can be derived by using a high and a low price-earnings ratio. In this manner a range of possible values is established for the market index. Once this range of values is established, the zones of value can be superimposed.

Although it is a favorite device of many security analysts, the estimated market price based upon an *EPS* estimate and a estimated *P/E* ratio may not be much of an improvement over the trend approach, basically for the same reason. In the trend appraoch, the past is expected to fully explain the future, but many times *EPS* and *P/E* ratios are extrapolations of the past trends. Consequently, this approach may be based on trend analysis and therefore has the same weakness as regression analysis. A moving average probably will provide as good results as any approach, but it will require some experimentation to determine the appropriate length for the moving average.

When the formula timing plans were originally conceived and had a wide following, that is, during the period 1929–53, these plans were reasonably successful. They were originally conceived to deal with a stock market cycle that did not have a strong upward trend. Under such market conditions, formula timing plans enabled the investor to sell as prices rose and to buy as prices fell. After 1953, however, stock prices began to show a strong upward trend, which the formula plans were not designed to handle. No matter which formula plan was used, forecasting market conditions was required to obtain best results from the plan. As a result, the fundamental reason for using formula plans was violated. Hence, the usefulness of formula plans was brought into question. As a result of this change in market conditions, formula plans are not widely used.

The popularity of formula plans began to wane in the early 1950s, and it is fair to say that their current use is very limited.

Summary

This chapter introduced the investment timing decision. The market tends to have a long-term trend component and a cyclical component. Technicians argue that there is a short-term component as well. The decision facing the investor is whether or not he should attempt to time his investments. A defensive approach means that the investor will not attempt to forecast stock market conditions. The aggressive investor, on the other hand, attempts to forecast market conditions. The two most common means are the use of business and economic statistics and the use of market statistics. Approaches using these data will be discussed in the next two chapters. In addition, it is important to distinguish buying and selling decisions based upon timing considerations from those based upon portfolio upgrading and reallocation.

The empirical evidence lends little support to the use of either a vigorous portfolio upgrading policy or to the use of portfolio reallocation. It appears that the investor should not be too concerned with portfolio upgrading since it appears that short-run trends in stock prices may not exist. If the market behavior of a stock is not as expected in the short run, one will not obtain substantial benefits by selling such stocks and purchasing those that have recorded good market behavior. This does not mean that some stocks should not be sold because they have not met expectations, but the basis for such a decision should probably be based upon changes in such fundamentals as sales and earnings growth rather than market performance. It appears that one should be cautious about portfolio upgrading and sell off stock only if it is clear that its prospects are very poor. Reallocation, on the other hand, appears to offer a method of improving the portfolio's return as long as there are no transactions costs. As soon as transaction costs are introduced, it seems that the benefits of a reallocation policy practically disappear.

Formula timing plans have been widely used during the last 50 years as defensive approaches to investment timing, but dollar-cost averaging appears to offer the most promising alternative. The true formula timing plans do not appear to offer a particularly attractive solution to the problem of investment timing. The constant dollar and constant ratio plans do not successfully deal with the uptrend in stock prices that has occurred since World War II. This result led to the development of the variable ratio plan and to the eventual abandonment of these plans by many financial institutions. Thus, the development of formula timing plans has gone full circle, and it appears that forecasting is unavoidable. Dollar-cost averaging, on the other hand, has properties that substantially improve the probabilities of obtaining a profit. Successful dollar-cost averaging only has two prerequisites. First, the prices of the stocks selected should be volatile. Second, the prices of the stocks selected should not be in a secular downtrend. For stocks that exhibit a strong uptrend along with volatility, dollar-cost averaging will lead to substantial profits. As a result, of all the approaches touched on in this chapter, only dollar-cost averaging appears to have features that strongly recommend its use.

Questions

1. What are the alternative approaches that may be taken toward investment timing? What premises would prompt an investor to adhere to a buy-and-hold policy?

2. What is the rationale for following a policy of portfolio upgrading? Reallocation?

3. On the basis of recent empirical studies, should the investor attempt to use either portfolio upgrading or reallocation as a basic portfolio policy? Under what conditions would a reallocation policy be worthwhile?

4. In many simulation studies—for example, studies of portfolio upgrading and reallocation—the effect of capital gains taxes is omitted. Why? Do you agree with this approach?

5. An investor owns 1,000 shares of a stock selling for $50 dollars per share. His cost was $2 per share in 1960. The problem is that the stock's prospects over the next five years are not good. It is expected that there will be no appreciation over that period, but the range of variation is expected to be between $60 on the high side and $40 on the low side. The investor's expected return over that period, therefore, is simply the dividend yield, or 3 percent. Currently, the investor's marginal tax rate is 36 percent. If he has an indefinite time horizon, what minimum return would be required to make switching worthwhile? Would you recommend switching into stocks promising a 7 percent return indefinitely?

6. Instead of assuming an indefinite time horizon, assume the investor in question 5 wants to recover his capital gains tax in five years. What is the minimum return required on an incoming stock for this portfolio?

7. Suppose you were considering the use of dollar-cost averaging. Further, suppose you were examining the following four stocks as possible candidates. The quarterly price history for the last five years is as follows

Quarter	Stock					Quarter	Stock			
	1	2	3	4			1	2	3	4
$t = 0$	42	44¼	101	80⅛		−10	52¼	44⅝	122⅛	45¼
−1	43½	45⅛	84⅛	70¼		−11	58⅛	46⅛	125	45⅞
−2	44⅛	47⅞	115¼	60⅜		−12	52	49	128⅜	43¼
−3	49¾	43⅜	80¼	50¼		−13	59½	48⅞	112	40⅛
−4	45⅝	40	75½	48⅜		−14	56¾	44	89⅞	37⅞
−5	44⅜	41⅞	60⅛	46¼		−15	54⅛	46⅛	126⅛	38⅛
−6	47	37⅝	62⅞	48⅞		−16	51⅞	51⅛	108⅛	35
−7	51⅛	34¼	96½	45⅝		−17	55⅝	55¼	114⅞	32¼
−8	52⅜	29	126⅝	39¾		−18	51	59⅞	106⅛	28
−9	56⅞	42¼	140	44⅞		−19	57¼	56¼	99¾	22½

If your expectations for the next five years are that these stocks will continue to perform in much the same fashion as in the previous five years, how would you rank these stocks on the basis of their suitability for a dollar-cost averaging program?

8. Formula timing plans were designed as a defensive approach to investment timing. What features of such formula timing plans as the constant dollar and constant ratio plans are supposed to capture the benefits of investment timing for the investor?

9. The constant dollar, constant ratio, and variable ratio plans do not have a wide following. Why is this true? Does the variable ratio plan actually comply with the basic reason for setting up these formula timing plans?

Selected References

Cohen, Jerome B., and Edward D. Zinbarg. *Investment Analysis and Portfolio Management*. Homewood, Ill.: Richard D. Irwin, 1967. Chapter 15.

Cottle, C. C., and W. T. Whitman. *Investment Timing: The Formula Plan Approach*. New York: McGraw-Hill, 1953.

Dince, Robert R. "Another View of Formula Planning." *Journal of Finance*, vol. 19, no. 4 (Dec., 1964), pp. 678–88.

Holt, Charles C., and John P. Shelton. "The Implications of the Capital Gains Tax for Investment Decisions." *Journal of Finance*, vol. 24, no. 4 (Dec., 1961), pp. 559–80.

Latane, Henry A., and William E. Young. "Test of Portfolio Building Rules." *Journal of Finance*, vol. 24, no. 4 (Sept., 1969), pp. 595–612.

Leffler, George L., and Loring C. Farwell. *The Stock Market*, 3d ed. New York: The Ronald Press, 1963. Chapter 33.

Levy, Robert A. "The Principle of Portfolio Upgrading." *Industrial Management Review*, vol. 9, no. 2 (Fall, 1967), pp. 82–96.

Tomlinson, Lucile. *Practical Formulas for Successful Investing*. New York: Wilfred Funk, 1953.

Chapter 19

Business and Economic Indicators

For those investors who undertake an aggressive policy toward investment timing, the major concern is finding a set of indicators that are reliable predictors of stock market conditions. The two types of statistics generally used are business and economic statistics and stock market statistics. Business and economic statistics can include a wide array of indicators of economic conditions, such as the rate of unemployment, interest rates, the growth of industrial production, and the growth of the money supply. Stock market statistics are more limited in their scope, being confined basically to prices of stocks and their volume. The focus of this chapter will be on the use of business and economic statistics to forecast turning points in the securities markets. Chapter 20 will discuss the various methods of using stock market statistics to predict the direction of stock prices.

Business and economic statistics are used to predict securities prices because it has been widely recognized that the level of business activity affects both stock and bond prices. Stock prices are generally directly affected by the level of business activity, while bond prices are inversely related. Recall that this fact was the basis for developing the formula timing plans. Consequently, it is widely believed that if business conditions can be accurately forecasted, securities prices can also be predicted, particularly at major turning points in the rate of change of business activity. The three different methods of forecasting business conditions are the National Bureau of Economic Research's leading, lagging, and coincident indicators, complex econometric forecasting models, and the use of monetary statistics. Each of these approaches will be discussed below.

Business Statistics

The use of business statistics to predict turning points in business activity was pioneered by the National Bureau of Economic Research (NBER). In their research they have developed three series of business statistics known as leading, lagging, and coincident indicators. Their research found that certain business series lead or lag turning points in business activity, and these series were designated as leading and lagging indicators. Furthermore, those series that closely parallel general business activity were designated coincident indicators. These indicators include a total of 72 series of which 36 were leading indicators, 25 were coincident indicators, and 11 were lagging indicators. From this list a short list of 25 series was developed. This list avoids duplications and includes the best performing of the leading, lagging, and coincident indicators. The following discussion will be confined to the short list, which is illustrated in Table 19-1. All these series are published by the United States Department of Commerce and are available in the publication *Business Conditions Digest.*

In developing the list of leading, lagging, and coincident indicators, the NBER ranked each series on a scale of 0 to 100 according to the following criteria:

1. Economic significance
2. Statistical adequacy
3. Historical conformity to business cycles
4. Consistency during business cycles
5. Smoothness
6. Promptness of publication

In addition, there were subordinate considerations that were applied. As a result, there were approximately 20 different criteria involved in the rating of the series. The end result was the determination of the leading, lagging, and coincident indicators, which were selected in descending order. The most recent list, which resulted from the Moore-Shiskin study in 1966, developed a full list of 88 indicators, but only 72 were leading, lagging, and coincident indicators. In addition, the NBER's short list of 25 indicators includes 12 leading indicators, seven coincident indicators, and six lagging indicators. This group was developed to provide a convenient summary of business conditions and it is this list, particularly the leading indicators, that will be discussed below.

Leading Indicators

In 1966 the series used to make up the leading, lagging, and coincident indicators were revised with new series replacing some of the old. The leading indicators included in the short list is a selective and generally unduplicated list of the leading indicators that may prove useful to the investor. Although the

TABLE 19-1 *The Leading, Lagging, and Coincident Indicators of Business Activity in the Short List*

Classification and series title (1)	First business cycle turn covered (2)	Timing at peaks and troughs — Business cycle turns covered (3)	Leads (4)	Lags (5)	Rough coincidences* (6)	Median lead(−) or lag(+) in months (7)
Leading indicators (12 series)						
1. Avg. workweek, prod. workers, mfg.	1921	19	13	4(2)	2	−5
30. Nonagri. placements, BES	1945	10	8	4(0)	1	−3
38. Index of net business formation	1945	10	8	3(1)	0	−7
6. New orders, dur. goods indus.	1920	20	16	7(1)	0	−4
10. Contracts and orders, plant and equipment	1948	8	7	2(0)	1	−6
29. New building permits, private housing units	1918	22	17	5(1)	1	−6
31. Change in book value, mfg. and trade inventories	1945	10	9	2(1)	0	−8
23. Industrial materials prices	1919	21	13	9(4)	2	−2
19. Stock prices, 500 common stocks	1873	44	33	14(2)	5	−4
16. Corporate profits after taxes, Q	1920	20	13	11(4)	2	−2
17. Ratio, price to unit labor cost, mfg.	1919	21	17	10(1)	3	−3
113. Change in consumer instalment debt	1929	14	11	4(0)	1	−10
Roughly coincident indicators (7 series)						
41. Employees in nonagri. establishments	1929	14	6	12(6)	2	0
43. Unemployment rate, total (inv.)	1929	14	4	8(3)	6	0
50. GNP in constant dollars, expenditure estimate, Q	1921	17	7	9(3)	3	−2
47. Industrial production	1919	21	9	13(9)	3	0
52. Personal income	1921	19	10	12(2)	5	−1
816. Mfg. and trade sales	1948	8	4	6(4)	0	0
54. Sales of retail stores	1919	21	5	7(1)	6	0
Lagging indicators (6 series)						
502. Unempl. rate, persons unempl. 15+ weeks (inv.)	1948	8	1	5(1)	6	+2
61. Bus. expend., plant and equip., Q	1918	20	2	16(5)	13	+1
71. Book value, mfg. and trade inventories	1945	10	2	7(0)	8	+2
62. Labor cost per unit of output, mfg.	1919	21	0	1(0)	14	+8
72. Comm. and indus. loans outstanding	1937	12	1	6(0)	7	+2
67. Bank rates, short-term bus. loans, Q	1919	21	2	5(1)	15	+5

* Rough coincidences include exact coincidences (shown in parentheses) and leads and lags of three months or less. Leads (lags) include leads (lags) of one month or more. The total number of timing comparisons, which can be less than the number of business cycle turns covered by the series, is the sum of the leads, exact coincidences, and lags. Leads and lags of quarterly series are expressed in terms of months.

Source: Geoffrey H. Moore and Julius Shiskin, *Indicators of Business Expansion and Contractions*. Occasional Paper No. 103. (New York: National Bureau of Economic Research, 1967), p. 68.

lead time has varied from series to series, this group of series has consistently been well-behaved leading indicators. The rationale for including each series will be discussed below.

Average Work Week for Production Workers   The average work week for production workers is generally accepted as a leading indicator because manufacturing firms are assumed to be sensitive to changes in business conditions. For example, it is common practice to reduce the work week to make necessary adjustments in production schedules. This is normally the first step in reducing the amount of output. If demand should continue to slacken, the firm will eventually begin to lay off personnel. As a result, a reduction in the work week for production personnel is considered to be a sensitive leading indicator of business activity.

Nonagricultural Placements   The labor force is made up of two segments, those workers already in the labor force and those workers entering the labor force. New positions increase and decrease as business activity ebbs and flows. Nonagricultural placements provide a particularly useful series that is only concerned with new positions that are available. Other aggregate statistics on employment may be misleading, since the labor force is constantly increasing. Nonagricultural placements forcuses on the new positions and therefore gives an indicator of business conditions and expectations.

New Business Formations   The formation of new businesses represents another aspect of the investment cycle. It is generally believed that new business formations are related to profits and profit margins. When profits and profit margins begin to improve at the beginning of a business upswing, new business formations increase as entrepreneurs see new opportunities open up. Once the business upswing gains momentum, profits and profit margins begin to narrow. As the business expansion slows, new business formations also slow with the result that the series of new business formations reach a peak at some point before the peak in the business cycle. New business formations turn up before the trough in business activity is reached.

New Orders in Durable Goods Industries   The previous series were based upon reactions to business conditions. New orders of durable goods, however, provide a series indicating the demand schedules facing durables manufacturers. Normally, it would be expected that this series would reflect business activity, since an increase in new orders would lead to a speed up in business output. However, economic analysis has not progressed beyond this point, because little is known about what stimuli start the process in motion. For example, little is known about the buying habits of consumers. Without a workable theory explaining those stimuli that lead to increases and decreases in purchases, little progress can be made in predicting changes in output. Currently, we must be satisfied with the new orders series for durable goods.

Contracts and Orders for Plant and Equipment The importance of new investment on economic growth is well recognized in economic theory. The inclusion of a series reflecting investment in new plant and equipment is therefore not surprising. This series is different from the series for the actual expenditures on new plant and equipment. This series represents the initial intent to expand plant and equipment. Expenditures for plant and equipment naturally follow the initial commitment, but there is a considerable lag. Contracts and orders for plant and equipment, however, is a leading indicator because of the indicator of intent. These are useful for the same reason that surveys of buying intent are useful in ascertaining consumer purchasing plans in the near term. Business is expected to expand plant and equipment in anticipation of rising demand. If demand has slowed, the need for new plant and equipment will also slow. As a result, this series may be an important leading indicator because contracts and orders represent a commitment, not just an intent.

New Building Permits for Private Housing Units New housing permits in many respects parallel the series for contracts and orders for plant and equipment. This series represents a tangible commitment on the part of households and investors. Further, it precedes the actual construction by a considerable period of time. This series reflects a multitude of factors; for example, interest rates and housing legislation affect the series. This series has important implications for other sectors of the economy. It has an important impact, for example, on employment, construction materials, household appliances, and furniture sales. As a result, this series reflects factors that may be signaling a turnaround in business activity long before it actually arrives. At the same time it has an impact on other sectors of the economy that will subsequently affect the economic environment.

Change in Manufacturing and Trade Inventories The rationale for this series is similar to that of several other series that represent the expectations of business firms. Inventory accumulation precedes an expected increase in sales. Conversely, as sales begin to fall off, inventories are pared down to accomodate the reduced sales level. Sometimes in the process of paring down inventories, there is a temporary build-up, but firms cut back production so that inventories can be worked down to an acceptable level. There is some evidence that inventory levels peak or trough somewhat before the peak or trough in business activity, indicating that business firms begin paring down inventories in advance of the peak and begin building inventories before the trough is reached.

Industrial Materials Prices This series is closely related to inventory levels and attempts to obtain insight into the demand schedules that firms face. The series is a daily index of the prices of 13 raw materials whose prices are very sensitive to changes in supply-demand conditions. The sensitivity of these key materials is used to determine the expectations of business firms. For example, if firms are building inventories as sales increase, this sensitive price series would reflect this upward pressure on prices. Conversely, if firms are reducing inventories, this series would fall, reflecting the fall-off in demand. Since this series is so closely related to inventories, it is expected to parallel the behavior of inventory levels very closely.

Stock Prices　Mainly as a result of the research of the NBER, stock prices are generally accepted to be a leading indicator of turning points in business activity. The rationale for stock prices leading business activity is controversial. One school of thought holds that stock prices are not a good leading indicator of business activity. Advocates of this point of view base their argument on the efficient markets hypothesis, which will be discussed in Chapter 21. Those who believe that stock prices are a leading indicator do not agree on the reason for it. One explanation is based upon the premise that professional investors would begin liquidating their stock holdings in advance of the actual downturn in business activity. Consequently, stock prices would begin to turn downward before the actual peak in business activity.

A second explanation that has been advanced closely parallels the first. This explanation holds that investors look to certain leading indicators as a basis for making their investment decisions. For example, the types of indicators being discussed in this section may be used. As a result, stock prices would be expected to be a leading indicator because investors have advance notice of turning points in business activity.

A third explanation, held by the neo-quantity school of economic thought, is that the rate of change of the money supply is an important driving force in the level of business activity in general and may also directly affect stock prices. This will be discussed more fully at the end of this chapter.

Corporate Profits After Taxes　Net profits, of course, are an important force behind business activity. As a result, both the investor and the firm are interested in the level of profits. If profits are expanding, firms are also expanding; as profits slow, the rate of expansion also slows. Near the peak of business activity, costs will have risen and profits may begin to level off. Once the decline in business activity gets under way, firms introduce many economy measures to slow the fall in profits. These measures, plus perhaps some buoyancy in sales, may be the beginning of a turnaround in profits. The growth of corporate profits is thus an important indicator of the business conditions. Corporate profit figures are available on a quarterly basis, and they are particularly useful in evaluating conditions in the corporate sector of the economy.

Change in Consumer Installment Credit　This series represents the net addition to the aggregate consumer installment credit. It represents the difference between new credit extended and existing credit that has been retired. Households presumably utilize consumer credit when they are optimistic about the future. An increase in consumer installment credit reflects the consumers' attitudes and expectations. This behavior in turn leads to increased production in many consumer durables. The result is an increase in output and employment. This series attempts to measure the expectations of the consumer, who is an important factor in determining the level of business activity. Although it is quite cyclical, this series consistently leads the turning points in business activity.

Composite Indexes

A major difficulty with attempting to follow a number of indicators to determine anticipated business conditions is that the various indicators may move in different directions. For example, how would one interpret a situation in which six of the leading indicators were moving upwards and six were moving downwards? A method was needed to resolve the confusion introduced by such contradictions. As a result, the diffusion indexes were developed to give a single indicator of the general direction of the various groups of indicators. A diffusion index indicates the proportion of the group of indicators that rose or fell during the month. For example, if seven of the leading indicators rose during a particular month, the diffusion index would be approximately 58 percent. If in the following month eight of the leading indexes rose, the diffusion index would be 67 percent. Diffusion indexes can also be complex. One version, which is published in *Business Conditions Digest* and is illustrated in Figure 19-1, converts a series that would normally fluctuate within a range of 0 to 100 percent to one that incorporates the underlying trend of the economic activity. This version is commonly known as "reverse trend adjusted."

Figure 19-1 presents this type of composite index for the leading, lagging, and coincident indicators for the period 1947–73. It also shows the major recessions during this period as shaded areas and the lead or lag the composite indexes had. By and large it appears that the leading, lagging, and coincident indicators did a reasonably good job. For the most part, the leading indicators peaked somewhat in advance of the downturn in business activity and turned upward somewhat in advance of the upturn in business activity. The turning points in the leading indicators generally led the turning point in business activity by a sufficient period of time for the investor to confirm that a turning point had actually occurred and to take the necessary action. In 1970, however, the leading indicators turned down approximately two months before the turning point in business activity, which probably was not enough time for the investor to act. Similarly, the leading indicators turned up one month before the upturn in business activity, which is a very short lead time. The coincident and lagging indicators, however, appear to have performed quite well. The coincident indicators appear to follow the turning points in business activity quite closely while the lagging indicators appear to have a reasonably long lag, especially in upturns in business activity. These indicators have thus appeared to function well.

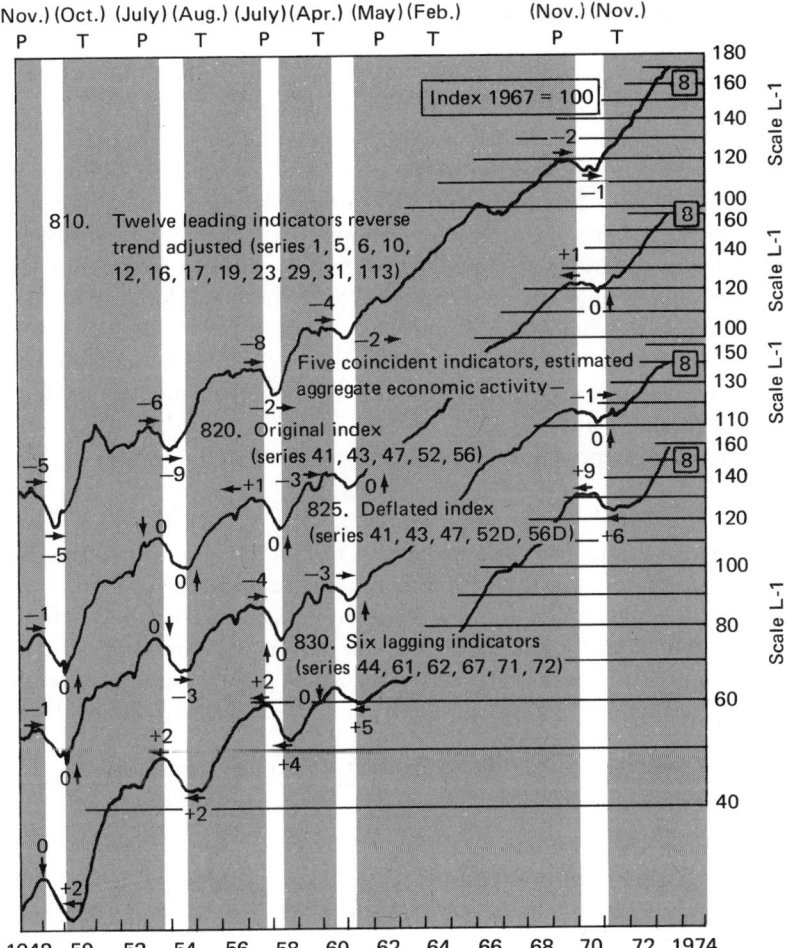

FIGURE 19-1 *Behavior of the Composite Indexes, 1947–73*

Source: *Business Conditions Digest* (Sept. 1973), p. 87.

The investor, therefore, may be able to use these composite series as indicators of business conditions. In particular, the composite index for the leading indicators appears to have worked well up to the recession of 1970. In the previous recessionary periods, this series gave sufficient lead time for the investor to confirm his suspicions and then act. In 1970 this did not occur, and it will be interesting to see whether this occurrence was unusual or whether it is an indication of the lead times in the future. If the leads are on the order of one and two months, the composite index for the leading indicators will not be as useful as it was in the past. To this point, however, it appears that the leading indicators, and to some extent the coincident and lagging indicators, may provide a method of predicting business conditions.

Macroeconomic Forecasting Models

The recent development of complex GNP forecasting models offers a method to predict the level of economic activity in the coming year. The actual features of some of these models were discussed in Chapter 11 and will not be repeated here. The major concern of the investor who attempts to use the forecasts of these models is the anticipated growth in the GNP in the coming year, and particularly whether a downturn in economic activity may be expected. Two important considerations are involved in such an analysis. First, an important distinction should be made between the GNP in nominal dollars and the GNP in real dollars. It is necessary to view the GNP in real dollars to determine whether the output of goods and services will decline in the coming year. Second, the accuracy of the forecasts of these large econometric models is of utmost importance, not only in terms of the GNP forecast but also in terms of forecasting turning points in economic activity.

Table 19-2 shows the GNP for the years 1969, 1970, and 1971 in nominal dollars and real dollars. In nominal dollars, both 1970 and 1971 showed increases, which might lead one to believe that output was expanding during these years. Reference to the bottom portion of Table 19-2, however, indicates that real output actually declined in 1970, dropping to $720 billion from $724.7 billion in 1969. This decline indicates that the increase in nominal GNP resulted from price increases and masked the fact that real output had declined in 1970. Any predictions of GNP should thus be in terms of real dollars. If predic-

TABLE 19-2 *National Income and Product Accounts, 1969–72*

National Income and Product		1969	1970	1971
Gross national product, total	bil.$	929.1	974.1	1,046.8
Personal consumption expenditures, total	do	579.6	615.8	662.1
Durable goods, total	do	89.9	88.6	100.5
Automobiles and parts	do	40.4	37.1	46.2
Furniture and household equipment	do	36.3	37.4	39.6
Nondurable goods, total	do	247.6	264.7	278.6
Clothing and shoes	do	50.3	52.6	57.0
Food and beverages	do	122.5	131.8	136.5
Gasoline and oil	do	21.1	22.9	24.4
Services, total	do	242.1	262.5	282.9
Household operation	do	33.7	36.1	39.2
Housing	do	84.0	91.2	99.7
Transportation	do	16.5	17.9	19.1
Gross private domestic investment, total	do	137.8	135.3	151.6
Fixed investment	do	130.4	132.5	149.3
Nonresidential	do	98.6	102.1	108.7
Structures	do	34.5	36.8	38.2
Producers' durable equipment	do	64.1	65.4	70.5
Residential structures	do	31.8	30.4	40.6
Nonfarm	do	31.2	29.7	40.1
Change in business inventories	do	7.4	2.8	2.2
Nonfarm	do	7.3	2.5	1.7

TABLE 19-2 *continued*

National Income and Product		1969	1970	1971
Net exports of goods and services	do	2.0	3.6	0
Exports	do	55.6	62.9	65.3
Imports	do	53.6	59.3	65.3
Govt. purchases of goods and services, total	do	209.7	219.4	233.0
Federal	do	99.2	97.2	97.6
National defense	do	78.4	75.4	71.4
State and local	do	110.6	122.2	135.5
By major type of product:				
Final sales, total	do	921.7	971.3	1,044.5
Goods, total	do	449.9	465.5	492.0
Durable goods	do	180.9	180.8	193.7
Nondurable goods	do	269.0	284.7	298.3
Services	do	377.4	410.3	443.3
Structures	do	94.4	95.5	109.2
Change in business inventories	do	7.4	2.8	2.2
Durable goods	do	4.5	−0.6	0.4
Nondurable goods	do	2.9	3.4	1.9
GNP in constant (1958) dollars				
Gross national product, total	bil.$	724.7	720.0	739.4
Personal consumption expenditures, total	do	469.3	475.9	491.8
Durable goods	do	84.8	81.4	89.5
Nondurable goods	do	202.7	207.3	211.4
Services	do	181.8	187.2	190.9
Gross private domestic investment, total	do	109.6	102.2	108.5
Fixed investment	do	103.2	99.9	106.3
Nonresidential	do	80.1	78.6	79.3
Residential strictures	do	23.1	21.3	27.0
Change in business inventories	do	6.4	2.3	2.1
Net exports of goods and services	do	0.1	2.4	−0.1
Govt. purchases of goods and services, total	do	145.6	139.4	139.2
Federal	do	73.8	65.4	62.2
State and local	do	71.9	74.0	77.0

Source: *Survey of Current Business* (June, 1972), p. S1.

tions in real terms are not available, the anticipated rate of inflation should be determined. This information will aid in determining the real GNP that is predicted for the coming year.

When the question of accuracy is raised, two aspects must be considered. First, the forecasts should be accurate, and normally this means that the smaller the difference between the forecast and the actual outcome, the better the forecast. The amount of acceptable error varies with the type of forecast being made. This applies particularly to GNP forecasts, which involve large magnitudes. For example, the actual GNP for 1972 was $1,155 billion, and the GNP for 1973 is expected to approach $1,260 billion. Forecasts of this magnitude probably involve error of $10 to $30 billion, which is a small percentage error and seems to indicate that these models are accurate. Much of the accuracy results from the magnitudes involved and the nature of the GNP. Therefore, evaluating the accuracy of GNP forecasts involves comparing the actual change in GNP with the forecasted change. For example, suppose the forecasted change is $100 billion, but the actual change is $80 billion. The error in this forecast is $20 billion, or 25 percent, which is relatively large.

The second aspect, and probably the more important one, is the accuracy of such models in forecasting turning points in the level of economic activity. A reversal in the growth of the real GNP normally characterizes either an "economic slowdown" or a recession. Currently, the apparent definition of a recession is two quarters in which the real GNP shows either a decline or no growth. Accurate GNP predictions are most useful for these turning points in economic activity because at these points the investor could make the necessary shifts in his portfolio. For example, if a recession were anticipated, stocks could be sold and bonds purchased. This action would lead to the realization of paper gains on the common stock portfolio, and it would also lead to appreciation of the bond portfolio as interest rates fell during the ensuing recession. The investor thus benefits in two ways. A more aggressive policy would be to sell the portfolio of stock and also sell certain stocks short. Regardless of the approach taken, accurate forecasts of turning points in economic activity would be of the utmost importance. The forecasts of turning points by these GNP forecasting models are probably the most important aspect to the investor who is attempting to time his investments.

Two studies of the accuracy of the GNP forecasts may shed some light on the relative accuracy of these forecasts. A study conducted by Victor Zarnowitz, which covered the period 1953–64, gives an indication of the accuracy of a number of these models. A more recent study conducted by Keith M. Carlson evaluates the accuracy of the Council of Economic Advisors' forecasts. The study by Zarnowitz divided the forecasts into eight sets for purpose of evaluation.[1] It was found that these forecasts were in error by about $10 billion on the average, or about 2 percent.[2] However, when the error was determined in terms of year-to-year change, it was found to be much larger, averaging about 40 percent of the year-to-year change. Thus, these models were not particularly accurate in predicting the change that might be expected in the GNP.

The study conducted by Keith M. Carlson shows the accuracy of the Council of Economic Advisors' forecasts for the period 1962–73.[3] The predicted change, the actual change, and the difference are shown in Table 19-3. It is clear that the year-to-year error varies considerably. On occasion the forecasts were quite accurate, as in 1964 and 1972. On other occasions, such as 1962, 1965, and 1971, the error was substantial, ranging from approximately 19 percent of the actual

[1] Victor Zarnowitz, *An Appraisal of Short-Term Economic Forecasts*. Occasional Paper No. 104. (New York: National Bureau of Economic Research, 1967).
[2] Ibid., p. 4.
[3] Keith M. Carlson, "The 1973 National Economic Plan: Slowing the Boom," *Federal Reserve Bank of St. Louis Review*, vol. 55, no. 3 (Mar., 1973), pp. 2–10.

TABLE 19-3 *Accuracy of Council of Economic Advisors' Forecasts, 1962–73*

	CEA projected change	Actual change	Error	Error/actual change
1962	9.4%	6.7%	2.7%	40.3%
1963	4.4	5.4	−1.0	18.5
1964	6.5	6.6	−0.1	1.5
1965	6.1	7.5	−1.4	18.7
1966	6.9	8.6	−1.7	19.8
1967	6.4	5.6	0.8	14.3
1968	7.8	9.0	−1.2	13.3
1969	7.0	7.7	−0.7	9.1
1970	5.7	4.9	0.8	16.3
1971	9.0	7.5	1.5	20.0
1972	9.4	9.7	−0.3	3.1
Average		7.2%	1.11%	15.9%

Source: Carlson, op. cit., p. 3.

change to as high as 40 percent. The average absolute error was 1.11 percent, and the average actual change was approximately 7.2 percent, which means the average error was in excess of 15 percent of the average change. It appears, therefore, that the CEA forecasts were more accurate than the forecasts studied by Zarnowitz. Nevertheless, it appears that the errors in forecasting year-to-year changes are still quite large.

Probably as important to the investor as forecasting the change in GNP is forecasting turning points in the growth of the GNP. In the Zarnowitz study, the record at turning points was not particularly satisfactory. Actual turning points were missed, and turning points were forecast that did not occur. Since there is little evidence on turning points in the data presented by the Carlson study, little can be concluded about turning point predictions from this study.

In summary, it appears that the relative error in the GNP forecasts will be very small, but the error in forecasting the change from year-to-year may be quite large, however. It is common to use the year-to-year change as the measure of accuracy, and probably the change is the appropriate consideration for the investor who is attempting to forecast security prices by means of GNP forecasts. The above discussion has been couched in terms of year-to-year changes; realistically, the investor should use quarterly data as an indicator of economic conditions. Quarterly data permit a more refined evaluation of economic conditions; downturns or upturns may be evident only by comparing quarter-to-quarter data, while annual data may obscure these turning points. However, Zarnowitz's study on turning points indicates that the GNP forecasting models have made both types of turning-point errors. That is, they forecasted turning points when they did not occur and did not forecast turning points when they did occur. This type of finding is not comforting to the investor. It follows, therefore, that while these models probably will prove useful, there is a possibility that turning points will be forecasted incorrectly.

Money Supply as a Predictive Tool

Recent years have witnessed the increased recognition of the monetarist, or neo-quantity, school of economic thought. This approach places a great deal of emphasis on the money supply as the driving force behind economic activity. In contrast the neo-Keynesians hold that investment expenditures play a major role in determining the level of economic activity. In the neo-Keynesian approach, the amount of investment undertaken depends upon the level of interest rates and firms' expectations. Low interest rates are believed to encourage firms to invest, but the neo-Keynesians also maintain that low interest rates will not assure increased levels of investment because firms may not see any need for additional plant and equipment based upon their current expectations. Consequently, if the monetary authority attempts to lower interest rates to stimulate investment, the desired new investment may not result. In such periods federal government fiscal policy is needed to provide the necessary economic stimulus.

Monetarists, on the other hand, disagree with this approach. Their position is that changes—especially large changes—in the money supply pervade the entire economy. Suppose, for example, that there is an increase in the money supply initiated by the Federal Reserve System. The monetarists agree that the initial effect will be to reduce interest rates, but they assert that this action is diffused through the entire range of assets, real and financial. In other words, the effect of the increase in the money supply must also affect the real sector. Since the return on financial assets has fallen, an imbalance in return has developed between real and financial assets. As a result, investment activity shifts from financial assets into real assets, and for this reason an increase or decrease in the money supply never affects only the financial sector. Consequently, the money supply is considered a potent economic force, and changes in the rate of growth of the money supply are necessary and sufficient for changes in nominal income.

With the growing interest in the monetarist point of view has come the recognition that the growth in the money supply may have considerable predictive power. If the money supply is the primary motivating force in the economy, it follows that it should have predictive value for many economic series, such as interest rates, stock prices, and GNP. In addition, it is a fairly simple approach to use, since the only variable involved is the rate of change in the money supply. At this point the controversy between the neo-Keynesians and the monetarists is unresolved, but there is a growing number who place substantial emphasis on the growth in the money supply as an indicator of the expected level of economic activity.

Money Supply and Business Activity

Recent empirical studies have shown a leading relationship between the rate of change in the money supply and the level of business activity. The data in Table 19-4 shows the lead time of the rate of change in the money supply in

TABLE 19-4 *Turning Points in the Rate of Change of the Money Supply and Business Activity*

In business downturns

Peaks in growth of money supply*			Peaks in business activity		Lead time in months
December	1918		January	1920	13
September	1922		May	1923	8
November	1924		October	1926	23
December	1928	(April 1928)	June	1929	6
July	1936	(June 1935)	May	1937	10
December	1951		July	1953	19
February	1955		July	1957	29
November	1958		May	1960	18
July	1968	(July 1967)	November	1969	16
					Range 29 to 6
					Average 15.8

In business upturns

Troughs in growth of money supply*			Troughs in business activity		Lead time in months
June	1921		July	1921	1
August	1923		July	1924	11
December	1926		November	1927	11
March	1932		March	1933	12
December	1937		June	1938	6
February	1949	(July 1948)	October	1949	8
November	1953	(March 1954)	August	1954	9
January	1958		April	1958	3
May	1960		February	1961	9
December	1969	(February 1970)	November	1970	11
					Range 12 to 1
					Average 8.1

* Computed using a six-month moving average
Source: Sprinkel, op. cit., p. 109.

upturns and downturns. The data covers a long period of time, 1918–71, and is derived from a study conducted by Beryl W. Sprinkel.[4] During this period of time, peaks and troughs in the rate of change (growth) in the money supply consistently led peaks and troughs in business activity. In downturns the peak in the growth of the money supply led peaks in business activity by an average of 15.8 months. However, this varied over a wide range. For example, in 1955 the growth in the money supply peaked 29 months before the peak in business activity that occurred in 1957. In 1928 the peak in the growth of the money supply preceded the peak in business activity by only six months. This range in lead times makes prediction somewhat difficult, but the fact that there is a consistent lead is encouraging.

[4] Beryl W. Sprinkel, *Money and Markets: A Monetarist View*, (Homewood, Ill.: Richard D. Irwin, 1970).

In upturns the trough in the growth in the money supply has also consistently led business activity, but the lead time is only 8.1 months on the average. The range is also much narrower, with the maximum lead of 12 months occurring in 1932 and the minimum lead of 1 month in 1921. Consequently, it appears that the growth in the money supply has a significantly different effect in downturns than in upturns. There appears to be much more uncertainty connected with predicting the downturn in business activity once the growth in money supply has reached a peak than when it has reached a trough. This means that there is a lot of slippage, which poses a distinct problem, although it does not appear to be nearly as significant in upturns as it is in downturns.

When it comes to forecasting the level of economic activity, the monetarists obviously believe that the growth in the money supply is the key variable. Predicting on the basis of the money supply, however, is rather intuitive. Based on the post–World War II experience, monetarists generally maintain that changes in the growth of the money supply are usually reflected in the level of business activity within six to nine months.[5] For example, if the money supply has been growing at a stable rate of 5 percent, the next six months can be expected to be very much like the past six months. If a significant change has occurred in the growth of the money supply, this is normally expected to be reflected in the next six to nine months. For example, suppose an expansion in business activity leads the Federal Reserve System to contract the money supply. By this rule of thumb, the business expansion would be expected to slow within six to nine months. If the Federal Reserve System continues to contract the growth in the money supply for 15 to 16 months, the monetarists would predict that a recession is eminent.[6] If the Federal Reserve System reversed the contraction of the money supply, business activity would be expected to accelerate within six to nine months.

Money Supply and Stock Prices

Up to this point, the focus has been on the relationship between the growth in the money supply and business activity. The common stock investor is really concerned with the effect of changing business conditions on the value of common stock. The important relationship is thus the predictive power of the growth in the money supply with respect to the level of stock prices. Table 19-5 illustrates the relationship between peaks and troughs in the growth of the money supply and peaks and troughs in stock prices. It is evident that this relationship is highly erratic, but nevertheless the growth in the money supply appears generally to lead changes in the level of stock prices.

Peaks in the growth of the money supply occurred generally in advance of the peak in stock prices, with the average lead of 8.8 months. The range of the lead was quite large, ranging from a maximum of 17 months to a minimum

[5] Ibid., p. 120.
[6] Ibid., p. 121.

TABLE 19-5 *Turning Points in the Rate of Change of the Money Supply and Stock Prices*

In stock market downturns

Peak in growth of money supply*		Peak in stock prices		Lead time in months
December	1918	October	1919	10
September	1922	March	1923	5
November	1924	February	1926	15
December	1928 (April 1928)	September	1929	9
July	1936 (June 1935)	March	1937	8
January	1945	May	1946	16
December	1951	January	1953	13
February	1955	July	1956	17
November	1958	July	1959	8
January	1962	December	1961	−1
January	1966 (October 1964)	January	1966	0
July	1968 (July 1967)	December	1968	5
				Range 17 to −1
				Average 8.8

In stock market upturns

Peak in growth of money supply*		Peak in stock prices		Lead time in months
June	1921	August	1921	2
August	1923	October	1923	2
December	1926	December	1926	0
March	1932	June	1932	3
December	1937	May	1938	5
February	1949 (July 1948)	June	1949	4
November	1953 (March 1954)	September	1953	−2
January	1958	December	1957	−1
May	1960	October	1960	5
September	1962	October	1962	1
November	1966	October	1966	−1
December	1969 (February 1970)	June	1970	6
				Range 6 to −2
				Average 2.0

* Computed using a six-month moving average
Source: Sprinkel, op. cit., p. 225.

showing the peak in the growth of the money supply lagging the peak in stock prices by one month. Troughs in the growth of the money supply, on the other hand, do not appear to precede the troughs in the stock market with the consistency exhibited in downturns. The average lead time is two months, and the range is much narrower, with a maximum of six months and a minimum lagging the trough in stock prices by two months. Consequently, there is reason to believe that the peak in the money supply will lead that in stock prices, but there are several cases where a lag actually occurred. It is difficult, therefore, to place a great deal of reliance on this relationship. Even so, this relationship may be useful, as will be shown below.

For the investor who is interested in using monetary statistics to time his investments, a two-step process may be formulated. The first step involves forecasting anticipated business conditions. Once the level of business activity has been predicted, the second step is to focus on predicting the level of the stock market. Monetary statistics appear to offer a promising approach for predicting the turning points in business activity. The evidence indicates that peaks and troughs in the growth rate of the money supply consistently lead peaks and troughs in business activity. In addition, the lead appears to be reasonably long, especially in business downturns, giving the investor ample warning. As a result, the first clue to a turning point in business activity should be provided by a peak or trough in the money supply. If there is clear evidence of a peak or a trough in the growth of the money supply, it may be useful to follow the leading indicators for confirmation of the anticipated turning point in business activity. Once these reach a turning point, a turning point in business activity may be anticipated shortly, and the investor must decide on the appropriate portfolio changes.

The problem of determining the turning points in the stock market is difficult; even after these forecasts have been made with some confidence, the investor's problem is not over. He must still make buy and sell decisions which themselves raise difficult questions. The solution to these can only be derived by an evaluation of all the facts available and relating these to the willingness of the investor to accept risk.

Summary

A common approach to investment timing is to adjust one's portfolio according to anticipated business conditions. When business conditions are expanding, selected common stocks may be expected to have the best performance. Conversely, when business activity slows and economic growth comes to a halt, high-quality bonds may be expected to appreciate as interest rates fall. Switching back and forth as conditions warrant appears to be a desirable strategy. The major obstacle to such an approach is being able to predict the turning points in business activity sufficiently in advance to take the appropriate action.

This chapter described three different methods for predicting major turning points in business activity: the NBER's leading, lagging, and coincident indicators, complex econometric forecasting models, and the growth of the money supply. The method using the NBER's leading, lagging, and coincident indicators has a wide following, and for the aggressive investor the leading indicators are of particular interest. Since the leading indicators include 12 different indicators that may move in different directions at any point in time, a diffusion index was developed to indicate how widespread the direction of movement is among the leading indicators. Econometric forecasting models can also be used to forecast the level of business activity. In general these models are quite accurate in predicting the absolute level of the GNP for the next year, but they are not nearly as accurate in forecasting the amount of the year-to-year change. In addition, these models do not seem to have a particularly good record in forecasting turning points. Although they may be useful to the aggressive investor, caution is required in their use.

An approach that has received considerable attention in recent years is based on the predictive ability of the rate of change in the money supply. If this approach is valid, monetary statistics, particularly the rate of change in the money supply, constitute an important predictive variable. The evidence appears to support the monetarists' contention that peaks and troughs in the rate of change in the money supply precede peaks and troughs in business activity by at least six months. This provides ample time for the investor to take the appropriate action. Unfortunately, the relationship between the growth in the money supply and stock prices is much less stable. A peak in the growth of the money supply does appear to precede a peak in the stock market, but the lead time is quite erratic. A direct comparison between these two series cannot be too heavily relied on.

A course of action that may lead to successful prediction of major turning points in the stock market is to use monetary statistics as the initial indicator of business conditions. If a peak or trough appears, the leading indicators may be closely followed for confirmation. Once confirmation is received, the appropriate change in the investor's securities portfolio may be undertaken. This approach appears to have merit, but there is little tangible evidence of the rewards that may be obtained. Another note of caution should also be raised with respect to the strategy of trading over the business cycle. First, as noted in Chapter 18, an investor may not wish to sell a particular stock even though he correctly anticipates a decline in stock prices. The investor may take this action for such reasons as capital gains taxes, long-run expectations, and aversion to risk, even though he may be able to improve his return by doing so. In addition, large institutional investors have difficulty making major switches in the mix of their portfolios. Generally these institutional investors will build up their cash reserves rather than undertaking major switching within the portfolio.

Questions

1. Contrast aggressive and defensive approaches to investment timing. Which approach would you undertake? Why?
2. What is the function of the diffusion index? Would it not be possible to simply refer to the leading indicators and not use the diffusion index?
3. Macroeconomic forecasting models can give the investor a general indication of the anticipated level of business activity. What information generated by these models is of particular interest to investors?
4. Can these macroeconomic forecasting models be of use to investors in predicting the level and direction of the stock market? Explain.

5. Suppose the Federal Reserve System sells $100 million of government securities. From a neo-Keynesian point of view, what would be the expected effect of this transaction? From the monetarist point of view?

6. How would you explain the apparent empirical fact that the change in the money supply is a fairly good predictor of business conditions?

7. Would you expect the rate of change in the money supply to be a good predictor of stock prices? Explain.

8. Suppose you own the following portfolio of stocks and have a cash reserve of $100,000 for investment in securities. Suppose you have decided to make buy and sell decisions on the basis of changes in the money supply and the diffusion index.

Stocks	*Cost/share*
(1) Polaroid	
(2) 3M	
(3) John Deere	
(4) Union Carbide	
(5) Safeway	
(6) Sears-Roebuck	
(7) Standard Oil (California)	
(8) Occidental Petroleum	
(9) American Home Products	
(10) Revlon	

a. Collect the necessary data for the past year.

b. Set forth specific policy guidelines indicating buy and sell decisions for different states of the market.

c. Under current conditions, what would you do?

Selected References

Anderson, Leonall C. "The State of the Monetarist Debate." *Federal Reserve Bank of St. Louis Review*, vol. 55, no. 9 (Sept., 1973), pp. 2–9.

Friedman, Milton. *The Demand for Money: Some Theoretical and Empirical Results.* Occasional Paper No. 68. New York: National Bureau of Economic Research, 1963.

———. *The Counter Revolution in Monetary Theory.* London: The Winncott Foundation, 1970.

Friedman, Milton, and Anna J. Schwartz. "Money and Business Cycles." Supplement to *Review of Economics and Statistics*, vol. 45, no. 1, Part 2 (Feb., 1963), pp. 32–65.

Hamburger, Michael J., and Lewis A. Kochin. "Money and Stock Prices: The Channels of Influence." *Journal of Finance*, vol. 27, no. 2 (May, 1972), pp. 231–50.

Homa, Kenneth E., and Dwight M. Jaffee. "The Supply of Money and Stock Prices." *Journal of Finance*, vol. 26, no. 5 (Dec., 1971), pp. 1045–67.

Keran, Michael W. "Expectations, Money and the Stock Market." *Federal Reserve Bank of St. Louis Review*, vol. 53, no. 1 (Jan., 1971), pp. 16–31.

———. "A Structural Model of the Stock Market." *Business Economics*, vol. 6, no. 4 (Sept., 1971), pp. 23–29.

Klein, Lawrence R., and Karl Brunner. "Commentary on 'The State of the Monetarist Debate.'" *Federal Reserve Bank of St. Louis Review,* vol. 55, no. 9 (Sept., 1973), pp. 9–15.

Moore, Geoffrey H., and Julius Shiskin. *Indicators of Business Expansions and Contractions.* Occasional Paper No. 103. New York: National Bureau of Economic Research, 1967.

Palmer, Michael. "Money Supply, Portfolio Adjustments and Stock Prices." *Financial Analysts Journal,* vol. 26, no. 4 (July–Aug., 1970), pp. 19–22.

Shapiro, Eli, Ezra Solomon, and William L. White. *Money and Banking,* 5th ed. New York: Holt, Rinehart, & Winston, 1968. Chapter 21.

Solomon, Ezra. "Economic Growth and Common Stock Values." *Journal of Business,* vol. 28, no. 3 (July, 1955), pp. 213–22.

Sprinkel, Beryl W. "Monetary Growth as a Cyclical Predictor." *Journal of Finance,* vol. 14, no. 3 (Sept., 1959), pp. 333–47.

———. *Money and Markets: A Monetarist View.* Homewood, Ill.: Richard D. Irwin, 1971.

Tobin, James. "Money and Income: Post Hoe Ergo Hoc." *Quarterly Journal of Economics,* vol. 84, no. 2 (May, 1970), pp. 301–30.

Trueblood, Lorman C. "The Dating of Postwar Business Cycles." *In 1961 Proceedings of the American Statistical Association: Business and Economic Section,* pp. 16–27.

Warburton, Clark. "The Misplaced Emphasis in Contemporary Business Fluctuation Theory." *Journal of Business,* vol. 19, no. 4 (Oct., 1946), pp. 199–221.

Zarnowitz, Victor. *An Appraisal of Short-Term Economic Forecasts.* Occasional Paper No. 104. New York: National Bureau of Economic Research, 1967.

Chapter 20

Predicting Stock Prices with Market Statistics

An approach that has focused more attention on investment timing than any other is technical analysis. Although not apparent from its name, technical analysis uses market statistics to the exclusion of other forms of data to determine the extent and direction of changes in the market and individual stocks. The type of market statistics used vary somewhat, but generally technical analysis focuses on security prices and volume of trading. In contrast to the fundamentalists, who place major emphasis on the operating performance of firms and industries, technicians ignore these data completely. Technical analysis includes a number of different techniques. One of the most popular and widely used is charting. The types of charts being used vary from the fairly basic line and bar charts to the more complex point-and-figure charts. These charts are interpreted in terms of formations that have specific meanings to the chartist. In addition to charting, technical analysis includes a number of other techniques; unlike charting many of these techniques cannot be applied to both the market and individual stocks. No matter which technique is used, however, the rationale for it follows from a basic set of premises.

Theoretical Foundation of Technical Analysis

Technical analysis has evolved as an alternative to fundamental analysis. The two approaches tend to use different types of data. In addition, the fundamentalist in many cases emphasizes the longer term while the technician takes a short-run point of view. It is common for the security analyst to attempt to forecast three to five years into the future. This approach presupposes a buy-and-hold policy by the investor. For example, many fundamentalists maintain that the investor should buy good quality stocks for the long term. An investor following this approach, therefore, would be oblivious to the short-run vagaries of the market. Technicians take the opposite approach on the premise that trading on short-run swings in the market is more profitable than a buy-and-hold policy. In addition, technicians hold that the key to successful trading is anticipating market developments. Fundamental data, according to the technician, arrives too late to be of value to the security analyst. The technician, on the other hand, can see the trends developing and be prepared to take advantage of these when they occur.

Beyond the question of timing, technicians raise basic questions about the data that is being used by the security analyst. First, many technicians believe that sufficient data is not available, while others do not believe that the published data disclose the relevant facts. Second, technical analysts argue that by focusing on fundamentals, security analysts overlook valuable psychological information available through the analysis of market statistics. The concern about the quality of the basic data used by the security analysts focuses on the accuracy of the forecasts of fundamental variables. Technicians argue that fundamentalists cannot forecast with any degree of accuracy and that even if accurate forecasts are made, they are of little benefit since the market's psychology plays an important role in determining the value of securities. Therefore, while the fundamentals may be accurately forecasted, the market's evaluation of securities may differ significantly from that predicted.

Much of the controversy between the technicians and fundamentalists can be traced to the basic premises of technical analysis. These may be summarized as follows:[1]

1. The market value of common stocks is determined by supply and demand.
2. The factors affecting supply and demand are complex. These factors influence the market and are reflected in the market value of stocks.
3. Trends in stock prices tend to persist for some time. Changes in these trends are the result of changes in the basic supply and demand relationships.

It is evident that technical analysis focuses on the market. No mention is made of earnings, dividends, or any other determinant of value. The value of a stock is the price for which it can be bought or sold. In some respects this view is hard to argue with, but it runs counter to the intrinsic-value concept of the fundamentalists. Furthermore, technical analysis is based on the premise that underlying supply and demand conditions follow trends that are reflected in the prices of common stock. It follows, then, that one should attempt to trade on the basis of these trends to obtain an above-average return. The fundamentalist, on the other hand, holds that anything can happen in the short-run; only over the longer run will the vagaries of the market average out.

[1] Robert D. Edwards and John Magee, *Technical Analysis of Stock Trends* (Springfield, Mass.: John Magee, 1964), Chapter 1.

Charting

Probably the most widely used form of technical analysis is charting. The types of charts used may be line, bar, or point-and-figure charts, but most technical analysts use either bar or point-and-figure charts. Bar charts represent the price range over a particular period of time. For example, the bar may represent the price range for a particular stock during one day. Point-and-figure charts are somewhat more complex in form, but their purpose is the same as other forms of charting.

Bar Chart Patterns

Categorizing the different types of bar chart patterns is somewhat arbitrary and may take several different forms. For example, bar chart patterns may be classified as bullish, bearish, and uncertainty patterns. Since bullish and bearish patterns are opposites, we will use a more general classification of reversal and consolidation patterns. This will enable us to view bullish and bearish patterns simultaneously in addition to the basic consolidation patterns that indicate uncertainty.

Reversal Patterns   Before describing the different types of reversal patterns, the basic concepts of resistance and support levels along with the role of trading volume must be pointed out. Fundamental to the interpretation of reversal patterns is the concept of support and resistance levels. Resistance levels refer to upward price movements. As stock prices move upward, resistance develops to further advances. This results from the underlying supply and demand conditions, since at some point it is believed that the advance of stock prices will be slowed by an increased supply of stock, hence a resistance level is reached. If an upward movement is to continue, the resistance level must be broken. Once a resistance level is broken, technicians expect the market to rise until it reaches a new resistance level. If the upward movement fails to break a resistance level, this is interpreted at least for the present as an indication that stock prices will decline. Subsequently, the resistance level may be broken, but in the interim a pullback from a resistance level would be considered a bearish sign. In a general downward movement, technicians begin talking in terms of support levels. The downward movement means that supply is greater than demand. At support levels demand increases to the point where the downward movement is stopped, at least temporarily. If the downward movement breaks through a support level, the downward movement is expected to continue until the next support level is reached.

It is clear that resistance and support levels are antithetical. The only difference is whether the price movement has been upward or downward. Yet it will be seen that these two concepts are fundamental to the interpretation of all bar chart patterns. In each case, a resistance or support level is a key element in the interpretation of a pattern, as illustrated in Figure 20-1.

The other key element is trading volume, which acts as confirmation for either an upside or downside breakout. Generally, heavy volume is required as confirmation of a particular breakout. For example, on the upside, a break-through of a particular resistance level on heavy volume would be considered bullish. On the other hand, a pullback on light volume would not be particu-larly bearish. On the downside, if there is a breakthrough of a support level on

FIGURE 20-1 *Reversal Patterns*

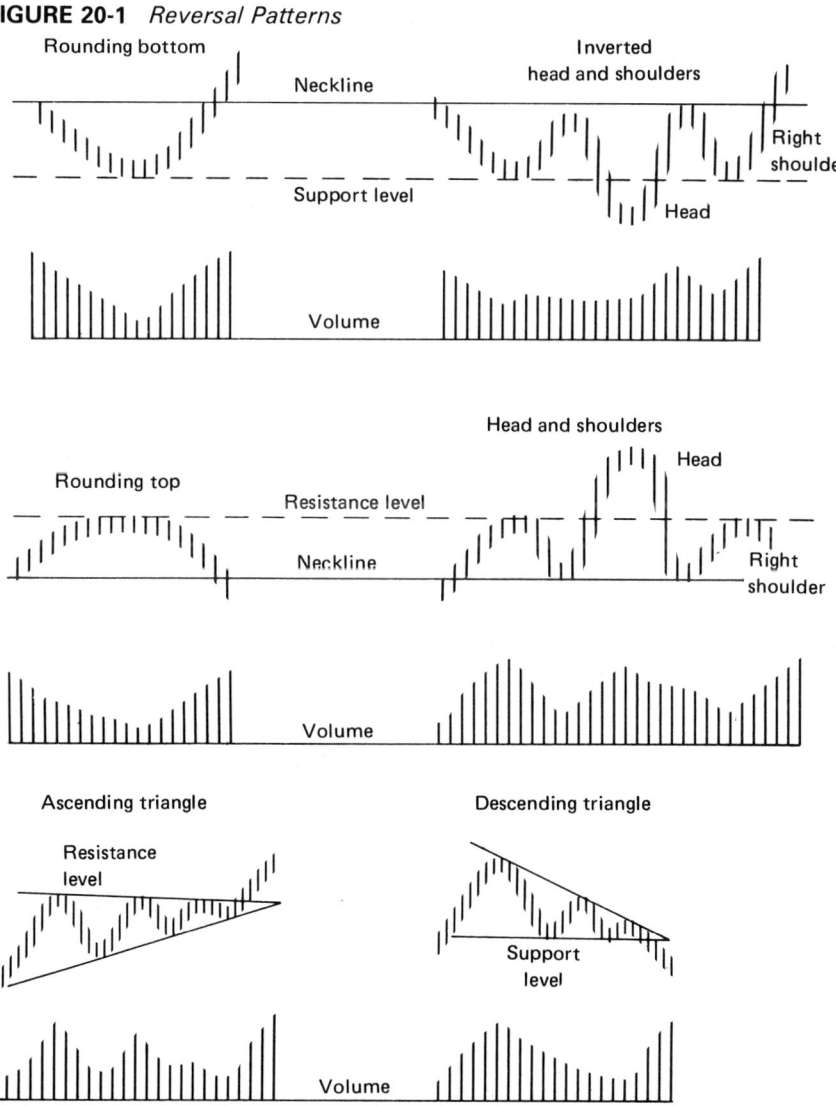

heavy volume, this is considered to be a bearish sign, but if the support level holds on light volume, this would not be considered a bullish sign.

Figure 20-1 illustrates three major reversal patterns. These are the rounding tops and rounding bottoms formations, head-and-shoulders formations, and the triangle formations. Rounding tops or bottoms are probably the simplest formations, since they represent a symmetrical change of direction. This symmetry is also reflected in the change in volume. Rounding tops or bottoms presumably represent a systematic change in the underlying supply and demand situation.

Head-and-shoulders formations are somewhat more complex and represent situations in which the change in the underlying supply and demand conditions are not as clear. The completed formation includes a head and two shoulders. The shoulders form a neckline, which may be considered a resistance level for a head-and-shoulders formation. Once the right shoulder of a head-and-shoulders formation is formed and there is a downside breakout on heavy volume, a downward movement is expected because the neckline, which was the resistance level, has not been broken. Conversely, the neckline constitutes a support level for an inverted head-and-shoulders formation. If the right shoulder is formed, and the neckline is not penetrated, an upward movement is expected. The key aspect of a head-and-shoulders or inverted head-and-shoulders formation is the emergence of the right shoulder. The formation of the right shoulder is evidence that the level represented by the head will not be penetrated at least immediately.

Triangle formations are the third major type of chart formation, but again the concept of resistance and support levels plays a primary role. The key to the direction of the breakout is which side of the triangle is horizontal. If the top of the triangle is horizontal, an upside breakout can be expected. The multiple tops indicate a resistance level, but the fact that the pullback from the resistance level has been getting less pronounced indicates that there will be an upside breakout. This is known as an ascending triangle. On the other hand, when the bottom side is horizontal, this is known as a descending triangle. The multiple bottoms in this case represent a support level; but again, since the upward movement from the support level is becoming successively smaller, a downward movement is expected.

Consolidation Patterns   An important aspect of technical analysis is the premise that the market goes through consolidation periods. After a steep drop, for example, the market may stabilize at a particular level. At this point investors are assumed to be analyzing the situation and developing their investment plans. Once these investors have reached individual decisions, a consensus emerges, which points to the future direction of the market. Casual observation of stock prices lends credence to this premise since there is evidence in both upward and downward movements of periods of pause in the general movement. The most common consolidation patterns are known as flags and pennants. Figure 20-2 illustrates upside and downside flags and pennants. These patterns represent pauses in the general upward and downward movement.

These consolidation patterns are particularly important to the chartist because the consolidation phase is expected to be followed by a new movement which may be a continuation of the past movement or a reversal.

An Evaluation of Bar Charts One of the difficulties of evaluating technical analysis is that there are very few empirical tests of the various tools of technical analysis available. This is true of charting as well as other forms of technical analysis. However, Robert A. Levy has conducted a test of the usefulness of bar charting.[2] His test was conducted on a sample of 548 stocks listed on the New York Stock Exchange for the period from July 3, 1964 to July 4, 1969. A total of 32 patterns were tested to determine whether a greater return could be obtained by trading on these patterns than utilizing a buy-and-hold policy. If charting is really worthwhile, a higher return should be obtained through its use than by using a naive buy-and-hold policy. The buy-and-hold policy was simulated by assuming that the investor could purchase a portfolio equivalent to the Standard and Poor's 500 Composite Index.

The major finding of Levy's study was that some patterns performed better than others, as might be expected, but the performance of neither the best nor

FIGURE 20-2 *Consolidation Patterns*

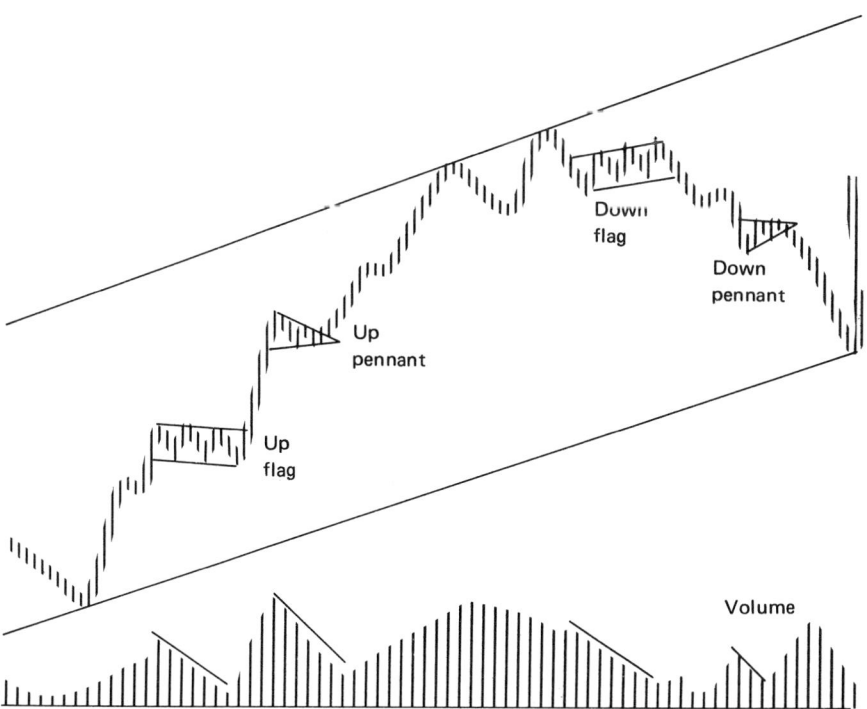

[2] Robert A. Levy, "The Predictive Significance of Five-Point Chart Patterns," *Journal of Business*, vol. 44, no. 3 (July, 1971), pp. 316–23.

the worst patterns was much different from the market in general. These results excluded commissions and transactions costs. Once these costs were taken into account, none of the 32 patterns tested showed any evidence of approaching the return of the market. Levy's study thus provides little support for the use of bar charts. As will be discussed in Chapter 21, technical analysis has received a severe challenge from the random walk hypothesis and the fair game model, as well as from the fundamentalists. The finding of Levy's study is consistent with what might be expected under the random walk hypothesis and the fair game model. A second finding of Levy's study has probably even more serious implications for bar charting, however. Levy found that bullish results were found in conjunction with generally accepted bearish patterns, and vice versa. In other words, the recognized bullish and bearish patterns did not reveal the anticipated market behavior at all. If this finding is confirmed by other studies, the credibility of bar charting is in serious doubt.

One important limitation of Levy's study is the omission of volume statistics. Recall that the technical analyst looks to volume as confirmation for a breakout. As a consequence, his study may be biased against the use of bar charts. Levy, however, believes that this is not the case. Neverthelss, the inclusion of the volume statistics would have eliminated this potential criticism of his study.

Point-and-Figure Charts

Point-and-figure charts were developed in the late 1950s and early 1960s and have become an important alternative to bar charts. Although the basic premises of technical analysis hold for point-and-figure (P & F) charts, the methodology involved is quite different from that of bar charts. First, the emphasis is on the direction of change. This means that point-and-figure chartists are not concerned with small changes. For example, for a stock selling at $50 per share, the P & F chartist may not be concerned with price movements of less than $1. Second, there is little concern with calendar time. P & F charting attempts to compress the price movement of a particular stock; calendar time, therefore, is not a relevant consideration. Finally, P & F charts are generally used only for individual stocks and not for the market as a whole.

The construction of P & F charts follows a generally accepted format, which may be summarized as follows:

1. Small price movements are ignored. However, what constitutes a small price movement is left to the judgment of the chartist.
2. The patterns are formed on arithmetic graph paper by marking the price movements in columns. Generally, X's are used for upward movements and O's for downward movements. As long as an upward or downward movement is in progress, only one column is marked, irrespective of calendar time.
3. There are no gaps in a column.

4. Each time there is a change in direction, a new column is used. That is, each time there is a reversal by an amount greater than some minimum amount, move to a new column.

To illustrate the construction of a P & F chart, suppose we consider a hypothetical ABC common stock selling for $50. For this stock suppose the chartist decides to use an X to indicate an upward price movement of a point or more and an O to indicate a downward price movement of a point or more. It should be pointed out that determining this minimum level is based upon the selling price of the stock. For low- and medium-priced stock, the minimum level may be $1. For high-priced stocks, this level may be higher, perhaps $3. Suppose for successive trading days, we have the following closing prices for ABC stock.

Date	Closing Price
May 1	40
May 2	40⅛
May 3	41¼
May 4	42¾
May 5	41¼
May 8	42
May 9	44
May 10	46¼
May 11	45⅛

Figure 20-3 illustrates the P & F chart for ABC common stock. On the far left, prices are shown in intervals of a point. The 5 in the first column opposite $40 is simply an indicator of the month. The price on May 2 is not large enough to

FIGURE 20-3 *A Point-and-Figure Chart for the Hypothetical ABC Stock*

Price							
48							
47							
46			X				
45			X	O			
44			X				
43			X				
42	X		X				
41	X	O					
40	5						

warrant an entry. However, X's are entered for May 3 and 4, indicating an upward price movement of more than a point; on May 5 an 0 is entered in the next column to indicate a reversal of more than a point. The downward reversal of May 5 is quickly ended. On May 8, 9, and 10 the stock rises to 46¼. This is indicated in column 3 by the X's. On May 11 there is another reversal of more than a point, and this is shown in column 4 by an 0. In this fashion the P & F chartist plots the movement of the ABC stock. Once a fairly substantial history has been developed, the key consideration becomes interpretation. P & F chartists look for breakouts from what is known as congestion areas. A congestion area is similiar to a consolidation pattern in bar charting, where the price of a stock appears to fluctuate within a narrow range. A breakout from the congestion area indicates the direction of the next move. The P & F chartist, like the bar chartist, waits for the breakout to indicate the direction of the next move.

To illustrate congestion areas consider the following P & F charts for the hypothetical ABC and XYZ common stocks. For the ABC common stock, the congestion area is represented by the first 10 columns in the chart. From this congestion area, there was an upside breakout, which is shown by the X's in column 11. The XYZ Corporation, on the other hand, illustrates a downside breakout from a congestion area. The first nine columns represent the congestion area, and the downside breakout is evident in column 10.

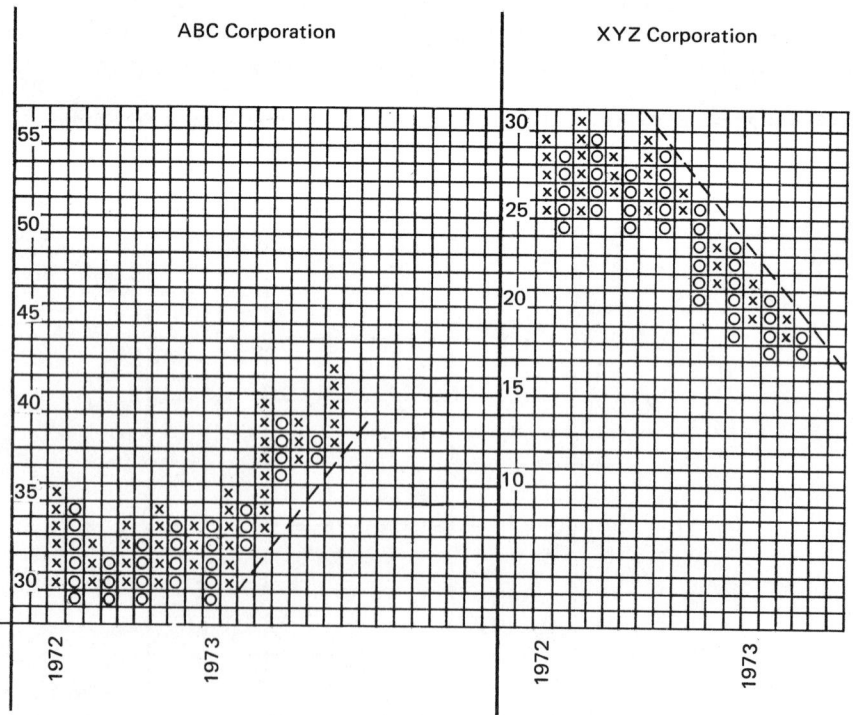

The most interesting aspect of P & F charts is the determination of the move once a breakout occurs. The size of the congestion area is believed to determine the amount of the next move. This is accomplished by counting the columns in the congestion area and multiplying by the scale used. For example, if there were 10 columns in a congestion area and the scale of 1 were used, then an upside breakout would be expected to carry 10 points above the congestion area. The opposite would be true if the breakout had been on the downside. P & F chartists cannot give a reasonable explanation for this rule of thumb, yet they hold that it provides accurate predictions.

Unfortunately, there do not appear to be any reliable studies of the return that may be obtained by using P & F charts. Therefore, little can be said about the type of returns an investor could expect from using P & F charts as opposed to a naive policy of buy-and-hold.

Indicators of the Market

Bar charts can be used to determine the direction of movement for individual stocks, while point-and-figure charts are generally used to evaluate individual stocks. However, a number of technical indicators have been developed to predict the general direction of the market. These indicators of expected market conditions do not indicate which individual stocks should be purchased or sold. As a result, the trader using these indicators is faced with making two important decisions. First, what is the intermediate-term outlook for the market? This decision depends upon the trader's interpretation of the forecasting method or methods used. Second, what stocks will be most affected by the anticipated market conditions? Having correctly predicted the direction of the market does not guarantee a trading profit. The trader must still select those stocks that are expected to be affected most by the predicted course of events. This often is the most difficult decision, but the technician has other techniques to aid in this decision, such as charting, which was discussed above, and the relative strength criterion, which will be discussed below,

Breadth of the Market

This indicator is sometimes referred to as the advance-decline line. It is based on the premise that the nature of the market can be ascertained by the pervasiveness of strength or weakness in the market. The market's strength is believed to ebb and flow, and therefore it is expected to go through consolidation periods. Unlike charting, however, the breadth indicator may give a clue to the future direction of the market before an actual breakout occurs. In a general upward or downward movement, the breadth indicator presumably will give an indication of the strength to that move.

Constructing a breadth-of-the-market indicator is quite simple, which is one of the major advantages of this indicator. All one needs to do is begin cumulating the net advances and declines of issues listed on the New York Stock Exchange. This information is readily available in the financial pages of many newspapers and business periodicals on either a daily or weekly basis. Normally the breadth indicator is calculated using daily data, but weekly data will give the same result. With this information the investor can determine the net advances or declines for a given period. These results are cumulated over time to form the breadth indicator.

To illustrate the construction of a breadth indicator, suppose we have the following advances and declines:

Day of week	Issues traded	Advances	Declines	Unchanged	Net difference
Monday	1,742	441	771	330	−330
Tuesday	1,744	180	1,380	184	−1,200
Wednesday	1,744	942	450	352	492
Thursday	1,732	911	499	322	412
Friday	1,733	763	632	338	131

Those stocks that remained unchanged are also included in the published information, but really do not play a role directly in the determination of the breadth indicator. Column 6 shows net difference of advances minus declines. In the first two days of the week, declines led advances by a sizable margin. However, this trend reversed itself later in the week with advances outdistancing declines in the remaining three days of the week.

As a result, if one were to begin a breadth indicator on Monday, the series for the week would be as follows:

Monday	−330
Tuesday	−1,530
Wednesday	−1,038
Thursday	−626
Friday	−495

In this manner, the investor would develop a breadth indicator. Once a sufficient history was developed, the investor could begin making decisions on the basis of the breadth indicator.

Use of the breadth indicator presents the problem of interpretation. A comparison of the breadth indicator with the leading market indexes indicates that it tends to parallel these indexes closely at both peaks and troughs. Yet there is always the problem of interpreting the breadth indicator and the possibility of a false signal. An example of this problem occurred in mid-1972, as illustrated by Clem Morgello.[3] From November 1971 to April 1972, the market indexes reflected a steep recovery of common stock prices, and in April 1972 it appeared as if these indexes were in a strong uptrend. However, in March 1972 the breadth indicator reached a peak and began declining while the Dow-Jones Industrial Average continued upward. The question that emerges is how to interpret these developments.

[3] Clem Morgello, "A Troubling Indicator," Newsweek, vol. 79, no. 19 (May 8, 1972), p. 102

Most technicians would interpret this development to mean that caution is required. When a divergence occurs between the breadth indicator and the leading stock market indexes, most technicians believe that a reversal is in the making. However, an added factor is that the breadth indicator has given false signals, as in 1963 and 1964. This situation illustrates the dilemma that may face the technician. In this situation most technicians would probably counsel caution, but the degree of concern would vary from technician to technician with some being more pessimistic than others. As it turned out, the leading market indexes continued upward, with the DJIA breaking 1,000 in late 1972. However, 1973 turned out to be a poor market year, with the DJIA falling back to a range of 880 to 980, and late in the year dropping to a low of 780 as the "energy crisis" developed. The breadth indicator may not have been wrong; it had been giving early indications of the market's difficulties.

The Disparity Index

The disparity index is normally used in conjunction with the breadth-of-the-market indicator. This indicator measures the disparity between the Dow-Jones Industrial Average and the Standard and Poor's 500 and is said to confirm a drop in the breadth indicator. The purpose of the disparity index is to determine whether the DJIA and the S & P's 500 have moved together. If not, a correction is expected to be forthcoming. For example, it is not uncommon for the DJIA to rise faster than S & P's 500. If this is the case, the proponents of the disparity index hold that the DJIA will correct itself, and the disparity index will measure the extent of the correction.

To determine the disparity index, one determines the ration of the current DJIA to a reconstructed DJIA. This reconstructed index represents the level of the DJIA under the assumption that it has risen at the same rate as the S & P's 500 over a given time period. The disparity index can be represented as follows:

$$DI_t = \frac{DJIA_t}{\widehat{DJIA}_t} \tag{20-1}$$

where

$$\widehat{DJIA}_t = DJIA_{t-1} + 10(\text{S \& P's 500}_t - \text{S \& P's 500}_{t-1}) \tag{20-2}$$

The reconstructed DJIA, $\widehat{DJIA}_t$, indicates the nature of the correction over the time period from time $t - 1$ to time t. This correction is always stated in terms of an expected change in the DJIA, and the expected correction can either be an increase or decrease in the DJIA.

To illustrate, suppose the DJIA has risen from 900 to 1,000 during the last year. Similarly, suppose that S & P's 500 has increased from 100 to 105 during the same period. Substituting into Equation 20-2 gives

$$DJIA = 900 + 10(105 - 100)$$

$$= 950$$

Substituting into Equation 20-1 gives a disparity index of

$$DI = \frac{1,000}{950} = 1.053$$

This indicates that the DJIA has risen faster than the S & P's 500, and therefore a decline of approximately 50 points should take place. It is generally believed that on advances the DJIA will lead the market as a whole. This view led to the emphasis on the DJIA. Conceivably the divergence could be just the opposite. In such a case, the correction in the DJIA would be on the upside.

Barron's Confidence Index

Barron's Confidence Index (BCI) is based on the premise that the professional investors can predict stock market conditions. Hence, the wise investor would do well to follow the lead of these investors. The BCI attempts to do this through the construction of an index of yields on high-quality and low-quality bonds. When the outlook is bouyant, the professional investors will presumably invest in lower quality bonds to take advantage of the higher yields. As the outlook becomes clouded, these investors become cautious. Finally, when these investors become convinced that conditions are worsening, they begin shifting away from low-quality bonds into high-quality bonds. This shifting with the outlook affects the yield spreads between high-quality and low-quality bonds. The BCI is based upon this relative yield spread.

The construction of the BCI is straightforward and notationally can be represented as follows:

$$BCI_t = \frac{Y_{Ht}}{Y_{Lt}} \times 100 \tag{20-3}$$

where Y_{Ht} is the average yield on Barron's 10 highest-quality bonds at time t, and Y_{Lt} is the yield on the Dow-Jones 40 low-quality bonds.

If the BCI reflected the switching back and forth between high- and low-quality bonds as expectations change, the BCI would tend to rise as optimism increased and fall as pessimism set in. The index, however, would never be expected to exceed 100, since the yield on high-quality bonds would never be expected to exceed that on low-quality bonds. The mechanics of the BCI can be illustrated by considering the following hypothetical data for three time periods:

	Time Period		
	1	2	3
Yield on Barron's High-Quality Bonds	8.0	6.5	7.0
Yield on Dow-Jone's Low-Quality Bonds	10.0	8.5	8.0
Ratio Y_H/Y_L	0.80	0.78	0.88
Barron's Confidence Index	80	78	88

Thus, the BCI was 80, 78, and 88, respectively, for the three time periods.

In time period 1, the spread between the yield on Barron's high-quality bonds and that on the Dow-Jones low-quality bonds is approximately 200 basis points. In period 2, yields on both high-quality and low-quality bonds declined substantially, but the yield spread remained the same, with the BCI falling from 0.80 to 0.78, giving a bearish signal. In period 3, however, the BCI reflects a return of optimism. The spread between the high-quality and low-quality bonds narrows to 100 basis points which indicates switching into low-quality bonds to take advantage of their high yields. As a result, the BCI rises to 0.88 and would be considered a bearish sign.

In evaluating the usefulness of the BCI, criticism has been raised on both conceptual and empirical grounds. Many believe that the rationale for the BCI is somewhat naive. These critics hold that many other factors affect the level of interest yields on high-quality and low-quality bonds. First, an important consideration is the long-run portfolio needs of investors. These needs are not determined by investment timing considerations so much as by other investment requirements such as income and stability of principal. Second, these critics argue that the BCI overlooks supply conditions. The supply of bonds on the market will have a definite effect on the yields of both high-quality and low-quality bonds, and critics of the BCI hold that this is significant enough to influence the yields on high-quality and low-quality bonds.

Finally, a damaging criticism of the BCI is the fact that the spread relationship between high-quality and low-quality bonds is not evidenced in other bond yield series. If the rationale for the BCI is sound, the same spread relationship should be found for other series of high-quality and low-quality bonds. Yet the evidence indicates that this is not the case, raising further questions about the soundness of this index.

The final test of the BCI is how well it has performed. Figure 20-4 shows the BCI and S & P's 500 stock index for the period 1960–73. Based on this period, two observations can be made. First, it is clear that swings in the BCI have been relatively minor, making interpretation difficult. A good indicator is one that will turn sharply at turning points—clearly indicating the turning point. The BCI does not appear to meet this criterion. For example, in 1966 the BCI did turn down, but the decline in the BCI was relatively small, making interpretation difficult. Second, its performance over the entire period appears mixed. In 1962 it gave no indication of the sharp downturn that occurred; in the following period up to 1966, on the other hand, it performed fairly well. In 1969–70, it appears to have lagged the market decline, being of little benefit to the investor during this period.

Since the rationale for the BCI is open to question, and since empirical verification is lacking, the usefulness of the BCI appears to be questionable.

Short-Interest Ratio

Unlike Barron's Confidence Index, the rationale for the use of the short-interest ratio does not depend upon accurate forecasts by professional investors. In fact, the proponents of the short-interest ratio do not care whether those selling short

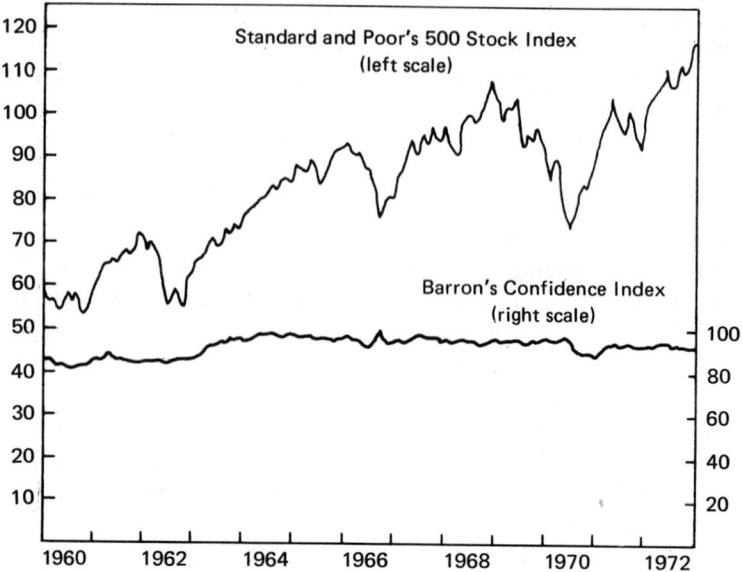

FIGURE 20-4 *Barron's Confidence Index and the Standard and Poor's 500 Stock Index, 1960–73*

Barron's Confidence Index © 1974 by Dow Jones & Company, Inc. Used with permission.

are right or wrong. The important consideration is the support that will be provided for the market by those who sell short. For example, an increase in the short interest is taken to mean support for the market, since these investors will have to cover their positions at some time in the future. A reduction in the short interest, on the other hand, means reduced demand in the future. Consequently, the proponents of the short interest are more concerned with the level of the short interest than with the forecasting ability of those selling short.

The actual calculation of the short-interest ratio is accomplished by determining the ratio of the number of shares sold short to the average daily trading volume. Data on the short interest is readily available for both the New York Stock Exchange and the American Stock Exchange in the financial section of several leading business periodicals. A graph of the short interest normally fluctuates within a narrow range. When the ratio approaches the upper bound, this is generally viewed as a source of support for the market. For example, in a falling market, an increase in the short interest is viewed as providing support to slow the descent. Conversely, when the ratio approaches the lower bound of the range, this means that the short interest is relatively low. This condition is interpreted to mean that there is little support for the market provided by short covering. For example, in a rapidly rising market, a reduction in the short interest is interpreted to mean little support for a continued rise.

Empirical studies have challenged the traditional use of the short-interest ratios. These studies have pointed out that strategies developed using the short-interest ratios have not outperformed the market, which seems to indicate that this indicator cannot be used to generate an above-average return for the investor.[4] Moreover, the typical relationship between the market indexes and the short-interest ratio has been found to be negative, which appears to indicate that the short sellers in the market can predict the general direction of specific stocks.[5] Consequently, an increase in the short interest should be interpreted as weakness and not strength in the market. These empirical studies raise questions about the use of the short-interest ratio that make it unclear whether the use of short-interest ratio can lead to an above-average return.

Odd-Lot Index

The previous two predictors were based upon the activities of professional investors in some manner. The use of odd-lot statistics, however, focuses on the investment behavior of the small investor, the odd-lot purchaser.. The odd-lot theory does not state that the small investor is wrong all the time, but only that odd-lot investors make mistakes at crucial times. The small investor attempts to do the right thing and succeeds most of the time. It is only at the peaks and troughs of the stock market cycle the odd-lot investors take the wrong course of action. In a rising market, the odd-lot investor is usually selling and taking some of this profit. However, as the peak draws near, it is believed that he suddenly begins to buy. At this point he presumably gets caught up in the general enthusiasm of a rising market. Conversely, in a declining market the odd-lot investor is believed to buy as prices are falling; then, near the trough in stock prices he suddenly panics and sells. The odd-lot theory maintains that only at turning points do odd-lot investors take the wrong course of action, and it is this activity that makes the odd-lot index a valuable indicator of subsequent stock market conditions.

In compiling the odd-lot series, the common practice is to use the ratio of odd-lot sales to odd-lot purchases. These sales and purchases are expressed in terms of the number of sales. This ratio is then used in conjunction with a leading stock market index, such as the S & P's 500 stock index. If the odd-lot theory holds, we can look for a change in the direction of the ratio near the peaks and troughs in the stock market cycle. In general the odd-lot index apears to have been a fairly good predictor of turning points in the trough of the market but of little value in determining downturns. A study by Stanley Kaish indicated that buy signals based on the odd-lot index would have led to above-average returns, but the sell signals were of little value to the investor.[6] Consequently, the usefulness of this indicator is greatly limited. Moreover, other

---

[4] Randall D. Smith, "Short Interest and Stock Market Prices," *Financial Analysts Journal*, vol. 24, no. 6 (Nov.–Dec., 1968), pp. 151–54.
[5] Joseph J. Seneca, "Short Interest: Bullish or Bearish?" *Journal of Finance*, vol. 22, no. 1 (Mar., 1967), pp. 67–71.
[6] Stanley Kaish, "Odd-lot Profit and Loss Performance," *Financial Analysts Journal*, vol. 25, no. 5 (Sept.–Oct., 1967), pp. 83–90.

studies have found it to be of little value in predicting turning points in the market, which raises more uncertainty about the usefulness of the odd-lot index.[7] All in all, the usefulness of the odd-lot index, like that of the BCI and the short-interest ratio, must remain in doubt.

Rate-of-Change Analysis

The final indicator of future market conditions that will be discussed here is commonly referred to as rate-of-change analysis. This technique involves the use of a moving average of a leading market index, such as S & P's 500 stock index. A major premise of technical analysis is that supply and demand determines the market value of common stocks, and the market will indicate the end of an uptrend in the market long before it occurs. This impending downturn becomes evident from the general slowing of the upward pressures. The proponents of rate-of-change analysis, therefore, believe that a moving average is useful in determining the strength of an upswing in the market. The most common method is to use a 200-day moving average, but there does not appear to be an obvious reason for selecting a moving average of this length.

FIGURE 20-5 *Rate-of-Change Analysis of the Standard and Poor's 500 Stock Index*

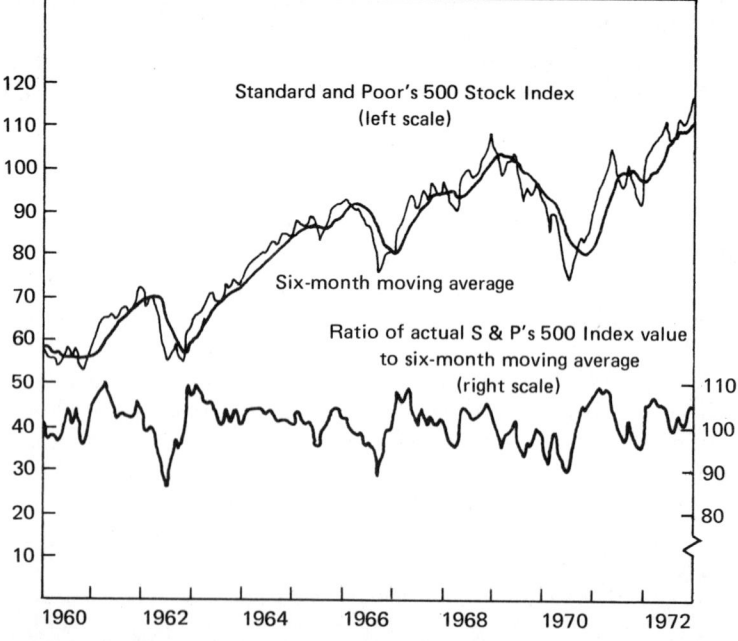

[7] For example, see Thomas J. Kewley and Richard A. Stevenson, "The Odd-Lot Theory as Revealed by Purchase and Sale Statistics for Individual Stocks," *Financial Analysts Journal*, vol. 23, no. 5 (Sept.–Oct., 1967), pp. 103–9.

Figure 20-5 illustrates the application of rate-of-change analysis to the S & P's 500 common stock index. A six-month moving average is used and is shown in the upper portion of Figure 20-5. The ratio of the actual S & P's index value to the six-month moving average is illustrated in the lower portion of Figure 20-5, and the ratio has been converted to index form referenced around 100. The crucial consideration in evaluating the ratio is its position relative to 100. When the S & P's 500 index falls below the six-month moving average value, these penetrations are an indication of a decline in the market. Furthermore, they have occurred early enough in the market's decline to permit the investor enough time to act and preserve most of the previous appreciation. Conversely, when 100 is penetrated from below, this is interpreted as indicating strength in the market. The ratio thus aids the technician in evaluating the market's activity, but its main function is to quantify the strength of the market.

In evaluating the rate-of-change analysis shown in Figure 20-5, several observations can be made. First, it appears that the ratio peaks well in advance of a downturn of the market index. This is evident for every bull market covered during the period 1960–73. Thus, the ratio appears to give ample warning of the impending downturn. For the period 1963–67, the ratio peaked in early 1963, but the downturn did not materialize until mid-1965, and it was quite mild. Generally, however, the lead time has not been so great. Second, there have been several false signals. For example, in mid-1969 and late 1971, the ratio penetrated 100 from below briefly and then turned downward. In both cases these may have been interpreted as indications of strength that did not materialize. Finally, there is the ever-present problem of interpretation. For example, even if the ratio does predict correctly, as in mid-1965 and early 1968, there is still the problem of estimating the extent of the market decline. In both these instances the decline was short-lived.

In summary, rate-of-change analysis appears to have a reasonably good record. All things considered, it and the breadth-of-the-market indicator are probably the best indicators of general market conditions examined in this section. Like all the other technical indicators, however, it is not infallible. It still presents problems of interpretation, and it has given false signals.

Relative Strength Criterion

Charting is a technique that can be applied to either individual stocks or to the market as a whole. The techniques discussed immediately above were designed to forecast future conditions for the market as a whole. However, even though the prospects for the market are predicted accurately, there still remains the question of which stocks to purchase or sell. A technique has been recently devised to answer this question. This technique is known as the relative strength criterion (RSC) and was first articulated by Robert A. Levy.[8] In some

[8] Robert A. Levy, "Relative Strength as a Criterion for Investment Selection," *Journal of Finance,* vol. 22, no. 5 (Dec., 1967), pp. 595–610.

respects this approach is similar to rate-of-change analysis since it attempts to determine the rate of change of a particular stock relative to its industry and the market. The basic premise of the RSC is that stocks that tend to outperform the market in an initial period will tend to do so in the subsequent period. Generally, this initial period is reasonably long, ranging from three to six months.

The RSC for a particular stock can be easily determined by comparing the price behavior for a particular stock with that of an industry index and a market index. Suppose we have the following information about the stock of the hypothetical ABC Corporation, the S & P's chemical index, and the S & P's 425 stock index.

Month	ABC	S & P's chemicals	S & P's 425	ABC/ chemicals	Chemicals/ market	ABC/ market
January 1	40	90	100	0.44	0.90	0.40
July 1	46	92	100	0.50	0.92	0.46

The period covered in this example is six months, with closing prices being used for the ABC stock.[9]

Casual inspection of columns 2, 3, and 4 indicates that both the ABC stock and the industry index have outperformed the market. This is confirmed by reference to the last two columns. Column 5 indicates that the ABC stock also outperformed its industry index. We can conclude, therefore, that the industry outperformed the market and that ABC is one of the better performing stocks within the industry grouping. We cannot say whether the ABC stock is the best performing stock in the industry until we obtain information on the other stocks in the industry. The RSC could be applied to other stocks in the industry and more generally to a large sample of stocks to determine those which had the best performance over the past six months. These stocks would be expected to continue to perform above-average in the next six months.

From the standpoint of verification, the RSC has been subjected to several tests. Unfortunately, agreement has not been reached on the usefulness of this approach. Levy, of course, was prominent in introducing this approach, and his results indicate that superior returns can be obtained by investing in stocks that have had superior performance in the past.[10] These results seem to indicate that the RSC is a worthwhile approach. A subsequent study by Donald E. Pursell confirmed the findings of Levy and concluded that the RSC is an excellent predictor of future stock prices.[11] Pursell gave particular attention to market conditions and found that RSC performed well despite market conditions. These two studies would seem to put the RSC on a solid empirical footing, but the question is nevertheless not settled.

A study conducted by Michael C. Jensen and George A. Bennington has cast doubt on the RSC.[12] Jensen and Benington's sample consisted of 1,952 stocks

[9] A variation of this approach is to use an average of the previous six months' prices. The rationale for averaging is to eliminate any unusual events that may temporarily affect a stock.
[10] Robert A. Levy, op cit.
[11] Donald E. Pursell, "The Relative Strength Hypothesis: A Computer Assisted Stock Selection Test," *Southern Journal of Business*, vol. 6, no. 3 (July, 1971), pp. 24–31.
[12] Michael C. Jensen and George A. Benington, "Random Walks and Technical Theories: Some Additional Evidence," *Journal of Finance*, vol. 25, no. 2 (May, 1970), pp. 469–81.

listed on the New York Stock Exchange for the period 1926–66. Substantial sampling was used to give the best opportunity for the benefits of RSC to be realized, but Jensen and Bennington conclude that the RSC did not yield substantially better results than a buy-and-hold policy. These findings are consistent with the results that would be obtained if the market were a fair game, which will be discussed in the next chapter. Because of the extensive nature of Jensen and Benington's study, the usefulness of the RSC as a valuable predictive tool must be considered unproven.

Summary

Technical analysis has been advanced on two grounds. First, it has been advanced as a timing device. Technicians hold that trading on intermediate swings in the market is more profitable than a buy-and-hold policy. Second, technical analysis is advocated by its proponents as an alternative to fundamental analysis. Throughout Parts II and III, the fundamental approach was taken to security evaluation. Technical analysis, however, is held to be superior to fundamental analysis because it is more profitable and more accurate. A close look at technical analysis raises certain questions about these claims. Certain techniques appear to have certain validity, such as the rate-of-change analysis and the breadth-of-the-market indicator. The usefulness of other techniques is unclear. Most notable within this group is bar charting. No conclusion can be reached on some indicators either because studies are not available or because empirical tests have reached conflicting conclusions. Within this group are such techniques as the odd-lot index, the short-interest ratio, point-and-figure charting, and the relative strength criterion.

Consequently, the investor who might be considering the use of technical techniques either to improve his return or as an alternative to fundamental analysis faces a formidable task. Add to this the evidence connected with the random walk and fair game models, which indicate that short-run trading techniques will not yield a higher return than a buy-and-hold policy, and the usefulness of technical analysis indeed appears in doubt. At this juncture there appears to be little evidence to support technical analysis. Some indicators did appear to give clues to a change in market direction, but it should be noted that these are not unequivocally accepted as valid indicators.

Questions

1. Much controversy in investment management surrounds the fundamental approach as opposed to the technical approach. What is the basis for this controversy?
2. What are the basic premises of technical analysis? What are the implications of these premises?

3. The concept of support and resistance levels is fundamental to bar chart reversal patterns. Explain why this is true.

4. What is the role of volume in bar chart reversal patterns?

5. The following price data for the stock of a certain corporation is for a 25-day period:

Day	Price	Day	Price
1	99	14	101¾
2	102½	15	103
3	99½	16	104⅝
4	97⅞	17	105
5	100¼	18	104¼
6	102	19	102¾
7	101¾	20	100
8	100	21	102⅝
9	105½	22	103
10	104¾	23	104⅞
11	103⅛	24	106¾
12	101¾	25	108¼
13	99⅞		

Using this information, construct a point-and-figure chart. Why did you select the particular scale you used? How would you interpret your chart? Do you have a prediction on the size of the move?

6. Empirical results show that both point-and-figure charts and bar charts give a better return than a simple buy-and-hold policy. Do you agree or disagree?

7. The disparity index is often used in conjunction with the breadth-of-the-market indicator.
   a. What is the breadth-of-the-market indicator?
   b. How is the disparity index used in conjunction with the breadth indicator?

8. Discuss the criticisms that have been leveled against the Barron's Confidence Index.

9. Suppose you had a research project that required you to evaluate the various market indicators. Your objective is to select as good a market indicator as possible. List those that you feel hold promise and those which do not. Give your reasons.

10. The relative strength criterion is a technical approach that can be applied to individual stocks.
    a. What is the underlying premise of the RSC? Is it any different in this respect than bar and point-and-figure charting?
    b. Do empirical studies tend to verify this approach as providing an above-average return?

Selected References

Blumenthal, Earl. *Chart for Profit*. Chicago: Chart for Profit Systems, 1965.

Cohen, Jerome B., Edward D. Zinbarg, and Arthur Treikel. *Investment Analysis and Portfolio Management*, rev. ed. Homewood, Ill.: Richard D. Irwin, 1973. Chapter 13.

Drew, Garfield A. *New Methods for Profit in the Stock Market*, 4th ed. Wells, Va.: Fraser Publishing Co., 1966.

Edwards, Robert D., and John Magee. *Technical Analysis of Stock Trends*, 5th ed. Springfield, Mass.: John Magee, 1964.

Granville, Joseph E. *A Strategy of Daily Stock Timing for Maximum Profit*. Englewood Cliffs, N. J.: Prentice-Hall, 1960.

Jensen, Michael C., and George A. Benington. "Random Walks and Technical Theories: Some Additional Evidence." *Journal of Finance*, vol. 25, no. 2 (May, 1970), pp. 469–81.

Kaish, Stanley. "Odd-Lot Profit and Loss Performance." *Financial Analysts Journal*, vol. 25, no. 5 (Sept.–Oct., 1969), pp. 83–90.

Kewley, Thomas J., and Richard A. Stevenson. "The Odd Lot Theory as Revealed by Purchase and Sale Statistics for Individual Stocks." *Financial Analysts Journal*, vol. 23, no. 5 (Sept.–Oct., 1967), pp. 103–9.

Latane, Henry A., and Donald L. Tuttle. *Security Analysis and Portfolio Management*. New York: The Ronald Press, 1970. Chapter 14.

Leffer, George L., and Loring C. Farwell. *The Stock Market*. New York: The Ronald Press, 1963. Chapter 34.

Levy, Robert A. "Conceptual Foundations of Technical Analysis." *Financial Analysts Journal*, vol. 22, no. 4 (July–Aug., 1966), pp. 83–89.

———. "Relative Strength as a Criterion for Investment Selection." *Journal of Finance*, vol. 22, no. 5 (Dec., 1967), pp. 595–610.

———. "Predictive Significance of Five-Point Chart Patterns." *Journal of Business*, vol. 44, no. 3 (July, 1971), pp. 316–24.

Markstein, David L. *How to Chart Your Way to Stock Market Profits* New York: Parker Publishing Co., 1966.

Pursell, Donald E. "The Relative Strength Hypothesis: A Computer Assisted Stock Selection Test." *Southern Journal of Business*, vol. 6, no. 3 (July, 1971), pp. 24–31.

Seneca, Joseph J. "Short Interest: Bearish or Bullish?" *Journal of Finance*, vol. 22, no. 1 (Mar., 1967), pp. 67–71.

Smith, Randall D. "Short Interest and Stock Market Prices." *Financial Analysts Journal*, vol. 24, no. 6 (Nov.–Dec., 1968), pp. 151–55.

Vaughn, Donald E. *Survey of Investment*. New York: Holt, Rinehart, & Winston, 1967. Chapters 18–22.

Chapter 21

Efficiency of the Capital Markets

The efficiency of the capital markets is of umost importance in investment management. If there are certain imperfections in the capital markets, the wise investor will attempt to utilize these to achieve a better-than-average return. Technical analysis is based on the premise that trends exist in the movement of stock prices. These trends are believed to persist. If they do exist, as hypothesized by technicians, this knowledge could be used to obtain an above-average return. The reason for this above-average return would be the imperfections in the stock market. As a result, whenever the question of efficiency is raised in connection with the capital markets, its importance to the investor hinges on whether an above-average return can be obtained by following a specified investment timing strategy.

Efficiency of the Stock Market

The term *efficiency* has several different meanings. In an economic sense, efficiency in the allocation of scarce resources means allocating these resources so that the best use is made of them. The mechanism for allocating these resources in capitalist countries is the pricing mechanism of the market system. Inherent in this system is the recognition that the parties involved must obtain an "economic profit" (commonly referred to as a normal return) on their capital investment, but not a "monopoly profit" (sometimes referred to as an above-average return). This same meaning applies to the allocation of funds among users within the economy. Generally, the term *allocational efficiency* is used to refer to the absence of abnormal profits among the nation's financial institutions as they allocate funds to the various users. Operational efficiency commonly refers to the actual cost of carrying on the allocational process—collecting funds from the savers within the economy and allocating these to the users.

From the investor's point of view, the major concern is whether an above-average return can be earned by following a trading strategy based on either business and economic indicators or market statistics. The investor's concern is the allocational efficiency of the securities markets. If they are efficient, the investor should be able to earn a normal return but not an above-average return. The controversy over the efficiency of the stock market really came into focus with the early empirical studies, which led to the random walk hypothesis (RWH). The RWH emerged from empirical tests of changes in stock prices which date back to 1900. Initially it was purely an empirical phenomenon without economic content, although the outcome was quite predictable mathematically. Tests showed that changes in stock prices were random. Once it was established that changes in stock prices were random, it remained to clothe this empirical phenomenon with economic content.

Fair Game Model

For all of its controversy, the RWH can be simply stated. It states that the changes in stock prices from one period to the next are independent. Notationally, the RWH can be represented as

$$P_{it} = P_{it-1} + \epsilon_{it} \qquad (21\text{-}1)$$

where P_{it} is the price of stock i at time t, P_{it-1} is the price of stock i at time $t - 1$, and ϵ_{it} is a normally distributed error term. Since ϵ_{it} is a normally distributed error term, knowing the price at time $t - 1$ will not provide any information about the change at time t. As a result, the history of stock price changes will not enable the investor to obtain an above-average return.

With the independence assumption, early random walk theorists also made some rather restrictive assumptions about probability density functions of price changes. Subsequent empirical studies found that these conditions were not met. As a result a less restrictive fair game model (FGM) was formulated. If the stock market is viewed as a fair game, assumptions about the underlying stochastic processes of stock prices are not needed. At the moment these processes are one of the unresolved issues of investment management.

Viewing the stock market as a fair game means that all available information is fully reflected in the current price of the stock, which implies that the investor cannot earn an above-average return based on currently available information. That is, the investor cannot expect to obtain an above-average return during time $t + 1$ based on the information available at time t. Such an interpretation does not require the specification of the underlying stochastic properties of stock prices. At the same time, it indicates that the investor cannot devise a strategy at time t based upon the information available that would lead to an above-average return over the period $t + 1$.

The implications of this FGM for trading strategies are clear. If the market is a fair game, a trading strategy using business and economic indicators or market statistics will not yield an above-average return. The FGM raises serious questions about the usefulness of technical analysis. It holds that technical analysis cannot lead to the above-average profit that many technicians believe will result. The FGM, however, does not necessarily constitute an attack on security analysis. As long as all available information is taken into account, there does not need to be agreement in its interpretation. Consequently, this does not mean security analysis is unnecessary. The only time there is a violation of the FGM would be when some analysts consistently analyze the available information and achieve superior returns.

Although studies are lacking, there appears to be little evidence to indicate that security analysts in general can consistently achieve superior returns. Nevertheless, the FGM raises an interesting question about the cost of research that should be undertaken. If indeed the FGM holds, perhaps portfolio managers should not undertake costly search operations for special situations. The key question here is whether the search will lead to inside information. If this is the case, it may be justified. Otherwise the FGM raises doubts. Some mutual fund managers have taken this point of view and spend a minimum on security analysis. Recent empirical studies point out that the best buys in mutual fund shares are the ones that have the lowest administrative costs.

Empirical tests of the efficiency of the stock market have generally taken three different forms. First, there are studies that have investigated historical price movements. Most of these studies were undertaken in connection with the RWH, but they have important implications for the more general FGM. These studies were generally concerned with determining whether price changes were independent. Second, with the development of the FGM, tests have been conducted to determine the speed of adjustment process to new information. Since the FGM postulates that the current common stock prices fully reflect all current information, it raises the question of how fast stock prices adjust to new information. Finally, studies have been conducted to determine the benefits that can be gained from inside information. The FGM states that current prices fully reflect all known information. Obviously, someone who has inside information would be expected to obtain an above-average return simply because this information is not reflected in the prices of stocks.

Tests Based on Historical Data

Most of the tests that analyzed historical data attempted to determine whether day-to-day changes in stock prices were independent. A number of methods are available to determine the independence of successive price changes. However, the following discussion will focus on the four common methods of the analysis of runs, distribution of price changes, serial correlation, and the use of filter rules.

Analysis of Runs Simply stated, the analysis of runs attempts to determine whether runs persist in successive price changes. Recall that technical analysis makes the assumption that trends in stock prices exist and tend to persist. If this were true, runs in successive price changes would be expected. The analysis of runs tests for the direction of successive price changes without considering the magnitude of these changes. For example, a stock might have the following pattern of runs in three successive periods: $(- - -)$, $(+ + +)$, or $(+ - +)$. In the first period—say, three successive days—closing prices fell, while in the second period, closing prices rose on three consecutive days. In the third, a pattern did not develop.

If successive price changes are not independent, for a large sample it would be expected that successive price changes would be approximately distributed according to a normal distribution. The data in Table 21-1 is taken from a study conducted by Eugene F. Fama involving daily data for the period of late 1957 to September 26, 1962, and the number of observations per stock in the sample ranged from about 1,200 to 1,700. The sample included the 30 stocks in the

TABLE 21-1 *Actual and Expected Number of Runs of 1-, 4-, 9-, and 16-Day Intervals*

	Daily		Four-day		Nine-day		Sixteen-day	
Stock	Actual	Expected	Actual	Expected	Actual	Expected	Actual	Expected
Allied Chemical	683	713.4	160	162.1	71	71.3	39	38.6
Alcoa	601	670.7	151	153.7	61	66.9	41	39.0
American Can	730	755.5	169	172.4	71	73.2	48	43.9
A.T.&T.	657	688.4	165	155.9	66	70.3	34	37.1
American Tobacco	700	747.4	178	172.5	69	72.9	41	40.6
Anaconda	635	680.1	166	160.4	68	66.0	36	37.8
Bethlehem Steel	709	719.7	163	159.3	80	71.0	41	42.2
Chrysler	927	932.1	223	221.6	100	96.9	54	53.5
Du Pont	672	694.7	160	161.9	78	71.8	43	39.4
Eastman Kodak	678	679.0	154	160.1	70	70.1	43	40.3
General Electric	918	956.3	225	224.7	101	96.0	51	51.0
General Foods	799	825.1	185	191.4	81	75.8	43	40.5
General Motors	832	868.3	202	205.2	83	85.8	44	46.8
Goodyear	681	672.0	151	157.6	60	65.2	36	36.3
International Harvester	720	713.2	159	164.2	84	72.6	40	37.8
International Nickel	704	712.6	163	164.0	68	70.5	34	37.6
International Paper	762	826.0	190	193.9	80	82.8	51	46.9
Johns Manville	685	699.1	173	160.0	64	69.4	39	40.4
Owens Illinois	713	743.3	171	168.6	69	73.3	36	39.2
Procter & Gamble	826	858.9	180	190.6	66	81.2	40	42.9
Sears	700	748.1	167	172.8	66	70.6	40	34.8
Standard Oil (Calif.)	972	979.0	237	228.4	97	98.6	59	54.3
Standard Oil (N.J.)	688	704.0	159	159.2	69	68.7	29	37.0
Swift & Co.	878	877.6	209	197.2	85	83.8	50	47.8
Texaco	600	654.2	143	155.2	57	63.4	29	35.6
Union Carbide	595	620.9	142	150.5	67	66.7	36	35.1
United Aircraft	661	699.3	172	161.4	77	68.2	45	39.5
U.S. Steel	651	662.0	162	158.3	65	70.3	37	41.2
Westinghouse	829	825.5	198	193.3	87	84.4	41	45.8
Woolworth	847	868.4	193	198.9	78	80.9	48	47.7
Averages	735.1	759.8	175.7	175.8	74.6	75.3	41.6	41.7

Source: Eugene F. Fama, "The Behavior of Stock-Market Prices," *Journal of Business,* vol. 38, no. 1 (Jan., 1965), p. 75.

Dow-Jones Industrial Average. The table does not consider the sign of the changes; it simply considers the length of the run. The sign is unimportant, since the major concern is whether dependence between successive changes may be expected to exist. It is clear that the actual and expected runs are not significantly different. The largest difference exists for daily changes, but the difference was not significant. However, the difference for the 4-day, 9-day, and 16-day intervals is very small. Thus, the distribution appears to conform fairly closely to a normal distribution.

These findings, therefore, seem to indicate that runs of stock price changes are normally distributed and give little evidence of dependence. Based on this test, then, there is little evidence that the historical information provides any useful information in obtaining an above-average return from a trading technique such as technical analysis.

Distribution of Price Changes   Another method of determining the nature of stock price changes is to investigate their distribution. If changes in stock prices are indeed random, the distribution of these changes for a large sample should be approximately normally distributed. Figure 21-1 illustrates the type of distribution that has been typically found. It is apparent that changes in stock prices do appear to be nearly normally distributed. This has led to the conclusion that the changes in stock prices are indeed independent.

However, reference to Figure 21-1 also illustrates a persistent phenomenon; that is, there appear to be too many observations in the tails of the distribution. Initially this was simply interpreted as sampling error. Its persistence, however, led to the recognition that the distribution of price changes did differ slightly from a normal distribution. Two alternative distributions that have

FIGURE 21-1 *A Comparison of the Frequency Distribution of Stock Price Changes*

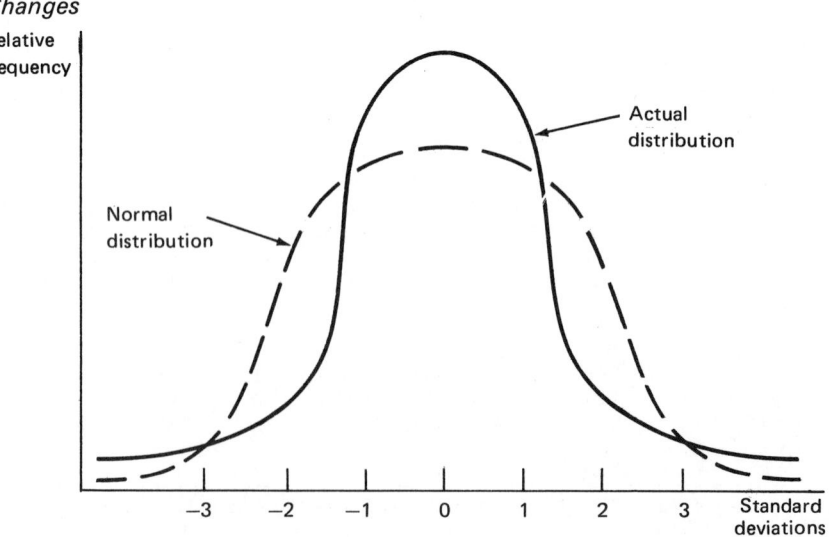

been advanced to explain the distribution of price changes are the stable pare-
tian distribution and the scaled t distribution. It is beyond the scope of this text
to discuss these studies. Nevertheless, it is generally recognized that price
changes are nearly normally distributed and hence random. The real issue now
is determining the nature of the distribution of price changes.

Serial Correlation   The final statistical test of historical data that will be discussed here is serial correlation. If successive price changes are independent,
the serial correlation between them should not be significantly different from
zero. Normally, testing for serial correlation takes the following form:

$$\Delta P_{it} = a_i + b_i \Delta P_{it-1} + \epsilon_{it} \tag{21-2}$$

where ΔP_{it} is the change in price of stock i at time t, a_i and b_i are constants, ΔP_{it-1}
is the change in price of stock i at time $t - 1$, and ϵ_{it} is a normally distributed
error term. This model simply tests to determine whether the price changes at
time $t - 1$ have any predictive value for changes at time t. Equation 21-2 is
formulated with only one explanatory variable. Hence, it assumes that the price
change at time t is fully explained by the change at time $t - 1$.

Results of tests for serial correlation have generally shown that the correlation between successive price changes was not significantly different from
zero. Typical of such studies are the results of a study by Eugene F. Fama,
which are reproduced in Table 21-2. The serial correlation coefficients were
determined for different periods ranging from 1 to 16 days. These correlation
coefficients for the 30 stocks in the sample are quite small, never exceeding
0.25, and generally they are much smaller than this. Fama's results, as well as
the results of other studies, have led to the conclusion that the serial correlation
between successive price changes has been too small to lead to trading profits.
The test for serial correlation thus provides little evidence to contradict the
hypothesis that successive stock price changes are independent.

Filters   Interest in filter techniques developed because of criticism leveled by
professional traders against the statistical techniques used to test for independence among successive price changes. The argument was that standard statistical tools were not sensitive enough to measure the type of dependence that
these traders see in their data. For example, the simple linear relationship
postulated by serial correlation models is not sophisticated enough to discern
the types of patterns that the chartist sees. Similarly, runs tests overlook the
magnitude of changes. For example, a stock may increase by $\frac{1}{2}$ one day, fall by
an $\frac{1}{8}$ on the following day, increase by $\frac{5}{8}$ on the succeeding day, and fall by $\frac{1}{4}$ on
the next day. The net result is that over the four day period the stock rose by $\frac{3}{4}$,
yet there is no evidence of a run in this data.

Filter techniques are a method to test these criticisms and further confirm or
reject the conclusions of the statistical tests for independence. Filters are a
trading technique expected to provide a return greater than a buy-and-hold
policy. Filter rules generally include the following features:

1. A filter of z percent is selected that will lead to a trading profit. For example, this may be a 1 percent, 2 percent, or 3 percent. The size of the filter is determined by the trader to maximize the trading profit.
2. A position is taken, either long or short, in stocks that have increased or decreased by z percent. For example, if a 3-percent filter is used, a stock is purchased once it moves up by 3 percent.
3. Stop-loss orders may be used in conjunction with filters. Generally the stop-loss order is placed z percent below the reference price for a long position.

TABLE 21-2   *First-Order Serial Correlation Coefficients for 1-, 4-, 9-, and 16-Day Changes in Log Price*

	Differencing interval (days)			
Stock	1	4	9	16
Allied Chemical	.017	.029	−.091	−.118
Alcoa	.118*	.095	−.112	−.044
American Can	−.087*	−.124*	−.060	.031
A.T.&T.	−.039	−.010	−.009	−.003
American Tobacco	.111*	.175*	.033	.007
Anaconda	.067*	.068	−.125	.202
Bethlehem Steel	.013	−.122	−.148	.112
Chrysler	.012	.060	−.026	.040
Du Pont	.013	.069	−.043	−.055
Eastman Kodak	.025	−.006	−.053	−.023
General Electric	.011	.020	−.004	.000
General Foods	.061*	−.005	−.140	−.098
General Motors	−.004	−.128*	.009	−.028
Goodyear	−.123*	.001	−.037	.033
International Harvester	−.017	−.068	−.244*	.116
International Nickel	.096*	.038	.124	.041
International Paper	.046	.060	−.004	−.010
Johns Manville	.006	−.068	−.002	.002
Owens Illinois	−.021	−.006	.003	.022
Procter & Gamble	.099*	−.006	.098	.076
Sears	.097*	−.070	−.113	.041
Standard Oil (Calif.)	.025	−.143*	−.046	.040
Standard Oil (N.J.)	.008	−.109	−.082	−.121
Swift & Co.	−.004	−.072	.118	−.197
Texaco	.094*	−.053	−.047	−.178
Union Carbide	.107*	.049	−.101	.124
United Aircraft	.014	−.190*	−.192*	−.040
U.S. Steel	.040	−.006	−.056	.236*
Westinghouse	−.027	−.097	−.137	.067
Woolworth	.028	−.033	−.112	.040

* Coefficient is twice its computed standard error
Source: Eugene F. Fama, "Efficient Capital Markets: A Review of Theory and Empirical Work," *Journal of Finance*, vol. 25, no. 2 (May, 1970), p. 393.

Through such a system of simple trading rules, the degree of dependence of successive price changes can be determined.

To illustrate the use of filters, consider the following filter rules:

1. Take a position in a stock that moves up or down by 5 percent or more.

2. The reference price becomes the new high closing price for long positions and the new low closing price for short positions. Otherwise the reference price is the initial cost of the stocks.

3. Positions are closed if subsequent daily prices are 5 percent or more below the reference price for long positions and 5 percent or more above the reference price for short positions.

4. Stop-loss orders are used to ensure that provisions of rule 3 are met.

The central decision in the use of filter rules is to determine the siee of the filter. Presumably the trader selects a filter that will maximize profits.

Once the filter rules have been selected, the trader follows them to the letter. Consider the use of the above filter rules in conjunction with a common stock that has just increased from 50 to 53. At this point the trader takes a long position at 53, with a stop-loss order placed at $50\frac{1}{2}$. On the following evening, the trader finds the closing price is $52\frac{7}{8}$. At this point he takes no action. On the next day, the stock closes at $53\frac{1}{4}$. This becomes the new reference price, and the stop-loss order is moved up to $50\frac{3}{4}$. Each time the stock reaches a new high with respect to the initial cost, the new high becomes a new reference price. In the following week, the stock fluctuates within a daily range but generally moves upward during the week, closing at $55\frac{3}{4}$. As the stock reaches new reference prices, the stop-loss order also moves upward, until at the end of the week it reaches 53.

It is evident from the above transactions that as the stock price moves above the initial cost, the stop-loss order plays an important role in obtaining a profit for the trader.[1] On the other hand, if the stock prices begin to fall, the stop-loss order limits the amount of the loss to approximately 5 percent. Stop-loss orders, therefore, play an important role in the use of filters. Note that the previous example was based upon a long position, but the mechanics for a short position are just the opposite of those described above.

A major consideration in the use of filters is determining the appropriate filter. There is no reason to believe that one particular filter is always better than others. Conceivably the filter used can be any size, from a very small one to a very large one. This same problem faced researchers attempting to test filters. As a consequence, filters ranging from 0.5 percent to 50 percent have been tested. The results of such studies appear to consistently indicate that above-average returns cannot be obtained with the use of filters. There is some evidence that small filters of up to 1.5 percent produce returns greater than

---

[1] Note that "almost" is a necessary qualifier, since the stop-loss order does not assure the price the trade will obtain. Once the market price reaches the price specified by the stop-loss order, it becomes a market order. The broker then attempts to obtain the best price possible but not necessarily the price stipulated by the stop-loss order. We are also ignoring transactions costs in this example.

those of a buy-and-hold policy excluding commissions.[2] Once commissions are considered, these profits for the most part disappear. Hence, an investor who must pay brokerage fees will not be able to benefit from filters. For filters greater than 1.5 percent, the returns ignoring commissions were less than the buy-and-hold policy. Filters thus do not appear to offer a profitable alternative to the trader.

These results seem to imply that the floor trader could use small filters to generate a trading profit. Floor traders must pay a clearinghouse fee, and if the specialist executes stop-loss orders, he receives a fee. Once these fees are taken into consideration, any potential profit may very well be eliminated by the number of trades. In general it appears that filters confirm the findings of the other statistical techniques. There appears to be little evidence to suggest that past stock price data can improve the expected return of the investor.

Adjustment to New Information

Early investigators of the RWH were concerned with historical data. As it became evident that the market was relatively efficient, the FGM emerged with its emphasis on information flows. The direction of inquiry broadened to include the adjustment of stock prices to new information. The question raised is, how long does it take for the market to adjust to new information? The types of information are diverse and generally assumed to reach the market in a random fashion. Consequently there are many different ways in which the adjustment process may be analyzed. However, the three types of information that have received extensive interest are stock splits, earnings per share, and world events. Stock splits have been the subject of substantial interest since the 1950s because of the interest in the effect of stock split on the relative value of split stocks. Interest in earnings per share and world events, however, are of fairly recent origin.

Stock Splits   There has been considerable interest in stock splits in the last two decades, but much of the attention has centered on the question of whether stock splits lead to an increase in the value of stocks. There seems to be no reason for a stock split in and of itself to increase the value of stocks, since the underlying fundamentals are unchanged. Complicating the analysis is the fact that dividends are usually increased at the time of the announcement of the stock split. The price of the stock may thus increase in the subsequent period reflecting the increased dividend. Separating the effect of these two factors becomes difficult.

Stock splits offer an unusual opportunity to evaluate the adjustment process of the stock market. If the stock market fully reflects all available information, it will adjust rapidly to the announcement of the stock split. On the other hand, if the market were inefficient, an investor could realize a profit by acquiring a

---

[2] For example, see Eugene F. Fama and Marshall E. Blume, "Filter Rules and Stock-Market Trading," *Journal of Business*, vol. 39, no. 1, part II (Jan., 1966), p. 237.

stock at the time of the split announcement. Essentially, the question is whether the split stocks turn in superior price performance after the split announcement. Several studies have been made recently of the behavior of stocks after the announcement of a stock split. The findings by W. H. Hausman, R. R. West, and J. H. Largay are probably the capstone to these studies.[3] Their study was designed to determine whether superior price performance occurred before or after the announcement. It was their contention that superior price performance actually took place before the stock-split announcement and not after. Consequently, the investor could not expect to achieve an above-average return by purchasing the stock after the announcement of the forthcoming split. Previous studies provided little conclusive evidence to support this view. Moreover, Keith B. Johnson had previously found some evidence that stock splits do increase the value of stocks.[4]

The results of the Hausman, West, and Largay study confirmed their hypothesis that the purchase of a stock on or near the day of the announcement of a split will not lead to superior returns. An interesting result of their study is the fact that there appeared to be abnormal price behavior approximately one month before the split, indicating that the purchase of split stocks approximately one month before the announcement of the split would lead to an above-average return. This leads to some interesting speculation about the reasons for this unusual activity. One explanation might be that insiders are buying at this time. An alternative explanation is that security analysts can predict such splits with considerable accuracy. Hence, investors are able to anticipate stock splits. It is difficult to say which of these two explanations is actually the case, but Hausman, West, and Largay favored the former explanation. Nevertheless, the results of this study appear to indicate that above-average returns cannot be obtained by purchasing split stock after the announcement date.

Earnings Reports An important type of published information is the earnings-per share-reports of firms, and investors have become quite sophisticated, focusing their attention on quarterly *EPS* reports. As a result, *EPS* reported in the annual report are generally anticlimactic and only serve to confirm the previously reported quarterly *EPS*. Evaluating quarterly reported *EPS* provides a method for determining the market's adjustment process to newly reported information. In many respects this question is very similar to that of stock splits. In the case of the stock split, we view the market's reaction to an unexpected event, that is, the announcement of the stock split. In the case of the quarterly *EPS* reports, the earnings report is expected. The question that remains is whether the reported quarterly *EPS* have any informational content that will enable the investor to earn an above-average return.

A study of Henry A. Latane, O. Maurice Joy, and Charles P. Jones was directed toward determining whether published quarterly *EPS* data contained

[3] W. H. Hausman, R. R. West, and J. A. Largay, "Stock Splits, Price Changes, and Trading Profits: A Synthesis," *Journal of Business*, vol. 44, no. 1 (Jan., 1971), pp. 69–77.
[4] Keith B. Johnson, "Stock Splits and Price Change," *Journal of Finance*, vol. 21, no. 5 (Dec., 1966), p. 686.

valuable information regarding the future short-run price movements.[5] Fundamental to their study was the contention that the stock market was efficient, but
adjustment to new information occurred with a lag. Consequently, quarterly
earnings data could be used to obtain an above-average return. They used two
tests in their study. First, they tested to determine whether an earnings-price
variable had any predictive power for the subsequent six-month period. Second, they tested to determine whether the ratio of the quarterly *EPS* to the
quarterly *EPS* for the same quarter a year ago had any predictive power. To
evaluate the usefulness of these two criteria, two samples of 350 and 416 stocks
were used. From these samples the 10 stocks with the largest increase in quarterly *EPS* ratios and *EP* ratios were selected. If their hypothesis was correct, the
investor would obtain a higher return by investing in these 10 stocks than by
investing in the S & P's 425 index.

The results of their study bear out their initial hypothesis. The investor could
obtain a higher return by investing in the 10 extreme performers in each quarter rather than the S & P's 425 index. It is interesting to note that a policy of
selling short those 10 stocks which had the largest decrease in quarterly *EPS* did
not provide an above-average return. Consequently, this procedure does not
appear to provide symmetrical results. These results are a direct contrast to
those for stock splits. Several aspects of the study on stock splits raise questions
about the Latane, Joy, and Jones study. First, the fact that above-average returns were obtained with the Latane, Joy, and Jones approach does not necessarily mean that the market adjusts to new information with a lag. It would have
been interesting to see whether there is unusual activity before the quarterly
earnings report. In the case of stock splits, there was unusual activity prior to
the announcement of the split, which meant the split was anticipated prior to its
occurrence. A similar situation may prevail for quarterly *EPS* data. Second, the
fact that Latane, Joy, and Jones did not find the same phenomena for stocks
whose *EPS* have fallen significantly raises the question of whether their
findings resulted from the effects of the elasticity of the stocks in the 10 stock
portfolios relative to that of the market. For example, if these portfolios were
made up of stocks with beta coefficients greater than 1.0, it would be expected
that these portfolios would outperform the market.

World Events Model   A method that may provide insight into the process of
adjustment to new information is the world events model. It is well known that
world crises have an important impact on the stock market. Consequently, a
study of their effects is extremely important since these events cannot be anticipated. Victor Neiderhoffer undertook a study of the impact of various world
events on stocks listed on the New York Stock Exchange.[6]

A study of this type is very difficult because the nature of the data is highly
qualitative. For this reason substantial definitional difficulties had to be over-

[5] Henry A. Latane, O. Maurice Joy, and Charles P. Jones, "Quarterly Data, Sort-Rank Routines, and
Security Evaluation," *Journal of Business*, vol. 43, no. 4 (Oct., 1970), pp. 427–39.
[6] Victor Niederhoffer, "The Analysis of World Events and Stock Prices," *Journal of Business*, vol. 44,
no. 2 (Apr., 1971), pp. 193–220.

come in the ranking of various types of world events. The period covered in Niederhoffer's study was 1950–66. The conclusions of this study are that there was an almost immediate reaction to major world events. If an isolated serious world event occurred—for example, President Eisenhower's heart attack—the market dropped significantly on the following day. If there was a crisis, such as the invasion of South Korea by North Korea, this brought about a marked drop in the market.

The reaction of the market on the days following an isolated world event appeared to be dependent on the results on the first day. Large decreases were more likely to be followed by large decreases. Similarly a large increase on the first day meant there was a greater chance of large increases in the following days. Generally these effects have their greatest impact during the first five days after a world event. These results appear reasonably consistent with the FGM. After a spectacular world event, one would expect a reaction, particularly if it could be classified as having serious consequences. Some investors would immediately sell while others would take some time to evaluate the possible outcomes. In any event, investors would make their decision in a very short period of time.

These findings seem to support the FGM. There are indications that the market adjusts very rapidly to new information, but during this adjustment period dependency among price changes do appear to exist, which is probably consistent with the premises of the FGM. It is an open question as to whether the investor can benefit from this dependency. It is conceivable, but these events are so irregular that it could hardly be used as a trading strategy. Moreover, there is little evidence on the profit that could be earned by following such a strategy after deducting transactions costs. It appears that the more desirable situation would be to have foreknowledge of the world event and correctly anticipate the direction of the market. However, this comes back to the basic question of having inside information, and of course the FGM is based upon the proposition that "insiders" will be able to profit from their inside information.

In summary, a method of determining the efficiency of the stock markets is to evaluate the adjustment process to new information. If the market is efficient, it will rapidly adjust to new information. Studies involving stock splits indicate that superior returns can only be obtained if the investor anticipated the stock split. It appears that unusual price behavior occurs about one month before the stock-split announcement. The increased price activity undoubtedly results because stocks that are split generally also increase their dividends. The increase in dividends, not the stock split, is responsible for any increase in stock price.

Quarterly *EPS* data present a somewhat different picture than that presented by the studies on stock splits. These data indicate that the market adjusts to new quarterly earnings reports with a lag. That is, the market adjusts slowly to new information, permitting the investor an opportunity to obtain an above-average return. This finding contradicts that of the stock-split study and raises some questions that need to be resolved. The world events model cannot add much to the above conclusions, but it does hold up the adjustment process in bold relief. It indicates that the market adjusts relatively quickly to events of world importance, and it presents little evidence that contradict the FGM's premise that the current prices of common stock fully reflect all available information.

Inside Information

It follows from the FGM that anyone with inside information will be able to obtain an above-average return, since this information is not reflected in stock prices. Little documentation exists on the returns that have resulted from insider activity. However, two studies are available indicating that inside information could lead to an above-average return. A study pointing out the influence of the specialist as an insider was conducted by Victor Niederhoffer and M. F. M. Osborne.[7] This study was concerned with the degree of correlation between successive transactions on the floor of the stock exchange. From the studies of the RWH, we would expect changes in price from transaction to transaction to be largely independent of one another. Contrary to the results for daily periods or longer, price changes for intraday transactions were found to be fairly highly correlated, and more surprisingly these were found to be negatively correlated. In other words, there appears to be an ebb and flow effect.

The results of this study indicate the correlation between price change at time t and $t-1$ was approximately -0.25. The explanation offered for this phenomenon involves barriers. It is believed that unexecuted limit orders tend to cluster in the specialists' books and act as barriers to the direction of price changes. These clusters of buy and sell limit orders are normally placed with the specialist. From this information the specialist has some valuable information on the sentiment prevailing in his particular stocks. As a result, the specialist has inside information which can lead to a superior return.

It is unclear whether the specialists have developed trading strategies based upon their "inside information," since the information needed for such studies is of a confidential nature. However, it is known that the specialists do trade in securities. Moreover, a technical indicator has been developed based upon the short selling of the specialists.[8] This indicator is based upon the premise that once short selling by the specialists exceeds 1.5 million shares in a given week, this is an indication of weakness in the market. This indicator has apparently performed quite well, at least until recently. Although specialists do trade —presumably successfully—it does not necessarily mean that they do so on the basis of the information in their books. Intuitively, however, it appears that this information would influence their decisions.

---

[7] Victor Niederhoffer and M. F. M. Osborne "Market Making and Reversal on the Stock Exchange," *Journal of the American Statistical Association,* vol. 61, no. 316 (Dec., 1966), pp. 897–916.
[8] William A. Kent, *The Smart Money* (Garden City, N. Y.: Doubleday, 1972).

A study by James A. Lorie and Victor Niederhoffer is available on insider trading that provides more insight into the benefits that can be gained from inside information.[9] Insiders are defined as officers, directors, and owners of 10 percent or more of the common stock listed on the new York and American Stock Exchanges. Lorie and Niederhoffer conclude that prompt and proper analysis of the data on insider trading can be profitable. This conclusion is consistent with the FGM. Their study covered the period of 1950–61 and used a random sample of 105 NYSE firms. They concluded that when insiders accumulate a stock intensively, that stock will outperform the market during the next six months. More importantly, insiders tend to be good predictors of major changes in stock prices. By and large they tend to buy before large price increases and sell before large price decreases. Finally, a change in insider activity tends to indicate a change in expectations concerning a particular stock. Thus, if insiders have been purchasing a particular stock on a regular basis and then start selling, this reversal probably indicates a change in expectations.

Consequently, the Lorie-Neiderhoffer study seems to confirm the fairly prevalent Wall Street view that insiders tend to benefit from their inside information. This finding is consistent with the FGM. It thus appears that the empirical verification of the FGM is all but complete.

Efficiency in the Bond Market

While the stock market is generally accepted to be efficient, the bond market is not generally believed to be nearly as efficient. This results mainly from the nature of the major participants, which are the federal government and the large financial institutions. Federal government transactions affect the bond market in many ways. For example, interest rates have been used as an indicator of economic conditions, with the result that monetary and fiscal policy have been geared to obtain the desired economic impact. Federal government debt management policies also have an important impact upon the bond market. Similarly, the Federal Reserve may be attempting to obtain a desired economic objective, for example, to expand or contract credit to spur or slow economic expansion. The impact of these two government agencies can lead to imperfections in the bond market.

In the private sector, large financial institutions are the leading purchasers of long-term bonds. Table 21-3 illustrates the dominant purchasers of corporate and foreign bonds during the period 1960–73. The figures do not include government debt instruments and therefore do not include the entire bond market. Nevertheless, they do illustrate the importance of financial institutions on the bond market. For corporate and foreign bonds, the leading purchasers are insurance companies, pension funds, and mutual funds. With these large financial institutions making up nearly 50 percent of the market, there is a

[9] James A. Lorie and Victor Niederhoffer, "Predictive and Statistical Properties of Insider Training," *Journal of Law and Economics*, vol. 11, no. 1 (Apr., 1968), pp. 35–54.

TABLE 21-3 *Purchasers of Corporate and Foreign Bond for Selected Years, 1960–72 (in $ Billions)*

Purchaser	1960	1965	1970	1972
Households	1.1	−0.8	12.6	4.9
State & local governments	1.1	5.1	0.2	0.0
Commercial banks	−0.2	0.0	0.5	1.7
Nonbank financial institutions	3.6	5.0	10.7	13.5
Rest of world	0.1	0.0	0.5	0.0
	5.7	9.3	24.5	20.1

Source: Federal Reserve Board's Flow of Funds Accounts.

greater potential for imperfections to develop in the bond market. The following discussion will cite only one example of these imperfections. Undoubtedly there are other instances of imperfections, but this example, which is taken from *Fortune's Guide to Personal Investing*, will be useful to illustrate that the bond market is not efficient in the fair game sense.[10]

The example illustrates how an investor in a high-tax bracket buying deep discount bonds on margin could earn an exceptionally high return with virtually no risk in May of 1969. At that time there were a number of Aaa and Aa deep discount bonds maturing in the mid-1970s. If the investor in the high-tax brackets purchased these and held them to maturity, he could be assured of an after-tax return of 6 percent or more. Consider R. J. Reynolds 3s of 1973 selling for 84⅛. Under the Federal Reserve rules in existence at that time, these bonds could be purchased on a 25 percent margin with the interest cost of 8 percent. Suppose an investor in the 50-percent tax bracket purchased 100 of these bonds. The total cost of the transaction would be $84,125, of which the investor would have to put up $21,031. The next interest cost—that is, the cost on the amount borrowed minus the interest paid on the bond—would be $10,385, which could be written off for tax purposes. Thus, the after-tax interest cost would be $5,192.

The profit realized on this transaction would be the capital appreciation minus capital gains taxes and the interest expense. These figures are summarized as follows:

Gross profit	Capital gains taxes	After-tax net interest cost	Net profit
$15,875	$3,969	$5,192	$6,714

A net profit of $6,714 gives an average rate of return of 6,714/21,031 = 0.319 or 31.9 percent. On an annual basis, that is an average return of approximately 7.2 percent with virtually no risk.

The reason that such investors could obtain this above-average return is that the major purchasers of bonds are financial institutions. These financial institutions are subject to special tax provisions and derive little benefit from the lower capital-gains tax rate. These institutions purchase for cash and hence do

---

[10] "Stealing in the Bond Market," *Fortune's Guide to Personal Investing* (Chicago: Time, Inc., 1969), pp. 132–34.

not obtain the benefits of margin buying. As a result, for certain investors there may be an opportunity to profit from the nature of the corporate bond market. This is in marked contrast to the stock market. In the stock market, it appears that one would have to look long and hard to find an opportunity for an above-average return and would probably accept substantial risk in doing so. In the bond market, an opportunity for an above-average return was readily available with low search costs and very little risk. This illustrates the types of opportunities that can emerge in an imperfect market.

Some Concluding Remarks

Studies of the efficiency of the stock market have tended to indicate that it is a fair game. In other words, all investors are on an equal footing when it comes to buying and selling stock in the markets, with the exception of those who have inside information. This means that the use of such special techniques as technical analysis will probably not lead to consistent above-average gains. It also means that the expected return for a given stock is the best unbiased estimator of the return that may be anticipated. It points out the necessity of portfolios, since this is the only way to be assured of obtaining the expected return over time. From an economic point of view, the stock markets represent a most desirable development, since imperfections represent a cost to society as a whole. Yet to the investor this efficiency is many times a source of frustration.

Imperfect markets permit enterprising individuals a greater opportunity for personal gain. The example from the corporate bond market illustrates this. The fact that the market appears efficient is a valuable bit of information for any investor. He should not generally expect to obtain an above-average return over time from investing in stocks. It is conceivable that the investor could obtain an above-average return, but the efficiency of the stock market greatly reduces the probability of doing so. For the investor contemplating such as an undertaking, careful consideration should be given to the costs of research. In an efficient market, costs of research to uncover unusual opportunities are not normally recovered. Consequently, an investor may not want to undertake extensive research activities.

Questions

1. The random walk hypothesis (RWH) has led to the development of the fair game model (FGM).
   a. Contrast the RWH with the FGM.
   b. Why is the FGM preferred to the RWH?
   c. What is the role of information in the FGM?
2. What are four ways in which historical data can be used to test the FGM? Explain each. What particular advantages do filters have over the others?

3. A successful investor believes the stock market is efficient but adjusts to new information with a sufficient lag for the astute investor to gain an above-average return.
   a. In what ways does this belief run counter to the FGM?
   b. Based upon the study by Hausman, West, and Largay on the adjustment process to stock-split announcement, would this investor's contention seem plausible?
   c. Based upon Neiderhoffer's world events model, would the adjustment process seem to occur over a fairly long period?

4. An investor believes that the stock market is perfect, meaning that it has no imperfections of any sort. Can you cite illustrations of imperfections that exist even though they may not be sufficient to lead to an above-average return?

5. Inside information appears to be a sufficient basis for obtaining an above-average return.
   a. Is this conclusion consistent with the FGM?
   b. What do empirical studies seem to indicate?
   c. The specialist may be viewed as having inside information. Explain.

6. What factors may be considered imperfections in the bond market?

Selected References

Bachelier, Louis. *Théorie de la Speculation*. Paris: Gauthier-Villars, 1900.

Cootner, Paul H. "Stock Prices: Random vs. System Changes." *Industrial Management Review*, vol. 3, no. 2 (Spring, 1962), pp. 24–45.

Cheng, Pao L., and M. King Deets. "Portfolio Returns and the Random Walk Theory." *Journal of Finance*, vol. 26, no. 1 (Mar., 1971), pp. 11–31.

Fama, Eugene F. "The Behavior of Stock Market Prices," *Journal of Business*, vol. 38, no. 1 (Jan., 1965), pp. 34–105.

————. "Efficient Capital Markets: A Review of Theory and Empirical Work." *Journal of Finance*, vol. 25, no. 2 (May, 1970), pp. 383–419.

Fama, Eugene F., and Marshall E. Blume. "Filter Rules and Stock-Market Trading." *Journal of Business*, vol. 39, no. 1, part II (Jan., 1966), pp. 226–41.

Fama, Eugene F., Lawrence Fisher, Michael C. Jensen, and Richard Roll. "The Adjustment of Stock Prices to New Information." *International Economic Review*, vol. 10, no. 1 (Feb., 1969), pp. 1–22.

Godfrey, Michael D., Clive W. J. Granger, and Oskar Morgenstern. "The Random-Walk Hypothesis of Stock Market Behavior." *Kyklos*, vol. 17 (1964), pp. 1–30.

Granger, Clive W. J., and Oskar Morganstern. "Spectral Analysis of New York Stock Market Prices." *Kyklos*, vol. 16 (1963), p. 1–26.

————. *Predictability of Stock Market Prices*. Lexington, Mass.: D. C. Heath, 1970.

Hausman, W. H., R. R. West, and J. A. Largay. "Stock Splits, Price Changes, and Trading Profits: A Synthesis." *Journal of Business*, vol. 44, no. 1 (Jan., 1971), pp. 69–77.

Johnson, Keith B. "Stock Splits and Price Change." *Journal of Finance*, vol. 21, no. 5 (Dec., 1966), pp. 675–86.

Latane, Henry A. O., Maurice Joy, and Charles P. Jones. "Quarterly Data, Sort-Rank Routines, and Security Evaluation." *Journal of Business*, vol. 43, no. 4 (Oct., 1970), pp. 427–39.

Lorie, James A., and Victor Neiderhoffer. "Predictive and Statistical Properties of Insider Trading." *Journal of Law and Economics*, vol. 11, no. 1 (Apr., 1968), pp. 35–54.

Neiderhoffer, Victor. "The Analysis of World Events and Stock Prices." *Journal of Business*, vol. 44, no. 2 (Apr., 1971), pp. 193–219.

Neiderhoffer, Victor, and M. F. M. Osborne, "Market Making and Reversal on the Stock Market." *Journal of the American Statistical Association*, vol. 61, no. 316 (Dec., 1966), pp. 897–916.

Niarchos, N. A., and C. W. J. Granger. "The Gold Sovereign Market in Greece—An Unusual Speculative Market." *Journal of Finance*, vol. 27, no. 5 (Dec., 1972), pp. 1127–36.

Owen, Joel. "Analysis of Variance Tests for Local Trends in the Standard and Poor's Index." *Journal of Finance*, vol. 23, no. 3 (June, 1968), pp. 509–14.

Pettit, R. Richardson. "Dividend Announcements, Security Performance, and Capital Market Efficiency." *Journal of Finance*, vol. 27, no. 2 (Dec., 1972), pp. 993–1008.

Reilly, Frank K., and Eugene F. Drzycimski. "Test of Stock Market Efficiency Following Major Events." *Journal of Business Research*, vol. 1, no. 1 (Summer, 1973), pp. 57–73.

Schmidt, Seymour. "A New Look at the Random-Walk Hypothesis." *Journal of Financial and Quantitative Analysis*, vol. 3, no. 3 (Sept., 1968), pp. 235–61.

Appendix

Table A-1 *Present Value of One Dollar at the End of N Years at Rth Percent*

N	1%	2%	3%	4%	5%	6%	7%	8%	9%	10%
1	.99010	.98039	.97087	.96154	.95238	.94340	.93458	.92593	.91743	.90909
2	.98030	.96117	.94260	.92456	.90703	.89000	.87344	.85734	.84168	.82645
3	.97059	.94232	.91514	.88900	.86384	.83962	.81630	.79383	.77219	.75132
4	.96099	.92385	.88849	.85481	.82271	.79210	.76290	.73503	.70843	.68302
5	.95147	.90573	.86261	.82193	.78353	.74726	.71299	.68059	.64993	.62092
6	.94205	.88798	.83749	.79032	.74622	.70496	.66635	.63017	.59627	.56448
7	.93273	.87056	.81310	.75992	.71069	.66506	.62275	.58349	.54704	.51316
8	.92349	.85350	.78941	.73069	.67684	.62742	.58201	.54027	.50187	.46651
9	.91435	.83676	.76642	.70259	.64461	.59190	.54394	.50025	.46043	.42410
10	.90530	.82035	.74410	.67557	.61392	.55840	.50835	.46320	.42241	.38555
11	.89634	.80427	.72243	.64958	.58469	.52679	.47510	.42889	.38754	.35050
12	.88746	.78850	.70139	.62460	.55684	.49698	.44402	.39712	.35554	.31863
13	.87868	.77304	.68096	.60058	.53033	.46884	.41497	.36770	.32618	.28967
14	.86998	.75788	.66113	.57748	.50507	.44231	.38782	.34046	.29925	.26333
15	.86137	.74302	.64187	.55527	.48102	.41727	.36245	.31524	.27454	.23940
16	.85284	.72846	.62318	.53391	.45812	.39365	.33874	.29189	.25187	.21763
17	.84440	.71417	.60502	.51338	.43630	.37137	.31658	.27027	.23108	.19785
18	.83604	.70017	.58740	.49363	.41553	.35035	.29587	.25025	.21200	.17986
19	.82776	.68644	.57030	.47465	.39574	.33052	.27651	.23171	.19449	.16351
20	.81957	.67298	.55369	.45639	.37690	.31181	.25842	.21455	.17843	.14865
21	.81145	.65979	.53756	.43884	.35895	.29416	.24152	.19866	.16370	.13513
22	.80342	.64685	.52190	.42196	.34186	.27751	.22572	.18394	.15018	.12285
23	.79547	.63417	.50670	.40573	.32558	.26180	.21095	.17032	.13778	.11168
24	.78759	.62173	.49194	.39013	.31008	.24698	.19715	.15770	.12641	.10153
25	.77979	.60954	.47762	.37512	.29531	.23300	.18425	.14602	.11597	.09230
26	.77207	.59759	.46370	.36069	.28125	.21982	.17220	.13520	.10640	.08391
27	.76443	.58588	.45020	.34682	.26786	.20737	.16093	.12519	.09761	.07628
28	.75686	.57439	.43709	.33348	.25510	.19564	.15041	.11592	.08955	.06935
29	.74937	.56313	.42436	.32066	.24295	.18456	.14057	.10733	.08216	.06304
30	.74195	.55208	.41200	.30832	.23138	.17412	.13137	.09938	.07537	.05731

Table A-1 *(Continued)*

N	11%	12%	13%	14%	15%	16%	17%	18%	19%	20%
1	.90090	.89286	.88496	.87719	.86957	.86207	.85470	.84746	.84034	.83333
2	.81162	.79719	.78315	.76947	.75614	.74316	.73051	.71819	.70617	.69445
3	.73119	.71178	.69305	.67497	.65752	.64066	.62437	.60863	.59342	.57870
4	.65873	.63552	.61332	.59208	.57175	.55229	.53365	.51579	.49867	.48225
5	.59345	.56743	.54276	.51937	.49718	.47611	.45611	.43711	.41905	.40188
6	.53464	.50663	.48032	.45559	.43233	.41044	.38984	.37043	.35214	.33490
7	.48166	.45235	.42506	.39964	.37594	.35383	.33320	.31393	.29592	.27908
8	.43393	.40388	.37616	.35056	.32690	.30503	.28478	.26604	.24867	.23257
9	.39093	.36061	.33289	.30751	.28426	.26295	.24341	.22546	.20897	.19381
10	.35219	.32197	.29459	.26975	.24719	.22668	.20804	.19107	.17560	.16151
11	.31729	.28748	.26070	.23662	.21494	.19542	.17781	.16192	.14757	.13459
12	.28584	.25668	.23071	.20756	.18691	.16846	.15198	.13722	.12401	.11216
13	.25752	.22918	.20417	.18207	.16253	.14523	.12989	.11629	.10421	.09346
14	.23200	.20462	.18068	.15971	.14133	.12520	.11102	.09855	.08757	.07789
15	.20901	.18270	.15989	.14010	.12290	.10793	.09489	.08352	.07359	.06491

Table A-1   *(Continued)*

N	11%	12%	13%	14%	15%	16%	17%	18%	19%	20%
16	.18829	.16312	.14150	.12289	.10687	.09304	.08110	.07078	.06184	.05409
17	.16963	.14565	.12522	.10780	.09293	.08021	.06932	.05998	.05196	.04507
18	.15282	.13004	.11081	.09456	.08081	.06914	.05925	.05083	.04367	.03756
19	.13768	.11611	.09807	.08295	.07027	.05961	.05064	.04308	.03670	.03130
20	.12404	.10367	.08678	.07276	.06110	.05139	.04328	.03651	.03084	.02608
21	.11174	.09256	.07680	.06383	.05313	.04430	.03699	.03094	.02591	.02174
22	.10067	.08264	.06796	.05599	.04620	.03819	.03162	.02622	.02178	.01811
23	.09069	.07379	.06015	.04911	.04018	.03292	.02702	.02222	.01830	.01510
24	.08171	.06588	.05323	.04308	.03493	.02838	.02310	.01883	.01538	.01258
25	.07361	.05882	.04710	.03779	.03038	.02447	.01974	.01596	.01292	.01048
26	.06631	.05252	.04168	.03315	.02642	.02109	.01687	.01352	.01086	.00874
27	.05974	.04689	.03689	.02908	.02297	.01818	.01442	.01146	.00913	.00728
28	.05382	.04187	.03265	.02551	.01997	.01567	.01233	.00971	.00767	.00607
29	.04849	.03738	.02889	.02238	.01737	.01351	.01053	.00823	.00644	.00506
30	.04368	.03338	.02557	.01963	.01510	.01165	.00900	.00698	.00542	.00421

Table A-1   *(Continued)*

N	21%	22%	23%	24%	25%	26%	27%	28%	29%	30%
1	.82645	.81967	.81301	.80645	.80000	.79365	.78740	.78125	.77519	.76923
2	.68301	.67186	.66098	.65036	.64000	.62988	.62000	.61035	.60093	.59172
3	.56448	.55071	.53738	.52449	.51200	.49991	.48819	.47684	.46583	.45517
4	.46651	.45140	.43690	.42297	.40960	.39675	.38440	.37253	.36111	.35013
5	.38555	.37000	.35520	.34111	.32768	.31488	.30268	.29104	.27993	.26933
6	.31863	.30328	.28878	.27509	.26214	.24991	.23833	.22737	.21700	.20718
7	.26333	.24859	.23478	.22185	.20972	.19834	.18766	.17764	.16822	.15937
8	.21763	.20376	.19088	.17891	.16777	.15741	.14777	.13878	.13040	.12259
9	.17986	.16702	.15519	.14428	.13422	.12493	.11635	.10842	.10109	.09430
10	.14865	.13690	.12617	.11636	.10737	.09915	.09161	.08470	.07836	.07254
11	.12285	.11221	.10258	.09383	.08590	.07869	.07214	.06617	.06075	.05580
12	.10153	.09198	.08340	.07567	.06872	.06245	.05680	.05170	.04709	.04292
13	.08391	.07539	.06780	.06103	.05498	.04957	.04473	.04039	.03650	.03302
14	.06934	.06180	.05512	.04922	.04398	.03934	.03522	.03155	.02830	.02540
15	.05731	.05065	.04482	.03969	.03518	.03122	.02773	.02465	.02194	.01954
16	.04736	.04152	.03644	.03201	.02815	.02478	.02183	.01926	.01700	.01503
17	.03914	.03403	.02962	.02581	.02252	.01967	.01719	.01505	.01318	.01156
18	.03235	.02790	.02408	.02082	.01801	.01561	.01354	.01176	.01022	.00889
19	.02674	.02286	.01958	.01679	.01441	.01239	.01066	.00918	.00792	.00684
20	.02210	.01874	.01592	.01354	.01153	.00983	.00839	.00717	.00614	.00526
21	.01826	.01536	.01294	.01092	.00922	.00780	.00661	.00561	.00476	.00405
22	.01509	.01259	.01052	.00880	.00738	.00619	.00520	.00438	.00369	.00311
23	.01247	.01032	.00855	.00710	.00590	.00491	.00410	.00342	.00286	.00240
24	.01031	.00846	.00695	.00573	.00472	.00390	.00323	.00267	.00222	.00184
25	.00852	.00693	.00565	.00462	.00378	.00310	.00254	.00209	.00172	.00142
26	.00704	.00568	.00460	.00372	.00302	.00246	.00200	.00163	.00133	.00109
27	.00582	.00466	.00374	.00300	.00242	.00195	.00158	.00127	.00103	.00084
28	.00481	.00382	.00304	.00242	.00193	.00155	.00124	.00100	.00080	.00065
29	.00397	.00313	.00247	.00195	.00155	.00123	.00098	.00078	.00062	.00050
30	.00328	.00257	.00201	.00158	.00124	.00097	.00077	.00061	.00048	.00038

Table A-2 *Present Value of One Dollar Per Year for N Years at Rth Percent*

N	1%	2%	3%	4%	5%	6%	7%	8%	9%	10%
1	0.99003	0.98037	0.97087	0.96154	0.95237	0.94339	0.93458	0.92593	0.91742	0.90909
2	1.97018	1.94150	1.91343	1.88608	1.85938	1.83337	1.80800	1.78326	1.75910	1.73553
3	2.94064	2.88379	2.82855	2.77506	2.72319	2.67298	2.62429	2.57708	2.53127	2.48683
4	3.90149	3.80759	3.71701	3.62985	3.54589	3.46505	3.38718	3.31211	3.23969	3.16984
5	4.85284	4.71328	4.57961	4.45177	4.32940	4.21231	4.10016	3.99269	3.88962	3.79076
6	5.79476	5.60121	5.41707	5.24207	5.07560	4.91725	4.76649	4.62286	4.48588	4.35523
7	6.72733	6.47177	6.23013	6.00198	5.78627	5.58231	5.38924	5.20634	5.03291	4.86839
8	7.65074	7.32521	7.01952	6.73266	6.46310	6.20971	5.97124	5.74661	5.53478	5.33490
9	8.56497	8.16192	7.78592	7.43524	7.10771	6.80161	6.51518	6.24686	5.99520	5.75899
10	9.47011	8.98225	8.53000	8.11080	7.72161	7.36000	7.02352	6.71005	6.41761	6.14454
11	10.36632	9.78649	9.25240	8.76038	8.30628	7.88678	7.49862	7.13893	6.80514	6.49503
12	11.25368	10.57496	9.95377	9.38496	8.86312	8.38375	7.94263	7.53604	7.16068	6.81366
13	12.13225	11.34795	10.63473	9.98553	9.39343	8.85259	8.35759	7.90374	7.48686	7.10333
14	13.00211	12.10579	11.29582	10.56301	9.89850	9.29488	8.74540	8.24420	7.78611	7.36666
15	13.86334	12.84881	11.93767	11.11826	10.37951	9.71215	9.10785	8.55945	8.06064	7.60605
16	14.71608	13.57722	12.56082	11.65216	10.83762	10.10579	9.44659	8.85134	8.31252	7.82368
17	15.56040	14.29137	13.16583	12.16554	11.27391	10.47716	9.76316	9.12161	8.54359	8.02153
18	16.39629	14.99150	13.75322	12.65916	11.68944	10.82750	10.05902	9.37186	8.75559	8.20139
19	17.22391	15.67792	14.32349	13.13381	12.08517	11.15802	10.33553	9.60357	8.95008	8.36489
20	18.04337	16.35086	14.87716	13.59018	12.46206	11.46982	10.59395	9.81812	9.12851	8.51354
21	18.85474	17.01062	15.41472	14.02902	12.82100	11.76398	10.83547	10.01677	9.29221	8.64867
22	19.65802	17.65744	15.93660	14.45097	13.16285	12.04148	11.06118	10.20072	9.44239	8.77152
23	20.45340	18.29161	16.44327	14.85670	13.48842	12.30328	11.27213	10.37103	9.58017	8.88320
24	21.24088	18.91330	16.93520	15.24682	13.79849	12.55026	11.46928	10.52873	9.70658	8.98472
25	22.02057	19.52281	17.41280	15.62194	14.09379	12.78326	11.65353	10.67475	9.82255	9.07702
26	22.79254	20.12038	17.87650	15.98263	14.37504	13.00307	11.82573	10.80995	9.92894	9.16093
27	23.55685	20.70624	18.32668	16.32944	14.64288	13.21044	11.98666	10.93514	10.02655	9.23721
28	24.31360	21.28059	18.76376	16.66292	14.89798	13.40607	12.13706	11.05106	10.11610	9.30655
29	25.06290	21.84367	19.18811	16.98357	15.14093	13.59063	12.27763	11.15839	10.19826	9.36959
30	25.80476	22.39574	19.60008	17.29189	15.37231	13.76474	12.40900	11.25776	10.27363	9.42690

Table A-2 *(Continued)*

N	11%	12%	13%	14%	15%	16%	17%	18%	19%	20%
1	0.90090	0.89286	0.88495	0.87719	0.86956	0.86207	0.85470	0.84746	0.84033	0.83333
2	1.71251	1.69005	1.66809	1.64665	1.62570	1.60523	1.58521	1.56564	1.54650	1.52777
3	2.44370	2.40182	2.36113	2.32162	2.28322	2.24588	2.20957	2.17426	2.13991	2.10648
4	3.10243	3.03734	2.97445	2.91370	2.85497	2.79817	2.74322	2.69005	2.63858	2.58873
5	3.69588	3.60477	3.51721	3.43306	3.35214	3.27429	3.19933	3.12716	3.05763	2.99061
6	4.23052	4.11140	3.99753	3.88865	3.78447	3.68473	3.58917	3.49759	3.40977	3.32551
7	4.71217	4.56374	4.42258	4.28828	4.16041	4.03856	3.92237	3.81152	3.70569	3.60459
8	5.14610	4.96763	4.79874	4.63884	4.48731	4.34358	4.20715	4.07756	3.95436	3.83716
9	5.53703	5.32824	5.13163	4.94635	4.77157	4.60654	4.45055	4.30301	4.16333	4.03096
10	5.88921	5.65021	5.42622	5.21610	5.01876	4.83322	4.65859	4.49408	4.33893	4.19247
11	6.20649	5.93769	5.68692	5.45271	5.23370	5.02864	4.83640	4.65600	4.48649	4.32706
12	6.49233	6.19436	5.91762	5.66027	5.42061	5.19710	4.98838	4.79322	4.61050	4.43921
13	6.74985	6.42354	6.12179	5.84235	5.58314	5.34233	5.11827	4.90950	4.71471	4.53268
14	6.98184	6.62816	6.30247	6.00206	5.72447	5.46752	5.22929	5.00805	4.80227	4.61056
15	7.19085	6.81085	6.46236	6.14215	5.84736	5.57545	5.32418	5.09157	4.87586	4.67547
16	7.37914	6.97398	6.60386	6.26505	5.95423	5.66849	5.40528	5.16235	4.93770	4.72956
17	7.54878	7.11962	6.72908	6.37285	6.04715	5.74870	5.47460	5.22233	4.98966	4.77463
18	7.70160	7.24966	6.83989	6.46741	6.12796	5.81784	5.53384	5.27316	5.03333	4.81219
19	7.83928	7.36577	6.93795	6.55036	6.19823	5.87745	5.58448	5.31624	5.07002	4.84349
20	7.96331	7.46944	7.02474	6.62312	6.25933	5.92884	5.62776	5.35274	5.10086	4.86958
21	8.07506	7.56200	7.10154	6.68695	6.31246	5.97313	5.66475	5.38368	5.12677	4.89132
22	8.17572	7.64464	7.16950	6.74294	6.35866	6.01132	5.69637	5.40990	5.14855	4.90943
23	8.26642	7.71843	7.22965	6.79205	6.39883	6.04424	5.72339	5.43212	5.16685	4.92452
24	8.34812	7.78431	7.28287	6.83513	6.43377	6.07262	5.74649	5.45095	5.18222	4.93710
25	8.42173	7.84313	7.32998	6.87292	6.46415	6.09709	5.76623	5.46690	5.19515	4.94759
26	8.48805	7.89565	7.37166	6.90607	6.49056	6.11818	5.78310	5.48043	5.20601	4.95632
27	8.54779	7.94255	7.40855	6.93515	6.51353	6.13636	5.79752	5.49189	5.21513	4.96360
28	8.60161	7.98442	7.44119	6.96066	6.53351	6.15204	5.80985	5.50160	5.22280	4.96967
29	8.65010	8.02180	7.47008	6.98303	6.55087	6.16555	5.82038	5.50983	5.22924	4.97472
30	8.69378	8.05518	7.49565	7.00266	6.56598	6.17720	5.82939	5.51680	5.23466	4.97894

Table A-2 (Continued)

N	21%	22%	23%	24%	25%	26%	27%	28%	29%	30%
1	0.82644	0.81967	0.81301	0.80645	0.80000	0.79365	0.78740	0.78125	0.77519	0.76923
2	1.50945	1.49153	1.47399	1.45681	1.44000	1.42353	1.40740	1.39160	1.37612	1.36094
3	2.07393	2.04223	2.01137	1.98130	1.95200	1.92343	1.89559	1.86844	1.84195	1.81611
4	2.54043	2.49363	2.44827	2.40427	2.36160	2.32018	2.27999	2.24096	2.20306	2.16624
5	2.92597	2.86363	2.80347	2.74538	2.68928	2.63507	2.58267	2.53200	2.48299	2.43557
6	3.24461	3.16691	3.09225	3.02047	2.95142	2.88497	2.82100	2.75938	2.70000	2.64274
7	3.50794	3.41550	3.32703	3.24231	3.16114	3.08331	3.00866	2.93701	2.86821	2.80211
8	3.72557	3.61926	3.51791	3.42122	3.32891	3.24072	3.15642	3.07579	2.99861	2.92470
9	3.90543	3.78628	3.67310	3.56550	3.46313	3.36565	3.27277	3.18421	3.09970	3.01900
10	4.05407	3.92318	3.79927	3.68185	3.57050	3.46480	3.36439	3.26892	3.17806	3.09154
11	4.17692	4.03539	3.90184	3.77569	3.65640	3.54349	3.43653	3.33509	3.23881	3.14734
12	4.27844	4.12737	3.98524	3.85136	3.72512	3.60595	3.49333	3.38679	3.28590	3.19026
13	4.36235	4.20276	4.05304	3.91239	3.78010	3.65551	3.53805	3.42718	3.32240	3.22328
14	4.43169	4.26456	4.10816	3.96160	3.82408	3.69485	3.57327	3.45873	3.35070	3.24867
15	4.48900	4.31521	4.15298	4.00129	3.85926	3.72607	3.60100	3.48339	3.37263	3.26821
16	4.53637	4.35673	4.18941	4.03330	3.88741	3.75085	3.62283	3.50264	3.38964	3.28324
17	4.57551	4.39076	4.21903	4.05911	3.90993	3.77052	3.64003	3.51769	3.40282	3.29480
18	4.60786	4.41866	4.24312	4.07993	3.92794	3.78612	3.65356	3.52945	3.41304	3.30369
19	4.63459	4.44152	4.26270	4.09672	3.94235	3.79851	3.66422	3.53863	3.42096	3.31053
20	4.65669	4.46026	4.27861	4.11026	3.95388	3.80834	3.67262	3.54580	3.42710	3.31579
21	4.67495	4.47563	4.29156	4.12117	3.96311	3.81614	3.67923	3.55141	3.43186	3.31984
22	4.69004	4.48822	4.30208	4.12998	3.97048	3.82234	3.68443	3.55579	3.43555	3.32295
23	4.70251	4.49854	4.31063	4.13708	3.97639	3.82725	3.68853	3.55921	3.43841	3.32535
24	4.71282	4.50700	4.31759	4.14281	3.98111	3.83115	3.69175	3.56188	3.44063	3.32719
25	4.72134	4.51393	4.32324	4.14742	3.98489	3.83425	3.69429	3.56397	3.44235	3.32861
26	4.72838	4.51962	4.32784	4.15115	3.98791	3.83670	3.69629	3.56560	3.44368	3.32970
27	4.73420	4.52428	4.33158	4.15415	3.99033	3.83865	3.69787	3.56688	3.44471	3.33054
28	4.73901	4.52810	4.33461	4.15657	3.99226	3.84020	3.69911	3.56787	3.44551	3.33118
29	4.74298	4.53123	4.33708	4.15853	3.99381	3.84143	3.70009	3.56865	3.44613	3.33168
30	4.74627	4.53379	4.33909	4.16010	3.99505	3.84240	3.70086	3.56926	3.44662	3.33206

Table B *Compound Sum of One Dollar for N Years at Rth Percent*

N	1%	2%	3%	4%	5%	6%	7%	8%	9%	10%
1	1.0100	1.0200	1.0300	1.0400	1.0500	1.0600	1.0700	1.0800	1.0900	1.1000
2	1.0201	1.0404	1.0609	1.0816	1.1025	1.1236	1.1449	1.1664	1.1881	1.2100
3	1.0303	1.0612	1.0927	1.1249	1.1576	1.1910	1.2250	1.2597	1.2950	1.3310
4	1.0406	1.0824	1.1255	1.1699	1.2155	1.2625	1.3108	1.3605	1.4116	1.4641
5	1.0510	1.1041	1.1593	1.2167	1.2763	1.3382	1.4025	1.4693	1.5386	1.6105
6	1.0615	1.1262	1.1940	1.2653	1.3401	1.4185	1.5007	1.5869	1.6771	1.7716
7	1.0721	1.1487	1.2299	1.3159	1.4071	1.5036	1.6058	1.7138	1.8280	1.9487
8	1.0828	1.1717	1.2668	1.3686	1.4774	1.5938	1.7182	1.8509	1.9925	2.1436
9	1.0937	1.1951	1.3048	1.4233	1.5513	1.6895	1.8384	1.9990	2.1719	2.3579
10	1.1046	1.2190	1.3439	1.4802	1.6289	1.7908	1.9671	2.1589	2.3673	2.5937
11	1.1157	1.2434	1.3842	1.5394	1.7103	1.8983	2.1048	2.3316	2.5804	2.8531
12	1.1268	1.2682	1.4257	1.6010	1.7958	2.0122	2.2522	2.5182	2.8126	3.1384
13	1.1381	1.2936	1.4685	1.6651	1.8856	2.1329	2.4098	2.7196	3.0658	3.4522
14	1.1495	1.3195	1.5126	1.7317	1.9799	2.2609	2.5785	2.9372	3.3417	3.7975
15	1.1609	1.3459	1.5579	1.8009	2.0789	2.3965	2.7590	3.1721	3.6424	4.1772
16	1.1726	1.3728	1.6047	1.8730	2.1828	2.5403	2.9521	3.4259	3.9702	4.5949
17	1.1843	1.4002	1.6528	1.9479	2.2920	2.6927	3.1588	3.7000	4.3276	5.0544
18	1.1961	1.4282	1.7024	2.0258	2.4066	2.8543	3.3799	3.9960	4.7170	5.5598
19	1.2081	1.4568	1.7535	2.1068	2.5269	3.0255	3.6165	4.3157	5.1416	6.1158
20	1.2202	1.4859	1.8061	2.1911	2.6532	3.2071	3.8696	4.6609	5.6043	6.7274
21	1.2324	1.5156	1.8603	2.2737	2.7859	3.3995	4.1405	5.0338	6.1087	7.4001
22	1.2447	1.5460	1.9161	2.3699	2.9252	3.6035	4.4303	5.4365	6.6585	8.1401
23	1.2571	1.5769	1.9735	2.4647	3.0715	3.8197	4.7404	5.8714	7.2577	8.9541
24	1.2697	1.6084	2.0328	2.5633	3.2250	4.0488	5.0723	6.3411	7.9109	9.8495
25	1.2824	1.6406	2.0937	2.6658	3.3863	4.2918	5.4273	6.8484	8.6229	10.8345
26	1.2952	1.6734	2.1565	2.7724	3.5556	4.5493	5.8072	7.3962	9.3989	11.9179
27	1.3082	1.7068	2.2212	2.8833	3.7334	4.8222	6.2137	7.9879	10.2448	13.1097
28	1.3212	1.7410	2.2879	2.9937	3.9200	5.1115	6.6487	8.6270	11.1668	14.4206
29	1.3345	1.7758	2.3565	3.1136	4.1160	5.4182	7.1141	9.3171	12.1718	15.8627
30	1.3478	1.8113	2.4272	3.2433	4.3218	5.7433	7.6121	10.0625	13.2673	17.4489

Table B *(Continued)*

N	11%	12%	13%	14%	15%	16%	17%	18%	19%	20%
1	1.1100	1.1200	1.1300	1.1400	1.1500	1.1600	1.1700	1.1800	1.1900	1.2000
2	1.2321	1.2544	1.2769	1.2996	1.3225	1.3456	1.3689	1.3924	1.4161	1.4400
3	1.3676	1.4049	1.4429	1.4815	1.5209	1.5609	1.6016	1.6430	1.6852	1.7280
4	1.5181	1.5735	1.6305	1.6890	1.7490	1.8106	1.8739	1.9388	2.0053	2.0736
5	1.6851	1.7623	1.8424	1.9254	2.0114	2.1003	2.1924	2.2877	2.3863	2.4883
6	1.8704	1.9738	2.0819	2.1950	2.3131	2.4364	2.5651	2.6995	2.8398	2.9860
7	2.0761	2.2107	2.3526	2.5023	2.6600	2.8262	3.0012	3.1855	3.3793	3.5832
8	2.3045	2.4760	2.6584	2.8526	3.0590	3.2784	3.5114	3.7588	4.0214	4.2998
9	2.5580	2.7731	3.0040	3.2519	3.5179	3.8029	4.1084	4.4354	4.7854	5.1598
10	2.8394	3.1058	3.3945	3.7072	4.0455	4.4114	4.8068	5.2338	5.6947	6.1917
11	3.1517	3.4785	3.8358	4.2262	4.6524	5.1172	5.6239	6.1759	6.7766	7.4300
12	3.4984	3.8960	4.3345	4.8178	5.3502	5.9360	6.5800	7.2875	8.0642	8.9160
13	3.8832	4.3635	4.8979	5.4923	6.1527	6.8858	7.6986	8.5993	9.5964	10.6993
14	4.3104	4.8871	5.5347	6.2613	7.0756	7.9875	9.0073	10.1471	11.4197	12.8391
15	4.7845	5.4735	6.2542	7.1378	8.1370	9.2655	10.5386	11.9736	13.5894	15.4069
16	5.3108	6.1304	7.0672	8.1371	9.3575	10.7479	12.3301	14.1288	16.1714	18.4883
17	5.8950	6.8660	7.9859	9.2763	10.7611	12.4676	14.4262	16.6720	19.2439	22.1859
18	6.5435	7.6899	9.0241	10.5750	12.3753	14.4624	16.8786	19.6729	22.9003	26.6231
19	7.2632	8.6127	10.1972	12.0555	14.2316	16.7764	19.7480	23.2141	27.2513	31.9477
20	8.0622	9.6462	11.5228	13.7432	16.3663	19.4606	23.1051	27.3926	32.4290	38.3372
21	8.9490	10.8038	13.0208	15.6672	18.8212	22.5743	27.0330	32.3232	38.5905	46.0046
22	9.9334	12.1002	14.7135	17.8606	21.6444	26.1862	31.6285	38.1413	45.9227	55.2055
23	11.0261	13.5522	16.6262	20.3611	24.8911	30.3759	37.0053	45.0068	54.6480	66.2466
24	12.2390	15.1785	18.7876	23.2116	28.6247	35.2361	43.2962	53.1079	65.0311	79.4958
25	13.5852	16.9999	21.2299	26.4612	32.9184	40.8738	50.6565	62.6673	77.3869	95.3950
26	15.0796	19.0399	23.9898	30.1658	37.8561	47.4136	59.2681	73.9474	92.0904	114.4739
27	16.7383	21.3246	27.1085	34.3889	43.5345	54.9998	69.3435	87.2578	109.5875	137.3686
28	18.5795	23.8836	30.6325	39.2034	50.0646	63.7997	81.1319	102.9641	130.4091	164.8422
29	20.6233	26.7496	34.6147	44.6918	57.5743	74.0076	94.9242	121.4976	155.1867	197.8107
30	22.8918	29.9595	39.1146	50.9486	66.2104	85.8488	111.0612	143.3670	184.6721	237.3726

Table B *(Continued)*

N	21%	22%	23%	24%	25%	26%	27%	28%	29%	30%
1	1.2100	1.2200	1.2300	1.2400	1.2500	1.2600	1.2700	1.2800	1.2900	1.3000
2	1.4641	1.4884	1.5129	1.5376	1.5625	1.5876	1.6129	1.6384	1.6641	1.6900
3	1.7716	1.8158	1.8609	1.9066	1.9531	2.0004	2.0484	2.0971	2.1467	2.1970
4	2.1436	2.2153	2.2889	2.3642	2.4414	2.5205	2.6014	2.6844	2.7692	2.8561
5	2.5937	2.7027	2.8153	2.9316	3.0518	3.1758	3.3038	3.4360	3.5723	3.7129
6	3.1384	3.2973	3.4628	3.6352	3.8147	4.0015	4.1959	4.3980	4.6083	4.8268
7	3.7975	4.0227	4.2593	4.5077	4.7684	5.0419	5.3287	5.6295	5.9447	6.2748
8	4.5949	4.9077	5.2389	5.5895	5.9605	6.3528	6.7675	7.2057	7.6686	8.1573
9	5.5599	5.9874	6.4438	6.9310	7.4506	8.0045	8.5947	9.2233	9.8925	10.6044
10	6.7274	7.3046	7.9259	8.5944	9.3132	10.0856	10.9153	11.8059	12.7613	13.7857
11	8.1402	8.9116	9.7489	10.6570	11.6415	12.7079	13.8624	15.1115	16.4621	17.9214
12	9.8496	10.8721	11.9911	13.2147	14.5519	16.0119	17.6052	19.3427	21.2361	23.2979
13	11.9180	13.2640	14.7490	16.3862	18.1899	20.1750	22.3586	24.7587	27.3946	30.2872
14	14.4208	16.1820	18.1413	20.3189	22.7374	25.4204	28.3954	31.6911	35.3391	39.3734
15	17.4491	19.7420	22.3138	25.1954	28.4217	32.0297	36.0621	40.5646	45.5874	51.1853
16	21.1134	24.0853	27.4459	31.2423	35.5271	40.3575	45.7989	51.9227	58.8077	66.5408
17	25.5472	29.3840	33.7585	38.7405	44.4089	50.8504	58.1645	66.4610	75.8619	86.5030
18	30.9121	35.8484	41.5229	48.0381	55.5111	64.0714	73.8689	85.0701	97.8619	112.4539
19	37.4036	43.7351	51.0731	59.5373	69.3889	80.7299	93.8134	108.8896	126.2418	146.1899
20	45.2583	53.3567	62.8199	73.8634	86.7361	101.7196	119.1430	139.3787	162.8519	190.0467
21	54.7624	65.0952	77.2684	91.5306	108.4202	128.1666	151.3115	178.4047	210.0788	247.0606
22	66.2625	79.4160	95.0401	113.5722	135.5252	161.4898	192.1655	228.3578	271.0017	321.1785
23	80.1775	96.8875	116.8993	140.8295	169.4066	203.4770	244.0500	292.2979	349.5920	417.5315
24	97.0147	118.2027	143.7861	174.6285	211.7582	256.3809	309.9431	374.1414	450.9736	542.7908
25	117.3876	144.2071	176.8568	216.5393	264.6975	323.0396	393.6277	478.9006	581.7561	705.6274
26	142.0389	175.9325	217.5337	268.5083	330.8721	407.0295	499.9067	612.9927	750.4651	917.3152
27	171.8669	214.6375	267.5662	332.9502	413.5901	512.8569	634.8811	784.6304	968.0996	1192.5083
28	207.9586	261.8574	329.1062	412.8582	516.9875	646.1995	806.2979	1004.3262	1248.8477	1550.2598
29	251.6297	319.4658	404.8005	511.9438	646.2341	814.2104	1023.9985	1285.5371	1611.0137	2015.3369
30	304.4714	389.7478	497.9041	634.8098	807.7932	1025.9041	1300.4766	1645.4878	2078.2080	2619.9360

Table C *Area Under a Normal Curve*

Z	0	1	2	3	4	5	6	7	8	9
0.0	.50000	.50399	.50798	.51197	.51595	.51994	.52392	.52790	.53188	.53586
0.1	.53983	.54380	.54776	.55172	.55567	.55962	.56356	.56749	.57142	.57534
0.2	.57926	.58317	.58706	.59095	.59483	.59871	.60257	.60642	.61026	.61409
0.3	.61791	.62172	.62552	.62930	.63307	.63683	.64058	.64431	.64803	.65173
0.4	.65542	.65910	.66276	.66640	.67003	.67364	.67724	.68082	.68439	.68793
0.5	.69146	.69497	.69847	.70194	.70540	.70884	.71226	.71566	.71904	.72240
0.6	.72575	.72907	.73237	.73565	.73891	.74215	.74537	.74857	.75175	.75490
0.7	.75804	.76115	.76424	.76730	.77035	.77337	.77637	.77935	.78230	.78524
0.8	.78814	.79103	.79389	.79673	.79955	.80234	.80511	.80785	.81057	.81327
0.9	.81594	.81859	.82121	.82381	.82639	.82894	.83147	.83398	.83646	.83891
1.0	.84134	.84375	.84614	.84849	.85083	.85314	.85543	.85769	.85993	.86214
1.1	.86433	.86650	.86864	.87076	.87285	.87493	.87697	.87900	.88100	.88297
1.2	.88493	.88686	.88876	.89065	.89251	.89435	.89616	.89795	.89972	.90147
1.3	.90320	.90490	.90658	.90824	.90987	.91149	.91308	.91465	.91620	.91773
1.4	.91924	.92073	.92219	.92364	.92506	.92647	.92785	.92921	.93056	.93188
1.5	.93319	.93447	.93574	.93699	.93821	.93942	.94062	.94179	.94294	.94408
1.6	.94520	.94630	.94738	.94844	.94949	.95052	.95154	.95254	.95352	.95448
1.7	.95543	.95636	.95728	.95818	.95907	.95994	.96079	.96163	.96246	.96327
1.8	.96407	.96485	.96562	.96637	.96711	.96784	.96855	.96925	.96994	.97062
1.9	.97128	.97193	.97257	.97319	.97381	.97441	.97500	.97558	.97614	.97670
2.0	.97725	.97778	.97830	.97882	.97932	.97981	.98030	.98077	.98123	.98169
2.1	.98213	.98257	.98299	.98341	.98382	.98422	.98461	.98499	.98537	.98573
2.2	.98609	.98644	.98679	.98712	.98745	.98777	.98809	.98839	.98869	.98899
2.3	.98927	.98955	.98983	.99009	.99036	.99061	.99086	.99110	.99134	.99157
2.4	.99180	.99202	.99224	.99245	.99265	.99286	.99305	.99324	.99343	.99361
2.5	.99379	.99396	.99413	.99430	.99446	.99461	.99476	.99491	.99506	.99520
2.6	.99534	.99547	.99560	.99573	.99585	.99597	.99609	.99621	.99632	.99643
2.7	.99653	.99663	.99673	.99683	.99693	.99702	.99711	.99720	.99728	.99736
2.8	.99744	.99752	.99760	.99767	.99774	.99781	.99788	.99795	.99801	.99807
2.9	.99813	.99819	.99825	.99830	.99836	.99841	.99846	.99851	.99856	.99860
3.0	.99865	.99869	.99874	.99878	.99882	.99886	.99889	.99893	.99896	.99900
3.1	.99903	.99906	.99910	.99913	.99915	.99918	.99921	.99924	.99926	.99929
3.2	.99931	.99934	.99936	.99938	.99940	.99942	.99944	.99946	.99948	.99950
3.3	.99952	.99953	.99955	.99957	.99958	.99960	.99961	.99962	.99964	.99965
3.4	.99966	.99967	.99969	.99970	.99971	.99972	.99973	.99974	.99975	.99976
3.5	.99977	.99978	.99978	.99979	.99980	.99981	.99981	.99982	.99983	.99983
3.6	.99984	.99985	.99985	.99986	.99986	.99987	.99987	.99988	.99988	.99989
3.7	.99989	.99990	.99990	.99990	.99991	.99991	.99991	.99992	.99992	.99992
3.8	.99993	.99993	.99993	.99994	.99994	.99994	.99994	.99995	.99995	.99995
3.9	.99995	.99995	.99996	.99996	.99996	.99996	.99996	.99996	.99997	.99997

Note: This table is constructed to give the total area under the normal curve going from $-\infty$ to $+\infty$.
To obtain the probability of being between O and Z subtract 0.5

Table D *Four-Place Common Logarithms*

N	0	1	2	3	4	5	6	7	8	9	1	2	3	4	5	6	7	8	9
											Proportional Parts								
10	0000	0043	0086	0128	0170	0212	0253	0294	0334	0338	4	8	12	17	21	25	29	33	37
11	0414	0453	0492	0531	0569	0607	0645	0682	0719	0756	4	8	11	15	19	23	26	30	34
12	0792	0828	0864	0899	0934	0969	1004	1038	1072	1106	3	7	10	14	17	21	24	28	31
13	1139	1173	1206	1239	1271	1303	1335	1367	1399	1430	3	6	10	13	16	19	23	26	29
14	1461	1492	1523	1553	1584	1614	1644	1673	1703	1732	3	6	9	12	15	18	21	24	27
15	1761	1790	1818	1847	1875	1903	1931	1959	1987	2014	3	6	8	11	14	17	20	22	25
16	2041	2068	2095	2122	2148	2175	2201	2227	2253	2279	3	5	8	11	13	16	18	21	24
17	2305	2330	2355	2381	2406	2430	2455	2480	2504	2528	2	5	7	10	12	15	17	20	22
18	2553	2577	2601	2625	2648	2672	2695	2718	2742	2765	2	5	7	9	12	14	16	19	21
19	2788	2810	2833	2856	2878	2900	2923	2945	2967	2989	2	4	7	9	11	13	16	18	20
20	3010	3032	3054	3075	3096	3118	3139	3160	3181	3202	2	4	6	8	11	13	15	17	19
21	3222	3243	3263	3284	3304	3324	3345	3365	3385	3404	2	4	6	8	10	12	14	16	18
22	3424	3444	3464	3483	3503	3522	3541	3560	3579	3598	2	4	6	8	10	12	14	15	17
23	3617	3636	3655	3674	3692	3711	3729	3748	3766	3784	2	4	6	7	9	11	13	15	17
24	3802	3820	3838	3856	3874	3892	3909	3927	3945	3962	2	4	5	7	9	11	12	14	16
25	3979	3997	4014	4031	4048	4065	4082	4099	4116	4133	2	3	5	7	9	10	12	14	15
26	4150	4166	4183	4200	4216	4232	4249	4265	4281	4298	2	3	5	7	8	10	11	13	15
27	4314	4330	4346	4362	4378	4393	4409	4425	4440	4456	2	3	5	6	8	10	11	13	14
28	4472	4487	4503	4518	4533	4548	4564	4579	4594	4609	2	3	5	6	8	9	11	12	14
29	4624	4639	4654	4669	4684	4698	4713	4728	4742	4757	1	3	4	6	7	9	10	12	13
30	4771	4786	4800	4814	4829	4843	4857	4871	4886	4890	1	3	4	6	7	9	10	11	13
31	4914	4928	4942	4955	4969	4983	4997	5011	5024	5038	1	3	4	6	7	8	10	11	12
32	5052	5065	5079	5092	5105	5119	5132	5146	5159	5172	1	3	4	5	7	8	9	11	12
33	5185	5198	5211	5224	5238	5250	5264	5276	5289	5302	1	3	4	5	6	8	9	10	12
34	5315	5326	5340	5353	5366	5378	5391	5403	5416	5428	1	3	4	5	6	8	9	10	11
35	5441	5453	5465	5478	5490	5502	5515	5527	5539	5551	1	2	4	5	6	7	9	10	11
36	5563	5575	5587	5599	5611	5623	5635	5647	5659	5670	1	2	4	5	6	7	8	10	11
37	5682	5694	5705	5717	5729	5740	5752	5763	5775	5786	1	2	3	5	6	7	8	9	10
38	5798	5809	5821	5832	5843	5855	5866	5877	5888	5900	1	2	3	5	6	7	8	9	10
39	5911	5922	5933	5944	5955	5966	5977	5988	5999	6010	1	2	3	4	5	7	8	9	10

Table D *(Continued)*

N	0	1	2	3	4	5	6	7	8	9	Proportional Parts 1	2	3	4	5	6	7	8	9
40	6021	6031	6042	6053	6064	6075	6085	6096	6107	6117	1	2	3	4	5	6	8	9	10
41	6128	6138	6149	6160	6170	6181	6191	6201	6212	6222	1	2	3	4	5	6	7	8	9
42	6232	6243	6253	6263	6274	6284	6294	6304	6314	6325	1	2	3	4	5	6	7	8	9
43	6335	6345	6355	6365	6375	6385	6395	6405	6415	6425	1	2	3	4	5	6	7	8	9
44	6435	6444	6454	6464	6474	6484	6493	6503	6513	6523	1	2	3	4	5	6	7	8	9
45	6532	6542	6551	6561	6571	6580	6590	6599	6609	6618	1	2	3	4	5	6	7	8	9
46	6628	6637	6646	6656	6665	6675	6684	6693	6703	6712	1	2	3	4	5	6	6	7	8
47	6721	6730	6739	6749	6758	6767	6776	6785	6794	6803	1	2	3	4	5	5	6	7	8
48	6812	6822	6831	6840	6849	6857	6866	6875	6884	6893	1	2	3	4	4	5	6	7	8
49	6902	6911	6920	6929	6937	6946	6955	6964	6972	6981	1	2	3	4	4	5	6	7	8
50	6990	6998	7007	7016	7024	7033	7042	7050	7059	7067	1	2	3	3	4	5	6	7	8
51	7076	7084	7093	7101	7110	7118	7127	7135	7143	7152	1	2	3	3	4	5	6	7	8
52	7160	7168	7177	7185	7193	7202	7210	7218	7226	7235	1	2	2	3	4	5	6	7	7
53	7243	7251	7259	7267	7275	7284	7292	7300	7308	7316	1	2	2	3	4	5	6	6	7
54	7324	7332	7340	7348	7356	7364	7372	7380	7388	7396	1	2	2	3	4	5	6	6	7
55	7404	7412	7419	7427	7435	7443	7451	7459	7466	7474	1	2	2	3	4	5	5	6	7
56	7482	7490	7497	7505	7513	7521	7528	7536	7544	7551	1	2	2	3	4	5	5	6	7
57	7559	7566	7574	7582	7589	7597	7604	7612	7619	7627	1	2	2	3	4	5	5	6	7
58	7634	7642	7649	7657	7664	7672	7679	7686	7694	7701	1	1	2	3	4	4	5	6	7
59	7708	7716	7723	7731	7738	7745	7753	7760	7767	7774	1	1	2	3	4	4	5	6	7
60	7782	7789	7796	7803	7810	7818	7825	7832	7839	7846	1	1	2	3	4	4	5	6	6
61	7853	7860	7868	7875	7882	7889	7896	7903	7910	7917	1	1	2	3	4	4	5	6	6
62	7924	7931	7938	7945	7952	7959	7966	7973	7980	7987	1	1	2	3	4	4	5	6	6
63	7993	8000	8007	8014	8021	8028	8035	8041	8048	8055	1	1	2	3	3	4	5	6	6
64	8062	8069	8075	8082	8089	8096	8102	8109	8116	8122	1	1	2	3	3	4	5	5	6
65	8129	8136	8143	8149	8156	8162	8169	8176	8182	8189	1	1	2	3	3	4	5	5	6
66	8195	8202	8209	8215	8222	8228	8235	8241	8248	8254	1	1	2	3	3	4	5	5	6
67	8261	8267	8274	8280	8287	8293	8300	8306	8312	8319	1	1	2	3	3	4	5	5	6
68	8325	8332	8338	8344	8351	8357	8363	8370	8376	8382	1	1	2	3	3	4	4	5	6
69	8389	8395	8401	8407	8414	8420	8426	8432	8439	8445	1	1	2	2	3	4	4	5	6

Table D *(Continued)*

N	0	1	2	3	4	5	6	7	8	9	Proportional Parts								
											1	2	3	4	5	6	7	8	9
70	8451	8457	8463	8470	8476	8482	8488	8494	8500	8507	1	1	2	2	3	4	4	5	6
71	8513	8519	8525	8531	8537	8543	8549	8555	8561	8567	1	1	2	2	3	4	4	5	5
72	8573	8579	8585	8591	8597	8603	8609	8615	8621	8627	1	1	2	2	3	4	4	5	5
73	8633	8639	8645	8651	8657	8663	8669	8675	8681	8686	1	1	2	2	3	4	4	5	5
74	8692	8698	8704	8710	8716	8722	8727	8733	8739	8745	1	1	2	2	3	4	4	5	5
75	8751	8756	8762	8768	8774	8780	8785	8791	8797	8802	1	1	2	2	3	3	4	5	5
76	8808	8814	8820	8825	8831	8837	8842	8848	8854	8859	1	1	2	2	3	3	4	5	5
77	8865	8871	8876	8882	8887	8893	8899	8904	8910	8915	1	1	2	2	3	3	4	4	5
78	8921	8927	8932	8938	8943	8949	8954	8960	8965	8971	1	1	2	2	3	3	4	4	5
79	8976	8982	8987	8993	8998	9004	9009	9015	9020	9023	1	1	2	2	3	3	4	4	5
80	9031	9036	9042	9047	9053	9058	9063	9069	9074	9080	1	1	2	2	3	3	4	4	5
81	9085	9090	9096	9101	9106	9112	9117	9122	9128	9133	1	1	2	2	3	3	4	4	5
82	9138	9143	9149	9154	9159	9165	9170	9175	9180	9186	1	1	2	2	3	3	4	4	5
83	9191	9196	9201	9206	9212	9217	9222	9227	9232	9238	1	1	2	2	3	3	4	4	5
84	9243	9248	9253	9258	9263	9269	9274	9279	9284	9289	1	1	2	2	3	3	4	4	5
85	9294	9299	9304	9310	9315	9320	9325	9330	9335	9340	1	1	2	2	3	3	4	4	5
86	9345	9350	9355	9360	9365	9370	9375	9380	9385	9390	1	1	2	2	3	3	4	4	5
87	9395	9400	9405	9410	9415	9420	9425	9430	9435	9440	1	1	2	2	3	3	4	4	4
88	9445	9450	9455	9460	9465	9469	9474	9479	9484	9489	0	1	1	2	2	3	3	4	4
89	9494	9499	9504	9509	9513	9518	9523	9528	9533	9538	0	1	1	2	2	3	3	4	4
90	9542	9547	9552	9557	9562	9567	9571	9576	9581	9586	0	1	1	2	2	3	3	4	4
91	9590	9595	9600	9605	9609	9614	9619	9624	9628	9633	0	1	1	2	2	3	3	4	4
92	9638	9643	9647	9652	9657	9661	9666	9671	9676	9680	0	1	1	2	2	3	3	4	4
93	9685	9690	9694	9699	9704	9708	9713	9717	9722	9727	0	1	1	2	2	3	3	4	4
94	9731	9736	9741	9745	9750	9754	9759	9764	9768	9773	0	1	1	2	2	3	3	4	4
95	9777	9782	9786	9791	9795	9800	9805	9809	9814	9818	0	1	1	2	2	3	3	4	4
96	9823	9827	9832	9836	9841	9845	9850	9854	9859	9863	0	1	1	2	2	3	3	4	4
97	9868	9872	9877	9881	9886	9890	9894	9899	9903	9908	0	1	1	2	2	3	3	4	4
98	9912	9917	9921	9926	9930	9934	9939	9943	9948	9952	0	1	1	2	2	3	3	4	4
99	9956	9961	9965	9969	9974	9978	9983	9987	9991	9996	0	1	1	2	2	3	3	4	4

Index